AUGUSTINE OF HIPPO

AUGUSTINE
OF HIPPO

a biography

by

PETER BROWN

faber and faber

LONDON · BOSTON

First published in 1967
by Faber and Faber Limited
3 Queen Square London WC1N 3AU
First published in this edition 1969
Reprinted 1975, 1979, 1985, 1988 and 1990

Printed in England by Clays Ltd, St Ives plc
All rights reserved

ISBN 0 571 09232 2

2 4 6 8 10 9 7 5 3

CONTENTS

PREFACE   *page* 9

PART I. 354–385

CHRONOLOGICAL TABLE A   16
1. AFRICA   19
2. MONICA   28
3. EDUCATION   35
4. 'WISDOM'   40
5. MANICHAEISM: (i) DUALISM   46
      (ii) *Gnosis*   53
6. FRIENDS   61
7. SUCCESS   65

PART II. 386–395

CHRONOLOGICAL TABLE B   74
8. AMBROSE   79
9. THE PLATONISTS   88
10. 'PHILOSOPHY'   101
11. *Christianae Vitae Otium*: CASSICIACUM 115
12. OSTIA   128
13. *Servus Dei*: THAGASTE   132
14. *Presbyter Ecclesiae Catholicae*: HIPP,O 138
15. THE LOST FUTURE   146
16. THE *'Confessions'*   158

PART III. 395–410

CHRONOLOGICAL TABLE C   184
17. HIPPO REGIUS   189
18. *Saluberrima consilia*   203
19. *Ubi Ecclesia?*   212

7

CONTENTS

20. *Instantia*   *page* 226
21. *Disciplina*   233
22. *Populus Dei*   244
23. *Doctrina Christiana*   259
24. 'SEEK HIS FACE EVERMORE'   270

PART IV. 410–420

CHRONOLOGICAL TABLE D   282
25. *Senectus Mundi*: THE SACK OF ROME   287
26. *Opus magnum et arduum*: WRITING THE
    'City of God'   299
27. *Civitas peregrina*   313
28. UNITY ACHIEVED   330
29. PELAGIUS AND PELAGIANISM   340
30. *Causa Gratiae*   353
31. *Fundatissima Fides*   365

PART V. 420–430

CHRONOLOGICAL TABLE E   378
32. JULIAN OF ECLANUM (i)   381
                        (ii)   387
33. PREDESTINATION   398
34. OLD AGE   408
35. THE END OF ROMAN AFRICA   419
36. DEATH   427
    BIBLIOGRAPHICAL TABLE   435
    INDEX   453

PREFACE

I have tried in this book to convey something of the course and quality of Augustine's life. Not only did Augustine live in an age of rapid and dramatic change; he himself was constantly changing. The historian of the declining Roman Empire can trace through his life the movements that would lead Augustine the schoolboy, weeping over the old story of Dido and Aeneas in a secure province, to end his life as the Catholic bishop of a North African port, that was blockaded by the war-bands of a tribe which had ultimately come from Southern Sweden. He can also seize some of the more elusive changes in the man himself: he will be constantly reminded, often by a stray detail — by nothing more, perhaps, than by a turn of phrase used in addressing a friend — of the long, inner journeys of Augustine. Most difficult of all, and most rewarding, the historian can attempt to seize that crucial area where external and internal changes touch each other. Augustine will have to meet the challenge of new environments; his style of life will be unconsciously transformed by long routines; and outside circumstances, in their turn, will take on a different meaning at different times, by being subtly charged with his personal preoccupations. By writing, by acting, by influencing an ever-increasing body of men, he will help to precipitate changes in the world around him, that were no less headlong than his own inner transformations. I shall be more than satisfied if I have given some impression of the subtle overlapping of these differing levels of change, and if, in so doing, I have encouraged others to believe, that it is possible to glimpse a figure in so distant a past in this way.

Inevitably, this perspective has led me to concentrate on some aspects of Augustine's life more than on others. Seeking to trace the changes I have traced, I am acutely aware that I have been led along the side of a mountain-face: I found myself, for instance, above the plains of Augustine's routine duties as a bishop, and far below the heights of his speculations on the Trinity. I trust, however, that my perspective will not be held deliberately to exclude whole areas of

9

PREFACE

Augustine's life, still less to diminish the richness of his thought. At least I can be confident that Augustine has been so excellently studied in the past generations, that if I have failed to do justice to many sides of his life, his thought, and his personality, others are to hand to remedy my omissions. The reader therefore should know, that many of the authors to whom I constantly refer, are for me far more than names, whose views support or complement my own: they are the giants on whose shoulders I have been honoured to perch.

The study of Augustine is endless — though fortunately well-signposted by modern bibliographical collections.[1] One can only emerge, as Augustine emerged from his study, reflecting that '*When a man hath done, then he beginneth*' (Ecclus. xviii, 6). I have chosen, therefore, whenever possible, to refer to those up-to-date treatments, that seemed to me to deal most exhaustively with the implications and divergent views that surround each question I have had to touch on. I am aware of having, thereby, omitted the work of some scholars, because their contributions, however important, have now been assimilated into modern Augustinian scholarship. This has also meant by-passing many controversies, to do justice to even one of which could have taken up an entire volume. I trust that the books and articles that I have included, will be like plants, which, when pulled up, will reveal the full ramifications of the root-system of modern studies of Augustine and his age.

My thanks go, first and foremost, to the Warden and Fellows of All Souls College, Oxford. Only the rare tranquillity of such a college could make it possible even to consider embarking on this work; only its distinctive atmosphere could refresh and stimulate me until it was completed. I have tried, throughout, to do justice to the high standards of Late Roman scholarship upheld by Professor A. Momigliano. I am most grateful to the many learned friends who encouraged me when writing, and who endeavoured to correct me, when I had written; especially to my teacher, the Reverend Dr. T. M. Parker, to the Reverend Professor H. Chadwick, and to Robert Markus. I have benefited greatly from the erudition of John Matthews and from his shrewd comments on certain facets of the age of Augustine. I am also very aware of a debt to my students, which is less easy to particularize. Every year, the enthusiasm and fresh interest with which a handful of

[1] Notably, C. Andresen, *Bibliographia Augustiniana*, 1962, T. Van Bavel, *Répertoire bibliographique de S. Augustin, 1950–1960* (Instrumenta Patristica, III), 1963 — 5502 titles! — and E. Lamirande, 'Un siècle et demi d'études sur l'ecclésiologie de S. Augustin', *Revue des études augustiniennes*, viii, 1962, pp. 1–124 — 988 titles. Every year, the *Revue des études augustiniennes* produces an exhaustive 'Bulletin augustinien', of some 400 titles.

PREFACE

undergraduates of the Modern History School of Oxford, crosses that rather lonely and precarious bridge flung out by their syllabus, between ancient and medieval history, between the disciplines of the historian, the theologian and the philosopher, have reinforced me in my own fascination with Augustine and his age.

The rigours of finally committing this book to paper would have been infinite, if I had not been able to rely on the scrupulous care, the interest, and the bibliographical acumen of Michael Walsh. The reader will thank him, as I do most warmly, for the chronological tables, and for the invaluable inventory of English translations of the works of Augustine. The index I owe to Father Charlier of Heythrop College. I have been fortunate to be able to turn to Mrs. Sheila Clayton for undaunted and highly intelligent typing. Last of all, my wife has enabled me to appreciate, in our shared labour throughout, the force of the remark of Augustine's, that 'a friend . . . is one with whom one may dare to share the counsels of one's heart'.

All Souls College,
Oxford.
June 1966

ABBREVIATIONS

In my footnotes, I have habitually used the following abbreviations of titles and standard editions:

Misc. Agostin. i = Morin, Sermones post Maurinos Reperti, *Miscellanea Agostiniana*, i, 1930

P. L. = J. P. Migne, *Patrologiae Cursus Completus, Series Latina* (volume number in Roman, column in Arabic numerals)

Vita = *Sancti Augustini Vita a Possidio episcopo* esp. inf. p. 409, n.4)

PART I
354-385

354	Augustine born at Thagaste.
361 Julian Emperor (to 363).	
364 Rogatist Schism.	
367 Ausonius tutor to Gratian at Trier.	
370	Returns to Thagaste from Madaura.
371	Goes to Carthage for first time.
372 Revolt of Firmus.	Patricius dies. Takes a concubine.
373 1.xii. Consecration of Ambrose.	Reading of *Hortensius*. ? Birth of Adeodatus.
374 Death of Firmus.	
375 17.xi. Death of Valentinian I.	Returns from Carthage to Thagaste to teach.
376	Death of friend; returns to Carthage.
378 9.viii. Defeat by Visigoths and death of Valens at Adrianople.	
379 Accession of Theodosius I. Consulship of Ausonius.	
380 ? Vindicianus Proconsul at Carthage.	Writes *De Pulchro et Apto* (not extant).
383 Revolt of Maximus (June). Faustus of Milevis arrives in Carthage. Ambrose in Trier (from Oct. to following Jan.). Famine in Rome.	Sails for Rome.
384 Symmachus Prefect of Rome. Altar of Victory controversy (summer). Dramatic date of Macrobius' *Saturnalia*.	Appointed Professor of Rhetoric in Milan (autumn).
385 Jerome (347–?420) sails from Ostia for the East, (August).	Monica arrives in Milan (late spring).

The works of Saint Augustine have been, or are being, translated in the following series:

> *A Library of the Fathers of the Holy Catholic Church*, Oxford, 1838–58.
> *The Works of Aurelius Augustinus*, Edinburgh, 1871–76.
> *The Fathers of the Church*, New York, 1947–.
> *Ancient Christian Writers*, Westminster, Maryland & Longmans, London, 1946–.
> *Library of Christian Classics*, London, 1953–55.

A Select Library of Nicene and Post-Nicene Fathers, New York, 1887–1902. (Drawn from the Oxford and Edinburgh translations. Only additional translations have been indicated in the tables).

Selected Sermons have been translated as follows:

> *Sermons on Select Lessons of the New Testament*, Oxford, 1844–45.
> *Commentary on the Sermon on the Mount with seventeen related Sermons*, New York, 1951.
> *Sermons for Christmas and the Epiphany*, London, 1952.
> *Sermons 184–265*, New York, 1959.

Select Letters have been published as follows:

> Edinburgh, 1872–73 (fairly complete); London, 1919 (small selections only); London, 1953 (a larger collection but not by any means complete); New York, 1951– (this is to be a complete series).

N.B. Some of the translations listed in the chronological table as published in London were published simultaneously in the United Kingdom and the United States of America.

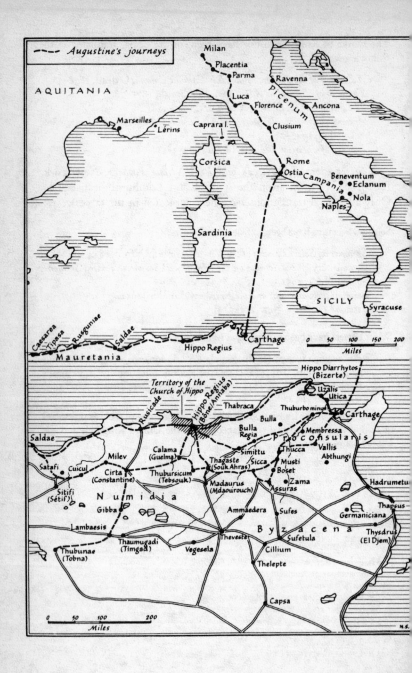

--- Augustine's journeys

AQUITANIA

Milan
Placentia
Parma
Ravenna
Picenum
Luca
Florence
Ancona
Clusium
Marseilles
Lérins
Caprara I.
Corsica
Rome
Ostia
Beneventum
Campania
Eclanum
Nola
Naples
Sardinia

SICILY
Syracuse

Caesarea
Tipasa
Rusguniae
Saldae
Hippo Regius
Carthage

Mauretania

0   50   100   150   200
Miles

Hippo Diarrhytos
(Bizerte)
Territory of the
Church of Hippo
Rusicade
Hippo Regius
(Bône/Annaba)
Uzalis
Utica
Thabraca
Thuburbo minus
Carthage
Saldae
Bulla
Membressa
Milev
Calama
(Guelma)
Bulla
Regia
Proconsularis
Satafi
Cuicul
Cirta
(Constantine)
Thubursicum
(Tebsouk)
Simittu
Thucca
Vallis
Abthungi
Thagaste
(Souk Ahras)
Sicca
Musti
Sitifi
(Sétif)
Numidia
Madaurus
(Mdaourouch)
Boset
Zama
Assuras
Hadrumetu
Gibba
Ammaedera
Sufes
Germaniciana
Thapsus
Lambaesis
Theveste
Byzacena
Thysdrus
(El Djem)
Thubunae
(Tobna)
Thaumugadi
(Timgad)
Vegesela
Sufetula
Cillium
Thelepte
Capsa

0   50   100   200
Miles

N.S.

I

AFRICA[1]

W hen Augustine was born there, in 354, the town of
Thagaste (modern Souk Ahras, in Algeria) had existed
for 300 years. It was one of the many nuclei of egregious
self-respect, which the Romans had scattered all over
North Africa: it called itself 'the most resplendent' council of
Thagaste.[2]

Since the first century B.C., an 'economic miracle' had transformed
the hinterland of North Africa.[3] Never again would prosperity be
extended so effectively over so wide an area. By the third century A.D.,
the high plains and valleys of the plateau — the old Numidia — where
Augustine was born, had been planted with grain, criss-crossed with
roads, settled with towns. Even farther south, beyond the Aures
mountains, a chain of forts guarded the boundary between intensive
cultivation and its absence, on the very edge of the Sahara. In that age
of affluence, the inhabitants of one area, of Thysdrus, the modern
El-Djem, had set up in the middle of the open plain, an amphitheatre
almost the size of the Colosseum at Rome; but the most typical
memorial of this 'boom' period comes from an inscription at Timgad,
a town far to the south of Thagaste, in what are now the desolate
highlands of southern Algeria: 'The hunt, the baths, play and laughter:
that's the life for me!'[4]

---

[1] P. Alfaric, *L'Évolution intellectuelle de S. Augustin*, 1918, is the most complete and
scientific account of Augustine's youth, and W. H. C. Frend, *The Donatist Church: a
movement of protest in Roman North Africa*, 1952, esp. pp. 25–75, is an outstanding study
of the African background of the age of Augustine.

[2] *Corpus Inscript. Lat.* VIII, 5145; 5146; 5150.

[3] v. esp. G. Ch.-Picard, *La civilisation de l'Afrique romaine*, 1959, pp. 45–102; cf. P. G.
Walsh, 'Massinissa', *Journ. Rom. Studies*, lv, 1965, pp. 151–155 (on the economic position
of pre-Roman Numidia).

[4] R. Cagnat, *Carthage, Timgad, Tébessa*, 1912, p. 70.

AFRICA

By the fourth century, the original expansion had come to a sinister halt. Schemes for building had stopped, the old public monuments had begun to crumble, 'shanty-towns' as chaotic as the winding lanes of the bazaars of an Arab town, had come to press in around the chequer-board avenues of the old Roman cities. The wealth of Africa had moved away from its former centres. Instead, forests of olive-trees had come to cover the hillsides of southern Numidia. Augustine could work all night in Africa, his lamp stocked with plentiful supplies of the coarse African oil: it was a comfort he would miss during his stay in Italy.[1] This oil came from little men, from villages which lacked the swagger of the Roman towns. These sturdy planters, suspicious of the outside world, living in tight-knit communities, whose habits had changed little since pre-historic times, had become the arbiters of the prosperity of Africa: 'Here lies Dion, a pious man; he lived 80 years and planted 4000 trees.'[2]

Augustine's Thagaste was perched on a plateau at the edge of this new Africa. It was administered from Carthage; but it had belonged to the old kingdom of Numidia. Our imaginations are dominated by the Africa of Carthage, the Africa of the Mediterranean coast. Augustine, however, grew up 200 miles from the sea, and 2,000 feet above it, cut off from the Mediterranean by great forests of pine, by high valleys of corn and olives. As a boy, he could only imagine what the sea was like by looking into a glass of water.[3]

This was a world of farmers. A town was a symbol of civilization; it was not a unit distinct from the countryside. For all their pride, these little Romes would have had populations of only a few thousand, living off the land in exactly the same way as the present inhabitants of a Spanish *pueblo* or a S. Italian township. It was on the land that the pleasures of life were sought by those who could afford them. On mosaics we can see the great country-houses of the African Romans: two-storied villas, surrounded by paddocks, fishponds, ornamental groves of cypresses. Their owners are shown, in the flowing robes of the age, hunting on horseback, and receiving the obeisance of a subservient peasantry. These men were the *patroni*, the 'protectors' of their community, in town and country alike. As they strode through the forum with their great retinues, the poor man was well-advised to rise and bow deeply to his lord.[4]

Misery also went with the land: the misery of 'bent backs', near

[1] *C. Acad.* I, iii, 6.
[2] *Inscriptions latines de la Tunisie*, no. 243; v. esp. Frend, *Donatist Church*, pp. 38–47.
[3] *Ep.* 7, iii, 6.   [4] *Enarr. in Ps.* 39, 28.

starvation, brutality like that of Tsarist Russia. A decade before Augustine's birth, Southern Numidia had witnessed a peasants' revolt, tinged, significantly, with a combative form of Christianity. Augustine, as a respectable member of a Roman town, was shielded from this misery. Indeed, as a schoolmaster, and later as a bishop, he was one of a very small class of men who had no direct contact with the land: he could even afford to talk nostalgically about gardening, to regard agriculture as 'bracing exercise'.[1] Tied to his desk in later years, he could only harbour distant memories of the long days in which he had roamed this countryside, hunting birds.[2]

To be a full member of a Roman town, Augustine had to be free and civilized: he did not have to be rich. His father, Patricius, was a poor man, a *tenuis municeps*, a burgess of slender means.[3] Augustine will grow up in a hard, competitive world, among proud and impoverished gentlefolk. A classical education was one of the only passports to success for such men; and he narrowly avoided losing even this. His early life will be overshadowed by the sacrifices his father made to give him this vital education: Patricius and his family had to go poorly-dressed;[4] he had to scrape; for one disastrous year Augustine found himself condemned to give up his studies at a pleasant 'university-town' at Madaura (or Madauros: modern Mdaourouch) to run wild in primitive Thagaste.[5] His cousins were less fortunate: they remained without a proper education;[6] and would have to face the poverty and boredom of a narrow world of unlettered squireens.

Yet Patricius could claim, perhaps as a relative, the patronage of a local grandee, Romanianus.[7] Romanianus would go frequently to Italy to defend his property at the Imperial court. He would return to Thagaste to show his power by giving wild-beast shows, and by patronizing young men such as Augustine. He would receive speeches and statues from his fellow-townsmen. He could expect titles and administrative positions from the Emperor.[8] In the very fluid world of the fourth century, luck and talent could close the gap between a Patricius and a Romanianus. By 385, Augustine will be a professor of rhetoric in Milan; he will be in a position to toy with the prospect of a rich heiress and a provincial governorship.[9] At that time he might well have reflected, as another successful African of his age had done: 'I grew up in the country, the son of a poor, uneducated father: in my

---

[1] *de Gen. ad litt.* VIII, viii, 15–18.   [2] *de quant. anim.* xxi, 36.   [3] *Conf.* II, iii, 5.
[4] *Serm.* 356, 3.   [5] *Conf.* II, iii, 5.   [6] *de beata vita*, i, 6.
[7] v. esp. *C. Acad.* II, i, 3 and Alfaric, *L'Évolution*, p. 7.   [8] *C. Acad.* I, i, 2.
[9] *Conf.* VI, xi, 19.

time, I have come, through my pursuit of literature, to live the life of a nobleman.'[1]

For men like Patricius and Romanianus did not think of themselves as 'Romans' for nothing. It is most unlikely that Augustine spoke anything but Latin. Between the exclusively Latin culture into which he had been so successfully educated, and any pre-existing 'native' tradition, there stretched the immeasurable qualitative chasm, separating civilization from its absence. What was not Roman in Africa, could only be thought of by such a man, in Roman terms. Augustine will use the word 'Punic' to describe the native dialects which most countrymen would have spoken exclusively, and which many townsmen shared with Latin. This was not because such men spoke the language of the ancient Carthaginians. Rather Augustine, an educated man, would instinctively apply this, the traditional, undifferentiated term, to any language spoken in North Africa that did not happen to be Latin.[2]

Yet, even the fully Latinized African of the fourth century remained somewhat alien. The opinion of the outside world was unanimous. Africa, in their opinion, was wasted on the Africans.[3]

In the days of their swaggering affluence in the second and third centuries, Roman culture had taken a significantly different turn in their hands. They strike us as 'Baroque' rather than classical men.[4] The gifted African for instance, delighted in the sheer play of words, in puns, rhymes and riddles: as a bishop, Augustine will be hugely admired by his congregation, for being superbly able to provide a display of verbal fireworks.[5] Such a man needed controversy. He throve on self-justification. He aimed to impress his fellows by eccentric turns of phrase, by vivid and far-fetched similes. At the age of seventy, this very African fire would still burn strong in Augustine: an opponent

[1] Aurelius Victor, *de Caesaribus*, XX, 5; v. the most interesting study of K. M. Hopkins, 'Social Mobility in the Later Roman Empire: the evidence of Ausonius', *Classical Quarterly*, n.s., 11, 1961, pp. 239–248.

[2] On this very difficult subject, v. the arguments of W. H. C. Frend, 'A note on the Berber background in the life of Augustine', *Journ. Theol. Studies*, xliii, 1942, pp. 188–191; Chr. Courtois, 'S. Augustin et la survivance de la punique', *Revue africaine*, 94, 1950, pp. 239–282; M. Simon, 'Punique ou berbère?', *Annuaire de l'Inst. de Philol. et d'Histoire Orientales et Slaves*, xiii, 1955, pp. 613–629 (=*Recherches d'Histoire Judéo-Chrétienne*, 1962, pp. 88–100); and the useful remarks of Picard, *La civilisation de l'Afrique*, pp. 393–395.

[3] *Totius orbis descriptio*, 62, ed. Müller, *Geographi Graeci minores*, 1861, p. 527.

[4] v. esp. the brilliant characterisation of Picard, *La civilisation de l'Afrique*, ch. VI, Le Baroque africain, pp. 291–353.

[5] Christine Mohrmann, 'S. Augustin écrivain', *Rech. augustin.*, i, 1958, pp. 43–66, esp. pp. 61–65.

had seemed to concede a point out of sheer embarrassment. 'Why, it looks as if your very ink had turned to rouge!'[1] The mosaics such men commissioned were bright, full of minutely observed details of daily life, a little grotesque.[2] Men like these could write novels: an unfailing eye for detail, for the picaresque, and an interest in the stirrings of the heart have ensured that the only two books of Latin literature that a modern man can place with ease beside the fiction of today were written by Africans — the *Golden Ass* of Apuleius and . . . *The Confessions* of Augustine. Augustine had been encouraged to weep gloriously at the tale of Dido and Aeneas, a very African interlude in the life of the upright founder of Rome;[3] and it is an African poet who will rectify the omissions of Vergil by writing the love letters of the deserted queen.[4]

The great African writers, however, were sudden meteors. The average African was more notorious as a lawyer. Augustine might have become one: 'that's a great thing, to have eloquence wielding great power, to have clients hanging on every word of the well-turned speech of their protector, pinning their hopes on his mouth. . . .'[5] Like the litigious country-gentlemen of the Elizabethan age, the 'good farmer' in Africa had, also, to be 'skilled in the law of the courts';[6] and, as among the Elizabethans, a dry, fierce legalism, a passionate dedication to manipulating the public forms of life by argument in the courtroom, was an effective complement, in the many, to fantasy and sensibility in the few. At exactly the same time, the leaders of the Christian church in Africa had imported this vigorous growth into their own controversies. A legal culture, hard-headed and relentless, had proliferated in its new clerical environment. Viewed by an Italian bishop who knew him well and heartily disliked his theology, Augustine was merely the latest example of an all-too-familiar figure, the *Poenus orator*, 'the African man of law'.[7]

Augustine, however, decided that he would rather be a schoolmaster. In this also, the Africans had shown their characteristic gusto. They worshipped education: simple men would cover their tombs with

---

[1] *C. Jul.* III, xiii, 26.

[2] A. Audollent, *Carthage romaine*, 1901, p. 665; J. Leclercq, 'Prédication et rhétorique au temps de S. Augustin', *Revue bénédictine*, lvii, 1947, pp. 117–131, esp. p. 126, notices identical qualities in an African sermon.

[3] *Conf.* I, xiii, 20.

[4] *Epistula Didonis ad Aeneam*, ed. Baehrens, *Poetae Latini Minores*, IV, pp. 271–277.

[5] *Enarr. in Ps.* 136, 3.

[6] Gsell and Joly, *Khamissa, Mdaourouch, Announa: I, Khamissa*, p. 29.

[7] *Op. Imp.* I, 48.

inscriptions in bad verse; the grandson of a Moorish soldier would boast that he was now 'a professor of Roman letters'; another had called himself 'the Cicero' of his little town. In Africa, Roman education had meant status for a crowd of little men. It was an atmosphere hostile to genuine talent. In Aquitaine and Upper Egypt, the fourth and fifth centuries were marked by sudden 'explosions' of literary talent.[1] In Africa, by contrast, the dust of erudition settled heavily on innumerable classical text-books, written by African professors.[2] Such men could pronounce '*homo*' correctly;[3] one would write a book on '*The Marriage of Mercury and Philology*'; another would prove his superiority to Augustine by taking him to task for writing 'Donatist' when the educated man said 'Donatian'.[4] Somehow, the superabundant energies of the second and third centuries had come to a halt: the Africa of the fourth century had become a stagnant and affluent backwater.[5]

In Thagaste at least, these sons of a dour and impoverished petty gentry would stick together, in their early life, in a common pursuit of advancement. Behind the single biography of Augustine we can also glimpse this 'collective biography' — the destinies of a remarkable group of young men determined to escape the inertia of a small African town. Many such friends were to stick together throughout their lives; the clique of earnest students was to become, in their middle age, a formidable group of bishops, controlling the destinies of the Catholic church in Africa. *Dulcissimus concivis*: 'my dearest friend, a fellow-townsman',[6] this phrase, used by Augustine as a bishop, will carry the ancient language of Roman public life into the new world of the Catholic hierarchy.

Yet, in the generation of Augustine, these old patterns were failing to satisfy men. The rich landowner, the adventurous student, the litigious bishop still had to 'sail away' to Italy from time to time: *navigare* is a constant theme in Augustine's works.[7] But they would not find their ambitions so easily satisfied. All the ambitious young men of

---

[1] e.g. Alan Cameron, 'Wandering Poets: a literary movement in Byzantine Egypt', *Historia*, xiv, 1965, pp. 470–509.

[2] *de util. cred.* vii, 17. [3] *Conf.* I, xviii, 29. [4] *C. Crescon.* II, i, 2.

[5] B. H. Warmington, *The North African Provinces from Diocletian to the Vandal Conquest*, 1954, p. 111. Against this negative judgement, we should set the high quality of the inherited resources of Roman Africa, shown, above all, in the mosaic-work (v. E. Marec, *Libyca*, i, 1953, 95–108) and in the resilience of pagan erudition (v. inf. pp. 300–302). For a significant revival of 'native' art-forms, v. W. H. C. Frend, 'The Revival of Berber Art', *Antiquity*, 1942, pp. 342–352.

[6] *Ep.* 84, 1.

[7] e.g. *Epp.* 21, 5 and 220, 4; *Serm.* 107, 8.

Thagaste will return to spend the rest of their lives in a thoroughly provincial setting, as the bishops of small African towns. For the Emperors had no need for the services of these Southerners. They had to stand guard over a threatened Northern frontier. Their court moved with the armies between Gaul, Northern Italy and the Danubian provinces. Africa, for them, was merely a reliable source of taxes, the heavily-administered granary of Rome. The men of Thagaste, Romanianus and his little band of clients, would find themselves not wanted: like the Anglo-Irish of the late eighteenth century, these representatives of a highly-civilized and prosperous society found themselves condemned to see their country sink to the state of a mere 'colony', administered by strangers from across the sea.[1]

Times had changed. In the fourth century the Roman Empire was facing the strain of perpetual warfare.[2] It was the prey of barbarian warbands in the North, challenged by the well-organized and militaristic kingdom of Persia in the East. The Emperors patrolled its frontiers at the head of regiments of heavy cavalry. They were acclaimed, with an enthusiasm that mounted with every disaster, as 'the Ever-Victorious', 'the Restorers of the World'. Taxation had doubled, even trebled, within living memory. The poor were victimized by an insane inflation. The rich defended themselves by unparalleled accumulations of property. The Emperor himself became a remote and awe-inspiring figure. His edicts were written in gold on purple paper; they were received with reverently covered hands, 'adored', and usually, circumvented. His servants could only rule by terror. A self-respecting man such as Patricius, coming from a class accustomed to being the unquestioned leaders of their locality, would find himself dwarfed by the great *nouveaux riches* and bullied by Imperial officials. He would have been threatened by the most ominous symptom of all in a civilized society: by a spectacular brutalization of the penal law. He could be flogged. An offence against the Emperor or his servants might bring ruin on a whole community of respectable burghers: it might leave them maimed by torture, reduced to the ranks of the beggars by crippling fines.[3]

Yet, as so often happens, this world on the edge of dissolution, had settled down to believe that it would last forever. The Jeremiahs of the declining Roman Empire will appear only in Augustine's old age; one cannot but be struck by the optimism of the men of Augustine's

---

[1] v. Warmington, *The North African Provinces*, pp. 106–108.
[2] v. esp. A. H. M. Jones, *The Later Roman Empire*, 1964 (3 vols.).
[3] *Ep.* 103, 3–4.

youth. Inscriptions in Africa will talk of 'golden times everywhere',[1] of 'the youthful vigour of the Roman name'.[2] A Christian bishop will regard Christianity and Roman civilization as coterminous: as if any Christian virtue could exist among the barbarians![3] A poetic administrator could write that Rome 'by living long has learnt to scorn finality'.[4] Rome, indeed, was still the 'Middle Kingdom'. For as in ancient China, educated men knew of no other civilized state. The Roman Empire was still upheld by the unquestioning loyalty of a class resembling the 'Mandarins' of Imperial China, by cultivated senators and bureaucrats whose ranks the young Augustine hoped to join.

Yet it is exactly in this aspect of Roman life that the most profound change of all had happened. The old patterns of Roman civilized life no longer entirely satisfied the cultivated man. They would even dress differently. The impeccable Roman toga, for instance, would still appear on statues of officials and great men. But the great men themselves would have worn a dress as flamboyant as any worn in the Arabian Nights: a tight tunic reaching down to the knees, heavily-embroidered at the hems; bright stockings; a huge cloak pinned above the right shoulder with a clasp of barbarian origin, its billowing silk sewn with gold thread, decorated with panels of colour appropriate to the rank of the wearer, or with figures, with flying dragons, and in the case of pious Christians, with scenes from the Bible. Nor would they have lived in the houses of the past, built foursquare around a court-yard; but in intricate palaces, bright with inlaid marble and rainbow-coloured mosaics, built from the inside out, to convey by their arcades, by halls on different levels, domed ceilings and a proliferation of heavy curtains, a new sense of privacy and opulent mystery. The expressions of Late Roman men, on their statues, often betray the most far-reaching change of all. These are no longer realistic portraits: their upraised eyes and immobile, lengthened features, show a preoccupation with the other world, with the inner life, that we would associate more readily with a Romanesque saint.

For the young Augustine, the traditional life will be only a veneer. At the height of his career as a professor of classical rhetoric, part of him at least, will listen to the teachings of Mani, a Persian visionary. His life will be changed by reading the works of Plotinus: a philosopher

[1] *Année épigraphique*, 1911, no. 217.
[2] J. M. Reynolds and J. B. Ward-Perkins, *The Inscriptions of Roman Tripolitania*, (British School at Rome), p. 134 no. 475.
[3] Optatus of Milevis, *de schism. Don.* II, 3 (P. L. xi, 1000A).
[4] Prudentius, *C. Symmachum*, II, 660.

'(who) seemed ashamed of being in the body'.[1] A great pagan senator, Praetextatus, will speak of his traditional Roman titles as 'bankrupt', of his mystical initiations as 'true blessedness'.[2]

Ambrose, sent to Milan as a Roman governor, will be ordained there as its Catholic bishop. Another nobleman, Paulinus, will suddenly disappear from the sheltered life of Aquitaine, to become a monk, leaving his friend, the old professor, Ausonius, puzzled. These incidents are omens for Augustine's future; he will be a traditional schoolmaster for eleven years of his life; a monk and a bishop for the remaining forty-four. As S. Jerome wrote of a small child in this new age: 'In such a world Pacatula has been born. Disasters surround her as she plays. She will know of weeping before laughter. . . . She forgets the past; she flees the present; she awaits with eagerness the life to come.'[3]

[1] Porphyry, *On the Life of Plotinus*, 1, (transl. S. MacKenna, *Plotinus: The Enneads*, 2nd ed. 1956, p. 1).

[2] *Corpus Inscript. Lat.* VI, 1779.

[3] Jerome, *Ep.* 128, 5.

2

MONICA

There is always something challenging about the way in which Augustine looked at things, and not least for his biographer. For his own masterpiece is an autobiography, the *Confessions*, which he wrote at the age of about 43, when he had become bishop of Hippo. This covers the first thirty-three years of his life. It is from this one book, that we gain most of what we know about Augustine's early youth. Yet no book undermines with such great artistry, the assumptions of a conventional biography. Augustine makes plain, throughout the *Confessions*, that the evolution of the 'heart' is the real stuff of autobiography;[1] and, viewed from this standpoint of the heart, much of the surface detail which a historian would demand of Augustine's youth, sinks into the background. When a young man, for instance, he lost a friend. We do not even know the name of this friend: what we do know is that 'My heart grew dark with grief, and wherever I looked, I saw only death. My own town became a torment to me and my own home a grotesque abode of misery. All we had done together was now a grim ordeal without him. My eyes searched everywhere for him, but he was not to be seen. I hated all places we had been together, because he was not in them, and they could no longer whisper to me "Here he comes!".'[2]

Yet when he considers a detail relevant to this analysis of the 'heart', Augustine will fasten upon it with astonishing perceptiveness. He saw no reason why men should forget how they had first behaved as babies. His parents had evidently palmed him off with pious stereotypes; so the middle-aged bishop would look for himself.[3] What he saw was not a 'little innocent': he had thrown himself on the breast with disturbing greed; he had exploded with anger whenever he failed to communicate his wishes; 'It is the physical weakness of a baby that makes it seem

[1] v. inf. p. 170.   [2] *Conf*. IV, iv, 9.   [3] *Conf*. I, vi, 8.

"innocent", not the quality of its inner life. I myself have seen a baby jealous: it was too young to speak, but it was livid with anger as it watched another baby at the breast.'[1] Yet he will also observe moments of unclouded bliss: 'I was made welcome into this world by the comfort of a woman's milk. . . . It was a good experience for them, that I drew so much good from them. . . . Later, I began to laugh: first, in my sleep, then, when I was awake.'[2] The *Confessions* is speckled in this way, with patches of warm light.

Yet we only know from passing references in the *Confessions* and from other works, that Augustine had at least one brother, Navigius, perhaps two sisters, and that his mother, Monica, must have been 23 when he was born. What Augustine remembered in the *Confessions* was his inner life; and this inner life is dominated by one figure — his mother, Monica.

Few mothers can survive being presented to us exclusively in terms of what they have come to mean to their sons, much less to a son as complicated as Augustine. The relationship between mother and son that weaves in and out of the *Confessions*, forms the thread for which the book is justly famous. Yet it takes two to make such a relationship. What Augustine says about Monica throws as much light on his own character as on that of his mother; and what he says is less important than the way in which he says it. Occasionally, we glimpse a genuinely impressive woman — very much what her son would have liked himself to be, as a bishop: restrained, dignified, above gossip, a firm peace-maker among her acquaintances, capable, like her son, of effective sarcasm.[3] She had been austerely brought up in a Christian family:[4] she clung to traditional practices in the African church, that educated men had always dismissed as 'primitive', to Sabbath fasts,[5] and meals at the tombs of the dead.[6] Yet she may not have been an entirely simple soul: she believed, for instance, that a good classical education, though pagan, would eventually make her son a better Christian.[7] Above all, she was a woman of deep inner resources: her certainties were unnerving; the dreams by which she foresaw the course of her son's life were impressive, and she was confident that she could tell, instinctively, which of these dreams were authentic.[8]

Yet, the balanced picture of Monica which Augustine provides in Book Nine of his *Confessions*, dissolves during most of the early books.

[1] *Conf.* I, vii, 11.   [2] *Conf.* I, vi, 7–8; cf. *de pecc. mer.* I, xxxv–xxxvii, 65–68.
[3] *Conf.* IX, ix, 21.   [4] *Conf.* IX, ix, 19.
[5] *Epp.* 36, xiv, 32 and 54, ii, 3; v. Frend, *Journ. Theol. Studies*, n.s., xv, 1964, p. 414.
[6] *Conf.* VI, ii, 2.   [7] *Conf.* II, iii, 8.   [8] *Conf.* VI, xiii, 23.

In Augustine's description of his early life, Monica appears, above all, as a relentless figure: 'She loved to have me with her, as is the way with mothers, but far more than most mothers.'[1] Whenever one of her sons went astray, 'She acted as if she was undergoing again the pangs of child-birth.'[2] This all-absorbing mother, deeply injured by her son's rebellions, is the Monica we usually see through Augustine's eyes. At the age of 28, a successful and conscientious young man, he will trick his mother by slipping off at night, to sail away to Rome, rather than face the guilt of leaving her behind: 'I have no words', he wrote, 'to express the love she had for me, and with how much more anguish she was now suffering the pangs of child-birth for my spiritual state than when she had given birth to me physically. I just cannot see how she could have been healed if my death in sin had come to pierce the entrails of her love.'[3] 'If the souls of the dead took part in the affairs of the living, if it was really they themselves who spoke to us, when we see them in our sleep . . . then my pious mother would not fail to visit me every night, that mother who followed me over land and sea that she might live with me.'[4]

Later Augustine realized that there had been an element of 'un-spiritual desire'[5] in Monica's devouring love for him: but, for all that, she had always been right; she had been the voice of God in his early life;[6] and he had never brought himself to say a hard word to her[7] — not even, that is, when she banned him from her house when he was a Manichaean heretic, or when, as a result of her arrangements, he found himself forced to part from a woman, with whom he had lived for fifteen years.

By contrast, Augustine's father, Patricius, is lost to us. Augustine, a man of many significant silences, will pass him over coldly. He was generous but 'hot tempered'.[8] Patricius had been immoderately proud of his son: he was admired by all for the sacrifices he made to complete Augustine's education.[9] Augustine records a scene in the baths, in which his father had been delighted to find that his son had reached puberty.[10] All that the son will say, in return, is that 'he saw in me only hollow things'.[11] Patricius died just after he had scraped together enough money to send his brilliant boy to Carthage: Augustine, who will soon experience and express deep grief at the loss of a friend, will mention his father's death only in passing.[12]

---

[1] *Conf.* V, viii, 15.
[2] *Conf.* IX, ix, 22.
[3] *Conf.* V, ix, 16.
[4] *de cura ger. pro mort.* xiii, 16.
[5] *Conf.* V, viii, 15.
[6] e.g. *Conf.* II, iii, 7; III, xi, 19 and xii, 21.
[7] *Conf.* IX, xii, 30.
[8] *Conf.* IX, ix, 19.
[9] *Conf.* II, iii, 5.
[10] *Conf.* II, iii, 6.
[11] *Conf.* II, iii, 8.
[12] *Conf.* III, iv, 7.

What Augustine remembered most vividly about his parents, was a subterranean tension. Monica had the measure of Patricius. She would tell her friends, sarcastically, that they were, after all, the 'slave-girls' of their husbands: it was not for them to 'rise up against their lord and master'.[1] Patricius never beat her, as other husbands beat their wives: she would wait, without saying a word to provoke him, until his anger abated. Then she would explain how she had been right. Patricius was unfaithful to her: she again waited, in silence, until, sure enough, he became a Christian.[2] Augustine's childhood Christianity was part of this tension: 'I was a believer like all my household, except father: but he could not cancel in me the rights of my mother's piety. . . . For she tried earnestly, my God, that You should be my father, not him. . . .'[3]

By remarks such as these, Augustine has deservedly brought down upon his own head the attentions of modern psychological interpreters. It is, however, one thing to take due note of a blatant childhood tension, that was still very much alive in Augustine's mind as he wrote the *Confessions* in middle age; and it is quite another, to follow this tension through, from its roots in Augustine's childhood, throughout a long and varied life. The unexpected combinations, ramifications and resolutions that a properly sophisticated knowledge of modern psychology would lead us to expect, escape the historian.[4]

Both parents, however, had one quality in common: determination. Patricius showed 'pigheaded resolution' to get his son educated;[5] Monica will live for another nine years, equally convinced, in her way, that 'the son of such tears could not be lost'.[6] Augustine was able to make this quality his own. It is no mean achievement to have done so. We can see the result, above all, in the manner in which he hounded his ecclesiastical opponents, and stuck firmly to his own ideas: Patricius and Monica, one feels, were highly-suitable parents for a Catholic bishop in fourth-century Africa.

Altogether, Augustine will grow up among men whose personal relationships strike us as singularly vehement. The inhabitants of Thagaste would live out of doors, in public. A man who got on badly

---

[1] *Conf.* IX, ix, 19. [2] *Conf.* IX, ix, 19. [3] *Conf.* I, x, 17.
[4] The studies known to me, notably B. Legewie, *Augustinus: Eine Psychographie*, 1925, E. R. Dodds, 'Augustine's Confessions: a study of spiritual maladjustment', *Hibbert Journal*, 26, 1927–1928, pp. 459–473, Rebecca West, *St. Augustine*, 1933 and C. Klegemann, 'A psychoanalytic study of the Confessions of St. Augustine', *Journal of the American Psychoanalytic Association*, v, 1957, pp. 469–484, show that it is as difficult as it is desirable to combine competence as an historian with sensitivity as a psychologist.
[5] *Conf.* II, iii, 5. [6] *Conf.* III, xii, 21.

with his wife, would spend all day in the forum, surrounded by friends and clients, his heart sinking, as the sun set and the time came for him to return home. 'I have enjoyed the clear sunlight for most of my days. . . . I was always pleasant to everybody; why should not everyone regret me?'[1]

This was a public life, in which a man was committed, above all, to maintaining his reputation: to 'live forever in the mouths of the people'[2] was the ambition of the successful African. Reading the inscriptions on their tombs, we realize that only Augustine, a Roman of Africa, could have thought, that a 'love of praise' had been sufficient to spur on the early Romans.[3] This public front was exceedingly fragile. Africans were expert at debunking their fellows. Augustine himself was a pastmaster of dry irony. Typical Africans, both Monica and Augustine's friend, Alypius, had their lives changed by a stray sarcasm that had suddenly deflated their immense sense of dignity.[4]

The life of a small town could be rent by long and rancorous feuds. A man would blench with anger as he heard the word 'mine enemy' sung in the Psalms.[5] It is not surprising that 'envy' should be one of the emotions which Augustine understood most deeply. We can appreciate its power among his fellow-Africans through scores of amulets against the evil eye.[6]

Exceedingly prickly, these men were, also, ferociously loyal to each other. Augustine, as we shall see, will hardly ever spend a moment of his life without some friend, even some blood-relative, close by him. No thinker in the Early Church was so preoccupied with the nature of human relationships; but then, few environments would have impressed their importance upon Augustine so vividly as the close-knit world in which he had grown up.

The deeper patterns of the imagination of these men can be seen in their religious beliefs. The Numidian inhabitants of the plateaux were closely related to the modern Berbers, a group that has always maintained a distinctive way of life. The name of Monica even, may be an outcrop of the earlier beliefs of her family, derived as it is from a local deity, the goddess Mon.[7] Like the Carthaginians, the Numidians had never worshipped the humane Olympian gods of classical Greece and Rome. Their gods had been 'High-Gods', worshipped on holy moun-

---

[1] *Inscriptions latines de l'Algérie*, II, no. 820.

[2] Epitaph of Vincentius the dancer: *Libyca*, iii, 1955, pp. 103–121.

[3] v. esp. Picard, *La civilisation de l'Afrique*, pp. 249–254, for the attitudes shown on African tombstones.

[4] *Conf.* VI, vii, 12 and IX, viii, 18.

[5] *Serm.* 90, 9 and 254, 4.

[6] Frend, *Donatist Church*, pp. 102–103.

[7] Frend, *Donatist Church*, p. 230.

tains, close relatives, through the Phoenicians, of the awesome Jehovah. The High God of Africa was Saturn: a 'Supreme Father', a 'Holy One', an 'Eternal One'. His religion was a religion of fear, of sacrificial atonement, of ritual purity. He sent his commands in dreams. Altogether, he was an exacting, ill-defined father, called, in reverent dread, 'The Old Man'. In Carthage, however, this terrifying father was eclipsed by a great, feminine deity, the *Dea Caelestis*, the 'Goddess of Heaven'; an all-absorbing, maternal figure, to whom even Christian parents wisely dedicated their children.[1]

The religion of the Christians in Africa, was also drastic. Ecstatic experiences were sought by drunkenness, chanting and wild dances.[2] Alcoholism, indeed, was widespread in the African congregations.[3] Dreams and trances were common:[4] simple peasants would lie for days in a coma;[5] and Monica, as we have seen, placed great reliance on her dreams.[6] These dreams were thought of as direct glimpses of another world, a world that pressed in, quite physically, to direct and inspire men in their sleep:[7] such dreams were 'great' dreams, particularly concerned with fearsome combats.[8] For two generations, the majority of African Christians had rallied to a caste of 'pure' bishops, rejecting the outside world as 'unclean': a group of their adherents were notorious for a combination of aggression against outsiders, and traditions of ritual suicide among themselves.[9] Equally drastic, Augustine and his friends found it easy to believe, for the time they were Manichees, that their bodies were split between absolute good and uncontrollable evil.[10]

It is easy to be glib about this 'African temperament'.[11] But it would be superficial to ignore the strength of the harsh and exacting patterns of behaviour current in a provincial society. At the age of 30, such patterns will not affect Augustine. Then his early life had reached its zenith: he was a classical rhetorician at Milan; he intended to reside in Italy. He would have been like a Westernized Russian in the nineteenth century, established in Paris. But he will soon return home to spend

[1] v. esp. J. Toutain, *Les cultes paiens dans l'Empire romain*, III, 1920, pp. 15–37.
[2] e.g. Frend, *Donatist Church*, pp. 174–175.   [3] e.g. *Serm.* 151, 4.
[4] e.g. *de Gen. ad litt.* XII, xvii, 35–38.   [5] *de Gen. ad litt.* XII, ii, 4.
[6] e.g. *Conf.* III, xi, 19 and VI, xiii, 15.
[7] *de Gen. ad litt.* X, xxv, 41–43. v. esp. P. Courcelle, *Les Confessions de S. Augustin dans la tradition littéraire: Antécédents et Posterité*, 1963, pp. 127–132.
[8] e.g. *Passio Maximiani et Isaac* (P.L. viii, 779–780).
[9] v. Frend, *Donatist Church*, pp. 172–176.
[10] v. inf. p. 50.
[11] v. the sound remarks of Picard, *La civilisation de l'Afrique*, pp. 293–297.

the rest of his life as a recluse, then as a priest, and later a bishop, among simple men in Africa: like the 'Holy Russia' of the nineteenth century, this world will close in around him; and, as is very often the case with educated men, it will close in all the more effectively for having once been rejected.

3

EDUCATION

Augustine grew up a sensitive boy, acutely anxious to be accepted, to compete successfully, to avoid being shamed, terrified of the humiliation of being beaten at school.[1] He would play in the fields around Thagaste. There he stalked birds,[2] watched the writhing tails torn off lizards;[3] he thought of thunder as the rattling of the heavy wheels of Roman coaches on the rough flagstones of the clouds.[4] Yet Augustine never mentions the wonderful spring flowers of Africa. His sense of smell was not particularly acute.[5] Mountains appear more often in his works: the light of the rising sun slipping down into the valleys;[6] the sudden view of a distant town from the wooded slopes of a pass.[7] Above all, he was surrounded by light. The African sunlight was the 'Queen of all Colours pouring down over everything'.[8] He was acutely alive to the effects of light. His only poem is in praise of the warm glow of the Easter Candle.[9]

There is, in all, little natural landscape around Augustine. Instead, there are faces: lively faces, with the great eyes of a Late Roman mosaic: eyes that betray the inner life of a man, hidden, except in them, by the heavy envelope of the flesh.[10] Above all, there will be many voices. Augustine's world is full of sounds: the chanting of the Psalms, songs at harvest time, and, most delightful of all, the entrancing speech of his fellow-men. 'Words, those precious cups of meaning'.[11] What is a good thing? 'The face of a man: regular features, a glowing complexion, a face lit up with good spirits'; and, of course, 'A speech, imparting its message with charm, well-tuned to touch the feelings of

---

[1] *Conf.* I, ix, 14. [2] *de quant. anim.* xxi, 36. [3] *de quant. anim.* xxxi, 62.
[4] *Enarr. in Ps.* 76, 20. [5] *Conf.* X, xxxii, 48. [6] *Enarr. in Ps.* 25, 9.
[7] *Conf.* VII, xxi, 27. [8] *Conf.* X, xxxiv, 51. [9] *de civ. Dei,* XV, 22.
[10] *de Gen. c. Man.* II, xxi, 32. [11] *Conf.* I, xvi, 26.

its hearers; the melodious rhythms and high sentiments of a good poem'.[1]

Augustine will be educated to become a master of the spoken word. The content of his education was barren. It was frankly pagan. It was surprisingly meagre: he would have read far fewer classical authors than a modern schoolboy. Vergil, Cicero, Sallust and Terence were the only authors studied in detail. It was exclusively literary: philosophy, science and history were, alike, ignored.[2] Its methods were, by modern standards, servile and myopic. It imposed a crushing load on the memory: a friend of Augustine's knew all Vergil and much of Cicero by heart.[3] The teacher would explain each text, word by word, much as an art-expert might pore over a painting with his magnifying-glass. It was quite impossible to teach a foreign language, such as Greek, by such methods. One shudders to think of the manner in which Homer must have been taught to Augustine in Thagaste. Augustine found that Greek bored him to distraction at just the same time as he had begun to 'revel' in the Latin Classics.[4] Augustine's failure to learn Greek was a momentous casualty of the Late Roman educational system: he will become the only Latin philosopher in antiquity to be virtually ignorant of Greek.[5] As a young man, he will set out, pathetically ill-equipped, on a traditional philosopher's quest for Wisdom. A cultivated Greek audience would have treated this exclusively Latin-speaking student from the university of Carthage as 'a dumb fool', acquainted as he was only 'with the opinions of Greek philosophers, or rather, with little snippets of these opinions, picked up, here and there, from the Latin dialogues of Cicero'; not 'with these philosophical systems as they stand, fully developed, in Greek books'.[6]

Yet the content of this education was not as important as its aim. This aim had remained unchanged for some 800 years. It was still being vigorously pursued in the fourth century, in the crowded, noisy school-rooms of the teachers of rhetoric,[7] as far apart as Bordeaux and Antioch: this was 'to learn the art of words, to acquire that eloquence that is essential to persuade men of your case, to unroll your opinions before them'.[8] The ideal product of this education was the orator, a man that is, who could 'give pleasure throughout his argument, by his vivacity,

---

[1] *de Trin.* VIII, iii, 4.

[2] Outstandingly the best studies are by H. I. Marrou, *S. Augustin et la fin de la culture antique* (1st ed. 1938), esp. pp. 1–104 and *History of Education in the Ancient World*, (transl. 1956).

[3] *de anim. et eius orig.* IV, vii, 9.   [4] *Conf.* I, xiii, 20.   [5] v. inf. pp. 271–273.

[6] *Ep.* 118, ii, 10.   [7] *de util. cred.* vii, 16.   [8] *Conf.* I, xvi, 26.

by the feelings at his command, by the ease with which words came to him, perfectly adapted to dress his message in style'.[1]

The great advantage of the education Augustine received was that, within its narrow limits, it was perfectionist. The aim was to measure up to the timeless perfection of an ancient classic. Vergil, for such people, had 'not only never made a mistake, but had never written a line that was not admirable'.[2] Every word, every turn of phrase of these few classics, therefore, was significant. The writer did not merely write: he 'wove' his discourse;[3] he was a man who had 'weighed the precise meaning of every word'.[4] We need only see how Augustine, as a bishop, will interpret the Bible as if everything in it were 'said exactly as it should be said',[5] to realize the lasting effect of such an education. Augustine will cite his new, Christian 'classic' 42,816 times (often from memory); he will choose every word he writes in a single short note:[6] he is a man who had been taught to manoeuvre, with infinite precision, in the cramped but supremely well-charted environment of an age-old tradition. Such a man could communicate his message to an educated Latin at the other end of the Roman world, merely by mentioning a classical figure, by quoting half a line of a classical poet.[7] It is not surprising that the group of men who had, by their education, come to conform so successfully to this rigidly-defined traditional standard of perfection, should have come, by the fourth century, to stand apart as a caste of their own. Despite the humble origins of many of them, a common mastery of Latin literature had raised this class 'above the common lot of men'[8] quite as effectively as that other class of 'superior men', the Mandarins of Imperial China.

Above all, this education would have taught Augustine to express himself. He was encouraged to weep, and to make others weep. He would win a prize at school for reliving, in an oration, the 'rage and pain' of Juno as she watched Aeneas sail from Carthage to Italy. 'What has that to do with me!', Augustine the bishop will write, at 43; 'Surely all this is so much smoke and wind'.[9] Yet, twenty years later he will still return to this, his first triumph: surely no one who knows his Vergil 'which we once read as boys, so that this great poet, held to be outstandingly the best, is absorbed at the earliest occasion', could fail to remember the scene.[10]

---

[1] *Conf*. V, vi, 11. [2] *de util. cred*. vi, 13. [3] *Conf*. XII, xxvi, 36.
[4] *de beata vita*, iv, 31. [5] v. inf. pp. 253 and 259–260.
[6] *de gest. Pel*. xxv, 51, explaining *Ep*. 146. [7] e.g. *Ep*. 40, iv, 7.
[8] pseudo-Jerome, *de virginitate*, 12 (P.L. xxx, 178A). [9] *Conf*. I, xvii, 27.
[10] *de civ. Dei*, I, 3.

EDUCATION

By the age of 15, Augustine had passed through the terrible floggings of his school at Thagaste. He had emerged as a gifted boy, driven hard by his parents, able to love what he was learning. He had developed, through this education, a phenomenal memory, a tenacious attention to detail, an art of opening the heart, that still moves us as we read his *Confessions*. At that time he was staying at Madaura. Madaura was a university-town with a distinctive atmosphere. It could boast the great Platonist and orator of the second century, Apuleius (known to us, above all, for his *Golden Ass*, but to Augustine as an eccentric philosopher who had dabbled in the black arts,[1] the author of '*On the God of Socrates*'.[2]) The teachers at Madaura were pagans: they loved the forum with its statues of the gods, as much as any College quadrangle;[3] they produced the greatest number of epitaphs in verse yet to be discovered in Roman Africa.[4]

By the next year, however, Augustine was back again at Thagaste. He had to wait for a year until Patricius had saved enough money to complete his education at Carthage.[5] This was a miserable year, marked by a disquieting act of vandalism,[6] and overshadowed by the sudden onslaught on an ambitious boy, who had hitherto been under constant pressure to succeed at school, of a belated adolescence.[7] The situation was made no easier by the 'enormous anxiety' with which Monica had warned him against dealings with women.[8] A son of less ambitious parents might have married at this age. Augustine will later blame Monica and Patricius (perhaps he felt resentful also at the time) for not having arranged a marriage to 'blunt the thorns'[9] of feelings that plainly distressed him greatly.

It is hardly surprising, therefore, that Augustine's arrival in Carthage, in 371, at the age of 17, should have been so memorable: 'I came to Carthage where the cauldron of illicit loves leapt and boiled around me'.[10] The cauldron was very much of Augustine's own boiling. Life was certainly more exciting in Carthage. The students were rowdy, as was only to be expected among boys who had come from little provincial towns all over Africa to their first experience of freedom in a big city. The freshmen and the teachers were terrorized by fraternities of 'old hands', the '*Eversores*'. Augustine, characteristically, was both shocked by their violence, and anxious to seem to 'belong' to them: for

---

[1] *Ep.* 138, iv, 19.   [2] as in *de civ. Dei*, books VIII and IX.   [3] *Ep.* 17, 2.
[4] Alfaric, *L'Évolution intellectuelle de S. Augustin*, pp. 13–15; Warmington, *The North African Provinces*, p. 104 and n. 1.
[5] *Conf.* II, iii, 5.   [6] *Conf.* II, iv, 9 sq.   [7] *Conf.* II, iii, 6.   [8] *Conf.* II, iii, 7.
[9] *Conf.* II, ii, 3.   [10] *Conf.* III, i, 1.

to be an '*Eversor*', an 'upsetter', was 'a notable way of being in the fashion'.[1]

Yet, the life of a big city meant little to Augustine compared with the long-delayed crisis of his adolescence. 'I was not yet in love, but I was in love with love, and, from the depths of my need, I hated myself for not more keenly feeling the need. . . . What I needed most was to love and to be loved; but most of all when I obtained the enjoyment of the body of the person who loved me. . . . I rushed headlong into love, eager to be caught. . . . Happily I wrapt those painful bonds around me; and, sure enough, I would be lashed with the red-hot iron rods of jealousy, by suspicions and fear, by bursts of anger and quarrels'.[2]

These were the days when Augustine could at last allow his feelings to luxuriate. He discovered the theatre: it was a world 'full of reflections of my own unhappiness, fuel to my raging fire'.[3] He loved, above all, to watch the parting of lovers: 'and I, an unhappy young man, loved to weep; and I went out of my way to find something to make me weep'.[4]

Yet within a year, all this was to change. Far from being the libertine that some authors have imagined, converted at the age of 32 from a life of unbridled sensuality, Augustine was, in reality, a young man who had cut the ebullience of his adolescence dangerously short. In the next two years, he clamped down firmly on his ebullient feelings. Patricius would die, probably at the end of Augustine's first year in Carthage: Monica will take over the strain of completing her son's education — another string to the heart.[5] Augustine will lapse into a 'second class' marriage at about this time. He will take a nameless woman as his concubine for the next 15 years: it was a perfectly respectable arrangement for a budding professor in the Later Empire.[6] He had, in this way, got what he wanted: he had, at last, been 'washed up on the shore of matrimony'.[7] Whether he particularly enjoyed the experience is another matter. Next, his son, Adeodatus, was born: this event, unwelcome at the time,[8] may well have had the 'sobering' effect which Augustine would later recommend to young husbands.[9]

Finally, at the age of 19, in 373, he will experience a profound change in his life: he will pass through his first religious 'conversion'.

[1] *Conf.* III, iii, 6.   [2] *Conf.* III, i, 1.
[3] *Conf.* III, ii, 2, v. Audollent, *Carthage romaine*, pp. 683–687, on the titles of such plays.
[4] *Conf.* III, ii, 4.   [5] *Conf.* III, iv, 7.   [6] v. inf. pp. 61–63.
[7] *Conf.* II, ii, 3.   [8] *Conf.* IV, ii, 3.   [9] *de bone coning.* iii, 3.

4

'WISDOM'

'In the usual course of the syllabus, I had reached a book by Cicero: its style was admired by almost all, though its message was ignored. This book, however, contains an exhortation to philosophy: it is called *"The Hortensius"*. This book, indeed, changed all my way of feeling. It changed my prayers to Thee, O Lord; it gave me entirely different plans and aspirations. Suddenly, all empty hope for my career lost its appeal; and I was left with an unbelievable fire in my heart, desiring the deathless qualities of Wisdom, and I made a start to rise up and return to Thee. . . . I was on fire, my God, on fire to fly away from earthly things to Thee'.[1]

For centuries now, the idea of philosophy had been surrounded with a religious aura. It involved far more than an intellectual discipline. It was a love of 'Wisdom'. 'Wisdom' would console and purify its devotees; it demanded, in return, self-sacrifice and moral readjustment. The wise man would realize who he was, where he stood in the universe, how that divine part of him, his rational soul, could transcend the lusts of his body and the illusory ambitions of daily life; for, as Cicero had said in his *Hortensius*, 'if the souls which we have are eternal and divine, we must conclude, that the more we let them have their head in their natural activity, that is, in reasoning and in the quest for knowledge, and the less they are caught up in the vices and errors of mankind, the easier it will be for them to ascend and return to Heaven'.[2] The exhortation to love 'Wisdom' had always been couched in such strongly religious terms. It is not surprising that by the fourth century, it had come to act as the bridgehead in traditional culture both

[1] *Conf.* III, iv, 7. The fundamental study of the role of Cicero in Augustine's evolution is M. Testard, *S. Augustin et Cicéron*, 2 vols. 1958; v. esp. i, pp. 20–35 for an excellent discussion of this incident.

[2] Cicero, *Hortensius*, fgt. 97 (*Opera*, IV, 3, ed. Müller, 1890, p. 325), cited by Augustine in *de Trin.* XIV, xix, 26.

for the idea of a religious conversion, and even of a conversion to a monastic life.[1]

Cicero had urged Augustine to seek Wisdom: 'I should not chase after this or that philosophical sect, but should love Wisdom, of whatever kind it should be; that I should search for it, follow hard upon it, hold on to it and embrace it with all my strength. That was what stirred me in that discourse, set me alight, and left me blazing'.[2]

The precise form of 'Wisdom' that Augustine might seek, would, of course, be very different from what Cicero would have recognized as 'Wisdom'. Augustine was a boy from a Christian household. In an age where only the writings of adults have survived, it is extremely difficult to grasp the nature of the 'residual' Christianity of a young man. One thing, however, was certain: a pagan wisdom, a wisdom without the 'name of Christ' was quite out of the question.[3] Paganism meant nothing to Augustine. In Carthage he will watch the great festivals that were still celebrated at the great temple of the Dea Caelestis: but he will do so in the manner of a Protestant Englishman witnessing the solemn Catholic processions of Italy — they were splendid and interesting; but they had nothing to do with religion as he knew it.[4] Moreover, Augustine grew up in an age where men thought that they shared the physical world with malevolent demons. They felt this quite as intensely as we feel the presence of myriads of dangerous bacteria. The 'name of Christ' was applied to the Christian like a vaccination. It was the only guarantee of safety. As a child, Augustine had been 'salted' to keep out the demons; when he had suddenly fallen ill, as a boy, he would plead to be baptized.[5] These Christian rites, of course, might influence a grown-up man's conduct as little as the possession of a certificate of vaccination; but they expressed a mentality that had cut off, as positively 'unhygienic', the pagan religion of the classical past.

In Carthage, Augustine had remained loyal to the Catholic church. He had already grown to love the solemn Easter vigils of the great basilicas.[6] A stranger from the provinces, he would, of course, go to church to find a girl-friend,[7] much as another stranger, the Genoese, Christopher Columbus, will meet his wife in Seville Cathedral.

Above all, the Christianity of the fourth century would have been presented to such a boy as a form of 'True Wisdom'. The Christ of the

---

[1] v. esp. A. D. Nock, *Conversion: the old and the new in religion from Alexander the Great to Augustine of Hippo*, 1933, pp. 164–186.
[2] *Conf.* III, iv, 8.   [3] *Conf.* III, iv, 8 and V, xiv, 25.   [4] *de civ. Dei*, II, 4, 14.
[5] *Conf.* I, x, 17.   [6] *C. Ep. Fund.* 8.   [7] *Conf.* III, iii, 5.

popular imagination was not a suffering Saviour. There are no cruci-
fixes in the fourth century. He was, rather, 'the Great Word of God,
the Wisdom of God.'[1] On the sarcophagi of the age, He is always
shown as a Teacher, teaching His Wisdom to a coterie of budding
philosophers. For a cultivated man, the essence of Christianity consisted in just this. Christ, as the 'Wisdom of God', had established a
monopoly in Wisdom: the clear Christian revelation had trumped and
replaced the conflicting opinions of the pagan philosophers; 'Here,
here is that for which all philosophers have sought throughout their
life, but never once been able to track down, to embrace, to hold
firm. . . . He who would be a wise man, a complete man, let him hear
the voice of God.'[2]

Augustine, therefore, turned, quite naturally, to the Bible, to find his
'Wisdom'.[3] It was a great disappointment. He had been brought up to
expect a book to be 'cultivated and polished':[4] he had been carefully-
groomed to communicate with educated men in the only admissible
way, in a Latin scrupulously modelled on the ancient authors.[5] Slang
and jargon were equally abhorrent to such a man; and the Latin Bible
of Africa, translated some centuries before by humble, nameless
writers, was full of both. What is more, what Augustine read in the
Bible seemed to have little to do with the highly spiritual Wisdom that
Cicero had told him to love. It was cluttered up with earthy and
immoral stories from the Old Testament;[6] and, even in the New Testament, Christ, Wisdom Himself, was introduced by long, and contra-
dictory, genealogies.[7]

Yet this Bible was the keystone of the Christian communities of
Africa. This African church was exceptionally narrow and conservative: many of its institutions and practices may have stemmed directly
from the Jewish synagogue; it was easy to regard the religion of its
congregations as a half-hearted compromise with the Old Testament.[8]
The bishops were exceptionally sensitive to any challenge to their
authority. This was not a vague authority 'in faith and morals', much
less was it the highly-sophisticated right to persuade and protect the
seeker after truth, that Augustine later would make of it; in the 370's,
as previously, the bishops' authority stemmed directly from their

[1] Serm. 279, 7.   [2] Lactantius, Divinae Institutiones, III, 30 (P.L. vi, 444–446).
[3] Conf. III, v, 9.   [4] Conf. III, iv, 8.
[5] v. esp. Christine Mohrmann, 'Le latin commun et le latin des chrétiens', Vigiliae
Christianae, 1, 1947, pp. 1–12, esp. pp. 1–3.
[6] Conf. III, vii, 12.   [7] e.g. Serm. 51, 5.
[8] v. C. Faust. XV, 1; v. esp. W. H. C. Frend, Martyrdom and Persecution in the Early
Church, 1965, p. 374.

possession of the 'Divine Law', the Scriptures, and from their duty to preserve and expound them. The Bible, in Africa, was the backbone of the Christian church, as rigid and demanding as the old Jewish Law, 'to alter one word of which must be accounted the greatest sacrilege.'[1] It was treated as a quarry for rigorous legal rulings; and to be a true Christian meant, quite simply, to accept this 'Law' in its entirety, without asking awkward questions.[2]

This oppressive environment had always tended to produce extreme reactions among some African Christians. A strong current of 'new', of 'spiritual' Christianity had always run against the massive literalism of the traditional church.[3] This 'new' Christianity had sloughed off the Old Testament as unspiritual and disgusting.[4] In such a Christianity, Christ did not need the witness of the Hebrew prophets: He spoke for Himself, directly to the soul, by His elevated message, by His Wisdom and His miracles.[5] God needed no other altar than the mind, particularly a mind such as the young Augustine's: 'A mind imbued with good arts and education.'[6]

These were the views of a group that had been particularly active among the half-Christian students and intelligentsia of Carthage.[7] Their missionaries were 'exceedingly well-spoken and fashionable'.[8] They enjoyed public debates, and could handle hecklers like accomplished Hyde Park orators.[9] Their demolition of the traditional Christian Scriptures was intelligent and persistent. They claimed, that 'putting aside the terror of authoritative commands to believe, they would lead all men who cared to hear them to God, and would free them from error, by a remarkably straightforward use of reason.'[10] Above all, they were a group of radical Christians.[11] To them, the Catholics were mere 'semi-Christians'.[12] Christ was a central figure in their system; and He appeared precisely as Augustine had been led to expect — as the principle of Wisdom *par excellence*.[13] This Christ enlightened men; He led them to a true knowledge of themselves; He had awoken Adam from his drunken slumber, to tell him precisely what

---

[1] *Acta Saturnini*, 18 (P.L. viii, 701B).   [2] v. inf. p. 218.

[3] This has been made particularly clear in the excellent study of W. H. C. Frend, 'The Gnostic-Manichaean tradition in Roman North Africa', *Journ. Eccles. Hist.* iv, 1953, pp. 13–26.

[4] *C. Faust.* IV, 1.   [5] *C. Faust.* XIII, 1.   [6] *C. Faust.* XX, 3.   [7] *de util. cred.* xiv, 32.

[8] *de util. cred.* i, 3.   [9] e.g. *C. Faust.* XXIII, 1.   [10] *de util. cred.* i, 2.

[11] The Manichees were more radical than the Gnostics, in that they originally claimed to be superior to Christianity, not merely to be the holders of the esoteric traditions of Christianity: v. esp. A. Böhlig, 'Christliche Wurzeln im Manichäismus', *Bull. de la soc. d'archéologie copte*, xv, 1960, pp. 41–61.

[12] *C. Faust.* I, 1.   [13] *C. Faust.* XX, 1–2.

Cicero would have told him in more classical terms: that is, that his soul was divine.[1] 'This name, Jesus, grace surrounds it.'[2] 'He came, He separated us from the Error of the World; He brought us a mirror, we looked, we saw the Universe in it.'[3]

These men were known as the Manichees. Their founder had been Mani, 'The Apostle of Jesus Christ.' Mani had received an inspired message in Mesopotamia, and had been executed, in 276 A.D., by the Persian government.[4] The spread of Mani's religion into the Christian Roman world is a remarkable symptom of the religious turmoil of the age. The later expansion of Manichaeism towards the Far East is even more astonishing.[5] By the 8th century A.D., a Manichaean state existed on the borders of the Chinese empire,[6] and, later, in the prosperous oasis of Turfan, linking Persia and the West with China. In Turfan, the Manichees left great monasteries, frescoes showing Mani and his austere followers, precious manuscripts whose miniatures show Manichaean rituals, known to us previously only from the works of Augustine.[7] In the thirteenth century, there were still Manichees in Fu-Kien.[8] Some of the most revealing Manichaean documents yet discovered are written in Chinese.[9]

The Manichaean missionaries had received from their founder a direct revelation of the true nature of God, of man, and of the universe, committed to great books — like Muhammad and the Koran. Mani had sent them forth to found the only truly universal church. Only they could teach a Wisdom that combined and transcended the partial and slipshod intuitions of all previous 'sects' — of the Christian

[1] *de Haeres.* 46, 5.

[2] Allberry, *Manichaean Psalmbook*, p. 185, 20.

[3] Allberry, *Manichaean Psalmbook*, p. 9. v. esp. J. Ries, 'Jésus-Christ dans la religion de Mani Quelques éléments d'une confrontation de saint Augustin avec un hymnaire christologique manichéen copte', *Augustiniana*, 14, 1964, pp. 437–454.

[4] H. C. Puech, *Le Manichéisme: son fondateur, sa doctrine* (Musée Guimet. Bibliothèque de diffusion, lvi), 1949, is outstandingly the best evaluation of Manichaeism. G. Widengren, *Mani and Manichaeism* (transl. Kessler), 1965, is more circumstantial, but less reliable. Chr. Baur, *Das manichäische Religionssystem*, 1831, largely based on the accounts of Augustine, remains indispensable. G. Bonner, *St. Augustine of Hippo, Life and Controversies*, 1963, pp. 157–192, is a learned and sympathetic account. J. Ries, 'Introduction aux études manichéennes', *Ephemerides Theologicae Lovanienses*, 33, 1957, pp. 453–482, and 35, 1959, pp. 362–409, is very helpful. A. Adam, *Texte zum Manichäismus* (Kleine Texte für Vorlesungen und Übungen, 175), 1954, is a useful collection of documents.

[5] v. A. Chavannes-P. Pelliot, 'Un traité manichéen retrouvé en Chine', *Journal asiatique*, sér. X, xviii, 1911, pp. 499–617, and sér. XI, i, 1913, pp. 99–199 and 261–394.

[6] Chavannes-Pelliot, *Journ. asiat.*, sér. XI, i, 1913, pp. 177–196.

[7] Illustrated in Widengren, *Mani*, esp. pls. 3–8, and chapter vii, pp. 107–116.

[8] Chavannes-Pelliot, *Journ. asiat.* sér. XI, i, 1913, pp. 340–349 — the report of an official, Lu Liu (1125–1209).

[9] v. esp. Chavannes-Pelliot, *Journ. asiat.* sér. X, xviii, 1911, pp. 499–617.

Evangelists in the Roman world, of Zoroaster in Persia, of Buddha in Central Asia.[1]

These missionaries had arrived in Carthage in 297 A.D. They were the 'Elect', a group of men and women pale with fasting, fenced in with elaborate taboos. They gathered around them congregations of 'Hearers' (the equivalent of the Christian 'catechumens'), who were content to admire the austerities of their spiritual heroes, the 'Elect', at a safe distance. These men brought with them an irresistible air of mystery:[2] complicated secret prayers;[3] the writings of Mani contained in gorgeous parchment volumes;[4] the hint of some deeper message veiled beneath their talk of 'Light' and 'Darkness'.[5] They would offer Augustine 'the open, undiluted truth'.[6]

> *I have tasted a sweet taste. I found nothing*
> *Sweeter than the word of Truth. Taste.*
> *I tasted a sweet taste. I found nothing sweeter*
> *than the taste of God. Taste.*
> *I tasted a sweet taste. I found nothing sweeter than Christ.*
> *Wisdom invites you, that you may eat with your Spirit.*[7]

What is 'Wisdom' for a 20-year-old, however, is not necessarily 'Wisdom' to a middle-aged man. 'Food in dreams', Augustine will comment later, 'is exactly like real food, yet it does not sustain us; for we are only dreaming.'[8]

[1] v. Adam, *Texte*, no. 3 d, pp. 6–7.   [2] *Conf.* III, vi, 11.   [3] *C. Fort.* 3.
[4] *C. Faust.* XIII, 18.   [5] *de beata vita*, i, 4.   [6] *de util. cred.* i, 2.
[7] Allberry, *Manichaean Psalmbook*, p. 158.   [8] *Conf.* III, vi, 10.

5

MANICHAEISM

(I) DUALISM[1]

Augustine was a 'Hearer' among the Manichees for some nine years. He could not have found his Wisdom among a more extreme group of men. The Manichees were a small sect with a sinister reputation. They were illegal; later, they would be savagely persecuted. They had the aura of a secret society: in foreign cities, Manichees would lodge only with members of their own sect;[2] their leaders would travel around a network of 'cells' scattered all over the Roman world. Pagans regarded them with horror,[3] orthodox Christians with fear and hatred. They were the 'Bolsheviks' of the fourth century: a 'fifth-column' of foreign origin bent on infiltrating the Christian church, the bearers of a uniquely radical solution to the religious problems of their age.

Only this group, Augustine thought, could answer the question that had begun to 'torment' him as soon as his 'conversion' to philosophy had caused him to think seriously: 'From what cause do we do evil?'[4] The Manichaean answer to the problem of evil is the core of the Manichaeism of the young Augustine. It was simple and drastic; it is fully known to us from the writings of Augustine; and in this century, we have been able to enter again into the intimate religious feelings of the Manichees, through the discovery, as far apart as Egypt and Sinkiang, of the impassioned liturgies of the Manichaean communities.[5]

Augustine attended the conventicles of the Manichees to hear the

[1] The best treatment is H. C. Puech, 'Der Begriff der Erlösung im Manichäismus' *Eranos Jahrbuch*, 1936, pp. 183–286.

[2] *Conf.* V, x, 19. [3] *de util. cred.* i, 2. [4] *de lib. arb.* I, ii, 4.

[5] The most impressive and revealing is the collection of Psalms in Coptic, almost contemporary with Augustine and coming also from a province in the Christian Roman Empire: ed. and transl. C. R. C. Allberry, *A Manichaean Psalmbook, (Part II)*, (Manichaean Manuscripts in the Chester Beatty Collection, vol. II), 1938; v. P.-J. de Menasce, 'Augustin manichéen', *Freundesgabe für Ernst Robert Curtius*, 1956, pp. 79–93.

great 'Letter of the Foundation' of Mani. At this solemn moment, the 'hearers' were 'filled with light'.[1] This 'illumination' was the first, the basic, religious experience of a Manichee: he was a man who had become acutely aware of his own state. It was as if he had been woken from deep sleep by a distant shout: . . . 'A man called down into the world saying: Blessed is he that shall know his soul.'[2]

Thus awoken, the Manichee would realize vividly, that he was not free. He could identify himself only with a part of himself, his 'good soul'.[3] So much of him plainly did not belong to this oasis of purity: the tensions of his own passions, his rage, his sexuality, his corrupt body, the vast, pullulating world of 'nature red in tooth and claw' outside him.[4] All this weighed upon him. It was obvious that what was good in him wished to be 'set free', to 'return', to merge again into an untroubled, original state of perfection — a 'Kingdom of Light' — from which it felt isolated. Yet it was equally plain that men had failed to carry out this, the only possible desire of their better nature. Therefore, this 'good soul' was plainly acting under duress: for some mysterious reason, it found itself 'imprisoned', 'retained', cramped and 'violated', pushed to and fro by a force which, temporarily, was stronger than itself.[5] 'Because it is a fact that we *do* sin against our wills . . . for this reason, we seek out a knowledge of the reason of things.'[6]

It was this 'knowledge of the reason of things' which the Manichees made plain to Augustine. Briefly, while everyone is aware of the intimate mingling of good and evil in himself and in the world around him, it was at the same time utterly repugnant to the religious man, and absurd to the rational thinker, that such evil should come from God. God was good, totally innocent. He must be protected from the faintest suspicion of direct or indirect responsibility for evil. This desperate 'piety towards the Divine Being'[7] accounts for the drastic nature of the religious system of the Manichees. They were dualists: so convinced were they that evil could not come from a good God, that they believed that it came from an invasion of the good — the 'Kingdom of Light' — by a hostile force of evil, equal in power, eternal, totally separate — the 'Kingdom of Darkness'. 'The first thing a man must do', says the Chinese Manichaean catechism, 'is to distinguish the Two

---

[1] C. Ep. Fund. 5.
[2] Allberry, *Manichaean Psalmbook*, p. 219. v. Puech, 'Begriff d. Erlösung', *Eranos Jahrbuch*, 1936, pp. 224–226.
[3] de ii anim. 1.   [4] C. Fort. 21.   [5] Conf. IV, xv, 26.   [6] C. Fort. 20.
[7] Simplicius, *Commentary on the Enchiridion of Epictetus*, 27, (Adam, *Texte*, no. 51, p. 74).

Principles (the Good and the Evil). He who would enter our religion must know that the Two Principles have natures absolutely distinct: how can one who is not alive to this distinction put into practice the doctrine?'[1]

On this issue, the Manichees were uncompromising rationalists. Augustine was confident, that as a Manichee, he could uphold the fundamental tenet of his religion by reason alone:[2] 'Where did these sins come from?' he would ask 'Whence did evil come at all? . . . If from a man, where did the man come from? If from an angel, whence the angel? And if you say, "From God . . .", then it would seem that all sin and evil were linked, as in an unbroken chain, to God Himself. This is the problem with which the Manichees think they can sweep the board, just by posing it — as if posing an awkward question meant knowing anything. If that were only the case, there would have been nobody more knowledgeable than myself.'[3]

Thus armed, Augustine, and the fellow-students he had won over to his new 'Wisdom', 'extremely intelligent young men and exceptionally argumentative,'[4] would have felt themselves invincible: 'I always used to win more arguments than was good for me, debating with unskilled Christians who had tried to stand up for their faith in argument. With this quick succession of triumphs the hot-headedness of a young man soon hardened into pigheadedness. As for this technique of argument, because I had set out on it after I had become a "Hearer" (among the Manichees), whatever I picked up by my own wits or by reading, I willingly ascribed to the effects of their teaching. And so, from their preaching, I gained an enthusiasm for religious controversy, and, from this, I daily grew to love the Manichees more and more. So it came about that, to a surprising extent, I came to approve of whatever they said — not because I knew any better, but because I wanted it to be true.'[5]

Augustine, the young Manichee, was a very clever young man. His conversion to Manichaeism coincided with a sudden, dramatic widening of his intellectual horizon. As a result of his 'conversion to philosophy', he had abandoned any intention of becoming a professional lawyer. Patricius, and Augustine's patron Romanianus, had plainly aimed high for the young man: they had intended him, as a lawyer, to join the Imperial civil service.[6] From the age of 20 onwards however, Augustine will be a dedicated teacher,[7] an austere devotee of 'Wisdom',

[1] Chavannes-Pelliot, *Journ. asiat.* sér. XI, i, 1913, p. 114. [2] e.g. *C. Fort.* 19.
[3] *de ii anim.* 10. [4] *de util. cred.* vi, 13. [5] *de ii anim.* 11.
[6] *Conf.* III, iii, 6. [7] *Conf.* IV, ii, 2.

anxious to increase his powers as a philosopher. Thus, Augustine's religious 'emancipation' from traditional religion, by becoming a Manichee, coincided exactly with an intellectual emancipation from his elders and betters in the university of Carthage, from the pretentious professors, whom he secretly despised.[1] To the amazement of his colleagues, he had mastered, on his own, a whole work of Aristotelian logic, the so-called *Ten Categories*. A revival of Aristotelian studies had been taking place in Rome, in a circle of cultivated aristocrats, supervised by a learned Greek professor.[2] The intelligentsia of a provincial city such as Carthage had been content to talk about this work of Aristotle, as 'something great and godlike';[3] only the young Augustine took up the challenge single-handed. It is hardly surprising therefore, that Augustine should have adopted a religion, which claimed to slough off any beliefs that threatened the independence of his very active mind.[4]

For as a Manichee, Augustine had been able to rid himself immediately, of ideas that cluttered up the religion of the conventional Christian. He was possessed of a vivid certainty:

> *I have known my soul and the body that lies upon it,*
> *That they have been enemies since the creation of the worlds.*[5]

There was no need to 'water-down' so intimate an awareness,[6] to obscure it with the clumsy scaffolding of Hebrew prophecies, that the Catholic Church had erected around the simple truth. The Manichee did not need to be ordered to believe.[7] He could grasp, for himself, the essence of religion. Immediacy was what counted most. The crucifixion of Christ spoke directly to such a man of the sufferings of his own soul.[8] His hero was Doubting Thomas, a man whose yearning for a direct, immediate contact with the divine secrets had not been spurned by Christ.[9]

Above all, as a serious and sensitive young man, Augustine could abandon the terrible father-figure of the Old Testament. The Manichaean system studiously avoided the acute ambivalence, that was later to be so important in the old Augustine's image of his God — a Father, that is, who could be, at one and the same time, a source of

---

[1] *Conf.* IV, xvi, 28.

[2] v. L. Minio-Paluello, 'The Text of the *Categoriae*: the Latin Tradition', *Classical Quarterly*, 39, 1945, pp. 63–74.

[3] *Conf.* IV, xvi, 28.

[4] Augustine the student would hardly have been impressed by the arguments of Augustine the priest, that professors were indispensable: *de util. cred.* vii, 16–17.

[5] Allberry, *Manichaean Psalmbook*, p. 56.   [6] *C. Faust.* XII, 1.

[7] *C. Faust.* XVI, 8.   [8] *C. Fort.* 7.   [9] *C. Faust.* XVI, 8.

tender generosity, and of punishment, vengeance and suffering.[1] In Manichaeism, the stern Jehovah of the Jews was rejected as a malevolent demon; and the Patriarchs, as dirty old men: '"*put forth thy hand over my loins, kill and eat, increase and multiply*", I knew', a Manichee would later write to Augustine, 'I knew that you always hated such stuff. I knew you were one who loved lofty things, things that shunned the earth, that sought out heaven, that mortified the body, that set the soul alive.'[2]

Manichaeism indeed, enabled Augustine to be a very austere, 'spiritual' young man. One may suspect that he had a need to feel so 'lofty'. For there was much in his life that continued to cause him acute guilt. Cicero, for instance, had written categorically in the *Hortensius*, (and Augustine, significantly, will remember the passage throughout his life): 'Are the pleasures of the body to be sought, which Plato describes, in all seriousness, as "snares, and the source of all ills"? . . . The promptings of sensuality are the most strong of all, and so the most hostile to philosophy. . . . What man in the grip of this, the strongest of emotions, can bend his mind to thought, regain his reason, or, indeed, concentrate on anything . . . ?';[3] 'and I, an unfortunate young man, wretched on the threshold of my adult life, used to pray, "Lord give me chastity and continence: but not now".'[4]

The elaborate avoidance of any intimate sense of guilt would later strike Augustine as the most conspicuous feature of his Manichaean phase. The Manichees were austere men. They were recognizable, at the time, by their pale faces; and, in modern literature, they have been presented as the purveyors of the bleakest pessimism. Yet they reserved this pessimism for only one side of themselves. They regarded the other side, their 'mind', their 'good soul', as quite untarnished: it was, quite literally, a crumb of the divine substance.[5] Their religion was directed to ensuring that this, the good part of themselves, would remain essentially untouched and unaffected by their baser nature. This baser nature would eventually be 'split off and shoved away from us, and, at the end of this existence, it will be defeated and wrapt up, all in a big, separate lump, as if in an eternal prison'.[6] The utterly alien

---

[1] v. esp. *C. Faust.* XXI, 1 and 3.

[2] *Ep. Secundini ad Aug.* Such attitudes are not confined to the fourth century; e.g. J. H. Newman, *Loss and Gain*, in which the hero exclaims: 'Surely the idea of an Apostle, unmarried, pure, in fast and nakedness, and at length a martyr, is a higher idea than that of one of the old Israelites, sitting under his vine and fig-tree, full of temporal goods, and surrounded by his sons and grandsons'.

[3] in *C. Jul.* IV, xiv, 72.   [4] *Conf.* VIII, vii, 17.   [5] *Conf.* IV, xvi, 31, cf. IV, xv, 26.

[6] *de Haeres.* 46, 6, (Adam, *Texte*, no. 49, p. 70).

force of evil therefore, could never do more than impinge externally on a good self, that would remain, forever, separate from it:

> *the vain garment of this flesh I put off, safe and pure;*
> *I caused the clean feet of my soul to trample confidently upon it.*[1]

Thus Augustine as a Manichee could enjoy the very real consolation, that for all his intense ambition, his disquieting involvement with his concubine, the pervasive sense of guilt that came so often to cloud his relations with his mother, at least the good part of him remained throughout, unsoiled:

> *I bent my neck beneath the yoke of virtue,*
> *in the time of my youth as the rebellion arose.*[2]

It is not the last time in the history of religious sentiment that a sensitive young man will cast his feelings in so drastic a mould: 'A brief anger had often invested him', James Joyce will write of his hero, 'but he was never able to make it an abiding passion, and had always felt himself passing out of it as if his very body were being divested with ease of some skin or peel. He had felt a subtle, dark and murmurous presence penetrate his being and fire him with a brief iniquitous lust: it too had slipped beyond his grasp, leaving his mind lucid and indifferent'.[3]

For Augustine, the need to save an untarnished oasis of perfection within himself formed, perhaps, the deepest strain of his adherence to the Manichees. Long after he had begun to appreciate the intellectual difficulties in the Manichaean system, its moral attitude still attracted him. After a frightening experience of illness in Rome, that had coincided with a crescendo of guilt in his relations with Monica, Augustine, now aged 29, about to be launched on a great career, will still be anxious to listen to the Manichaean 'Elect': 'For I still held the view that it was not I who was sinning, but some other nature within me. . . . I very much preferred to excuse myself and accuse some other thing that was in me, but was not I. But in truth,' the Catholic bishop will add, 'I was a complete whole: it was my impiety that divided me against myself.'[4]

The price which the Manichees had seemed to pay for this total

[1] Allberry, *Manichaean Psalmbook*, p. 99.
[2] Allberry, *Manichaean Psalmbook*, p. 97.
[3] James Joyce, *Portrait of the Artist as a Young Man* (Jonathan Cape, 1944, p. 70), cf. Puech, 'Begriff d. Erlösung', *Eranos Jahrbuch*, 1936, pp. 206–207.
[4] *Conf.* V, x, 18.

disowning of the bad, was to render the good singularly passive and ineffective. As a bishop, Augustine will emphasize this aspect of Manichaeism: for it is the one element in the Manichaean system that he would come to reject most forcibly.[1] Every writing of Mani illustrates this attitude, in which good is essentially passive, impinged upon by the violent activity of the bad.[2] For the Manichee, the existing universe, in which good and bad were so disastrously mingled, had arisen from a headlong invasion of the good — the 'Kingdom of Light' — by the bad — the 'Kingdom of Darkness'. This 'Kingdom of Light' had been utterly at rest, entirely ignorant of any tension of good and evil. So divorced from evil was the 'ruler' of the 'Kingdom', the 'Father of Light', that he was defenceless against it: he could not even enter into conflict with the invaders, without undergoing a drastic and belated transformation of his being.[3] By contrast, the 'Kingdom of Darkness' was the active force; it impinged, it violated, it was driven in upon the 'Land of Light'; its ravenous powers were blind; they had been directed only by the uncontrollable cries of greed emitted by their fellows.[4] When Augustine wrote a treatise of aesthetics at the age of 26, he will reflect, in an acceptable, classical, form, this exotic and potent myth. Here again, the Good is a 'monad', 'like a mind without the tension of male and female'; while it is evil that is active, 'a divided thing', 'reasonless', 'anger and lust'.[5]

Thus, throughout Manichaeism, it is the good that is condemned to be passive. The Christ of the Manichee was, above all, the 'Suffering Jesus',[6] 'Crucified throughout the whole visible universe.'[7] The height of Manichaean piety was to realize that one's good part was totally merged and identified with this violated divine essence, to identify one's fate entirely with a Saviour who was, himself, being saved.[8] 'I am in everything; I bear the skies; I am the foundation; I am the life of the world; I am the milk that is in all trees; I am the sweet water that is beneath the sons of matter.'[9] Yet, outside this intimate, sensitive involvement, the forces of evil would rage unmodified and (to Augustine's later horror) apparently uncontrolled by any power of

[1] v. esp. *Op. Imp.* I, 97.

[2] Chavannes-Pelliot, *Journ. asiat.*, sér. X, xviii, 1911, p. 546. The Chinese tractate makes plain that the Manichaean story of the invasion of the Kingdom of Light by the Kingdom of Darkness was held to be mirrored exactly in the experience of the individual: his good, isolated soul is invaded by an uncontrollable, alien force of evil.

[3] e.g. Adam, *Texte*, no. 7, p. 16, and Alexander of Lycopolis, *de placitis Manichaeorum*, 3: the good God was 'destitute of the evil necessary to cope with the invasion of Evil'.

[4] Adam, *Texte*, no. 5b, p. 13.   [5] *Conf.* IV, xv, 24.   [6] *C. Faust.* XX, 2.

[7] *Enarr. in Ps.* 140, 12.   [8] *C. Fort.* 18; *Enarr. in Ps.* 140, 12.

[9] Allberry, *Manichaean Psalmbook*, p. 54.

good: 'I weep for my soul saying: May I be saved from this, and from the terror of the beasts that devour one another.'[1]

The Manichee found himself in an acute dilemma. His religion promised the believer that, once 'awoken', he would be in complete control of his essential identity, and able to secure his release. It had told him that part of him would always remain untarnished; and it offered a harsh ritual that would further 'precipitate' the irreducible good stuff of his soul. Yet this confidence was constantly eroded by the powerful myths of the sect itself, myths that made the good seem utterly abandoned and helpless before the onslaught of evil: oppressed, violated, messed-up, its God of so untarnished an innocence as to be dangerously shorn of His omnipotence. The older Catholic bishop knew his Manichaeism only too well. He will put his finger on this one weak spot, and will use it to drive a former Manichaean friend to breaking-point in a public debate.[2]

Yet just this Manichaeism had been Augustine's religion as a growing man. It had provided him with an extreme and distinctive mould for his feelings. More than anything, perhaps, it had enabled the young Augustine to disown, for a time, and at a heavy cost, disquieting qualities that he would only later come to accept, both in his God and, one may suspect, in himself. These were the hard, 'paternal' qualities associated with the omnipotent Father of Catholic belief: a Father capable of righteous anger, of inflicting punishment, His unique goodness separated by an unbridgeable gulf from the intimate guilt of His sons.

(II) GNOSIS

In 375, Augustine returned from Carthage to teach literature at his home-town. He brought his new 'Wisdom' with him. To an African Catholic, the Manichees were the 'heretics' *par excellence*. Monica was appalled. She shut Augustine out of her house.[3] Characteristically, she relented only after she had been made certain, through a dream, that in the long run her son would come back to her religion. A bishop she had consulted, was also certain that Augustine would not long remain a Manichee. He himself, he told her, had been brought up as a Manichee; had religiously copied out the great authoritative books of Mani, and had soon found their contents impossible to accept.[4]

[1] Mary Boyce, *The Manichaean Hymn Cycle in Parthian*, 1954, p. 83.
[2] *C. Fort.* 33-37.   [3] *Conf.* III, xi, 19.   [4] *Conf.* III, xii, 21.

These great books, seven in all, formed the spine of Manichaeism. They would preserve the identity of the sect for some 1200 years, in environments as different as Carthage and Fu-Kien.[1] But for an educated man in the late classical world, the revelations contained in them were irreducibly exotic: they were a 'Persian fairytale'.[2]

In 375, however, Augustine could confidently propagate his Manichaean 'Wisdom' among educated Romans. For the Manichaeism of Africa in the 370's and early 380's, was rather like Communism in England in the 1930's: it had spread rapidly and, despite an exotic and highly doctrinaire core, it could still mean many things to many people. The Manichaeism of Augustine was the Manichaeism of a specific group, of the cultivated intelligentsia of the university of Carthage and of the small-town notables of Thagaste. Many of his fellow-students joined Augustine immediately at Carthage; and in a small town such as Thagaste, far from the watchful eyes of the Catholic authorities, it was easy to win over the eminent Romanianus and Romanianus' relative, Alypius. Such men were the 'Fellow travellers' of Manichaeism. Romanianus plainly saw nothing strange in supporting this illegal sect, and, at the same time, litigating at the court of the Catholic Emperors who had banned it.[3] Many of these 'Fellow Travellers' came straight from paganism. Manichaeism claimed to be the true 'Church of the Gentiles' in Africa: it attracted pagans disturbed by the rise of Christianity, for it disowned the authoritarian methods of the established church and the crudities of the Old Testament.[4] It fitted easily into that wide penumbra of Christianity, in which learned men would pore over what they took to be oracles of the Sibyl that had prophesied the coming of Christ.[5] In the 370's, this Manichaeism of cultivated men seems to have come to the fore in Africa, with Augustine and his friends as its most active representatives. The men to whom Augustine will later write in order to undo the beliefs he had himself propagated, are a tribute to the success of this wing of the Manichaean movement. They are, all of them, stalwart schoolmasters, deaf to any appeal other than to reason, capable of understanding the idea of authority only if introduced to them tactfully, in terms of their professional use of authoritative text-books as an aid to learning.[6]

---

[1] The Emperor Diocletian, in 297 (Adam, *Texte*, no. 56, pp. 82–83), and Lu Liu, in 1166 (Chavannes-Pelliot, *Journ. asiat.* sér. XI, i, 1913, p. 349), both single out these books to be burnt. On these books, v. Widengren, *Mani*, pp. 74–81 and 110–113.

[2] e.g. *de util. cred.* xviii, 36.   [3] v. inf. p. 90.   [4] *C. Faust.* XIII, 1.

[5] *C. Faust.* XIII, 1: Flaccianus, whom Augustine knew at Carthage at that time, had a copy of such Oracles: *de civ. Dei* XVIII, 23, 6.

[6] *de util. cred.* vii, 17.

This group, however, may have been somewhat peripheral to the movement as a whole. Other Manichees were far more doctrinaire. They would regard themselves exclusively as the reformers of Christianity. Some, indeed, managed to remain crypto-Catholics. Augustine would later discover, as a bishop, that one of his deacons had even continued to attend Manichaean services as a 'Hearer';[1] and a young man once joined Augustine's monastery at Hippo, after he had been impressed by the ascetic ideas contained in Apocryphal scriptures circulated by the Manichees.[2] Other such 'reformers' were less furtive. When Augustine became a bishop they would openly challenge him on his own territory, as interpreters of S. Paul, rather than as exponents of a rationally-based 'Wisdom'. These men formed the hard core of African Manichaeism: they came to the fore as soon as renewed persecution (in 386) and the desertion of Augustine and his impressive circle, had shaken the faith of the 'Fellow Travellers'.[3]

Both these groups contained educated men. Other Manichees were not educated. The movement had attracted many small men, respectable artisans and merchants.[4] The merchants, indeed, were the most effective missionaries of Manichaeism: in China and Central Asia, Manichaeism soon flickered out after the Mongols had destroyed the great commercial empires of the oases of the Gobi desert.[5] In the Roman Empire, also, the spread of Manichaeism may well have come to a halt with the recession of commerce.[6]

People such as these found it easier to accept the florid revelations of Mani as the literal truth than their more educated fellows. Many of these simple followers were exceptionally austere. As members of the 'Elect' they were the equivalents, in the Manichaean communities, of the sturdy Egyptian fellahin, who, as hermits, had become the wonder of the Christian world. These men, 'unpolished and primitive', were the most dedicated of all; and, not surprisingly in such a movement, they were particularly admired by sophisticated intellectuals.[7]

Augustine's disillusionment with the Manichees began as soon as he had come into contact with these 'fundamentalist' groups. It was they

[1] *Ep.* 236. [2] *Ep.* 64, 3.
[3] v. J. Ries, 'La Bible chez S. Augustin et chez les manichéens', *Rev. études augustin.* ix, 1963, pp. 201–215.
[4] e.g. the names given in the abjuration of a Manichee (in P.L. xlii, 518).
[5] Adam, *Handbuch der Orientalistik*, I Abt., viii, 2, pp. 118–119.
[6] Possidius, *Vita*, XV, 5: a rich Manichaean merchant, Firmus. v. *Enarr. in Ps.* 136, 3, on the exceptional freedom of movement enjoyed by a merchant.
[7] *de mor. Man.* (II), xx, 74.

who had upheld, without compromise, the revelations entrusted to them in the great books of Mani.

Mani was a religious genius. He had shared with all previous Gnostic thinkers, a vivid sense of man as a shameful mixture of two opposing forces: but he explained this mixture in terms of a fully-detailed description of the physical universe. The universe itself, for Mani, was a result of this mixture; the good news given by the Manichees, was that the visible world was a gigantic 'pharmacy', in which the pure essence of the ruined fragments of the Kingdom of Light would be 'distilled'.[1] The Manichee, therefore, was entirely embedded in the visible world. Every physical process around him was happening for his salvation. He might appear to worship the Sun, like a pagan,[2] bending the knee to it,[3] turning towards it as he prayed.[4] A pagan however, would have felt himself far below the Sun. To a pagan, men were creatures 'bound to human bodies and subject to desire, grief, anger . . . the late born, hindered by so many desires';[5] while the Sun was, plainly, a 'visible god', a superhuman mind, revolving as it did, in perfect rhythm, far above the world.[6] A Manichee would have seen in the Sun nothing less than the visible brilliance of a part of himself, a fragment of his own good substance in the last stage of its distillation, ready to merge again into the 'Kingdom of Light'.[7] He would have experienced the thrill of being involved in an ineluctable process, 'objective', 'scientifically' described in the books of Mani:

> *The Light shall go to the Light,*
> *the fragrance shall go to the fragrance . . .*

> *. . . The Light shall return to its*
> *place, the Darkness shall fall and not rise again.*[8]

No other 'Apostle of Jesus Christ' could tell the faithful 'in what way the visible universe has been constructed, and what is really happening throughout it'.[9] No religious system, indeed, had ever treated the visible world so drastically, and with such literalism, as an externalization of an inner, spiritual conflict.[10]

The picture of the universe that emerged was not, of course, the

---

[1] Chavannes-Pelliot, *Journ. asiat.* sér. X, xviii, 1911, p. 515.   [2] *C. Faust.* XX, 1.
[3] *de mor. Man.* (II), viii, 13.   [4] *C. Fort.* 3.
[5] Plotinus, *Ennead,* II, 9, 5 (MacKenna, 2, p. 136).
[6] Plotinus, *Ennead,* II, 9, 4 (MacKenna, 2, p. 135).
[7] *C. Faust.* XX, 1.   [8] Allberry, *Manichaean Psalmbook*, p. 215.   [9] *C. Fel.* I, 9.
[10] This, the 'Nature and Cause of the Mingling', was the heart of Manichaeism; it may have been kept secret from the newly-converted: *de ii anim.* 16.

world to which an educated Roman was accustomed: for it had been drastically distorted by Mani's religious preoccupations.[1] The clash between the contents of the Manichaean books, and the observed facts of the physical universe, was almost inevitable. For the Manichees would never concede that their picture of the universe was a 'Myth' symbolizing some deeper truth.[2] The waxing and waning of the Moon, for instance, was not merely the distant image of some spiritual event: it was, quite literally, caused by the influx of released fragments of 'Light' flowing upwards from the world. The moral discipline of a Manichee, his sense of being enabled to pursue a spiritual struggle to its glorious conclusion, depended on his accepting Mani's explanation of the movements of the physical universe as the literal truth.

Augustine was turning his attention to the physical universe, at just the time when he had settled down as a Manichee. He was determined to continue his studies as a philosopher.[3] He soon returned from Thagaste to Carthage; and by 380, he had written his first book — the 'On the Beautiful and the Fitting'. He had continued to quarry the work of Cicero for philosophical information.[4] Even the 'Hortensius', had he noticed it, contained information on the nature of eclipses that might have contradicted the Manichees.[5] He had, also, dabbled in astrology. An anxious young man, this had offered him an 'art', contained in impressively 'scientific' books, that could put him in touch with the impersonal, omnipotent forces governing his destiny.[6] In the fourth century as in the Renaissance, science and 'pseudo-science' went hand in hand: an eminent and shrewd doctor whom Augustine met at this time, had also once considered these astrological books as a viable alternative to the works of Hippocrates.[7] The information about the movements of the stars contained in these books was perfectly accurate. Late Roman astrologers needed empirical observations in order to cast correct horoscopes, just as Rudolf II of Bohemia will need the tables of Tycho Brahe, and the fussy Emperor of China, the superior astro-

[1] Mani, for instance, distorted the traditional astronomical data on which astrological beliefs were based: v. Widengren, *Mani*, ch. iv, 4, pp. 69–72, esp. p. 72.

[2] *C. Faust.* XV, 6.

[3] The importance of Augustine's reading of second-hand manuals of philosophical opinions is rightly stressed by A. Solignac, 'Doxographies et manuels dans la formation philosophique de S. Augustin', *Rech. augustin.*, i, 1958, pp. 113–148.

[4] v. esp. Testard, *S. Augustin et Cicéron*, i, pp. 64–68. The best introduction to the possible contents of this book is the note of A. Solignac to *Les Confessions*, transl. Tréhorel and Bouissou, *Bibliothèque augustin.*, ii sér., 13, pp. 671–673. v. most recently, Takeshi Katô, 'Melodia interior. Sur le traité *De pulchro et apto*', *Rev. études augustin.*, xii, 1966, pp. 229–240.

[5] e.g. *de civ. Dei*, III, 15, 39, on solar eclipses.   [6] *Conf.* IV, iii, 4.   [7] *Conf.* IV, iii, 5.

labes of the Jesuits.[1] The Manichees had condemned astrology: it was amateurish dabbling compared with the 'objective' Wisdom of their own books.[2] Augustine, however, quickly realized that the astronomical calculations of the astrologers were true; and he was a man who wanted nothing but the truth.[3]

He was told that only the most spectacular leader of the Manichees could help him, Faustus of Milevis. To judge from this man's pamphlets, he had addressed his appeals to the educated group to which Augustine himself belonged:[4] he had gained a vast reputation for learning, conveniently maintained by his frequent absences on missionary journeys.[5] Here indeed was a 'Top Party Member', who would explain everything. When Faustus arrived in Carthage, in 383, Augustine could see for himself what sort of man controlled the movement in the Latin world: 'I found at once that the man was not learned in any of the liberal studies save literature, and not especially learned in that, either. . . .'[6]

Faustus was not greatly interested in the intricacies of the revelations of Mani.[7] He represented the wing of Manichaeism that stood for a 'reformed' Christianity: he claimed to be living the life of a 'true' Christian by following the example of Christ as drastically as would S. Francis.[8] Faustus indeed, is a remarkable example of the type of leader thrown up by the religious turmoil of the fourth century. He was a poor man's son from Milevis,[9] and so, self-taught. He will settle down, with Augustine as his tutor, to learn more of the classics. For these would be his passport to the cultivated and influential men who might support his movement.[10] But Faustus had as good as lost the support of Augustine as a Manichee. Next year, Augustine would move away from Carthage to Rome.[11] The moral ideas of Manichaeism might still attract him; but he would seek his 'Wisdom' from a more convincing, more purely classical source.

Yet, more was at stake than a conflict between a 'Persian' religious system, and a Greco-Roman view of the physical world. Many educated Latins of the fourth century found themselves accepting non-

---

[1] They had even been anticipated, in the 8th century, by Manichaean astronomers: Chavannes-Pelliot, *Journ. asiat.*, sér. XI, i, 1913, pp. 152–153 and 161.

[2] ed. H. J. Polotsky, *Manichäische Homilien*, 1934, p. 30, 3.

[3] *Conf.* V, iii, 3 and 6; cf. *de doct. christ.* II, xxi, 32.

[4] v. esp. P. Monceaux, 'Le manichéen Fauste de Milev.: Restitution de ses "Capitula",' *Mém. Acad. des Inscript. et Belles Lettres*, 1924.

[5] *Conf.* V, iii, 3.   [6] *Conf.* V, vi, 11.   [7] *Conf.* V, vii, 12.

[1] *C. Faust.* V, 1.   [9] *C. Faust.* V, 5.

[10] *Conf.* V, vii, 13.   [11] v. inf. p. 68.

classical myths as part of their religion. Viewed by a conservative pagan, Augustine had merely stepped out of the frying-pan into the fire, in passing from the Mesopotamian and Hebrew folk-tales of the Old Testament, to the Mesopotamian revelations of Mani.[1] On a deeper level, Manichaeism had disillusioned Augustine, by being an essentially static religion. 'I could make no progress in it':[2] from the old Augustine, this was the definitive condemnation of the Manichaean system. The Manichees had avoided the tensions of growth on all levels. Morally, they claimed to do no more than 'set free' the good part of themselves, by disassociating themselves from whatever conflicted with their comforting image of a fragment of untarnished perfection lodged within them. The Manichaean discipline therefore, was based on an exceedingly *simpliste* view of the way a man acts. It was extremely optimistic: for it assumed that no reasonable man, once 'awoken' to his true state could possibly fail to set about liberating his own soul by following their solemn routines:[3] 'If he knows how to observe the rituals, he will awaken: the fragment of luminous mind in him will return to its full purity; and the "foreign" nature of good that resides, temporarily, in his body will disengage itself from all dangers. . . .'[4] The complexities of doubt, of ignorance, deep-rooted tensions within the citadel of the will itself, are deliberately ignored in Manichaeism. With all their talk of 'setting-free', the Manichees had no room, in their religious language, for more subtle processes of growth — for 'healing', for 'renewal'.[5]

It was the same on the intellectual level. To a classical man, 'Wisdom' was the fruit of a prolonged intellectual discipline and of personal growth. Compared with this ideal, it became clear to Augustine as he grew older, that the Manichees were merely presenting him with a *Gnosis* in its crudest form: he had run up against an esoteric and exotic 'secret' revelation, that claimed to by-pass the exigencies and excitements of a classical philosopher's quest for truth.[6]

As a Manichee, Augustine had been an austere young man, who had found a ready use for his great intelligence. His religion inspired the first book he ever wrote. He had been brought in touch with a genuine metaphysical preoccupation concerning the nature of evil. He would have continued to regard himself as a good Christian. But he will have to pass through the 'Wisdom' of a pagan exponent of the thought

[1] *C. Faust.* XIII, 17.　　　　　　　　　[2] *Conf.* V, X, 18.
[3] *C. Fel.* II, 8. This is clearly seen by Bonner, *St. Augustine*, pp. 174–175.
[4] Chavannes-Pelliot, *Journ. asiat.*, sér. X, xviii, 1911, p. 546.
[5] *de mor. Man.* (II), xi, 22.　　　　　　[6] v. esp. *de mor. eccl. cath.* (I), xxv, 47.

of Plato — the great Plotinus — before he can write to his former teachers: 'Let them deal harshly with you, who do not know with what labour truth is found ... who do not know with what pain the inner eye of a man is healed that he may glimpse his Sun.'[1]

[1] *C. Ep. Fund.* 2.

6

FRIENDS

Augustine will never be alone. When he returned to Thagaste, he formed a core of abiding friendships. Boys who had grown up with him as fellow-students now rallied to him as Manichees.[1] They were a singularly intelligent and priggish group of young men. They had been attracted by the austerity of the Manichees:[2] one of them, indeed, would reckon his adherence, as a young man, to Manichaeism as the only period in his life in which he had been chaste.[3] Augustine, who had lapsed into monogamy, was a rarity among these celibates. They thought that music was a divine gift;[4] they would discuss together the nature of beauty;[5] they felt themselves above the circus.[6] Augustine knew to perfection how to keep such friendships 'on the boil by the heat of shared enthusiasms'.[7] 'All kinds of things rejoiced my soul in their company — to talk and laugh, and to do each other kindnesses; to read pleasant books together; to pass from lightest jesting to talk of the deepest things and back again: to differ without rancour, as a man might differ with himself, and when, most rarely, dissension arose, to find our normal agreement all the sweeter for it; to teach each other and to learn from each other; to be impatient for the return of the absent, and to welcome them with joy on their homecoming; these, and such-like things, proceeding from our hearts as we gave affection and received it back, and shown by face, by voice, by the eyes, and by a thousand other pleasing ways, kindled a flame which fused our very souls together, and, of many, made us one.'[8]

In all this, of course, one figure is notably absent — Augustine's concubine. Our curiosity about her is a very modern preoccupation,

---

[1] de ii anim. 11 and 24; cf. de mor. Man. (II), xix, 71.   [2] Conf. VI, vi, 12.
[3] Ep. 259, 3.
[4] de mor. Man. (II), v, 16. cf. Allberry, Manichaean Psalmbook, p. 168, 20.
[5] Conf. IV, xii, 20.   [6] Conf. VI, vii, 12.   [7] Conf. IV, iv, 7.   [8] Conf. IV, x, 13.

which Augustine and his cultivated friends would have found strange. Why, after all, had God chosen to make a woman to live with Adam? 'If it was company and good conversation that Adam needed' Augustine will answer, 'it would have been much better arranged to have two men together, as friends, not a man and a woman.'[1] Eve could bear Adam's children; this unnamed woman bore Augustine's son — Adeodatus. It is only Adeodatus that we know of. We catch a glimpse of him some years after his mother had vanished. At the age of sixteen 'His intelligence filled me with a kind of awe'. When he died, soon afterwards, there are no more echoes of him in Augustine's writings: 'I had no part in that boy but the sin.'[2]

This woman lived with Augustine until 385, when he dismissed her on becoming betrothed to a young heiress. Concubinage of this kind was a traditional feature of Roman life. Even the Catholic church was prepared to recognize it, provided that the couple remained faithful to one another.[3]

For a full marriage was prohibitively complicated: it demanded that the partners should be of equal status, and it involved complex dynastic arrangements. As a provincial professor 'on the make', Augustine had no wish for anything but a 'second-class' marriage with a concubine. He had little inclination to tie himself, by a premature match, to some family of impoverished gentlefolk at Thagaste;[4] to find himself liable to serve as a member of the town-council, to collect taxes, to organize circus-shows, to make sure that the public baths were properly heated. After all, the greatest rhetorician in the Greek East in this age, Libanius of Antioch, was quite content with just such an arrangement: 'an excellent woman, if not of free birth,' 'the mother of my son, and better than any servant(!).'[5]

A respectable arrangement, of course, need not be a particularly civilized one. No Late Roman gentleman, for instance, wrote poems to his concubine. She would be his housekeeper, the mother of his sons, of considerably lower class than himself. Throughout her partner's Manichaean enthusiasms, Augustine's concubine may have remained a Catholic catechumen;[6] their son was called Adeodatus, 'given by God.'

---

[1] *de Gen. ad litt.* IX, v, 9.   [2] *Conf.* IX, vi, 14.

[3] v. *Serm.* 312, 2, for Augustine's later attitude: 'If you have no wives, you may not have concubines, women whom you will later dismiss in order to marry a wife.' This is precisely what Augustine himself had done.

[4] e.g. *Conf.* II, iii, 8, 'fettered to a wife'.

[5] Libanius: *Autobiography (Oration I)*, ed. and transl. A. F. Norman, 1965, §278, p. 143. v. esp. p. 231, on her status. As with Augustine, only her son, Cimon, is ever mentioned by name.

[6] v. inf. p. 89.

FRIENDS

This is the Latin form of the Punic, Iatanbaal; with its religious associations, it was a popular name among Carthaginian Christians.[1] Nor does Augustine seem to have been particularly happy about the needs that bound him to this woman: he would remember their relationship as 'the mere bargain of a lustful love'.[2] In an atmosphere charged with the presence of Monica, who lived with her son for much of this time, Augustine's disquiet is not, perhaps, so very surprising: 'What is the difference?' he would tell another young man, oppressed with a mother, 'Whether it is in a wife or a mother, it is still Eve (the temptress) that we must beware of in any woman.'[3]

In 385, however, it was not moral scruples that led Augustine to abandon his concubine. It was ambition. Augustine had to marry an heiress. A man such as Libanius could afford to be faithful to his concubine until her death: for he was a respectable figure, from a wealthy family, firmly-entrenched as the spokesman of the vested-interests of the great Eastern city of Antioch. Augustine, making his career in the Latin West, could never hope to achieve such a safe position. In a small provincial town in Africa, the only alternative to a career that took him far away from his background, was poverty and boredom; and the only chance of permanent success, an alliance with those great families, who, in distant Rome and Milan, controlled the destinies of men of talent from the provinces.[4] The unnamed concubine will be sent back to Africa, an obscure victim of the high Catholic principles and great snobbery of the Milanese.[5]

The small-town life of Thagaste, indeed, would never satisfy Augustine. But what shook him out of his home-town was a purely private matter — the terrible blow of a friend's death. This friend of Augustine's had become a Manichee: 'he wandered, in his soul, along with me; and my soul could do nothing without him.'[6] For Augustine was an imperialist in his friendships. To be a friend of Augustine's, meant only too often becoming a part of Augustine himself: 'we depended too much upon each other.'[7] When this friend was lying unconscious, his Catholic family baptized him. Augustine, waiting at his bedside, was not worried by such primitive precautions. He was confident that his friend would join him in laughing off the ceremony: but when he regained consciousness, 'he reacted as if I were his deadly

---

[1] I. Kajanto, *Onomastic Studies in the Early Christian Inscriptions of Rome and Carthage* (Acta Instituti Romani Finlandiae, II, 1) 1963, pp. 102 and 115.

[2] *Conf.* IV, ii, 2.　　　[3] *Ep.* 243, 10.

[4] *Sol.* I, x, 17–xi, 19, is a particularly revealing statement of what Augustine had hoped to gain.

[5] *Conf.* VI, xv, 25. v. inf. pp. 88–89.　　　[6] *Conf.* IV, iv, 7.　　　[7] *Conf.* IV, iv, 8.

enemy, and, in a sudden and unexpected show of independence, warned me that I should stop this talk if I wished to remain his friend.'[1] A few days later, he died suddenly, when Augustine was absent. The double rejection of his friend's death and his acceptance of Catholic baptism, quite unmanned Augustine: 'I fled my home town.'[2] He wished, so desperately, to return to Carthage, that he overrode the wishes of his patron, Romanianus.[3] This time he was not coming to a 'cauldron': in 376, at the age of 22, he came to Carthage as the capital of Africa, the spring-board of a career.

[1] *Conf.* IV, iv, 8.   [2] *Conf.* IV, vii, 12.   [3] *C. Acad.* II, i, 3.

7

SUCCESS

'Time takes no holiday. It does not roll idly by, but through our senses works its own wonders in the mind. Time came and went from one day to the next; in its coming and its passing it brought me other hopes and other memories. . . .'[1]
Carthage, in 376, was still the second city in the Western Empire.[2] Its marvellous artificial harbour was ringed with colonnades; its regular avenues shaded with trees; its waterfront open to the wide world.[3] On the 'Maritime Parade', Augustine could see the skeleton of a whale large enough to shelter 12 men;[4] a mosaic showing the Sciopods, the weird inhabitants of lands far beyond the Roman Empire;[5] in the bookstalls that lined the street, he could pick up centuries-old writings of Gnostic heretics, a source of distress, later, to the older bishop, but an exciting discovery for the crowds of curious browsers.[6]

Augustine would have taught rhetoric in the centre of the public life of the town. His schoolroom would have been sheltered from the bustle of the forum by only a curtain. It was too public for Augustine. His pupils were mainly rowdy young bloods, sent by their wealthy families from all over Africa (and even, in one case, from the Greek East),[7] to acquire a 'proper' education — that is, a smattering of Cicero. If he was to go beyond Carthage in his career, Augustine would have to look up the hill above the Forum, the Byrsa. For there was the palace of the Proconsuls. Arriving from beyond the seas for short periods, these men were important figures in the life of the town. They were a reassuring sight for a young teacher of rhetoric: for these

---

[1] *Conf.* IV, viii, 13.
[2] Salvian, *de gubernatione Dei*, VII, 16 (P.L. liii, 143). On Carthage in the fourth century, v. esp. G. Charles-Picard, *La Carthage de saint Augustin*, 1965.
[3] v. Audollent, *Carthage romaine*, pp. 211–223.   [4] *Ep.* 102, vi, 31.
[5] *de civ. Dei*, XVI, 8.   [6] *Retract.* II, 58.
[7] *Epp.* 117 and 118, on Dioscurus; v. inf. p. 299.

aristocrats were connoisseurs of literature, influential patrons who regarded a good classical education as the best qualification for high office.

The Later Roman Empire was a military autocracy. At just this moment in Augustine's career, however, the cultivated aristocrats of Gaul and Italy were enjoying a momentary 'thaw'. Their former Emperor, Valentinian I, had been a grim soldier. He had surrounded himself with professional administrators who had little sympathy for the old traditions; he was said to feed the victims of purges to his pet bears; he would burst out with 'shift his block'; and he had allowed his military commanders to victimize the upper classes of Africa.[1] Yet this simple man had been anxious that his son should be well-educated. On Valentinian's death, Ausonius, an elderly professor of rhetoric from Bordeaux, found himself the favourite of a boy Emperor whose tutor he had been, and so became the figurehead of an alliance of lettered conservatives, determined to make the best of the new dispensation. The son and son-in-law of Ausonius would come to Carthage as Proconsuls in the years when Augustine began his courses as a teacher of rhetoric.[2] He could have no better omen for his career.

In Rome also, the great senators were anxious to count 'men enthusiastic for wisdom' among their friends. Symmachus, for instance, was a senator who owed his reputation and influence to his literary talents. He, also, had come to Carthage as Proconsul, in the same year as Augustine, as a student, had passed through his conversion to 'Wisdom'.[3] Men such as Symmachus and his Roman friends thought of themselves as the 'élite of the human race'. They would be only too glad to patronize, and eventually to co-opt, a man such as Augustine. They needed teachers for their sons, well-trained spokesmen for their grievances, amateur administrators duly impressed by the vast prestige of their traditional way of life. These men represented the peak of Augustine's ambition as a young man ... 'a country estate, a house, gardens watered by clear streams, the soft glow of marble in contrasting shades. To live this way helps me towards a quiet old age, turning over the learned writings of the ancient masters'.[4] Without such men, Augustine might well have remained in Carthage; and he would never have passed, at a crucial moment in his career, from Rome to Milan, at the

[1] The best study is A. Alföldi, *A Conflict of Ideas in the Later Roman Empire*, 1952, pp. 28–95.

[2] A. C. Pallu-Lessert, *Fastes des provinces africaines*, ii, 1901, pp. 83–88.

[3] Pallu-Lessert, *Fastes*, ii, pp. 78–80.

[4] Naucellius, in *Epigrammata Bobiensia*, ii, no. 5, ed. Munari, 1955, p. 55.

behest of Symmachus, to meet the Christian version of these great men, Symmachus' own cousin, S. Ambrose.[1]

At Carthage, Augustine soon made contact with distinguished outsiders. He won a prize for a set-poem, and became a friend of the Proconsul who had crowned him, Vindicianus.[2] Vindicianus was a successful court doctor (which is hardly surprising, seeing that he was adept at curing indigestion and avoided painful surgery).[3] He was not a polished speaker, but lively and vigorous: a heartening example of a man who had risen by his talents. This 'shrewd old man'[4] was quite prepared to unbend before Augustine, warning him 'like a father' against astrology;[5] bound together by a common love of the classics, the poet and the proconsul could meet as equals.

For such men, all roads still ran to Rome. In around 380 Augustine will dedicate his first book, a treatise on aesthetics, to Hierius, an orator in Rome. Augustine knew Hierius only by reputation. Like himself, Hierius was a provincial (even, indeed, a Greek-speaking Syrian) who had become a master of Latin. Like Augustine, also, he claimed to be a philosopher as well as a rhetorician.[6] He and his brother would gravitate around the pagan circle of Symmachus, as Augustine and his pupils would do for a short moment.[7]

Augustine's two deepest friends — Alypius and Nebridius — stand for the different aspects of his life. Alypius, a boyhood friend from a leading family in Thagaste, is the man of action.[8] He was cut out to be an administrative lawyer.[9] He will be powerfully attracted by the slaughter of the gladiatorial shows. Typically, he admired the Manichees, above all, for their chastity, having himself had an unfortunate sexual experience in his youth.[10] Later in Milan, he will be unmoved by Augustine's intellectual uncertainties, and will appear instead as a persistent advocate of an upright 'blessed life'. When he is finally converted from the world, he will take his decision quietly,[11] and will walk barefoot on the frozen ground, as the logical consequence of his adhesion to this, his new course of action.[12] Solemn, well-known for his courtesy, given to calm and obstinate resolutions, an authoritarian,

---

[1] On the ideals of this class, v. esp. Alföldi, *A Conflict*, pp. 96–124.

[2] v. Pallu-Lessert, *Fastes*, ii, pp. 93–94; K. Deichgräber, s.v. 'Vindicianus', *Pauly-Wissowa Reallexikon*, IX, A. 1 (ii, xvi), 1961, coll. 29–36.

[3] Ep. ad Valentinianum, in *Corpus Medicorum Latinorum*, V, ed. Wiedermann, 1916, cc. 5 and 9, pp. 23–24.

[4] *Conf.* VII, vi, 8.   [5] *Conf.* IV, iii, 5.   [6] *Conf.* IV, xiv, 21.

[7] v. most recently, L. Herrmann, 'Hierius et Domitius', *Latomus*, xiii, 1954, pp. 37–39.

[8] *Conf.* VI, vii, 11.   [9] *Conf.* VI, x, 16.   [10] *Conf.* VI, xii, 20.

[11] *Conf.* VIII, xii, 30.   [12] *Conf.* IX, vi, 14.

Alypius will remain Augustine's *alter ego* for the rest of their lives.

Augustine's other friend, Nebridius, came from another, more leisured and more gentle world. He charmed Augustine, who always speaks of him as *dulcis*, his sweet friend.[1] Unlike Alypius and Augustine, he did not need to be a careerist. A wealthy, pagan Carthaginian, he could afford to live a life of studious retirement, not unlike the *dilettante* senators of Rome. He followed Augustine from Carthage to Milan, merely to live in the company of his brilliant friend.[2] He will die in 390, after Augustine and he himself had retired, as recluses, to their respective homes at Thagaste and Carthage. It is the end of a truly intimate friendship. Seventeen years later, Augustine will remember him: 'While reading in your letter', he will tell a bishop, 'and pondering its contents so far as my limited time permitted, the memory of my friend Nebridius came back to me. While he was a most diligent and eager student of difficult problems, he had a great aversion to giving a short answer to a great question. If anyone insisted on doing this, he was exceedingly displeased: and if he was not prevented by respect for the age or rank of the person involved, he would indignantly rebuke the questioner with stern looks and words; for he considered him unworthy to be investigating matters such as these who did not know how much might be said, or should be said, on a subject of great importance.'[3]

By 382, the time had come for Augustine to move from Carthage. He was disillusioned with the Manichees: they were, in any case, a persecuted sect, living in fear of denunciation.[4] He disliked teaching such rowdy students. Alypius had already gone ahead of him to Rome, as an administrative lawyer.[5] Well-connected friends now promised Augustine 'better earnings' and 'high honours'.[6] Above all, the Roman students seemed to be better-disciplined. In Rome, they were made aware of being on the august threshold of the Imperial civil service; and, as potential recruits, the students, (especially the many Africans who had flocked to Rome), were strictly supervised by the Emperor.[7]

Augustine had reckoned without Monica. 'She, indeed, was in dreadful grief at my going and followed me right to the coast. Then she clung to me, passionately determined that I should either go back to home with her or take her to Rome, but I deceived her with the pretence that I had a friend whom I did not want to leave until he had

[1] *Conf.* VIII, vi, 13 and IX, iii, 6.   [2] *Conf.* VI, x, 17.   [3] *Ep.* 98, 8.
[4] *de mor. Man.* (II), xix, 29.   [5] *Conf.* VI, viii, 13.   [6] *Conf.* V, viii, 14.
[7] *Codex Theodosianus*, XIV, 9, 1 (370).

sailed off with a fair wind. Thus I lied to my mother — and such a mother! . . . She would not return home without me, but I managed with some difficulty to persuade her to spend the night in a place near the ship, where there was an oratory in memory of St. Cyprian. That night I stole away from her. She remained, praying and weeping. . . . The wind blew and filled our sails and the shore dropped from our sight. She went home, and I to Rome.'[1]

After such an incident, it is hardly surprising that Rome was a disappointment. Augustine spent a miserable year in the Eternal City. He fell dangerously ill on his arrival: as he remembered it, in the *Confessions*, this 'scourge of illness' is fused with the account of his desertion of Monica, in a passage of mounting desperation.[2] As for the students, they were in the habit of cheating their teachers, simply by abandoning them when the time came to pay their fees.[3]

Yet, Augustine was not entirely disappointed. At the end of the year, he had attracted the notice of Symmachus. Another provincial who had come to Rome to make his fortune in the same way as Augustine, the Antiochene Ammianus Marcellinus, had not been so lucky. This man, the last great historian of Rome, found himself excluded from the charmed world which Augustine was able to enter: the Roman aristocrats struck him as ostentatious boors, their libraries 'closed like a tomb'. When food became short, these men were prepared to deport all foreign 'professors of the liberal arts', while retaining 3000 dancing girls![4]

Augustine, however, avoided the fate of the less fortunate Ammianus. For Symmachus, as Prefect of the City, had been ordered to choose a professor of rhetoric for the city of Milan.[5] As the Imperial court resided in Milan, this was an important appointment. A professor of rhetoric would deliver the official panegyrics on the Emperor and on the consuls of the year. These speeches would have been carefully tuned to publicizing the programmes of the court, so that the successful rhetorician would have found himself, in many ways, a 'Minister of Propaganda'.[6]

Symmachus chose Augustine for this vital post. The choice was made on the strength of a speech performed before him; but Symmachus had already been approached by Manichaean friends to appoint

[1] *Conf.* V, viii, 15. [2] *Conf.* V, ix, 16. [3] *Conf.* V, xii, 22.
[4] Ammianus Marcellinus, *Res gestae*, XIV, 6, 1. v. esp. A. Cameron, 'The Roman Friends of Ammianus', *Journ. Rom. Studies*, liv, 1964, pp. 15–28.
[5] *Conf.* V, xiii, 23.
[6] For the opportunities and perils of such a position, v. Cameron, 'Wandering Poets', *Historia*, xiv, 1965, pp. 497–507.

their protégé.[1] Up to the last, the Manichees had looked after their own: Augustine had lodged with a Manichaean 'Hearer'; and as we have seen, he had good, personal reasons, in his sad mood, to frequent the austere 'Elect'.[2]

The Roman Manichees could well approach a conservative pagan such as Symmachus as a potential ally. The growth of an intolerant Catholicism had thrown together the representatives of the old religion and these new heretics. A Roman Manichee, Secundinus, who later wrote to Augustine, plainly regarded the philosophical Romans of Cicero's 'Dialogues' as preferable to the disgusting Jewish superstitions of Catholicism.[3] In a city where, for instance, scenes from the Old Testament predominate markedly in the family-vault of one Christian senator, to reject the Old Testament, as the Manichees did, may well have seemed equivalent to opposing Christianity as Symmachus knew it.[4]

In the autumn of 384, Symmachus had every reason to welcome a non-Catholic in so important a post.[5] Earlier in the year, he had petitioned the Emperor to reverse a decision, made a few years previously, to 'disestablish' the traditional pagan religion of Rome — in reality, to abolish it, by cutting the vital link between pagan ceremonies and their public funds. Symmachus' petition was a carefully worded appeal for toleration: 'Not by one way alone can man attain to so great a Mystery.'[6] He had been trumped by his own relative, Ambrose, established on the threshold of the court as bishop of Milan: Ambrose had written direct to the boy-Emperor, Valentinian II, reminding him that he was a catechumen of the Catholic Church, that 'the gods of the nations are demons', and that he would be debarred from Ambrose's church if he granted the requests of Symmachus.[7] Smarting under so dramatic a snub to the traditional religion, Symmachus may well have been glad to ensure that a man such as Augustine, known to him as a member of a violently anti-Catholic sect, would be in a position to speak before the Emperor.

Augustine went to Milan as the protégé of Symmachus. He may have taught a son of Symmachus' boyhood friend.[8] His ambition would

[1] *Conf.* V, xiii, 23.   [2] v. sup. p. 51.

[3] *Ep. Secundini ad Aug.* v. sup. p. 50. cf. the refutation of Justinus, a cultivated Roman Manichee, ascribed to Marius Victorinus, in P.L. viii, 990–1010.

[4] v. esp. A. Ferrua, *Le pitture della nuova catacomba di Via Latina*, 1960.

[5] P. Courcelle, *Recherches sur les 'Confessions'*, 1950, pp. 78–79.

[6] Symmachus, *Relatio*, III, 10.   [7] Ambrose, *Ep.* 17, 1 and 13.

[8] J. Rougé, 'Une émeute à Rome au IVe s.', *Rev. études anciennes*, 63, 1963, p. 61. Augustine's pupils were being educated for senatorial careers: *de ord.* II, viii, 25.

be fostered, at just this time, by a typical correspondent of Symmachus, Marcianus — a poet, a Greek scholar, a future Prefect of Rome, even, perhaps, a future apostate from Christianity.[1] He may well have read and admired, at least, the style of Symmachus' famous appeal for toleration.[2] He certainly delivered the panegyric of Symmachus' friend, Bauto, a Frankish general, himself a pagan.[3] Symmachus' net was widely-spread: even Ponticianus, the African civil servant, whose meeting with Augustine will provoke the 'conversion' of Augustine and Alypius from the 'world', was — for all his piety and tales of the lives of hermits — yet another successful protégé of Symmachus![4]

Nor was Symmachus unaware of the advantage he had bestowed on the young African: 'the highroad to office', he once wrote, 'is often laid open by literary success'.[5] Milan was the political capital of an important part of the Western Empire.[6] A typical residence of the Emperors in this time of constant emergency, it owed its importance to its strategic position on the roads leading over the Alps. Diplomats and secret agents came there from as far apart as Trier, to the North, and Persia, to the East. The barbarian soldiers around the palace would have been a sinister reminder of a strange, untamed world beyond the Alps. Only wooden stockades on the passes into modern Jugoslavia, stood between this prosperous new city and barbarian warbands that would soon wander with impunity throughout the Balkans.

A brilliant society had grown up around the court. Poets would come to Milan from as far away as Alexandria;[7] and the works of Greek philosophers would be read both by the clergy of the Milanese church, and by great landowners in villas within sight of the Alps. Such men would study the revived philosophy of Plato; they would write both on classical metre and on the nature of the universe.[8] Even the Catholicism of the town was eminently respectable: the sermons of Ambrose were 'learned',[9] his major work was modelled carefully on Cicero,[10] his ideas betrayed the influence of contemporary exponents of

---

[1] *Ep.* 258. He may well be the Marcianus described in Chastagnol, *Les Fastes de la Préfecture urbaine*, no. 117, pp. 268–269.

[2] *Sol.* I, xiii, 23. v. *Retract.* I, 4, and *de vera religione*, xxviii, 51 (*tam grande secretum*).

[3] Courcelle, *Recherches*, pp. 79–83.

[4] v. inf. p. 107, and Symmachus, *Ep.* I, 99 and V, 32.   [5] Symmachus, *Ep.* I, 20.

[6] v. esp. L. Ruggini, *Economia e società nell' italia annonaria*, 1962. A. Piganiol, *L'Empire chrétien* (Histoire romaine, IV, 2), 1947, pp. 230–252, provides a brilliant picture of the political and religious situation of the 380's.

[7] Claudian; v. Cameron, 'Wandering Poets', *Historia*, xiv, 1965, pp. 495–496.

[8] Manlius Theodorus; v. inf. p. 90.   [9] *Conf.* V, xiii, 23.

[10] e.g. O. Hiltbrunner, 'Die Schrift "de officiis ministrorum" des hl. Ambrosius und ihr ciceronisches Vorbild', *Gymnasium*, 71, 1964, pp. 174–189.

Plato.[1] Even the sarcophagi of such Christians show an exquisite classical taste.[2]

For Augustine, Milan meant new interests, new learning, great chances of success. For a year he threw himself into its life with vigour and whole-hearted ambition. Yet in the long run, it became for him a symbolic city, with an unexpected figure at its centre. In his *Confessions*, Carthage had first appeared to Augustine as his 'cauldron' — the Latin *sartago* deliberately echoes *Karthago*.[3] Now Milan will take on its own, peculiar significance: *et veni Mediolanum ad Ambrosium episcopum*; 'And I came to Milan . . . to Ambrose, the bishop.'[4]

---

[1] Ambrose's contact with contemporary Neo-Platonism may be wider even than the reading of Plotinus revealed by Courcelle, *Recherches*, pp. 93–138. v. also Courcelle, 'Nouveaux aspects du platonisme chez saint Ambroise', *Rev. études latines*, 34, 1956, pp. 220–239; 'De Platon à Saint Ambroise par Apulée', *Revue de Philologie*, n.s. xxxv, 1961, pp. 15–28; and the important survey, 'Anti-Christian arguments and Christian Platonism', *The Conflict between Paganism and Christianity in the 4th century*, ed. Momigliano, 1963, pp. 151–192, esp. p. 165.

[2] e.g. the beautiful example surviving in San Ambrogio in Milan, illustrated in C. Mohrmann and F. Van der Meer, *Atlas of the Early Christian World*, 1958, no. 186, p. 77.

[3] *Conf.* III, i, 1.   [4] *Conf.* V, xiii, 23.

PART II
386-395

386 Affair of the Basilicas in Milan (Feb.).
 17.vi. Finding of Ss. Gervasius and Protasius.
 Ambrose in Trier (summer or autumn).
 Purge of Manichees at Carthage.
	Reads the *libri Platonicorum* (June?).
	 Visited by Ponticianus. Conversion (end of August).
	 Goes to Cassiciacum (September).
	   Contra Academicos (November).
	   De Beata Vita.
	   De Ordine (December).
	   Soliloquia (winter).

387 Maximus invades Italy (autumn).	Returns to Milan (early March). 24.iv. Baptism. *De immortalitate animae*. Begins *De Musica*. Vision of Ostia. Death of Monica.

388	Goes to Rome from Ostia.
	 Stays in Rome until latter part of year.
	   De quantitate animae.
	   De libero arbitrio (Bk. 1).
	 /90 *De moribus ecclesiae catholicae et de moribus Manichaeoru*
	
	 Returns to Carthage, then to Thagaste.
	 /89 *De Genesi contra Manichaeos*.
	 /96 *De diversis quaestionibus*.

389 Baptism of Paulinus of Nola.	*De Magistro*. /91 *De vera religione*.
390	? Deaths of Adeodatus and Nebridius.
391 24.ii. General edict against paganism (*Cod. Theod.* xvi, 10, 10.). Aurelius becomes bishop of Carthage.	Arrives in Hippo to found monastery (spring). Ordained priest. /92 *De utilitate credendi*. /92 *De duabus animabus contra Manichaeos*. /95 *De libero arbitrio* (Bks. 2–3).

392 15.v. Death of Valentinian II.
 Eugenius proclaimed Emperor (August).
	28/29.viii. Debate in Hippo with Fortunatus.
	   Acta contra Fortunatum Manichaeum.
	 Writes to Jerome asking for Latin translations of Greek con taries on the Bible.
	 /420 *Ennarrationes in Psalmos*
	    (commentaries on the first 32 psalms had been writt 392).

393 24.vi. Donatist council at Cebarsussa; Maximian goes into schism. Optatus, Donatist bishop of Timgad.	3.xii. Council of Hippo. Preaches *De fide et symbolo*. *De Genesi ad litteram imperfectus liber*.

905   *Against the Academicians*, Milwaukee, 1942; *Answer to Sceptics*, NY., 1948; *St Augustine against the Academicians*, Ld., 1950.
959   *The Happy Life*, St Louis, 1939 & NY., 1948.
977   *Divine Providence and the problem of evil*, NY., 1948.
869   *Soliloquies of St Augustine*, Ld., 1910; *Soliloquies of St Augustine*, Edinburgh, 1912; *Soliloquies*, NY., 1948; (in) *Basic Writings of St Augustine I*, NY., 1948; (in) *Augustine: earlier writings*, Ld., 1953.

1021   *The immortality of the soul*, NY., 1938; *The immortality of the soul*, NY., 1947; (in) *Basic Writings I*, NY., 1948.
1081   *On Music*, NY., 1947.

1035   *The magnitude of the soul*, NY., 1947; *The greatness of the soul*, Ld., 1950.
1221   (in) *Augustine: earlier writings*, Ld., 1953; *The problem of free choice*, Ld., 1955.
1309   (in) *On the Manichaean Heresy*, Edinburgh, 1872; (in) *Basic Writings I*, NY., 1948 (only first part); *The Catholic and Manichaean ways of life*, NY., 1966.

173
11

1193   *Concerning the Teacher*, NY., 1938; *The teacher*, Ld., 1950; (in) *Augustine: earlier writings*, Ld., 1953; (in) *Basic Writings I*, NY., 1948.
121   *Augustine: earlier writings*, Ld., 1953.

65   (in) *Seventeen short treatises of St Augustine*, Oxford, 1847; *On the advantage of believing*, Oxford, 1885; *The advantage of believing*, NY., 1947; (in) *Basic Writings I*, NY., 1948.
93   (in) *Nicene and Post-Nicene Fathers*, 4, NY., 1901.
SEE ABOVE ad ann. 388.

111   (in) *Nicene and Post-Nicene Fathers*, 4, NY., 1901.

67 & *Expositions on the Book of the Psalms* (6 vols.), Oxford, 1847–57; *St Augustine on the*
1   *Psalms* (2 vols. so far), Ld., 1960–.

181   (in) *Seventeen short treatises*, Oxford, 1847; *On Faith and the Creed*, Edinburgh, 1873; *On Faith and the Creed*, Oxford, 1886; (in) *Augustine: earlier writings*, Ld., 1953; *Faith and the Creed*, NY., 1955.

219

394 Donatist Council at Bagai. Suppression of Maximianist Schism. 6.ix. Defeat of Eugenius. 25.xii. Ordination of Paulinus.	Suppression of *Laetitia* at Hippo. *Psalmus contra partem Donati.* *De sermone Domini in monte.*

Death of Ausonius ca. 394.	26.vi. I Council of Carthage.
	 Lectures on the *Epistle to the Romans* at Carthage.
	 /95 *Expositio 84 propositionum epistolae ad Romanos.*
	      Epistolae ad Romanos inchoata expositio.
	      Expositio epistolae ad Galatas.
	      De Mendacio.

395 17.i. Death of Theodosius. Emperors: Arcadius (East) Honorius (West) 395–404 Claudian the poet *floruit*.	Augustine is consecrated as successor to Bishop Valerius.

· 23
· 1229   *The sermon on the mount expounded*, Edinburgh, 1873; *The Lord's sermon on the mount*, Ld., 1948; *Commentary on the Lord's sermon on the mount*, NY., 1951.

· 2063
· 2087
· 2105
· 487   (in) *Seventeen short treatises*, Oxford, 1847; *Lying*, NY., 1952.

8

AMBROSE[1]

When Augustine arrived in Milan, in the autumn of 384, he was a disillusioned man. The certainties of his youth had dissolved. In such a mood, he turned, yet again, to Cicero.[2] In his philosophical dialogues, Cicero had made available, in Latin, the sceptical views of the 'New Academy'. These doctrines had been elaborated, in the second century B.C. by Carneades, a formidable Greek logician, in opposition to the Stoics. The Stoics had claimed that a man could know exactly the nature of the world around him and so could act wisely and in perfect certainty in the light of this knowledge.[3] The sceptics — called the *Academici*, 'the Academics' — had denied that knowledge could be gained with such ease.[4] The wise man, in Cicero's opinion, should learn to walk more warily: his greatest virtue lay in suspended judgement: his greatest peril, in unheeding adherence to any single opinion.

No religious movement in the fourth century A.D. was more exposed to this shrewd criticism than the Manichees. They had claimed to offer absolute certainty, straightforward and unambiguous to any rational

[1] The most comprehensive study of Ambrose is F. Homes-Dudden, *The Life and Times of St. Ambrose*, 2 vols., 1935. P. Courcelle, *Recherches sur les Confessions de S. Augustin*, 1950, has laid the foundations of all modern views on Augustine's evolution in Milan; he has amplified and defended his position in *Les Confessions de S. Augustin dans la tradition littéraire: Antécédents et Posterité*, 1963, esp. pp. 19–88.

The interpretation of books V to VIII of the *Confessions* is decisive for this period, hence the importance of two sound commentaries, M. Pellegrino, *Les Confessions de S. Augustin*, 1960, and A. Solignac in *Les Confessions*, (transl. Tréhorel and Bouissou), *Bibliothèque augustinienne*, sér. ii, 13–14, 1962.

[2] *Conf.* V, x, 19. v. Testard, *S. Augustin et Cicéron*, i, pp. 81–97.

[3] v. esp. E. R. Dodds, *The Greeks and the Irrational* (Univ. Calif. Paperbound, 1963), p. 239.

[4] The best statement of the Academic position is by R. Holte, *Béatitude et Sagesse: S. Augustin et le problème de la fin de l'homme dans la philosophie ancienne*, 1962, esp. pp. 42–

man.[1] The 'Wisdom' contained in their books described the exact reality of the universe: all a man need do, was to act in conformity with this knowledge. Thus, in supporting the Manichees so fervently, Augustine had been guilty of the crowning temerity described by Cicero: the hot-headed partisanship of a schoolboy for a sect.[2] It is hardly surprising, then, that Cicero's 'New Academy' should have come, for a time, to lend intellectual respectability to Augustine's disillusionment.

Later, Augustine will transcend this position, and deal harshly with it.[3] Yet this comparatively short period of uncertainty is one of the most crucial and little-known turning-points of his life. For it brought home to Augustine the ideal of 'Wisdom' as a prolonged quest. Cicero had never abandoned this ideal. Far from it: the wise man's quest for wisdom was all the more heroic for being a forlorn hope:

> *On a huge hill,*
> *Cragged and steep, Truth stands, and he that will*
> *Reach her, about must, and about must go.*[4]

The Manichees had offered Augustine a 'ready-made' Wisdom. He now began to appreciate the great attractions of a life-time of philosophical discipline, spent in modestly rejecting false opinions.[5]

Once the way to Wisdom was seen as a quest, Augustine was led to wonder by what means this quest could be carried out. The Academics had seemed to him to deny that the human mind could ever reach truth. Augustine never adopted this radical view whole-heartedly. The alternative which he continued to consider throughout this time came more naturally to him: that men might use some 'authority' to point the way to truth.[6]

Augustine's reading of Cicero may even have helped him to come to this conclusion. For Cicero had deployed his scepticism only against the doctrinaire philosophers of his age: he was far too much of a Roman to attack the established religion of his ancestors.[7] In the same way, Augustine's scepticism would have swept away the doctrinaire assertions of the Manichees, while leaving intact the submerged

---

[1] v. sup. p. 59.   [2] Cicero, *Academica*, II, iii, 8.

[3] v. the learned translation and commentary of J. O'Meara, *St. Augustine: Against the Academics* (Ancient Christian Writers, 12), 1950, and Holte, *Béatitude et Sagesse*, pp. 73–109.

[4] Donne, *Sat.* iii.   [5] *C. Acad.* III, vii, 15.   [6] *de util. cred.* viii, 20.

[7] v. Cicero, *de natura deorum*, I, xxii, 61: the 'Academic' Cotta is also the priest who held it 'to be a duty most solemnly to maintain the rights and duties of the established religion'.

bedrock of *his* ancestral religion — the Catholicism of Monica. This accounts, perhaps, for the ease with which Augustine decided to become a catechumen of the Church of Milan.[1] He may have taken this decision when his mother arrived in Milan in the late spring of 385.[2] He had no reason to resist the strong external pressures towards such an act of politic conformity. He had a career to make, and Monica was arranging a match for him with a Catholic heiress.[3] The court was Christian; Ambrose, as Catholic bishop, dominated Milan; while, to be a catechumen at that time, would not have committed Augustine very deeply to the Catholic Church. It was a politic gesture of conformity; and, once a catechumen, he could have postponed indefinitely the decisive step of being baptized.

Augustine had lost his confidence. As he told a Manichaean friend, seven years later: 'At that time, there was no one more open to being taught than I was. . . .'[4] It was a significant moment for any man to make his first acquaintance with S. Ambrose.

Ambrose was some 14 years older than Augustine, and had been bishop of Milan for 11 years. On the surface, he is the most striking representative of the Roman governing class of his age — that is, of men whose position depended less on their patrician birth, than on their ability to grasp and hold power in a ruthless society. The son of an administrator, he had been residing in Milan as governor of the province (Liguria), when he was suddenly seized upon to be bishop of the city. The Catholic populace of Milan stuck to their choice. Augustine owed his appointment to the court. But this court was isolated in Milan: it was full of suspect foreigners, Goths, Arian heretics, tolerators of pagans. Its authority was overshadowed, in the West, by the usurpation of another Emperor; and in the city itself, by the formidable Ambrose. Throughout 386, Ambrose would show his power in his inimitable manner. In February, the Emperor's mother, Justina, had ordered Ambrose to surrender a church for use by the Arian members of the court. Ambrose showed himself to be far less inhibited than his cousin, Symmachus, in defending the traditional property of his religion. With studied deference, he flatly refused to give up the church. It became an issue of 'court' against 'city', with Ambrose making little effort to check the hatred of the Milanese for their Gothic garrison. The leading courtiers were placed under a curfew lest they join this 'usurper'; and, as the Gothic troops surrounded the basilica in which Ambrose stood with his congregation, it seemed as if a

[1] *Conf.* V, xiv, 25. [2] Courcelle, *Recherches*, pp. 86–87.
[3] *Conf.* VI, xiii, 23. [4] *de util. cred.* viii, 20.

general massacre might ensue. But the court lost its nerve and gave way. As children played with the tattered shreds of the hangings that marked the basilica as confiscated, Imperial property, the boy, Valentinian, rounded on his followers, saying that 'If Ambrose gave you word, you would hand me over in chains to him'. 'We priests' Ambrose had said, 'have our own ways of rising to Empire. Our infirmity is our way to the throne. For *When I am weak, then am I powerful*.'[1]

By June 17th, the triumph of Ambrose was complete. He had built a basilica. A 'certain burning feeling' made him certain that he would find the relics of some martyrs with which to dedicate the building. After a short search, the complete bodies of SS. Gervasius and Protasius were unearthed and carried in triumph to the new church. Overcome by the emotion he had himself provoked, Ambrose could hardly speak. When he did, he told the crowds, that the martyrs would lie in the great sarcophagus, which he, a typical Roman, had prepared for himself beneath his altar in this his basilica — the *Basilica Ambrosiana*. 'These are the sort of influential men whose support I am securing.'[2]

Such a man would have had little interest in Augustine. He knew the type only too well: the man who would become a Christian to marry a wife, and bend his knees in church to get a position from the Christian court.[3] He greeted Augustine formally on his arrival, as befitted a bishop, and with more affability, perhaps, than Augustine had expected from this distant, paternal figure: 'and I first began to love him ... as a man who showed me kindness.'[4] But, when Ambrose's sermons had begun to worry Augustine, it was impossible to approach the bishop. Ambrose was always busy with important people (on one occasion, it seems, two Persian noblemen came the whole way to Italy to talk with this great man).[5] When Augustine could make his way through such crowds, he found Ambrose disconcertingly remote — suddenly drawn into himself at the end of the day, and reading a book in complete silence: 'When he read, his eyes travelled over the page and his heart sought out the sense, but voice and tongue were silent. No one was forbidden to approach him, nor was it his custom to require that visitors should be announced: but when we came into him we often saw him reading, and always to himself; and after we had sat long in

---

[1] v. Homes-Dudden, *St. Ambrose*, i, pp. 270–293.

[2] v. Homes-Dudden, *St. Ambrose*, i, pp. 298–319.

[3] Ambrose, *In Ps.* cxviii, 20, 48 (P.L. xiv, 1490).

[4] *Conf.* V, xiii, 23.

[5] Paulinus of Milan, *Vita S. Ambrosii*, 25, ed. M. Pellegrino (Verba Seniorum, n.s. i), 1961, pp. 88–89.

silence, unwilling to interrupt a work on which he was so intent, we would depart again.'[1]

It was in church, on Sundays, that Augustine would have seen this passionate little man, much as we can still see him, on a mosaic:[2] a frail figure, clasping the *codex* of the Scriptures, with a high forehead, a long melancholy face, and great eyes.[3] Here we have the other side of Ambrose, a side far less well known than the man of action. It was this other side which was destined to influence Augustine.[4] Here, the studied vehemence of his political life appears as a feminine intensity. At that time, Ambrose introduced exciting new Eastern melodies, so that his congregation should chant the Psalms as they were besieged by the Imperial troops.[5] He had 'bewitched' the Catholics with his new hymns.[6] He was the most enthusiastic advocate of absolute virginity, 'the one thing that separates us from the beasts.'[7] His sermons are studded with the language of the Song of Songs: 'kissing' — so seldom mentioned by Augustine — recurs constantly in Ambrose:[8] 'What then is this: "*Let him kiss me with the kisses of his mouth*"? Think of the Church, now hanging for innumerable ages on its Lord's coming ... or of the soul, rising free from the body, having turned away from sensuality and the sweet pleasures of its flesh, and cast off the cares of this worldly life. Now it begs for a full breath of the Divine Presence, and is tormented, that it should come so late, is troubled, and feels the deep hurt of charity ... and so declares the cause and her impatience, saying: *Let him kiss me with the kisses of his mouth*. It is not one kiss that she wants, but many, to satisfy her longing.'[9] He can describe the calmed sea: 'When it no longer breaks upon the shore, but wins it over and greets it as a friend with peaceful caresses.'[10]

Augustine, as a 'professional', was anxious to hear this distinctive oratory. He found it delightful: less 'soothing and entertaining' than that of Faustus, but 'far more learned'.[11] It is a significant difference. Ambrose had enjoyed all the advantages of an upper-class education in Rome itself. There was nothing 'provincial' about him. Thus, unlike

---

[1] *Conf.* VI, iii, 3.   [2] *Conf.* VI, iii, 4.

[3] v. A. Ratti, 'Il piu antico ritratto di S. Ambrogio', *Ambrosiana*, ch. xiv, 1897.

[4] v. Homes-Dudden, *St. Ambrose*, ii, pp. 442–476.   [5] *Conf.* IX, vii, 15.

[6] Ambrose, *c. Auxentium*, 34 (P.L. xvi, 1017).

[7] Ambrose, *In Ps.* lxi, 21 (P.L. xiv, 1175) cf. *Conf.* VI, iii, 3.

[8] v. M. Tajo, 'Un confronto tra s. Ambrogio e s. Agostino a proposito dell'esegesi del Cantico dei Cantici', *Rev. études augustin.*, vii, 1961, pp. 127–151.

[9] Ambrose, *de Isaac*, iii, 18 (P.L. xiv, 506).

[10] Ambrose, *Hexaemeron*, III, v, 21 (P.L. xiv, 177).   [11] *Conf.* V, xii, 23.

Augustine, he could read Greek fluently. He could comb the books of a brilliant new generation of Greek bishops and a whole tradition of Greek Christian scholarship, to give his congregation some of the most learned and up-to-date sermons in the Latin world.[1] Nor did he have any scruples about borrowing from the pagans: he gloried in being able to parade his spoils from the pulpit — this 'gold of the Egyptians' was fair prize.[2]

Augustine may have heard his opening sermons on the Book of Genesis. He would have been impressed by the extraordinary self-confidence of the man. He himself had just owed his emancipation from the Manichees to the opinions of the 'philosophers', painfully scraped together from manuals and the works of Cicero.[3] But in this field, Ambrose showed himself a complete master of the situation:[4] he could parade all the great 'names' and their opinions, only to dismiss them with contempt; how could these frail quibblings stand against the word of Moses, who had spoken 'mouth to mouth' with God? In any case, what was true in these philosophers was merely plagiarized from their predecessors in time, the Hebrew prophets.[5]

Ambrose first impressed Augustine by being able to defend the Old Testament against Manichaean criticisms.[6] With some relief Augustine now heard how it was possible to see the Patriarchs in a different light: what had once appeared to him, when a Manichee, as a collection of formidable and disgusting *bons pères de famille*,[7] were presented by Ambrose as a stately procession of authentic 'philosophers', each one symbolizing the state of a soul purified by wisdom.

Later, Augustine seems to have realized what was the key to Ambrose's attitude: 'I noticed, repeatedly, in the sermons of our bishop ... that when God is thought of, our thoughts should dwell on no material reality whatsoever, nor in the case of the soul, which is the one thing in the universe nearest to God.'[8]

Ambrose's religion was radically other-worldly. For him, a man was his 'soul'. His body was merely a 'tattered garment': 'We ourselves are different from what we merely own.'[9] In going against his 'soul', a

[1] v. esp. G. Lazzati, *Il valore letterario dell'esegesi ambrosiana* (Archivio ambrosiano, xi), 1960, and L. F. Pizzolato, *La 'Explanatio Psalmorum XII' : Studio letterario sulla esegesi di Sant'Ambrogio* (Archivio Ambrosiano, xvii), 1965.

[2] v. Holte, *Béatitude et Sagesse*, pp. 119–124.   [3] v. sup. p. 57.

[4] Not that his sources were any less second-hand: v. J. Pépin, *Théologie cosmique et théologie chrétienne (Ambroise, Exaém.* I, 1, 1–4), 1964, pp. 45–58.

[5] v. Holte, *Béatitude et Sagesse*, p. 131.   [6] *Conf.* VI, iv, 6.

[7] v. sup. p. 50.   [8] *de beata vita,* i, 4.

[9] Ambrose, *Hexaemeron,* VI, 7, 42 (P.L. xiv, 258).

man ceased to exist: in 'returning' to its God, the 'soul' must cast off everything else, like washing the mud off gold. Nothing else matters: our body is only the passive instrument of the soul. 'The enemy is right inside you, the cause of your erring is there, inside, I say, shut up in ourselves alone.'[1] One thought runs through Ambrose's preaching: beneath the opaque and rebarbative 'letter' of the Old Testament, this 'spirit', the hidden meaning, calls to our spirit to rise and fly away into another world.[2]

It is difficult nowadays to enter into the extent to which this other-worldliness must have appeared as quite revolutionary to Augustine.[3] With the exception of the Platonists, most thinkers in the ancient world, the most religious included, were 'materialists' in the strict sense. For them, the divine was also an 'element', though infinitely more 'fine', more 'noble' and less 'mutable'.[4]

Man was related to this living force that seemed to permeate the universe: and so it was his position in a physical world, infused with divine energy, that concerned most thinkers, not the intangible depths of his soul. These assumptions brought traditional philosophers, such as the Stoics, into the same field of ideas as the Manichees and even, it appears, perfectly orthodox Catholics in Africa and elsewhere.[5] Previously, Augustine had met the Catholics only on that level: he thought that they could only think of God as crudely limited to a human form, and so that his own materialism appeared more 'advanced', in that he regarded the 'Kingdom of Light' as a subtle, living material, contained in the whole world like a 'force'.[6] Now, he was disillusioned with the Manichaean cosmology, and especially with their explanation of the 'mixing' of the two Kingdoms.[7] He no longer wished to think of this good 'force' as having been invaded and violated by an opposing element: but he was still quite unable, or unwilling, to think himself out of a materialist position. For a moment,

---

[1] Ambrose, *Hexaemeron*, I, viii, 31 (P.L. xiv, 140).

[2] This aspect of the thought of Ambrose has been excellently characterized by Holte, *Béatitude et Sagesse*, pp. 165–175.

[3] v. the most stimulating study of F. Masai, 'Les conversions de S. Augustin et les débuts du spiritualisme de l'Occident', *Le Moyen Âge*, 67, 1961, pp. 1–40.

[4] v. esp. P. Henry, 'Introduction' to MacKenna, *Plotinus, The Enneads* (2nd ed. 1956, p. xxxix): 'The belief that the soul is immaterial was far from being shared by all the Greeks. In this respect Plato, Aristotle, and Plotinus are fairly isolated from the main Greek tradition and a long way from that rarefied materialism which Armstrong calls 'the pneumatic type of thought' and which, envisaging the soul as tenuous matter, has representatives through the whole range of Greek thought from Homer to the Stoics, not to mention the Manichaeans. . . .'

[5] *Conf.* V, x, 19.　　[6] *Conf.* V, x, 20.　　[7] *Conf.* VII, ii, 3, v. sup. p. 52.

he came close to the solution of the Stoics, by which an inviolable divine 'fire' permeated the universe, which lay bathed in this element like a sponge in the depths of a boundless ocean.[1]

Ambrose, therefore, introduced Augustine to some totally new ideas. Augustine found himself in the position of a man, 'influenced by an authoritative statement, and prepared to say that there was something "immaterial", but unable to think other than in terms taken from material things.'[2] It was an issue on which Cicero, and with him the greater part of the ancient philosophical tradition, could offer him no assistance.[3] The story which Augustine tells in the *Confessions* of his dilemmas in dealing with this problem is one of the most dramatic and massive evocations ever written of the evolution of a metaphysician; and his final 'conversion' to the idea of a purely spiritual reality, as held by sophisticated Christians in Milan, is a decisive and fateful step in the evolution of our ideas on spirit and matter.[4]

But this is to anticipate. Augustine may have arrived gradually at these ideas; and it is exceptionally difficult to assess the precise influence of Ambrose in provoking this evolution. It is impossible to date Ambrose's surviving sermons (a small proportion of those he actually preached) with sufficient certainty.[5] It may even be misleading thus implicitly to limit Ambrose's influence on Augustine to specific doctrines and statements picked up from specific sermons.[6] What Augustine tells us in the *Confessions*, however, is a charmingly authentic description of the state of mind into which Ambrose had thrown him: 'To-morrow, I shall find it: it will be all quite clear and I shall grasp it. Faustus will come and explain everything. And those mighty Academics — is it true that nothing can be grasped with certainty for the directing of this life? No: we must search the more closely and not despair. For now the things in the Scriptures which used to seem absurd are no longer so. . . . I shall set my foot on that step on which my parents placed me as a child, until I clearly find the truth. But where shall I search? When shall I search? Ambrose is busy. I am myself too busy to read. And in any event, where can I find the

---

[1] *Conf.* VII, i, 2.

[2] *de mor. eccles. cath.* (I), xxi, 38.   [3] v. Testard, *S. Augustin et Cicéron*, i, p. 111.

[4] Masai, 'Les conversions de S. Augustin', *Le Moyen Âge*, 67, 1961, p. 29.

[5] v. Courcelle, *Recherches*, pp. 98–102 (on the *Hexaemeron*) and pp. 122–124 (on the *de Isaac* and the *de bono mortis*), is challenged by Theiler, *Gnomon*, 75, 1953, p. 117. v. also the views of Testard, *S. Augustin et Cicéron*, i, esp. pp. 85–89.

[6] The absence of any reference in the *Confessions* and in the *de utilitate credendi* to Ambrose's sermons as a source of Neo-Platonic ideas is striking: v. esp. J. O'Meara, 'Augustine and Neo-Platonism', *Rech. augustin.* i, 1958, pp. 91–111 at p. 100.

books? Who has them, or when can I procure them? Can I borrow them from anyone? I must appoint set times, set aside certain hours for the health of my soul. A great hope has dawned: the Catholic faith does not teach things I thought and vainly accused it of. . . . Do I hesitate to knock, that other truths may be opened?

'My pupils occupy the morning hours, but what do I do with the rest? Why not do this? But if I do, when shall I have time to visit powerful friends of whose influence I stand in need, or when prepare the lessons I sell to my pupils, or when refresh myself by relaxing my mind from too close preoccupation with my heavy concerns?'[1]

When Monica arrived, Augustine's relations with the distant challenging figure of Ambrose became yet more complicated: 'she hastened to church more zealously than ever and drank in the words of Ambrose as a fountain of water . . . she loved that man as an angel of God, because she had learnt that it was by him that I had been brought so far as to that wavering state I was now in. . . .'[2]

We are dealing, here, with a relationship between two people whose eddies may escape the historian. The influence of Ambrose on Augustine is far out of proportion to any direct contact which the two men may have had. We may only glimpse the charged quality of their relationship in one scene, not mentioned in the *Confessions*: 'When my mother followed me to Milan', he once told a correspondent, 'she found the church there not fasting on Saturdays. She began to be troubled, and to hesitate as to what she should do: upon which I, though not taking a personal interest in such things, applied on her behalf to Ambrose for his advice. He answered me that "he could only teach me to do what he himself did, for, if he knew of any better rule, he would have observed it." I had thought that he was intending just to tell us to give up fasting on Saturdays merely by an appeal to authority, without giving any reason [and, evidently, Augustine had turned away, feeling snubbed]. . . . But he followed after me, and said "When I go to Rome, I also fast on Saturday: when here, I do not. If you go to any church, observe the local custom. . . ." As for me, on frequently thinking back on this statement I have always treated it as if it were an oracle from heaven.'[3]

[1] *Conf.* VI, xi, 19.   [2] *Conf.* VI, i, 1.   [3] *Ep.* 54, ii, 3.

9

THE PLATONISTS

Augustine had every reason to feel out of his depth in Milan. Even his African accent was noticeable;[1] and Ambrose was only one among the many highly-cultured men who could make this provincial feel that his previous opinions were ill-founded and misplaced. Nor had Ambrose greatly helped Augustine. In his sermons, he had drawn on the works of the pagan philosophers rather as we would draw on a spiritual anthology, adapting their conclusions to make a point as an orator and a moral teacher.[2] The Manichees, however, had made Augustine into a tenacious, if ill-read, metaphysician. He wanted complete certainty on ultimate questions. He might have 'heard' that a man was solely responsible for his evil actions:[3] but, as a Manichee, he had been encouraged to ask *why* such evil actions should happen at all — a very different and more fundamental question.[4]

For a time, Augustine seems to have been content just to suspend judgement. His first year in Milan must have been devoted to pushing his interests as a *rhetor*, surrounded by friends who had just reached the centres of power, and who had begun to experience the excitements and regrets of success.

Augustine's mistress was the first casualty of his exciting new life: she made way for an heiress obtained for Augustine by his mother; 'this was a blow which crushed my heart to bleeding. I loved her dearly.'[5]

In Milan, however, well-to-do people gave little thought to such things. To abandon one's concubine, in order to take a wife in legitimate matrimony, was 'not bigamy, but a sign of moral improvement'.[6]

---

[1] *de ord.* II, xvii, 45.   [2] v. Lazzati, *Il valore letterario dell'esegesi ambrosiana*, pp. 88–91.
[3] Ambrose, *Hexaemeron*, I, viii, 31 (P.L. xiv, 151).   [4] *Conf.* VII, iii, 5.
[5] *Conf.* VI, xv, 25.   [6] Leo, *Ep.* 167 (P.L. liv, 1205).

(These are the words of that very Roman man, Pope Leo.) Ambrose also knew how to speak to the great landowners in his congregation on this delicate topic: Abraham, he said, had been wise to cast off his low-born concubine; did they want 'marriages beneath their class', 'children to whom they could not pass on their land', their noble wives snubbed by serving maids?[1] The family which was prepared to accept Augustine as a son-in-law would take no such risk: the professor's concubine had to leave Milan, a good two years before the marriage was to take place.[2]

Thus, this nameless woman will return to Africa, 'vowing never to know a man again.'[3] In all probability she had been a good Catholic throughout her life with Augustine; and, by this vow, she intended either to become eligible for baptism, or to be re-admitted to the Eucharist.[4]

A well-bred gentleman would not mention his concubine. Later, when Augustine will announce his 'conversion' to his Milanese patrons, he will only mention having abandoned an advantageous marriage.[5] It was to take him a good decade before he allowed himself to feel again about her, to write about her in the 'Confessions', and to envisage her in another work:

'This problem often arises: If a man and a woman live together without being legitimately joined, not to have children, but because they could not observe continence; and if they have agreed between themselves to have relations with no one else, can this be called a marriage? Perhaps: but only if they had resolved to maintain until death the good faith which they had promised themselves, even though this union did not rest on a desire to have children. . . . But if one or the other of these conditions is lacking, I cannot see how their alliance can be called a marriage. Indeed, if a man takes a woman only for a time, until he has found another who better suits his rank and fortune: and if he marries this woman, as being of the same class, this man would commit adultery in his heart, not towards the one whom he had married, but towards her with whom he had lived without being legitimately married. The same can be said for the woman. . . . Nevertheless, if she was faithful to him, and if, after his marriage to another, she herself gave no thought to marriage, but abstained from all sexual relations, I would not dare to accuse her of adultery — even

---

[1] Ambrose, de Abraham, I, iii, 19 and iv, 26 (P.L. xiv, 427 and 431–2).
[2] Conf. VI, xv, 25.　　　　[3] Conf. VI, xv, 25.　　　　[4] de fide et oper. xix, 35.
[5] K. Holl, 'Augustins innere Entwicklung', Abh. preuss Akad. d. Wiss. 1922, (Philos. Hist. Kl. no. 4), 1923, p. 11, is harsh and just.

though she may have been guilty, in living with a man who was not her husband.'[1]

Moving delicately on the fringes of a great court, Augustine and his friends were touched by sentiments appropriate to courtiers in the Later Empire, as at other times: regrets for their vain ambitions, a studied admiration of the life of leisure. When Augustine was preparing a propaganda speech in honour of the Emperor, he and his circle will, of course, admire the more natural happiness of a drunken beggar;[2] and, following a current fashion, they toyed with the idea of living a 'Perfect Life', a *beata vita*, in a philosophical community.[3] So, ten of them, including Romanianus, would decide to pool their considerable resources so that they could all live together as friends, having retired from such cares of the world.[4] The scheme failed, the wives of the prospective recluses had objected(!), and their life in Milan continued much as before, through 385 and well into 386. Augustine continued to move among the local teachers: one, Verecundus, was glad to employ Nebridius as his assistant. Alypius took to giving advice on private cases after his third term as a lawyer in the financial administration.[5] The great lawsuit, which had brought Romanianus to Milan, dragged on, with Romanianus becoming ever more anxious.

Litigation in the Later Roman Empire involved an assiduous quest for patrons; and Romanianus must have counted on the support of leading Milanese citizens to secure a favourable settlement at the Imperial court. It may be in this way, as the *protégé* of Romanianus, and the tutor of his son, Licentius, that Augustine first made the acquaintance of these remarkable people.

We know of them from the letters and books which Augustine wrote late in 386: they are Zenobius,[6] Hermogenianus[7] and Manlius Theodorus.[8] The most notable, Manlius Theodorus, was a particularly cultured and influential man. He had retired from active life some three years previously, in about 383, and, in his country retreat, he had begun to write books on philosophy and a treatise on classical metre. Later, he will emerge to become consul, in 399.[9]

These men were united by intellectual interests which Augustine

[1] *de bono coniug.* v, 5.   [2] *Conf.* VI, vi, 10.   [3] *Conf.* VI, viii, 17.

[4] *Conf.* VI, xiv, 24.   [5] *Conf.* VIII, vi, 13.   [6] *Ep.* 2 and the *de ordine*.   [7] *Ep.* 1.

[8] *de beata vita*. It is the outstanding merit of P. Courcelle to have drawn attention to the existence of such a group in his *Les lettres grecques en Occident de Macrobe à Cassiodore*, 1948, pp. 119–129. A. Solignac in *Les Confessions, Biblio. augustin.*, sér. ii, 14, pp. 529–536, provides a useful summary.

[9] v. esp. Courcelle, *Les lettres grecques*, pp. 122–128 and *Recherches*, pp. 153–156.

came to share. The discovery of the nature and range of their interests is one of the most exciting events in modern research on Augustine: it has done nothing less than put his famous 'conversion', a lonely and intimate story as told in the *Confessions*, into perspective, as one event among many in the intellectual life of a brilliant capital.

These men thought of themselves as taking part in a Renaissance of philosophy. A century before, the authentic doctrine of Plato had been rediscovered: the clouds had parted, and this, 'the most refined and enlightened' teaching in philosophy, could shine out in its full brilliance, in the works of Plotinus — a soul so close to his ancient master that in him Plato seemed to live again.[1] Such men even had dreams, in which philosophers expounded 'Platonic maxims' to them in their sleep.[2] We call this movement 'Neo-Platonism': but the participants called themselves 'Platonists', *Platonici*, pure and simple — that is, the direct heirs of Plato.

Plotinus, an Egyptian Greek, had taught in Rome and had died in 270. His difficult and allusive discourses, now known as *The Enneads*,[3] were edited by his disciple Porphyry, also a Greek, from Tyre. The two men were very different. Plotinus was an amateur: a highly-intuitive man, arguing intensely, but obscurely, among sterile academics. He annoyed his pupils by insisting on threshing out each problem on its own merits as it arose, for days, if needs be, rather than give the usual course of set lectures on philosophical systems.[4] A man of massive detachment, he had once shocked and thrilled his scrupulous friends by saying, of a festival, that 'It is for those Beings to come to me, not for me to go to them.'[5]

Porphyry, by contrast, was a thoroughly-trained academic.[6] Augustine always calls him '*doctissimus*' and 'the most notable pagan philosopher'. He turned Plotinus' discovery of Plato into text-books, and made from it a coherent system, intensely religious and otherworldly. He is the first systematic theologian in the history of thought.[7]

---

[1] *C. Acad.* III, xviii, 41.   [2] *de civ. Dei*, XVIII, 18, 57–60.

[3] Translated by S. MacKenna, *Plotinus: The Enneads*, (2nd ed. 1956 and 3rd ed. 1962) with an illuminating introduction by P. Henry. The best biographical study of Plotinus is by R. Harder, *Kleine Schriften*, 1960, pp. 257–295. E. R. Dodds, 'Tradition and Personal Achievement in the Philosophy of Plotinus', *Journ. Rom. Studies*, l, 1960, pp. 1–7 and P. Hadot, *Plotin ou la simplicité du regard*, 1963, provide brilliant characterizations of the thought of Plotinus.

[4] Porphyry, *On the life of Plotinus*, 13, (MacKenna, 2, p. 9).

[5] Porphyry, *Life of Plotinus*, 10, (MacKenna, 2, p. 8).

[6] v. Harder, *Kleine Schriften*, p. 260.

[7] v. esp. H. Dörrie, 'Porphyrius als Mittler zwischen Plotin und Augustin', *Miscellanea Mediaevalia I: Antike und Orient im Mittelalter*, 1962, pp. 26–47, esp. pp. 41–43.

The title of a lost work of his which enjoyed great popularity at the time, 'De Regressu Animae', 'The Return (to Heaven) of the Soul', could well be the motto of the religious life of Milan: it is a motto summed up in a verse which Manlius Theodorus wrote for his sister, a nun, buried in the Ambrosian Basilica: 'Who, having no thought of mortal things within her mortal mind, has always loved the road that led to Heaven.'[1]

Porphyry, unlike Plotinus, was an unquiet and erratic man. He had been attracted to Christianity, then written the 'Against the Christians', a work for which he was to be notorious in the next century. At the age of 70, this writer of a treatise 'On abstinence', who had once 'conceived a hatred for the human body', suddenly married a widow, the mother of eight children. Throughout his life, he had been troubled by the insufficiency of a purely rational quest for God. He had dabbled in a collection of the utterances of mediums, the so-called 'Chaldaean Oracles',[2] and had once hoped to find, in phenomena as diverse as seances and Indian yogi, some 'Universal Way' that would set free the soul.[3]

Looking back on these two men, Augustine saw Plotinus as a great, impersonal mind, 'drawing out the hidden meaning of Plato.'[4] He and his contemporaries, pagan and Christian alike, entered far closer into the disquietudes of Porphyry. He seemed a microcosm of the tensions of serious pagan intellectuals. Augustine will present him as a Faust-like figure, whose urgent sense of the need for a divine liberator of the soul had kept ill company with a fascination with the occult.[5]

But Augustine's new acquaintances belonged to a different age from these two pagan Greeks.[6] In Milan, much of the articulate and fashionable Platonism was Christian. This highly significant change had begun in Rome, in the mid-century. There, an African professor of rhetoric, Marius Victorinus, had suddenly joined the Christian church. He also translated Plotinus and other Neo-Platonic writings into Latin.[7] Thus, the books made available by translation to less educated

[1] v. esp. Courcelle, 'Quelques symboles funéraires du néo-platonisme latin', Rev. études anciennes, 46, 1944, pp. 65–93, esp. pp. 66–73.

[2] v. esp. H. Lewy, Chaldaean Oracles and Theurgy. Mysticism, Magic and Platonism in the Later Roman Empire, 1956.

[3] On the evolution of Porphyry, v. the convincing reconstruction of P. Hadot, 'Citations de Porphyre chez Augustin', Rev. études augustin., vi, 1960, pp. 205–244, esp. pp. 239–240.

[4] e.g. de civ. Dei, X, 2, 7.   [5] e.g. de civ. Dei, X, 24.

[6] P. Henry, Plotin et l'Occident, (Spicilegium Sacrum Lovaniense, 15), 1934, is fundamental.

[7] v. the excellent introduction of P. Hadot to Marius Victorinus: Traités théologiques sur la Trinité, (Sources chrétiennes, 68), 1960, esp. pp. 7–76.

men such as Augustine, were provided by a man known to have died as a Christian.[1] Victorinus had even known a Milanese priest, Simplicianus, who was now an old and experienced man.[2] Since Simplicianus seems to have directed the theological studies of Ambrose, the Catholic bishop of the town had come within range of this movement; and Simplicianus, as the 'spiritual father' of Ambrose, had come to act as the *éminence grise* of a most audacious attempt to combine Platonism and Christianity.[3]

Like all exciting and self-confident movements, these Christian Platonists had their own view of the past, a view which seems naïve and bizarre in retrospect, but which was capable of opening up intriguing horizons to Augustine. After a long, esoteric existence, the philosophy of Plato, reconciled with that of Aristotle, had emerged as 'the one absolutely true philosophical culture'.[4] To a Christian Platonist, the history of Platonism seemed to converge quite naturally on Christianity. Both pointed in the same direction. Both were radically other-worldly: Christ had said, '*My Kingdom is not of this world*'; Plato had said the same of his realm of ideas.[5] For Ambrose, the followers of Plato were the 'aristocrats of thought'.[6]

It is into this movement that Augustine was about to enter. It was a movement with distinctive features among Latin-speakers. In the West, Platonism had become a philosophy for amateurs: often, the works of the Platonists would be read only in translation, as Augustine would do.[7] Victorinus and Augustine were remarkably alike: both men were products of an exclusively literary culture; for both of them, philosophy was an 'outside' interest, which deepened hand in hand with their interest in religion.[8] They lacked both the caution and the exclusiveness of established professors of philosophy such as continued to exist in Athens and Alexandria.[9] Like Cicero before them, these Latin amateurs never committed themselves entirely to the ideas they handled. They felt, however obscurely, that there was more to life than meta-

---

[1] *Conf.* VIII, ii, 2.   [2] *Conf.* VIII, ii, 2.

[3] v. esp. Courcelle, *Recherches*, pp. 137–138 and 168–174.

[4] *C. Acad.* III, xix, 42. v. most recently, R. Walzer, 'Porphyry and the Arabic Tradition', *Porphyre*, (Entretiens, Fondation Hardt, XII), 1965, pp. 275–299, esp. p. 288.

[5] *C. Acad.* III, xix, 42.

[6] Ambrose, *Ep.* 34, 1 (P.L. xvi, 1119). Holte, *Béatitude et Sagesse*, pp. 111–164, is a brilliant account of this tradition in Early Christian writers.

[7] *Conf.* VII, ix, 13; VIII, ii, 2.

[8] But v. Courcelle, *Les Confessions*, pp. 69–70, on the very vague meaning of '*orator*'.

[9] Thus H. I. Marrou, 'Synesius of Cyrene and Alexandrian Neo-Platonism', *The Conflict between Paganism and Christianity in the Fourth Century*, pp. 126–150, provides an essential doublet to Augustine in Milan.

physical systems: and, like Cicero, they tried whether as Catholics or as pagans, to reconcile the ideas they had picked up from the Greeks with the traditional religion of their elders.

Some time, perhaps in the early summer of 386,[1] Augustine was introduced to these new ideas. He obtained 'through a certain man, puffed up with overweening haughtiness ... a few books of the Platonists'.[2] It is typical of Augustine, that in his *Confessions*, this profound change in his thought should be merely hinted at in those few, unflattering strokes. We do not know who this man was. We do not know whether Augustine avoided naming him because he was still alive.[3] Nor do these reticent ideograms give any clue as to why Augustine should have obtained the books. It has been suggested, ingeniously but without sufficient foundation, that Augustine had been prompted to get hold of the writings of the Platonists because he had noticed the specifically Platonic tone of some of the sermons of Ambrose.[4] It may even be that, when Augustine and his friends had announced their intention of living a life in retirement as an intellectual community, some colleague made sure that they should spend their time reading the 'right' books.

We can only reconstruct with difficulty what books these were and who wrote them. They seem to have included many treatises of Plotinus, in the Latin translation of Marius Victorinus, and, possibly, one work at least, now lost, by Porphyry.[5] But Augustine, with an artist's touch, seems to have deliberately dwarfed the number of the books he had received and the time which he took to absorb them: for in this way he could convey, in his *Confessions*, the impression of the quite disproportionate impact which such few writings, obtained for him, as he now saw it, by God's providence through such an un-promising agency, had made on his religious ideas.

As with many immensely fertile thinkers, it is difficult to imagine Augustine as a reader. Yet, what happened at this crucial time, and in the years that follow, was a spell of long and patient reading, apparently

[1] Courcelle, *Recherches*, p. 280, (June).   [2] *Conf.* VII, ix, 13.

[3] As suggested by Courcelle, *Les Lettres grecques*, pp. 126–128: I am not convinced.

[4] As suggested by Courcelle, *Recherches*, pp. 133–138, but v. sup. p. 86.

[5] On the treatises of Plotinus read by Augustine, v. esp. P. Henry, *Plotin et l'Occident*, 1934, pp. 78–119, and on Plotinus and Porphyry, v. Courcelle, *Recherches*, pp. 157–167, and *Les Confessions*, pp. 27–42. I would agree with Hadot, 'Citations de Porphyre', *Rev. études augustin.*, vi, 1960, p. 241, in placing Plotinus, not Porphyry, at the centre of Augustine's reading in 386.

A. Solignac, in *Les Confessions, Biblio. augustin.*, sér. ii, 13, pp. 683–689, provides an instructive juxtaposition by printing passages from *Confessions* VII parallel to passages from the *Enneads*.

aided by some discussions.[1] Such reading included treatises of Plotinus, one of the most notoriously difficult writers in the ancient world. It was a reading which was so intense and thorough that the ideas of Plotinus were thoroughly absorbed, 'digested' and transformed by Augustine. Ambrose, who also read Plotinus, patently ransacked his author: it is possible to trace literal borrowings from Plotinus in the bishop's sermons. For Augustine, however, Plotinus and Porphyry are grafted almost imperceptibly into his writings as the ever present basis of his thought. He made his masters his own to such an extent, he picked out their main preoccupations with such uncanny perceptiveness, that he felt he could elaborate their thought in very different terms. Thus Augustine, an amateur philosopher who knew no Greek, appears as one of the few thinkers who could master the Neo-Platonic authors with an originality and independence of mind unequalled in an age in which many far better educated men prided themselves on being 'Platonists'.

Among the treatises by Plotinus, Augustine may well have read a short one entitled 'On Beauty'. It would have affected him intimately: for it dealt with a subject on which he had written, seven years before, in the *de pulchro et apto*; and, in the opening paragraphs, Plotinus dismissed the particular theory of beauty that Augustine then defended.[2] From this disconcerting beginning, Plotinus' enthusiastic exposition would have swept Augustine into the heart of the Platonic system: 'What loftier beauty there may be yet, our argument will bring to light.'[3]

Plotinus began by challenging the obvious: '. . . What is it that attracts the eye of those to whom a beautiful thing is presented . . . ?

'Almost everybody declares [as Augustine had done himself] that the symmetry of parts towards each other and towards a whole . . . constitutes the beauty recognized by the eye, that, in visible things, as indeed in all else, universally, the beautiful thing is essentially symmetrical, patterned.

'But think what this means. . . . All the loveliness of colour and even the light of the Sun, being devoid of parts and so not beautiful by symmetry, must be ruled out of this realm of beauty. And how comes

[1] I am indebted to the challenging approach to Augustine's absorption of Plotinus suggested by R. J. O'Connell, '*Ennead* VI, 4 and 5 in the works of St. Augustine', *Rev. études augustin.*, ix, 1963, pp. 1–39.

[2] *Conf.* IV, xv, 24. v. sup. p. 57, n. 4.

[3] v. G. Mathew, *Byzantine Aesthetics*, 1963, pp. 17–21, for a fine appreciation of Plotinus' ideas.

gold to be a beautiful thing? And lightning by night and the stars, why are these so fair?

'Again, since the one face constant in symmetry, appears sometimes fair and sometimes not, can we doubt that beauty is something more than symmetry, that symmetry itself owes its beauty to a remoter principle?'[1]

This new way of seeing things, persistently and passionately argued by Plotinus, impressed Augustine deeply. In his *Confessions*, he wrote a monumental summary of this train of thought, in his own, more sober and direct language:

'For I wondered how it was that I could appreciate beauty in material things ... and what it was that enabled me to make correct judgements about things that are subject to change, and to rule that one thing ought to be like this, another like that. I wondered how it was that I was able to judge them in this way, and I realized that, above my own mind, which was liable to change, there was the never-changing true eternity of truth. ...

'The power of reason, realizing that in me, too, it was liable to change, led me to consider the source of its own understanding. It withdrew my thoughts from their normal course ... so that it might discover what light it was that had been shed upon it when it proclaimed for certain that what was immutable was better than that which was not, and how it had come to know the immutable itself. For unless by some means, it had known the immutable, it could not possibly have been certain that it was preferable to the mutable. And so, in an instant of awe, my mind attained to the sight of the God who *is*.'[2]

Augustine will insist on this train of thought. Within a few months of his reading of the Platonic books, he will describe it to Nebridius as the 'exceptionally well-known argument'.[3]

For what had obsessed Plotinus, was the contrast between the changing and the changeless. In the 'here' of the world known to his senses, he was haunted by the timeless quality of a 'there' of another world, which his mind could grasp with abiding certainty in judging qualities such as goodness and beauty. This other world provided the basis of the world of the senses. It charged the passing spectacle of material things with an intensity and a permanence, that they could not possess in their own right. For things known to the senses can also be judged to be 'good' and 'beautiful'; and, in perceiving this quality in them, Augustine now saw them with the eyes of a Platonist, as depending for their existence on eternal principles.

[1] *Ennead*, I, vi, 1, (MacKenna 2, pp. 56–57).   [2] *Conf.* VII, xvii, 23.   [3] *Ep.* 4, 2.

Why was it that the beauty of the physical world was so superficial, so ephemeral, so saddening a depletion, a 'running out' of some concentrated 'inner' source of beauty, available to his mind alone? This was the problem which Plotinus thought that he shared with philosophers of all ages. The soul itself to him mirrored this process of depletion. For the soul 'falls': it loses touch with its deepest activity, and seeks beauty in the outside world, that it can no longer find in itself. Thus the transitory world of the senses imposes itself upon the soul's attention; the 'fallen' soul charges this world with a specious concreteness by focusing too narrowly upon it, to the exclusion of the deep, elusive echoes of its own inner beauty. What might be seized 'within', whole and simple in a moment of insight, has to be painfully sought in the outside world, again and again, on every level of the mind's activity. It is groped for by the long, pedestrian processes of discursive reasoning. It is further externalized by the artist, when he struggles to impose an abiding form on the transient, material stone of a statue. Even the statesman, imposing order on his city, is for Plotinus yet another such philosopher *manqué*: for he also seeks in the changeable world outside himself a satisfaction, which only his inner world can provide.[1]

Plotinus' universe therefore has a centre, which the mind can barely touch: 'All flows so to speak from one fount, not to be thought of as some one breath or warmth, but rather as one quality englobing and safeguarding all qualities — sweetness with fragrance, wine-quality, and the savours of everything that may be tasted, all colours seen, everything known to touch, all that ear may hear, all melodies, every rhythm.'[2] What we see around us is a disintegrated communication of this concentration of the whole. It is as if an artist, faced with the execution of a single theme, should lose his 'nerve': he becomes ever more diffuse, more literal; the first intensity goes. The vision has become scattered; but it is that same vision that he is striving to communicate.

The poignant sense that the average man, bound to the obvious world of the senses, is moving in twilight, that the knowledge he claims to possess is merely the last, dim state of an ineluctable progression of declining stages of awareness, is the hall-mark of Plotinus' view of the universe. Yet these declining stages are intimately related to each other: each stage depends on a 'superior' stage, because this 'superior' stage is fundamental to it, as the source of its consciousness. The

[1] Dodds, 'Tradition and Personal Achievement', *Journ. Rom. Studies*, l, 1960, p. 5.
[2] *Ennead*, VI, vii, 12, (MacKenna 2, pp. 570–571).

'inferior' stage is unlike its predecessor. It cannot 'know' it, any more than a literal-minded man can ever really capture the thought of an intuitive man. But instinctively each stage seeks to complete itself by 'touching' its superior, the alien but related source of its own consciousness. Thus the outward-going diffusion of the One coincides with a continuous tension of every part to 'return' to the source of its consciousness. This tension for completion is what links the One directly to each manifestation of Its intensity, and, most notably for Plotinus and his disciple Augustine, to the human mind that yearns to be complete.

Such, briefly, is the Neo-Platonic doctrine of *procession* outwards, and its corollary, a *turning* inwards.[1] The idea is as basic to the thought of the age of Augustine as is the idea of Evolution to our own.[2] It brought pagan and Christian thinkers together within a single horizon of ideas. For Plotinus, the Intellect was an all-important Mediating Principle: 'touching' the One, it turned outwards at the same time, as the source of the Many. It was easy to see in this fundamental, Mediating Principle, a philosophical exploration of the *Word* of the Gospel of S. John; and this is how Plotinus was read by cultured Christians in Milan: — '. . . I read — not, of course, word for word, though the sense was the same and it was supported by all kinds of different arguments — that: "*In the beginning was The Word, and The Word was with God, and The Word was God . . .*".'[3]

'The books also tell us that your only-begotten Son abides forever in eternity with you; that before all time began, He was; that He is above all time and suffers no change: that of his fullness our souls receive their part and hence derive their blessings: and that by partaking in the Wisdom which abides in them they are renewed, and this is the source of their Wisdom. . . .'[4]

Augustine read the Platonic books when he was still emerging from ways of thought that had led him to favour the Manichees. He had, for instance, found it impossible to think of God as both present to him, and, at the same time, separate.[5] As a Manichee, he had favoured a particularly drastic answer to this problem: the individual was entirely merged with the 'substance' of a good God, and everything that could not be identified with this fragment of perfection, he had split off as

[1] v. esp. Dodds, 'Tradition and Personal Achievement', *Journ. Rom. Studies*, l, 1960, pp. 2–4.

[2] E. Bréhier, *La Philosophie de Plotin*, rev. ed. 1961, p. 35; v. esp. pp. 35–45.

[3] *Conf.* VII, ix, 13.

[4] *Conf.* VII, ix, 14.

[5] v. esp. O'Connell, '*Ennead* VI, 4 and 5', *Rev. études augustin.*, ix, 1963, pp. 13–14.

absolutely and irredeemably evil.[1] Plotinus was able to help Augustine out of this dilemma. One of his most laborious treatises had been devoted to conveying that the spiritual world was fundamental to the world of place and time, while still remaining distinct from it.[2] More important still for Augustine, Plotinus had argued, constantly and passionately, throughout his *Enneads*, that the power of the Good always maintained the initiative: the One flowed out, touching everything, moulding and giving meaning to passive matter, without itself being in any way violated or diminished. The darkest strand of the Manichaean view of the world, the conviction that the power of the Good was essentially passive, that it could only suffer the violent impingement of an active and polluting force of evil, was eloquently denied by Plotinus: 'Evil is not alone: by virtue of the nature of good, the power of Good, it is not Evil only: it appears necessarily bound around with chains of Beauty, like some captive bound in fetters of gold: and beneath these it is hidden, so that, while it must exist, it may not be seen by the gods, and that men need not always have evil before their eyes, but that when it comes before them they may still not be destitute of images of the Good and Beautiful for their Remembrance.'[3]

For, Plotinus' universe was a continuous, active whole, which could admit no brutal cleavages and no violent irruptions. Each being in it drew strength and meaning from its dependence on this living continuum. Evil, therefore, was only a turning away into separateness: its very existence assumed the existence of an order, which was flouted while remaining no less real and meaningful. It was the self-willed part that was diminished, by losing contact with something bigger and more vital than itself.[4]

This view of evil overlaps without coinciding with Augustine's later elaboration. But Plotinus had been provoked by a similar challenge (he had written against the Christian Gnostics, the direct spiritual ancestors of the Manichees); and, to a former Manichee, such as Augustine, his views were quite sufficient to provoke a dramatic change of perspective.[5]

[1] v. sup. pp. 47 and 52.

[2] O'Connell, '*Ennead* VI, 4 and 5', *Rev. études augustin.*, ix, 1963, pp. 8–11.

[3] *Ennead*, I, viii, 15, (MacKenna 2, p. 78).

[4] *Ennead*, VI, vi, 12, (MacKenna 2, p. 541). v. O'Connell, '*Ennead* VI, 4 and 5', *Rev. études augustin.*, ix, 1963, pp .18–20.

[5] Plotinus, also, had been a 'convert' to authentic Hellenism from a form of Gnosticism, even if his evolution was less dramatic than Augustine's and his Gnosticism less radical. v. esp. H. C. Puech, 'Plotin et les gnostiques', *Les Sources de Plotin*, (Entretiens, Fondation Hardt, V) 1960, pp. 161–174, and the important treatment of this evolution in E. R. Dodds, *Pagan and Christian in an Age of Anxiety*, 1965, pp. 24–26.

It is this revolution which is, perhaps, the most lasting and profound result of Augustine's absorption of Neo-Platonism. It did nothing less than shift the centre of gravity of Augustine's spiritual life. He was no longer identified with his God: this God was utterly transcendent — His separateness had to be accepted. And, in realizing this, Augustine had to accept, that he, also, was separate and different from God: 'I realized that I was far away from you. I was in the land when all is different from You, and I heard Your voice calling: "I am the Food of full-grown men. Grow and you shall feed on me. But you shall not change me into yourself. . . . Instead, you shall be changed into me".'[1]

Just as Augustine could no longer identify himself with the good, so he could no longer reject all that did not measure up to his ideals as an absolute, aggressive force of evil. He could distance himself: the sense of intimate, passive involvement in all the good and evil of the world, gave way, under the influence of the Platonic books, to a view in which evil was only one, small aspect of a universe far greater, far more differentiated, its purposes more mysterious and its God far more resilient, than that of Mani. . . . 'I no longer desired a better world, because I was thinking of creation as a whole: and in the light of this more balanced discernment, I had come to see that higher things are better than the lower, but that the sum of all creation is better than the higher things alone.'[2]

<hr/>

[1] *Conf.* VII, x, 16. [2] *Conf.* VII, xiii, 19.

10

PHILOSOPHY

Some months later, in the autumn of 386, Augustine could write to Romanianus: 'We never ceased to sigh for Philosophy, and thought of nothing but of that form of life which we had agreed to live among ourselves. This we did continuously, though with less keenness, thinking that it was enough just to entertain the prospect. Since that flame which was to burn us up entirely had not yet flared up, we thought that the glow that warmed us slowly was the greatest there could be. Suddenly, some substantial books appeared . . . and sprinkled on this little flame a few small drops of precious ointment. They started up an incredible blaze, incredible, Romanianus, quite incredible, more than you might perhaps believe if I told you. What can I say? It was more powerful than I, myself, can bring myself to believe. After this, how could honour, human pomp, desire for empty fame, the consolations and attractions of this dying life, move me. Swiftly, I turned completely in upon myself.'[1]

Augustine's reading of the Platonic books had done one thing which everyone could understand: they had brought Augustine to a final and definitive 'conversion' from a literary career to a life 'in Philosophy'. This conversion was bound to affect Augustine's public and private life. Beyond this, nothing could be certain. If it was possible for a young man, in Carthage, in the 370's, to read an exhortation to Philosophy by Cicero . . . , and straightway to become a Manichee, the repercussions of having read Plotinus in Milan could be no less unpredictable. 'Conversion' is a very wide term: how drastically would this reorientation alter Augustine's life? 'Philosophy', also, could mean many things: what would be the precise nature of this 'Philosophy'? As it is, Augustine's 'conversion to Philosophy' is one of the most fully-documented records of such a change in the ancient world; its

[1] *C. Acad.* II, ii, 5.

course was one of the most complex: and the final form that emerged, one of the most idiosyncratic.

One thing was certain: Augustine could renounce the sceptical position of the New Academy. The first work that he wrote from his philosophical 'retreat' in Cassiciacum, was directed against such scepticism. In thus declaring that it was possible to find a 'true philosophy', Augustine may well have taken up a position against many purely literary men in Milan. For in the late fourth century, the professional Latin *rhetor*, caught between Christianity and paganism, would have been glad, as Augustine had once been glad, to have Cicero to shelter behind, against the cold winds of philosophical dogmatism and clerical orthodoxy.[1]

In abandoning his neutral position, however, Augustine would have found himself in troubled waters. The thought of sophisticated men in Milan was 'post-Plotinian', much as that of our own age is 'post-Freudian'. These common ideas, far from bringing pagans and Christians closer, had divided them with all the bitterness of a family quarrel: for well over a century, they had fought each other for a share in the inheritance of Plato.[2] The Christians would welcome, in the Platonists, a fine description of the structure of the spiritual universe; but pagan Platonists regarded the Christian myth of redemption — an Incarnation, a Crucifixion and a Resurrection of the body — as a barbarous innovation on the authentic teachings of their master. To them, it was as if some vandal had set up a vulgar and histrionic piece of Baroque sculpture beneath the ethereal dome of a Byzantine church. The more 'liberal' pagan Platonists had hoped to 'civilize' the Christian churches by writing '*In the beginning was the Word*' in golden letters on their walls; but they would not tolerate even S. John when he said that '*The Word was made flesh*'.[3] In Milan, they had provoked Ambrose to write a pamphlet by claiming that Christ had derived all that was good in His teachings from reading Plato![4]

These differences, however, were only symptoms of an even more profound tension over an issue that coincided only partially with the confessional division between pagans and Christians. The issue was one of spiritual autonomy: to what extent could a man be expected to work out his own salvation by his own power alone? Plotinus had been

---

[1] *Ep.* 135, 1: it is not surprisingly, the opinion favoured by a pagan literary circle in 411; v. inf. pp. 300–301.

[2] This tension is supremely well documented by Courcelle, 'Anti-Christian Arguments and Christian Platonism', *The Conflict between Paganism and Christianity*, pp. 151–192.

[3] *de civ. Dei*, X, 29, 99; v. esp. Courcelle, *Les Confessions*, pp. 73–74.

[4] *Ep.* 31, 8.

definite on this issue: his last words had been, 'I am striving to give back the Divine in myself to the Divine in the All'.[1] 'Nor does this divine self await liberation ... ; it awaits only discovery, there is no "drama of redemption".'[2] The Platonists had always felt able to offer a vision of God that a man might gain for himself, by himself, through the unaided, rational 'ascent' of his mind to the realm of ideas. This claim of immediate achievement had fascinated a previous Christian convert, the philosopher Justin, in the second century;[3] and now for a moment, it seems to have fascinated Augustine.

The tradition of individual autonomy could produce 'Christians' who were merely tolerant of the organized life of their church. For a time, Marius Victorinus had passed through such a phase: 'Privately, as between friends, though never in public, he used to say to Simplicianus: "I want you to know that I am now a Christian." Simplicianus used to reply: "I shall not believe it, or count you as a Christian until I see you in the Church of Christ." At this, Victorinus would laugh and say: "Is it then the walls of a church that make a Christian?"'[4] It is interesting that Simplicianus should have chosen this particular anecdote to tell to Augustine, when first approached by him. We may suspect that the shrewd old priest had summed up his visitor: he saw in Augustine a man like Victorinus — a professor of rhetoric, an admirer of the pagan Platonists, at best, merely tolerant of Catholicism.

At just that precise moment in Milan, in 386, walls certainly did make a Christian. In February, Augustine's mother was besieged, with her bishop, within the walls of the Catholic basilica;[5] and, from his *cathedra*, Ambrose had dared the eunuchs of the court to execute him rather than hand over those precious walls. But in June, while astonishing things were happening in Ambrose's new basilica, while possessed men were howling before the relics of SS. Gervasius and Protasius, Augustine still stood aloof:[6] 'There are some men' he wrote later, 'who consider themselves able to refine themselves on their own, in order to contemplate and remain in God. ... They can promise themselves such refinement through their own efforts, because a few of them really were able to carry their minds beyond all created things and touch, however partially, the light of unchanging truth.

---

[1] Porphyry, *Life of Plotinus*, 2, (MacKenna 2, p. 2).

[2] Dodds, 'Tradition and Personal Achievement', *Journ. Rom. Studies*, l, 1960, p. 7.

[3] v. Justin, *Dialogue with Trypho*, ii, 3–6.

[4] *Conf.* VIII, ii, 4.   [5] *Conf.* IX, vii, 15.

[6] v. esp. Courcelle, *Recherches*, pp. 157–167. G. Madec, 'Connaissance de Dieu et action de grâces', *Rech. augustin.*, ii, 1962, pp. 273–309, esp. pp. 279–282, is a perceptive treatment of this crucial period.

Accordingly, they look down upon the mass of Christians who live on faith alone, as not being yet able to do as they do. . . .'[1]

Thus, in the summer of 386, Augustine refused, for the last time in his life, to resist the temptations of complete spiritual autonomy. As the Manichees had once claimed to do, it really seemed as if this Philosophy would both be able to solve Augustine's metaphysical anxieties and to offer a way to self-fulfilment independent of an external authority. 'I chattered away' he wrote, 'as somebody in the know'. *Garriebam quasi peritus.* 'Had I continued to be such an expert, I should have gone to my destruction.'[2] *Peritus . . . periturus*: such is the tantalizingly succinct judgement of Augustine the bishop on this crucial moment.

The mood passed in a matter of a few months. But it was far from inevitable, that Augustine should finally have decided in favour of Catholicism. Pagan Platonism was a force to be reckoned with in the 380s; and the great alternative that Augustine considered for that short time, continued to haunt him throughout his life. It is shown in his continued fascination with the dilemma of the pagan Platonists, his anxious insistence on a discipline of authority as a pre-requisite for contemplation, in his acute awareness of the spiritual dangers of a failed mystic.[3] All this shows how a man's character is decided, not only by what actually happens in his life, but, also, by what he refuses to allow to happen.

Augustine, however, would never be another Plotinus; perhaps he lacked the massive tranquillity of the great pagan. Just as the Manichaean 'Wisdom' did not come to him only as an 'inner' knowledge, but also as an elaborate moral regime, which enabled him for many years to master his sense of guilt and involvement in the flesh,[4] so he now turned to find a discipline to complement the lucid spirituality of the Platonists.

It is not really surprising that he should have turned to the writings of S. Paul.[5] Ambrose had ensured that Augustine could again regard

---

[1] *de Trin.* IV, xv, 20.   [2] *Conf.* VII, xx, 26.

[3] e.g. *de quant. anim.* xxxiii, 75; *de mor. eccl. cath.* (I), vii, 11. While one may not be convinced that Augustine's view of Christ, at this crucial time, reflects exactly the opinion of Christ held by Porphyry and his pagan followers (v. Courcelle, 'S. Augustin "photinien" à Milan, *Conf.* VII, 19, 25', *Ricerche di storia religiosa*, i, 1954, pp. 225–239 and *Les Confessions*, pp. 33–42, with the criticisms of Hadot, 'Citations de Porphyre', *Rev. études augustin.*, vi, 1960, p. 241), it is impossible to deny that he passed through a phase of 'autonomous' Platonism, whose exponents had regarded themselves as superior to Christianity; v. esp. Courcelle, 'Les sages de Porphyre et les "viri novi" d'Arnobe', *Rev. études latines*, 31, 1953, pp. 257–271, esp. pp. 269–270.

[4] v. sup. pp. 50–51.   [5] *Conf.* VII, xxi, 27.

the Christian Scriptures as an authoritative source of Wisdom. In any case, Paul was in the air: Simplicianus would try to draw Ambrose to meet these interests by preaching on Paul as well as on the mysteries of the Old Testament.[1] The African Manichees had appealed constantly to Paul as the prophet of Mani *par excellence*, although they read him rather as an Apocryphal Scripture, picking out only what was consistent with Mani's authoritative canon of Holy Books.[2] In any case, Augustine had always lived sufficiently within the sphere of Christianity for his imagination to be caught quite as much by an Apostle as by a pagan sage: both, for him, were *viri magni*, 'The Great Men', of his curiously mixed past.[3] Thus, when Augustine read Paul at that time, he would have been reading a text which, as a Manichee, he had known of in bits and pieces. Now the time had come to see it as a unity; and inevitably, the unity that emerged was coloured by Augustine's preoccupations. 'Because even if a man "*takes pleasure in the Law of God in his inner Self*" what about "*the other law — which I see in my members?*" What shall be done with "*O wretched man that I am!*": Who shall "*set him free?*"[4]

When Augustine finally approached the priest Simplicianus (perhaps in late July 386), he had already moved imperceptibly towards Catholic Christianity. He was, indeed, an enthusiastic convert to 'Philosophy'; but this 'Philosophy' had already ceased to be an entirely independent Platonism. It had been 'fortified', in a highly individual way, by the more sombre teachings of S. Paul; and it had come to be identified, on a far deeper level, with 'the religion woven into our very bones as children' — that is, with the solid Catholic piety of Monica.[5]

Augustine had been trying to 'stand still'.[6] He wanted some guarantee of permanence and stability. This accounts for the main feature of his 'Philosophy': it was a Platonism whose immediate gains were to be made permanent; and such permanence could be gained only by abdicating a large measure of self-reliance. The methods, the aims and the final satisfactions of the wise man remained those upheld by the Platonists. But Augustine would embark on his life 'in Philosophy' as a convalescent: the therapy which the Platonic tradition had always demanded of anyone who would rise above the world of the senses, would no longer depend on himself alone, but on an 'invisible doctor',[7] that is, on God. And this God was no lonely aristocrat: this therapy had been made available to the mass of men by an act of *popularis*

---

[1] Ambrose, *Ep.* 37, 1 (P.L. xvi, 1085) v. inf. pp. 153–154. [2] *Conf.* VII, xxi, 27.
[3] *C. Acad.* II, ii, 5. [4] *Conf.* VII, xxi, 27.
[5] *C. Acad.* II, ii, 5. [6] *Conf.* VIII, i, 1. [7] *Sol.* I, xiv, 25.

clementia[1] — that is, by the Incarnation of Christ and by the preservation of divine scriptures in a universal church. These considerations form the first sketch of Augustine's idea of the Catholic church.
Yet so rich in paradoxes is this crucial stage in Augustine's life, that it
can be suggested, plausibly, though without carrying complete
conviction, that Augustine might have seen his own dilemma and its
solution, reflected as in a distant mirror, in the works of that other,
unquiet soul, Porphyry, the great enemy of the Christians. For
Porphyry, also, had hoped for a 'Universal Way', open to the mass of
men.[2]

These, and similar, considerations had led Augustine to approach
Simplicianus: 'By now he was an old man, and I thought that in all the
long years he had spent to such good purpose following Your Way, he
must have gained great experience and knowledge. I hoped that if I
put my problems to him, he would draw upon his experience and his
knowledge to show me how best a man in my state of mind might walk
upon Your Way.

'I saw that the church was full, yet its members each followed a
different path in the world. But my own life in the world was
unhappy. . . .'[3]

Augustine, indeed, had to face the prospect of some bitter renunciations, if he wished to become, at one and the same time, a baptized
Catholic and a Philosopher. In Milan, ideas of forms of life which we
are now accustomed to keep separate, overlapped and intermingled
inextricably in the imagination of Augustine and his friends. The ideal
of philosophical retirement was as stringent as any call to the monastic
life: it would mean breaking off his career, his marriage, all forms of
sexual relations; while the renunciations which the Catholic church
demanded in its mysteries of baptism, were also thought of as heroic, as
nothing less than the death of an old life. Augustine's friend, Verecundus, for instance, would not be baptized as a Christian just because
he was a married man, even though his wife was a Christian.[4] A heroic
break with the world was all that these enthusiasts could envisage for
themselves on becoming baptized. It is hardly surprising, therefore,
that the majority of Christians in the Later Roman Empire fought shy
of baptism; that Constantine, the first Christian Emperor and, with

---

[1] *C. Acad.* III, xix, 42; *de ord.* II, x, 29.

[2] The case is persuasively stated by J. O'Meara, *The Young Augustine*, 1954, pp. 143–155,
and *Porphyry's Philosophy from Oracles in Augustine*, 1959; but see the weighty reserves
of Hadot, 'Citations de Porphyre', *Rev. études augustin.*, vi, 1960, pp. 205–244, (with
O'Meara's comment, pp. 245–247).

[3] *Conf.* VIII, i, 1–2.   [4] *Conf.* IX, iii, 5.

him, many others, were baptized only on their death bed; and that Ambrose preached in vain, with macabre urgency, for his flock to pass through this spiritual 'death' to the world: 'How long with your *delights*; how long with your *revelling*? The day of judgement draws ever nearer: while you postpone this grace, death approaches. Who shall say, then: Now, I am not free, I am busy. . . .'[1]

'. . . the only answers I could give were the drowsy words of a lie-a-bed — "Soon." "Presently." "Let me wait a little longer." But "soon" was not soon and "a little longer" grew much longer.'[2]

At the end of August, the little group received a visitor who had been at the court of Trèves, Ponticianus, a fellow-African, a member of the Imperial reserve of Special Agents.[3] This pious man was surprised to find a copy of S. Paul on Augustine's table. He took to telling Augustine and Alypius about the monks of Egypt and of how the story of their founder, S. Anthony, had moved two of his colleagues at Trèves to leave the world:[4]

'This was what Ponticianus told us. But while he was speaking, O Lord, You were turning me around to look at myself. . . . I saw it all and stood aghast, but there was no place where I could escape from myself. . . .

'. . . Many years of my life had passed — twelve, unless I was wrong — since I had read Cicero's *Hortensius* at the age of 19, and it had inspired me to study philosophy. But I still postponed my renunciation of this world's joys. . . .

'I turned upon Alypius. My looks betrayed the commotion of my mind as I exclaimed: "What is the matter with us? What is the meaning of this story? These men have none of our education, yet they stand up and storm the gates of heaven while we, for all our learning, lie here grovelling in this world of flesh and blood! . . ."[5]

'. . . I broke off and turned away, leaving Alypius to gaze at me speechless and astonished. . . . There was a small garden attached to the house where we lodged. . . . I now found myself driven by the torment in my breast to take refuge in this garden, where no one could interrupt that fierce struggle, in which I was my own contestant, until it came to its conclusion. . . . I tore my hair and hammered my forehead with my fists; I locked my fingers and hugged my knees. . . .[6]

'I was held back by mere trifles, the most paltry inanities, all my old attachments. They plucked at my garments of flesh and whispered:

---

[1] Ambrose, *de Helia vel de ieiunio*, xxii, 85 (P.L. xiv, 764).   [2] *Conf.* VIII, v, 12.

[3] *Conf.* VIII, vi, 12.   [4] *Conf.* VIII, vi, 15.

[5] *Conf.* VIII, vii, 18.   [6] *Conf.* VIII, viii, 20.

"Are you going to dismiss us? From this moment we shall never be with you again, for ever and ever. From this moment you will never again be allowed to do this thing, or that, for evermore." What was it, my God, when they whispered "This thing" or "that"? Things so sordid and so shameful that I beg You in Your mercy to keep the soul of Your servant free from them. . . .

'And again, continence seemed to say: "Close your ears to the unclean whispers of your body. It tells you of things that delight you, but not of such things as the Law of the Lord your God has to tell."

'In this way I wrangled with myself, in my own heart, about my own self. And all the while Alypius stayed at my side, silently awaiting the outcome of this agitation that was now in me. . . .[1]

'I probed the hidden depths of my soul and wrung its pitiful secrets from it, and when I mustered them all before the eyes of my heart, a great storm broke within me, bringing with it a great deluge of tears. I stood up and left Alypius so that I might weep and cry to my heart's content. . . . I moved away far enough to avoid being embarrassed even by his presence.

'Somehow I flung myself down beneath a fig-tree and gave way to the tears which now streamed from my eyes, the sacrifice that is acceptable to you. . . . For I felt that I was still the captive of my sins, and in my misery I kept crying "How long shall I go on saying 'Tomorrow, tomorrow'? Why not now? Why not make an end of my ugly sins at this moment?"

'I was asking myself these questions, weeping all the while with the most bitter sorrow in my heart, when all at once I heard the sing-song voice of a child in a nearby house. Whether it was the voice of a boy or a girl I cannot say, but again and again it repeated the refrain "Take it and read, take it and read". At this I looked up, thinking hard whether there was any kind of game in which children used to chant words like these, but I could not remember ever hearing them before. I stemmed my flood of tears and stood up, telling myself that this could only be a divine command to open my book of Scripture and read the first passage on which my eyes should fall. For I had heard the story of Anthony, and I remembered how he had happened to go into a church while the Gospel was being read and taken it as a counsel addressed to himself when he heard the words: *Go home and sell all that belongs to you.* . . .

'So I hurried back to the place where Alypius was sitting, for when I

---

[1] *Conf.* VIII, xi, 27.

stood up to move away I had put down the book containing Paul's Epistles. I seized it and opened it, and in silence I read the first passage on which my eyes fell: "*Not in revelling and drunkenness, not in lust and wantonness, not in quarrels and rivalries. Rather, arm yourselves with the Lord Jesus Christ, spend no more thought on nature and nature's appetites.*" I had no wish to read more and no need to do so. For in an instant, as I came to the end of the sentence, it was as though the light of confidence flooded into my heart and all the darkness of doubt was dispelled.

'I marked the place with my finger or by some other sign and closed the book. My looks now were quite calm as I told Alypius what had happened to me. He too told me what he had been feeling, which of course I did not know. He asked to see what I had read. I showed it to him and he read on beyond the text which I had read. I did not know what followed, but it was this: *Find room among you for a man of over-delicate conscience. . . .*

'Then we went in and told my mother, who was overjoyed. And when we went on to describe how it had all happened, she was jubilant with triumph and glorified You, *who are powerful enough, and more than powerful enough, to carry out your purpose beyond all our hopes and dreams. . . .* You converted me to yourself, so that I no longer desired a wife or placed any hope in this world, but stood firmly upon the rule of faith, where you had shown me to her in a dream so many years before. And you *turned her sadness into rejoicing*, into joy far fuller than her dearest wish, far sweeter and more chaste than any she had hoped to find in children begotten of my flesh.'[1]

In any case, Augustine had come to the end of his career. During the summer he had developed some illness of the chest, a *dolor pectoris*, which affected his voice, and so would have made it impossible to continue his work.[2] It would be of great importance to know the exact nature of this sudden development: such knowledge might reveal the stress under which Augustine had been living.[3] Some, for instance, have suggested that this 'pain' was a bout of asthma, which is often a psychosomatic illness;[4] and it is more than probable, that in these tense months, Augustine had come to develop the physical manifestations of a nervous breakdown. It is perhaps most revealing, that although

---

[1] *Conf.* VIII, xii, 28–30.   [2] *Conf.* IX, ii, 4.

[3] B. Legewie, 'Die körperliche Konstitution und Krankheiten Augustins', *Misc. Agostin.*, ii, 1930, pp. 5–21, esp. pp. 19–20, is duly cautious.

[4] v. Klegeman, 'A psychoanalytic study of the Confessions', *Journ. Amer. Psychoanalytic Assoc.*, v, 1957, p. 481.

Augustine suffered from frequent ill-health in his later life, this 'pain in the chest', a pain which seemed to strike him just where he was most implicated in his career as a public speaker, and in just that part of the body which he later came to regard as the symbolic resting-place of a man's pride,[1] is never again mentioned.

So it is that, at the time of the Vintage Holidays, the *Feriae Vindemiales*, a time always welcomed by teachers as a Vacation that might be dedicated to creative leisure, Augustine and a small, strangely assorted group, his son, his mother, his brother and cousins, Alypius, Licentius and Trygetius, a young nobleman, retired to a country-villa lent them by Verecundus at Cassiciacum, perhaps, the modern Cassiago, near Lake Como, in the beautiful foothills of the Alps.[2]

Augustine was an ill man: but his convalescence did not affect the sudden spate of books that announced to learned circles in Milan, the delights of his new-found life 'in Philosophy' — a work against the Academics, for Romanianus; a religious discourse, on the *Perfect Life*, for Manlius Theodorus; for Zenobius, a Pythagorean essay on the *Order* of the Liberal Arts as a stepping-stone to a contemplation of the order of the Universe.[3]

These works have been scrutinized minutely for evidence of Augustine's evolution in the previous months: but it is easy to forget that they also throw light on a more profound aspect of the evolution of a man, that is, on the nature of the future that Augustine thought he had won for himself.

Augustine had now found a field of intellectual activity that assured him of fruitful progress: as he told a friend, he 'had broken the most hateful bonds that had held me away from the breast of Philosophy — the despair of finding Truth, Truth which is the nourishing food of the soul'.[4] And this voracious intellect felt that he had gained his future through the religion of his mother: 'It is by your prayers — I know it and admit it without hesitation — that God has given me a mind to place the Discovery of Truth above all things, to wish for nothing else, to think of nothing else, to love nothing else. And I never cease to believe that it is your prayers which will enable us to achieve so great a good. . . .'[5]

---

[1] *de Gen. c. Man.* II, xvii, 26.

[2] On the location of Cassiciacum, v. Pellegrino, *Les Confessions de S. Augustin*, p. 191, n. 2.

[3] J. Nørregaard, *Augustins Bekehrung*, 1923, though outdated on the circumstances of Augustine's conversion, remains an invaluable study of the religious ideas that appear in the Cassiciacum dialogues.

[4] *Ep.* 1, 3.   [5] *de ord.* II, xx, 52; cf. *de beata vita*, i, 6.

Augustine felt that he was exploring a 'Philosophy' which was both fully-integrated and well-signposted: the *sacra* and *mysteria*, the rites and dogmas, of the Catholic church summed up completely the truths which the mind of a philosopher might one day grasp.[1] Augustine's Platonic universe admitted of no brutal cleavages between the traditional authority of the Catholic religion and his own reason. Like M. Jourdain, who had talked prose all his life without realizing it, Augustine's philosopher, with his 'very subtle reasonings' would, in fact, be talking theology.[2]

We can appreciate the sense of confidence which this view gave Augustine when we read a small discourse, the '*De Beata Vita*', 'The Happy Life', which he dedicated to Manlius Theodorus. Manlius Theodorus was known to be an admirer of Plotinus.[3] He was, also, a good Catholic. In dedicating 'one of my most religious' works[4] to such a man — a book impeccably orthodox on the Trinity and prefaced by solemn warnings against academic pride[5] — Augustine may well have sought to make an honourable amend to the men around Ambrose for his flirtations with more dubious intellectuals, among them 'the man . . . of overweening haughtiness', in the past summer.[6] The discourse is made to end with the audience realizing that, in defining the sources of the Happy Life, they had in fact described the Catholic Trinity;[7] and so, Monica can close a pious evening, by chanting a hymn of S. Ambrose, *Fove precantes Trinitas*.[8] At the beginning of that same year, such hymns must have been sung by the Catholic populace during their resistance to the Court.[9] It is not often in the history of thought, that a philosophical dialogue can culminate in such a way with a fighting-song.

Augustine had regained a sense of purpose. 'Believe me', he wrote to Romanianus, 'rather, believe Him who said, "*Seek and ye shall find*": such comprehension is not to be despaired of; and it shall come to be more self-evident than are the properties of numbers.'[10] '*Seek and ye shall find*' is one of the very few Scriptural citations used in Augustine's first works. This particular citation had been a common tag among the Manichees;[11] and so it appears quite naturally in a work written to Romanianus and his fellow-Africans, all of them former Manichaean sympathizers.[12] *Plus ça change, plus c'est la même chose*: the least

[1] e.g. *de ord.* II, v, 16.
[2] v. esp. Holte, *Béatitude et Sagesse*, pp. 303–327.
[3] *de beata vita*, i, 4.
[4] *de beata vita*, i, 5.
[5] *de beata vita*, i, 3.
[6] v. sup. pp. 94 and 102–104.
[7] *de beata vita*, iv, 34.
[8] *de beata vita*, iv, 35
[9] *Conf.* IX, vii, 15.
[10] *C. Acad.* II, iii, 9.
[11] *de mor. eccl. cath.* (I), xvii, 31.
[12] *C. Acad.* II, iii, 8.

surprising thing about Augustine, at this time, was that he should have identified Philosophy with some form of Christianity. Ever since his first, abortive 'conversion to Philosophy' at Carthage, Augustine had moved within a horizon in which Christianity and Wisdom were thought of as coinciding. But the difference between a Manichaean version of Christianity and this Christian Platonism is enormous: the Manichees excluded any process of growth and intellectual therapy; they had claimed to offer him an esoteric 'Wisdom' which would make him pure.[1] Augustine had found that this 'Wisdom' had enabled him to 'make no progress',[2] while he now felt that he had entered into a life 'in Philosophy' in which progress was assured.

It is this confident sense of being able to develop his intellect creatively within the framework of the Catholic church that would have made Augustine seem strange even to so cultured a bishop as Ambrose. The reading of the Platonic books had ensured one thing: Augustine, who had come to Milan as a disillusioned careerist, not averse to falling back on the established religion of his parents, did not, in the end, make an act of unconditional surrender to the Catholic bishop. He was very definitely not a *type croyant*, such as had been common among educated men in the Latin world before his time. He did not believe that philosophy had proved sterile, and, so, that the methods of the philosophers could be replaced by a revealed Wisdom. Ambrose, for all his use of pagan authors, seems to have taken this old-fashioned view. He thought of himself first and foremost as a bishop, whose duty it was to understand and communicate to his flock the 'sea' of the Scriptures. Anything that could not be poured into this single mould was valueless. He once wrote to a philosopher who was perplexed by the problem of the nature of the soul, a problem which was to obsess Augustine at Cassiciacum, that he should read the Book of Esdras.[3] He answered the letter in which Augustine, in asking to be baptized, had also laid bare his perplexities, (if only this letter had survived!), by recommending him to read the Book of Isaiah. Augustine found the book quite incomprehensible![4] Later, Ambrose even came to believe that Julian the Apostate had lapsed from Christianity when he had 'given himself over to Philosophy';[5] and this is exactly what Augustine, in a series of works and letters, proudly proclaimed himself to be doing in Cassiciacum! The difference between the two men is a symptom of a change of momentous consequence in

[1] *de mor. eccl. cath.* (I), xxv, 47. v. sup. pp. 59–60.   [2] *Conf.* V, x, 18.
[3] Ambrose, *Ep.* 34, 2 (P.L. xvi, 1119).   [4] *Conf.* IX, v, 13.
[5] Ambrose, *de obitu Theodosii*, 51 (P.L. xvi, 1466).

the culture of the Christian church. Ambrose, the fully educated bishop who read Greek, still belongs to the old world. He felt himself intimately bound to the vast prestige of the Christian scholarship of the Greek world, above all, to the great Origen of Alexandria. Augustine, the amateur, felt far more free to follow his own course: and, paradoxically, in so doing, he came closer than did Ambrose to the spirit of the early Christian schools of Alexandria,[1] and so, to a firm belief that a mind trained on philosophical methods could think creatively within the traditional orthodoxy of the church. The revolution is all the more radical because Augustine, at the time, seems to have taken his own position entirely for granted: 'for I am ust the sort of man who is impatient in his longing not only to take what is true on faith, but to come to understand it.'[2]

A sense of purpose and continuity is the most striking feature of Augustine's 'Conversion'. Seen in his works at Cassiciacum, this 'conversion' seems to have been an astonishingly tranquil process. Augustine's life 'in Philosophy' was shot through with S. Paul; but it could still be communicated in classical terms. The highest rewards of such a life were, almost automatically, reserved for those who had received a traditional, classical education.[3]

This sense of continuity is all the more surprising, as Augustine had already heard of an alternative to a classical life 'in Philosophy': that of the monks of Egypt. The asceticism of such men had involved much purely physical mortification, and a decisive breach with the forms of classical culture. But the heroic example of S. Anthony had left Augustine's intellectual programme unaffected. He intended to remain an educated man: as he wrote to Zenobius, some men deal with the wounds inflicted on them by the senses by 'cauterizing' them 'in solitude', while others 'apply ointment to them' by means of the Liberal Arts.[4] Plainly Augustine, surrounded by his relatives and pupils, his library in Cassiciacum well stocked with traditional textbooks,[5] had chosen the more gentle treatment of the Liberal Arts.

The modern historian of Late Roman culture is in a better position than his predecessors to understand the tranquil synthesis of great traditions, that is so marked a feature of the works which Augustine wrote at Cassiciacum: they reflect the catholic tastes and broad sympathies of a group of Milanese Christians. Augustine's own tranquillity of mind, however, may have had deep, personal roots.

---

[1] v. Holte, *Béatitude et Sagesse*, pp. 177–190, is a brilliant assessment.
[2] *C. Acad.* III, xx, 43.
[3] e.g. *de ord.* I, vii, 20; II, v, 15 and xvi, 44.
[4] *de ord.* I, i, 2.
[5] e.g. *de ord.* I, ii, 5.

These are only revealed ten years later in Augustine's *Confessions*, that work of deep psychological authenticity, rather than in the formal, literary works of the time of his 'conversion'. In his formal works, Augustine wrote as one public figure to other public men: he is a professor in retirement, and so his illness, the reason for this retirement, is mentioned,[1] as are the effects of his retirement on his public career, that is, his abandonment of a rich marriage and the prospects of a governmental post: but the classic scene in the garden in Milan is passed over in silence. Yet it is only in this scene that we can glimpse the depth of the reorientation which was taking place in Augustine. It affected parts of him which bore little relation to his public life as a literary man: it affected the nature of his painful involvements with women, and, of course, his even more intimate relation with his mother.

When Augustine retired to Cassiciacum, a change had already taken place in him on that deep level. Because of it, Augustine felt a free man again, able to pursue his interests with new energy and certainty. So intimate a readjustment did not need to be expressed in histrionic gestures, such as had been fashionable among the less balanced admirers of the monks, the learned Jerome among them.[2] Instead, one has the impression that the sudden, sanguine creativity of Augustine's new 'Life in Philosophy' mirrors the feelings of a man who, for a few precious years, could feel at last that he had regained a lost innocence.

[1] e.g. *de ord.* I, ii, 5.
[2] v. H. von Campenhausen, *The Fathers of the Latin Church*, (transl. 1964), pp. 184–188.

II

CHRISTIANAE VITAE OTIUM: CASSICIACUM[1]

When Augustine retired to Cassiciacum, in September 386, he would have appeared to be following a long-established and delightful tradition: delivered from the cares of a public career, he was about to enter upon a life of creative leisure, dedicated to serious pursuits. This was the ancient ideal of *otium liberale*, of a 'cultured retirement';[2] and looking back upon this period of his life, Augustine could speak of it as a time of *Christianae vitae otium*, a 'Christian otium'.[3] This ideal was to form the background of Augustine's life from that time until his ordination as a priest, in 391.

In the late fourth century the tradition of *otium* had taken on a new lease of life. It had become more complex, and, often, far more earnest. On their great estates in Sicily, the last pagan senators continued to re-edit manuscripts of the classics (as Augustine did, for part of the time, in Cassiciacum). One such country villa even came to be known as 'The Philosopher's Estate'.[4] And they had been joined by more troubled figures: a century earlier, Porphyry had retired to the same island to recover from a nervous breakdown and to write his bitter treatise 'Against the Christians'.[5] Many had come to think that this essentially private life might be organized as a community. Augustine

[1] The historian is particularly fortunate to possess two brilliant analyses of Augustine's programme at Cassiciacum and of its position in Late Antique culture, by H. I. Marrou, *S. Augustin et la fin de la culture antique*, 1938, pp. 161–327, esp. pp. 161–186, and R. Holte, *Béatitude et Sagesse*, 1962, notably pp. 73–190 and 303–327.

[2] *de ord.* I, ii, 4.

[3] *Retract.* I, i, 1.

[4] v. A. Ragona, *Il proprietario della villa romana di Piazza Armerina*, 1962, pp. 52 sq.

[5] S. Mazzarino, 'Sull'*otium* di Massiminiano Erculio', *Rend. Accad. dei Lincei*, s. 8, viii, 1954, pp. 417–421.

and Romanianus had already toyed with the idea;[1] Plotinus had once planned a 'City of Philosophers' called Platonopolis.[2] Later, in Augustine's middle age, Dardanus, a retired Prefect, would turn his village in the Basses Alpes into a Christian version of this philosophers' Utopia, called 'Theopolis', 'City of God.'[3] Indeed, some of the first monasteries in the West were these 'lay monasteries' of sensitive pagans and Christians.

For at least a year, Augustine had regarded some form of this life 'in Philosophy' as the only possible life for himself.[4] But he had intended to retire gracefully into such a life. He would marry a rich and, so he hoped, a well-educated heiress. He would serve the short spell of routine administration required of a cultured local governor. Supported by his wife's estates[5] and protected by the senatorial privileges of a former administrator, he would have found himself free, in a few years, to follow his dream.[6] Life, however, proved more complicated. The retreat of the little group to Cassiciacum was quite precipitate: within a few months, Augustine had abandoned his marriage, his public position, his hopes of financial security and social prestige. His friends may well have been puzzled, especially his patron, Romanianus. A slight note of embarrassment lingers in the very formal language of Augustine's dedication to him of his first work. It may well have been difficult to communicate what had, also, been a stormy religious conversion, in terms of a gracious withdrawal from public life, such as might have satisfied Cicero.

Perhaps the ancient tradition of *otium liberale* appealed to Augustine just because his life had, recently, been far too complicated. He needed a firm, traditional mode of life, such as was provided in Cassiciacum, both dignified and explicable in the eyes of the learned circles of Milan. The estate belonged to Verecundus, a professor who shared in the current enthusiasm for a life in retirement. An illustrious precedent for such a retirement had been set by Manlius Theodorus.[7] Later, this retreat could be thought of as a fitting subject for a mediocre poem: it could be described as a country idyll, spent among school books, within sight of the Alps.[8]

Augustine's writings, also, are closely linked to his past life. We would be rash to scrutinize them for traces of the future bishop. They

---

[1] v. sup. p. 90. v. Courcelle, *Les Confessions*, pp. 21–26.
[2] Porphyry, *Life of Plotinus*, 12, (MacKenna 2, p. 9).
[3] H. I. Marrou, 'Un lieu dit "Cité de Dieu",' *Aug. Mag.*, i, 1954, pp. 101–110.
[4] *C. Acad.* II, ii, 4.   [5] *Sol.* I, x, 17.   [6] *de beata vita*, i, 4.
[7] v. sup. p. 90.   [8] *Ep.* 26, 4 (the poem of Licentius).

represent the payment of intellectual debts contracted in Milan over the past year:[1] the *De Beata Vita* takes up discussions that may have been held in the house of Manlius Theodorus;[2] the *De Ordine* was written in answer to a poem by Zenobius.[3] Thus, Augustine's first surviving works, preserved, originally, on the shelves of his episcopal library, far away in Hippo, are the only fragments that remain of that marvellous society of Christian laymen in Milan. Augustine's readers were confident that the history of philosophy had culminated in their own movement.[4] They were proud of the literary achievement of their own times.[5] They themselves could write dialogues in the manner of Cicero.[6] They included aesthetes,[7] able to appreciate the techniques of mosaic;[8] poets, who wrote on philosophical themes, such as on the beauty of the universe,[9] and who anticipate Boethius by seeking, in philosophy, to exorcize the fear of death:[10] they also knew what it was to take in the smells of a rose-garden.[11]

This environment gives Augustine's early works a quality unique in his life: his dialogues are content to show the sunny surface of his thought, and the studied charm of his personal relationships. In such a mood, he is ready to believe the best of people. Romanianus has been defeated in a lawsuit. But Augustine can extend his sympathy even to Romanianus' rival, another *grand seigneur*: 'I must confess that he has a certain grandeur of soul, lying dormant. . . . From this there springs his way of keeping open house, the charming wit which enlivens his social gatherings, his elegance, his grand manner, his impeccable good taste. . . . Believe me, we should despair of no-one, and least of all of such men. . . .'[12] As for Romanianus, he is like a dark thundercloud. Every now and then, his friends have a chance of seeing him lit up by a sudden bright flash: if only his soul was free to shine out in its full brilliance, it would astonish everyone![13]

But it is Augustine, and not Romanianus, who is opaque. He is a tired, sick man. He must speak slowly and deliberately to avoid excitement.[14] He thinks late in the dark;[15] and, in the mornings, he prays frequently, in the passionate manner of Late Roman men, 'with tears.'[16] He is open, as seldom later, to the natural beauties around him: the rhythm of running water in the bathhouse;[17] two cocks fighting in the morning sunlight;[18] the clear skies of an Italian autumn: 'the day' he

[1] *C. Acad.* II, ii, 3. [2] *de beata vita*, vii, 16. [3] *de ord.* I, vii, 20.

[4] *C. Acad.* III, xix, 42. [5] *Sol.* II, xiv, 26. [6] *de ord.* I, xi, 31.

[7] *de ord.* I, ii, 4. [8] *de ord.* I, i, 2 and 4. [9] *de ord.* I, vii, 20.

[10] *Sol.* II, xiv, 26. [11] *de ord.* II, xi, 33. [12] *C. Acad.* II, ii, 6.

[13] *C. Acad.* I, i, 2. [14] *C. Acad.* III, vii, 15. [15] *de ord.* I, iii, 6.

[16] *de ord.* I, viii, 22. [17] *de ord.* I, iii, 6. [18] *de ord.* I, viii, 25.

writes 'was of such limpid clarity that nothing seemed to fit so perfectly the serenity that was to dawn in our own minds'.[1] In this fragile mood, the physical pain of toothache was the supreme degradation; by it, the body refused to leave him alone with his thoughts.[2]

By the end of his stay, the openness of the dialogues is replaced by a mood of intimate self-searching, in his *Soliloquia*, his 'Conversations with Myself'. 'Of a sudden, someone spoke to me — perhaps it was myself, perhaps some other, outside me or within, I do not know. (For that is what I strive, above all else, to know.)'[3] The self-portrait that emerges is drawn by a sombre examination of his weaknesses: 'How sordid, filthy and horrible a woman's embraces seemed to you, when we were discussing the desire for a wife. But that very night, when you lay awake, turning it over in your mind — it was different from what you supposed. . . . But do not cry! Take heart: you have already cried so much; it has only added to the illness in your chest.'[4]

Only a few figures in Augustine's circle emerge in the dialogues. Monica is in charge of the household. She is as awesome as ever, seeming to draw upon hidden resources of absolute certainty. She can dismiss a whole philosophical school in a single vulgar word;[5] and her son has established her, with great intensity, as an oracle of primitive Catholic piety.[6] Augustine's eldest brother, Navigius, makes a surprising, and unique, appearance: he has a bad liver,[7] and he is the only one of the group who persistently refuses to see the point of what his younger brother is saying.[8] The only relationship that is clearly illuminated in these pages is that with Romanianus' son, Licentius. For Licentius was the 'star' pupil, whose intellectual grooming interested Augustine's principal readers, the friends of the boy's father.[9] Thus while his own son, Adeodatus, emerges only slightly in these dialogues, Licentius felt the full weight of Augustine's intensity.

It is not an entirely happy relationship. Licentius was a boy with a fine sense of the surface of things. He was an enthusiastic poet: he is obsessed by the unaccustomed rhythms of the Ambrosian chant, (and shocks Monica by singing a psalm in the lavatory).[10] He can observe and describe minutely the way in which autumn leaves choke the course of a stream: a fact which Augustine had entirely failed to notice.[11] The impact of Augustine's abstract, dialectical mind seems only to have inhibited him, 'like a cold douche.'[12] The occasional touch of sarcasm,

---

[1] *C. Acad.* II, iv, 10.
[2] *Sol.* I, xii, 21.
[3] *Sol.* I, i, 1.
[4] *Sol.* I, xiv, 25–26.
[5] *de beata vita*, iii, 16 and 20.
[6] e.g. *de beata vita*, ii, 10.
[7] *de beata vita*, ii, 14.
[8] *de beata vita*, ii, 7.
[9] *C. Acad.* II, iii, 8.
[10] *de ord.* I, viii, 23.
[11] *de ord.* I, iii, 7.
[12] *de ord.* I, ix, 28.

which made Augustine so formidable, would leave him crestfallen.[1]
Eventually, the two will drift apart. A passionate letter which Augustine
wrote to Licentius some eight years later shows that the austere ideal
of a life 'in Philosophy' had failed to hold this budding poet.[2] He
intended to make his fortune in Rome, with the support of pagan
senators, and was capable of dreaming — such was the strength of the
old world — that he would be a consul and a pagan pontiff. The poem,
which he wrote to Augustine shows traces of the influence of another,
far more brilliant writer — Claudian, a Greek from Alexandria, who
had come to Italy and would establish himself as the greatest Latin
poet of the 'Silver Age' of Rome.[3] Claudian, also, was an admirer of
Manlius Theodorus, and would reside, for a time, in Milan. His
brilliant career, and the influence which his art could exercise on a
younger man such as Licentius, shows that in advocating a life 'in
Philosophy', Augustine was not deserting an exhausted literary culture:
rather, he was attempting to swim against an equally strong and self-
confident current in Later Roman life. One wonders what sort of
poetry Licentius would have written under the influence of Augustine.
It would have been philosophical poetry, completely spiritualized; so
that the story of the lovers Pyramis and Thisbe would appear as a
rarefied allegory of the love of the wise man for wisdom.[4]

The group lived in a state of continuous intellectual excitement. One
day, the boys had found a centipede, and the whole company gathered
round to watch the way in which its chopped-up portions continued
to move of their own accord across a writing-tablet. Problems immediately sprang to mind: is the animating soul of the beast also
divisible? Is it, therefore, a material thing, that can be chopped up?
Heaven forbid, that 'one little worm' should thus disprove the Platonic
doctrine of the immaterial nature of the soul! The boys are sent to their
studies, to sharpen their minds for such problems; and Alypius and
Augustine talk all afternoon about the implications of what they had
just seen.[5]

Taken all together, however, Augustine had gathered together an
ill-assorted company for a life of philosophical *otium*: a pious old
woman, two uneducated cousins,[6] and two private pupils, aged about
16.[7] The dialogues that emerge from such a group show very clearly

[1] e.g. *de ord.* I, iii, 9 and *C. Acad.* II, xiii, 29.   [2] *Ep.* 26.
[3] A. K. Clarke, 'Licentius, Carmen ad Augustinum, ll. 45 seqq., and the Easter Vigil',
(Studia Patristica, viii), *Texte u. Untersuchungen*, 93 [to appear].
[4] *de ord.* I, v, 12 and vii, 24.   [5] *de quant. anim.* xxxi 62–63.
[6] *de beata vita*, i, 6.   [7] *de ord.* I, ii, 5.

one of Augustine's greatest gifts as an artist: an instinctive ability to create an interesting new form from the most unlikely materials. It was a masterful stroke of literary showmanship to turn this strange company into vehicles perfectly adapted to communicate an ideal of philosophy by and for the amateur. For Augustine's 'true Philosophy' was also the religion of a universal church. It must therefore be widened to take in all kinds of mind: a sort of universal franchise of wisdom had to be established. And Augustine's circle was well-chosen to communicate just such a message — that the 'highest pitch' of wisdom was available to any moderately educated and serious mind.

As a teacher among pupils, Augustine could set the pace in any discussion; and to his boys, he could emphasize the necessity of an exacting preliminary training.[1] Indeed, in these dialogues, Augustine emerges as one of the many thinkers who have chosen to express their ideals as part of a programme of moral education. His pupils were urged not to spend their whole day among books, but to leave time to be 'with themselves', just thinking.[2] Augustine insisted that they should learn, thereby, to prize their own powers of thought, their *ingenium*;[3] it is the first sign, in Augustine's first work, of his great respect for the faculty of sheer, hard ratiocination. They would 'brush up' this faculty by 'playing at philosophy'.[4] The works produced by this training would be read in Milan, not as original works of philosophy, but as *apéritifs*,[5] as 'painted, golden doors to the inner court of wisdom'.[6]

Inevitably, therefore, these dialogues have all the vices of their virtues. The little group at Cassiciacum is not above an inverted snobbery: the youths proudly proclaim total ignorance of Greek thinkers![7] Dialogues which betray amateur philosophers at work can be most painful reading. There are digressions, inconsequential trains of thought, and a general misuse of argument.[8] These dialogues nevertheless succeed in communicating consistently a lively faith that, 'really great things, when discussed by little men, can usually make such men grow big.'[9]

It is easy to dismiss such works as immature. But we do this partly because Augustine himself matured so quickly; and, in following Augustine, we have left his early works behind. Plainly the methods which he proposed at the time — a rigorous preliminary training which would culminate in a contemplation of the Trinity and of the

---

[1] e.g. *C. Acad.* I, iii, 8.   [2] *de ord.* I, iii, 6.   [3] e.g. *C. Acad.* II, vii, 17.
[4] *C. Acad.* II, ix, 22.   [5] *C. Acad.* I, i, 4.   [6] *de ord.* I, xi, 31.
[7] *C. Acad.* I, iii, 7.   [8] v. Marrou, *S. Augustin et la fin de la culture antique*, pp. 242–243.
[9] *C. Acad.* I, ii, 6.

beautiful order of the universe — could only provide keys that would open a limited number of problems; and Augustine, in going on to pose totally new problems, will have to adopt totally new methods.[1] But not everyone grew up as fast as Augustine: when, at the end of his life, his *City of God* — such a different book! — was beginning to circulate, educated men were still anxious to obtain a copy of the *Against the Academics*.[2]

From Cassiciacum, Augustine had advocated nothing less than an intellectual programme: to his admirers, it appeared as 'a truly great vision for a life's work'.[3] The programme was not original.[4] It was only posed in a particularly extreme form. Augustine's first requisite was discipline. To answer metaphysical questions and to contemplate 'such a God',[5] the mind must receive a proper training, an *eruditio*. To be able to do without such a training would be 'a scarcely credible stroke of good fortune'.[6] Here we can see an echo of Augustine's sense of his own humiliating intellectual flounderings,[7] and of his awareness of the high standards of his Milanese readers.[8] But this anxiety is hardened by the fanaticism of a true philosopher — a passion for a single method, within which all problems might be fruitfully posed and answered, and outside which no problems would exist. It is typical of Augustine, however, that in a matter of two years, this method will be partially abandoned in favour of yet other means of disciplining his restless mind.

Augustine's programme is sketched fully in his dialogue *On Order*. The traditional education was to be expanded to its full range, thus including the abstract sciences, geometry, and the mathematical groundwork of astronomy. But these Liberal Arts were treated merely as a preparatory stage for philosophical contemplation. Such contemplation, of course, was entirely religious: Augustine's pupils might busy themselves with Vergil and with textbooks on the Liberal Arts by Varro, but he had found a place, also, for Monica. Her natural austerity, reinforced by old age, would enable her to seize the 'soul' of this knowledge, while leaving its 'body' to the pedants.[9] It is in his sharp-

---

[1] v. inf. pp. 175–176.

[2] Letter to Firmus, in *Corpus Christianorum*, Series Latina, xlvii, 1955, p. iv. On the continuity of Augustine's ideas on knowledge and culture, v. esp. R. Lorenz, 'Die Wissenschaftslehre Augustins', *Zeitschrift für Kirchengeschichte*, 67, 1956, pp. 29–60 and 213–251.

[3] *de ord.* II, x, 28.

[4] v. esp. Solignac, 'Doxographies et manuels', *Rech. augustin.*, i, 1958, p. 122, and n. 26.

[5] *de ord.* I, vii, 20.   [6] *Sol.* I, xiii, 23.   [7] *de ord.* II, v, 17.

[8] *Sol.* II, xiv, 26.   [9] *de ord.* II, xvii, 45.

ness and sense of an over-riding purpose that Augustine foreshadows the medieval world.[1] All this knowledge, which could once be treated as the rich accompaniment of the life of a cultured gentleman, is now seen, by Augustine, as a pure, disembodied structure, subject to absolute laws of truth, that all point to a final certainty: 'There are a sort of men who are well trained in the Liberal Sciences, but this does not content them. They do not hold back until they behold in its greatest extent and perfection, the full blaze of Truth, whose splendour, even now, shimmers beneath the surface of such sciences.'[2]

The 'well-trained soul'[3] would handle with confidence the problems which had once baffled Augustine. He would understand the meaning of evil in the universe; he would 'dare' to prove the immortality of the soul; he would contemplate the 'wealth of meaning' in the Trinity; and by the mysteries of the Catholic Church he would be fortified 'more secretly and more firmly'[4] (that is, in a different language but to the same end) in those truths which, one day, he may apprehend with the same perfect intellectual satisfaction as the quality of numbers.[5] The life of philosophy, which the sceptics had held to be a way of shadows, is now seen to be full of light. This is the heart of Augustine's message from Cassiciacum: 'This Philosophy it is, which promises that it shall demonstrate with limpid clarity the most true and hidden God, and deigns, step by step, to show Him forth, as if through clouds suffused with light.'[6]

In these dialogues we are still only on the surface of Augustine's thought. He had to choose easy subjects for discussion.[7] But he was no mere popularizer: he spent much of his time grappling with the problems raised by the Neo-Platonic books. He was determined to reason out the nature of the soul; and this problem was a genuine metaphysical obsession which will form the undercurrent to his work for the next four years.[8] We know surprisingly little about this aspect of Augustine's life at Cassiciacum. He must have continued to read the Neo-Platonists, but the stages of this absorption are lost to us. This reading, however, culminated in a sketch of a series of proofs of the immortality of the soul, the *De Immortalitate Animae*.[9] But it was only a sketch; and in reading it again as an old man, Augustine confessed that, 'On

---

[1] v. esp. Marrou, *S. Augustin et la fin de la culture antique*, p. 211, (and p. 275: it is 'medieval', also, in the extent of its omissions).

[2] *Sol.* II, xx, 35. [3] *de ord.* II, xix, 50. [4] *de ord.* II, v, 15–16.
[5] *de ord.* II, vii, 24. [6] *C. Acad.* I, i, 3. [7] *Retract.* I, 3.
[8] *de beata vita*, i, 5.

[9] v. esp. O'Connell, 'Ennead VI, 4 and 5', *Rev. études augustin.*, ix, 1963, pp. 1–2, for the importance of this work as evidence of Augustine's absorption of Plotinus.

first reading, the reasoning is so involved and compressed as to be quite obscure. I still cannot concentrate when I read it — and I can only just make sense of it myself!'[1] This book is the first of Augustine's many 'left-overs'. He will never be a systematic thinker in the manner of Porphyry: his life will be littered with lines of thought that are not worked through to their conclusion, and with abandoned literary enterprises. It is the heavy price he would pay for being so prodigal and flexible a writer.

The abortive demonstration was to crown a daring literary innovation, the *Soliloquia*.[2] Even the title of this work was new. It is Augustine's first intimate self-portrait, written for a circle of friends. Typically, it begins with a long prayer; equally typically, it continues with a prolonged argument between his *Reason* and his *Soul*, in which Augustine, at last, felt free to give himself the intellectual drubbing which he knew would have been impossible to give without offending the tender feelings of an opponent.[3]

Augustine valued and remembered this work more than any other of the time. It betrays tensions between the two elements of his thought, that will remain unresolved for very many years. His God is the god of the philosophers: He is the founder of the harmonies of the universe; and His relation to men is as absolute and necessary as the form of a geometrical theorem. . . . 'God, whose kingdom is the world of which the senses know nothing . . . from Whom to turn away is to fall, to turn towards, to rise again, to remain in Whom is to stand still . . . God, Whom no man loses, but when deceived; no one seeks, but when reminded; Whom no one finds, but when made pure.' But He is also the God of S. Paul: 'by Whom *we overcome the Enemy* . . . by Whom we yield not to adversities . . . by Whom *Death is swallowed up in victory*. . . .'[4] In this prayer, we have an unmistakeable sign of what will become distinctive in Augustine's religious attitude — a sharp note of unrelieved anxiety about himself and a dependence on his God, expressed more woodenly than in the language of the *Confessions*, but, nevertheless, quite recognizable: 'I shall apply myself', says Soul, 'with diligence and close attention — that is, if no shadows creep in upon me, or, what I fear most deeply of all, if those shadows stir my pleasure'. 'Believe in God' says Reason: 'give yourself over to Him as much as you are able. Do not wish for your own will to be yours and at your own disposal; but proclaim yourself His slave — the slave of a merciful and capable master.'[5] It is this abiding fear of the dark which drove

---

[1] *Retract.* I, 5. [2] *Retract.* I, 5. [3] *Sol.* II, vii, 14.
[4] *Sol.* I, i, 3. [5] *Sol.* I, xv, 30.

Augustine, as the autumn turned to an ugly Northern winter, to return to Milan to seek to wash away his sins in baptism.

In Milan, Augustine, Adeodatus and Alypius became *competentes*: that is, they joined those who 'begged' baptism at the hands of Ambrose on the next Easter (on the night of April 24–25, 387). As a *competens*, Augustine would have received solemn instructions from Ambrose himself. Ambrose never spared himself in directing this momentous initiation;[1] and Augustine was, plainly, deeply affected by what he heard when, after the main celebration of the Liturgy, the *competentes* assembled in the baptistry adjoining the main basilica to hear their bishop:[2] 'Are we so out of touch with our feelings as not to remember how conscientiously and with what anxiety we heard those who taught us the catechism laid down for us, when we begged the sacraments of that fount of life?'[3]

The catechism of Milan was still an awesome discipline, calculated to intimate, to converted pagans, mysteries which, until that moment, had been hidden from the outside world: even the Lord's Prayer was not 'handed over' to the believer until he had passed through his initiation.[4] Augustine heard, and remembered, solemn warnings against polytheism and idolatry;[5] the precise way in which God had taken on human flesh would have been laid down;[6] and the hard and, to many pagans quite alien, doctrine of personal retribution after death, would have been brought home to the listeners repeatedly. At Easter, the rite of baptism itself emphasized the momentous nature of the transformation which Augustine was undergoing. On the eve of the Resurrection, Augustine and the throng of other *competentes*, of all ages and both sexes, would troop to the Baptistry beside the main basilica of Ambrose. Passing behind curtains, Augustine would descend, alone, stark naked, into a deep pool of water. Three times, Ambrose would hold his shoulders beneath the gushing fountain. Later, dressed in a pure white robe, he would enter the main basilica ablaze with candles; and, amid the acclamations of the congregation, he and his fellow neophytes would take their place on a slightly raised floor[7] by the altar, for a first participation in the mysteries of the Risen Christ. The theme of 'putting off the old', of 'putting on the new', of rebirth and rising again from death, of the consequent ascent of the soul to heaven

---

[1] Paulinus, *Vita Ambrosii*, 38, (ed. Pellegrino, pp. 104–105).
[2] v. esp. B. Parodi, *La catachesi di S. Ambrogio*, 1957 and Homes-Dudden, *Saint Ambrose*, i, pp. 336–342.
[3] *de fide et oper.* vi, 9.   [4] Parodi, *La catachesi*, p. 66.   [5] *de quant. anim.* xxxiv, 77.
[6] Courcelle, *Recherches*, p. 213.   [7] Parodi, *La catachesi*, p. 19.

made possible by the descent of Christ to earth, reverberated in Augustine's imagination. In the next years, he wove his own, refined Platonic doctrine of the ascent of the soul from the 'old man' of the senses, around this elemental and mysterious action.[1]

Seen from outside, Augustine was a rare, but quite recognizable, type. We can see him mirrored in the advice which Augustine later gave to a priest in Carthage: 'I certainly must not omit another case, that of a fully-educated man who has decided to become a Christian, and has come to you in order to be made one (by baptism). He must have made himself acquainted with most of the Scripture and Christian writings, and has been instructed by this reading. He has now come merely to be able to take part in the Sacraments. For such men are in the habit of enquiring into religious matters and of communicating and discussing with others what they think beforehand, and not just at the time when they come to be baptized as full Christians.'[2]

Now a new world closed in around the devotee of Philosophy.[3] He was told how a doorkeeper of the Basilica had been healed by the body of S. Gervasius.[4] He went to visit the monastery in the neighbourhood of the town, presided over by a learned and holy priest.[5] He saw Ambrose, surrounded by the bishops of the neighbourhood, stern men, leading small, self-conscious communities. Among them was Filastrius, the bishop of Brescia: this old man was compiling a catalogue of 156 heresies. Among them appear 'those who say that there is an infinite number of worlds'.[6] This doctrine may, recently, have been popularized in Milan by none other than Manlius Theodorus:[7] such is the distance between the two poles of Augustine's life.

Augustine's links with Ambrose continued to be maintained on two levels: one level is represented by Monica, and the other by Christian Platonists such as Manlius Theodorus, to whom Augustine speaks of Ambrose as 'our bishop'.[8] The fact that Manlius Theodorus had preceded Augustine into a philosophical retirement, and had not concealed his admiration for Plotinus,[9] ensured that Augustine was not the only man to read the *Enneads* in those years. Ambrose may well have taken this new movement into account at much the same time as Augustine. It is possible that Ambrose preached the series of sermons, 'On Isaac and the Soul' and 'On Jacob and the Happy Life',

---

[1] *de quant. anim.* i, 4.   [2] *de cat. rud.* viii, 12.   [3] Courcelle, *Recherches*, p. 217.
[4] *Conf.* IX, vii, 16.   [5] *Conf.* VIII, vi, 15 and *de mor. eccl. cath.* (I), xxxiii, 70.
[6] Filastrius, *de Haeres.*, c. 115 (P.L. xii, 1239).
[7] Courcelle, *Les lettres grecques*, p. 123. This could be an open question among Christians, v. Pépin, *Théologie cosmique et théologie chrétienne*, pp. 77–78.
[8] *de beata vita*, i, 4.   [9] *de beata vita*, i, 4.

in the early months of 387.[1] In these sermons he drew heavily on much the same treatises of Plotinus as Augustine had read. To the *cognoscenti* in his audience, these impressive sermons would have amounted to a public baptism of Plotinus and his philosophy.

When he looked back on his last days in Milan, Augustine allowed the perspective of his emotions to predominate exclusively. In the *Confessions* we have the authentic words of a convert: 'The days were not long enough as I meditated and found wonderful delight in meditating upon the depth of Your design for the salvation of the human race. I wept at the beauty of Your hymns and canticles, and was powerfully moved at the sweet sound of Your Church's singing. Those sounds flowed into my ears, and the truth streamed into my heart: so that my feeling of devotion overflowed, and the tears ran from my eyes, and I was happy in them.'[2]

Yet, at exactly the same time, Augustine was doggedly pursuing his great intellectual programme: 'I was attempting to write text books of the sciences, questioning those who did not object to such an education, in the desire of reaching, or coming upon a road with definite, easy stages, that would lead the mind from material things to the immaterial.'[3] All that survives of this strange venture is the book *De Musica*, a treatise, not on music, but a literary and technical examination of metre. Such works were fashionable in Milan: Manlius Theodorus had written one such;[4] and the first 5 books that lead up to Augustine's own impressive conclusion in its last book, are so commonplace that they may have been seized upon by teachers and abridged as a manual.[5] Thus, an academic text-book is the last contribution of a future bishop to the intellectual life of Milan.

By that time, however, Augustine's plans for the future had become more definite. The Africans had come to form a tight, almost monastic group: Alypius had already gained a reputation for his austerities.[6] They were joined, in Milan, by another future bishop and fellow-townsman — Evodius (later bishop of Uzalis), a retired member of the secret police, whose duties had (not surprisingly) caused him to reject the world.[7] Augustine intended to return to his home town. There, he would live a secluded life with his mother, his son, and a few

---

[1] While Courcelle, *Recherches*, pp. 106–122, has established the Plotinian content of these sermons, their chronology remains uncertain: v. Theiler, *Gnomon*, 75, 1953, pp. 117–118.

[2] *Conf.* IX, vi, 14. [3] *Retract.* I, 6.

[4] *de metris*, ed. Keil, *Grammatici Latini*, vi, 1874, pp. 585–601.

[5] v. esp. Marrou, *S. Augustin et la fin de la culture antique*, pp. 570–579.

[6] *Conf.* IX, vi, 14. [7] *Conf.* IX, viii, 17.

friends of similar dedication, supported, presumably, by a small family property administered by his elder brother and Monica. They had come a long way from the grandiose community-venture which had once appealed to Romanianus. The exact nature of these plans is unknown to us; they were probably uncertain at the time.[1] It is in this way that Augustine, his son, his mother and some friends, will follow the road to the south which, within two years, had been taken by his rejected mistress, herself, also, returning to a life of continence in her harsh native land.

[1] *Conf.* IX, viii, 17.

12

OSTIA

As the party made for the sea, the distant civil war, which had overshadowed the public life of Milan for years, finally reached Italy. The fleet of the usurper, Maximus, a general who had been in command at Caernarvon, was blockading the harbours of Rome; the Emperor Theodosius, a pious Galician general who ruled in Constantinople, was preparing to crush his rival. Because of this blockade, the little group of Africans was brought to a halt in Ostia.

Ostia is one of the few towns whose life in the fourth century has been revealed to us by the archaeologist.[1] The vulgar, bustling life of the old Empire had ebbed away, leaving the town forlorn and rarified. The great occasional residences of Roman noblemen protruded, incongruously, among derelict streets. Augustine may well have stayed in the houses of the Christian members of this nobility, away from the crowds of the harbour-area of Porto.[2] An Italica, to whom he will later write on the Vision of God,[3] appears there as a name stamped on a leaden drain pipe;[4] a consul will later write an epitaph for Monica.[5] This stay in Ostia may well have been Augustine's first contact with a formidable Christian clan, the Anicii, the wealthiest family in the Empire, whose palace was one of the marvels of Rome.[6] If this is so, we have some indication of the standing of Augustine and his friends in the eyes of the outside world. It was considerable: they were protégés

[1] v. esp. the learned study of R. Meiggs, *Roman Ostia*, 1960, esp. pp. 83–101, 211–213 and 258–262.
[2] *Conf.* IX, x, 23.   [3] *Epp.* 92 and 99, v. inf. p. 190, n. 4.
[4] v. Meiggs, *Roman Ostia*, pp. 212–213, would make her the wife of a Faltonius Adelfius.
[5] Meiggs, *Roman Ostia*, p. 400.
[6] *Ep. Secundini ad Augustinum.* Solignac, in *Les Confessions, Biblio. augustin.*, sér. ii, 14, p. 535, identifies the Hermogenianus of *Ep.* 1 with a member of the Anicii.

of the great Ambrose; all of them had retired from office in the capital of the Empire.

In one house at Ostia, a room, perhaps a salon for philosophical discussions, had been lined, a century before, with statues of a philosopher. The philosopher may well be Plotinus himself.[1] Here was a figure to suit Augustine's mood: a contemplative, with raised eyes and a face strained with the upward movement of the soul.

It is against this background that great events in the inner life of Augustine occurred. One day, Augustine and his mother 'stood alone, leaning in a window, which looked inwards to the garden within the house where we were staying. There we talked together, she and I alone, in deep joy. . . . And while we were thus talking of His Wisdom and panting for it, with all the effort of our heart we did for one instant attain to touch it; then, sighing and leaving the first fruits of our spirit bound to it, we returned to the sound of our own tongue, in which words must have a beginning and an end. . . . What we said is this: "If to any man the tumult of the flesh grew silent, silent the images of earth and sea and air; and if the heavens grew silent, and the very soul grew silent to herself, and, by not thinking of self, mounted beyond self; if all dreams and images grew silent, and every tongue and every symbol — everything that passes away . . . and in their silence He alone spoke to us, not by them, but by Himself: so that we should hear His word, not by any tongue of the flesh, not in the voice of an angel, not in the sound of thunder, nor in the darkness of a parable — but that we should hear Himself . . . should hear Himself and not them." '[2]

Within a fortnight, Monica was dead. During her nine days of illness, she withdrew inside herself entirely; she only emerged to bless her sons, to tell Augustine that never in her life had she heard one sharp word from him, and to tell Navigius how she no longer cared that she would not be buried beside Patricius in her native soil.[3]

'I closed her eyes. An immeasurable sorrow flowed up into my heart and would have overflowed in tears. But my eyes, under the mind's strong constraint, held back their flow and I stood dry-eyed. In that struggle it went very hard with me. As she breathed her last, the

[1] v. Meiggs, *Roman Ostia*, p. 393, and H. P. L'Orange, 'The Portrait of Plotinus', *Cahiers archéologiques. Fin de l'Antiquité et Moyen-Âge*, v, 1951, pp. 15-30.

[2] *Conf.* IX, x, 23-25. P. Henry, *La Vision d'Ostie. Sa place dans la vie et l'oeuvre de S. Augustin*, 1938 is fundamental. For a challenging analysis of Augustine's description, v. A. Mandouze, 'L'extase d'Ostie: possibilités et limites de la méthode de parallèles textuels', *Aug. Mag.* i, 1954, pp. 67-84.

[3] *Conf.* IX, xi, 27-28.

child Adeodatus broke out into lamentations. We checked him and brought him to silence. . . .[1]

'Because I had now lost the great comfort of her, my soul was wounded and my very life torn asunder, for it had been one life — made of hers and mine together.[2] . . . When the boy was quieted and ceased weeping, Evodius took up the Psalter and began to chant — with the whole household making the responses — the psalm "*Mercy and judgement I will sing unto Thee, O Lord*". And when they heard what was being done, many of the brethren and religious women came to us — those whose duty it was to make arrangement for the burial; while, in another part of the house, where it could be properly done, I discoursed with friends who did not wish to leave me by myself . . . listening closely to me, they thought that I lacked all feeling of grief . . . but I knew what I was crushing down in my heart. For I was very much ashamed that these human emotions could have such power over me . . . and I felt a new grief at my grief, and so was afflicted by a double sorrow.[3]

'When the body was taken to burial, I went and returned without tears. During the prayers . . . while the body, as the custom there is, lay by the grave before it was actually buried — during those prayers I did not weep. Yet all that day I was heavy with grief within and in the trouble of my mind I begged of You in my own fashion to heal my pain; But You would not. . . . The idea came to me to go and bathe, for I had heard that the bath — which the Greeks call βαλανεῖον — is so-called because it "drives anxieties from the mind" (a bath in Ostia still bears an inscription of that time, advertising a 'soothing wash'[4]) . . . (But) the bitterness of my grief had not sweated out of my heart. Then I fell asleep, and woke again to find my grief not a little relieved. And as I was in bed and no one about, I said over those true verses that your servant Ambrose wrote of you: *Deus creator omnium* . . . .

'And then, little by little, I began to recover my former feeling about Your handmaid, remembering how loving and devout was her conversation with You, how pleasant and considerate her conversation with me, of which I was thus suddenly deprived. And I found solace in weeping in Your sight both about her and for her, about myself and for myself. . . .'[5]

So Monica was buried in Ostia. Medieval pilgrims copied the epitaph in verse above her tomb: one, Walter, a canon of Arrouaise in Northern France, was allowed to take home part of her body — 'There are so

[1] *Conf*. IX, xii, 29.   [2] *Conf*. IX, xii, 30.   [3] *Conf*. IX, xii, 31.
[4] Meiggs, *Roman Ostia*, p. 475.   [5] *Conf*. IX, xii, 32–33.

many saints in that wilderness' he wrote 'that we could not easily decide where we should lay them to rest as was fitting'.[1] 'In the summer of 1945, two boys, playing in a small courtyard beside the church of S. Aurea in Ostia, began to dig a hole to plant a post for their game. They disturbed a fragment of marble: it contained part of the original inscription.'[2]

Augustine and Evodius returned to Rome, to wait until the blockade had lifted. In late 388, they arrived in Carthage. There Augustine met, among many former acquaintances and new, Catholic admirers, a pupil, an Eulogius Favonius. Eulogius had stayed at home, and had become a teacher in the schools at Carthage. When he was preparing a lecture on a set book of Cicero, he was perplexed by an obscure passage: that night, he dreamt of Augustine; and, in this dream, Augustine had solved the problem for him.[3] Eulogius the schoolmaster had been living the old life, in the old way: it is strange to think that only four years had elapsed since Augustine had done just the same thing, in just the same town.

[1] Meiggs, *Roman Ostia*, p. 525.   [2] Meiggs, *Roman Ostia*, p. 400.
[3] *de cura ger. pro mort.* xi, 13.

13

SERVUS DEI: THAGASTE

Thagaste could never be another Cassiciacum. Even during his stay in Rome, Augustine's writings show a new determination.[1] From that time onwards, he intended to live a secluded life no longer, as in Milan, on the fringe of a society of intellectual laymen, but directly in the shadow of the organized life of the Catholic church. Thus, when Alypius and Augustine arrived in Carthage, in late 388, they already belonged to an ill-defined, but quite recognizable, group of men: they were *Servi Dei*, 'Servants of God'. As such, they were visited by the local clergy, were lodged, with honour, in the house of a pious official;[2] and good Catholic laymen would write to ask for their prayers.[3] These *servi Dei* had owed their position in the Latin church less to any connexion with an organized monastic life, than to the pressure of a fashion in perfection. They produced some of the most remarkable men of their time. They differed widely — so widely, indeed, that, a generation later, Pelagius, the great challenger of Augustine, will arrive in Carthage in exactly the same guise as Augustine had arrived: in Augustine's description of him, we can see what Augustine once was; a *servus Dei*,[4] a baptized, dedicated layman, determined to live, in the company of bishops, priests and noble patrons, the full life of a Christian.[5]

The little group finally settled on Augustine's portion of the family estates in Thagaste.[6] Their community could still mean many things to

[1] v. J. Burnaby, *Amor Dei: A Study of the Religion of St. Augustine*, 1938, p. 88, on the *de moribus ecclesiae catholicae*: 'He has already made his own many of those texts which will be the pivots of his Christianity, and already uses them pivotally'.

[2] *de civ. Dei*, xxii, 8, 48.   [3] *Ep.* 20, 2.   [4] *Ep.* 186, i, 1.

[5] v. inf. p. 341. For the quality of Augustine's life at this time I am particularly indebted to the sound and differentiated studies of G. Folliet, notably, 'Aux origines de l'ascétisme et du cénobitisme africain', *Studia Anselmiana*, 46, 1961, pp. 25–44, esp. pp. 35–44.

[6] Possidius, *Vita Augustini*, III, 1–2 [From henceforth cited as *Vita*].

many people. To Nebridius, now returned to Africa and living with his mother in his country-house near Carthage, Augustine's circle had remained a gathering of philosophers: 'It gives me the greatest pleasure to keep hold of your letters as if they were my own eyes. Some shall speak to me of Christ, some of Plato, some of Plotinus.'[1] The two men remained separated by illness, which made it impossible for either to travel along the gruelling highroad of the Mejerda valley: but, as philosophers, they prided themselves on being able to live happily with their own minds.[2] Even the threat of death — a threat very close to Nebridius — can appear of no significance to them.[3] The ideal which Augustine upholds to Nebridius is to 'grow god-like in their retirement', *deificari in otio*: the phrase may have been taken from the works of Porphyry.[4] A 'Spiritual Anthology' composed by his friends at the time can include the work of a pagan sage, Fonteius of Carthage, who was later baptized as a Christian: 'Act, O wretched mortals', he says, 'lest the evil spirit befoul this dwelling-place; lest, when mixed into the senses, it should besmirch the holiness of the soul and cloud over the light of the mind. . . .'[5] This harsh passage shows how close Augustine and his circle still moved along the borderline of Christian and pagan religious sentiment.

Yet, although Augustine's ideal might be that of a Neo-Platonic recluse, the only alternative he can now envisage to this ideal, is the active life of a Catholic bishop.[6] For, in Thagaste, he had been brought face to face with the organized life of the African church. In Milan this did not happen: he was a foreigner, moving among the many intellectual circles of a big city. Now this neutral middle-distance had disappeared: in Thagaste, Augustine was a local man, returned home to a small community, in a province where the Catholic church was particularly self-conscious of its position among powerful enemies — pagans, Manichees, Donatist schismatics. At any moment, these small communities might attempt to recruit their local 'talent'. Soon Alypius will become bishop of Thagaste, his home town. He would always cut a more impressive figure than Augustine in provincial society; and, in a sense, he had merely replaced his relative[7] Romanianus as a distinguished 'patron' of Thagaste. Augustine was careful to avoid towns where the bishopric was vacant, for fear of similar 'conscription'. At

---

[1] *Ep.* 6.   [2] *Ep.* 9, 1 and 10, 1.   [3] *Ep.* 10, 2; cf. *de vera rel.* xlvii, 91.

[4] v. G. Folliet, ' "Deificari in otio", Augustin, *Epistula* X, 2'. *Rech. augustin.*, ii, 1962, pp. 225–236.

[5] *de div. quaest.* lxxxiii, 12; *Retract.* I, 26.   [6] *Ep.* 10, 2.

[7] v. *Ep.* 26, 3 and 32, 5, on the blood relationship between Alypius and Romanianus.

that time, Augustine told a correspondent, sharply, that he should remember how he was 'an African, writing for Africans, both of us living in Africa'.[1] The reminder is equally applicable to Augustine: always susceptible to 'atmosphere', Augustine was, yet again, changing his mode of life.

In Thagaste, Augustine was caught up with his African past as a Manichee. The tension between Catholics and Manichees had been particularly acute in Africa: they were the 'heretics' *par excellence*. So it is not surprising that Augustine's works against the Manichees should have become more decisively 'ecclesiastical' in this environment: his first commentary on Genesis 'against the Manichees', is also his first ecclesiastical pamphlet; he wrote it in a simple, readily-intelligible style.[2] The remarkable summary of his position, *'On True Religion'*, was carefully written and produced[3] in order to impress upper-class Manichaean sympathizers, such as Romanianus. Augustine seems to have taken pains to have it circulated, and went out of his way to provoke debates.[4] The relations between the Catholic Church and the Manichees seemed to have reached a crisis in just these years. The most obvious symptom of this crisis was an official 'purge' of Manichees in Carthage, in 386.[5] Thus, the fact that Augustine and his friends in Thagaste were ex-Manichees, energetically proposing their own solution to the Manichaean problem, would have given them considerable importance in the eyes of the authorities of the African church.

The centre of gravity of Augustine's thought had begun to shift. He had returned to Africa without his text-books,[6] and his schemes for an intellectual programme based on the Liberal Arts now seemed distant. Even the conclusions of his dialogue with Adeodatus, *'On the Master'*, were immediately applied, in his defence of the Catholic Church, to the dogma of the Incarnation:[7] this dogma was to form the pivot of a philosopher's religion.[8] We can see this change most clearly in Augustine's correspondence with Nebridius. Nebridius, with his pagan background, is still fascinated by problems raised on the fringe of Neo-Platonism and the occult: has the soul a 'vehicle'?[9] Can celestial powers influence our thoughts?[10] Augustine soon came to regard such 'curiosity' as the parting of the ways between pagan and Christian Platonism.[11] His speculations are already subordinated to a firm scale of

---

[1] *Ep.* 17, 2.   [2] *de Gen. c. Man.* I, i, 1.   [3] *Ep.* 15, 1.   [4] e.g. *Ep.* 19.
[5] *C. litt. Petil.* III, xxv, 30.   [6] *Ep.* 15, 1.   [7] *de Mag.* xi, 38.
[8] *Epp.* 11, 2; 12; 14, 4, and *de vera relig.* l, 99.   [9] *Ep.* 13, 1.   [10] *Ep.* 8.
[11] *de vera relig.* iv, 7.

priorities: with great severity, he leads Nebridius' questions back to the central mysteries of the Christian faith;[1] his little group must repudiate everything in philosophy that was not consistent with the Catholic creed, while believing that there was nothing in this creed that could not be contemplated by a philosopher.[2] Augustine will reject, with considerable ill-humour, the broad-minded approaches of a 'liberal' pagan — Maximus, a teacher at his former school in Madaura;[3] indeed, taken all together, this new *Platonicus* returned from Milan would have appeared as a formidably single-minded man.

The two years which Augustine spent at Thagaste are marked by even more significant, though more mysterious, changes. At this time, Augustine was a contemplative. His view of the Days of Creation in his commentary on Genesis is a faithful mirror of his own state of mind: he was still contemplating the 'lights in the firmament', 'spiritual meanings', shining clear and distant before the mind: outside, however, there lay the 'beasts of the sea and air', a fuller life of action, which had not yet dawned for him, with the 'whales' of great deeds, cleaving the rough waters of the world, and the words of preachers 'flying' through the air.[4]

But such a disembodied, tranquil life might soon seem very empty. By the end of these years, death had intervened. Nebridius and Adeodatus died. We do not know when: this double blow is one of the most significant blanks in Augustine's life. In his dialogue, 'On the Master', Adeodatus had appeared very like his father: intelligent, rather pert, far better equipped than Licentius had been to see through the dialectical traps prepared for him by his father.[5] In the last book he ever wrote, Augustine will quote a passage from Cicero that, perhaps, betrays the hurt of this loss: 'Surely what Cicero says comes straight from the heart of all fathers, when he wrote: "*You are the only man of all men whom I would wish to surpass me in all things*".'[6] It may well be that grief and a sense of emptiness now pressed Augustine into a more active life. He was no longer content to 'live sweetly with the mind'.[7] 'Let us put off all empty duties, and take on useful ones. As for exemption from care: I do not think that any can be hoped for in this world.'[8] In the year before he was made a priest in Hippo, Augustine may already have tried to fill out his life — to organize his community, to found the personal relations within it upon a permanent code of behaviour, to be responsible for the spiritual well-being of many other

[1] *Ep.* 11, 2. [2] *de vera relig.* vii, 12. [3] *Epp.* 16 and 17.
[4] *de Gen. c. Man.* I, xxv, 43. [5] *de Mag.* iii, 5, and v, 14. [6] *Op. Imp.* VI, 22.
[7] *Ep.* 10, 1. [8] *Ep.* 18.

people, and to exercise some real measure of authority over them. As a result, the group of like-minded enthusiasts that had gathered around him in his retirement, came, by slow and subtle stages, to resemble a 'monastery', with Augustine as a 'spiritual father'.

There must, inevitably, be a large element of speculation in this view of Augustine. His relations with the monastic movement at that time, are most obscure. In Milan and Rome he had visited the first 'monasteries',[1] and had heard distant, somewhat romantic, tales of the great communities of Egypt.[2] But it is unlikely that he now thought of 'founding' a 'monastery' immediately on his arrival in Thagaste: the old forms of a life of scholarly retirement, reinforced by his ecclesiastical status as a *servus Dei*, probably seemed sufficient. What we do know, however, is the way in which the monastic life had come to appeal to him: the monks seemed to him to have succeeded in living in permanent communities, where all personal relationships were moulded by the dictates of Christian charity,[3] presided over by men who exercised a permanent, fatherlike authority over willing charges.[4]

Such a life had already begun to influence Augustine in his first year in Thagaste. Instinctively, he wanted to be something more than a contemplative: Nebridius might urge him to live alone with God; but Augustine is determined to be very much in charge of his own community, and allows himself to be tied to Thagaste by 'those whom I feel it would be wrong to desert'.[5] By 391, the transformation is complete. Augustine, who, a year before, had refused to travel to see his dying friend Nebridius, now took the highroad that led from the hills down to the ancient sea port of Hippo. An acquaintance, a member of the secret police, like Evodius, had wished to talk with him about abandoning the world.[6] Augustine was prepared to go out of his way to gain a new recruit. He had even arrived in Hippo 'looking for somewhere to found a monastery'.[7] He intended that the life of this 'monastery' should be devoted to the reading of the Scriptures.[8] Immersion in the Scriptures would have equipped Augustine and his followers more fully for an active life in the African church. It would have brought them into line with the culture of the average clergyman. It is not the first time in Augustine's life that grief, and some inner discontent, drove him from the small, tight society of his home town down into a wider and more busy world.

[1] *de mor. eccl. cath.* (I), xxxiii, 70.   [2] *de mor. eccl. cath.* (I), xxxi, 67.
[3] *de mor. eccl. cath.* (I), xxxiii, 73.   [4] *de mor. eccl. cath.* (I), xxxi, 67.
[5] *Ep.* 10, 1.   [6] *Vita*, III, 3–5.
[7] *Serm.* 355, 2.   [8] *Ep.* 21, 3.

SERVUS DEI: THAGASTE

Much had changed in the past three years. When Augustine arrived in Hippo, in the spring of 391, he was a lonely man, entering middle age, who had lost much of his past and who was groping, half-consciously, for new fields to conquer.

14

PRESBYTER ECCLESIAE CATHOLICAE: HIPPO

Thirty-five years later Augustine told his congregation what had happened to him on his arrival in Hippo:

'I, whom you see, with God's grace, as your bishop — I came as a young man to this city, as many of you know. I was looking for a place to set up a monastery, to live with my "brethren". I had given up all hope in this world. What I could have been, I wished not to be: nor did I seek to be what I am now. For I chose to be *humble in the house of my God* rather than to *live in the tents of sinners*. I kept apart from those who loved the world: but I did not think myself the equal of those who ruled over congregations. At the Lord's Feast, I did not take up a higher position, but chose a lower and more retiring place: and it pleased the Lord to say "Rise up".

'I feared the office of a bishop to such an extent that, as soon as my reputation came to matter among "servants of God", I would not go to any place where I knew there was no bishop. I was on my guard against this: I did what I could to seek salvation in a humble position rather than be in danger in high office. But, as I said, a slave may not contradict his Lord. I came to this city to see a friend, whom I thought I might gain for God, that he might live with us in the monastery. I felt secure, for the place already had a bishop. I was grabbed. I was made a priest . . . and from there, I became your bishop.'[1]

The incident was a common one in the Later Empire.[2] It passed over quickly: in a sermon, the bishop, Valerius, spoke pointedly of the urgent needs of his church;[3] the congregation turned to find, as they

[1] *Serm.* 355, 2.
[2] J. Gaudemet, *L'Église dans l'Empire romain* (iv–ve. s), (Histoire du droit et des institutions de l'Église en Occident, III), 1958, pp. 108–111.
[3] *Vita*, IV, 1.

expected, Augustine standing among them in the nave; with the persistent shouting required for such a procedure, they pushed him forward to the raised throne of the bishop and the benches of the priests, which ran around the curved apse at the far end of the basilica. The leading Catholic citizens of Hippo would have gathered around Augustine, as the bishop accepted his forced agreement to become a priest in the town.[1] What was happening seemed perfectly natural to them: twenty years later they would try, without success, to kidnap in this way another passing 'star'.[2] They merely assumed that Augustine had burst into tears because he had wanted to be a bishop, and now found himself condemned to the inferior rank of a priest.[3] Characteristically, Augustine's immediate reaction was that he stood condemned: his God had *'laughed him to scorn'*, and he wept from the shame of having once thought ill of clergymen and their congregations.[4]

The man responsible for this change of fortunes, the bishop Valerius, was a figure quite as eccentric as Augustine himself. He was an elderly Greek, who spoke Latin with difficulty,[5] and was quite unable to understand the Punic dialect of the country-folk of his diocese.[6] His community desperately needed a voice. The Catholics in Hippo were a harassed minority. The rival church, that of the 'party of Donatus', was predominant both in the town and the surrounding countryside. It was supported by prominent local landowners[7] and enjoyed the tacit recognition of local officials. Its bishop had been able, at about this time, to impose a boycott on his rivals: he had forbidden the bakers to bake bread for the Catholics.[8] (Anyone who has been in a Mediterranean town will know the importance of the oven which stands in the centre of every little neighbourhood.) What is more, the Manichees had established themselves with great success on the fringes of the demoralized Catholic congregation. Their 'priest', Fortunatus, had even known Augustine at Carthage.[9] This fact alone, would have singled Augustine out for consideration by the worried bishop.

The situation called for unprecedented measures; and Valerius had the courage of his eccentricity. Not only did he 'press-gang' Augustine to be his priest: he insisted that he should preach. Within two years, Valerius' new acquisition was patiently explaining the Creed to the assembled Catholic bishops of Africa! By allowing Augustine to preach, Valerius had infringed on a jealously-guarded privilege of the

---

[1] *Vita*, IV, 2. [2] v. inf. p. 294. [3] *Vita*, IV, 2.

[4] *Ep.* 21, 2. [5] *Vita*, V, 3. [6] *Ep. ad Rom. incoh. expos.* 13.

[7] On Donatism and Augustine's later relations with this rival church, v. inf. pp. 212 sq.

[8] *C. litt. Petil.* II, lxxxiii, 184. [9] *Vita*, VI, 1.

African hierarchy — that the bishop alone, seated on his raised throne, should expound the Catholic Scriptures.[1] Later, Valerius showed that he was capable of intriguing vigorously to keep hold of his protégé. In 395, he wrote secret letters to the primate of Carthage to have Augustine consecrated as his co-adjutor:[2] again, he was acting in defiance of the canons; and, this time, of the canons of no less a council than Nicaea, which he, as a Greek, might, of all people, have been expected to know.[3] Before that, he had once hidden Augustine for fear that a delegation from a neighbouring town might abduct him as their new bishop.[4] He welcomed Augustine's proposal to set up a monastery; and put the garden-enclosure of the main church at his disposal.[5] He, therefore, ensured both that this unprecedented institution was officially recognized in Africa, and that a group of extraordinary men — many of them former Manichees[6] — should settle in his town. Valerius acted as a Greek: he was accustomed both to monks and to priests who might preach. But his stubborn and intricate manoeuvres were not calculated to make either himself or his brilliant new priest popular among the more conservative local bishops. At the moment of Augustine's consecration as a co-adjutor bishop, in 395, the storm of irritation which had gathered for a long time suddenly burst, as we shall see.[7]

It is possible to credit Valerius with the perceptiveness of a foreigner. The local Catholic church in Africa had come to a standstill: divided by schism, exposed to the Manichaean heresy, its bishops had settled down as local dignitaries with limited gifts and ambitions.[8] They were content to secure official privileges and seemed capable of displaying energy only in litigation. (For Augustine, at Thagaste, the life of a bishop seemed to consist entirely of business-trips; and the duties of a priest seemed roughly those of a legal agent.)[9] In church, they would be content to celebrate the Liturgy: outside it, they would arbitrate in law-suits. In every way, the rival church, that of the Donatists, was more active. The greatest African exegete was a Donatist, Tyconius, a man whose work was to influence Augustine profoundly.[10] Only the Donatists seem to have undertaken the difficult task of converting the hill-villages around Hippo and in the interior.[11]

In this 'dumb' church, Valerius' new priest was nothing if not articulate. Augustine began by teaching the catechism. Short addresses, intricate and concise, fell from him with ease.[12] Soon he was in the public

---

[1] *Vita*, V, 3. [2] *Vita*, VIII, 2. [3] *Ep.* 213, 4.
[4] *Vita*, VIII, 1. [5] *Serm.* 355, 2. [6] Notably, Alypius and Fortunatus.
[7] v. inf. p. 203. [8] Frend, *Donatist Church*, pp. 245–246.
[9] *Ep.* 21, 5. [10] v. inf. p. 272. [11] v. inf. pp. 192–193. [12] *Serm.* 214 and 216.

eye. On the 28th of August 392, he stood opposite his former friend, Fortunatus the Manichee, in the hall of a public bath house, for a formal debate.[1] Before a large audience of all creeds,[2] Augustine opened with the words:

'I now think an error what I had previously thought to be the truth. Whether I am right in my opinion, I desire to hear from you.'[3]

At the end of two days, he had harried Fortunatus until he had not a word to say, and was forced to leave the town for good.[4] The Manichees had placed great faith in such public encounters.[5] Now Augustine had beaten his former masters at their own game. He soon tried, with far less success, to apply these methods to the Donatist bishops, by challenging them to a debate. But they, more prudently, kept out of the way of a 'professional',[6] and may have viewed such novel tactics with genuine distrust. As a popular movement, the Donatists had relied on the popular song.[7] In 394, Augustine could meet them with just such a song: his '*A.B.C. against the Donatists*'. This was yet another of Augustine's highly unconventional works. The song was a mere jingle: each couplet began with a letter of the alphabet, and ended with the constant refrain, 'You who take your joy in peace, now is the time to judge what's true.'[8] Even the rhythm was popular: Augustine deliberately abandoned the metre of a classical poem and had, instead, adopted a style which shows how close the Latin of the streets had come to resembling a Romance language in pronunciation.[9] Twenty years before, Augustine had been crowned for writing a classical set-piece, a *carmen theatricum*.[10] Now, a gulf which will separate two civilizations, almost two languages, had opened between the student and the Catholic priest. The poem is a symptom of the resilience and extreme unconventionality which Augustine will show as an ecclesiastical campaigner.

In December 393, the General Council of Africa met for the first and last time in Hippo. This was an important occasion.[11] The assembled bishops would have had their first chance of seeing Augustine. On December 3rd, he expounded the Creed to them. This address — '*On*

---

[1] *C. Fort.* 1.   [2] *Vita*, VI, 2.   [3] *C. Fort.* 1.   [4] *Vita*, VI, 7–8.

[5] e.g. *de ii anim.* ix, 16, and the evidence collected in Brown, 'St. Augustine's attitude to religious coercion', *Journ. Rom. Studies*, liv, 1964, at p. 109 n. 13.

[6] *Ep.* 34, 6.   [7] *Ep.* 55, xviii, 34.   [8] On this v. Bonner, *St. Augustine*, pp. 253–258.

[9] *Retract.* I, 19.   [10] *Conf.* IV, ii, 3.

[11] Perhaps the summoning of this council and the programme of reform embarked upon by it had been planned by Augustine and Aurelius his friend, the new bishop of Carthage: F. L. Cross, 'History and Fiction in the African Canons', *Journ. Theol. Studies*, n.s. xii, 1961, pp. 227–247, esp. pp. 229–230.

the Faith and the Creed' — is Augustine's *'On True Religion'* as presented, no longer to a disinterested layman such as Romanianus, but to an assembly of bishops. It is compressed, greatly simplified, and now ribbed with Scriptural citations; but it is marked by the same precocious certainty of touch. The difficulties of simple men — and to judge by some of the problems treated in passing, Augustine's audience must have included some very simple bishops indeed — are confidently resolved. The Creed is shown as a coherent whole, perfectly satisfying and intelligible. Augustine is still inspired by a great hope: that a powerful and pious intelligence might yet play on this highly compressed document in such a way as to make every statement in it translucent with understanding.

Augustine's ideal at this time was a 'lamp': an intellect, shining with truth, set upon a body reduced to complete submission.[1] For his congregation, Augustine was, and remained, the man who knew. He can tell them the hidden meanings of the Bible.[2] He can unravel the significance of a number.[3] He can immediately pay off a promise to answer Manichaean criticisms of the Old Testament.[4] He always remains sharp, questioning, gesticulating to convey his inmost meaning, never at a loss for words: 'We should understand what this Psalm means. Sing it with human reason, not like birds. Thrushes, parrots, ravens, magpies and the like are often taught to say what they do not understand. To know what we are saying — that was granted by God's will to human nature. We know only too well the way bad, loose-living men sing, as suits their ears and hearts. They are all the worse for knowing only too well what they are singing about. They know they are singing dirty songs — but the dirtier they are, the more they enjoy it. . . . And we, who have learnt in the Church to sing God's words, should be just as eager. . . . Now, my friends, what we have all sung together with one voice — we should know and see it with a clear mind.'[5] Occasionally, as when he preaches on marriage, Augustine strikes a chill note that would remind his delighted audience that their priest was also a Neo-Platonist, who lived among monks; and who could seriously expect them to love the sexuality of their wives and the physical bonds of their families only as a Christian must love his enemies.[6]

Augustine was never to live alone in Hippo. As a priest, he would return from his duties to preside over the Monastery in the Garden.[7]

[1] *Vita*, V, 5; *de serm. Dom. in monte*, I, xvii ,17.   [2] *de serm. Dom. in monte*, II, xx, 68.
[3] *de serm. Dom. in monte*, I, iv, 12.   [4] *Serm*. I, 1   [5] *Enarr. in Ps*. 18, 2.
[6] *de serm. Dom. in monte*, I, xv, 41, (later revised by him: *Retract.* I, 19, 5).   [7] *Vita*, V, 1.

Later, when fully occupied as a bishop, he would envy the monks their regular life of prayer, reading and manual labour.[1] Adam and Eve were fortunate to work in a garden: 'When all is said and done, is there any more marvellous sight, any occasion when human reason is nearer to some sort of converse with the nature of things, than the sowing of seeds, the planting of cuttings, the transplanting of shrubs, the grafting of slips? It is as though you could question the vital force in each root and bud on what it can do, and what it cannot, and why.'[2]

This monastery was still recruited from among Augustine's past friends. Evodius and Alypius were there. Inevitably, however, a permanent institution, such as a monastery, would attract younger men, whose tastes, culture and past history did not resemble that of Augustine and his friends. Such a man was Possidius — a straightforward and pertinacious disciple. It is paradoxical that Possidius should have written the only contemporary biography of Augustine; and that he should have chosen to present his complex hero largely in terms of the tranquil, uncomplicated life that he had created for others.[3]

Inevitably, these *servi Dei* came to form an influential group within the African church. Their most remarkable supporter was Aurelius, whom Augustine had known as a deacon in Carthage, in 388, and who became bishop of the city in 392. As president of the first regular and prolonged series of 'total' councils in the history of the African church, Aurelius came to use his authority to the full as 'Primate' of Africa. Augustine is always careful to address him as *Auctoritas tua*, 'Your Authority.' This forceful and dominant figure was destined to give 'a sword' to the reforms of Augustine.[4]

Not only did Aurelius patronize Augustine's community;[5] he actively encouraged Augustine to form a centre of brilliant men in the ecclesiastical province of Numidia. He was pleased that Alypius had stayed in Hippo 'as an example to those who would leave the world'.[6] His encouragement was amply rewarded. Augustine's *monasterium* in Hippo became a 'seminary' in the true sense of the word: a 'seed-bed' from which Augustine's protégés were 'planted out' as bishops in the leading towns of Numidia.[7]

This sudden influx of new men would have affected the balance of forces in the province dramatically. The ecclesiastical world of Africa remained a small one, in which most bishops knew each other, and a bishop was a well-known personality in the small towns. The men

---

[1] *de opere mon.* xxix, 37.   [2] *de Gen. ad litt.* VIII, viii, 16.   [3] v. inf. p. 409.
[4] *Ep.* 22, 2.   [5] *Ep.* 22, 9.   [6] *Ep.* 22, 1.
[7] *Vita*, XI, 1–4, mentions 10 in all.

who came from Augustine were not only dedicated figures, susceptible to his inspiration: many of them were spectacular personalities in their own right. The average Donatist and Catholic bishop had remained a provincial figure: the Donatist spokesmen in Numidia, for instance, had been local, small-town lawyers and schoolmasters.[1] But the 'world' from which many members of Augustine's monastery had been converted, was often the wider and more ruthless world of the Imperial bureaucracy.[2] Some of these humble *servi Dei*, indeed, had been members of the dreaded secret police;[3] and in their new life of poverty they could count on the support of some of the greatest landowners in the Western Empire.

Soon Alypius, whose characteristic of *humanitas*,[4] his never failing *savoir faire*, enabled him to take such initiatives, presumed on his acquaintance with a Roman relative of Paulinus of Nola, to approach this *doyen* of the monastic movement of the day.[5] Paulinus was the sole remaining heir of one of the oldest and richest families of the time: he had owned 'kingdoms' of estates in Gaul and Spain. He had recently retired with his wife, Therasia, to a monastic retreat in his senatorial mansion at Nola, in Campania. Later, Augustine hoped that this 'lion' of the ascetic movement might make a special visit to Africa to support the cause of the monks: this wish shows to what an extent the new group looked outside the provincial church of Africa for encouragement and inspiration.[6]

By 395, Paulinus could write that the impossible had happened in Africa. Augustine had become a bishop without difficulty, as had his other correspondents, Aurelius, Alypius, Profuturus and Severus.[7] All of them were *servi Dei*, all of them intimate friends of Augustine. By such men, the '*horn of the Church*' was raised high, a fact which boded ill for the '*horns of the sinners*', for the Manichees and the Donatists.[8] This is the beginning of a dramatic revolution in the history of African Christianity.

The sudden constellation of able men in one province is the symptom

---

[1] Well characterized by P. Monceaux, *Histoire littéraire de l'Afrique chrétienne*, vi, 1922.

[2] e.g. Evodius and Alypius; v. esp. Monceaux, *Hist. littér.*, vii, 1923, pp. 35–62.

[3] v. sup. p. 126.   [4] *Ep.* 2.

[5] *Ep.* 24. On Paulinus, v. esp. P. Fabre, *S. Paulin de Nole et l'amitié chrétienne*, 1949, and the detailed study of Paulinus' relations with Augustine in P. Courcelle, 'Les lacunes dans la correspondance entre s. Augustin et Paulin de Nole', *Rev. études anciennes*, 53, 1951, pp. 253–300, and *Les Confessions*, pp. 559–607.

[6] e.g. *Ep.* 27, 6 and 31, 4.

[7] v. O. Perler, 'Das Datum der Bischofsweihe des heiligen Augustinus', *Rev. études augustin.*, xi, 1965, pp. 25–37.

[8] *Ep.* 32, 2.

of an even more profound change in the life of the Roman Empire. Paulinus mentions the elevation of Augustine and his friends in the course of a letter to Romanianus and Licentius. Romanianus and his son had come to Italy again. As befitted a member of the traditional Roman governing class, he had come to press his son's fortunes in Rome. Ten years previously, he had been followed by a whole group of serious, ambitious provincials, in search of honour and power in Italy, with Augustine among them. Now, most of these men had come to retire for ever to little provincial towns in Africa. They must have seemed to have condemned themselves to living in a backwater. Yet, this news from Italy is the last we hear of Romanianus and his son. They disappear from history, and it is Augustine, Aurelius and Alypius, bishops wielding power in little towns, over little men, who will influence the lives of their fellow-provincials far more intimately than ever Romanianus could have done, with his many lawsuits and his distant ambitions. It is in such ways that all roads no longer ran to Rome.

15

THE LOST FUTURE[1]

A decade elapsed between Augustine's first works after his conversion and the writing of his best-known masterpiece, the *Confessions*. In this decade, Augustine moved imperceptibly into a new world.

For, from 386 to 391, in Italy and in Thagaste, Augustine was still firmly rooted in the old world. The ideal on which he based his life still belonged to the Platonic tradition of the ancient world. He would be a '*sapiens*', a wise man, living a life of contemplation, determined, as were his pagan contemporaries in the same tradition, 'to grow godlike in their retirement'.[2] We meet such philosophers in some sarcophagi of the time: austere, tranquil figures, sitting among a small circle of admiring disciples, a book open on their knees — the highest human type that the classical culture of Late Antiquity thought it could produce.[3] Educated Christians thought of their saints as having achieved much the same ideals as contemporary pagans had ascribed to the philosophers. When Augustine, therefore, spoke of the quality

[1] Compared with the erudition lavished, recently, on the two years of Augustine's conversion, the changes of his thought in the following decade have received singularly little attention. The excellent study of A. Pincherle, *La formazione teologica di S. Agostino*, 1947, is a notable exception. The following articles, also, have drawn attention to some of the more significant changes in Augustine's ideas: E. Cranz, 'The Development of Augustine's ideas on Society before the Donatist Controversy', *Harvard Theol. Rev.*, xlvii, 1954, pp. 255–316; M. Löhrer, *Der Glaubensbegriff des heiligen Augustins in seinen ersten Schriften bis zu den Confessiones*, 1955, and G. Folliet, 'La typologie du sabbat chez s. Augustin', *Rev. études augustin.*, ii, 1956, pp. 371–390.

For this, and successive treatments of the religious ideas of Augustine, I am especially indebted to the brilliant exposition of J. Burnaby, *Amor Dei: a study of the Religion of St. Augustine*, 1938, notably pp. 25–82.

[2] *Ep.* 10, 2. v. sup. p. 133.

[3] e.g. G. Rodenwalt, 'Zur Kunstgeschichte der Jahre 220 bis 270', *Jahrbuch des deutsch. archäolog Inst.* 51, 1936, pp. 104–105, and H. P. L'Orange, 'Plotinus–Paul', *Byzantion*, 25–27, 1955–1957, pp. 473–483.

of the life achieved by his heroes, the Apostles, we can see exactly what he was hoping for himself: '*Blessed are the peacemakers*.' 'For those are peacemakers in themselves, who, in conquering and subjecting to reason . . . all the motions of their souls, and having their carnal desires tamed, have become, in themselves, a Kingdom of God. . . . They enjoy the peace which is given on earth to men of good-will . . . the life of the consummate and perfect man of wisdom. . . . All this can reach fulfilment in this present life, as we believe it was reached by the Apostles.'[1] Such ideas were deeply ingrained: they show in the controlled, distant faces of any contemporary mosaic; and, some thirty years later, educated bishops were still supposed to be shocked by the suggestion of the old Augustine, that even Saint Paul might still have been 'greatly tainted by sexual desires'.[2]

Ten years later, this great hope had vanished. 'Whoever thinks', Augustine will then write, 'that in this mortal life a man may so disperse the mists of bodily and carnal imaginings as to possess the unclouded light of changeless truth, and to cleave to it with the unswerving constancy of a spirit wholly estranged from the common ways of life — he understands neither What he seeks, nor who he is who seeks it.'[3]

Augustine, indeed, had decided that he would never reach the fulfilment that he first thought was promised to him by a Christian Platonism: he would never impose a victory of mind over body in himself, he would never achieve the wrapt contemplation of the ideal philosopher. It is the most drastic change that a man may have to accept: it involved nothing less than the surrender of the bright future he thought he had gained at Cassiciacum.[4]

To reduce such a change, as some neat scholars have done, to a sloughing-off of 'Neo-Platonism' and the discovery of some 'authentic' Christianity, is to trivialize it. The mould into which Augustine had poured his life as a convert was capable of holding educated Christians of different temperaments, in different parts of the Roman world, for the whole of their lives. Yet Augustine broke this mould in a decade — one suspects, partly because it could not withstand the terrific weight of his own expectations of it. In a decade, hard thought and bitter

---

[1] *de serm. Dom. in monte*, I, ii, 9.   [2] *C. Epp. Pelag.* I, viii, 13.
[3] *de cons. evang.* IV, x, 20.
[4] v. sup. p. 122.

This crucial change should not obscure the continuity of Augustine's Neo-Platonism. It remains fundamental to his thought, and provides the key to a proper understanding of it, as has been clearly shown both by R. Holte, *Béatitude et Sagesse*, and, recently, by R. Lorenz, 'Gnade und Erkenntnis bei Augustinus', *Zeitschr. für Kirchengesch.*, 75, 1964, pp. 21–78.

experience subtly transformed the whole quality of his life; and, in following this deep change, we can appreciate the momentum of the new ideas that had forced themselves upon Augustine as he sat down, around 397, to review and re-interpret his past life in the *Confessions*. For Augustine would pass voraciously from problem to problem: what begins, perhaps, as the dangerous disillusionment of a perfectionist, emerges in the *Confessions*, as a new view of man, a reassessment of his potentialities, an exciting and profound discovery of the true sources of his motivation.

In the first place, Augustine came to appreciate the sheer difficulty of achieving an ideal life. We can see this awareness forcing itself upon him as a priest, and especially in the works he wrote against the Manichees, between 392 and 394. For it would be naïve to expect that, faced with a sect with whom he had always had a peculiarly intense relationship, liable to be confronted in a man such as Fortunatus, with living reminders of his own past as a Manichee, Augustine would develop only those parts of his system that directly contradicted his opponents. Far from it: by a subtle attraction of opposites, the Manichees would succeed in bringing to the forefront of Augustine's mind certain problems that the Platonists of the time had failed to answer.

Above all, there was the burning problem of the apparent permanence of evil in human actions. This problem had placed Augustine in an awkward position. For, previously, he had taken up his stand on the freedom of the will; his criticism of Manichaeism had been a typical philosopher's criticism of determinism generally. It was a matter of common sense that men were responsible for their actions; they could not be held responsible if their wills were not free; therefore, their wills could not be thought of as being determined by some external forces, in this case, by the Manichaean 'Power of Darkness'.[1] This was, of course, a dangerous line of argument: for it committed Augustine, in theory at least, to the absolute self-determination of the will; it implied an 'ease of action', a *facilitas*,[2] that would hardly convince such sombre observers of the human condition as the Manichees. At this time, indeed, Augustine was, on paper, more Pelagian than Pelagius: Pelagius will even quote from Augustine's book '*On Free Will*' in support of his own views.[3] So, paradoxically, the great opponent of Augustine's old age had been inspired by those

---

[1] Notably in *de ii anim.* 13–15.

[2] *de lib. arb.* I, xiii, 29. This is the obvious conclusion drawn by Augustine's interlocutor; already Augustine answers by reminding him that the matter is more complex.

[3] *de lib. arb.* III, vi, 18, in *de natura et gratia*, lviii, 69.

treatises of the young philosopher, in which Augustine had defended the freedom of the will against a Manichaean determinism.[1]

For what Augustine could not explain so easily, was the fact that in practice, the human will did not enjoy complete freedom.[2] A man found himself involved in seemingly irreversible patterns of behaviour, subject to compulsive urges to behave in a manner contrary to his good intentions, sadly unable to undo habits that had become established.

Thus, when Manichees pointed to the fact that the soul did not, in fact, enjoy complete freedom to determine its own behaviour, they could appeal both to the obvious and to the authority of S. Paul. In his public debate, Fortunatus would insist on this point: 'It is plain from this that the good soul . . . is seen to sin, and not of its own accord, but following the way in which "*the flesh lusteth against the spirit and that which you wish not, that you do.*" And, as Paul says elsewhere: "*I see another law in my members*".'[3]

This direct challenge had to be met. It led Augustine to open up a new approach to the problem of evil. He would explain the permanence of evil in the human will in purely psychological terms: in terms of the compulsive force of habit, *consuetudo*, which derived its strength entirely from the working of the human memory. The pleasure derived from past actions is 'inflicted' on the memory, and so perpetuated.[4] But this process of perpetuation does not strike Augustine as straightforward: for by reason of 'some mysterious weakness',[5] the pleasure of every past evil act is amplified and transformed by being remembered and repeated. Thus, a compulsive habit can soon set in.

It is in this way that Augustine is led to see man bound by the continuity of his inner life. In a passage of great force, Augustine likens the soul caught by the weight of habit to Lazarus, lying four days dead in the tomb.[6] The shift of emphasis implied in this symbolism is far-reaching: it is no longer possible to speak of a man's body as the only 'tomb' of his soul; Augustine has been forced to consider the mysterious manner in which he could create his own tomb in his memory.

Augustine was helped in this growing awareness of the intractable elements in behaviour by his experience as a priest in Hippo. For the Africans were notorious swearers of oaths. Augustine's early sermons show how he had to combat this vice in his congregation,[7] and to

[1] v. inf. p. 386, n. 1.   [2] Burnaby, *Amor Dei*, p. 187.   [3] *C. Fort.* 21.
[4] *de serm. Dom. in monte*, I, xii, 34.   [5] e.g. *de Musica*, VI, v, 15.
[6] *de serm. Dom. in monte*, I, xii, 35.
[7] *de serm. Dom. in monte*, I, xvii, 51; *Ep. ad Gal. expos.* 9.

think about it in himself.[1] This campaign against swearing, indeed, would have brought him up against the compulsive force of certain habits, quite as much as any modern campaign against smoking might do. Augustine, therefore, will draw upon immediate experience when he answers the question posed by Fortunatus: 'In our present state, we do have the free power to do or not to do anything, before we are caught up in any habit. When we have used this freedom to do something, the sweetness and pleasure of the act holds our soul, and it is caught in the sort of habit that it cannot break — a habit that is created for itself by its own act of sin. We see around us many men who do not want to swear, but, because their tongue has picked up the habit, words escape from their lips which they are just unable to control. . . . If you want to know what I mean, start trying not to swear: then you will see how the force of habit goes on its own way.'[2]

Like a single cloud that grows to darken the whole sky, this sense of the force of past habit deepens in Augustine.[3] *Consuetudo carnalis*, 'a force of habit directed towards the ways of the flesh,' will stand like a black bar, framing his description of every contemplative experience in the *Confessions*. A decade previously, such transitory experiences of contemplation had seemed to be the initial stages of a development that might culminate, in this life, in 'a place of rest' . . . 'the full enjoyment of the absolute and true good, breathing the clear air of serenity and eternity'.[4] Now Augustine is resigned never to know more than glimpses: 'And sometimes You fill me with a feeling quite unlike my normal state, an inward sense of delight, which, if it were to reach fulfilment in me, would be something entirely different from my present life. But my heavy burden of distress drags me back: I am sucked back to my habits, and find myself held fast; I weep greatly, but I am firmly held. The load of habit is a force to be reckoned with!'[5]

A sense of intractable obstacles to perfection will lead Augustine to a new humility, perhaps even to a measure of tolerance:

'O pig-headed souls!', he can exclaim to the Manichees in 390: 'Give me a man . . . who stands up to the senses of the flesh, and to the blows which it rains on the soul; who stands up to the habitual thinking of men . . . who "carves away at his spirit".' (The last exhortation is taken straight from Plotinus.)[6] Ten years later he must write: 'Let them deal harshly with you, who do not know with what effort truth is found and with what difficulty errors are avoided; let them deal harshly with

---

[1] *Vita*, XXV, 2; *Serm.* 180, 10 and 307, 5.

[2] *C. Fort.* 22.

[3] e.g. *de serm. Dom. in monte*, I, iii, 10.

[4] *de quant. anim.* xxxiii, 76.

[5] *Conf.* X, xl, 65.

[6] *de vera relig.* xxxiv, 64.

you, who do not know how rare and how exacting it is to overcome imaginations from the flesh in the serenity of a pious intellect, let them deal harshly with you, who do not know with what pain the inner eye of a man is healed, that he may glimpse his Sun.'[1]

With such a mood growing upon him, Augustine turned once again to S. Paul. By June 394, he was giving 'lectures' on the Epistle to the Romans to his friends at Carthage.[2] He even intended to write a complete commentary on the Epistles of S. Paul: it is yet another of Augustine's great abandoned projects.[3] In turning his attention to S. Paul, Augustine was intervening in a problem that had begun to preoccupy many of his contemporaries. The last decades of the fourth century in the Latin church, could well be called 'the generation of S. Paul': a common interest in S. Paul drew together widely differing thinkers, and made them closer to each other than to their predecessors. In Italy, Paul had already received commentaries from the Christian Platonist, Marius Victorinus, and from an anonymous layman, probably a retired bureaucrat, known to us as 'Ambrosiaster'. In Africa, an interest in Paul had brought the Donatist layman, Tyconius, closer to Augustine than to his own bishops. Above all, at that time, Augustine had the most radical and self-confident of Paul's expositors in mind, the Manichees: they were responsible for most of the specific questions which Augustine had to resolve for his audience at Carthage.[4] Given this widespread interest, it is not surprising that, at exactly the same time as Augustine was speaking on Paul in Carthage, his future opponent, Pelagius, was presenting a radically different Paul to the circle of his friends in one of the great palaces of Rome.[5]

Augustine did not 'discover' Paul at this time. He merely read him differently. Previously, he had interpreted Paul as a Platonist: he had seen him as the exponent of a spiritual ascent, of the renewal of the 'inner' man, the decay of the 'outer';[6] and, after his baptism, he had shared in Paul's sense of triumph: 'Behold all things have become new.' The idea of the spiritual life as a vertical ascent, as a progress towards a final, highest stage to be reached in this life, had fascinated Augustine in previous years. Now, he will see in Paul nothing but a single, unresolved tension between 'flesh' and 'spirit'. The only changes he could find were changes in states of awareness of this tension: ignorance of its existence 'before the Law'; helpless realization of the extent of the

---

[1] C. Ep. Fund. 2.
[2] The Expositio quarundarum propositionum ex Ep. Apostoli ad Romanos; Retract. I, 22.
[3] Retract. I, 24, 1.
[4] e.g. Propp. ex Ep. ad Rom. 13 and 49.
[5] v. inf. p. 342.
[6] e.g. de quant. anim. xxviii, 55 and de vera relig. lii, 101.

tension between good and evil 'under the Law'; a stage of utter dependence on a Liberator 'under grace'. Only after this life would tension
be resolved, 'When death is swallowed up in victory.' It is a flattened
landscape: and in it, the hope of spiritual progress comes increasingly
to depend, for Augustine, on the unfathomable will of God.

Yet Augustine fought a stubborn losing battle against regarding
men as utterly helpless. While he was a priest, he insisted that men's
unaided efforts counted for something. Men could not overcome their
limitations; but they could take the initiative in believing in God and
in calling on Him to save them.[1] When asked what was the one,
unforgivable sin against the Holy Ghost, Augustine would answer
firmly, at this time, that it was despair.[2]

For some years, he remained perched between two worlds. There
was no more talk of an 'ascent' in this life. 'Remember . . . you have
postponed your vision.'[3] A new image will make its appearance: that
of a long highway, an *iter*.[4] The moments of clear vision of truth that
the mind gains in this life, are of infinite value; but they are now the
consolations of a traveller on a long journey: 'While we do this, until
we achieve our aim, we are still travelling.' These moments are no more
than points of light 'along this darkening highway'.[5] Augustine,
himself, always resented travelling: he always associated it with a sense
of protracted labour and of the infinite postponement of his dearest
wishes; and these associations will colour the most characteristic image
of the spiritual life in his middle age.[6]

Nevertheless, there is a heroic refusal to countenance the despair
that 'gnaws at men'. 'It will not be held against you, that you are
ignorant against your will, but that you neglect to seek out what it is
that makes you ignorant; not that you cannot bring together your
wounded limbs, but that you reject Him that would heal them. No man
has been deprived of his ability to know that it is essential to find out
what it is that it is damaging not to be aware of; and to know that he
should confess his weakness, so that He can help him who seeks hard
and confesses.'[7]

It is important to stress Augustine's hesitations at this time. He was
surrounded by men who were more 'Augustinian' than himself. *Servi
Dei* like Paulinus and Evodius had already made a cult of human
frailty; they regarded themselves as worthless, as 'dust and ashes', as

[1] *de serm. Dom. in monte*, I, xviii, 55; *Propp. ex Ep. ad Rom.*, 44.
[2] *Ep. ad Rom. in incoh. expos.* 14.   [3] *de lib. arb.* II, xvi, 42.
[4] *de lib. arb.* II, xvi, 41.   [5] *de lib. arb.* II, xvi, 41.
[6] v. inf. p. 202 and p. 210.   [7] *de lib. arb.* III, xix, 53.

having been 'predestined' by God alone. Yet these expressions of impotence lacked a philosophical basis; they belonged more to the world of ascetic sensibility than to theology.[1] Augustine, however, was a responsible thinker, still preoccupied by a need to define himself over against the Manichees. He would move all the more cautiously. He would carefully sift Paul for his true meaning, and he would turn, significantly enough, to the African tradition of S. Cyprian and Tyconius for the 'better treatments' that would enable him to make up his mind.[2] The very deliberation of his first steps would make Augustine's final interpretation of Paul all the more impressive: in a decade he had already worked through many layers of Pauline theology (and each layer could have lasted a lesser man for a lifetime) in order to come out with his own revolutionary synthesis. In this we can see the hallmark of a genius: Augustine possessed the relentless ability to work out in precise and cogent detail, an intuition that had already been hovering in a partial, confused form, at the back of the minds of his contemporaries.

Even the circumstances of Augustine's final step are dramatic. Around 395, he had been approached with a handful of 'problems' by none other than Simplicianus of Milan. Augustine's answer was exceedingly painstaking:[3] he was plainly aware that his opinions would be carefully appraised by the old man to whom he owed so much.[4] Yet both men had changed in the past decade. In Milan, Augustine and Simplicianus had met as metaphysicians: they had found common ground between the Platonists and S. John in their description of the structure of the spiritual universe.[5] Now Simplicianus will pose a totally different kind of question: why was it that God had said 'I have hated Esau'? It is a long journey from the contemplation of a Logos, whose existence can be 'hinted at by innumerable rational proofs', to this acute posing of the unfathomable nature of individual destinies. And Augustine will provide Simplicianus with what Ambrose had been unable to provide. For when Simplicianus had approached his bishop for his opinions on Paul, Ambrose had merely replied that Paul presented no problems, that it would be just a matter of 'reading him aloud'.[6] À mesure qu'on a plus d'esprit, on trouve plus des hommes originaux! Ambrose was not as clever as Augustine: and he was very

---

[1] e.g. *de lib. arb.* III, iii, 7, where it is Evodius, not Augustine, who exclaims, 'His will is my necessity'.

[2] Pincherle, *La formazione*, pp. 175 sq., provides a particularly valuable discussion.

[3] *Ad Simplicianum de diversis quaestionibus*: transl. with an introduction by G. Bardy, *Bibliothèque augustinienne*, sér. i, 10, 1952, pp. 383–578.

[4] *Ep.* 37, 2.   [5] v. sup. p. 93.   [6] Ambrose, *Ep.* 37, 1 (P.L. xvi, 1085).

much the traditional, educated bishop of his time. For him, the main problem was still to understand the 'spiritual' message of the Old Testament in terms of allegories evolved by the Alexandrian school.[1] But, in the next four years, Origen will fall out of favour. The Latin church will find itself without any 'classic' of Christian scholarship, with which to solve its problems. It was a time of fruitful intellectual confusion. In this hiatus, only two men were to create their own theology using ideas more current in the Latin world than among the Greeks, and expressing them in terms of their meditations on S. Paul. These were Augustine and that other revolutionary, Pelagius.

Augustine later regarded his solution of the main problem posed by Simplicianus, as having been 'revealed' to him by God:[2] 'To solve the question, I had previously tried hard to uphold the freedom of choice of the human will; but the Grace of God had the upper hand. There was no way out but to conclude that the Apostle (Paul) must be understood to have said the most obvious truth, when he said: "*Who has made you different? What have you got that you did not first receive? If you have received all this, why glory in it as if you had not been given it?*".'[3]

Augustine had, indeed, given Simplicianus 'no way out'. His answer to the 'Second Problem' is a classic of his ruthless dialectical technique. It is this ability to exclude all alternatives to his own interpretation, as being logically inconsistent with a single *intentio*,[4] a basic meaning of S. Paul, that enabled Augustine to do what Ambrose could never have done: he derived from a seemingly unambiguous text, an intricate synthesis of grace, freewill and predestination. For the first time, Augustine came to see man as utterly dependent on God, even for his first initiative of believing in Him: '*Work out your salvation in fear and trembling: for it is God who works in you, both that you should wish and act with a good will.*'[5]

Augustine had come to this conclusion through a reassessment of the nature of human motivation. It is this psychological discovery which gives cogency to the interpretation that he placed on Paul. Briefly, Augustine had analysed the psychology of 'delight'. 'Delight' is the only possible source of action, nothing else can move the will. Therefore, a man can act only if he can mobilize his feelings, only if he

[1] Ambrose, *Ep.* 76, 1 (P.L. xvi, 1314). v. esp. Lazzati, *Il valore letterario dell'esegesi ambrosiana*, pp. 46–47.

[2] *de praed. sanct.* iv, 8; but v. inf. p. 280 for the precise meaning of this.

[3] *Retract.* II, 27.

[4] *Ad Simpl. de div. quaest.* I, qu. ii, 2, 5 and 10.

[5] *Phil.* 2, 12 and 13: *Ad Simpl. de div. quaest.* I, qu. ii, 12.

154

is 'affected' by an object of delight.[1] Ten years before, this element had been notably lacking in Augustine's programme for a 'well-trained soul': such a soul would have risen to truth by academic disciplines, supported by 'sparkling little chains of argument'. Now, 'feeling' has taken its rightful place as the ally of the intellect.[2]

But 'delight' itself is no longer a simple matter. It is not a spontaneous reaction, the natural thrill of the refined soul when confronted with beauty.[3] For it is just this vital capacity to engage one's feelings on a course of action, to take 'delight' in it, that escapes our powers of self-determination: the processes that prepare a man's heart to take 'delight' in his God are not only hidden, but actually unconscious and beyond his control:[4] 'The fact that those things that make for successful progress towards God should cause us delight is not acquired by our good intentions, earnestness and the value of our own good will — but is dependent on the inspiration granted us by God. . . . Surely our prayers are, sometimes, so lukewarm, stone-cold, indeed, and hardly prayers at all: they are so distant in our thoughts that we do not even notice this fact with pain — for if we were even to feel the pain, we would be praying again.'[5]

Augustine came to view 'delight' as the mainspring of human action; but this 'delight' escaped his self-control. Delight is discontinuous, startlingly erratic: Augustine now moves in a world of 'love at first sight', of chance encounters, and, just as important, of sudden, equally inexplicable patches of deadness: 'Who can embrace wholeheartedly what gives him no delight? But who can determine for himself that what will delight him should come his way, and, when it comes, that it should, in fact, delight him?'[6] In only a few years, Augustine's *Confessions* will show that a work of art could spring from such a dictum.

For a crucial change had taken place in Augustine. Ten years previously, surrounded by his eager friends, he had enjoyed the most pleasant illusion a gregarious man could enjoy: he could take his friends for granted; he could know a good man when he saw one; he moved in a circle of equals, of superior souls — serious, upright, well-educated, admirable within a single, widely-accepted, ideal of the perfect man. Now he is no longer so sure: 'This choice of God is certainly hidden

[1] *Ad. Simpl. de div. quaest.* I, qu. ii, 13.   [2] e.g. *de Musica*, VI, xvii, 59. cf. *Ep.* 4, 2.
[3] e.g. *Ennead* I, vi, 4, (MacKenna 2, p. 59). This is seen very clearly by Burnaby, *Amor Dei*, p. 89.
[4] *Ad. Simpl. de div. quaest.* I, qu. ii, 22.   [5] *Ad. Simpl. de div. quaest.* I, qu. ii, 21.
[6] *Ad. Simpl. de div. quaest.* I, qu. ii, 21.

from us. . . . Even if it should be perceptible to some men, I must admit that, in this matter, I am incapable of knowing. I just cannot find what criterion to apply in deciding which men should be chosen to be saved by grace. If I were to reflect on how to weigh up this choice, I myself would instinctively choose those with better intelligence or less sins, or both; I should add, I suppose, a sound and proper education. . . . And as soon as I decide on that, He will laugh me to scorn.'[1]

If Augustine could not take his friends for granted any longer, still less could he understand himself in terms of his old ideals. We met him, at Cassiciacum, as a man certain of his future: his books are all of them programmes; even his reminiscences are no more than a list of those obstacles to perfection, which he hoped soon to surmount. In the *Confessions*, he is a man who has lost this certain future: as we shall see, he is obsessed by the need to understand what had really happened to him in his distant past.

A new tone has come to suffuse Augustine's life. He is a man who has realized that he was doomed to remain incomplete in his present existence, that what he wished for most ardently would never be more than a hope, postponed to a final resolution of all tensions, far beyond this life. Anyone who thought otherwise, he felt, was either morally obtuse or a doctrinaire.[2] All a man could do was to 'yearn' for this absent perfection, to feel its loss intensely, to pine for it. '*Desiderium sinus cordis*': 'It is yearning that makes the heart deep.'[3] This marks the end of a long-established classical ideal of perfection: Augustine would never achieve the concentrated tranquillity of the supermen that still gaze out at us from some mosaics in Christian churches and from the statues of pagan sages. If to be a 'Romantic', means to be a man acutely aware of being caught in an existence that denies him the fullness for which he craves, to feel that he is defined by his tension towards something else, by his capacity for faith, for hope, for longing, to think of himself as a wanderer seeking a country that is always distant, but made ever-present to him by the quality of the love that 'groans' for it, then Augustine has imperceptibly become a 'Romantic':[4] and the *Confessions* which he wrote soon after, when he was the Catholic bishop of Hippo, will be a monumental statement of that most rare mood:

---

[1] *Ad. Simpl. de div. quaest.* I, qu. ii, 22.   [3] v. esp. Burnaby, *Amor Dei*, pp. 52–73.

[2] *Tract. in Joh.* 40, 10.

[4] Compare the fine presentation of Burnaby, *Amor Dei*, pp. 52–73, with two brilliant evocations of parallel feelings in Late Roman art and thought: G. Mathew, *Byzantine Aesthetics*, pp. 21–22, and P. Hadot, *Plotin*, pp. 73–75.

'Let me leave them outside, breathing into the dust, and filling their eyes with earth, and let me enter into my chamber and sing my songs of love to Thee, groaning with inexpressible groaning in my distant wandering, and remembering Jerusalem with my heart stretching upwards in longing for it: Jerusalem my Fatherland, Jerusalem who is my mother. . . .'[1]

[1] *Conf.* XII, xvi, 23.

16

THE 'CONFESSIONS'[1]

Augustine had come to live in a circle of men who shared a lively curiosity about other people. In the late fourth century, it had become increasingly difficult to take the course of the life of one's fellow-men for granted. Conventional careers, traditional ties of class and education, had failed to hold many. Paulinus of Nola was among them. He had suddenly abandoned the immemorial life of a country-gentleman in Aquitaine, to become, first, a monk, then priest and later bishop in a far-away town. He and his friends needed to explain and justify the dramatic changes in their lives: what would interest Paulinus in a new friend was not only '*Of what family are you, from what great house do you come?*' but in what way had he been 'made separate' by God, in what way he had come to live a life so very different from the old life of a Roman.[2]

The changes that had happened to these men, the course of their 'conversion', the quality of the new life they had adopted, would be a subject of absorbing interest to anyone who had shared such an experience. Augustine's table at Hippo was surrounded by such men. They would talk, not about things, but about people. Two friends of Paulinus arrived one day: they came 'as another kind of letter from you, that could hear and give us in return a most sweet part of your

<hr>

[1] P. Courcelle, *Les Confessions de S. Augustin dans la tradition littéraire: Antécédents et Postérité*, 1963, provides a magisterial introduction both to the influence of the *Confessions* in European literature and to the vast resources of modern scholarship mobilized around this single text. I am particularly indebted to the excellent study of G. N. Knauer, *Die Psalmenzitate in Augustins Konfessionen*, 1955, a model study of an important aspect of the literary qualities and style of the *Confessions*; to the commentaries of M. Pellegrino and A. Solignac (cit. sup. p. 79, n.); and to the text and notes of J. Gibb and W. Montgomery, *The Confessions of St. Augustine*, (Cambridge Patristic Texts), 1908. Bonner, *St. Augustine*, pp. 42–52, has provided a judicious and well-documented summary of conflicting views on the historical value of the *Confessions*.

[2] *Ep.* 24, 2 (to Alypius).

presence . . . in their eyes and expressions we could read you . . . written in their hearts'.[1] And in the same manner, Augustine had once hung on the words of a chance acquaintance in Milan, Ponticianus, as he talked about total strangers at opposite ends of the Roman world: about a hermit in Upper Egypt, S. Anthony, and about the impact which a description of his life had on courtiers taking an afternoon's stroll outside Trèves.[2]

Augustine, therefore, already found himself with an audience used to intimate biography, and so, ripe for autobiography. The stories that circulated about people concerned the events of their inner life: in Africa, for instance, a simple woman, S. Perpetua, had already left an account of her experiences in prison, that spoke straight from the heart: 'And so I managed to have my (newborn) child stay with me in prison: straightway I became better and was relieved by the task of looking after my little baby; and the prison suddenly was made for me a palace, and I would rather have been there than anywhere else.'[3]

Early Christians, however, had been overshadowed by death: when they wrote of themselves, martyrdom, the impending climax of their lives, had caused their past to pale into insignificance. The biographer of S. Cyprian, for instance, could pass over the first forty years of his hero's life, and concentrate on merely the last four years before his martyrdom: this, his 'new' life after baptism, was considered his true life, and the only one that might interest Christian readers of the third century.[4] By the time of Augustine, the Church had settled down in Roman Society. The Christian's worst enemies could no longer be placed outside him: they were inside, his sins and his doubts; and the climax of a man's life would not be martyrdom, but conversion from the perils of his own past.

Wandering, temptations, sad thoughts of mortality and the search for truth:[5] these had always been the stuff of autobiography for fine souls, who refused to accept superficial security. Pagan philosophers had already created a tradition of 'religious autobiography' in this vein: it will be continued by Christians in the fourth century, and will reach its climax in the *Confessions* of S. Augustine.

Augustine, therefore, did not need to look far to find an audience for the *Confessions*. It had been created for him quite recently, by the

[1] *Ep.* 31, 2. v. inf. p. 200.   [2] *Conf.* VIII, vi, 14–15.
[3] *Passio Ss. Perpetuae et Felicitatis*, 3, ed. P. Franchi De'Cavalieri, (*Röm. Quartalschrift*, 5, Supplementheft), 1896, p. 110.
[4] Pontius, *Vita Cypriani*, 2, (P.L. iii, 1542).
[5] v. esp. Courcelle, *Les Confessions*, pp. 91–100.

amazing spread of asceticism in the Latin world. The *Confessions* was a book for the *servi Dei*, for the 'servants of God';[1] it is a classic document of the tastes of a group of highly sophisticated men, the *spiritales*, the 'men of the spirit'.[2] It told such men just what they wanted to know about — the course of a notable conversion;[3] it asked of its readers what they made a habit of asking for themselves — the support of their prayers.[4] It even contained moving appeals to the men who might join this new élite: to the austere Manichee[5] and the pagan Platonist, still standing aloof from the crowded basilicas of the Christians.[6] We know some of the men who were impressed by the *Confessions* when they first appeared in Rome. They seem a mixed group: Paulinus, Secundinus, a cultured Manichee,[7] Pelagius.[8] Yet they are joined by the common bond of that quest for perfection which characterized the amazing generation of the end of the fourth century.

No other member of this group of *servi Dei*, however, wrote a book that even remotely resembles the *Confessions*. Their interest in each other might seem to promise the most intimate self revelation. For Paulinus of Nola, for instance, Christian friendships were 'made in Heaven': God had 'predestined' such friends for each other by their common break with the past; all they did was to 'recognize' each other in a flash.[9] Their soul was their 'inner self';[10] and this soul could be poured out, in a single letter, to a fellow-member of the 'City of God'.[11] Augustine's contemporaries, however, will confine this charming, and highly romantic, ideal of friendship to the etiquette of letter-writing (and, perhaps, to the world of clerical gossip). Augustine, by contrast, grasped at it desperately. For him, it was the only way he had of justifying the astounding novelty of the book he was writing. He felt compelled to reveal himself: he was glad to have an audience whose ideal of friendship had prepared them to listen without contempt, as he insisted on telling them what it was like to steal pears as a teenager, to have cast off a mistress, to be still in doubt as to which temptation he might yet not resist.

Paulinus was a cold and lonely man. He was content to recreate among his new Christian correspondents a form of 'instant' friendship

---

[1] e.g. *Conf.* IX, ii, 4.
[2] e.g. *Conf.* V, x, 20. cf. *Ep.* 30, 2.
[3] e.g. *Conf.* IX, i, 1. cf. *Ep.* 24, 1.
[4] e.g. *Conf.* IX, xiii, 37 and X, iv, 5. cf. *Ep.* 24, 5.
[5] *Conf.* VIII, x, 23 and IX, iv, 10.
[6] *Conf.* VIII, ii, 3–5.
[7] *C. Ep. Secundini*, 11, (refers him to a book in the possession of Paulinus).
[8] *de dono persev.* XX, 53.
[9] *Ep.* 24, 1. cf. 30, 2.
[10] *Ep.* 27, 1.
[11] *Ep.* 24, 1.

that was free of the labour (and the dangers) of long acquaintances,[1] an intimacy of like souls that bye-passed the embarrassment of self-revelation, an emphasis on the spirit, that rather poignantly denied the yearning of the body for the physical presence of his friends.

Augustine, the warmer man, still 'yearned': 'yearning' is the hall-mark of his warmest letters.[2] A good Platonist, he might agree that the physical presence of a friend was 'a tiny thing': but he had the courage to admit how much he 'greatly craved'[3] this 'tiny thing' — a face, eyes that could still speak of a soul hidden in the envelope of flesh,[4] impatient gestures.[5] Yet, even when this contact occurred, Augustine still despaired of ever being able to communicate all he felt to anyone else: for a conversation, to him meant dragging vivid thoughts 'through the long, twisting lanes of speech'.[6]

He had come to feel these tensions ever more deeply. Men, he now thought, were, perhaps, too frail to bear the weight of revealing themselves to their fellows. The fallen race was too deeply flawed for its members to communicate freely.[7] The idea of a Christian fellowship in a 'City of God', of which Paulinus spoke so glibly, as if it already existed in this world, in a scattered élite of bishops and monks, had become for Augustine a desperate hope, a hope deferred to a future life.[8]

In the *Confessions* we will meet a naturally expansive man, very much the son of the 'exceedingly open-handed' Patricius, a man who needed to have friends around him, who could never quite be content with a world of disembodied souls, turning in despair away from human communication to God. He would at least tell Him what no other ancient man had told others of himself: 'Let me, then, speak . . . dust and ashes, yet let me speak. . . . It is to Your mercy that I speak, not to man — not to man who would mock me.'[9]

Augustine wrote his *Confessions* at some time around 397, that is, only a few years after he had become a bishop in Africa. The Mediterranean itself and 'a long stretch of soil and salt' now cut off Augustine and his African circle of *servi Dei* from the 'spiritual' men to whose acquaintance they felt entitled. They had been formed in Italy, and baptized by none other than S. Ambrose. By their standards, Africa was a backward and isolated province; they would even need books

---

[1] v. esp. P. Fabre, *S. Paulin de Nole et l'amitié chrétienne*, 1949, pp. 137–154, and esp. pp. 387–390.

[2] e.g. *Ep.* 27, 1. v. inf. pp. 210–211. [3] *Ep.* 28, 1. [4] *de div. quaest.* LXXXIII, 47.
[5] e.g. *Ep.* 267. [6] *de cat. rud.* x, 15. [7] *Enarr. ii in Ps.* 30, 13.
[8] v. sup. p. 156. [9] *Conf.* I, vi, 7.

from the libraries of such 'spiritual' men — Alypius will approach
Paulinus of Nola,[1] and Augustine, Jerome, for translations of Greek
authors.[2] Above all, they felt they had lost contact with the average
servus Dei by becoming bishops. A decade previously, Augustine had
regarded the combination of monk and bishop as well-nigh impossible;[3]
and Paulinus, a mere priest at the time, was still impressed by such a
combination in Alypius.[4] Augustine and Alypius, indeed, were types
of the future: the monk-bishop would grow in importance in the Latin
Church; and in the *Confessions*, Augustine had already provided a
classic statement of the ideal of such a man.

The *Confessions* is very much the book of a man who had come to
regard his past as a training for his present career. Thus, Augustine will
select as important, incidents and problems that immediately betray the
new bishop of Hippo. He had come to believe that the understanding
and exposition of the Scriptures was the heart of a bishop's life.[5] His
relations with the Scriptures, therefore, come to form a constant theme
throughout the *Confessions*. His conversion to the Manichees, for
instance, is now diagnosed, not in terms of a philosophical preoccupation with the origin of evil, but as a failure to accept the Bible.[6] We
see Ambrose through the eyes of a fellow-professional: we meet him as
a preacher and exegete, facing the Christian people in the basilica,[7] not
as the connoisseur of Plotinus. Augustine remembered how, in his
early days in Milan, he had seen the distant figure of Ambrose as a
bishop, from the outside only.[8] Now a bishop himself, he will ensure
that he will not be seen in this way: he will tell his readers exactly how
he still had to struggle with his own temptations; and in the last three
books of the *Confessions*, as he meditates on the opening lines of the
book of *Genesis*, he will carry his readers with him into his thoughts as
he, also, sat in his study, as he had once seen Ambrose sit, wrapt in the
silent contemplation of an open page.[9]

Not every bishop, of course, had the same view of his function as
Augustine. Alypius, for instance, plainly valued himself as the professional lawyer of the Catholic episcopate; he would appear in
Thagaste, as the searching judge of the Christian community.[10] So,
with an unexpected sense of fun, Augustine will tell the world how, as

---

[1] *Ep.* 24, 3. [2] *Ep.* 28. v. inf. p. 271.
[3] v. inf. p. 205; e.g. *de mor. eccl. cath.* (I), xxxii, 69. [4] *Ep.* 24, 2.
[5] v. inf. p. 262; v. esp. *Conf.* XI, ii, 2. [6] e.g. III, v, 9, as against *de lib. arb.* I, ii, 4.
[7] *Conf.* VI, iv, 6. [8] *Conf.* VI, iii, 3.
[9] *Conf.* VI, iii, 3: 'quid spei . . . quid luctaminis . . . quid solaminis', cf. *Conf.* X; 'et
occultum os eius . . . quam sapida gaudia de pane tuo', cf. *Conf.* XI–XIII.
[10] *Conf.* VI, ix, 15; v. inf. p. 201 for Alypius' characteristics.

a student, Alypius had once been mistaken for a burglar — a salutary experience for a future judge.[1]

No matter how much Augustine wished to share the ideals of a group, he remained irreducibly eccentric. He had still a lot to explain about himself. He was known for his anti-Manichaean works;[2] yet he was accused by a senior colleague, of being a crypto-Manichee.[3] He had been baptized by Ambrose;[4] but his writings betrayed a deep acquaintance with pagan Platonists. Even his conversion, by comparison with the histrionics of many of his contemporaries, had been notably unspectacular: for he had merely retired punctiliously from a chair of rhetoric in Milan, at the end of term, on grounds of ill-health.[5] A pupil of his at the time, Licentius, could still write about their stay in Cassiciacum, as if it had been a delightful, classical house-party.[6] Licentius would visit Paulinus: and when Augustine describes Paulinus to him, we see, perhaps, what Augustine would have liked himself to have been — a simple man, a 'servant of God', whose conversion from the world had been dramatic, but fundamentally uncomplicated.[7] Augustine's evolution had not been so simple; and he did not make it seem so. The *Confessions* would not have allayed the doubts of limited, pious men, who dreaded the Manichees and disliked a Greek philosophy they failed to understand.[8] No book, for instance, conveyed so vividly to Christian readers, the impact of the disquieting fascination of the *Platonici*.[9] Augustine the *servus Dei*, Augustine the bishop, had remained very much Augustine; and his *Confessions* could not have communicated this to his friends with greater charm, persuasiveness, and with a determination all the more unanswerable for being addressed not to a human audience, but to God.

While Augustine had many good reasons for introducing himself, at just such a moment in his career, to his fellow-Christians, only a very profound, inner reason would have led him to write a book such as the *Confessions*: he was entering middle age. This has been considered a good time for writing an autobiography. Around 397, Augustine had reached a watershed in his life. Since 391, he had been forced to adjust himself to a new existence, as a priest and bishop. This change had affected him deeply.[10] It had already driven him to anxious self-examination: a letter written after his ordination as a priest, to Aurelius of

---

[1] *Conf.* VI, ix, 14.
[2] *Ep.* 24, 1.
[3] *C. litt. Petil.* III, xvi, 19; *C. Crescon.* III, lxxx, 92. v. inf. p. 203.
[4] *Ep.* 24, 4.
[5] *Conf.* IX, ii, 4.
[6] *Ep.* 26, 4.
[7] *Ep.* 26, 5.
[8] Courcelle, *Les lettres grecques*, p. 132: 'Ce demi-savant qui raille les Platoniciens de son temps. . . .'
[9] *Conf.* VII, xx, 26.
[10] v. inf. pp. 204–211.

Carthage, already strikes a tone similar to that of the *Confessions*;[1] and now that he had become a bishop, he wanted urgently, to unburden himself to Paulinus of Nola, before the 'chain' of his office 'bit into' him.[2] On a deeper level, as we have just seen, the ideals on which he had hoped to build his life, had been set aside: the first optimism of his conversion had disappeared, leaving Augustine a man 'made deeply afraid by the weight of my sins'.[3] The kind of life which Augustine had set himself to live in his prime would not last him into old age. He must base his future on a different view of himself: and how could he gain this view, except by reinterpreting just that part of his past, that had culminated in the conversion, on which he had until recently placed such high hopes?

The *Confessions*, therefore, is not a book of reminiscences. They are an anxious turning to the past. The note of urgency is unmistakable. 'Allow me, I beseech You, grant me to wind round and round in my present memory the spirals of my errors. . . .'[4]

It is also a poignant book. In it, one constantly senses the tension between the 'then' of the young man and the 'now' of the bishop. The past can come very close: its powerful and complex emotions have only recently passed away; we can still feel their contours through the thin layer of new feeling that has grown over them. Augustine is still hardly able to understand the quite unexpected emotions that had accompanied the death of Monica, the sudden numbing of all feeling, the febrile talking, the unnatural self-control, the crushing shame of having wept so little for the mother who had 'wept so many years for me'.[5] 'Now my heart is healed from that wound . . .';[6] but it is only after the bewildering experience has surged up before us in the pages of the *Confessions*, that Augustine can distil a new feeling from it. Monica, the idealized figure that had haunted Augustine's youth like an oracle of God, is subtly transformed, by Augustine's analysis of his present feelings on remembering her death, into an ordinary human being, an object of concern, a sinner like himself, equally in need of mercy.[7]

Death had come to stand between Augustine and his youth. Cassiciacum, a place of rest among mountains, has deepened into an image of Paradise. So many of his friends of that time had left him for '*the mountain of abundance. Thy mountain, the mountain of richness*'.[8]

[1] esp. *Ep.* 22, 9.　　[2] *Ep.* 31, 4.　　[3] *Conf.* X, xliii, 70.
[4] *Conf.* IV, i, 1.　　[5] *Conf.* IX, xii, 33.　　[6] *Conf.* IX, xiii, 34; cf. IV, v, 10.
[7] *Conf.* IX, xii, 34.
[8] *Conf.* IX, iii, 5: a particularly exquisite play of associations; Knauer, *Psalmenzitate*, p. 123.

Even his own son was now only a name in a book: 'You took his life from this earth; and I can remember him now without apprehension, for I have nothing to fear for him as a boy, as a young man, nor for what he might have become as a grown man.'[1]

Augustine had been forced to come to terms with himself. The writing of the *Confessions* was an act of therapy.[2] The many attempts to explain the book in terms of a single, external provocation, or of a single, philosophical *idée fixe*, ignore the life that runs through it. In this attempt to find himself, every single fibre in Augustine's middle age grew together with every other, to make the *Confessions* what it is.

Death and disillusionment (the dangerous disillusionment of a former perfectionist), stood between Augustine and his rich past. He could so easily have cut himself off from it, and allowed himself to be cast, high and dry, on a lonely eminence of authority. Instead, he wrote the *Confessions*: and as an old man of about 74, he will still be able to look back, along the dry catalogue of his works, to recapture, in the 'Thirteen books of my Confessions', a moment of insight and tender feeling: 'as for me, they still move me, when I read them now, as they moved me when I first wrote them.'[3]

Our appreciation of the *Confessions* has suffered from the fact that they have become a classic. We tend to accept or dismiss them according to our own standards, as if Augustine were still our contemporary. In paying Augustine this compliment, we forget that a Late Roman man who first opened his copy of the *Confessions*, would have found them a startling book: traditional forms of literary expression, that he had taken for granted, would flow into it only to be transformed beyond recognition.

At first sight, it was easy to place the *Confessions*: they were patently the work of a Neo-Platonic philosopher. They were, for instance, written in the form of a prayer to God that was common to a long tradition of religious philosophy. For the God of the Platonists was an Unknown God, so far above the human mind that the philosopher could only increase his knowledge of Him by committing himself entirely to Him. Philosophical enquiry, therefore, verged on the concentrated quality of an act of prayer; and the search for wisdom was infused by a yearning to receive enlightenment, by tapping its very source in the human consciousness — by establishing a direct relation-

[1] *Conf.* IX, vi, 14.
[2] v. esp. E. R. Dodds, 'Augustine's Confessions', *Hibbert Journal*, 26, 1927–1928, p. 460.
[3] *Retract.* II, 32.

ship with God. 'In venturing an answer, we first invoke God Himself, not in loud words, but in that way of prayer which is always within our power, leaning in soul towards Him by aspiration, alone towards the alone.'[1] Even to commit such an inward prayer to words, was considered a therapy: it was a 'turning about of the heart, a purging of the inner eye'.[2]

Prayer, therefore, was a recognized vehicle for speculative enquiry. Augustine had begun one of his first philosophical works, the *Soliloquia*, with a prayer;[3] he would end his speculative masterpiece, the *De Trinitate*, with another.[4] The *Confessions* were to be read right through in this spirit. They were a prolonged exploration of the nature of God, written in the form of a prayer, to 'stir up towards Him the intellect and feelings of men'.[5] The fact that they were couched in the form of a prayer, far from relegating them to a work of piety, would have increased their value as a philosophical exercise: *da mihi, Domine, scire et intellegere*, 'Give me, O Lord, to know and understand'.[6] In such a way the Platonist would strain upwards, believing that the opaque, 'outer' formulae of his words of prayer were laden with meanings, which in wordless 'inner' contemplation, might become clear in the 'dawn light'[7] of truth in his mind. Milton, in the opening lines of *Paradise Lost*, will be the last exponent of this great tradition of philosophical self-expression:

> *So much the rather, Thou Celestial Light,*
> *Shine inward and the mind through all her powers*
> *Irradiate, there plant eyes, all mist from thence*
> *Purge and disperse, that we may see and tell*
> *Of things invisible to mortal sight.*[8]

Yet such prayers were usually regarded as part of a preliminary stage

---

[1] Plotinus, *Ennead*, V, i, 6, (MacKenna 2, p. 374). Despite this example, prayer of this sort is not very common in Plotinus' expositions. The attitude continued into Arab times: v. R. Walzer, 'Platonism in Islamic Philosophy', *Greek into Arabic*, 1962, pp. 248–251.

[2] *de serm. Dom. in monte*, II, iii, 14; cf. *de Mag.* i, 2.

[3] e.g. *Sol.* I, i, 2–6, and the revealing statement of *Sol.* I, ii, 7: 'What do you wish to know? Everything I have said in prayer'.

[4] *de Trin.* XV, xxviii, 51.   [5] *Retract.* II, 32.

[6] *Conf.* I, i; 1. cf. Tiberianus, *Versus Platonis*, ed. Baehrens, Poetae Latini Minores, III, p. 268, l. 26 sq. 'da nosse volenti'.

[7] *Conf.* XI, xxvii, 34.

[8] To this tradition one must add the more specifically Judaeo-Christian idea of the 'Sacrifice of Praise': praise of God in His works (v. esp. Madec, 'Connaissance de Dieu et action de grâces', *Rech. augustin.*, ii, 1962, pp. 302–307), and in His acts of mercy in delivering His people: v. J. Ratzinger, 'Originalität und Überlieferung in Augustins Begriff der "Confessio",' *Rev. études augustin.*, iii, 1957, pp. 375–392.

in the lifting of the philosopher's mind to God. They had never been used, as Augustine would use them throughout the *Confessions*, to strike up a lively conversation with Him: 'Plotinus never gossiped with the One as Augustine gossips in the *Confessions*.'[1] Just as a dialogue builds up a lasting impression of the speakers, so Augustine and his God emerge vividly in the prayers of the *Confessions*: God, in the little phrases with which He is approached — *Deus cordis mei*, 'God of my heart',[2] *Deus dulcedo mea*, 'God, my sweetness',[3] *O tardum gaudium meum*, 'O my late joy';[4] Augustine, as the eager listener, breathless, fussy, an impenitent poser of awkward questions,[5] above all, gloriously egocentric. No other writer could have crowned a hackneyed Manichaean argument on the origin of evil with 'who, then, has sown in me this seedbed of bitterness — in me, me who was made all of one piece by You, my most sweet God'.[6]

The *Confessions* are a masterpiece of strictly intellectual autobiography. Augustine communicates such a sense of intense personal involvement in the ideas he is handling, that we are made to forget that it is an exceptionally difficult book. Augustine paid his audience of *spiritales* the great (perhaps the unmerited) compliment of talking to them, as if they were as steeped in Neo-Platonic philosophy as himself. His Manichaean phase, for instance, is discussed in terms of ideas on which the Platonists regarded themselves as far in advance of the average thought of their age, the ideas of a 'spiritual' reality, and of the omnipresence of God.[7] Augustine had frankly regarded such subjects as far too difficult to discuss in his average works against the Manichees.[8] Yet, while the *Confessions* are marked by a particularly austere tone, this Neo-Platonic tradition has come to play around incidents in Augustine's experience, that are conveyed as vividly as any novel. In the course of the philosopher's prayer, we can now meet a gang of small boys: 'There was a pear-tree on a plot near our vineyard. . . . We had been playing in the fields long after night had fallen, as was our wicked habit. Off we went to shake down the fruit and carry it away: we filched great loads of pears, not to eat, but just to throw at pigs.'[9] We meet Monica standing at the quayside at Carthage: 'The wind rose and filled our sails, the shore slipped from our sight and on that shore, in the morning light, she stood in a frenzy of grief.'[10]

[1] Dodds, 'Augustine's Confessions', *Hibbert Journal*, 26, 1927–1928, p. 471.
[2] *Conf.* VI, i, 1; v. Knauer, *Psalmenzitate*, p. 55, n. 1.   [3] *Conf.* I, vi, 9.
[4] *Conf.* II, ii, 2; v. esp. Knauer, *Psalmenzitate*, pp. 31–74.   [5] e.g. *Conf.* VIII, iii, 6.
[6] *Conf.* VII, iii, 5; cf. *de ii anim.* 11.   [7] v. sup. p. 85 and p. 99.
[8] e.g. *Conf.* V, x, 20–xi, 21.   [9] *Conf.* II, iv, 9.   [10] *Conf.* V, viii, 15.

Yet these incidents are always placed in relation to the most profound philosophical concepts available to a Late Antique man: they embodied, for Augustine, the great themes of the Neo-Platonic tradition in its Christian form; they are suffused with a sense of the omnipresence of God, and they illustrate the fatal play of forces in a wandering soul, the tragedy of a man 'disintegrated' by the passing of time.[1] Augustine allows his past self to grow to the dimensions of a 'classic' hero: for these experiences summed up for him, the condition of 'my race, the human race'.[2] Every incident in this book, therefore, is charged with the poignancy of a Chinese landscape — a vivid detail perched against infinite distances: 'In the shadow of that day, on which she was to leave the world — a day which You had known, not us — it so happened, I believe through Your arrangement, by Your hidden ways, that I and my mother stood alone, leaning at a window that looked upon the enclosed garden of the house in which we lodged: it was at Ostia, on the Tiber.'[3]

Augustine enjoyed the immense advantage of being rooted in a mature tradition. For the Neo-Platonists provided him with the one, essential tool for any serious autobiography: they had given him a theory of the dynamics of the soul that made sense of his experiences.

The *Confessions* are a manifesto of the inner world: 'Men go to gape at mountain peaks, at the boundless tides of the sea, the broad sweep of rivers, the encircling ocean and the motions of the stars: and yet they leave themselves unnoticed; they do not marvel at themselves.'[4] A man cannot hope to find God unless he first finds himself: for this God is 'deeper than my inmost being',[5] experience of Him becomes 'better' the more 'inward'.[6] Above all, it is man's tragedy that he should be driven to flee 'outwards', to lose touch with himself, to 'wander far' from his 'own heart': 'You were right before me: but I had moved away from myself. I could not find myself: how much less, then, could I find You.'[7]

This emphasis on the fall of the soul as a turning outwards, as a loss of identity, as becoming 'a partial thing, isolated, full of cares, intent upon the fragment, severed from the whole'[8] is a clear echo of the thought of Plotinus. The *Confessions*, indeed, are the high-watermark of Augustine's absorption of the *Enneads*: in them, he will talk the language of his master with greater conviction and artistry than in any

---

[1] *Conf.* XI, xxix, 39. [2] *Conf.* II, iii, 5. [3] *Conf.* IX, x, 23. [4] *Conf.* X, viii, 15.
[5] *Conf.* III, vi, 11. [6] *Conf.* X, vi, 9. [7] *Conf.* V, ii, 2.
[8] Plotinus, *Ennead* IV, viii, 4, (MacKenna 2, pp. 360–361); cf. *Conf.* II, i, 1.

other of his works.[1] But all this has been transformed. The 'soul' of Plotinus is very much a cosmic, archetypal soul; its 'Fall' merely forms the shadowy background of the human condition, as it now strikes the philosopher. With Augustine this 'fall' is intensely personal: he sees it as a field of forces in the heart of each man, an agonizing weakness that forced him to flee from himself, a 'fall', a 'wandering', that showed itself in a hundred precise incidents of his past life.[2] The profound, abstract intuitions of Plotinus have come to provide the material for a new, classic language of the unquiet heart:

'I carried about me a cut and bleeding soul, that could not bear to be carried by me, and where I could put it, I could not discover. Not in pleasant groves, not in games and singing, nor in the fragrant corners of a garden. Not in the company of a dinner-table, not in the delights of the bed: not even in my books and poetry. It floundered in a void, and fell back upon me. I remained a haunted spot, which gave me no rest, from which I could not escape. For where could my heart flee from my heart? Where could I escape from myself? Where would I not dog my own footsteps? Still — I left my hometown.'[3]

It is often said that the *Confessions* is not an 'autobiography' in the modern sense. This is true, but not particularly helpful. Because, for a Late Roman man, it is precisely this intense, autobiographical vein in the *Confessions*, that sets it apart from the intellectual tradition to which Augustine belonged.

It is more important to realize that the *Confessions* is an autobiography in which the author has imposed a drastic, fully-conscious choice of what is significant. The *Confessions* are, quite succinctly, the story of Augustine's 'heart', or of his 'feelings' — his *affectus*. An intellectual event, such as the reading of a new book, is registered only, as it were, from the inside, in terms of the sheer excitement of the experience, of its impact on Augustine's feelings: of the *Hortensius* of Cicero, for instance, he would never say 'it changed my views' but, so characteristically, 'it changed my way of feeling' — *mutavit affectum meum*.[4]

---

[1] The importance of the theme of the wandering of the soul from God has been rightly emphasized by G. N. Knauer, 'Peregrinatio Animae. (Zur Frage der Einheit der augustinischen Konfessionen)', *Hermes*, 85, 1957, pp. 216–248. Its Plotinian basis has been presented in the highly provocative study of R. J. O'Connell, 'The Riddle of Augustine's "Confessions": A Plotinian Key', *International Philosophical Quarterly*, iv, 1964, pp. 327–372. Another theme, 'the conversion to the heart', to one's inner life, a marked feature of the pagan Plotinus, significantly absent in the Christian Origen, (v. P. Aubin, *Le problème de la 'conversion'*, 1963, esp. pp. 186–187), is crucial to the *Confessions*: e.g. *Conf.* IV, xii, 18.

[2] This important difference is clearly stated by J. Burnaby, *Amor Dei*, pp. 119–120.

[3] *Conf.* IV, vii, 12.   [4] *Conf.* III, iv, 8.

The emotional tone of the *Confessions* strikes any modern reader. The book owes its lasting appeal to the way in which Augustine, in his middle-age, had dared to open himself up to the feelings of his youth. Yet, such a tone was not inevitable. Augustine's intense awareness of the vital role of 'feeling' in his past life had come to grow upon him.[1]

Surprisingly enough, therefore, the austere answer to the *Second Problem* of the *Various Problems for Simplicianus* is the intellectual charter of the *Confessions*.[2] For both books faced squarely the central problem of the nature of human motivation. In both books, the will is now seen as dependent on a capacity for 'delight', and conscious actions as the result of a mysterious alliance of intellect and feeling: they are merely the final outgrowth of hidden processes, the processes by which the 'heart' is 'stirred', is 'massaged and set' by the hand of God.[3]

Had Augustine written his autobiography in 386, it would have been a very different book: different layers of his past experience would have struck the new-fledged Platonist as important. We might have had a book that was far more circumstantial: it would have contained much information that is passed over as irrelevant in the *Confessions* — more precise details of the books he had read, of the views he had held, of the fascinating men he had met in Milan. But it is most unlikely that such a book could have conveyed so consistently the sheer resilience of those inner strands of feeling that had once bound Augustine to the world around him, to his opinions, to his friends, to the delights of his past life. It may well not have included the mighty emotional upheaval in the garden in Milan; and we may never have caught a glimpse of Augustine's concubine, in the bright, narrow focus of his 'heart': 'In the meantime my sins multiplied: and the woman with whom I used to sleep was torn from my side, as an obstacle to my marriage. The heart, to which she stuck fast, was cut and wounded in me, and oozed blood.'[4]

The life of feeling was what really counted in personal growth. This conviction now led Augustine in Book IX of the *Confessions* to pierce far beneath the surface of his life at Cassiciacum. What was important to him now were the emotions of the convert, conjured up with classic authenticity. These were the 'inner goads' that had 'tamed' Augustine;[5] for they had lasted for him, while the hopes contained in the intellectual programmes of the time had been eroded, and the *Dialogues*, now

---

[1] v. sup. pp. 154–155.   [2] v. sup. pp. 153–154.   [3] e.g. *Conf.* VI, v, 7.
[4] *Conf.* VI, xv, 25; cf. *Ep.* 263, 2, on the implications of this image.   [5] *Conf.* IX, iv, 7.

'smelling of the class-room',[1] had come to rest on his bookshelf — high and dry, full of the names of dead friends.

Seeing that Augustine wrote his *Confessions* 'remembering my wicked ways, thinking them over again in bitterness',[2] it is amazing how little of this bitterness he has allowed to colour his past feelings. They are not made pale by regret: it is plainly the autobiography of a man who, even as a schoolboy, had known what it was to be moved only by 'delight', to be bored by duty, who had enjoyed fully what he had enjoyed: ' "One and one is two, two and two is four," this was a hateful jingle to me: and the greatest treat of all, that sweet illusion — the Wooden Horse full of armed men, Troy burning and the very ghost of Creusa.'[3] After all, where better than in the pages of the *Confessions* can one read of the eternal dilemma of a young man, 'witty and polished'? 'I had not yet been in love and I was in love with loving. . . . I set about finding an occasion to fall in love, so much in love was I with the idea of loving.'[4]

Augustine analyses his past feelings with ferocious honesty. They were too important to him to be falsified by sentimental stereotypes. It is not that he had abandoned strong feeling: he merely believed it possible to transform feelings, to direct them more profitably. This involved scrutinizing them intently. For instance, he had once enjoyed crying at the theatre: now, it was only by trying to understand why he had behaved in this paradoxical way as a student in deriving pleasure from sharing the simulated grief of two actors, that he could define in a convincing way, how he would now behave as a Christian bishop when faced by genuine suffering: 'Should we then cut off all feeling for suffering? Certainly not! Therefore, at times, let us still find sorrow welcome.'[5]

He was fascinated by the precise quality of human feelings. We meet him observing the behaviour of babies at the breast;[6] and, as he touches in passing on the attitudes of contemporaries to a long engagement, we can catch in the language of this bishop of Hippo, some distant echo of courtly love: 'It is the custom that a couple, once engaged, should not be married straight away; lest the man, as a husband, should hold cheap the woman for whom he had not sighed throughout the long delays of courtship.'[7]

Above all, Augustine will twice handle, with unique insight, the most complex of all emotions — grief and mourning. Friends, in romantic fiction, were prepared to die together: 'But a mysterious

[1] *Conf.* IX, iv, 7.   [2] *Conf.* II, i, 1.   [3] *Conf.* I, xiv, 22.   [4] *Conf.* III, i, 1.
[5] *Conf.* III, ii, 3.   [6] *Conf.* I, vi, 9 sq. v. sup. pp. 28–29.   [7] *Conf.* VIII, iii, 7.

feeling quite contrary to this obsessed me: my very loss of interest in living took the form of an oppressive fear of dying. I believe that, the more strongly I loved him, the more I hated and feared, as a relentless enemy, death, that had snatched him away. I thought death capable of suddenly devouring all men, because he had taken this loved one. That is how I felt, as I remember it. . . . For I felt his soul and mine to be one soul in two bodies and so looked on life with horror, because I did not wish to live as only half myself: and so it may well be that I feared death, lest, in dying, I should bring about the total extinction of that man I loved so much.'[1]

In the *Confessions*, however, the evocation of Augustine's feelings forms part of the wider study of the evolution of his will. Every step Augustine takes in his career, for instance, is firmly embedded in an exhaustive analysis of his motives. When describing how he wrote his first book, he will strike despair into modern scholars by refusing to tell us what it was he said in it,[2] and will, instead, dwell at length on the complex motives involved in his having dedicated it to an unknown professor: 'Who can map out the various forces at play in one soul, the different kinds of love. . . . Man is a great depth, O Lord; You number his hairs . . . but the hairs of his head are easier by far to count than his feelings, the movements of his heart.'[3]

Nothing shows Augustine's preoccupation with the will more clearly than the way in which he recounts his adolescence. His African readers tended to think that a boy was innocent until he reached puberty: 'as if' Augustine once said, 'the only sins you could commit were those in which you use your genitals'.[4] These, indeed, are the sins that seem to have interested the average reader of the *Confessions* ever since. Augustine, however, treats them as not very important: in his eyes they paled into insignificance before a single act of vandalism. The pointless robbing of a pear-tree is what really interests this great connoisseur of the human will:[5] he will analyse this one incident with fascinated repulsion; 'For what could I not have done, seeing that I could enjoy even a gratuitous act of crime?'[6]

For, in the *Confessions* we are faced with the full force of Augustine's new awareness of the limitations of human freedom. The 'gratuitous act' of a young hooligan is a sad paradigm for freewill. Men were free

[1] *Conf.* IV, vi, 11.   [2] v. sup. p. 57, n. 4.   [3] *Conf.* IV, xiv, 22.
[4] *de Gen. ad litt.* X, xiii, 23.
[5] 'Rum thing to see a man making a mountain out of robbing a peartree in his teens', Oliver Wendell Holmes to Harold Laski, Jan. 5th, 1921 ,*Holmes–Laski Letters* (I), ed. M. de W. Howe, 1953, p. 300.
[6] *Conf.* II, vii, 15.

only 'to throw themselves headlong'.[1] By such destructive acts of will, they had even crippled their own capacity to act creatively. For when a man came to wish to choose the good, he found himself unable to follow his conscious choice wholeheartedly: for his previous actions had forged a 'chain of habit' in which he was held fast, 'not in another's shackles, but in the iron links of my own will.'[2] The strength of this 'chain' obsesses Augustine throughout the *Confessions*. Five years of sad experience in battling with the hardened wills of his congregation have flowed into this book: even in the miniature biographies of Alypius and Monica,[3] the sins that God has 'cured' are 'besetting sins' — extreme cases of compulsive habits.

Thus, in Book VIII of the *Confessions*, the problem of the will leaps into focus. For here, with all his difficulties resolved, with a 'definite feeling of sweetness' claiming his loyalty to the Catholic faith, we meet Augustine still trapped in the habits of a lifetime: it is as if we had thought we had reached a plateau, only to find this last peak towering gigantic before us. 'The enemy had control of my will, and from that had made a chain to bind me fast. From a perverted act of will, desire had grown, and when desire is given satisfaction, habit is forged; and when habit passes unresisted, a compulsive urge sets in: by these close-knit links I was held'[4] ... 'To set out and arrive at my goal was only a matter of having a will to go: but it meant a wholehearted and un-divided act of will, not this stumbling to and fro with a maimed will, wrestling with it as one part rose while the other slipped to the ground.'[5]

The sombre preoccupation of Augustine with the manner in which a man could imprison himself in a 'second nature' by his past actions makes the *Confessions* a very modern book. In so many ancient and medieval biographies, for instance, we meet heroes described in terms of their essential, ideal qualities. It is almost as if they had no past: even their childhood is described only in terms of omens of the future 'peak' of their life — S. Ambrose plays at being a bishop, S. Cuthbert refused to turn cartwheels. We meet them full face: it is as if they had sloughed off, in their past, all that did not point directly to the image of perfection to which they conformed.

By contrast, we twice meet Augustine firmly held in his past: in the Garden of Milan, and in the terrible day that followed the death of his mother.[6] For Augustine regarded a man's past as very much alive in his present: men were different from each other precisely because their

---

[1] *Conf.* IV, i, 1. [2] *Conf.* VIII, v, 10. [3] *Conf.* VI, viii, 13 and IX, viii, 18.
[4] *Conf.* VIII, v, 10. [5] *Conf.* VIII, viii, 19. [6] esp. *Conf.* IX, xii, 32.

wills were made different by the sum total of unique, past experiences.[1] When Augustine struggles with himself in the garden, what is at stake is no generalized 'force of evil', no extraneous 'matter' that had 'splashed mud' on the pure metal of the soul: it is a tension in the very memory itself, a battle with the precise quality of past experiences: 'Habit was only too strong for me when it asked: "Do you think you can do without *these* things?"' [2] Thus, when Augustine describes his friends, we feel we know them, in those few strokes, far better than many more famous ancient men. For he has connected their past with their present; he has seen them as moulded by precise experiences reaching back even to childhood — Monica would have been a drunkard, if, at the age of 6, she had not been called a 'little tippler';[3] Alypius would not have been so chaste if he had not had an unsatisfactory experience of sex when a boy.[4]

Augustine emphasized this experience of the force of habit because he now thought that such an experience proved conclusively that change could only happen through processes entirely outside his control: 'That was all, just not to wish what I wanted, and to want what You wished. But where was my free-will in that gruelling time: from what deep recess was it called-up, at that turning-point, in which I bent my neck to Your light yoke.' [5]

It is not surprising that the *Confessions*, suffused as they are with a dramatic sense of God's interventions in Augustine's life, are studded with the language of the Psalms. This was, in itself, a startling literary innovation: for the first time, a work of self-conscious literary art had incorporated, (and most beautifully), the exotic jargon of the Christian communities.[6] But for Augustine, far more was at stake than a new literary form. He had gradually entered a new world of religious sentiments, he had undergone experiences which he could only express in the language of the Psalms. It was the language of a man who addressed a jealous God, a God Whose 'hand' was always ready to 'stretch out' over the destinies of men. Like any gentleman of feeling in the ancient world, the Psalmist had a 'heart';[7] but he also had 'bones'[8] — that is, a part of himself that was not just a repository of feeling, but

---

[1] *de div. quaest.* LXXXIII, 40. [2] *Conf.* VIII, xi, 26. [3] *Conf.* IX, viii, 18.
[4] *Conf.* VI, xii, 20. [5] *Conf.* IX, i, 1.
[6] v. esp. Chr. Mohrmann, 'Comment s. Augustin s'est familiarisé avec le latin des Chrétiens', *Aug. Mag.* i, 1954, pp. 111–116, and 'Augustine and the Eloquentia', *Études sur le latin des Chrétiens*, i, 1958, pp. 351–370.
[7] E. de la Peza, *El significado de 'cor' en San Agustin*, 1962, and *Rev. études augustin.*, vii, 1961, pp. 339–368.
[8] Knauer, *Psalmenzitate*, p. 151.

was the 'core of the soul',[1] with which God dealt directly, in His rough way, 'exalting' and 'crushing'. A classic description of sophisticated distaste for the business of the world, will now end on a harsher note: 'Because of this, *You were breaking my bones asunder* with the rod of Your discipline.'[2]

Augustine was always concerned to bring together the 'God of Abraham, of Isaac and of Jacob', and the 'God of the Philosophers'. No book shows this fusion with greater literary art than the *Confessions*. But in no other book can we see so clearly what this tension meant for Augustine: it meant an ability to move on innumerable levels of religious feeling, including the most primitive. For when Augustine uses the language of the Psalms in its most direct and dramatic form, when he speaks of the 'hand' of God 'stretching forth' to 'snatch' him, he is thinking, more often than not, of Monica.[3] For it is in the *Confessions* that we meet Monica the visionary: and through her eyes we see Augustine, as simple African Christians had always seen their heroes, as a man 'predestined',[4] the course of his life already ineluctably marked out by God, and communicated to His faithful servants in a series of vivid dreams.[5] This old tradition will harbour some at least of the many roots of Augustine's grandiose theory of predestination: and, as with so many very clever people, such simple roots were all the stronger for being largely unconscious.

The *Confessions* are one of the few books of Augustine's, where the title is significant. *Confessio* meant, for Augustine, 'accusation of oneself; praise of God.'[6] In this one word, he had summed up his attitude to the human condition: it was the new key with which he hoped, in middle age, to unlock the riddle of evil. The old key had proved insufficient. His method at the time of his conversion had been summed up in the title of a book — *De Ordine*, 'On Order':[7] in 386, Augustine had hoped that his 'well-trained soul' might grasp how evil merged into the harmony of the universe, as black cubes enhance the pattern of a mosaic-pavement.[8] Yet, when he wrote '*On the Free-Will*', only a few years before he turned to write the *Confessions*, he had found the problem posed again, in agonizing terms: man was responsible for his actions; but, at the same time, he was helpless, dislocated by some ancient fall. How could this state be reconciled with the goodness and

---

[1] *Enarr. in Ps.* 138, 20.   [2] *Conf.* VI, vi, 9.

[3] e.g. *Conf.* III, xi, 19.   [4] e.g. *Passio Marculi*, (P.L. viii, 760D and 762–763).

[5] v. esp. Courcelle, *Les Confessions*, pp. 127–128.

[6] *Serm.* 67, 2.   [7] v. sup. pp. 121–123.

[8] *de ord.* I, i, 2.

the omnipotence of God? A 'well-trained soul' could not answer such a question: what Augustine now wanted was a 'pious seeker'.[1] For to be 'pious' meant refusing to solve the problem simply by removing one of the poles of tension. These poles were now seen as firmly rooted in the awareness of the human condition of a man of religious feeling — and how better expressed for him than in the language of the Psalms? Man's first awareness, therefore, must be of a need to be healed: but this meant both accepting responsibility for what one is, and at one and the same time, welcoming dependence on a therapy beyond one's control. 'They should cry with the very bone and marrow of their inmost experience: "*I have said, o Lord, have mercy on me: heal my soul; for I have sinned before thee.*" In this way, by the sure routes of divine mercy, they would be led into wisdom.'[2]

In writing the *Confessions*, Augustine insisted that his reader should be 'led into wisdom' by this, his new method. The pace of the *Confessions* is determined by the growth of Augustine's awareness of the need to confess. The avoidance of 'confession' now struck Augustine as the hallmark of his Manichaean phase: 'it had pleased my pride to be free from a sense of guilt, and when I had done anything wrong not to *confess* that it was myself who had done it, that You might *heal my soul*.'[3] In Milan, it was different: even Augustine's language changes; the brutal imagery of external impingement changes to the more tender terms of growing inner pain, even to the medical language of the inner 'crisis' of a fever. For by that time Augustine had accepted responsibility for his actions; he is aware of guilt: 'I had not gone down into that world of the dead where no man *confesses* to You.'[4] But if denial of guilt was the first enemy, self-reliance was the last. The massive autonomy of Plotinus is now thrown into the sharpest relief by Augustine's new preoccupation with confession. Once he had been excited by the common ground between the Platonists and S. Paul; in 386, they seemed to merge naturally, to form 'so splendid a countenance of Philosophy'.[5] Now he sees only the danger of the Platonists obscuring the one 'countenance' that mattered: 'the countenance of true piety, the tears of confession.'[6]

Augustine wrote the *Confessions* in the spirit of a doctor committed only recently, and so all the more zealously, to a new form of treatment. In the first nine books, therefore, he will illustrate what happens when this treatment is not applied, how he had come to discover it, and,

[1] e.g. *de lib. arb.* III, ii, 5.   [2] *de lib. arb.* III, ii, 5.   [3] *Conf.* V, x, 18; cf. IV, iii, 4.
[4] *Conf.* VII, iii, 5; cf. *de vera relig.* lii, 101.   [5] *C. Acad.* II, ii, 6.
[6] *Conf.* VII, xxi, 27.

skipping a decade, he will demonstrate, in Book Ten, its continued application in the present.

It is this theme of *Confession* that would make Augustine's treatment of himself different from any autobiography available, at the time, to his readers. For the insistence on treatment by 'confession' has followed Augustine into his present life. The amazing Book Ten of the *Confessions* is not the affirmation of a cured man: it is the self-portrait of a convalescent.

This one book of the *Confessions* would have taken Augustine's readers by surprise: when it was read in Rome, for instance, Pelagius was 'deeply annoyed' by its tone. For what the conventional Christian wanted, was the story of a successful conversion. Conversion had been the main theme of religious autobiography in the ancient world. Such a conversion was often thought of as being as dramatic and as simple as the 'sobering up' of an alcoholic.[1] Like all too many such converts, the writer will insist on rubbing into us that he is now a different person, that he has never looked back. Seen in such a light, the very act of conversion has cut the convert's life in two; he has been able to shake off his past. Conversion to philosophy or to some religious creed was thought of as being the attainment of some final security, like sailing from a stormy sea into the still waters of a port: S. Cyprian treats his conversion to Christianity in just these terms;[2] so did Augustine when at Cassiciacum.[3] The idea is so deeply ingrained, that it comes quite naturally from the pen of a classic 'convert' of modern times, Cardinal Newman. In the late fourth century, also, the drastic rite of baptism, coming as it often did in middle age, would only have further emphasized the break with one's past identity, that was so marked a feature of the conventional idea of conversion.

The tastes of Augustine's age demanded a dramatic story of conversion, that might have led him to end the *Confessions* at Book Nine. Augustine, instead, added four more, long, books. For, for Augustine, conversion was no longer enough. No such dramatic experience should delude his readers into believing that they could so easily cast off their past identity. The 'harbour' of the convert was still troubled by storms;[4] Lazarus, the vivid image of a man once dead under the 'mass of habit',[5] had been awoken by the voice of Christ: but he would still have to 'come forth', to 'lay bare his inmost self in confession', if he

---

[1] Nock, *Conversion*, pp. 179–180.　　[2] Cyprian, *Ep.* 1, 14, (to Donatus), (P.L. iv, 225).
[3] *C. Acad.* II, i, 1; *de beata vita*, i , 1. Paulinus also sees Augustine in these terms: e.g. *Ep.* 25, 3.
[4] *Enarr. in Ps.* 99, 10.　　　　　　　[5] v. sup. p. 149.

was to be loosed.[1] 'When you hear a man confessing, you know that he is not yet free.'[2]

It was a commonplace among Augustine's circle of *servi Dei* to talk of oneself as 'dust and ashes'. But Book Ten of the *Confessions* will give a totally new dimension to such fashionable expressions of human weakness. For Augustine will examine himself far less in terms of specific sins and temptations, than in terms of the nature of a man's inner world: he is beset by temptations, above all because he can hardly grasp what he is; 'there is in man an area which not even the *spirit of man* knows of.'[3]

Augustine had inherited from Plotinus a sense of the sheer size and dynamism of the inner world. Both men believed that knowledge of God could be found in the form of some 'memory' in this inner world.[4] But, for Plotinus, the inner world was a reassuring continuum. The 'real self' of a man lay in its depths; and this real self was divine, it had never lost touch with the world of Ideas. The conscious mind had merely separated itself from its own latent divinity, by concentrating too narrowly.[5] For Augustine, by contrast, the sheer size of the inner world, was a source of anxiety quite as much as of strength. Where Plotinus is full of quiet confidence, Augustine felt precarious. 'There is, indeed, *some light in men*: but let them walk fast, walk fast, *lest the shadows come*.'[6] The conscious mind was ringed with shadows. Augustine felt he moved in 'a limitless forest, full of unexpected dangers'.[7] His characteristic shift of interest to the abiding 'illnesses' of the soul,[8] his scrupulous sense of life as '*one long trial*'[9] had placed beside the mystical depths of Plotinus, a murmurous region: 'This memory of mine is a great force, a vertiginous mystery, my God, a hidden depth of infinite complexity: and this is my soul, and this is what I am. What, then, am I, my God? What is my true nature? A living thing, taking innumerable forms, quite limitless. . . .'[10] 'As for the allurement of sweet smells' for instance, 'I am not much troubled. . . . At least, so I seem to myself: perhaps I am deceived. For there is in me a lamentable darkness in which my latent possibilities are hidden from myself, so that my mind, questioning itself upon its own powers, feels that it cannot rightly trust its own report.'[11]

---

[1] *Serm.* 67, 2. [2] *Enarr. ii in Ps.* 101, 3; cf. *Enarr. iii in Ps.* 32, 16.
[3] *Conf.* X, v, 7. [4] *Conf.* X, xxiv, 35 — xxv, 36.
[5] e.g. Plotinus, *Ennead* IV, iii, 30, (MacKenna 2, p. 286). v. Dodds, 'Tradition and Personal Achievement in Plotinus', *Journ. Rom. Studies*, l, 1960, pp. 5–6.
[6] *Conf.* X, xxiii, 33; cf. *de vera relig.* lii, 101. [7] *Conf.* X, xxxv, 56.
[8] *Conf.* X, iii, 3. [9] *Conf.* X, xxviii, 39. [10] *Conf.* X, xvi, 25.
[11] *Conf.* X, xxxii, 48.

It was a traditional theme to expose one's soul to the commands of God, knowing that He 'searched the hearts of men'.[1] But it was most unusual to insist, as Augustine does, that no man could ever sufficiently search his own heart, that the 'spreading, limitless room' was so complex, so mysterious, that no one could ever know his whole personality; and so, that no one could be certain that all of him would rally to standards, which the conscious mind alone had accepted. Augustine's sense of the dangers of identifying himself exclusively with his conscious good intentions, underlies the refrain that so shocked Pelagius: 'command what you wish, but give what You command.'[2] For 'I cannot easily gather myself together so as to be more clean from this particular infection: I greatly fear my hidden parts, which Your eyes know, but not mine. . . .[3] Behold, I see myself in You, my truth . . . but whether I may be like this, I just do not know. . . . I beseech You, God, to show my full self to myself.'[4]

Nothing could be more vivid than an inner self-portrait sketched by a man, who had not allowed himself to be lulled into certainty about what he was really like: 'which side will win I do not know. . . . I just do not know.'[5] He still has sexual dreams: they worry him because of the emotion of consent and of subsequent guilt that occurs even in his sleep.[6] Greed, however, is a far more acute and revealing source of disquiet for him. He had watched with fascinated sympathy the insatiable voracity of little babies.[7] He still felt himself on a slippery slope: he speaks with the harshness and the fear of someone for whom the boundaries between a measured appetite and a shadow of sheer greed were still not safely fixed.[8] With the delight of music, by contrast, he is fortified by his own, positive experiences. The beautiful chanting of a Psalm might cause his mind to wander: but he was prepared (as he would never be prepared at table), to risk enjoying himself: 'I feel that all the various emotions of the heart have rhythms proper to them in verse and song, whereby, by some mysterious affinity, they are made more alive.'[9]

[1] v. esp. H. Jaeger, 'L'examen de conscience dans les religions non-chrétiennes et avant le Christianisme', *Numen*, vi, 1959, pp. 176–233.

The unique quality of the *Confessions* has led some scholars to suggest a Manichaean prototype in the annual confession at the Bema feast, v. esp. A. Adam, 'Das Fortwirken des Manichäismus bei Augustinus', *Zeitschrift für Kirchengeschichte*, 69, 1958, pp. 1–25, notably pp. 6–7. However, I find the objections of J. P. Asmussen, *Xᵘ ĀSTVĀNĪFT, Studies in Manichaeism*, (Acta Theologica Danica, VII), 1965, esp. p. 124, decisive against this view.

[2] *Conf.* X, xxix, 40; *de dono persev.* xx, 53.
[3] *Conf.* X, xxxvii, 60.
[4] *Conf.* X, xxxvii, 62.
[5] *Conf.* X, xxviii, 39.
[6] *Conf.* X, xxx, 41.
[7] *Conf.* I, vii, 11.
[8] *Conf.* X, xxxi, 47.
[9] *Conf.* X, xxxii, 49.

We have entered the world of a very sensitive man. The garish colours of the past have become muted; his temptations appear almost, at times, a charming absence of mind. The 'lust of the eyes', for instance, stirs for Augustine only while he sits for a moment in the limpid African sunlight, the countryside bathed in a light, that was itself the 'Queen of Colours', and finds himself regretting that he must go indoors: 'I miss it; and if I am long deprived of it, I grow depressed.'[1] 'I no longer go to the games to see a dog chasing a hare; but if, in crossing the fields, I come upon the same thing, the chase may easily draw me upon itself, forcing me from my path, not by moving my horse, but by diverting my heart. Indeed, unless You quickly showed me my infirmity and admonished me . . . I would simply stand gaping at it. What is to be said of me? A lizard catching flies or a spider eating them as they fall into his net still can hold me absorbed when I sit in my room.'[2]

But the most characteristic anxiety of Augustine, was the manner in which he still felt deeply involved with other people: 'For I have a certain ability to explore myself in other tensions; but in this I have hardly any at all.'[3] Having read the life of this extremely inward-looking man, we suddenly realize, to our surprise, that he has hardly ever been alone. There have always been friends around him. He learnt to speak 'amid the cooing of nurses, the jokes of laughing faces, the high spirits of playmates'.[4] Only a friendship could make him lose 'half my soul';[5] and only yet more friendship would heal this wound.[6] Seldom do we find him thinking alone: usually he is 'talking on such subjects to my friends'.[7] Augustine has hardly changed in this: in middle age he remains delightfully and tragically exposed to 'that most unfathomable of all involvements of the soul — friendship'.[8]

After the distant storm of the garden in Milan, after this anxious peering into dark potentialities, the remaining three books of the *Confessions* are a fitting ending to the self-revelation of such a man: like soft light creeping back over a rain-soaked landscape, the hard refrain of 'Command' — 'Command what You wish' — gives way to 'Give' — 'Give what I love: for I do love it.'[9] For Augustine, progress in wisdom, measured now by the yardstick of his understanding of the Holy Scriptures, could only depend upon progress in self-awareness:[10] these 'first shafts of light of my illumination'[11] as he meditates on the

---

[1] *Conf.* X, xxxiv, 51. [2] *Conf.* X, xxxv, 57. [3] *Conf.* X, xxxvii, 60.
[4] *Conf.* I, xiv, 23. [5] *Conf.* IV, vi, 11. [6] *Conf.* IV, ix, 14.
[7] *Conf.* IV, xiii, 20. [8] *Conf.* II, ix, 17. [9] *Conf.* XI, ii, 3.
[10] v. inf. pp. 262–263. [11] *Conf.* XI, ii, 2.

opening lines of the Book of Genesis, illustrate directly the effects of the therapy he has just undergone. It is this therapy of self-examination which has, perhaps, brought Augustine closest to some of the best traditions of our own age. Like a planet in opposition, he has come as near to us, in Book Ten of the *Confessions*, as the vast gulf that separates a modern man from the culture and religion of the Later Empire can allow: *Ecce enim dilexisti veritatem, quoniam qui facit eam venit ad lucem.* 'For behold, *You have taken delight in truth*: and he that *does truth comes to the light*. I desire to *do truth* in my heart, before Thee, by confession: with my pen, before many witnesses. . . .'[1]

[1] *Conf.* X, i, 1.

PART III
395-410

396 Death of Valerius. Romanianus returns to Italy (early summer).	*Ad Simplicianum de diversis quaestionibus.* *Contra epistolam quam vocant fundamenti.*
395–398 Revolt of Gildo, Count of Africa.	*De agone christiano.* *De doctrina christiana* (finished 426).
397	26.vi. II Council of Carthage. 28.viii. III Council of Carthage. Debates with Donatist Bishop Fortunius at Thubursicum Bure.
4.iv. Death of Ambrose. Succeeded by Simplicianus.	/400 *Quaestiones evangeliorum.* /98 *Contra Faustum Manichaeum.* /401 *Confessiones.*
398 Defeat of Gildo. Execution of Optatus, Don. bp. of Timgad.	*Contra Felicem Manichaeum* (December).
399 19.iii. Imperial agents close the pagan shrines in Africa. Consulship of Manlius Theodorus.	27.iv. IV Council of Carthage. *De natura boni contra Manichaeos.* *Contra Secundinum Manichaeum.* *Adnotationes in Job.* /400 *De catechizandis rudibus.* /419 *De Trinitate.*
400	Preaches *De fide rerum quae non videntur.* *De consensu evangelistarum.* *Contra epistolam Parmeniani.* /01 *De baptismo contra Donatistas.* *Ad inquisitiones Januarii* (= *Epp.* 54-5). *De opere monachorum.*
401 Election of Pope Innocent I (401–March, 417).	15.vi. V Council of Carthage. Goes to Assuras and Musti to investigate former Maximianist clerg 13.ix. VI Council of Carthage. At Hippo Diarrhytus for election of Bishop (late September). *De bono conjugali.* *De sancta virginitate.*
Crispinus, Donatist bishop of Calama, held responsible for attack on Possidius.	/05 *Contra litteras Petiliani.* /14 *De Genesi ad litteram.*
402 Defeat of Goths in Italy. Death of Symmachus.	7.viii. In Milevis for the VII Council.
403 Bishop of Bagai set upon by Donatists and badly wounded.	25.viii. VIII Council of Carthage. Preaches in Carthage at intervals until 8.xi.

VOL.	COL.	
40 ·	11	(in) *Augustine: earlier writings*, Ld., 1953, (Bk. 1 only).
42 ·	173	(in) *On the Manichaean Heresy*, Edinburgh, 1872.
40 ·	289	(in) *Seventeen short treatises*, Oxford, 1847; *The Christian Combat*, NY., 1947.
34 ·	15	*On Christian Doctrine*, Edinburgh, 1873; *Christian Instruction*, NY., 1947.
35 ·	1321	
42 ·	207	(in) *On the Manichaean Heresy*, Edinburgh, 1872.
32 ·	659	(there are innumerable translations, but the best is:) *The Confessions of St Augustine*, translated by F. J. Sheed, Ld., & NY., 1943 (regularly reprinted).
42 ·	519	
42 ·	551	(in) *Basic Writings, I*, NY., 1948; (in) *Augustine: earlier writings*, Ld., 1953.
		(in) *Nicene and Post-Nicene Fathers, 4*, NY., 1901.
42 ·	577	
34 ·	825	
40 ·	309	(in) *Seventeen short treatises*, Oxford, 1847; *On catechizing*, Edinburgh, 1873; *Instructing the unlearned*, Oxford, 1885; *A treatise on the manner of catechizing the uninstructed*, Ld., 1902; *A treatise on the catechizing of the uninstructed*, Ld., 1912; *St Augustine's 'De catechizandis rudibus'*, Ld., 1913; *The first catechetical instruction*, Ld., 1946.
42 ·	819	*On the Trinity*, Edinburgh, 1873; (in) *Basic Writings II*, NY., 1948 (selections only); (in) *Augustine: Later writings*, Ld., 1954; *The Trinity*, NY., 1963.
40 ·	171	(in) *Seventeen short treatises*, Oxford, 1874; *Concerning faith of things unseen*, Oxford, 1885; *On faith in things unseen*, NY., 1947.
34 ·	1041	*The harmony of the evangelists*, Edinburgh, 1873.
43 ·	33	
42 ·	107	(in) *On the Donatist Controversy*, Edinburgh, 1872.
33 ·	199	
40 ·	547	(in) *Seventeen short treatises*, Oxford, 1847; *The work of monks*, NY., 1952.
40 ·	373	(in) *Seventeen short treatises*, Oxford, 1847; *The good of marriage*, NY., 1955.
40 ·	397	(in) *Seventeen short treatises*, Oxford, 1847; *Holy Virginity*, NY., 1955.
43 ·	245	(in) *On the Donatist Controversy*, Edinburgh, 1872.
34 ·	245	

404 Bishop of Bagai goes to Ravenna to ask for stern measures against the Donatists.	26.vi. IX Council of Carthage.
405 12.ii. 'Edict of unity' against the Donatists (Cod Theod xvi, 5, 8).	*De unitate ecclesiae.* 23.viii. X Council of Carthage. /06 *Contra Cresconium grammaticum.*
406 Vandal invasion of Gaul.	/11 *De divinatione daemonum.*
407 Usurpation of Constantine III.	XI Council held at Thubursicum (late June). 407–408. Begins *Tractatus in Joh. Ev.*
408 Theodosius II becomes Emperor in the East (May). Fall of Stilicho (Aug.). Riot in Calama when Possidius tried to break up pagan procession. Alaric enters Italy (Oct.).	16.vi. XII Council of Carthage. 13.x. XIII Council of Carthage. (Augustine's presence uncertain at these.) *Epistola 93* to Vincentius, Donatist Bishop of Cartenna. /09 *Quaestiones expositae contra paganos* (= ep. 102). /12 *De utilitate je junii.*
409 Alaric beleaguers Rome. Donatists enjoy toleration.	15.vi. XIV Council of Carthage (presence uncertain). *Ep.* 101 to Memor. Macrobius, Donatist bishop, re-enters Hippo.

P.L.		TRANSLATIONS
VOL.	COL.	
43 ·	391	
43 ·	445	
40 ·	581	*The divination of demons*, NY., 1955.
		SEE BELOW ad. ann. 414.
33 ·	321	
33 ·	370	
40 ·	707	*The usefulness of fasting*, NY., 1952.
33 ·	367	

17

HIPPO REGIUS[1]

When Augustine became Catholic bishop in Hippo Regius, the town had existed for over a thousand years.[2] It was the second port of Africa. To a traveller by sea from Carthage, a long row of cliffs would suddenly give way for some miles to the rich, flat plain of the river Seybouse. Hippo Regius would have stood out at the far end of this plain, covering two little hillocks, a natural harbour formed by the mouth of the river, and backed, on the west, by a high mountainous headland, the Djebel Edough.

Augustine was very much a newcomer in an ancient town. Even the streets were not the regular avenues of Roman 'new' towns in the hinterland, such as his own Thagaste: they were narrow, twisting lanes, paved by the Phoenicians with massive, irregular blocks.[3] What was Roman, was splendid and already very old. The exceptionally large forum was crowded with statues: the name of a Proconsul mentioned by Tacitus, sprawled across the spacious flagstones;[4] Suetonius, the biographer of the first Emperors, stood among the local worthies.[5] The town had been a *civitas Romana*, a 'city of Roman citizens', for two hundred years. Roman life had been established on a magnificent scale: there was a theatre to seat some five to six thousand, a great public bath, a classical temple crowning the hill on the site of an ancient sanctuary of Baal-Hammon. The values of a Roman pagan city, that Augustine would attack in his *City of God*, would have met his eye, frozen in stone, in hundreds of inscriptions. This pagan past had somehow lost its soul by the late fourth century; the works of Cicero were no longer sold in the bookshops of the town;[6] but it

[1] F. Van der Meer, *Augustine the Bishop*, (transl. Battershaw and Lamb), 1961, is a brilliant evocation of Augustine and his environment.
[2] v. esp. E. Marec, *Hippone-la-Royale: antique Hippo Regius*, 1954.
[3] Marec, *Hippone*, p. 68.   [4] Marec, *Hippone*, pp. 71–72.   [5] Marec, *Hippone*, p. 79.
[6] *Ep.* 118, ii, 9.

would have been impossible to ignore the sheer physical presence of the past in the buildings that covered the main hill, from the theatre at its foot to the forum and the temple on its crest. These solid reminders of the affluence of pagan times would outlast Christianity in North Africa. The brick core of the public baths was standing long after the old city had been silted over: Arab travellers would call them the 'glisia Rumi', the 'church of the Roman', mistaking them for the cathedral of 'Augodjin, a great doctor of the Christian religion'.[1]

To reach the part of the town where Augustine lived in his 'Christian quarter', consisting of his main church with adjacent baptistry, a chapel, the bishop's house, and perhaps a monastery in a building overlooking the bishop's garden,[2] you would have had to leave the main hill, and would have walked a good half mile towards the harbour. The main church was partly built on the deserted site of a dyer's yard; it was about a third of the area of the mighty forum; it was less than a century old. This simple building, that had been enlarged suddenly, with the official recognition of Christianity three generations previously,[3] was an upstart, inserted at a safe distance from the traditional centre of the public life of Hippo, from the temple and the forum. Nonetheless, Augustine was strategically placed in just that quarter, where the hold of the old public life of Hippo had already weakened. For only a minute's walk away, there were the villas of the rich. These were the private, residential suburbs, overlooking the harbour. For at least a century, no one had spent large sums of money on the public buildings around the forum, as had been the custom in the 'boom' days of the town. Instead, great wealth was spent, significantly, indoors, on opulent mosaic floors as rich as oriental carpets, that show the life of men who had prospered as private landowners, at a time when the public finances of the Roman towns were being shaken by repeated economic crises. Some owners of mansions did not even live regularly in Hippo: Augustine's church abutted a magnificent house, managed by a senatorial lady who lived in Rome;[4] a pious Christian and an absentee, the public life of the forum, with its pagan associations, would have interested this lady as little as it did Augustine.[5]

---

[1] Marec, *Hippone*, p. 89.

[2] v. esp. E. Marec, *Monuments chrétiens d'Hippone*, 1958; H. I. Marrou, 'La Basilique chrétienne d'Hippone', *Rev. études augustin.*, vi, 1960, pp. 109–154, and Van der Meer, *Augustine*, pp. 19–25.

[3] Marec, *Monuments*, p. 43.

[4] *Ep.* 99, 1, to Italica. v. sup. p. 128, and P. R. L. Brown, 'Aspects of the Christianisation of the Roman Aristocracy', *Journ. Rom. Studies*, li, 1961, pp. 5–6, esp. n. 37.

[5] v. Marec, *Libyca*, i, 1953, pp. 95–108.

The harbour lay beyond this quarter. The Mediterranean still brought men from the East, as it had in the days of the Phoenicians: Greek sailors with strange oaths;[1] a Syrian;[2] it had even brought Augustine's own predecessor, Valerius.[3] Above all, the regular shipping in the port would have enabled Augustine to remain in touch with a far wider world than if he had remained at Thagaste, in the land-locked hinterland. Augustine's letters would sail with the cornships to Italy — to Paulinus of Nola, and, later, to the bishops of Rome.[4]

Yet, like so many ancient men, Augustine feared the sea. He never dared to sail along the rocky coast to Carthage;[5] he always regarded the seaborne merchant as a speculator, taking the most hair-raising risks.[6] Hippo, in fact, did not depend exclusively on the sea. It owed its wealth to the one commodity that was always lacking in sufficient quantities in the Mediterranean, food.[7] Augustine's congregation consisted of 'farmers',[8] men who owned or tilled the wonderfully fertile plain of the Seybouse: even those who owned no land would spend their time in little garden-plots outside the town.[9] The inhabitants of Hippo were prosperous, not because they used the sea to trade, but because they had more than enough food. The vineyards along the valley of the Seybouse were carefully maintained;[10] the foothills of the Djebel Edough would have been dark with olive-groves; the plain was bright with corn. Augustine knew more about the technique of grafting olives than did S. Paul;[11] and when he mentions clouds and rain, he will always talk of them as a farmer would, as a singular mercy of God,[12] like the sudden mist that forms over the Djebel Edough after weeks of intolerable sunshine, a blessed omen of rain.

Corn was the basis of the wealth of Hippo. Dependence on corn is not an unmixed blessing. Corn can ruin the small man, and make the fortune of the big profiteer. Corn was the basis of the great estates in the plain, centred around villas stocked with tasteful classical statuary,[13]

---

[1] *Serm.* 180, 5.   [2] *de civ. Dei*, xxii, 8.

[3] *Vita*, v, 2. Note also that a citizen of Hippo was a deacon in an Eastern church: *de gest. Pel.* xxxii, 57; *Ep.* 177, 15.

[4] e.g. *Ep.* 149, 34.

[5] v. esp. O. Perler, 'Les voyages de S. Augustin', *Rech. augustin.*, i, 1958, pp. 5–42, esp. p. 36.

[6] *Serm.* 64, 5; but v. *Enarr. in Ps.* 136, 3, on the advantages of being a merchant.

[7] Wine and oil, of course, were less bulky; v. A. H. M. Jones, *The Later Roman Empire*, ii, 1964, p. 845: but Hippo had the advantage of being a port. For the importance of the trade in cereals, v. L. Ruggini, 'Ebrei e orientali nell' Italia settentrionale (iv–vi s.)', *Studia et Documenta Historiae et Juris*, xxv, 1959, pp. 236–241. This prosperity survived into Arab times; e.g. v. Ibn Haukal (A.D. 970), cited in Piesse, *Itinéraire de l'Algérie*, 1885, p. 429.

[8] *Serm.* 87, 2.   [9] *Serm.* 361, 11.   [10] *Enarr. in Ps.* 136, 5.   [11] *Enarr. in Ps.* 146, 15.

[12] *Enarr. in Ps.* 59, 2.   [13] Marec, *Hippone*, p. 16, pl. 6 (at Duzerville).

whose owners would sacrifice to the demons for a shortage and high prices.[1] Corn filled the countryside with its most depressed and violent elements — the serf-like tenant farmer and the seasonal labourer.[2] Corn, above all, attracted the unwelcome attention of the Imperial administration. An official charged with the compulsory purchase of grain resided in Hippo;[3] too much of the harvest drained away into his state warehouses for transport to Rome and to the army. Even Augustine, in the *City of God*, dared to wish that things had been better arranged;[4] while his congregation, especially the local traders, showed their opinion by lynching the commander of the local garrison.[5]

This countryside indeed, was to present Augustine with an intractable problem. Inside Hippo, the law and order of a 'Roman city' could, at least, be expected to exist.[6] Outside, the great landowners would not hesitate to use 'strong arm' methods: Augustine wrote to one 'recommending' that he should refrain from burning down the church of a priest who had crossed him in a lawsuit.[7]

Worst of all, there were the hill-villages surrounding the plain, especially those of the granite mass of the Djebel Edough. Here 'Punic' was spoken, not Latin; here the great landowners would hunt boar, even lions, in wild country;[8] here villages of poor men, with never enough land to go round, had acquired a solid identity against the civilized life of the plain. One, composed of Donatists, murdered and beat up its Catholic priests;[9] another formed a community vowed to absolute continence, and recruited its members by adopting the children of neighbouring villages.[10] These poor men would always press down into the plains: perhaps they formed the core of those bands of roving fanatics, the Circumcellions, whose warcry of 'Praise be to God' was feared more than the roaring of their mountain-lions.[11]

Augustine did what he could in this situation. He tried to secure priests who spoke the local dialect,[12] and such priests might act, like the landowners, as the spokesmen and protectors of little communities.[13] But Augustine was forced, increasingly, to rely on those who exercised the real power in that rough-and-ready land — the great landowners themselves: the Catholic churches would be established near their

[1] *Enarr. in Ps.* 70, 17.
[2] Ch. Saumagne, 'Ouvriers agricoles ou rôdeurs de celliers? Les circoncellions d'Afrique', *Annales d'hist. écon. et sociale*, 6. 1934, pp. 351–364.
[3] *Corpus Inscript. Lat.* VIII, 5351, and Marec, *Hippone*, p. 108.   [4] *de civ. Dei* V, 17.
[5] *Serm.* 302, 16.   [6] *Ep.* 35, 3.   [7] *Ep.* 251.
[8] *Mai.* 126, 12, (*Misc. Agostin.*, i, p. 366.)   [9] *Ep.* 209, 2.   [10] *de Haeres.* 87.
[11] *Enarr. in Ps.* 132, 6.   [12] *Epp.* 84 and 209, 2.   [13] *Ep.* 224, 3.

villas;[1] and their influence, often brought to bear as directly as a good flogging administered to refractory tenants,[2] would further the Catholic cause. Augustine, a conscientious and mild man in the oasis of Roman order at Hippo, will have feet of clay in the vast stretch of countryside that came within his care.[3]

Hippo was isolated by its very prosperity. Situated in a rich, coastal plain, it did not need to take part in the more primitive life of the hinterland. Augustine would feel this isolation. Hippo was administered from Carthage; his lay friends resided in Carthage by preference; he would go there frequently, to attend the councils assembled by Aurelius. There is no direct evidence that, as he followed the Mejerda valley to Carthage,[4] Augustine ever made the detour into the mountains, to visit again his 'fatherland after the flesh', Thagaste:[5] high mountains, a harsher climate,[6] maybe some inner reserve, kept him away.

Yet Augustine was a bishop in the ancient ecclesiastical province of Numidia. The affairs of his colleagues forced him to take an interest in cities that lay a week's journey inland, such as Milevis and Cirta, and in events that took place in a countryside he never visited, of whose ways he remained ignorant,[7] and which seemed very wild indeed, viewed from the shelter of a 'Roman city' on the Mediterranean coast.

As Christian bishop, Augustine had become a public figure in a town where much of life was public, explicit, guided by long traditions of correct behaviour. Life was lived in the open air. Sharp differences of wealth and status were emphasized as conspicuously as possible: Augustine will show little interest in the plastic arts, but will emphasize the importance of dress 'by which the ranks of men are distinguished';[8] and in an age of ostentatious costumes, the simple black robe, the *birrus*, which Augustine wore as a 'servant of God', would have marked him out in a particularly public manner.[9] Tensions were explicit, even ritualized: the town would be divided into rival 'factions' at the theatre;[10] one town would actually 'let off steam' by staging an annual pitched

---

[1] *de civ. Dei* XXII, 8. Augustine seems to have experienced less difficulty than other bishops of his time in persuading the owners of estates to build churches. *Serm.* 18, 4 is the only evidence of opposition.

[2] v. esp. *Epp.* 58; 89, 8; 139, 2; Brown, 'Religious Coercion in the Later Roman Empire', *History*, xlviii, 1963, p. 286, n. 35; pp. 290 and 303, esp. n. 196.

[3] v. inf. pp. 241–242.

[4] v. esp. Perler, 'Les voyages', *Rech. augustin*, i, 1958, pp. 26–27.

[5] *Ep.* 124, 1; 126, 7.   [6] *Ep.* 124, 1.   [7] Frend, *Donatist church*, p. 234.

[8] *de doct. christ.*, II, xxv, 39.

[9] e.g. *Enarr. in Ps.* 147, 8: the reaction of a crowd to the conspicuous dress of a *servus Dei*.

[10] *Serm.* 198, 3.

battle between rival *quartiers*;[1] and the warring religious groups, pagans against Christians, Donatists against Catholics, would have seemed little different to an outsider. This clearly patterned existence survived after death. The cemetery was just another Hippo, placed at a decent distance from the living, dominated by the vaults of rich families in Numidian marble, where the ancestors were in their proper place, and expected to be visited every year for a solemn meal.[2]

Thus, Augustine stepped into a position where certain things were expected of him. One of the most important and elusive aspects of his life in Hippo, is the extent to which Augustine lived up to the traditional expectations of the average townsman, and the degree to which he flouted and transformed them. Augustine's life, as seen in his letters and sermons, seems an unchanging routine, a form of 'slavery' imposed upon him,[3] a 'packload'.[4] Notwithstanding his unchanging pastoral routine, Augustine lived through a generation of rapid changes, many of which were provoked by his own initiative, and by that of his Catholic colleagues. During Augustine's episcopate, Hippo became a Christian town;[5] Augustine drove out his Christian rivals, the Donatists; his position in the face of influential local men changed dramatically.[6] All these are stages in the rise to power of a group of new men, men with ideas and policies that were frequently at a tangent to the traditional assumptions of a Roman townsman, and at times overtly hostile to them. Thus, Augustine's impact on the tight world of Hippo will mark a significant stage in the end of the civic life of an ancient town.

Late Roman men expected to be looked after by influential private patrons.[7] The State was oppressive and corrupt; but it covered a far narrower area of a citizen's life than it does today. The individual sought protection against the outside world, redress of grievances, and pursued his advantages, above all in the 'family', and beyond the family by submitting his fortunes to a powerful man, who might be the head of a little empire of allies, clients, dependants, freedmen and slaves, stretching across the Mediterranean. As a bishop, Augustine

---

[1] *de doct. christ.* IV, xxiv, 53.   [2] *Enarr. i in Ps.* 48, 13; *Serm.* 86, 6.   [3] *Ep.* 122, 1.
[4] *Ep.* 85, 2 'so holy a burden'. v. M. Jourjon, ' "Sarcina", un mot cher à l'évêque d'Hippone', *Rech. sc. relig.*, 43, 1955, pp. 258–262.
[5] e.g. *Serm.* 196, 4.   [6] v. inf. p. 242.
[7] No student of the functioning of modern Mediterranean societies need be surprised by the importance of this mentality in the Later Empire: v. esp. J. Davis, 'Pasatella: an economic game', *Brit. Journ. of Sociology*, xv, 1964, pp. 191–205, esp. pp. 202–205, on the role of the *Padroni*, the *famiglia* and the *familiari* in a S. Italian town. On the Later Empire, v. esp. L. Harmand, *Le Patronat sur les collectivités publiques des origines au Bas-Empire*, 1957, and W. Liebeschuetz, 'Did the Pelagian Movement have social aims?', *Historia*, xii, 1963, pp. 227–241, esp. pp. 227–232 and 241.

found himself, in this way, at the head of a 'family': the Christian community of his town, which he speaks of often as the *familia Dei*.[1] Ever since the official recognition of Christianity, the bishop took his place among the influential men, who were expected and actually encouraged to look after their own: Augustine would visit jails to protect prisoners from ill-treatment; he would intervene, tactfully but firmly, to save criminals from judicial torture and execution;[2] above all, he was expected to keep peace within his 'family' by arbitrating in their lawsuits.[3]

Augustine did not inherit a ready-made position of strength. The Christian bishop of fourth century Africa was very different from the ecclesiastical magnates of medieval times, with their precise jurisdictions. In intervening to protect members of his flock, he was acting as any Late Roman patron might be expected to act; and so he had to compete with well-established rivals.[4] Citizens of Hippo would often prefer to turn for help to a great pagan senator, such as Symmachus,[5] rather than to Augustine. He would find himself forced to wait around all morning in a governor's waiting-room.[6] Many of the great local men, indeed, began by being hostile to him; some were Donatists,[7] others were pagans. We would like to have known the opinions of a certain 'notable landowner of Hippo', a pagan, who once praised Augustine's learning 'with a touch of sarcasm'.[8] Altogether, Augustine started with none of the advantages of a born aristocrat; and he will establish his position, over the course of years, by fighting hard for it.

It was, therefore, only in his more humble capacity as an arbitrator in lawsuits, that Augustine found himself a vital figure in the community. For he offered the one thing everyone wanted: a free, quick and uncorrupt settlement of cases. The Christian bishop was empowered to impose a settlement, by arbitration, on consenting parties.[9] Augustine was mobbed: crowds of litigants, pagans and heretics quite as much as Catholic Christians, would keep him busy from the early morning, often until the late afternoon.[10] It was the one aspect of his routine in Hippo, which Augustine heartily resented: 'O with what

---

[1] e.g. *Ep.* 177, 1: *familia Christi.*   [2] *Vita* xix, 6-xx.

[3] This would even include arbitrating in disputes on rents between landowners and their tenants: *Ep.* 247.

[4] This is true of most Christian bishops in the fourth century, e.g. S. Giet, 'Basile, était-il sénateur?', *Rev. d'Hist. ecclés.*, 60, 1965, pp. 429-443, esp. pp. 442-3.

[5] Symmachus, *Ep.* IX, 51.   [6] *Serm.* 302, 17.   [7] v. inf. pp. 226 and 240.   [8] *Ep.* 136, 2.

[9] v. esp. F. Martroye, 'S. Augustin et la compétence de la juridiction ecclésiastique au Vᵉ siècle', *Mém. soc. nat. des antiquaires de France*, 7ᵉ ser., x, 1911, pp. 1-78, and J. Gaudemet, *L'Église dans l'Empire romain*, 1958, pp. 229-252.

[10] *Vita*, xix, 1-5.

disgust at obstreperous crowds and with what longing it is said: *"Get hence from me, wicked men: and I shall gaze upon the commandments of my God. . . ."* Certainly he must mean those who fight each other stubbornly in our court, and, when they set out to oppress good men, spurn our judgements, and make us fritter away time we could devote to providing divine things. . . . It is as if the Psalmist was swatting them away like flies dancing before his eyes.. .."[1]

Yet, this constant task of arbitration deeply influenced Augustine's attitude to his own position as a bishop. The need to get quickly to the bottom of a complex case, and to impose a firm, clear settlement in the light of Christian principles, was no mean training for an ecclesiastical polemist. Augustine would often write as if he were closing a case in his court: *causa finita est.*[2] Above all, the authority by which he imposed settlements was deeply tinged with distinctive, religious ideas. Sitting in the *secretarium* that adjoined his basilica, so not far from the sacred altar, with a copy of the Sacred Scriptures close to hand, Augustine thought of himself as the successor of the upright judges of Israel. And, in delivering judgement, he would always look forward, with terror, to the Last Judgement.[3]

The God of the African Christians was very much the awe-inspiring Judge.[4] A streak of this primitive terror was strong in Augustine; even when he seemed to be very far from his roots, as a successful *rhetor* in Milan, he was haunted by 'fears of death and Judgement'.[5] Now, in Africa, this fear would always be very close to him: a future bishop, one of Augustine's colleagues who had eloped with a nun, was deterred from sleeping with her by the sudden terror of God sent in a dream.[6] The men who crowded round Augustine expected such sanctions. Augustine, sensitive as ever, would soon catch their mood. When faced with an insoluble quarrel between two members of his clergy, on which the whole community was divided, he would send both to a shrine in Italy, where perjuries were detected by Divine judgement: we are entering the medieval world of the ordeal.[7]

This real terror of the Last Judgement was the backbone of

---

[1] *Enarr. xxiv in Ps.* 118, 3–4.

[2] e.g. *Ps. c. Don.* 38; *Serm.* 131, 10; cf. *Ep.* 193, ii, 4 and *c. Jul.* III, xxi, 45.

[3] e.g. *Ep.* 77, 2 and *Enarr. in Ps.* 25, 13. v. esp. H. Jaeger, 'Justinien et l'episcopalis audientia', *Rev. hist. de droit français et étranger*, 4e ser., xxxviii, 1960, esp. pp. 217–231, and 'La preuve judiciaire d'après la tradition rabbinique et patristique', *Recueils de la Société Jean Bodin*, xvi, 1964, pp. 415–594.

[4] e.g. *de cat. rud.* xiii, 18: in a brief catechism, three items, the unity of the church, temptations, the conduct of the Christian, are to be 'impressed forcefully, in the light of the Judgement to come'.

[5] *Conf.* VI, xvi, 26. [6] *de VIII Dulcitii qu.*, vii, 3. [7] *Epp.* 77 and 78.

Augustine's authority in the Christian community. He did not use this fear crudely, to terrorize his flock. More subtle and more effective, he took the full load of responsibility on himself: on that terrible day, he would be responsible to God for the sins of them all.[1] It was an approach perfectly adapted to the solemn paternalism, with which Augustine ruled his recalcitrant 'family'. It also gave him a crushing sense of mission and responsibility, which was notably lacking in the secular society of the Western Empire: as often as not, a provincial governor would be a blue-blooded nonentity, appointed for a short time only, to act as the figurehead of an ill-paid clerical staff; by contrast, the Christian bishop would have stood out as a permanent figure in the life of every town, a man dedicated to his authority, and responsible only to a God who was all the more present for being invisible: 'before Whom our heart is open and bare, Whose Judgement we fear, for Whose help we hope, in this life and the next.'[2]

Despite this high sense of his office, however, the average Christian bishop could have been coopted readily into the little oligarchies of great landowners, who counted for something in the life of their cities.[3] The African church had always had 'senior' laymen;[4] now these were senators, 'noble Christian laymen.' Such men would visit Augustine and discuss their problems with him on Sunday mornings before he went in to church.[5] They would act as the representatives of the community: at tense moments, these important men would come up to the apse, and negotiate alone with the bishop.[6] They would help Augustine to decide difficult cases.[7] Augustine would need their support; and they would need the bishop, for, as legal guardian of minors, he might affect their dynastic policies.[8] Just as the splendid houses of the rich pressed in around Augustine's church, so this small group would claim to take its place as the natural leaders of a community of poor, illiterate farmers when Hippo became a Christian town; and just as these men, as Christians, still trod on the frankly pagan mosaic floors laid down by their fathers, so they would want to see in Augustine just another influential man, rooted in the old traditions of their town. They would make of him yet another civic notable with religious duties.

Absorption into the established patterns of life could have happened only too easily. Many bishops were married men; their sons would

---

[1] e.g. *Serm.* 17, 2. [2] *Ep.* 104, ii, 9.

[3] v. *Serm.* 137, 14. They would expect the bishop to collude in landgrabbing.

[4] v. esp. P. G. Caron, 'Les *Seniores Laici* de l'Église africaine', *Rev. intern. des Droits de l'Antiquité*, vi, 1951, pp. 7–22, and W. H. C. Frend, 'The *Seniores Laici* and the origins of the Church in N. Africa', *Journ. Theol. Studies*, n.s., xii, 1961, pp. 280–284.

[5] *de div. daem.* i, 1; ii, 6. [6] *Ep.* 126, 1. [7] *Serm.* 355, 3. [8] *Epp.* 252–255.

have continued the old life, even to the extent of celebrating the public games that marked their entry into the town council.[1] Such bishops would treat their office as an 'honour', carrying privileges like any other civic title;[2] they could act as landowners on a large scale — the church at Hippo owned estates twenty times as great as the 'tiny plot' that Augustine had once possessed in Thagaste;[3] they were men of classical education. Only too often the pagan dignitaries of neighbouring towns, would attempt to approach Augustine as one of themselves, as a man 'schooled in all branches of cultures',[4] 'A great man, an educated man; but why a Christian?'[5]

Augustine would reject the expectations such men had of him. He had chosen his company differently. He surrounded himself with 'servants of God' in black robes. Augustine insisted that his priests should live with him in a monastic establishment in the bishop's house. They would thus be deliberately isolated from the life of the town by vows of poverty, celibacy, and by a strict rule.[6] They would be educated in the Christian Scriptures alone.[7] In time, many of the members of Augustine's monastery would become bishops elsewhere; they, in turn, would group similar monastic establishments around themselves.[8] In so doing, they preserved the Catholic clergy as a distinct caste, involved neither by marriage nor by economic interest in the life of their town; and, indirectly, they would drive yet another wedge into the old unity of a Roman city.

Attitudes to the use of wealth, for instance, would have shown clearly the difference in outlook between Augustine's circle and the average Roman. For a Late Roman man, wealth was there to be spent ostentatiously. It was considered ignoble to save.[9] Augustine would attempt to canalize this tradition of lavish giving, in favour of alms to the Christian poor;[10] and he would himself show *humanitas*, an openhanded courtesy, by giving a banquet to the poor on the anniversary of his ordination,[11] and in entertaining his many visitors.[12] But compared with traditional occasions for showing generosity, almsgiving seemed too indiscriminate: it cemented no ties of mutual obligation, as in the

[1] *Breviarium Hipponense*, xi, (P.L. lxvi, 424/5). [2] *Ep.* 208, 2.
[3] *Ep.* 125, 1; 126, 7; cf. *Vita*, xxiii, 1–xxiv, 7. v. Jones, *Later Roman Empire*, ii, 904–910.
[4] *Ep.* 90. [5] *Enarr. in Ps.* 39, 26.
[6] v. Van der Meer, *Augustine*, pp. 199–234 and, now, the admirable survey of R. Lorenz, 'Die Anfänge des abendländischen Mönchtums im 4. Jahrhundert', *Zeitschr. für Kirchengesch.*, 77, 1966, pp. 1–61, esp. pp. 39 sq.
[7] v. inf. pp. 266–267. [8] v. Frend, *Donatist Church*, pp. 246–247.
[9] e.g. Claudian, *In Prob. et Olybr. cons.*, esp. ll. 42–49; cf. *Serm.* 355, 5.
[10] *Serm.* 259, 5; *Enarr. in Ps.* 75, 26. [11] *Serm.* 339, 3. [12] *Serm.* 355, 5.

great exchange of gifts between friends, clients and allies on the feast of the Kalends of January;[1] and it was neither as public nor as competitive, as the extraordinary circus displays presented by the local magnates.[2] By comparison, Augustine spoke of almsgiving as something as impersonal as stockbroking — as a judicious transfer of capital from this unsafe world to the next.[3]

There would be no truce between Augustine and traditional ways of spending wealth in the circus-shows. These shows had become a way of showing that the old Roman way of life had survived, much as, after 1945, notable families would reappear in their boxes at the opera house in Eastern European capitals, to show that, despite all appearances, everything was as it had been. Yet in the years of mounting anxiety that followed the sack of Rome in 410, Augustine would preach bitterly against rich men who would ruin themselves to maintain such displays;[4] he would be glad to see a ruined amphitheatre;[5] and he would even welcome public disasters as a way of forcing a puritanical 'austerity' on the upholders of a rival order.[6] Augustine wrote in this vein to leading town councillors and responsible administrators, at a time when nothing less was at stake than the demoralization of a whole class and, with it, the disappearance of the old Roman ways in the African towns. These letters are some of the most shabby documents of the relations of Christianity to the civilization of the ancient world.

In choosing his company as he did, however, Augustine arranged that he would never be alone. He needed company. Even his most intimate experience of contemplation, he had in the presence of his mother; and now he ensured that in his bishop's palace at Hippo, he would always be the centre of a tight group of like-minded friends. Augustine maintained to the last the natural clannishness of Africans. His widowed sister would settle in Hippo to take charge of the women 'servants of God';[7] as did his niece[8] and his nephew, Patricius.[9]

He had established an austere monastic routine, with a strict vegetarian diet,[10] and an absolute prohibition on female visitors.[11] When, as an old man, Augustine considered what possible sins so perfect a man as Ábel the Just might yet have committed, he imagined that he might possibly have 'sometimes laughed a little too heartily, or forgot himself so much as to play pranks . . . ; he may have helped himself to too

---

[1] *Serm.* 198, 2–3.   [2] *Enarr. in Ps.* 147, 12.
[3] *Frang.* 9, 4, (*Misc. Agostin.*, i, p. 235); *Serm.* 345, 3.
[4] *Frang.* 5, 5, (*Misc. Agostin.*, i, p. 216); *Enarr. in Ps.* 147, 7.
[5] *Denis* 24, 13, (*Misc. Agostin.*, i, p. 153); v. inf. p. 297.
[6] *Ep.* 138, ii, 14.   [7] *Vita*, xxvi, 1.   [8] *Vita*, xxvi, 1.
[9] *Serm.* 356, 3.   [10] *Vita*, xxii, 2.   [11] *Vita*, xxvi, 1–2.

many apples, had indigestion from eating too much, or thought of something else when he was praying':[1] strange peccadilloes, yet ones that mattered to Augustine and his friends in the rarified moral climate of their establishment.[2]

Nevertheless, this monastery was unlike the ascetic communities isolated in the Egyptian desert: books were read, study was pursued, learned conversation took place in a pleasant garden, in a town whose port brought many travellers.[3] By the end of Augustine's life, visitors had become so many, that a hostel was built to lodge them.[4] These visitors would meet around the table in Augustine's house: there were hermits from little islands off Sardinia;[5] Gothic monks;[6] but for the absence of Augustine on one occasion, there might even have been Pelagius himself.[7] If we knew what these men talked about, we would know far more about Augustine's relations with the outside world. For, in the ancient world, the man who carried the letter was quite as important as the letter itself: he might be an intimate friend or a trusted servant, and in this way full of personal news.[8] Unfortunately for us, the surviving letter itself is often no more than a visiting-card, a *salutatio*, consisting of a few, well-turned phrases.

Good conversation counted for more than food at this table,[9] and around it many reputations would have been made — and lost:

'He wrote the following verses on the table, warning against the common plague of gossip:

> *Whoever thinks that he is able,*
> *To nibble at the life of absent friends,*
> *Must know that he's unworthy of this table,*

... Once, when some intimate friends of his, fellow bishops, were forgetful enough of his verses as to gossip, he upbraided them so sternly that he lost his temper, and said that either they should rub these verses off the table, or that he would get up and go to his room in the middle of the meal.'[10]

Augustine needed the constant response and reassurance of a circle

---

[1] *de nat. et gratia*, xxxviii, 45.

[2] e.g. *Conf.* X, xxi, 43–47, on greed; *Ep.* 95, 2, on laughing.

[3] P. Monceaux, 'S. Augustin et S. Antoine', *Misc. Agostin.*, ii, 1931, pp. 61–89.

[4] *Serm.* 356, 10.   [5] *Ep.* 48.   [6] *de civ. Dei*, XVIII, 52, 59.

[7] *de gest. Pel.* xxii, 46.

[8] e.g. *Epp.* 31, 2 and 200; cf. *Ep.* 184, a brief *salutatio* from Pope Innocent.

[9] *Vita*, xxii, 6; cf. *C. Jul.* IV, xiv, 71.

[10] *Vita*, xxii, 6–7. He had plainly underestimated Monica's virtues in being above gossip before he came to live among clergymen: *Conf.* IX, ix, 21.

of friends: both to know that he was loved,[1] and to know that there was someone worth loving,[2] encouraged him greatly to love in return. 'I must confess that I throw myself headlong upon their charity, especially when I am depressed by the tensions of the world.'[3] At this time, he found no difficulty in calling a friend 'half of my soul'.[4] His idea of friendship, a complete harmony of minds and purpose,[5] was ideally suited to maintain a tight group of dedicated men.[6] A letter which Severus of Milevis once wrote to him is a fulsome echo of his own ideals: 'Sweetest brother, it is good for me to be with you through your writings. I rejoice to be bound more closely to you, and, if I may say so, to cling as wholeheartedly as I can to you, and gain my strength from the overflowing richness of your breasts. . . .'[7] Augustine's reply is characteristic: seasoned with wit, bristling with problems, paradoxical, almost coquettish, plainly glad to be surrounded by such 'greedy' men:[8] 'As for me, when praise is given me by one who is very near and dear to my soul, I feel as if I were being praised by part of myself.'[9]

In this way, Augustine allowed his friends to complement him. Alypius, for instance, will always be at his side in conducting the ecclesiastical politics of Numidia: he will prompt him on technical points;[10] he will carry Augustine with him into more drastic courses;[11] later, he will use his *savoir faire* to 'tip' officials at the Imperial court.[12] Once when the two friends were divided over an embarrassing incident, (Alypius had been booed by the congregation of Hippo for having kept from them a millionaire settled at Thagaste, whom they had hoped to lure to their own town, by ordaining him as a priest),[13] we see Augustine as the weaker of the two men. Alypius is firm and narrow: he bases his case on a clear principle of Roman law.[14] Augustine is compromised by his need to placate his flock, and wants to discuss the problem in general terms; and his intellectual sensitivity smells not a little of casuistry.[15]

This group, however, will gradually disperse. Severus, Possidius, Evodius, Alypius, Profuturus will all go away from Hippo, to become

---

[1] *de cat. rud.* iv, 7. [2] *de Trin.* VIII, ix, 13. [3] *Ep.* 73, iii, 10.

[4] *Conf.* IV, vi, 11, from Horace, *Ode* I, 3, 8; cf. *Ep.* 270. v. Courcelle, *Les Confessions*, p. 22 n. 5.

[5] e.g. *Ep.* 258, 4, citing Cicero. v. Testard, *S. Augustin et Cicéron*, ii, p. 135; v. esp. M. A. MacNamara, *Friendship in St. Augustine*, (Studia Friburgensia), 1958, esp. ch. iv.

[6] Any discussion of love of one's neighbour begins, with Augustine, in terms of a relationship to a friend: e.g. *de doct. christ.* I, xx, 20–xxiii, 22; cf. *Ep.* 109, 2 (from Severus of Milevis).

[7] *Ep.* 109, 1. [8] *Ep.* 110, 1. [9] *Ep.* 110, 4. [10] *Ep.* 44, iii, 6.
[11] v. inf. p. 233. [12] v. inf. p. 362. [13] v. inf. p. 294.
[14] *Ep.* 125, 3 — on the validity of a forced oath. [15] *Ep.* 125, 4

the bishops of distant cities. Augustine will even become reconciled to travelling; for only in travelling, could he recreate his old relationships.[1] The friends would often arrange to travel together to the many councils in Carthage and Numidia.[2] Then, at least, in the long hours on horseback, Augustine would find himself speaking again to a friend 'as if to myself'.[3] But for the rest of the time, Augustine would have to stay in Hippo. His letters to his friends become full of the nagging details of ecclesiastical business: petty rivalries between their communities,[4] the eccentric behaviour of their country clergy; and Augustine found that he had 'only a few drops of time',[5] in which to reply to their own short notes.[6]

Augustine will also have to resign himself increasingly to a purely African circle of episcopal colleagues. The other men to whose friendship he felt entitled — Paulinus at Nola, Jerome in Bethlehem — remained far away. He would have to content himself with 'knowing their soul in their books'.[7] This phrase might be a polite cliché for some Later Roman correspondents; but as we have seen, it forced Augustine to commit himself to writing the *Confessions*. For this book, at least, could carry his soul across the sea to the friends whose absence tantalized him. It is the touching reaction of a man drifting against his will into a world of impersonal relationships.[8]

The slow dissolution of the old group of intimate friends is one of the silent tragedies of Augustine's middle age: 'But when you yourself begin to have to surrender some of the very dearest and sweetest of those you have reared, to the needs of churches situated far from you, then you will understand the pangs of longing that stab me on losing the physical presence of friends united to me in the most close and sweet intimacy.'[9] Augustine, indeed, will have to abandon the secluded cultivation of a group of friends to become a public figure. He will spend his middle age in a bitter campaign against fellow-Christians, the Donatist schismatics: and in the profound adjustment that he made to becoming a severe and aggressive figure of authority, we can trace some of the deepest sources of Augustine's activity in the following decades.

---

[1] *Enarr. in Ps.* 119, 6; v. Perler, 'Les Voyages', *Rech. augustin.*, i, 1958, p. 35.
[2] v. Perler, 'Les Voyages', *Rech. augustin.*, i, 1958, p. 30.   [3] *Ep.* 38, 1–2.
[4] e.g. *Epp.* 62–63.   [5] *Ep.* 261, 1.   [6] *Ep.* 84.
[7] *Ep.* 40, 1.   [8] v. sup. pp. 160–162.   [9] *Ep.* 84.

18

SALUBERRIMA CONSILIA

Augustine had become a bishop in a land that was the forcing-ground of extreme views on the position of the bishop in the Christian community. The hero of both groups of African Christians — Catholics and Donatists — was a bishop: Cyprian of Carthage.[1] The division between Catholics and Donatists had occurred, not because of any profound disagreement in doctrine, but, rather, because of the rival claims of two groups of bishops to have lived up to the ideal of a bishop's office as exemplified by S. Cyprian. It meant that, by 395, over three hundred bishops on each side, faced each other in little towns. Each stood at the head of a community which regarded their bishop as a member of a priestly caste, as in the Old Testament;[2] they would provide him with 'sanctuaries built up on steps, thrones draped with honorific cloth, processions and the chanting of crowds of consecrated virgins'.[3] The sense of honour, always acute in Africans, seemed particularly brittle in their clergy: a converted Donatist priest who learnt that he was not allowed to retain his office as a Catholic, stood 'burning with indignation and pain ... until he burst out into sobs';[4] and when Augustine cried bitterly on being made a priest, the congregation at Hippo was certain that he wept in this way from the dishonour of not having been made a bishop immediately.[5]

Augustine, a comparative outsider, had been forced, against his conscious intention, into this intense and prickly world. Even his consecration as a bishop created a scandal. Megalius of Calama, the senior bishop of Numidia, treated him as a suspicious upstart, and refused for a time to ordain him. Augustine, he said, was a crypto-

---

[1] v. esp. Bonner, *St. Augustine*, pp. 276–278, on the cult of S. Cyprian in Africa.
[2] Diehl, *Inscriptiones Latinae Christianae veteres*, i, 1961, no. 2435; cf. *C. Ep. Parm.* II, viii, 15.
[3] *Ep.* 23, 3.   [4] *Enarr. ii in Ps.* 36, 11.   [5] *Vita*, iv, 2.

Manichaean; he had been sending love-philtres to an eminent married lady.[1] It was a famous scandal. The 'eminent lady' may have been none other than the wife of Paulinus of Nola, to whom Augustine had sent a token of blessed bread. Paulinus may well have broken off relations for a time with this dubious new friend, as a result of such a rumour.[2] Fortunately, the incident blew over. But Augustine was deeply hurt by it. Even after Megalius' death, he will still speak of the dangers of 'hatred'.[3] To whose hatred did he refer? To the ill-tempered and suspicious old man? or to his own sensitive resentment?

Yet this ugly incident was only one of the many impingements to which Augustine was exposed on becoming a priest, and then a bishop in the African church. The manner in which he adjusted himself does not only throw a vivid light on his character: it helps to understand the personal animus behind his views on the nature of the Catholic Church and its problems in Africa. As always with Augustine, these views would not have been so carefully considered, nor so vehemently maintained, if they had not been partly the fruit of a constant effort to embrace and resolve tensions of which he was acutely aware in himself.

It is easy to concentrate on the more superficial differences between Augustine's sheltered life in Thagaste, and his life in the Church of Hippo. Augustine, the contemplative philosopher, became a priest. In the long run, his intellectual interests would be transformed by his new duties. But this was a slow change. When Augustine came to Hippo, he was already a mature Christian thinker. The change between his life as a layman and that of a priest was far less abrupt than that of many of his contemporaries. Ambrose, for instance, had stepped straight from a governorship into a bishopric, with no intervening period of theological meditation. By contrast, Augustine had imperceptibly acquired a semi-ecclesiastical position over four years; the quality of his thought evolves comparatively slowly, and for reasons that are only partly connected with his abrupt change in environment.[4]

The real change was more intensely personal. In 391, Augustine had been thrust out of a life of contemplation into a life of action.[5] Not only would he suffer from the obvious strain of new duties, and from constant new demands on his time and energy. He had to face a far more painful

---

[1] *C. litt. Petil.* III, xvi, 19; *C. Crescon.* III, lxxx, 92.

[2] Courcelle, *Les Confessions*, p. 567.   [3] *Ep.* 38, 2.

[4] v. sup. ch. 15.

[5] v. *de civ. Dei* XIX, 19, for Augustine's contrast of the two lives. v. esp. Burnaby, *Amor Dei*, pp. 60–73, and A. Wucherer-Huldenfeld, 'Mönchtum u. kirchl. Dienst bei Augustinus nach d. Bilde d. Neubekehrtens u. d. Bischofs', *Zeitschr. f. kathol. Theol.*, 82, 1962, 182–211.

adjustment than mere loss of leisure. He had to return to a life which resembled only too closely the life of a minor public figure, such as he had rejected with great abruptness, in 386. His career in Milan had been a *ventosa professio* — 'a puffed-up occupation';[1] but it was easy for the life of an African bishop, also, to be a 'puffed-up existence', *ventosa tempora*.[2] In Milan he had suddenly rejected his past career, and with it very much a part of himself, with horror and contempt. He had cut himself off from an environment that had seemed to bring into play emotions that affected him intimately: great ambition, a love of praise, a need to dominate others, an immense sensitivity to insult. The slightest hint of competitiveness among his pupils in Cassiciacum provoked a passionate outburst.[3] When he wrote about Adam and Eve, in Thagaste, Eve stood for the 'active' part of the soul: the labile, passionate part, that courted impingement, and reached out for objects of its desire; it was very much the rejected, feminine element, from which temptation always came. Adam, the masculine element, a mind rigidly collected upon itself in the life of contemplation, was the part with which Augustine wished to identify himself.[4] It seemed inconceivable to Augustine that he should expose himself again, even in the interests of the Church, to what he had so recently rejected with such horror. Bishops and priests, he thought, must be particularly strong men to put up with the impingement of 'men who are not healed, but stand in need of healing' ... 'it is most difficult, in their position, to hold to the best way of life, and to keep the soul at peace and calm'.[5]

Now, in Hippo, Augustine was again exposed to what he regarded as his previous besetting weaknesses. For a bishop was a figure of authority. If he was to be effective, he had, at least, to be admired; he must concern himself with his reputation.[6] In a divided community, he had to take the initiative. This meant being aggressive, and feeling angry: Evodius will lose his temper in his first interview with the Donatist bishop of Hippo.[7]

Augustine, indeed, had to draw on aspects of his own character that he had always regarded with infinite disquiet. In Book Ten of the *Confessions*, he faced this fact with exceptional honesty: he may no longer be vengeful when insulted,[8] but love of praise, the need to feel admired and loved by others, still caused him to be 'roasted daily in the oven of men's tongues'.[9] One feels that the tensions that sprang from

---

[1] *C. Acad.* I, i, 3. [2] *Ep.* 23, 6. [3] *de ord.* I, x, 29.
[4] *de Gen. c. Man.* II, xi, 15 and xiv, 21. [5] *de mor. eccl. cath.* (I), xxxii, 69.
[6] *Ep.* 22, ii, 7, cf. *de serm. Dom. in Monte*, II, i, 1; *Ep. ad Gal. expos.* 59, cf. *Serm.* 46, 6.
[7] *Ep.* 33, 3. [8] *Conf.* X, xxxvi, 58. [9] *Conf.* X, xxxvii, 60; cf. *Ep.* 95, 2–3.

his relations to others, his need to influence men, his immense sensitivity to their response to him, were far more deeply-rooted and insidious, than the more obvious temptations of greed and sexuality.[1] His acute awareness of the motive-force of a 'love of praise' in his ecclesiastical rivals, the Donatist bishops,[2] and in the ancient, pagan Romans,[3] shows both how vividly he had experienced the emotion in himself, and how sternly he had repressed it: for 'no one who has not declared war on this enemy can possibly know how strong it is'.[4]

Immediately after his ordination as a priest, Augustine wrote a desperate letter to his bishop, Valerius, begging for some time to retire to study the Scriptures. He did not do this to equip himself as a theologian. This was unnecessary. What he needed now, was to apply 'medicine' to his soul.[5] The letter is all the more poignant, for having been written some short time after Augustine had thrown himself enthusiastically into his active life as a priest. The experience had come to him as a galling revelation of his own limitations: 'I found it far, far more than I had thought. . . . I just had not known my powers: I still thought they counted for something. But the Lord laughed me to scorn and, by real experience, wished to show me to myself.'[6]

This short period of anxious retirement,[7] is vital in Augustine's later life. The *saluberrima consilia* — 'the most healthy advice'[8] — which he drew from the Scriptures, will eventually crystallize into an ideal of ecclesiastical authority, that will dominate Augustine's life until his death. Plainly, what he absorbed at this time, were the lessons of the active life of S. Paul. He will identify himself passionately with the ideal of authority shown in the letters of Paul to his wayward communities: 'insisting in season and out of season,' committed to impinge constantly on his flock and its enemies, driven by the objective 'terror' of the Holy Scriptures.

In a letter which he wrote immediately afterwards to Aurelius of Carthage, he felt he could 'talk aloud to himself'.[9] The extent of Augustine's adjustment to a life of authority revealed in this letter, is quite awe-inspiring. For Augustine was determined to make Aurelius use the 'sword of authority'[10] as an active reformer. The text which he had once read, for himself alone, in the sheltered garden in Milan, is turned outwards, and applied to the habits of a whole Church.

---

[1] He certainly regarded such failings as universal: *Enarr. in Ps.* 1, 1. [2] e.g. *Ep.* 23, 3.
[3] v. inf. p. 310.   [4] *Ep.* 22, 8.   [5] *Ep.* 21, 3.   [6] *Ep.* 21, 2.
[7] v. esp. Pincherle, *La formazione teologica di S. Agostino*, pp. 70–71.
[8] *Ep.* 21, 6.   [9] *Ep.* 22, 2. v. sup. p. 143.
[10] *Ep.* 22, 2 seq. v. sup. p. 141, n. 11.

'*Drunkenness, chambering and wantonness*' are referred precisely to the respectable African custom of banquets for the dead.[1]

What Augustine is discussing with Aurelius, is nothing less than the precise way in which the new spiritual élite of the African church could abolish one of its most deeply-rooted customs: the 'gay celebrations' — the *laetitiae* — which took place on the anniversaries of the martyrs.[2] For men of the mettle of Augustine and Aurelius, such customs smacked of 'license and evil freedom'.[3] It is the first time that we see the way in which Augustine and his colleagues will set about changing the habits of whole communities, by a carefully premeditated mixture of firmness and persuasion.[4]

In 394, the *laetitia* that accompanied the feast of S. Leontius of Hippo (the first martyr bishop of the town) was discontinued. Augustine avoided a serious commotion only by preaching until he was exhausted. 'I did not provoke their tears with my own; but when I said the things I said, I confess I was quite caught up in their weeping and could not control myself.'[5] He had carefully planned an even more drastic scene, had he failed in his first appeal: having read from the prophet Ezechiel that '*A watchman is absolved if he gives the cry of danger*', he would have rent his clothes in front of his congregation.[6]

But now, this passion had become impersonal. It is not Augustine, the ambitious *rhetor*, nor the exacting friend who speaks: 'If any threats are made, let them be made from the Scriptures, threatening future retribution, that it should not be ourselves who are feared in our personal power, but God in our words.'[7] '*Voce ecclesiae loquor*', 'I speak with the voice of the Church'.[8] It is an ominous circumvention of the complexities of individual anger and aggression. It will only be a matter of time before this impersonal intensity will overstep the frontiers of the Catholic Church and make itself felt against its rivals. The Donatist Church appeared to Augustine as yet another aberration of 'mere human custom'.[9] Within a decade Augustine and his friends will find themselves bringing about its destruction by harsh police-measures. 'The honour of this world passes away', a Donatist bishop

---

[1] *Ep.* 22, 2.

[2] J. Quasten, ' "Vetus superstitio et nova religio" ', *Harvard Theol. Rev.*, xxxiii, 1940, pp. 253–266, and Van der Meer, *Augustine*, pp. 498–526.

[3] *Ep.* 22, 3.

[4] *Ep.* 22, 5. The measures, in fact, were less drastic than those taken by Ambrose: meals at the tombs of the dead were controlled, not abolished.

[5] *Ep.* 29, 7.

[6] *Ep.* 29, 8. v. Van der Meer, *Augustine*, pp. 498–526, and Bonner, *St. Augustine*, pp. 116–119.

[7] *Ep.* 22, 5.   [8] *Serm.* 129, 4.   [9] *Ep.* 23, 2.

will be told by his new neighbour, the Catholic priest of Hippo, 'grasping at high office passes. . . . I do not intend to spend a puffed-up existence in ecclesiastical positions: my thoughts are on the day when I must render my account for the sheep committed to me by the Prince of Shepherds. . . . Understand my fear . . . for I fear deeply.'[1]

'But, of course, only those who have personality and emotions know what it means to want to escape from these things.'[2] Augustine was the son of a violent father, and of a relentless mother. He could uphold what he considered objective truth with a notable innocence of his own aggressiveness: he will, for instance, badger the elderly and eminent Jerome in a singularly humourless and tactless manner.[3] He was capable of swingeing sarcasm: he even admired this quality in S. Paul, and regarded it as a legitimate weapon for the Christian.[4] These qualities were needed in his life as a bishop; and we do see Augustine accepting and refining them to the best of his ability.

He found to his great relief that such hard-edged qualities could find expression in the Catholic Church without doing irreparable damage to his fellows. Augustine was immensely impressed by the resilience of the Catholic Church: it was *desuper texta*, 'knit through and through from above';[5] the 'sound constitution' of its peace could allow for considerable argument on central theological problems without disrupting the unity of the group;[6] and there were always plenty of external enemies to fight.

Above all, Augustine was able to accept his role as a stern figure of authority. He did not find it easy. When he comments on the verses of Psalm 54 — '*darkness has overwhelmed me. . . . O that I had the wings of a dove, that I might fly away and be at peace*' — this 'darkness' is not the tender depression of a recluse; it stands for the 'clouds' of sheer anger that gathered in Augustine's mind as he faced the intractable mass of his congregation: 'setting right warped, misshapen men who, willy-nilly, belong to one's responsibility; and on whom all human zeal and insistence is spent in vain.'[7]

It is no easy thing for a man as exacting with himself as Augustine, to avoid despising the masses he was determined to reform. Augustine avoided this contempt. 'The man you cannot put right is still yours: he is part of you; either as a fellow human being, or very often as a member of your church, he is inside with you; what are you going to

---

[1] *Ep.* 23, 3 and 6. [2] T. S. Eliot, *Selected Essays*, p. 21. [3] v. inf. p. 274.
[4] *Ep.* 138, ii, 13. [5] v. esp. M. Pontet, *l'Exégèse de S. Augustin*, p. 444.
[6] *de Bapt.* I, iv, 5.
[7] *Enarr. in Ps.* 54, 8 and 9; cf. *Enarr. iii in Ps.* 30, 5 and *Ep. ad Gal. expos.* 35.

do?'[1] 'Therefore, brother, among these shocking conditions, there is only one remedy: do not think ill of your brother. Strive humbly to be what you would have him be; and you will not think that he is what you are not.'[2] The animus that Augustine will show against the leaders of the Donatist church only reflects the stern effort he had made, to master his own tendencies to despise or disown his fellow-men. For he had once, himself, tended to disown the 'fleshly' rank and file of the African Church. He had viewed them with evident distaste from his rarefied haven at Thagaste;[3] and, as 'more learned and better', he had allowed himself to criticize the Catholic clergy.[4] Now he suspected that the Donatists had attempted to achieve a similar spurious innocence, by refusing to coexist with 'impure' colleagues.[5] He found it difficult to forgive them for having done frankly what he had only been tempted to feel.

To 'coexist' with one's fellows, however, also meant taking an active interest in reforming their ways. For this reason, the power of *correptio*, of admonition, which Augustine exercised as a bishop, preoccupied him deeply. Even in his early works as a priest, Augustine will constantly attempt to define the uneasy boundary between severity and aggression. The role of anger in delivering a rebuke, for instance, is examined with scrupulous honesty.[6] 'Love wholeheartedly: then do what you like' is an epigram which, in twenty years, will appear in its harshest form, as a justification of persecution by the Catholic Church;[7] but it begins with a sincere attempt by a sensitive man to embrace the complexity of human relationships, in which anger and aggression had come to have a necessary place.[8]

More tender changes had taken place in Augustine. Love and friendship, for instance, are no longer thought of as exclusively the property of like-minded souls living together as a self-conscious élite. In Milan, this ideal was unquestioned among the narrow circle of cultured gentlemen to which Augustine had attached himself. Just as truth might be found by the sincere, cultivated man, as easily as the sun growing in brightness at the edge of a passing haze, so also a friend might be known, 'as a flash of lightning lights up a whole cloud.'[9] It was the same at Thagaste: Augustine will come to know a new acquaintance, 'as if the bandages of the flesh had been torn away.'[10] Now,

---

[1] *Enarr. in Ps.* 54, 8. [2] *Enarr. ii in Ps.* 30, 7; cf. *Enarr. in Ps.* 25, 5.

[3] e.g. *de mor. eccl. cath.* (I), xxxiv, 75. [4] *Ep.* 21, 2. [5] v. inf. p. 222.

[6] *de serm. Dom. in Monte* I, ix, 24, II, ix, 34; *Ep. ad Gal. expos.* 57. [7] *In i Ep. Joh.* vii, 8.

[8] e.g. *Serm.* 88, 19–20. v. esp. J. Gallay, ' "Dilige et quod vis fac" ', *Rech. sc. relig.* xliii, 1955, pp. 545–555.

[9] *C. Acad.* II, i, 2. [10] *Ep.* 19.

a wide horizon will stretch beyond such little circles. In Hippo, men will seem more opaque; but somehow more real. For love has come to embrace a whole community; and so has come to include a large measure of acceptance — of the alien, of the unpromising, of the unknown and the unknowable in human character. As Augustine faced his congregation, perched up on his *cathedra*, he will realize how little he would ever penetrate to the inner world of the rows of faces: '*One depth calleth to another*.'[1] And Augustine's insistence on revealing his most intimate tensions in the *Confessions*, is in part a reaction to his own isolation: it is, also, a deliberate answer to a deep-seated tendency of African Christians to idealize their bishops. In a world of long-established clerical stereotypes, it is a manifesto for the unexpected, hidden qualities of the inner world — the *conscientia*.[2]

Thus the virtue of coexisting with a mixed company of men, whose merits and destinies have to be accepted as hidden from us, are the qualities which Augustine came to value most in his middle age — *tolerantia, patientia*.[3] It is as if a mist had suddenly descended on Augustine's landscape, blurring the obvious contours of good and bad. Like a winter between the sea and high hills, Augustine found himself in 'rain and fog'.[4] He must get on with the labour of sowing his seed; and must be prepared to extend infinite respect to potentialities that might lie quite dormant until revealed in the 'summer season' of the next life.[5]

Augustine disliked the winter season[6] as much as he loathed travelling. It is some measure of his changed outlook, that in his middle age both the images of travelling, of *peregrinatio*,[7] and of foul weather,[8] come to sum up the life of a Christian on earth.

For the man who had once thought that he could reach an ideal of perfection fixed for him by the philosophical culture of his age, in the company of friends of recognizable quality, unambiguously marked out for the higher life by education and serious intentions, becomes filled with Romantic longings for states he would never achieve in this life, for friends he would never entirely know.[9] In his correspondence with his friends, Augustine now seems to be straining across vast distances. He will never see Paulinus: 'I grieve that I do not see you;

---

[1] *Enarr. in Ps.* 41, 13; v. Pontet, *l'Exégèse de S. Augustin*, pp. 107–108.
[2] v. sup. p. 178; cf. *Serm.* 252, 7.   [3] *de serm. Dom. in Monte*, I, v, 13; *Serm.* 47, 16.
[4] *Serm.* 46, 23.   [5] *Enarr. iii in Ps.* 36, 9 and 14; *de lib. arb.* III, xxii, 65.
[6] *Ep.* 124, 1.
[7] e.g. *Enarr. in Ps.* 137, 12, v. sup. p. 152; v. Perler, 'Les Voyages', *Rech. augustin.*, i, 1958, p. 35.
[8] *Enarr. iii in Ps.* 36, 14.   [9] e.g. *Ep.* 101, 4.

but I take some comfort in my pain. I have no patience with that spurious "strength of character" that puts up patiently with the absence of good things. Do we not all long for the future Jerusalem? . . . I cannot refrain from this longing: I would be inhuman if I could. Indeed, I derive some sweetness from my very lack of self-control; and, in this sweet yearning, I seek some small consolation.'[1]

[1] *Ep.* 27, 1.

19

UBI ECCLESIA?[1]

The imagination of African Christians of the time of Augustine had become riveted on the idea of the Church. This Church was the '*strong woman*'.[2] 'It would not be decent for us', Augustine said, 'to speak of any other woman.'[3] In a land which, to judge from Monica, had a fair share of formidable mothers, the *Catholica*, the Catholic Church was The Mother: 'One Mother, prolific with offspring: of her are we born, by her milk we are nourished, by her spirit we are made alive.'[4]

This Church was thought of as a preserve of safety and cleanliness in a world ruled by demonic powers.[5] It existed to protect the believer. The African came to church, less because he was 'thirsty . . . and heavy laden', but because he wished to survive in a battlefield: the Psalms of deliverance from the hands of enemies predominate notably in their inscriptions.[6] The rite of baptism, therefore, was thought of as a drastic purification: with the bishop's 'spell', Christ, the 'Great Fish', slipped into the water of the baptismal pond;[7] for a week afterwards, the initiates would wear special sandals, lest their 'pure' feet touch the earth.[8] They wished to find that their Church was what it was said to

[1] W. H. C. Frend, *Donatist Church*, ch. xx. pp. 315–332, is a classic juxtaposition of Donatist and Catholic attitudes; his *Martyrdom and Persecution in the Early Church* 1964, has added a further dimension to the contrast. P. Monceaux, *Histoire littéraire de l'Afrique chrétienne*, notably vols. v–vii, 1920–1923, remains indispensable for the literature of the controversy. R. Crespin, *Ministère et Sainteté: Pastorale du clergé et solution de la crise donatiste dans la vie et la doctrine de S. Augustin*, 1965, is a valuable study of Augustine's reaction to Donatism.

[2] *Serm.* 37, 2, citing *Prov.* 31, 10.

[3] *Serm.* 37, 1. (His audience knew, and enjoyed, this theme: *Serm.* 37, 17.)

[4] Cyprian, *de unitate*, 5; cf. Aug. *Ep.* 34, 3, on a young man who had both beaten his mother and abandoned the Catholic Church.

[5] Frend, *Donatist Church*, p. 113.

[6] e.g. Diehl, *Inscript. Lat. Christ. vet.*, i, no. 2413, 2415 and 2415A.

[7] Optatus of Milevis, *de schism. Don.* III, 2, (P.L. xi, 990). [8] *Ep.* 55, xix, 29.

be in the *Song of Songs*: that it was morally 'without spot or wrinkle'; that they had come into a 'shut-in garden, a sealed fountain, a well-spring of living water, a paradise (an oasis) bearing the fruit of apples'.[1] 'This is the door of the Lord', they wrote on the lintel of a church in Numidia, 'the righteous shall enter in.'[2] 'The man who enters', however, wrote Augustine, 'is bound to see drunkards, misers, tricksters, gamblers, adulterers, fornicators, people wearing amulets, assiduous clients of sorcerers, astrologers. . . . He must be warned that the same crowds that press into the churches on Christian festivals, also fill the theatres on pagan holidays.'[3]

It was a disconcerting double-image. The Africans' view of the church had depended on their being able to see in it a group different from the 'world', an alternative to something 'unclean' and hostile. The spread of Christianity in Africa, by indiscriminately filling the churches, had simply washed away the clear moral landmarks that separated the 'church' from the 'world'. In the conditions of the third century, S. Cyprian could well expect his convert or his penitent, to find himself 'among the saints';[4] Augustine knew only too well that he was just as likely to rub shoulders with the most notorious landgrabber of the neighbourhood.[5]

Ever since 311, the African Christians had been divided on the attitude they should take, to the contrast between the ideal holiness of the church, and the actual quality of its members. The issue, briefly, was this. The Donatists had claimed, against the Catholics that, as the church was a unique source of holiness, so no sinner could have a part in it. The Church had to survive in its full holiness: it was a 'true vine', and like a vine, it had to be drastically pruned.[6] It could only survive as pure, if unworthy bishops were excluded: for the guilt of a bishop automatically rendered ineffective the prayers by which he baptized and ordained.[7] What is more, this guilt actually threatened the identity of the true Church: it created an anti-church, a sinister *Doppelgänger*, a 'Church of Judas', held together by the 'original taint' of its founders.[8]

---

[1] *Song of Songs*, 4, 12–13.   [2] Diehl, *Inscript. Lat. Christ. vet.*, i, No. 2421.

[3] *de cat. rud.* xxv, 48.   [4] Cyprian, *Ep.* 70, 2.   [5] *Serm.* 164, 8.

[6] pseudo-Aug., *C. Fulgentium*, 26, (P.L. xliii, 774). The most illuminating treatment of Donatist attitudes to the Church is by J.-P. Brisson, *Autonomisme et christianisme dans l'Afrique romaine*, 1958, pp. 123–153. Donatist pamphlets of the time of Augustine have been reconstructed by Monceaux, *Hist. littér.*, v, pp. 309–339.

[7] Cyprian, *Ep.* 65, iv, 1. v. inf. p. 218.

[8] *C. litt. Petil.* II, xi, 25. This ambivalent view of the religious community, the good group always dogged by a bad imitation, has been traced back to the Dead Sea Scrolls (Frend, *Martyrdom and Persecution*, p. 61), and forward, to late medieval popular belief

Both sides appealed to the authority of S. Cyprian;[1] but they applied his answers to very different questions. The times had changed. What was at stake in the late fourth century, was the attitude which the Church should take up to the 'world' at large; and their concern with the inner composition of their respective churches was important only because it determined this attitude.

The problem was acutely relevant. Christianity was the only religious group that had expanded in Roman society. Both churches had played a dramatic role in bringing about the end of paganism in Africa. They were faced by the fundamental problem of the relationship of any group to the society in which it lives. Briefly, the Donatists thought of themselves as a group which existed to preserve and protect an alternative to the society around them. They felt their identity to be constantly threatened: first by persecution, later, by compromise. Innocence, ritual purity, meritorious suffering, predominate in their image of themselves. They were unique, 'pure': 'the Church of the righteous who are persecuted and do not persecute.'[2]

The Catholicism of Augustine, by contrast, reflects the attitude of a group confident of its powers to absorb the world without losing its identity. This identity existed independently of the quality of the human agents of the Church: it rested on 'objective' promises of God, working out magnificently in history, and on the 'objective' efficacy of its sacraments.[3] This Church was hungry for souls: let it eat, indiscriminately if needs be.[4] It is a group no longer committed to defend itself against society; but rather, poised, ready to fulfil what it considered its historic mission, to dominate, to absorb, to lead a whole Empire. '*Ask Me, and I shall give the uttermost parts of the earth as Thy possession.*'[5] It is not surprising, therefore, that Africa, which had always been the home of articulate and extreme views on the nature of the Church as a group in society, should, once again, in the age of Augustine, become the 'cockpit of Europe', for this, the last great debate, whose outcome would determine the form taken by the Catholic domination of the Latin world until the Reformation.

---

and Luther: J. Ratzinger, 'Beobachtungen z. Kirchenbegriff d. Tyconius', *Rev. études augustin.*, ii, 1958, p. 181, n. 45.

[1] v. esp. Brisson, *Autonomisme et christianisme*, pp. 138–153 and 178–187. v. *de Bapt.* I, xviii, 28; V, xvii, 22.

[2] The claim of the Donatist statement of their case in 411: *Coll. Carthag.* iii, 258, (P.L. xi, 1408–1414, at 1408B).

[3] v. esp. Brisson, *Autonomisme et christianisme*, pp. 153–178, and Crespin, *Ministère e Sainteté*, pp. 209–284.

[4] *Serm.* 4, 19.   [5] *Ps.* 2, 7–8.

Until the time of Augustine, the tide of feeling in this debate had flowed consistently towards the Donatist attitude. Their case was, very briefly, this:[1]

Around 311, the African communities found themselves in a position similar to that of members of a Resistance movement whose country had begun to settle down to the complexities and compromises of peacetime. Too many bishops, it was thought, had 'collaborated' during the last, the Great, Persecution of Diocletian, in 303–305. They had handed over copies of the Holy Scriptures to be burnt by the pagan magistrates. This craven act, the *traditio*, the 'handing-over' of the Holy Books, would have deprived the guilty bishop, the *traditor*, of all spiritual power. It was believed that Caecilian, bishop of Carthage, had been ordained by such a *traditor*. It was a simple matter for 80 Numidian bishops, in 311, to declare his ordination invalid, and to elect another bishop in his place. This 'pure' bishop of Carthage was soon succeeded by another, Donatus: and, it was he, who, as rival bishop of Carthage, gave his name to what we call 'The Donatist Church' — the *pars Donati*, 'the party of Donatus.'

Caecilian held on against his rivals. The case of the Numidians was extremely flimsy: many of them, also, had been *traditores*. The rest of the Latin Church was more prepared to tolerate 'collaborators'. Above all, the Roman Emperor himself, Constantine, had become a Christian. He wanted to patronize a unified and respectable church. Caecilian was the existing bishop: Constantine, therefore, supported him against what appeared to non-Africans as exaggerated and parochial grievances.[2]

Thus the support enjoyed by Caecilian was widespread, but distant; that of Donatus, confined to Africa, but firmly-rooted. Each side was confident of victory; both ended by drifting into irreconcilable division. Around 347, the 'party of Caecilian' resorted to violence.[3] An Imperial commissioner, Count Macarius, frightened Africa into submission to the Catholic Church. He was praised by the Catholics as an 'agent of a holy task':[4] the torn garment of African Christianity had been decently and briskly 'sewn up'.[5] But the schism would never be healed again, except by renewed force. In Numidia, the 'Time of Macarius' was remembered by Donatists, in the same way as the 'Time of Cromwell' was remembered in Ireland. This solution based on force had been transient. The short reign of a pagan Emperor, Julian the

---

[1] v. esp. Frend, *Donatist Church*, pp. 3–23; 141–168.
[2] Monceaux, *Hist. littér.*, v, p. 18, citing Aug. *Ep.* 43, v, 14.
[3] Frend, *Donatist Church*, pp. 177–192. [4] P.L. viii, 774.
[5] Optatus of Milevis, *de schism. Don.* III, 9, (P.L. xi, 1020).

Apostate (361–363) upset it, by bringing renewed tolerance for the Donatists. Now it was the turn of the Catholics to be all but buried in the avalanche.

Only after this setback, did the Catholics deign to argue with their rivals. '*On the Donatist Schism*', by Optatus, Catholic bishop of Milevis,[1] contained the first appeal on either side for direct negotiation between rival bishops. But Optatus wrote a generation too late. The 'Time of Macarius' and the revanche of the Donatists in the reign of Julian, now stood like a wall between the contemporaries of Optatus, and the exact sequence of events in Carthage in 311. The rights and wrongs of the 'case of Caecilian' could never sway men as potently as did their own direct experience of violence at the hands of Christian 'brothers'.[2]

In this way then, the Donatist Church had become the dominant church in Numidia: 'You say (to a Donatist): "You are perishing in your heresy, in this schism of yours: you will come straight to damnation."'

— ' "What has that to do with me" (he would reply): "as I lived yesterday, so I shall live today; what my parents were, so I intend to be." '[3]

Augustine came to the problem of Donatism from the outside. Thagaste was a Catholic stronghold; he had been a Manichee;[4] he returned to Africa even more a foreigner in spirit, for the future pattern of his life had been set 'across the waters', in Milan. He did not even read the same translation of the Bible as his opponents.[5] Above all, his ideal of the Catholic Church had already grown to majestic proportions outside the African tradition. It had developed in a polemic against Manichees and pagan Platonists, that had no place in the writings of Cyprian. He had defended the Catholic Church as a philosopher: only the *auctoritas*, the persuasive force of this venerable, international institution, seemed to be able to hold and purge the minds of men.[6] The Catholic Church, indeed, was essential to what Augustine most dearly valued in himself, the continuing search for truth. Now he returned to Africa to find that this church had been divided by nothing

[1] transl. O. R. Vassall-Philips, *The Work of S. Optatus bishop of Milevis against the Donatists*, 1917. Monceaux, *Hist. littér.*, v, pp. 241–306, remains the best characterization.

[2] Forcefully described by Frend, *Donatist Church*, pp. 191–192.

[3] *Enarr. in Ps.* 54, 20.

[4] v. W. H. C. Frend, 'Manichaeism in the Struggle between St. Augustine and Petilian of Constantine', *Aug. Mag.*, ii, 1954, pp. 859–866.

[5] *Retract.* I, 20, 5.

[6] v. esp. Holte, *Béatitude et Sagesse*, pp. 303–327; Bonner, *St. Augustine*, pp. 231–235.

more important than the rancours of its bishops. 'Snap out of it! I am not dealing with an obscure problem', he would tell them, 'I am not dealing with some hidden mystery, where no human mind, or very few, can make headway. The matter is as clear as day.'[1] The Donatist bishops expounded the same Bible as himself, they professed the same creed, they celebrated an identical liturgy; yet they refused to see the obvious truth about the Catholic Church — '*They go down with open eyes into Hell.*'[2]

Sympathetic to the Manichees, who held out 'the unvarnished promise of Truth',[3] Augustine studiously withheld his sympathy from the Donatists. It has recently become fashionable to make this bitter conflict between fellow-Christians palatable by explaining it away: to say that the religious differences were only the expression of the social and ethnic cleavages of Roman North Africa; and that the Donatists represented a popular tradition which Augustine, as a Romanized townsman, could not be expected to understand.[4] In fact, no great differences in class, race or education separated Augustine from the Donatist bishops, whose views he caricatured in his pamphlets. In any case, such a theory adds little to our understanding of what, for Augustine, was all-important: that is, that watershed of ideas and highly personal assumptions, which in his own mind, separated him from his Donatist rivals.

Augustine rapidly absorbed the African tradition that Catholics shared with Donatists.[5] Yet he approached it from a different direction, with a highly personal training as a philosopher, and with an attitude that had evolved in the course of his own adjustment to becoming a bishop. He will transform the firm and narrow ideas of his contemporaries, and so his writings against the Donatists will mark a final stage in the evolution of Early Christian ideas on the church, and its relation with society as a whole.

If we are to understand what it was like to be a Donatist, we should read their versions of the *Acts* of the martyrs of the Great pagan Persecution, and their descriptions of persecutions by the Catholics.[6] For these were the novels of Augustine's day.

---

[1] *Ep.* 43, iii, 6. [2] *Enarr. in Ps.* 54, 16. [3] *C. Ep. Fund.* 4.
[4] Notably by Frend, *Donatist Church*, pp. 229–238. I am unconvinced: v. Brown, 'Religious Dissent in the Later Roman Empire: the case of North Africa', *History*, xlvi, 1961, pp. 83–101. Many aspects of Dr. Frend's thesis have been criticized in detail by E. Tengström, *Donatisten u. Katholiken: soziale, wirtschaftliche u. politische Aspekte einer nordafrikanischen Kirchenspaltung*, (Studia Graeca et Latina Gothoburgensia, xviii), 1964.
[5] v. esp. J. Ratzinger, *Volk u. Haus Gottes*, 1954.
[6] *Monumenta ad Donatistarum historiam pertinentia*, P.L. viii, 673–784.

In the *Acts*, the Donatists admired an attitude such as the orthodox Jew had to the Torah.[1] Their religion also was thought of as a 'Law'. Like the Maccabees, whose example moved them profoundly, their martyrs had died for 'their holy laws'.[2] 'I care for nothing but the Law of God, which I have learnt. This I guard, for this I die; in this I shall be burnt up. There is nothing in life other than this Law.'[3]

The feeling of having defended something precious, of preserving a 'Law' that had maintained the identity of a group in a hostile world, these are potent emotions. Such feelings had preserved, and would preserve, the amazing integrity of Judaism. In the lines of any Donatist manifesto, we can still sense the power of such feelings: they had led the Christian Church, always thought of as a 'True Israel', embracing in its past also Moses, the prophets, and the Maccabees, to victory in Africa. Such a Church was '*catholic*' in what the Donatists regarded as the most profound sense of the word: for it was the only church that had preserved the '*total*' Christian Law.[4]

A church could only preserve the Christian 'Law' in its entirety by remaining 'pure'. The Donatists were not 'Puritans' in the Northern European sense. Augustine (who was far closer to that modern type) expected his readers to believe, that the Donatists had claimed such personal purity for themselves: and it gave scope to his journalistic talents to show that some of their leading bishops were far from being 'saints'.[5]

The Donatist idea of 'purity' drew its strength from a different source. It was the purity of the group in its relationship to God, that mattered. This group, like the ancient Israel, enjoyed a special relationship with God: for its prayers only were heard by Him.[6] The anxiety, that genuinely haunted the Donatist bishops, was that, by tolerating any breach in a narrow and clearly defined order of ritual behaviour, they might alienate God from His Church.[7] They will always quote those passages of the prophets of Israel in which they tell of how God had closed His ears to His Chosen People because of their sins.[8]

Anyone who reads a Donatist pamphlet, or, indeed, a work of S.

---

[1] v. W. H. C. Frend, *Martyrdom and Persecution*, esp. p. 362, on the possible links between Judaism and African Christianity.
[2] *Macc.* 7, 9: *C. litt. Petil.* II, viii, 17, (Monceaux, *Hist. littér.*, v, p. 312).
[3] *Acta Saturnini*, 4, (P.L. viii, 692).
[4] *C. litt. Petil.* II, xxxviii, 90 and *Coll. Carthag.* iii, 102, (P.L. xi, 1381D).
[5] e.g. *C. Ep. Parm.* II, iv, 8. v. inf. p. 228.
[6] v. esp. *Acta Saturnini* 20, (P.L. viii, 702–703).
[7] e.g. *C. Ep. Parm.* II, vii, 12; cf. the citations in *Acta Saturnini* 19, (P.L. viii, 702).
[8] e.g. *C. Ep. Parm.* II, iii, 6.

Cyprian,[1] will be struck by the power of the idea of ritual purity that stemmed straight from the Old Testament: the fear of a sudden loss of spiritual potency through contact with an 'unclean' thing,[2] and the elemental imagery of the 'good' and the 'bad' water.[3] Such ideas had lost little of their force in fourth century Africa. Even the sophisticated Roman still regarded religion as a precise code of rites, designed to establish the correct relationship of the community to its God (or gods). Augustine shared this attitude: rebaptism genuinely shocked him as a 'sacrilege', for it 'defaced' the correct, Catholic rite.[4] The Donatist enthusiasts carried clubs called 'Israels';[5] they would 'purify' Catholic basilicas with coats of whitewash; they would destroy the altars of others.[6] Such men could understand, far better perhaps than Augustine with his sophisticated, 'spiritual' exegesis of the Old Testament, the urgent need for 'separation', for the active, physical destruction of the 'unclean', that runs as a constant refrain through the pages of the Bible.[7]

Logically, the emphasis on the need to form a small 'pure' group, might seem to favour any minority which claimed to be holier than its neighbours. Augustine will emphasize the existence of 'splinter-groups' in Donatism, which in his opinion had crumbled their church into 'so many crumbs'.[8]

Such splinter-groups, however, were not very frequent in Donatism. The basic Donatist idea was of a Chosen People, that had preserved its identity without compromise with the 'impure' world. Far from fostering a 'minority mentality', such an idea could gain the unwavering support of a whole province. It contained the secret of a success unparalleled in the history of the Early Church. For like Nonconformity in Wales, the Donatist Church had won over a provincial society, isolated, self-respecting, suspicious of the outside world, to its form of Christianity.

For the Donatist Church was 'pure' in an obvious and not particularly exacting sense: it had kept itself pure *from* a single, unspeakable crime, from *traditio*, the sacrificing of the Christian 'Law'; that is, from

---

[1] Brisson, *Autonomisme et christianisme*, pp. 89–105.

[2] e.g. *Isaiah* 52, 11.

[3] e.g. Fulgentius in Monceaux, *Hist. littér.*, v, pp. 335–339.

[4] e.g. *Enarr. in Ps.* 145, 16; v. *C. Faustum* XIX, 11.

[5] *Enarr. in Ps.* 10, 5.

[6] Optatus of Milevis, *de schism. Don.* VI, 1–3, (P.L. xi, 1063–1072); cf. Aug. *Ep.* 29, 12.

[7] M. Simon, 'Le judaisme berbère dans l'Afrique ancienne', *Rev. d'hist. et de philos. relig.*, xxvi, 1946, 1–31 and 105–145 (= *Recherches d'Hist. Judéo-Chrétienne*, 1962, pp. 30–87, esp. pp. 46–47).

[8] *C. Ep. Parm.* II, xviii, 37.

a crime committed by total strangers in a conveniently distant past.[1] Its caste of 'pure' bishops were often eminent men in Roman towns that had maintained their prestige.[2] In the eyes of their congregations, these bishops stood for the uninterrupted succession of the 'Church of the Martyrs': a Donatist priest would be told by an angel the precise 'line of descent of Christianity' that culminated in the bishop of his town.[3] In a society that valued sheer physical continuity in life and death (Monica, after all, had once wished to 'rejoice in grandsons after the flesh',[4] and had hoped to be buried in her home soil),[5] these bishops were thought of as the 'sons of the martyrs' as surely as the despised Catholics were the 'sons of Caecilian'.[6] The memory of these martyrs would be constantly relived, beside their graves, by pilgrimages, and by uproarious festivals that crystallized the tenacious loyalty of simple men for venerated ancestors.[7]

The archaeologist is in the best position to appreciate the strength of Donatism in Numidia; for it is, appropriately enough, in the ground, that we can see the traces of those strong roots, which a community of farmers and small townsmen had created for their religion.[8] There were the 'great churches', Timgad and Bagai[9] — huge basilicas, with great warehouses, shrines and a hostel for pilgrims.[10] In the shadow of these 'holy cities' of Donatism, the hillsides were studded with villages that had gained a new sense of importance from the new religion. They could now boast a bishop of their own;[11] they would combine to build churches;[12] these churches would become the centre of intense loyalties;[13] and so they would unite, as only a village could, to repel outsiders.[14] They were 'the flock of the Lord', 'brought to lie down in the South.'[15]

Such, briefly, were the ideas that had formed the Donatist church. These ideas enjoyed the widespread support of simple men; and yet in the age of Augustine, they were also held by sophisticated men.

---

[1] v. R. Crespin, *Ministère et Sainteté*, pp. 221–225, and A. C. de Veer, in *Rech. augustin.*, iii, 1965, pp. 236–237. Augustine chose to overlook this vital distinction: he has persuaded too many modern historians of Donatism, but may not have convinced his Donatist opponents. The distinction is, of course, a fine one; a Donatist layman, for instance, failed to make it: e.g. *C. Crescon.*, III, vii, 7.

[2] v. Brown, 'Religious Dissent', *History*, xlvi, 1961, pp. 91–92.   [3] *Ep.* 53, i, 1.

[4] *Conf.* VIII, xii, 13.   [5] *Conf.* IX, xi, 28.   [6] *Coll. Carthag.* iii, 221, (P.L. xi, 1402A).

[7] *C. Ep. Parm.* III, vi, 29. v. esp. H. I. Marrou, 'Survivances paiennes dans les rites funéraires des donatistes', *Extrait de la Collection Latomus*, ii, 1949, pp. 193–203.

[8] v. esp. Frend, *Donatist Church*, pp. 211–212.   [9] *Enarr. in Ps.* 21, 26.

[10] Frend, *Donatist Church*, p. 209.

[11] Brown, 'Religious Dissent', *History*, xlvi, 1961, p. 95.

[12] *Année épigraphique*, 1894, 25 and 138; Warmington, *The North African Provinces*, p. 84 and n. 4.

[13] *Ep.* 44, vi, 14.   [14] *Ep.* 209, 2.   [15] *Song of Songs* 1, 7; v. *Serm.* 46, 35.

Augustine felt that such ideas were inadequate because they were essentially static. The Donatist church was a group on the defensive: it was immobilized by anxiety to preserve its identity. The Church, a Donatist bishop had said, was like the Ark of Noah. It was well-tarred inside and out. It was watertight: it kept within itself the good water of baptism; it had kept out the defiling waters of the world.[1]

For Augustine, it was not enough for the Christian church to preserve a holy 'Law'. This attitude would have condemned Christianity, as in Augustine's eyes it had condemned the Donatist church, to remaining isolated, like the old Israel, content to guard a static alliance of 'obedience' between itself and God. Instead, he presented the Catholic Church as the heir of a will, about to take over a vast property.[2] The Church's expansion was foreordained. The Donatist opinion, that the unworthiness of some of its members had placed this expansion in jeopardy, that it had, for the moment at least, reduced the 'true' Church to Africa, drew from Augustine some of his most angry outbursts.[3] For to claim this was tantamount to allowing the free will of frail human beings to stand in the way of the omnipotence and foresight of God: 'Who shall remove the preordained course (the *praedestinatio*) of God?'[4] It is in such outbursts, that we recognize clearly the future exponent of the doctrine of the predestination of the elect.[5] Augustine would turn upon this great rival church the ominous contempt of a man, who knew that the ineluctable course of history was on his side: 'The clouds roll with thunder, that the House of the Lord shall be built throughout the earth: and these frogs sit in their marsh and croak — We are the only Christians!'[6]

However, such a rapidly expanding church could never claim to be 'holy' in any sense that was immediately apparent. Here the Donatists could appeal to the obvious. If the church was defined as 'pure', if it was the only body in the world in which the Holy Spirit resided, how could its members fail to be 'pure'? Augustine, however, was a man steeped in Neo-Platonic ways of thought. The whole world appeared to him as a world of 'becoming', as a hierarchy of imperfectly-realized forms, which depended for their quality, on 'participating' in an Intelligible World of Ideal Forms. This universe was in a state of constant, dynamic tension, in which the imperfect forms of matter

[1] *Ep. ad cath.* v, 9.
[2] v. esp. *Enarr. in Ps.* 21, 28 f., in the racy translation of Edmund Hill, *Nine Sermons of St. Augustine on the Psalms*, 1958, pp. 56–60.
[3] e.g. *Enarr. ii in Ps.* 101, 8.   [4] *Enarr. iii in Ps.* 32, 14; cf. *C. Ep. Parm.* I, iv, 6.
[5] e.g. *Ep. ad cath.* ix, 23.   [6] *Enarr. in Ps.* 95, 11.

strove to 'realize' their fixed, ideal structure, grasped by the mind alone. It was the same with Augustine's view of the Church. The rites of the church were undeniably 'holy', because of the objective holiness of a Church which 'participated' in Christ.[1] The 'true church' of Augustine is not only the 'body of Christ', the 'heavenly Jerusalem', it is also deeply tinged with the metaphysical ideas of Plotinus:[2] it is the 'reality', of which the concrete church on earth is only an imperfect shadow.[3] Thus, the men who received and administered these rites merely strove imperfectly to realize this holiness, 'according to a certain shadow of the reality.'[4]

Thus the rites of the church take on an objective and permanent validity. They exist independently of the subjective qualities of those who 'participate' in them: in a way which Augustine never claimed to understand, the physical rites of baptism and ordination 'brand' a permanent mark on the recipient, quite independent of his conscious qualities.[5] At the same time as he wrote '*On Baptism*', Augustine wrote his *Confessions*. In them also, the youth of a Catholic boy is portrayed as studded with reminders of the potency of the sacraments: his Manichaean friend, who had been baptized when unconscious, comes to his senses strangely changed;[6] even his intellectual development is now seen as penetrated, at every turn, by the mysterious force of the 'Name of Christ'.[7]

Augustine endowed the concrete rites of the Catholic Church with a mysterious and enduring validity. Yet he did so in order to make the Church itself a field of innumerable, personal evolutions. The individual Catholic was only 'guarded' by his sacraments: he still had before him the long processes of spiritual growth.[8] Once the visible church is seen in this way, the type of relationship that could be established between its members becomes immeasurably more complex and dynamic. For, as Augustine saw it, the Donatists had solved the problem of evil in the men around them, merely by refusing to establish any relationship with it. They had withdrawn from contact with an 'unclean' society into a coterie of their equals. For Augustine, inno-

---

[1] e.g. *Ep.* 261, 2.

[2] e.g. *Conf.* XII, xi, 12–13. v. J. Pépin, ' "Caelum Caeli" ', *Bulletin du Cange*, 23, 1953, esp. pp. 267–274, and J. Lamirande, *L'Église céleste selon S. Augustin*, 1963, (with the suggestive comments of A. H. Armstrong, *Journ. Theol. Studies*, n.s., xvi, 1965, pp. 212–213).

[3] A. Wachtel, *Beiträge z. Geschichtstheologie d. Aurelius Augustinus*, 1960, pp. 118–119.

[4] *C. Ep. Parm.* II, iv, 8. [5] *de Bapt.* IV, xxiii, 30.

[6] *Conf.* IV, iv, 8. [7] *Conf.* III, iv, 8.

[8] *de Bapt.* I, xv, 24; III, xiv, 19; and IV xv–xvi, 23, on theological misconceptions in the convert similar to those held by Augustine himself in Milan: v. *Conf.* VII, xix, 25.

cence was not enough. It was only 'one third' of the full range of human relationships to which the good Christian had to expose himself.[1] He must perform a threefold task: he must himself become holy; he must coexist with sinners in the same community as himself, a task involving humility and integrity; but he must also be prepared, actively, to rebuke and correct them.[2] The stern qualities which the Donatists would merely direct to those outside their group, would, in the Catholic Church, be turned inwards: a 'foreign policy' directed exclusively against the 'world' outside the church, becomes a 'home front' against the 'worldly' within the Church.

Augustine's critique of what he considered to be the Donatist attitude contains far-reaching assumptions. For it treated the Catholic community as essentially a community made up of two layers. This community would always contain a large, even a predominant, element of seemingly intractable human material, surrounding a core of 'true' members. The dividing-line between 'true' and 'false' members was, of course, invisible: this core would later harden into Augustine's 'defined number of the elect'.[3] But Augustine both envisaged such an élite, and had no doubts about the practical duties which every Catholic clergyman had to perform: over against the mass of men, they must not only be innocent, not only tolerate their fellows, but they must also be prepared, whenever possible, to take the offensive with measured severity, and an active, paternal authority; 'for the rod has its own kind of charity.'[4]

While the Donatist view of the Church had a certain rock-like consistency, Augustine's Church was like an atomic particle: it was made up of moving elements, a field of dynamic tensions, always threatening to explode.

His view of the Church had perched it on the brink of a war of conquest. In Augustine's thought, tenacious bonds could be seen to run out from this institution, throughout Roman society. The bishops already ruled large communities; and Augustine had as good as admitted that such communities would only respond to a measure of severity.[5] In the late fourth century, it was easy for such an ideal of active authority to overstep the boundaries of the Catholic communities proper. Already, invisible tentacles, the sacraments of baptism and ordination administered in schism by the Donatists, linked the remaining Christians in Africa to their true owner, the Catholic Church.[6]

[1] C. Ep. Parm. II, xxi, 40. [2] C. Ep. Parm. II, xxi, 41. [3] e.g. C. Ep. Parm. III, iv, 25.
[4] C. Ep. Parm. III, i, 3; cf. C. Ep. Parm. III, v, 26. [5] Ep. 22, 5.
[6] de Bapt. IV, ix, 13 and xi, 17.

For these sacraments were like the tattoos which soldiers in the Imperial armies had branded on the back of their hands,[1] so as to identify deserters: in the same way, Christ the Emperor of the Catholic Church was entitled to recall to the ranks of His Church, those who had received His brand.[2]

This image reflects the quality of Augustine's age. It was a harsh age, that thought, only too readily, in terms of military discipline and uniformity. The Emperors were also devout Catholics: it would only be a matter of a decade before they would decide to round up 'spiritual' deserters from the ranks of the Catholic Church.[3]

C'est le premier pas qui coûte. Augustine had already taken a decisive step almost ten years before he wrote his first pamphlets against the Donatists. Ultimately, the Donatists regarded their church as an alternative to society, as a place of refuge, like the Ark. Augustine believed that the Church might become coextensive with human society as a whole: that it might absorb, transform and perfect, the existing bonds of human relations. He was deeply preoccupied by the idea of the basic unity of the human race. God had made all men from one man, Adam, in order to show, that 'nothing is more rent by discord than this human race, in its flawed state; though nothing was so plainly intended by its Creator for living together'.[4] The idea of a common kinship in Adam is the mould into which Augustine, in his middle age, will pour his continuing preoccupation with friendship, with the true relations between human beings.[5] The poignant sense of the need to regain some lost unity is perhaps the most distinctive strand in Augustine's mystique of the Catholic Church. The Donatists might be content to find themselves in the Ark: Augustine was concerned with a deeper problem; the human race was divided, communication between fellow men in society was difficult; the image of the Division of Tongues at the Tower of Babel came to dominate his thought.[6] The Catholic Church was a microcosm of the re-established unity of the human race: it had already united all the tongues of men at Pentecost;[7] and we should never forget that Augustine, in founding his monastery, wished to recreate around him exactly the same community, as the Apostles had created when they received this gift of the Holy Spirit.[8]

---

[1] *Serm.* 317, 5.

[2] *de Bapt.* I, iv, 5 and III, xix, 25. v. esp. M. Ch. Pietri, in *Mélanges d'archéol. et d'hist.*, 74, 1962, 659–664: a Christian is shown on his sarcophagus, 'enrolling' like a soldier.

[3] e.g. *C. Gaud.* xx, 23. The recipient was, himself, an officer; v. inf. p. 335.

[4] v. esp. *de civ. Dei* XII, 28; cf. *Serm.* 268, 3.   [5] e.g. *de bono coniug.* i, 1; cf. *Serm.* 90, 7.

[6] e.g. *Enarr. in Ps.* 54, 9.   [7] *Serm.* 269, 2, and 271; cf. *Enarr. in Ps.* 95, 15.

[8] *Serm.* 356, 1.

Such a monastery was to be a microcosm of the ideal human relationships that might be partially re-established in the Catholic Church.

A man who feels intensely that the existing bonds of men in society are somehow dislocated, but that the group to which he belongs can consolidate and purify them, will regard the society around him as so much raw material to be absorbed and transformed. He will be very different from the man who feels that he can only create an alternative to this society — a little 'Kingdom of Saints', sheltering beneath a bishop, the only possessor of a divine Law in a hostile or indifferent world.[1]

Augustine's writings against the Donatists betray his increasing absorption of the common stock of ideas available to African Christians — above all, of the idea of the Church as a clearly distinguished group in society, marked out as the sole possessor of a body of 'saving' rites. Behind these ideas, however, there still lurks the great 'mirage' of his early middle age, all the more potent for never having to be analysed in controversy. This was his image of the Catholic Church as it had appeared to him in Milan and in Rome. It was not the old church of Cyprian, it was the new, expanding church of Ambrose, rising above the Roman world like 'a moon waxing in its brightness'.[2] It was a confident, international body, established in the respect of Christian Emperors, sought out by noblemen and intellectuals,[3] capable of bringing to the masses of the known civilized world the esoteric truths of the philosophy of Plato,[4] a church set, no longer to defy society, but to master it. *Ecclesia catholica mater christianorum verissima*: 'The Catholic Church, most true Mother of Christians. . . .

'It is You who make wives subject to their husbands . . . by chaste and faithful obedience; you set husbands over their wives; you join sons to their parents by a freely granted slavery, and set parents above their sons in pious domination. You link brothers to each other by bonds of religion firmer and tighter than those of blood. You teach laves to be loyal to their masters . . . masters . . . to be more inclined to persuade them than to punish. You link citizen to citizen, nation to nation, indeed, You bind all men together in the remembrance of their first parents, not just by social bonds, but by some feeling of their common kinship. You teach kings to rule for the benefit of their people; and You it is who warn the peoples to be subservient to their kings.'[5]

---

[1] *ep. ad cath.* xiii, 33.   [2] Ambrose, *Ep.* 18, 24, (P.L. xvi, 1020).
[3] *de util. cred.* vii, 18-19   [4] *de vera relig.* iv, 6.   [5] *de mor. eccl. cath.* (I), xxx, 63.

20

INSTANTIA

As a bishop, Augustine sat all morning arbitrating in law-suits. He would have to deal mainly with intricate and rancorous cases of divided inheritances. It was a rare thing for brothers to agree about their property;[1] and Augustine would listen for hours while families of farmers argued passionately about every detail of their father's will.

The atmosphere of a courtroom will follow Augustine into church when he preached against the Donatists. He will read out the Testament of God, that Christ and His church should have 'the uttermost parts of the earth as Thy possession'; and with the same unnerving confidence as Monica had once displayed her own marriage contract,[2] Augustine would now produce the 'marriage contract' of Christ and His Church.[3] Altogether, Augustine's campaign against the Donatists shows little trace of oecumenical moderation. It drew its strength from the bitter obstinacy of small men committed, as it were, to a long family law-suit.

From 393 onwards, Augustine and his colleagues took the offensive against the Donatist church. They had good reason to do so. In Hippo, the Catholics were in a minority: they had recently been boycotted;[4] Augustine's first appeal to local notables was snubbed.[5] For Donatism, not Catholicism, was the established church of Numidia. It seemed to Donatists as if the 'peace of the Church' had come,[6] and that only a few concessions needed to be made to complete the absorption, by their 'purified' church, of the despised and weakened 'church of the *traditores*'.[7] In Hippo, for instance, mixed marriages had been common

---

[1] *Serm.* 359, 1; cf. 358, 2 and 47, 21, on the strong feelings evoked by a disputed will.
[2] *Conf.* IX, ix, 19.　　[3] *Serm.* 238, 2–3.　　[4] *C. litt. Petil.* II, lxxxiii, 184.
[5] *Ep.* 35, 1.　　[6] Tyconius, *Liber Regularum*, ed. Burkitt, p. 61 and p. xvii.
[7] v. Monceaux, *Hist. littér.*, v, p. 170.

among the great local landowners.[1] It was normal to become a Donatist to make headway in a law-suit.[2] 'God is both here and there: what difference does it make? This division is the result of men's past quarrels; God can be worshipped everywhere.'[3] Even the previous Catholic bishop of Carthage, Genethlius, had accepted this impasse. He had gained a reputation for tolerance among the Donatists.[4]

Tolerance, however, was the one thing Augustine could not afford in Hippo: for all the pressures of social life in his town seemed to favour the gradual erosion of his Catholic minority by their dominant brethren. His campaign, therefore, is marked by the extremist qualities of a man fighting an uphill battle for his position against forces of conservatism and common human feeling.

Augustine and Aurelius were committed, also, to a policy of internal reform of the Catholic Church. The decisions drafted at Hippo in 393 had been unpopular: many bishops had ignored them.[5] When Augustine had suppressed the *laetitia* in 394, the strength of the popular reaction had almost 'capsized the boat'.[6] Such 'chaff' in his congregation might well be blown outside the Church altogether at the next, cold wind of reform.[7] A policy of internal change might easily have created a new schism, if it could not be linked with the prospect of a campaign against a formidable rival.

By 397, we can see how far Augustine's resolve had taken his colleagues. The links which bound the Catholic clergyman to the society around him were cut away: even the sons of clergymen were forbidden to make mixed-marriages;[8] and the clergy themselves were forbidden to make any donation, to leave any legacy to a non-Catholic, not even to a blood-relative.[9] These frankly confessional principles would drive a wedge into African society. At just this time, Augustine received a letter from a relative, Severus. Severus was a Donatist: 'What profit is there in temporal good health and in the ties of blood, if we willingly spurn the eternal inheritance of Christ. . . . But this opinion is not mine, who am nothing. . . . They are the words of Almighty God Himself: whoever rejects Him, in this world, as Father, will find Him, in the next, as Judge.'[10]

It has sometimes been said that Donatism was a popular 'movement of protest', which threatened the basis of Roman law and order in Africa. This view does not do justice to the situation created by

[1] *Ep.* 33, 5. [2] *Serm.* 46, 15. [3] *Serm.* 46, 15. [4] *Ep.* 44, v, 12.
[5] *Breviarium Hipponense*, (P.L. lxvi, 418). [6] *Serm.* 252, 1.
[7] *Enarr. in Ps.* 54, 18; cf. *Serm.* 46, 15. [8] *Brev. Hippon.* xii, (P.L. lxvi, 424/5).
[9] *Brev. Hippon.* xiv, (P.L. lxvi, 425). [10] *Ep.* 52, 4.

Augustine and his colleagues between 393 and 405. In this period, the only 'movement' came from on top: it is the sudden self-assertion of the Catholic Church and the hardening of the Imperial authority against all non-Catholics in Africa. We shall trace the full course of a vicious circle only too familiar in modern history — doctrinaire persecution from above, which, in turn, can only be resisted by mounting violence from below.[1]

Augustine took the field as the voice of the Catholic Church. His polemic against the Donatists betrays an unsuspected flair for journalism.[2] His caricature of contemporary Donatism is put together with such an eye for circumstantial detail, that it is far too often accepted at its face value, even today. At the time, however, it formed part of a use of propaganda unparalleled in the history of the African church. For Augustine publicized theological arguments in the form of a commentary on contemporary events, constantly repeated and simplified for a semi-literate audience.[3] He sensed the popular tone of the controversy, and exploited it with gusto. He will begin his campaign by writing a popular song;[4] and he will tell his readers, among many other titbits of provincial gossip, of how an elderly bishop was once made to dance upon his own altar-table, with dead dogs tied around his neck.[5]

In this way, Augustine exploited the problems which had faced the Donatists in their position of dominance. In 394–395, for instance, they had successfully suppressed a schism of their own, that of the followers of Maximian.[6] In doing this, they had appealed to Imperial laws against heretics, in order to regain the basilicas held by the Maximianist bishops; and they had re-absorbed these bishops without rebaptizing them. Augustine laboured every detail of this incident.[7] While the Donatists could not absorb their own schismatics without appearing inconsistent, the Catholics could.[8] Their forcible solution of the Maximianist schism provided Augustine with an ominous precedent: it was a 'mirror'[9] in which the Donatist might contemplate the fate that his own church deserved from the hands of the Catholics.[10]

Both churches, by that time, had a record of violence. The Catholics

[1] v. Brown, 'Religious Coercion in the Later Roman Empire: the Case of North Africa', *History*, xlviii, 1963, pp. 283–305, esp. pp. 295–297, and Tengström, *Donatisten u. Katholiken*, esp. pp. 66–90.

[2] Augustine had to justify this journalistic approach: v. *Enarr. iii in Ps.* 36, 18.

[3] e.g. *Ps. c. Don.* 79 sq. and *Retract.* II, 55.   [4] v. sup. p. 141.

[5] *C. Ep. Parm.* III, vi, 29.   [6] v. Frend, *Donatist Church*, pp. 213–214.

[7] v. the excellent treatment of A. C. de Veer, 'L'exploitation du schisme maximianiste par S. Augustin dans sa lutte contre le Donatisme', *Rech. augustin.*, iii, 1965, pp. 219–237.

[8] *C. litt. Petil.* II, xx, 44.   [9] *C. Crescon.* III, lviii, 69.

[10] v. *Enarr. ii in Ps.* 36, 19; and *Enarr. in Ps.* 57, 15.

were fatally implicated in their record of persecution at the 'Time of Macarius'; and Augustine could get round this awkward memory only by publicizing the sporadic brutalities of an extreme wing of the Donatist church, the Circumcellions.[1] This strange movement resembled the marabouts or dervishes of modern North Africa: bands of holy men and women moving through the country-villages on an endless pilgrimage, keeping alive the memory of the martyrs at enthusiastic gatherings around their whitewashed shrines[2] — a combination of gipsy and itinerant Hot Gospeller.[3] Any attempt by Augustine and his colleagues to upset the *status quo* by sending preachers to Donatist areas, and later by using force against Donatist churches, was held in check by such bands. Compared with the mounting pressure of the Catholic persecutions, the violence of the Circumcellions would always seem erratic and aimless; and in Hippo at any rate, such violence reached a climax only as an answer to the use of force by the Catholics.[4] But such incidents 'made headlines'. They will ensure that Augustine's account of Donatism came to be perpetuated by tales of 'atrocities', as shocking as those reported, vividly, and it must be added, avidly, by English newspapers at the time of the Irish peasant agitation of the last century: barns and churches destroyed;[5] the brutal and ingenious maiming of renegades from 'The Cause';[6] the midnight descent of the armed gang on an isolated cottage.[7]

Whatever Augustine might write about the Donatist church at large, in Hippo, at least, he was faced at the outset by a situation resembling a Cold War: 'You hold on to what you have got; you have your sheep, I have mine; don't you interfere with my sheep; I don't interfere with yours.'[8] Augustine, therefore, wished to take the initiative without incurring the odium of appearing the aggressor. Thus his letters to neighbouring Donatist bishops are scrupulously polite; but they are like the diplomatic notes of one Great Power to another in a Cold War. Augustine will wait until he has a legitimate grievance; armed with this grievance, he will offer a conference; and he will imply that if a conference is refused, he will feel free to let the world know his side of the case.[9] It is hardly surprising, that the local Donatists rejected such transparently diplomatic approaches.

---

[1] e.g. *Enarr. in Ps.* 10, 5.

[2] W. H. C. Frend, 'The *cellae* of the African Circumcellions', *Journ. Theol. Studies*, n.s., iii, 1952, pp. 87–89, is the most revealing treatment of this aspect of the movement.

[3] On this exceedingly complex, and obscure, subject, v. most recently, Tengström, *Donatisten u. Katholiken*, pp. 24–78.

[4] v. inf. p. 241.   [5] *Ep.* 111, 1.   [6] *Ep.* 105, ii, 3.

[7] *Ep.* 108, vi, 19.   [8] *Enarr. in Ps.* 21, 31.   [9] e.g. *Epp.* 23; 33; 34; 35; 49; 51.

On one occasion however, in 397, Augustine and Alypius were able to visit Fortunius, the elderly Donatist bishop of Thubursicum Bure.[1] They were welcomed by an excited crowd, and the two rivals parted on good terms; and Augustine admitted that, 'in my opinion, you will have difficulty in finding among your bishops another whose judgement and feelings are so sound as we have seen that old man's to be'.[2]

Such encounters were rare, and they were only possible in the small world of Augustine's diocese. He had to allay the suspicions of his neighbours, if he was to make any headway with his rivals. He would, for instance, solemnly disown any intention of resorting again to the use of force, as in the 'Time of Macarius'.[3] This diplomatic concession would later embarrass Augustine.[4] For, in those years, and especially from 399 to 401, he had paid frequent visits to Carthage. Here he would have found himself in a less quiet world, and would move among more ruthless men. Above all, he would have been directly affected by the political excitements of that time.

In 398, a local usurper, Gildo, the Moorish Count of Africa, was suppressed by the Emperor Honorius. The atmosphere of a 'purge' hung heavily over the reconquered province. Nothing was too bad to say about the unsuccessful rebel and his associates. A Donatist bishop, Optatus of Timgad, the *doyen* of the Donatist church in Numidia, had been one of Gildo's adherents.[5] As the bishop of a town of military importance, it is hardly surprising that Optatus had paid court to Gildo.[6] But it is typical of Augustine's ruthless journalism, that the Donatist bishop should be made to appear as a close ally of a man about whom everyone could now safely echo the official propaganda in calling him 'a most monstrous enemy of the Roman order'.[7]

The successful Emperor, Honorius, was a devout Catholic: his troops had even considered themselves protected by the ghost of S. Ambrose.[8] The new Count of Africa was expected to choose his friends more carefully: no Donatist bishop, but Severus, Catholic bishop of Milevis, an intimate friend of Augustine, would dine at his table.[9]

The first religious group to feel the effects of this sudden hardening of authority, were not, however, the Donatists. Paganism, quite as

---

[1] *Ep.* 44. [2] *Ep.* 44, vi, 13. [3] *Ep.* 23, 7. [4] *Retract.* II, 5.

[5] *Ep.* 76, 3; *C. litt. Petil.* II, xcii, 209.

[6] Frend, *Donatist Church*, pp. 208–229, seems to exaggerate the significance of this 'alliance'; v. E. Tengström, *Donatisten u. Katholiken*, pp. 75–77 and 84–90.

[7] *C. Ep. Parm.* I, xi, 17; compare Claudian, *De Bello Gildonico*, esp. i, 94, (ed. Platnauer, Loeb, i, p. 104).

[8] Orosius, *Hist.* vii, 36. [9] *de civ. Dei* XXI, 4, 92.

much as Donatism, was the traditional enemy of the Catholic bishops. Early in 399, special Imperial agents arrived in Africa to close pagan shrines.[1] Religious riots broke out: in Sufes, some 60 Christians were killed;[2] in the countryside, the Catholic mobs showed themselves quite as violent in 'cleansing' the great estates of pagan shrines, as had the Circumcellions.[3] Augustine and his colleagues stood at the centre of this storm. In Carthage, he would preach to great crowds amid cheers of 'Down with the Roman gods'.[4] It is the first time we see him, a peace-loving man, intensely sensitive to violence, thoroughly caught up in the excitement which his own passionate certainty had done so much to provoke. For the Catholic church had shown once again, that it was the only body in Africa that had the legal recognition of the Emperor: 'You must know, my friends, how the mutterings (of the pagans) join with those of heretics and Jews. Heretics, Jews and pagans — they have come to form a unity over against our Unity.'[5]

Many leading pagans found it advisable to conform to the Catholic Church. One such, Faustinus, wished in this way to gain office in Carthage. Yet in a sermon of considerable charm, Augustine will invite his congregation to accept even such a transparently politic conversion.[6] Sermons such as this are a 'dress rehearsal' of Augustine's later justification of the forced conversion of Donatist communities. It is hardly surprising, therefore, that a Donatist observer, Petilian, bishop of Cirta, would now dismiss the continued offers of negotiation from the Catholics as mere 'war waged with kisses'.[7]

This excitement, indeed, affected Augustine deeply. He felt that he lived at a long-foretold turning-point of history. For centuries, the pagan Emperors had persecuted the Church; within a generation, these same Emperors had uprooted the vast edifice of gods which the Romans had spread over the world.[8] It had all happened, he said, '*valde velociter*' — 'extremely fast'.[9] Reading his Bible, Augustine had come to see the events around him as part of an ineluctable process, foretold a thousand years before, by David in the Psalms, and by the prophets of Israel.[10] The Catholic Church had spread throughout the world: 'it was written; it has come true.'[11] It was the same with the Roman

---

[1] *de civ. Dei* XVIII, 54.   [2] *Ep.* 50.   [3] *Serm.* 62, 13.   [4] *Serm.* 24, 6.

[5] *Serm.* 62, 18; v. Brown, 'St. Augustine's Attitude to Religious Coercion', *Journ. Rom. Studies*, liv, 1964, pp. 107–116, at pp. 109–110.

[6] *Morin* i, (*Misc. Agostin.* i, pp. 589–93).   [7] *C. litt. Petil.* II, xvii, 38.

[8] *Serm.* 24, 6.   [9] *Enarr. in Ps.* 6, 13.   [10] *Enarr. in Ps.* 62, 1.

[11] v. *Ep.* 232 and *C. Faust.* XIII, 7, (written at about this time; this is the principal argument used to impress a pagan).

Emperors. They also had learnt to 'serve the Lord with fear and trembling', by suppressing the enemies of His Church.[1]

Thus, when Augustine published his first long tract against the Donatists, at just this time, probably at Carthage, he had already come a long way from his first tactful moves as a local figure in Hippo. The Christian Emperor had a right to punish 'impieties'. The storm cloud of a forcible suppression of Donatism might still be distant; but its outline was clearly visible.[2] The most ominous feature of this tract was the deadly sense of urgency betrayed by its author: 'The mass of men keep their heart in their eyes, not in their heart. If blood comes spurting out of the flesh of a mortal man, anyone who sees it is disgusted; but if souls lopped off from the peace of Christ die in this sacrilege of schism or heresy . . . a death that is more terrifying and more tragic, indeed, I say plainly, a more true death than any other — it is laughed at, out of force of habit.'[3]

[1] v. esp. *Enarr. iii in Ps.* 32, 9 sq.   [2] *C. Ep. Parm.* I, viii, 15–x, 16.
[3] *C. Ep. Parm.* I, viii, 14.

21

DISCIPLINA

Thirty years had passed since Augustine first came to Carthage as a student. Now, in 403, he arrived as a famous man, well-hated by his enemies. 'For what am I?' he told the Catholic congregation, 'Am *I* the Catholic Church? . . . It is enough for me to be within it. You (Donatists) slander my past evil ways. You think this a great thing to do, do you? I am more severe on my own misdeeds than ever you have been. You raked them up: I have condemned them. These belong to the past. They are all known, especially in this town. . . . Whatever I was then, that is past, in the Name of Christ. What they now criticize in me, they know nothing of. O, there are many things in me which they could fasten on: it would thrill them to know about them! Much still happens in my thoughts — fighting against my evil promptings, a day-long tension; the Enemy almost continuously wishing to make me fall. . . .

'Brothers, say to the Donatists just this: "Here is Augustine . . . a bishop in the Catholic Church. . . . What I have learnt to look to, above all, is the Catholic Church. I shall not put my trust in any man." '[1]

The Donatists had been ruthless in defending themselves. Converts to Catholicism among their clergy were, especially, treated without mercy. The bishop of Bagai was set upon and left for dead by the congregation he had deserted to become a Catholic. Towards the end of 404, he had set out on his own initiative to seek retribution from the Imperial court.[2] Faced with such violences, many of Augustine's colleagues wanted a quick and firm solution, similar to the persecution of Count Macarius.[3] Alypius may even have come to stand against Augustine on this issue.[4]

Augustine did not want to go so far. He was no liberal. Even his

---

[1] *Enarr. iii in Ps.* 36, 19. [2] Frend, *Donatist Church*, pp. 262–263.
[3] *Ep.* 93, v, 16–17. [4] In citing the example of Thagaste: *Ep.* 93, v, 16.

early disclaimers of a wish to persecute were dictated more by diplomacy than by principle. But he was a very conscientious bishop; and, in 404, he still did not think that the Catholic Church could absorb the Donatist congregations which it might win by force. There would be too many *ficti* — too many 'feigned' Catholics.[1] At Hippo, he felt that the quality of his own congregation had already been seriously diluted by the semi-pagans who had joined the church *en masse*, when Christianity became the established religion.[2] They had brought with them the primitive rites, such as feasting the dead, which Augustine had combated ten years before as a priest.[3] Thus, he had every reason to view with genuine reluctance the prospect of this steady trickle of pagan 'hypocrisy', turned into a flood of resentful Donatists, used to becoming solemnly drunk on the feast-days of their martyrs.

Such prudent arguments could still prevail in the Catholic Council of 404:[4] the bishops only asked for police-protection.[5] But the bishop of Bagai had already reached the Imperial court with an independent story of 'atrocities'.[6] By June 405 a drastic 'Edict of Unity' was posted to Carthage: the Donatists were branded as 'heretics', and so brought under general laws against heresy.[7]

For all its bombast, this Edict was faithful to the general principle of Roman legislation on religion. It touched only externals. No Donatist, as yet, was forced to join the Catholic Church. Rather, the Donatist Church was 'disbanded', like a modern political party that has been declared illegal. The Donatist bishop would be removed, his church would be taken over by the Catholics; and Augustine would be faced with the unpleasant and arduous task of absorbing a leaderless congregation.[8]

Augustine, characteristically, accepted the change of policy which this Edict involved as an act of Providence.[9] Earlier in the year, he had

---

[1] *Ep.* 93, v, 17. v. Brown, 'St. Augustine's Attitude', *Journ. Rom. Studies*, liv, 1964, p. 111.

[2] e.g. *Serm.* 10, 4; *Enarr. in Ps.* 7, 9. The motives of such a pagan are vividly described in *Serm.* 47, 17.

[3] *Ep.* 29, 9.

[4] *Commonitorium* of the Council of 404, (P.L. xi, 1203C). The Emperors are asked not to apply the laws depriving heretics of legal rights lest they provoke feigned conversions among prospective litigants.

[5] *ibid.* P.L. xi, 1202–1204.   [6] *Ep.* 88, 7.

[7] Principally *Cod. Theod.* XVI, 5, 38; 6, 4–5 and 11, 2, (in P.L. xi, 1208–1211). v. Frend, *Donatist Church*, pp. 263–265.

[8] v. esp. Brown, 'Religious Coercion', *History*, xlviii, 1963, pp. 285–7 and 292–3.

[9] *Ep.* 185, vii, 26.

even written to Paulinus on the way in which God 'speaks' through events beyond one's control.[1] In fact, Augustine had already moved half of the way towards accepting coercion as a means of solving the Donatist schism; and the new circumstances created by the Edict merely crystallized an attitude which had been evolving for a long time. But the new policy had to be defended, aggressively, against a coherent and easily-understood battery of criticism, manned with equal zeal by leading Donatist bishops[2] and by simple schoolmasters:[3] that it was unheard-of for a Christian to advocate a policy of persecution;[4] that Augustine had gone back on his word.[5] Augustine, in replying to his persistent critics, wrote the only full justification, in the history of the Early Church, of the right of the state to suppress non-Catholics.

Some profound and ominous changes had taken place in Augustine's attitude to the church and society in his first ten years as a bishop. His ideas on grace and predestination, for instance, had grown more deeply-rooted in him. He would fall back on them now, to palliate the situation in which he found himself. He had to absorb communities of reluctant Donatists: but he could reassure himself with the belief, that God's grace was able to bring about a change of heart even in men who had been forced into the Catholic Church. He would, therefore, leave the problem of feigned conversions to God: to object to the Catholic policy because it provoked such feigned conversions became, in his opinion, tantamount to denying the 'Power of God',[6] Who would seek out His own among the masses who had conformed with a bad grace to the Catholic church.

Theory and practice had gone hand in hand to reinforce Augustine's change of mind. When he returned from Italy, fifteen years previously, Augustine had found the average African community alien, and so 'indigestible'. But he had grown more used to the customs and habits of mind which were common to the rank and file of both churches and so the task of absorption did not seem quite as difficult.[7]

Furthermore, when Augustine had become a priest he had retained some optimism about the power of man's free will: the act of faith was still an act of conscious choice, and so it was dependent upon human

---

[1] *Ep.* 80, 3.

[2] Petilian of Cirta in *C. litt. Petil.* II, lxxix, 175–xcvii, 223, (Monceaux, *Hist. littér.*, v, cc. 46–58, pp. 323–326).

[3] Cresconius the *grammaticus*; v. esp. *C. Crescon.* III, li, 57.

[4] *C. litt. Petil.* II, xciii, 214.   [5] Implied in *Ep.* 93, i, 1 and v, 17.

[6] *C. Gaud.* xxv, 28; cf. *Ep.* 89, 7 and *C. mend.* vi, 11.

[7] Brown, 'St. Augustine's Attitude', *Journ. Rom. Studies*, liv, 1964, p. 111.

agencies, such as correct and reasonable instruction. He had attempted to reform popular piety at this time, because he believed that by persuasion[1] and by removing habits that gave rise to false opinions,[2] he might turn a congregation of unthinking Christians into good, 'spiritual' Catholics.[3] Now he was less sure. There seemed to be a great disparity between human circumstances and intentions, and the invincible purpose of an omnipotent God. The ability of the Catholic church to expand rapidly, by force if needs be, came to depend less on what a mere, conscientious bishop might judge to be practicable. For the backbone of this church had come to consist in an unfathomable relationship between God and the 'defined number' of His elect: in whatever way these elect entered the concrete, imperfect Church on earth, '*God is able to graft them in again.*'[4]

For a Donatist, Augustine's attitude to coercion was a blatant denial of traditional Christian teaching: God had made men free to choose good or evil; a policy which forced this choice was plainly irreligious.[5] The Donatist writers quoted the same passages from the Bible in favour of free will, as Pelagius would later quote.[6] In his reply, Augustine already gave them the same answer as he would give to the Pelagians: the final, individual act of choice must be spontaneous; but this act of choice could be prepared by a long process, which men did not necessarily choose for themselves, but which was often imposed on them, against their will, by God.[7] This was a corrective process of 'teaching', *eruditio*, and warning, *admonitio*, which might even include fear, constraint, and external inconvenience: 'Let constraint be found outside; it is inside that the will is born.'[8]

Augustine had become convinced that men needed such firm handling. He summed up his attitude in one word: *disciplina*. He thought of this *disciplina*, not as many of his more traditional Roman contemporaries did, as the static preservation of a 'Roman way of life'.[9] For him it was an essentially active process of corrective punishment, a

---

[1] e.g. *de mor. eccl. cath.* (I), xxxiv, 76.   [2] *Ep.* 22, 3.   [3] *Ep.* 29, 4 and *Serm.* 5, 4.
[4] *Rom.* 12, 23; *Ep.* 87, 9, (used, previously, in relation to Donatist ordinations, *Ep.* 61, 2); cf. *Ep.* 98, 5.
[5] *C. litt. Petil.* II, lxxxiv, 185; *Coll. Carthag.* iii, 258, (P.L. xi, 1413C); *C. Gaud.* xix, 20.
[6] e.g. *Eccles.* 15, 17–18 in *C. litt. Petil.* II, lxxxiv, 185, and *Eccles.* 15, 14 in *C. Gaud.* xix, 20; cf. de Plinval, *Pélage*, p. 94.
[7] v. esp. *C. litt. Petil.* II, lxxxiv, 185.
[8] *Serm.* 112, 8. v. Brown, 'St. Augustine's Attitude', *Journ. Rom. Studies*, liv, 1964, pp. 111–112.
[9] v. esp. W. Dürig, 'Disciplina: Eine Studie z. Bedeutungsumfang des Wortes i.d. Sprache d. Liturgie u. d. Väter', *Sacris Erudiri*, 4, 1952, pp. 245–279.

'softening-up process', a 'teaching by inconveniences' — a *per molestias eruditio*.[1] In the Old Testament, God had taught His wayward Chosen People through just such a process of *disciplina*, checking and punishing their evil tendencies by a whole series of divinely-ordained disasters.[2] The persecution of the Donatists was another 'controlled catastrophe' imposed by God, mediated, on this occasion, by the laws of Christian Emperors;[3] in Augustine's mind, it was no more than a special instance of the relationship of the human race as a whole, to its stern Father, who would 'whip the son He receives',[4] and indiscriminately enough at that; like the man who beat his family every Saturday night 'just in case'.[5]

Furthermore, the situation of the Catholic Church in Africa, placed by force at the head of unwilling communities, had come close to that of the People of Israel under the 'yoke' of the Law of Moses. Augustine insisted that the Law, also, had been imposed on the majority of the Israelites, quite frankly, by force: they had been compelled, by fear, to remain in a compact unity under the Law, even though the Law's significance had been understood and loved by only the very few 'spiritual' men among them.[6] Yet Augustine regarded this blatantly coercive régime as having fulfilled an important function: the Jews had been deterred from the worse sins of polytheism; and it was only among the Jews at Jerusalem, the centre of the physical, enforced unity of the old Israel, that the 'spiritual' unity of the Church had been distilled, at Pentecost.[7]

As for the severities and violent deeds with which the Law had been upheld in the Old Testament, such incidents had long ceased to shock Augustine. He had excused them, against the Manichees, years before he would cite them as precedents for persecution against the Donatists.[8] He had changed his mind on one point only. Ten years previously, he had thought that the ages before the coming of Christianity had belonged to a more primitive 'stage of moral evolution';[9] and that, in his own days, Christianity was a purely 'spiritual' religion. It had risen entirely above the physical sanctions and the enforced observances of

---

[1] *Enarr. xvii in Ps.* 118, 2; cf. *Ep.* 93, ii, 4. v. esp. A. M. La Bonnardière, *Recherches de chronologie augustinienne*, 1965, p. 36 and 37 n. 3.

[2] *Ep.* 173, 3, cf. *Enarr. in Ps.* 136, 9; *Tract. in Joh.* 5, 2.   [3] *Ep.* 105, iv, 12–13.

[4] *Prov.* 3, 12.   [5] e.g. *de urbis excidio*, 1. v. inf. p. 293.

[6] *de serm. Dom. in Monte*, I, xx, 64; *de util. cred.* iii, 9; *Ep. ad Gal. expos.* 22; *Enarr. in Ps.* 138, 28.

[7] *de doct. christ.* III, vi, 10.

[8] e.g. *de serm. Dom. in Monte*, I, xx, 63–65; *C. Adim.* 17; *C. Faust.* XXII, 20, cf. *Ep.* 44, iv, 9.

[9] *de div. qu.* lxxxiii, 53; cf. *C. Faust.* XXII, 23.

that 'shadowy' past.[1] Now Augustine was no longer so sure. The 'spiritual' element might be predominant in the Catholic Church; but he now felt that its unity had come to embrace a vast number of 'carnal' men, who lived at exactly the same moral level as the ancient Israelites, and so would still only respond to fear.[2] This was a profoundly pessimistic conclusion. The history of mankind now showed no obvious sign of an irreversible ascent, by 'stages', towards a 'spiritual' religion: the human race still lay, 'like a great invalid',[3] at all times in need of what a great Liberal historian once called, with great distaste, 'the plaster of Paris' of authority.[4]

Augustine's view of the Fall of mankind determined his attitude to society. Fallen men had come to need restraint. Even man's greatest achievements had been made possible only by a 'strait-jacket' of unremitting harshness. Augustine was a great intellect, with a healthy respect for the achievements of human reason. Yet he was obsessed by the difficulties of thought, and by the long, coercive processes, reaching back into the horrors of his own schooldays, that had made this intellectual activity possible; so 'ready to lie down'[5] was the fallen human mind. He said he would rather die than become a child again. Nonetheless, the terrors of that time had been strictly necessary; for they were part of the awesome discipline of God, 'from the school-masters' canes to the agonies of the martyrs,' by which human beings were recalled, by suffering, from their own disastrous inclinations.[6]

The test of such an attitude is what Augustine thought might happen if ever the pressures of society were relaxed: 'the reins placed on human licence would be loosened and thrown off: all sins would go unpunished. Take away the barriers created by the laws! Men's brazen capacity to do harm, their urge to self-indulgence would rage to the full. No king in his Kingdom, no general with his troops, ... no husband with his wife, nor father with his son, would attempt to put a stop, by any threats or punishments, to the freedom and the sheer sweet taste of sinning.'[7] A man who had recently analysed, with evident fascination and horror, the strength of the motives that had once led him, in his teens, to a quite gratuitous act of vandalism by stealing pears, would not be likely to underestimate the dangerous force of the 'sweet taste of sinning'.[8]

---

[1] *de vera relig.* xxvi, 48–49. v. Brown, 'St. Augustine's Attitude', *Journ. Rom. Studies*, liv, 1964, pp. 112–114.

[2] e.g. *de Bapt.* I, xv, 23–24; *Serm.* 4, 12; *de cat. rud.* xix, 33.   [3] *C. Faust.* XXXII, 14.

[4] H. A. L. Fisher, *History of Europe*, 1936, Preface.   [5] *de civ. Dei* XXII, 22, 34.

[6] *Conf.* I, xiv, 23.   [7] *C. Gaud.* XIX, 20; cf. *Ep. ad cath.* XX, 53.

[8] v. sup. p. 172.

This oppressive sense of the need for restraint may alarm a modern man more than it did Augustine's contemporaries. What shocked the Donatists, however, was the way in which Augustine seemed prepared to break down the barriers, firmly fixed in the imagination of the average Early Christian, between the 'sacred' and the 'profane', between the purely spiritual sanctions exercised by the Christian bishop within the Church, and the manifold (and at times, horrific) pressures of Roman society, as administered by the Emperors.[1]

True to their defensive attitude, the Donatists were not hostile to the State; they just thought they could ignore it in what mattered most, in the preservation of an untainted Divine Law.[2] The bishop filled their narrow horizons: he was the only proper source of alms,[3] of exhortation, of spiritual penalties.[4] God, they said, had sent prophets, not kings, to warn the people of Israel;[5] for 'in the Church alone should the commands of the Law be taught to the people of God'.[6]

Augustine, by contrast, had as much as admitted that man, in his fallen state, required more than purely spiritual pressures to keep him from evil.[7] A part of his power as a bishop to 'warn' wayward sheep among the Christians of Africa had been devolved on the 'terror' of Imperial laws; and the 'Apostolic discipline'[8] of the bishop had been diffused throughout society, from Emperors issuing laws, to heads of families flogging their Donatist dependants into submission to the Catholic Church.[9]

It may be that first impressions had been the most lasting for Augustine. His first contact with the disciplinary aspects of Catholicism had been through the lay fanaticism of his mother: it was Monica, not the local bishop, who had 'excommunicated' Augustine, as a young Manichee, by refusing to have him with her in her house.[10] Altogether, this was an ominous change: for given the studied generality of Augustine's comments on the 'restraining' and 'warning' functions of human society as a whole, it would be difficult for his successors to

[1] e.g. Gaudentius, Donatist bishop of Timgad, draws the distinction firmly: *C. Gaud.* xxiv, 27.

[2] v. esp. W. H. C. Frend, 'The Roman Empire in the eyes of Western Schismatics during the 4th century', *Miscellanea Historiae Ecclesiasticae*, 1961, pp. 9–22.

[3] This is the precise occasion of the famous remark of Donatus,'What has the Emperor to do with the Church?': the Emperor had distributed alms on his own initiative. Optatus of Milevis *de schism. Don.* III, 3, (P.L. xi, 998–1000).

[4] *C. Ep. Parm.* I, x, 16. [5] *C. Gaud.* xxxiv, 44. [6] *C. Crescon,* I, x, 13.

[7] *Ep.* 89, 7, 'human authority'; cf. *Enarr. in Ps.* 149, 14. [8] *Serm.* 94.

[9] e.g. *Serm.* 182, 2; 302, 19; cf. *Enarr. in Ps.* 85, 16. For direct pressures applied by landowners, v. sup. pp. 192–193.

[10] *Conf.* III, xi, 19; cf. *C. Ep. Parm.* III, ii, 16.

distinguish between the strictly religious forces making for the unity of the Catholic Church and the social pressures that would buttress this unity in a nominally Christian society.

Augustine may be the first theorist of the Inquisition;[1] but he was in no position to be a Grand Inquisitor. For unlike a bishop of the Middle Ages, he was not bent on maintaining the *status quo* in a totally Christian society. He was faced not by small sects, feared and hated by the whole community, but by a body of Christians as large as his own congregation, and in many ways very similar to it. Thus, for Augustine, religious coercion remained a genuinely corrective treatment: it was a brusque way of winning over 'hardened' rivals, rather than an attempt to stamp out a small minority. He had to remain tactful and conscientious: 'For if they were only being terrorized, and not instructed at the same time, this would be an inexcusable tyranny on our part.'[2] Any other interpretation of his duties in such a situation shocked Augustine deeply. A Spanish priest, Consentius, who was frightened by a 'fifth column' of heresy in his church, later wrote to Augustine to ask whether he would approve of the use of *agents provocateurs* to obtain the names of heretics. Augustine was furious at this 'ingenious hunting with lies' . . . 'instead of being snared with falsehoods, it would be easier for their error to be uprooted by truthful arguments; and it is up to you to get down to writing these'.[3]

After 405 indeed, Augustine had practised what he would preach to Consentius. Many of his colleagues managed at one and the same time to be efficient suppressors of Donatism and great scoundrels.[4] The Catholic bishop of Hippo Diarrhytos (Bizerte), kept his rival in jail for years and tried to have him executed.[5] He even built an enlarged basilica, named after himself, to celebrate this famous victory; and Augustine would preach at its dedication — so close did he find himself to ruthless men![6] At Hippo, however, Augustine was free to act in character: he covered the walls of the Donatist basilica with posters stating, yet again, the eminent reasonableness of his case.[7]

Despite Augustine's conscientious behaviour, violence could not be avoided. The Imperial laws fell erratically on African society. They drove a wedge between rich and poor, town and countryside. The Donatists lost their bishops and the support of the upper classes.[8] One

[1] v. esp. H. Maisonneuve, 'Croyance religieuse et contrainte: la doctrine de S. Augustin', *Mél. de science relig.* xix, 1962, pp. 49–68.
[2] *Ep.* 93, ii, 3. [3] *C. mend.* vi, 11. [4] *Ep.* 85 (to bishop Paulus).
[5] *Coll. Carthag.* i, 142, (P.L. xi, 1318A). [6] *Serm.* 359.
[7] *Retract.* ii, 27; v. Brown, 'Religious Coercion', *History*, xlviii, 1963, p. 293.
[8] v. Brown, 'Religious Coercion', *History*, xlviii, 1963, pp. 290–292.

landowner, Celer, had had poems inscribed in his honour in the forum.[1] Now he found that, as a Donatist, he could not hold office, that he could not protect his property by litigation nor pass it on to his heirs by valid testament.[2] After 405 therefore, such men found it wise to conform to the established religion. The pressures of a common social life, of mixed marriages, of respectability, which, in more tolerant days, had militated against Augustine and in favour of the Donatists, now brought the leading citizens of Hippo to heel around Augustine, as the Catholic bishop, supported by Catholic Emperors.[3]

Outside Hippo, it was different. The Donatists had established a numerous and obstreperous country clergy in the estates and villages around Hippo. These priests would now ally with the Circumcellions to meet force with force. Circumcellion terrorism kept the Donatist churches open throughout the 'Penal Days'.[4] When the Donatist bishop, Macrobius, reappeared in Hippo, around 409, he had plainly been forced for four years to live as an outlaw in the primitive villages of his diocese: he now arrived at the head of a mob of countrymen whose language he did not even speak.[5] It was a strange fate to have befallen a respectable and well-educated citizen of Hippo!

For the towns, therefore, the new policy may have taken a course not very different from that outlined so plausibly by Augustine: the laws imposed external 'inconveniences', such as would make respectable men think twice before remaining Donatists; they would have merely tipped the balance in favour of Augustine. Outside Hippo, however, religious coercion had been met by violence; and the dissolution of the Donatist church threatened to degenerate into the bloody repression of a peasants' revolt in embryo.[6] Catholic landowners would not trouble to hand Circumcellions over to Augustine to be 'instructed': they merely dealt with them on the spot 'like any brigands'.[7] Imperial officials, also, moved by a primitive, Roman horror of 'sacrilege', would automatically impose the death penalty on Donatists convicted of mutilating priests or destroying churches.[8]

Augustine opposed the death-penalty in principle, for it excluded the possibility of repentance.[9] He also wished to avoid it for tactical reasons: the wave of murders had provided the Catholics with authentic martyrs; he had no wish to bestow a similar opportunity for

---

[1] *Epp.* 56, 57 and 139, 2; v. Marec, *Hippone*, p. 77.

[2] The career of Romanianus shows how much a well-to-do African needed to defend his property by litigation and by visits to the Imperial court: v. also *Serm.* 107, 8.

[3] e.g. Celer, sup. n. 65, and Donatus, *Ep.* 112, 3.

[4] *Ep.* 108, v, 18.

[5] *Ep.* 108, v, 14.

[6] v. esp. *Ep.* 108, v, 18.

[7] *Ep.* 88, 9.

[8] *Epp.* 133; 134; 139, 1–2.

[9] e.g. *Ep.* 153, 18.

righteous suffering on his rivals.[1] A passionate and shrewd letter written to the Proconsul of Africa in 408, shows Augustine's high principles; but it also betrays his inability to put a halt to many executions.[2]

The Imperial laws, however, had one unexpected result for Augustine. They forced him to the fore, for the first time, as an influential local figure. As Catholic bishop, it was he who would administer the property of the Donatist churches; he would draw up lists of Donatists; he would receive them, personally, as converts; he would be constantly busy ensuring that the laws were applied.[3] For some of his colleagues, this was a lonely and dangerous eminence. Possidius, as we shall see, tried to use his new authority under the Imperial laws to suppress a pagan public procession in Calama: when he was attacked by a pagan crowd, his congregation quietly stood aside — they plainly thought that their bishop and his clergy had over-reached themselves.[4]

Augustine, by contrast, gained from this change. It was now over a decade since, as a priest, he had debated with Fortunatus the Manichee. Then the two former friends had met on neutral ground, in a public bath-hall, in front of an audience of all religions.[5] Now, when another Manichee, Felix, arrived in Hippo, Augustine will meet him from his bishop's throne in the apse of the Catholic basilica. Augustine will address him, not only as a debater, but rather like a Justice of the Peace. 'I cannot do much against your power' Felix replied, 'for the bishop's position is wonderfully powerful. . . .'[6]

Augustine had changed. Around 408 he was challenged by a distant correspondent, Vincentius of Cartennae (Ténès), to justify his present views on coercion.[7] More was at stake, in that letter, than a theory of persecution: it was the quality of Augustine's distant past. For the two men had been students together in Carthage. Augustine the Manichee (for the only Father of the Church to write at length on persecution had himself been a member of a persecuted sect), had become Catholic bishop in Hippo. Vincentius had returned even farther West, to become the leader of a Donatist splinter-group, the sect of Rogatus. 'I knew you, my excellent friend' Vincentius wrote, 'as a man dedicated to peace and uprightness, when you were far removed from the Christian

[1] *Ep.* 139, 2.

[2] *Ep.* 100; v. Brown, 'Religious Coercion', *History*, xlviii, 1963, pp. 300–301.

[3] v. Brown, 'Religious Coercion', *History*, xlviii, 1963, pp. 302–304.

[4] *Ep.* 91, 8 and 10. v. inf. p. 288.   [5] v. sup. p. 141.

[6] *Gesta cum Felice*, i, 12; v. Brown, 'Religious Coercion', *History*, xlviii, 1963, pp. 304–305.

[7] *Ep.* 93.

faith. In those days you were occupied with literary pursuits. But since your conversion, I am told . . . you have come to devote all your time and energy to theological controversies.'[1]

Augustine was now an ageing man. 'You know me now', he replied 'to yearn even more for rest and to be more earnest in seeking it than when you knew me in my young days in Carthage.'[2] We catch a glimpse of Augustine, at just this time, in a long, depressed letter to Paulinus of Nola:

'What shall I say as to the infliction and remission of punishment in cases where we have no other desire but to forward the spiritual welfare of those we have to decide whether or not to punish? . . . What trembling we feel in these things, my brother, Paulinus, O holy man of God! What trembling, what darkness! May we not think that with reference to such things it was said: *Fearfulness and trembling are come over me, and horror overwhelmed me. And I said: "O that I had wings like a dove; for then I would fly away and be at rest."* '[3]

---

[1] *Ep.* 93, xiii, 51. [2] *Ep.* 93, i, 1. [3] *Ep.* 95, 3.

22

POPULUS DEI[1]

Augustine preached to men who thought they knew what the Christian life consisted of. The world in which they lived was situated 'in the lowest depths of the universe',[2] a tiny pocket of disorder beneath the harmonious stars.[3] This world was ruled by hostile 'powers', above all, by the 'Lord of this world', the Devil.[4] The Christian, therefore, found himself committed to a wrestling-match, an *agon*. The ring was clearly defined: it was the 'world', the *mundus*. The enemy was specific and external to him, the Devil, his angels and their human agents. The 'training' provided by his church had equipped the Christian for the due reward of victory in any competition — a 'crown', in the next world.[5] Simple men in the time of Augustine would still die for their beliefs, inspired by such ideas: Donatist martyrs would have visions of crowns;[6] they would dream of fighting a wrestling match of horrible violence;[7] they would long to escape from this 'double prison, the flesh and the world'.[8]

Augustine never questioned the broad outlines of these beliefs. The idea of a world cut off from perfection, and shared by human beings with hostile 'powers', was part of the 'religious topography'[9] of all Late Antique men. Augustine merely turned the Christian struggle

---

[1] I am particularly indebted to the sensitive and learned study of M. Pontet, *L'Exégèse de S. Augustin prédicateur*, 1945.

[2] *Serm.* 18, 1.

[3] v. esp. E. R. Dodds, *Pagan and Christian in an Age of Anxiety*, 1965, pp. 7–8.

[4] *de agone christ.* i, 1; cf. Dodds, *Pagan and Christian*, pp. 12–17.

[5] *de agone christ.* i, 1. v. G. Sanders, *Licht en Duisternis in de christelijke Grafschriften*, ii, 1965, pp. 896–903.

[6] *Passio Maximiani et Isaac*, (P.L. viii, 768C).

[7] *Passio Maximiani et Isaac*, (P.L. viii, 779D–780A).

[8] *Passio Marculi*, (P.L. viii, 764A).

[9] e.g. *de agone christ.* iii, 3: the Devil and his angels could never live in the 'heavenly' region of the stars.

inwards: its amphitheatre was the 'heart';[1] it was an inner struggle against forces in the soul; the 'Lord of this world' becomes the 'Lord of desires' — of the desires of those who love this world, and so come to resemble demons committed to the same emotions as themselves.[2] 'The Devil is not to be blamed for everything: there are times when a man is his own devil.'[3] In the same way, victory comes to depend on adherence to some inner source of strength: on 'remaining in Christ', interpreted as an abiding principle within the self.[4] For, when this 'inner' Christ 'sleeps', the boat of the soul is rocked by desires for the world: when this Christ 'wakes in the soul', it becomes calm again.[5]

Once again, in his sermons as in his *Confessions*, we meet Augustine as the authentic follower of Plotinus. Faced by a similar popular view of the religious life among his fellow-pagans, Plotinus also had turned inwards. He had insisted that the 'ascent' of the soul was not, crudely, a physical journey from the demon-haunted world to the pure light of the Milky Way,[6] but that it involved the realization of some latent principle within the inner world.[7] Plotinus, of course, reached a diametrically opposite conclusion from Augustine on the nature of this inner principle: what for Plotinus was the divine within the soul itself, becomes for Augustine, Christ, a principle separate from the soul, a principle, that is, not only 'deeper than my inmost being' but also 'high above my highest peak'.[8] But both men stand out together, against the background of the current religious ideas of their age. And what Plotinus had struggled to convey to a select classroom in Rome, the Christians of Hippo and Carthage could hear any Sunday in the sermons of Augustine. They could even have read a booklet, deliberately written in simple Latin for them, 'On the Christian Struggle', *De Agone Christiano*.[9] With such an influence at work, Latin Christian piety could never be the same again.

For, the contours of Augustine's thought in his sermons, are laid down by his deep attachment to Neo-Platonism. Love of the world, for instance, will be condemned, not because the 'world' is the haunt of demons, but because it is by definition, for the Neo-Platonic

[1] *de agone christ.* ii, 2. v. esp. A. M. La Bonnardière, 'Le combat chrétien', *Rev. études augustin.*, xi, 1965, pp. 235–238, for the development of this theme against the Manichees.
[2] *de agone christ.* i, 1 and ii, 2.
[3] *Frang.* 5, 5, (*Misc. Agostin.* i, pp. 212 sq.); cf. *Enarr. in Ps.* 136, 9.
[4] *de agone christ.* i, 1.   [5] *Enarr. in Ps.* 147, 3; *Frang.* 5, 6, (*Misc. Agostin.*, i, p. 217).
[6] E. Bréhier, *La Philosophie de Plotin*, pp. 26–32.   [7] P. Hadot, *Plotin*, pp. 25–39.
[8] *Conf.* III, vi, 11. v. esp. A. H. Armstrong, 'Salvation, Plotinian and Christian', *The Downside Review*, 75, 1957, pp. 126–139.
[9] *Retract.* II, 29.

philosopher incomplete, transient, overshadowed by Eternity.[1] All the
sadness of the ancient philosophers will flood into Augustine's language
as he talks of this transience. Human existence is 'a speck of rain
compared with Eternity'.[2] 'From when I started speaking until this
moment, you realize you have grown older: you cannot see your hair
growing; and yet, while you stand around, while you are here, while
you do something, while you talk, your hair keeps on growing on you
— but never so suddenly that you need a barber straight away: so your
existence fades away — you are passing.'[3] 'Let a few years go by: let
the great river slip forward, as it always does, passing through many
places, washing, always, through some new tombs of the dead.'[4]

Augustine's view of the Christian life is determined by this antithesis
of transience and eternity. At times, the Crucifixion will appear in this
light, as a reminder of the necessary boundary, already drawn with
such passion by Plotinus,[5] between the incomplete, unfulfilled, disintegrated existence of a 'here', and the fullness, the permanence, the
unity of a 'there': 'He may wish to be happy here, when complete
happiness does not exist here. Happiness is a real thing, good and great:
but it has its proper region. Christ came from that region of happiness;
not even He could find it here. . . .'[6]

The Christian, therefore, could not be thought of as approaching
God as a successful wrestler might approach an impartial judge to
claim a prize.[7] He must come with the yearning of the uncomplete to
be filled, of the transient to gain stability. Such yearning might pierce
through the rites of the African church, and transform their traditional
associations. The Christians of Hippo came to be baptized, chanting
the Psalm '*Like as the hart desireth the waterbrooks*'.[8] They would have
expected to be told about the cleansing powers of the waters that flowed
into the baptismal basin. Instead, their bishop told them how to yearn
for something more fundamental: for God, thought of as a fountain,
just as Plotinus had called the One 'an inexhaustible, ever-flowing
spring'.[9] And Augustine will speak to them with the certainty of a
contemplative. 'Behold, sometimes we are made glad by a certain inner
sweetness. Yes, our mind has been able to catch a glimpse, for a fleeting
instant, of something above change. . . . Now I have a sense throughout my being of something beyond time.'[10] 'O greedy men, what will
satisfy you, if God Himself will not.'[11]

---

[1] *de agone christ.* i, 1.   [2] *Enarr. ii in Ps.* 101, 9.   [3] *Enarr. in Ps.* 38, 12.
[4] *Denis*, 23, 3, (*Misc. Agostin.*, i, p. 139).   [5] Bréhier, *La Philosophie de Plotin*, p. 31.
[6] *Serm.* 19, 4.   [7] *Frang.* 2, 6, (*Misc. Agostin.*, i, pp. 196–197).
[8] *Psalm 41*; v. Van der Meer, *Augustine*, pp. 347–387.   [9] *Enarr. in Ps.* 41, 1.
[10] *Enarr. in Ps.* 41, 10; cf. *de agone christ.* ix, 10.   [11] *Serm.* 158, 7.

Augustine knew how to play on an audience's fear of Hell.[1] But a sense of the loss of a loved one, not of punishment, is what he wished most to communicate: 'A girl might say to her lover, "Don't wear that sort of cloak": he won't. If she tells him in winter: "I like you best in your short tunic," he would rather shiver than offend her. Surely she has no powers to inflict punishment on him? ... No, there is only one thing he fears: "I shall never look at you again." '[2]

The congregations who heard Augustine preach were not exceptionally sinful. Rather, they were firmly rooted in long-established attitudes, in ways of life and ideas, to which Christianity was peripheral. Among such men, the all-demanding message of Augustine merely suffered the fate of a river flowing into a complex system of irrigation: it lost its power, in the minds of its hearers, by meeting innumerable little ditches, by being broken up into a network of neat little compartments.[3]

Even the religious imagination of these men was rigidly compartmented. There were two worlds: this world and the next. Each was governed by its own rulers. The pagan gods, therefore, were almost impossible to banish: for they were not the classical Olympians, they were faceless 'powers'. These 'powers' had increasingly come to pour into the gap that had widened between the daily concerns of a man — his illnesses, his anxieties, his ambitions, his acute sense of being the object of malign influences — and a Supreme God, Whom pagan and Christian philosophers alike had conspired to make too grandiose and too remote for the humble business of living at peace in this world.[4] Augustine found himself checkmated by this split in the imagination of his hearers. Christianity, they had been told, was otherworldly. They would keep it so. Christ was eminently suitable as a god of the next world: He was to be worshipped for eternal life;[5] His rites and emblems — baptism and the sign of the Cross — would be infallible pass-words to open the next world to the believer.[6] But this world had to be controlled by traditional and well-tried means: by astrologers, by soothsayers and by amulets.

On the level of the family, also, Augustine found his path barred by immemorial attitudes. Augustine's congregation was not notably dissolute. Far from it: a small African town of the fourth century could be a narrow, puritanical community. It consisted of tightly-knit families in which the mother played a dominant role.[7] Disrespect for

[1] e.g. *Serm.* 161, 4.
[2] *Serm.* 161, 10.
[3] v. esp. Van der Meer, *Augustine*, pp. 46–75 and 129–198.
[4] *Enarr. ii in Ps.* 26, 19.
[5] *Enarr. in Ps.* 40, 3.
[6] *de fide et oper.* i, 1.
[7] *de serm. Dom. in Monte*, II, ii, 7 (the wives control the money of the household).

one's mother would shock both Augustine and his hearers deeply.[1] What a man did in his own home, however, was considered his own business. He would despise prostitutes; he would avoid adultery; but (like the young Augustine!) he would think nothing of taking a concubine: ' "Surely I can do what I like in my own house?" I tell you, No: you cannot. People who do this go straight to Hell.'[2]

Above all, Augustine had to combat the deeply ingrained double morality of such men. It was a double morality fortified by laws against the adulterous wife that had become even more oppressive in the Christian era.[3] Augustine would insist that the wives, also, should expect their husbands to be faithful. It is on this issue, which affected the traditional structure of family life most intimately, that we see Augustine and his flock in head-on collision:

'I do not want Christian married women to lie down under this. I solemnly warn you, I lay down this rule, I command you. I command you as your bishop; and it is Christ Who commands in me. God knows, in whose sight my heart burns. Yes, I say, I command you. . . . For so many years, now, we have baptized so many men to no effect, if there are none here who preserve the vows of chastity they took. . . . Far be it from me to believe that this is so. It would have been better not to have been your bishop than that this should have been the case. But I hope and I believe the opposite. It is part of my sorry situation that I am forced to know all about adulterers, and cannot be informed about the chaste. The virtues in you that give me joy are hidden from me, while what distresses me is only too well-known.'[4]

There was one other split in the moral ideas of his hearers which Augustine could do nothing to heal: for it was a split within Christian ethics itself. The Christian communities had come increasingly to accept a dangerous degree of 'moral specialization': one life was left for the 'perfect', another for the average Christian.[5] And it was just this widening gulf between an ascetic élite and a passive rank and file which brought the Christianization of the Roman world to a halt.

Augustine and his friends were deeply involved in the movement for the 'perfect' life in the West. He experienced all the excitement of sharing in a dramatic revolution of standards of conduct among the few. News of notable feats of renunciation by Roman aristocrats would come to him from all over the Mediterranean.[6] While his defence

---

[1] e.g. *Serm.* 323, 1.   [2] *Serm.* 224, 3.
[3] *Serm.* 9, 4.   [4] *Serm.* 392, 4 and 6.
[5] v. esp. N. H. Baynes, 'The Thought World of East Rome', *Byzantine Studies*, pp. 26–27, and Jones, *Later Roman Empire*, ii, pp. 979–985.
[6] e.g. *Ep.* 94, 3–4. v. inf. p. 294.

of married life was conscientious,[1] his treatise on virginity was quite lyrical;[2] and he will even betray traces of outraged gallantry in defending the reputation of nuns who had been raped in the Sack of Rome.[3] Like many men wrapt up in a successful movement, the rapid advances of their own ideas on a narrow front, would have seemed to compensate, even to eclipse, the failure of their society as a whole: ' "In the old days" you say, "there were never such great grabbers of other men's property": ah, but ... in the old days there were never men who gave away their own.'[4]

A society that admires nothing less than a saint can be demoralizing for the ordinary sinner. The tendency was to be content with a vicarious holiness by isolating and admiring a recognizable caste of 'holy' men and women, who lived a life, the demands of which were conceived of as so superhuman as to be safely unrelated to one's own life as a man of the world. In Augustine's church, for instance, the dedicated virgins would have been screened by a balustrade of pure white marble:[5] the congregation plainly wanted to see such a visible talisman of sanctity, safely placed between themselves and the raised benches of their 'holy' bishops and clergy.[6] But at the other end, there stood another group, the solid, immovable mass of the *paenitentes*, the 'penitents', who had been excluded from communion by the rigorous penitential discipline of the African church. They showed no inclination to submit themselves again to the high demands of the Christian life. Here stood the average men of the Later Empire, once pagans, now baptized Christians, kept at arm's length partly because they could console themselves with the thought that the perfectionism of the bishop and his monks could only be for the very few: 'You are thinking that I am saying what I always say; and you go on doing what you always do. ... What shall I do — now that I seem just a cheap old song to you. Change, change, I beseech you. The end of life is always unpredictable. Each man walks with a chance of falling. I beseech you brothers, even if you have forgotten about yourselves, at least take some pity on me.'[7]

A bishop could approach his flock armed with many sanctions. The Last Judgement and eternal punishment were the 'old wives' tales of the Christians'[8] *par excellence*. 'It happens very rarely, indeed never, that someone comes wanting to be a Christian who has not been smitten by some fear of God.'[9] Augustine would use this fear; he would

[1] *de bono coniug.* (401). [2] *de sancta virg.* (401). [3] *de civ. Dei*, II 2, 28.
[4] *Enarr. in Ps.* 80, 1; cf. *Enarr. in Ps.* 136, 8. [5] *Corpus Inscript. Lat.* VIII, 17810.
[6] *Serm.* 91, 5; *Mai.* 94, 7, (*Misc. Agostin.*, i, p. 339). [7] *Serm.* 232, 8.
[8] *Enarr. in Ps.* 134, 20. [9] *de cat. rud.* v, 9; cf. *Enarr. in Ps.* 149, 14 and 85, 17.

turn the celebration of the anniversary of his own consecration into a sombre affair: 'I do not care whether you expect some well turned phrases today. It is my duty to give you due warning in citing the Scriptures. *Do not be slow to turn to the Lord, nor delay from day to day, for His wrath shall come when you know not.* God knows how I tremble on my bishop's throne when I hear that warning. I cannot be silent; I am forced to preach on it. Filled with fear myself, I fill you with fear.'[1]

In fact, the moments when Augustine stands outside his flock and threatens them in this way are rare. For he was well aware, that as the Catholic bishop, he had gathered a whole new group around himself, the 'Christians' of Hippo;[2] and that consciously or unconsciously, the preacher had to keep his audience united by meeting them half-way on many issues.

Augustine always thought of himself as living among a new 'people' — the *populus Dei*, the 'people of God', the direct successors of a compact and distinctive tribe, the 'people of Israel'. It was not for him to inveigh against Roman society as a whole: it was his first duty to look after his own, to maintain the identity and the morale of his 'people', the Catholic congregation.

Thus, like the old 'people of Israel', the congregation was a mixed body. Differences in wealth and behaviour were only too public among them. Notably insensitive to infidelity and fornication,[3] the average Catholic had a sharp eye for the land grabber, for the usurer and the drunkard.[4] Like the Psalmist in the old Israel, what moved him was less any modern 'class feeling', directed against the dominance of a group of rich, selfish men in the social life of the town, than the galling fact that such notorious sinners had got away with it: '*I was angry at sinners, seeing the peace of sinners.*'[5]

Augustine had to keep his flock together. It must not be disrupted by envy. He had, therefore, to protect unpopular members rather than exclude them. His deep sense of the compulsive force of habit, for instance, made him more lenient to drunkards than his congregation might have wished.[6] Above all, there is little doubt that his need to preserve the sense of unity in his flock, especially against Donatist criticism, led him to gloss over, even perhaps to collude with, the very real divisions between rich and poor. Augustine will rarely stand out

---

[1] *Frang.* 2, 8, (*Misc. Agostin.*, i, p. 199.)   [2] *Serm.* 302, 19.   [3] *Serm.* 224, 2.
[4] *Enarr. in Ps.* 127, 11 and *Serm.* 88, 25 and 224, 1: a catalogue of sins which the baptized must avoid.
[5] *Psalm* 72, 3; e.g. *Denis* 21, 2, (*Misc. Agostin.*, i p 125).
[6] *Serm.* 17, 3; cf. *Serm.* 151, 4.

against the rich in the manner of Ambrose.[1] Ambrose would tell his flock bluntly, that 'Naboth's vineyard may be an old story; but it is happening every day'.[2] He could inveigh against the local landowners of Milan in the manner of a born patrician, who both knew intimately what it was to be very rich in the Later Empire, and so could despise men who thought of nothing but becoming yet richer.[3] Augustine, by contrast, will often plead for a truce to such unwelcome tensions: 'It is not a matter of income, but of desires. . . . Look at the rich man standing beside you: perhaps he has a lot of money on him, but no avarice in him; while you, who have no money, have a lot of avarice.'[4] 'Strive for unity, do not divide the people.'[5]

Thus, to feel part of a group mattered far more to Augustine than to denounce his congregation from the outside. He knew that he might follow the example of S. Cyprian in taking advantage of a time of public calamity to denounce the sins of his congregation.[6] Yet, when such a time of calamity came with the sack of Rome, he will prefer to join in with his hearers, addressing them as 'fellow-citizens of Jerusalem', talking to them, not of the punishment they would deserve at the Last Judgement, but of their future life, all together, in 'that sweet City'.[7]

This is the secret of Augustine's enormous power as a preacher. He will make it his first concern to place himself in the midst of his congregation,[8] to appeal to their feelings for him, to react with immense sensitivity to their emotions, and so, as the sermon progressed, to sweep them up into his own way of feeling.[9] He could identify himself sufficiently with his congregation to provoke them to identify themselves completely with himself.

Augustine would not even have been physically isolated from his audience, as a modern preacher would be, who stands in a pulpit above a seated congregation. The congregation of Hippo stood throughout the sermon, while Augustine usually sat back in his *cathedra*. The first row, therefore, would have met their bishop roughly at eye level, at only some 5 yards' distance.[10] Augustine would have spoken directly

---

[1] But v. esp. *Serm.* 61, 13: a witty appeal on behalf of the beggars outside the church.

[2] Ambrose, *de Nabuthe*, i, 1, (P.L. xiv, 731).

[3] L. Ruggini, *Economia e società nell' Italia annonaria*, 1962, shows how much can be learnt about the economic life of Milan from the sermons of Ambrose (v. esp. pp. 10–16).

[4] *Enarr. in Ps.* 51, 14; cf. *Enarr. in Ps.* 72, 26.

[5] *Enarr. in Ps.* 72, 34. v. esp. H. Rondet, 'Richesse et pauvreté dans la prédication de S. Augustin', *Rev. ascét. et myst.*, xxx, 1954, pp. 193–231.

[6] *C. Ep. Parm.* III, ii, 16.   [7] *Enarr. in Ps.* 61, 7. v. inf. p. 315.

[8] *de cat. rud.* xiii, 18–19, advice to a priest giving addresses on the catechism.

[9] e.g. *Tract. in Joh.* 35, 9.

[10] For what follows, v. esp. Van der Meer, *Augustine*, pp. 405–467.

to them, quite extempore: the natural flow of vivid, pure Latin would occasionally lapse, with charming self-consciousness, into an unclassical term, or it would run into a jingle of rhymed phrases and puns, to delight the ear of an illiterate audience.[1]

But there could be little room in Augustine's approach, for the relaxed mood of the contemplative. An audience will identify itself only with an excited man: and Augustine would be excited for them; vehement yearnings for peace,[2] fear,[3] and guilt[4] — these are the emotions to which Augustine's audience reacted with shouts and groans.[5] This could be dangerous. When Augustine preached against Pelagianism, for instance, we can see, only too clearly how Pelagius, the austere upholder of the autonomy of the conscious mind, was outflanked by a man who could put himself in touch with the more sinister currents of feeling in a large crowd, with their pervasive sexual guilt,[6] and with their terror at the unsearchable ways of God.[7]

Sermons such as these, however, were usually exceptional performances before the excited crowds at Carthage. Augustine was certain of his basic role. It was not to stir up emotion: it was to distribute food. The Scriptural idea of 'breaking bread', of 'feeding the multitude', by expounding the Bible, an idea already rich with complex associations, is central to Augustine's view of himself as a preacher.[8] The little boy who had once supplied his 'gang' with stolen tit-bits,[9] would find himself, as a bishop, still constantly giving: 'I go to feed so that I can give you to eat. I am the servant, the bringer of food, not the master of the house. I lay out before you that from which I also draw my life.'[10] As he told Jerome, he could never be a 'disinterested' Biblical scholar: 'If I do gain any stock of knowledge (in the Scriptures), I pay it out immediately to the people of God.'[11]

For Augustine and his hearers, the Bible was literally the 'word' of God. It was regarded as a single communication, a single message in an intricate code, and not as an exceedingly heterogeneous collection of separate books. Above all, it was a communication that was intrinsically so far above the pitch of human minds, that to be made available to our senses at all, this 'Word' had to be communicated by means of an intricate game of 'signs' (very much as a modern therapist makes contact with the inner world of a child in terms of significant patterns

[1] v. Van der Meer, *Augustine*, pp. 412–432.
[2] e.g. *Enarr. in Ps.* 147, 20.
[3] e.g. *Serm.* 131, 5.
[4] e.g. *Serm.* 151, 8.
[5] v. Pontet, *L'Exégèse de S. Augustin*, pp. 43–44.
[6] *Serm.* 151, 8. v. inf. p. 388.
[7] *Serm.* 26, 13.
[8] e.g. *Serm.* 95, 1.
[9] *Conf.* I, xix, 30.
[10] *Frang.* 2, 4, (*Misc. Agostin.*, i, p. 193).
[11] *Ep.* 73, ii, 5.

emerging in play with sand, water and bricks): 'Wisdom's way of teaching chooses to hint at how divine things should be thought of by certain images and analogies available to the senses.'[1] And so, by this method, the most bizarre incidents of the Old Testament could be taken as 'signs', communicating in an allusive manner, something that would be made explicit in the New.[2]

Once it is thought possible for something larger than our conscious awareness to be capable of active communication, whether this be the 'whole' personality, conscious and unconscious of the modern psychoanalyst, or the ineffable 'Word' of the Early Christian exegete, an attitude similar to that of Augustine occurs quite naturally. For this communication is regarded as betraying itself by 'signs' — by the imagery of dreams, by bizarre remarks, by slips of the tongue; in fact, by *absurdities*,[3] which served as warnings to the exegete and to Freud alike, of the existence of hidden, complex depths.

The exegete, therefore, faced with the Bible conceived of as a communication of this kind, will train himself to listen for the single, hidden 'will' that had expressed itself in the deliberate selection of every word of the text:[4] for in a sacred text, 'everything was said exactly as it needed to be said.'[5] Thus the first question he must ask is not 'what', 'what was the exact nature of this particular religious practice in the ancient Near East?' but *'why'* — 'why does this incident, this word and no other, occur at just this moment in the interminable monologue of God; and so, what aspect of His deeper message does it communicate? Like the child who asked the basic question: 'Mummy, *why* is a cow?', Augustine will run through the text of the Bible in such a way that every sermon is punctuated by '*Quare . . . quare . . . quare*' 'Why? . . . why? . . . why?'

We shall see that Augustine's attitude to allegory summed up a whole attitude to knowledge.[6] But his hearers might have had less sophisticated reasons for enjoying the sermons of their bishop. For, seen in this light, the Bible became a gigantic puzzle — like a vast inscription in unknown characters.[7] It had all the elemental appeal of the riddle: of that most primitive form of triumph over the unknown which consists in finding the familiar hidden beneath an alien guise.

---

[1] *C. Faust.* xxii, 34.
[2] v. esp. Pontet, *L'Exégèse de S. Augustin*, pp. 149–194 and 257–383.
[3] e.g. *Enarr. in Ps.* 77, 26–27. v. esp. J. Pépin, *Mythe et Allégorie*, 1958, pp. 483–4 and 'A propos de l'histoire de l'exégèse allégorique: l'absurdité, signe de l'allégorie', (Studia Patristica, i), *Texte u. Untersuchungen*, 63, 1957, pp. 395–413.
[4] *de doct. christ.* II, v, 6; cf. *Serm.* 71, 13.
[5] *Enarr. in Ps.* 145, 12.
[6] v. inf. pp. 260–262.
[7] *C. Faust.* xii, 37.

The African, particularly, had a Baroque love of subtlety. They had always loved playing with words; they excelled in writing elaborate acrostics; *hilaritas* — a mixture of intellectual excitement and sheer aesthetic pleasure at a notable display of wit — was an emotion they greatly appreciated.[1] Augustine would give them just this: he could hold them spellbound while he explained why there were 13 Apostles and only 12 thrones on which they would sit.[2] Augustine was able to communicate to a congregation his contemplative ascent to God;[3] he could reduce the inhabitants of a whole town to tears;[4] but he would have owed his position as a 'star' preacher to the quite characteristic way in which he would settle back in his chair, and like the inspired teacher that he had always been, get his listeners to identify themselves with his own excitement at unravelling a difficult text: 'Let me try to winkle out the hidden secrets of this Psalm we have just sung; and chip a sermon out of them, to satisfy your ears and minds.'[5] 'I confess, this *is* a problem. *Knock and it shall be opened to you*: knock, by concentrating hard; knock by showing a keen interest; knock even for me, by praying for me, that I should extract something from it worth while telling you.'[6]

In the unselfconscious routine of these sermons we can come as close as is possible to the foundations of Augustine's qualities as a thinker. Seen in action at such close range, the cumulative impression is quite overwhelming. He is very much the product of a culture that admired a complete mastery of texts combined with great dialectical subtlety in interpretation.[7] His memory, trained on classical texts, was phenomenally active.[8] In one sermon, he could move through the whole Bible, from Paul to Genesis and back again, *via* the Psalms, piling half-verse on half-verse. This method of exegesis indeed, which involved creating a whole structure of verbal echoes, linking every part of the Bible, was particularly well-suited to teaching this hitherto quite unknown text, to an audience used to memorizing by ear.[9] And, like a schoolmaster, Augustine tended to present the Bible as a series of cruxes. He never relaxes for a moment the impression of a mind of terrifying acuteness. This hard intellectual quality, tenacious to the

---

[1] e.g. *Ep. ad Rom. incoh. expos.* 13; cf. *de cat. rud.* xiii, 18, where the same device is recommended as one of the only ways to arouse the interest of a *grammaticus*.

[2] *Enarr.* 49, 9; cf. *Serm.* 249, 3. [3] e.g. *Enarr. ii in Ps.* 26, 8.

[4] *de doct. christ.* IV, xxiv, 53. [5] *Enarr. ii in Ps.* 30, 1.

[6] *Frang.* 5, (*Misc. Agostin.*, i, 212). [7] v. esp. *de doct. christ.* IV, xx, 39.

[8] Quintilian, *Inst.* XI, 2, 1: memory is 'the treasure-house of eloquence'.

[9] e.g. *Enarr. in Ps.* 121, 8, 'Let us be their book of the Scriptures'; cf. *Enarr. in Ps.* 35, 19 and *Serm.* 232, 1.

point of quibbling, was what Augustine plainly valued most in himself, and communicated most effectively to his audience. It was the secret of his everyday style — the 'subdued' style: 'When it resolves exceptionally difficult problems, comes out with an unexpected demonstration, shows that the speaker can bring out singularly penetrating formulations, as if out of the blue; when it hits on an adversary's weak point, and can expose as fallacious an argument that had seemed unanswerable — all this with a certain stylish touch . . . this can provoke such enthusiastic applause that you would hardly take it for "subdued." '[1]

But, above all, there is Augustine's amazing power of integration. He could communicate to perfection the basic idea of the 'Word' in the Bible, as an organic whole. His beautiful sermons on the Psalms are quite unique in Patristic literature. For, for Augustine, each Psalm had a 'single body of feeling that vibrates in every syllable'.[2] Each Psalm, therefore, could be presented as a microcosm of the whole Bible — the clear essence of Christianity refracted in the exotic spectrum of a Hebrew poem. Augustine seldom wanders: he 'unwinds'.[3] A single incident, the juxtaposition of Christ and John the Baptist — is 'unravelled', so that the associations of John's statement '*He must grow and I must diminish*' spread throughout the whole Bible and come to be reflected even in the rhythm of the seasons: 'There are many things that could be said about S. John the Baptist, but I would never be finished with telling you, nor you with listening. Now let me round it off in a nutshell. Man must be humbled, God must be exalted.'[4]

This sense of the particular incident as the vehicle through which an organic whole can find expression accounts for the beauty of Augustine's exegesis. For, as in the incidents of his own life in the *Confessions*, significance suddenly comes to light on a tiny detail. The Father of the Prodigal Son 'falls upon his shoulders': it is Christ placing His yoke on the Christian, and in a flash we see the incident as Rembrandt would see it; every line of the heavy figure of the old man charged with meaning. 'In some sense or other, Importance is derived from the immanence of infinitude in the finite.'[5]

---

[1] *de doct. christ.* IV, xxvi, 56. [2] *Enarr. in Ps.* 70, 1. [3] *Enarr. in Ps.* 147, 2 and 23.
[4] *Guelf.* 22, 5, (*Misc. Agostin.*, i, p. 515). Such exegesis, of course, is not based on mere 'free-association'. The 'associations' are, in this case, given by the liturgical traditions surrounding the Feast of John the Baptist. Thus, many allegories used by Augustine as a preacher would have been as familiar to his congregation, through traditional preaching, through the liturgy, and, in the case of Africa, through polemic on the nature of the Church (e.g. *Ep. ad cath.* v, 9), as the figures in political cartoons in a modern newspaper.
[5] A. Whitehead, *Modes of Thought*, 1938, p. 28.

Augustine preached in this manner for 39 years. The experience influenced him deeply. For Augustine approached his position as a preacher with considerable misgivings. He was a contemplative in the austere tradition of Plotinus. He came near to regarding speech itself as a falling-away of the soul from its inner act of contemplation.[1] 'Nothing can be better, nothing more sweet for me than to gaze upon the Divine treasure without noise and hustle: this is what is sweet and good. To have to preach, to inveigh, to admonish, to edify, to feel responsible for every one of you — this is a great burden, a heavy weight upon me, a hard labour.'[2]

As is so often the case with him, Augustine used this tension so creatively just because he could feel so strongly the opposing poles within himself. Thus communication fascinated him: 'For my own way of expressing myself almost always disappoints me. I am anxious for the best possible, as I feel it in me before I start bringing it into the open in plain words: and when I see that it is less impressive than I had felt it to be, I am saddened that my tongue cannot live up to my heart.'[3]

The huge pressure built up by the need to communicate will do nothing less than sweep away the elaborate scaffolding of ancient rhetoric. For, as Augustine came to see it at the end of his life, rhetoric had consisted of polishing an end-product, the speech itself, according to elaborate and highly self-conscious rules.[4] It ignored the basic problem of communication: the problems faced by a man burning to get across a message, or by a teacher wanting his class to share his ideas.[5] Immediacy was Augustine's new criterion. Given something worth saying, the way of saying it would follow naturally, an inevitable and unobtrusive accompaniment to the speaker's own intensity:[6] 'the thread of our speech comes alive through the very joy we take in what we are speaking about.'[7] The impact, also, was immediate: for the speaker's style was not thought of as a harmonious assemblage of prefabricated parts, which the connoisseur might take to pieces, but rather as the inseparable welding of form and content in the heat of the message, so that 'it is a waste of time to tell someone what to admire, if he does not himself sense it'.[8] If we read, in the *Confessions*, some passage of full-blooded lyricism and compare it with the stilted language in which the same ideas are expressed in one of Augustine's more

---

[1] On this, v. esp. M.-F. Berrouard, 'S. Augustin et le ministère de la prédication', *Rech. augustin.*, ii, 1962, pp. 447–501, esp. p. 499 n. 131; cf. *Enarr. in Ps.* 139, 15.

[2] *Frang.* 2, 4, (*Misc. Agostin.*, i, p. 193).   [3] *de cat. rud.* ii, 3.

[4] *de doct. christ.* IV, vii, 21.   [5] *de doct. christ.* IV, x, 24–xii, 28.

[6] *de doct. christ.* IV, xx, 42.   [7] *de cath. rud.* ii, 4.   [8] *de doct. christ.* IV, vii, 20.

'classical' philosophical dialogues, we can immediately see that the Latin language has been fused, has caught alight, in the almost-daily flame of Augustine's sermons.[1] It is just this intensity which Augustine came to love in the Hebrew prophets. His ear was sensitive to the charm of an exotic language, to a syntax that was after all not so distant from the Punic he could have listened to (and to which he would often refer as some substitute for his ignorance of Hebrew),[2] to the strange appeal of the reiterated phrases of the Psalms,[3] to the names of the towns of Israel that studded a passage 'like great lights'.[4] But he saw in the prophets, above all, men like himself: men with a message to bring home to a whole 'people' — *'a hammer shattering the stones'.*[5]

Augustine lived through the emotions to which he appealed. In his middle age, he became increasingly preoccupied with the idea of a 'Mystical Body' of Christ: a body of which Christ was the Head and all true believers the members.[6] For a Platonist, the unity of a body was, above all, a unity of sensations: the soul was the core of the body, for it alone was the centre in which all the emotions of the body were experienced.[7] It was this doctrine, which enabled Augustine to put himself in touch with the vast reserves of feeling contained in the Hebrew Scriptures.[8] For seen in this light, the Psalms were the record of the emotions of Christ and His members. Just as He had taken on human flesh, so Christ had, of his own free will, opened Himself to human feeling.[9] These feelings are only hinted at in the Gospels. Often, the Christ of Augustine's sermons is the pale, impassive figure of a Late Roman mosaic; His Crucifixion is a solemn, measured act of power — 'the sleep of a lion'.[10] But when he turns to the Psalms, Augustine will draw from them an immensely rich deposit of human emotions: for here was Christ, speaking directly in the person of the passionate King David. The song of the desperate fugitive from the wrath of Saul, is the inner story of the Passion: *'Heaviness fell upon me; and I slept.'*[11] 'His voice in the Psalms — a voice singing happily, a voice groaning, a voice rejoicing in hope, sighing in its present state —

---

[1] e.g. compare *Enarr. in Ps.* 9, 3 and *de lib. arb.* II, 35 with *Conf.* X, vi, 8.

[2] e.g. in *Enarr. in Ps.* 136, 18.   [3] *Enarr. in Ps.* 71, 2.   [4] *de doct. christ.* IV, vii, 17.

[5] *Jerem.* 23, 29, in *de doct. christ.* IV, xiv, 30. v. esp. H. I. Marrou, *S. Augustin et la fin de la culture antique*, pp. 521–540, and E. Auerbach, 'Sermo humilis', *Literary Language and its Public in Late Latin Antiquity and in the Middle Ages*, (transl. Manheim), 1965, pp. 27–66.

[6] v. esp. E. Mersch, *Le corps mystique du Christ*, ii, 3rd ed. 1951, esp. pp. 84–138.

[7] e.g. *Enarr. in Ps.* 30, 1.   [8] v. Pontet, *L'Exégèse de S. Augustin*, pp. 395–411.

[9] *Enarr. in Ps.* 93, 19.   [10] *Serm.* 37, 2.   [11] *Enarr. in Ps.* 6,11.

we should know this voice thoroughly, feel it intimately, make it our own.'[1]

Augustine's voice, also, will take on richer tones in his later middle age, and especially in the amazing sermons on the 'City of God', preached when he was sixty. His sense of the bonds of human feeling will become more acute; and a greater awareness of the pleasures of his audience, of their capacity for love and fear, will seep into his preaching. In these sermons, we begin to hear the songs of Africa.[2] The 'sweet melody' of a Psalm sung in the streets,[3] the 'serenades',[4] above all, the strange rhythmic chant of the labourers in the fields. It is this chanting in the countryside that will, at last, provide Augustine, the austere Neo-Platonic bishop, with an image worthy of the fullness of the Vision of God: 'So men who sing like this — in the harvest, at the grape-picking, in any task that totally absorbs them — may begin by showing their contentment in songs with words; but they soon become filled with such a happiness that they can no longer express it in words, and, leaving aside syllables, strike up a wordless chant of jubilation.'[5]

[1] *Enarr. in Ps.* 42, 1.   [2] e.g. *Serm.* 9, 6 sq.   [3] *Enarr. in Ps.* 132, 1.
[4] *Enarr. in Ps.* 64, 3.   [5] *Enarr. ii in Ps.* 32, 8.

23

DOCTRINA CHRISTIANA[1]

As he sat as a bishop on his *cathedra* with a book open across his knees, Augustine would have found himself in a position not very different from that to which he had been accustomed in his previous career. He was once again a teacher, expounding a venerated text. In the first surviving portrait of him, we see him sitting, a typical educated man of his age, his eyes fixed on a book.[2] Even when he looked around him in church, he saw on the walls, not the brilliant innovations of Later Roman mosaic-work, but only yet more open pages; the scenes and the verses he had written under them would be the 'book' of his congregation.[3] A Late Roman man of letters to the core, even the world of nature was only God's 'dumb show':[4] what interested him far more was the spoken word, the speech of God committed to a book, 'an eloquence, teaching salvation, perfectly adjusted to stir the hearts of all learners.'[5]

We cannot help noticing the extent to which the 'Divine eloquence' of God is the eloquence of a Late Roman writer. For no one else would have made such a cult of veiling his meaning. Such a man lived among fellow-connoisseurs, who had been steeped too long in too few books.[6] He no longer needed to be explicit: only hidden meanings,[7] rare and difficult words[8] and elaborate circumlocutions,[9] could save his readers

---

[1] H.-I. Marrou, *S. Augustin et la fin de la culture antique*, pp. 331–540, is fundamental; see most recently G. Strauss, *Schriftgebrauch, Schriftauslegung und Schriftbeweis bei Augustin*, (Beiträge z. Gesch. d. bibl. Hermeneutik, 1), 1959, and R. Holte, *Béatitude et Sagesse*, pp. 303–386.

[2] v. esp. H.-I. Marrou, *MOYCIKOC ANHP. Étude sur les scènes de la vie intellectuelle figurants sur les monuments funéraires romains*, 1938. The portrait of Augustine is shown in colour in *Miscellanea Agostiniana*, ii, facing p. 1, with comments by G. Wilpert, pp. 1–3, and, plain, in Van der Meer, *Augustine*, pl. 11, facing p. 216. (v. the dust-jacket of this book)

[3] *Serm.* 319, 7.   [4] *Enarr. i in Ps.* 103, 1.   [5] *Ep.* 55, vii, 13.

[6] Quintilian, *Inst.* VIII, 2, 20, already admits this.   [7] v. *Conf.* XII, xxvi, 36.

[8] v. *Ep.* 102, vi, 33.   [9] *de civ. Dei* X, 20.

from boredom, from *fastidium*, from that loss of interest in the obvious, that afflicts the overcultured man.[1] He would believe (with André Gide, among others) that the sheer difficulty of a work of literature made it more valuable — a sinister way of thinking in an age when educated men tended to form a caste, rebuffing the outsider by their possession of the ancient authors. Above all, the narrow canon of acknowledged classics had been charged with a halo of 'Wisdom': an intellectual agility quite alien to a modern man, would have to be deployed constantly to extract the inexhaustible treasure that, it was felt, must lie hidden in so cramped a quarry.[2]

Thus, when Augustine wished to justify the allegorical method of interpretation, by which he extracted such profound meanings from so singularly opaque and unwieldy a text as the Old Testament, he could always appeal to the tastes of his audience. But this general taste does not fully explain Augustine's attachment to the allegorical method. For, despite its diffused penumbra, a general fashion in cryptic expression, the allegorical method proper had been confined to a precise area of ancient culture, to the philosophical interpretation of sacred texts, pagan, Jewish and Christian.[3]

The idea of allegory had come to sum up a serious attitude to the limitations of the human mind, and to the nature of the relationship between the philosopher and the objects of his thought. This was a distinctive relationship. The religious philosopher explored a spiritual world that was of its very nature 'ever more marvellous, ever more inaccessible.'[4] It should not be rendered 'insipid with veracity' by bald statements; but rather the mind must move from hint to hint, each discovery opening up yet further depths. The worst enemies of such inquiry, of course, were superficiality, the dead-weight of common-sense, habitual stereotypes that made a man cease to be surprised and excited, and thus veiled the most vertiginous complexities with a patina of the obvious. Take the problem of Time: 'We are forever talking about time and times. . . . They are the plainest and commonest words, yet, again, they are profoundly obscure and their meaning is still to be discovered.'[5]

---

[1] *Conf.* XIII, xx, 27; *Ep.* 137, 18; *de civ. Dei* X, 20; v. esp. Marrou, *S. Augustin et la fin de la culture antique*, pp. 469–503.

[2] e.g. *de Gen. ad litt.* I, xxi, 41.

[3] v. esp. J. Pépin, *Mythe et Allégorie*, 1958, and 'S. Augustin et la fonction protréptique de l'allégorie', *Rech. augustin.*, i, 1958, pp. 243–286.

[4] *Conf.* XI, xxxi, 41; cf. *Serm.* 169, 18.

[5] *Conf.* XI, xxii, 28; cf. *Tract. in Joh.* 14, 5: 'If, however, you say: "That's all there is to know", you are lost'. 'It is this instinctive conviction, vividly poised before the imagina-

The Bible had been similarly 'veiled' by God in order to 'exercise' the seeker. It was an acid test in just the same way as a philosophical problem might be: the superficial would be content with the obvious, with the 'letter'; only the profound man could grasp the deeper meaning, the 'spirit'. No one could accuse Augustine of wanting to be superficial. While Ambrose might regard the 118th Psalm as 'as clear as the midday sun',[1] to Augustine it would appear 'all the more profound the more obvious it seems'.[2] For beneath the deceptive simplicity of the Hebrew constructions, he had chosen to see the great complexity of his own views on grace and free will, veiled to the unenquiring mind, a source of wonder to the philosopher.

This was the function which many ancient philosophers had assigned to allegory;[3] it could easily lapse into a justification of effort for effort's sake. Augustine, however, went further: he produced a singularly comprehensive explanation of why allegory should have been necessary in the first place. The need for such a language of 'signs' was the result of a specific dislocation of the human consciousness. In this, Augustine takes up a position analogous to that of Freud. In dreams also, a powerful and direct message is said to be deliberately diffracted by some psychic mechanism, into a multiplicity of 'signs' quite as intricate and absurd, yet just as capable of interpretation, as the 'absurd' or 'obscure' passages in the Bible. Both men, therefore, assume that the proliferation of images is due to some precise event, to the development of some geological fault across a hitherto undivided consciousness: for Freud, it is the creation of an unconscious by repression; for Augustine, it is the outcome of the Fall.[4]

For the Fall had been, among many other things, a fall from direct knowledge into indirect knowledge through signs. The 'inner fountain' of awareness had dried up: Adam and Eve found that they could only communicate with one another by the clumsy artifice of language and gestures.[5] Above all, Augustine was preoccupied by the coexistence of this necessary but defective means of knowledge by 'signs', with flashes of direct awareness. He had remained a philosopher in the

tion, which is the motive power of research — that there is a secret, a secret which can be unveiled', A. N. Whitehead, *Science and the Modern World*, Lowell Lectures, 1925, (Mentor Books, p. 13).

[1] Ambrose, *In Ps. 118 Expos.*, Prolog., (P.L. xv, 1197).   [2] *Enarr. in Ps.*, Prooem.
[3] v. Pépin, 'S. Augustin', *Rech. augustin.*, i, 1958, esp. pp. 277–285.
[4] v. esp. R. Holte, *Béatitude et Sagesse*, pp. 335–343; J. Pépin, *Mythe et Allégorie*, 69–71, for a differentiated discussion of modern parallels.
[5] *de Gen. c. Man.* ij, 32. v. esp. U. Duchrow, ' "Signum" u. "Superbia" beim jungen Augustin', *Rev. études augustin.*, vii, 1961, pp. 369–372.

Platonic tradition. Wise men, pagan as well as Christian, had been able to rise above material things to 'an ineffable reality grasped by the mind alone', 'for a moment, like a blinding light, a lightning flash through heavy darkness.'[1] Yet Augustine had found such experiences painfully transient: 'You did beat back the weakness of my gaze, blinding me too strongly, and I was shaken with love and dread. . . . And I learned that *Thou hast corrected men for iniquity and Thou didst make my soul shrivel up like a moth*.'[2] The idea of the Vision of God, constantly expressed by Augustine through the Psalms, will become tinged with distant echoes of just that mixture of fascination and terror, which, in the ancient Near East, had always surrounded the 'countenance of God'.

The remedy was plain: 'For the meantime, let the Scriptures be *the countenance of God*.'[3] The gulf which separated a direct awareness of God from a human consciousness dislocated, as it were 'repressed', by the Fall, had been mercifully bridged through the Bible, by a marvellous proliferation of imagery. It was as if the eye had sought rest from the blinding African sun in the cool glow of a night sky.[4]

This was the mould into which Augustine had poured his intellectual life in middle age: a mind that had once hoped to train itself for the vision of God by means of the Liberal Arts, would now come to rest on the solid, intractable mass of the Christian Bible. For this reason, the last three books of his *Confessions* are in many ways the most strictly autobiographical part of the whole book. In taking the form of an allegorical exegesis of the opening verses of Genesis, they show exactly what Augustine had come to regard as the essence of his life as a bishop: 'Grant me, then, space for my meditations on the hidden things of Your Law, nor close them fast against those who knock. Not for nothing have You willed so many pages to be written in veiled secrets. . . . Complete Your work in me, O Lord, and open these pages to me.'[5] There is no doubt that, as Augustine would use the Bible, it

[1] *de civ. Dei*, IX, 16.

[2] *Conf.* VII, x, 16. v. esp. P. Courœlle, *Les Confessions*, pp. 43–58, for Philo, through Ambrose, as a possible source for this crucial idea.

[3] *Serm.* 22, 7.

[4] e.g. *Conf.* XIII, xviii, 23; *Enarr. in Ps.* 138, 14. One must remember the intense religious associations of the night-sky to an ancient man: this was a world of divine intelligences, visible to human eyes.

[5] *Conf.* XI, ii, 2. La Bonnardière, *Rech. de chronologie augustin.*, 1965, p. 180: 'Car si Saint Augustin est un théologien, il est un théologien de la Bible: son enseignement sourd directement de l'Écriture. Dans la mesure où l'on ne fait pas sa place à ce fait primordial, on se prive, dans l'étude des oeuvres de Saint Augustin, d'un éclairage qui non seulement a la valeur scientifique que peut posséder tout fait bien attesté, mais surtout fournit le meilleur moyen de compréhension de l'oeuvre augustinienne'.

was the fuel of a blast furnace: for in interpreting so much of it as an allegory, Augustine was finding in it all that he had always valued in his intellectual activity — hard labour, the excitement of discovery, and the prospect of endless movement in a philosopher's quest for Wisdom: 'The presentation of truth through signs has great power to feed and fan that ardent love, by which, as under some law of gravitation, we flicker upwards, or inwards, to our place of rest. Things presented in this way move and kindle our affection far more than if they were set forth in bald statements. . . . Why this should be, is hard to say: . . . I believe that the emotions are less easily set alight while the soul is wholly absorbed in material things; but when it is brought to material signs of spiritual realities, and moves from them to the things they represent, it gathers strength just by this very act of passing from the one to the other, like the flame of a torch, that burns all the more brightly as it moves. . . .'[1] Some twenty years later, Augustine had already piled up a vast commentary on Genesis, the *De Genesi ad litteram*, and had ransacked the Scriptures in the opening books of his *De Trinitate*. He could write from his own experience: 'For such is the depth of the Christian Scriptures that, even if I were attempting to study them and nothing else, from boyhood to decrepit old age, with the utmost leisure, the most unwearied zeal, and with talents greater than I possess, I would still be making progress in discovering their treasures. . . .'[2]

Augustine wrote this, in 411, to a young pagan, who was steeped in the classics. It was the most direct challenge he could have made to such a man: for Augustine implied that the Christians, too, possessed a classic as inexhaustible and as all-absorbing as Vergil or Homer had been to the pagans. Their Bible also, could form a man for all he needed in this life. Its text alone, could become the centre of a whole auxiliary literature. In an age when culture was thought of exclusively in terms of the understanding of a classical text, the Bible was nothing less than the basis of a 'Christian culture', a *doctrina Christiana*.[3]

Not only would the study of the Bible in this way, involve theological speculation through an allegorical method, it could demand a whole range of literary interests unknown to classical readers — a knowledge of Hebrew, of the history of the ancient Near East, even of the plants and animals of Palestine.[4] It would also continue old

---

[1] *Ep.* 55, xi, 21. [2] *Ep.* 137, 3.
[3] v. esp. H.-I. Marrou, *S. Augustin et la fin de la culture antique*, esp. pp. 357–385 and 549–560.
[4] *de doct. christ.* II, xxxix, 59.

methods: throughout the Dark Ages, the classical schoolmaster, the *grammaticus*, would find that his vital position in culture, as the exponent of the precise interpretation of a text by grammatical methods, had been assured by the *imprimatur* of the bishop of Hippo.[1] Thus, an ambitious programme of new learning is latent in a work which Augustine began to write in his middle age, the *De Doctrina Christiana* — started in 396 but left unfinished until 427.[2]

The *De Doctrina Christiana*, however, was not a far-reaching scheme for independent Biblical studies. For Augustine lived in an age oppressed by reverence for the 'expert'. He believed in dragons because he had read of them in books.[3] 'Christian scholarship', for him, tended to become little more than the acquisition of manuals by acknowledged 'experts'.[4]

Yet this book is one of the most original that Augustine ever wrote. For it dealt, explicitly, with the ties that had bound educated Christians to the culture of their age. It did this with such intellectual sharpness that it cut forever, in Augustine's mind at least, the Gordian knot that had bound him to his past education. It is no small thing to be able to transcend one's own education, especially an education that enjoyed as exclusive a prestige as the classical education of the Later Roman Empire. In Cassiciacum, surrounded by young aristocrats, feeling a little out of place among the polished Christians of Milan, Augustine had not dreamt that he could transcend this education: it might be subordinated to a quest for Wisdom; but it remained intact, massive and irremovable as the foothills of the Himalayas.

For there had seemed to be simply no alternative to such a culture. It was, of course, possible to be religious without being educated: quite apart from Monica, Augustine had met many such figures, thrown up by the spiritual turmoil of the age: Faustus, the Manichee, is a good example,[5] as were S. Anthony and his followers in Egypt.[6] Yet he admired such men with the particular sort of admiration which sophisticated men reserve for people quite alien to themselves. It was genuinely difficult for him to conceive of a 'wise' man who was not a

---

[1] v. esp. Grabmann, 'Der Einfluss d. heil. Augustinus auf die Verwertung und Bewertung d. Antike im Mittelalter', *Mittelalterliches Geistesleben*, ii, 1936, pp. 1–24, esp. pp. 9–18.

[2] The earliest existing manuscript may go back to the time of Augustine himself: W. M. Green, 'A Fourth Century Manuscript of Saint Augustine?' *Rev. bénédictine*, 69, 1959, pp. 191–197.

[3] *de Gen. ad litt.* III, ix, 13.

[4] *de doct. christ.* II, xxxix, 59; v. Marrou, *St. Augustin et la fin de la culture antique*, pp. 411–413.

[5] v. sup. p. 58.   [6] *Conf.* VIII, viii, 19.

man of classical education: he reacted much as a modern doctor would react to wart-healers — such activities happened outside an age-old tradition of correct, scientific knowledge; they could at best be exercised only by a knack, and, at worst for a Late Roman man, by commerce with demons.[1]

As long as there was nothing to put in its place, Christian critics of a classical education were all the more confused and bitter for lacking constructive alternatives, and for being bound by strong, half-conscious ties to the old world. In the fourth century, Christians and pagans alike had been drawn into the conflict with equal, blind violence. Christian rejection of the classics was met by a pagan 'fundamentalism': the conservatives crudely 'divinized' their traditional literature; the classics were treated as a gift of the gods to men.[2] Christians, for their part, would play in with this reaction by 'diabolizing' the same literature. Many, indeed, wanted to end this tension by denying culture altogether: unexpectedly sophisticated men were glad to hear of monks who had been taught to read by the Holy Ghost alone.[3]

Augustine was surprisingly uninvolved in this confused situation.[4] He regarded the last solution, that of by-passing education, as quite ridiculous.[5] The great Jerome would wake trembling from a dream in which Christ had called him a 'Ciceronian not a Christian'.[6] Augustine was untroubled by nightmares. He avoided them in a characteristic manner: by hard thinking and by the application of a few basic formulae.

He began by remarking that culture was the product of society: it was a natural extension of the fact of language.[7] It was so plainly the creation of social habits as to be quite relative. There could be no absolute standards of classical 'purism':[8] he even noticed that, for many Africans, the alien Latin of the Psalms had come, by the passage of time, to seem 'better' Latin than that of the classics.[9] In the same way, religion, also, was a specific product of the need to communicate: pagan rites and sacrifices were no more than a similar, 'agreed language'

---

[1] c. Acad. I, vii, 19–21 — on the case of a clairvoyant in Carthage.

[2] v. esp. N. H. Baynes, 'The Hellenistic Civilisation and East Rome', Byzantine Studies, pp. 15–16.

[3] de doct. christ., Prooem. 4; v. esp. U. Duchrow, 'Zum Prolog v. Augustins "De Doctrina Christiana" ', Vigiliae Christianae, 17, 1963, pp. 165–172.

[4] Brilliantly put by H.-I. Marrou, S. Augustin et la fin de la culture antique, pp. 354–356.

[5] de doct. christ. Prooem. 5 sq.

[6] v. P. Antin, 'Autour du songe de S. Jérôme', Rev. études latines, 41, 1963, pp. 350–377.

[7] de doct. christ. II, iv, 5; cf. Conf. I, xii, 19–xiii, 21.

[8] de doct. christ. II, xiii, 19.   [9] de doct. christ. II, xiv, 21.

between men and demons.[1] Outside this context they were not a source of infection to the Christian: in the *Aeneid*, Vergil could 'describe' pagan sacrifices without arousing a tremor of religious awe in the pagan, or religious horror in the pious Christian.[2] Thus, at a stroke, much of classical literature, and indeed the habits of a whole society, were secularized. Consistent to the last, Augustine will even apply his distinctions to the smallest details of dress. Possidius, new from the austerities of Augustine's monastery, had tried to abolish ear-rings among his flock. This streak of Puritanism was common in African Christianity. Augustine intervened firmly: amulets worn to placate demons must go; but ear-rings worn to please human men could stay.[3]

Augustine, indeed, is the great 'secularizer' of the pagan past. Areas of Roman life, in which the gods still seemed to lurk, reassuring the conservative and frightening the Christian, are stripped of their religious aura for both sides. They are reduced to purely human dimensions: they were only 'traditional forms laid down by men; adjusted to the needs of human society, with which we cannot dispense in this life'.[4] Augustine will even treat the Roman Empire in this way. As a Christian, he could have reacted to it as the harlot of the Apocalypse;[5] as a Catholic bishop, making use of its legislation, he could have become an hysterical Imperialist.[6] (One often feels that the two attitudes were somehow related in the minds of many of Augustine's colleagues: the Empire was such a force that it could only be totally denigrated or totally idealized.) In the *City of God*, however, Augustine will judge the Empire on its merits as a purely human institution: he will reduce it to the level of any other state, in order to beat out the gods from its history;[7] and he will discuss its contribution to the life of a Christian in terms so general, as to assume that the Empire's function might be taken over by any other state.[8] It is a rare thing to come across a man of sixty, living on the threshold of a great change, who had already come to regard a unique culture and a unique political institution as replaceable, in theory at least.

Behind this change in Augustine's attitude to culture, there lies the change in the quality of his own life. Immensely sensitive to environment and to human contact, he now moved among men, many of whom were entirely uneducated. In a sense, he had 'come home'. His edu-

[1] *de doct. christ.* II, xxiv, 37. [2] *de doct. christ.* II, xx, 30.

[3] *Ep.* 245, 2; cf. *de doct. christ.* II, xx, 30 and xxv, 38. [4] *de doct. christ.* II, xl, 60.

[5] v. inf. p. 293.

[6] e.g. the shocked comments of Optatus of Milevis on the claim of Donatus, as a bishop, to be closer to God than the Emperor: *de schism. Don.* III, 3, (P.L. xi, esp. 1101A).

[7] *de civ. Dei*, IV, 7; v. inf. p. 309. [8] e.g. *de civ. Dei* XIX, 17, 47–58.

cation, after all, had only been half of him. Not all members of his family had been educated.[1] Furthermore, in the monastery at Hippo, he had created an environment in which uneducated men were the equals of the sophisticated: Possidius, for instance, was 'fed on the good bread of the Lord', quite innocent of the Liberal Arts.[2] Visiting an old bishop in his deathbed, Augustine, characteristically wrapt up in his campaigns against Donatism, had told him that the Church needed him, that he should go on living: 'If never, good' the old man replied, 'if sometime, why not now?' 'And Augustine was struck by this old man and praised him as one who feared God — and he had only grown up on a farm and had little book-learning.'[3]

As at Cassiciacum, Augustine was determined to be the educationalist of his circle. But his circle now consisted of the clergy and devout laymen of Africa: the sons of the nobility, who in Milan, would be groomed as 'well trained souls', were now replaced by young men 'fearing God; made meek by piety, who seek the will of God'.[4]

Yet, despite this new freedom, there is an element of strenuously maintained detachment in Augustine's attitude. His whole programme of learning was subtly moulded by the anxiety not to recreate, in the study of the Bible and in preaching, the crippling self-consciousness of the traditional education. The *De Doctrina Christiana* seems a very modern book for this reason. Augustine will give a large place in education to the 'natural', and will be genuinely concerned lest the 'gifted' man be trammelled by rules and regulations. He will play off 'talent' against 'education'.[5] Above all, he will attempt to by-pass the most self-conscious element in Late Roman education, the obsession with the rules of eloquence: a good ear, a knack, and the social fact of hearing good Latin spoken is what Augustine offers by way of training as a substitute for the schools of rhetoric in which he had once made his career.[6]

Augustine never faced the problem of replacing classical education throughout the Roman world. He merely wished to create for the devotees of true 'Wisdom' an oasis of literary culture, that was distinguished by being unselfconscious, unacademic, uncompetitive, and devoted to the understanding of the Bible alone. Indeed, like many such 'withdrawals' on Augustine's part, it tacitly took for granted the

---

[1] *de beata vita* i, 6.   [2] *Ep.* 101, 1.   [3] *Vita*, xxvii, 9–10.
[4] *de doct. christ.* II, ix, 14.
[5] *de doct. christ.* II, xxxvii, 55. v. esp. Marrou. *S. Augustin et la fin de la culture antique,* pp. 515–519.
[6] *de doct. christ.* IV, iii, 5; cf. III, xxix, 40–41.

resilience of the old ways. He hoped to gain some inner detachment from the traditional culture; but he assumed that it would continue. He felt under no obligation to perpetuate his attitude by creating an education of his own. Typically, he refused to codify his very interesting views on style: this would have reminded his readers too vividly of his previous career as a schoolmaster.[1] What Augustine seems deliberately to have forgotten, was that a culture requires a framework of rules and organized teaching. His own superbly unaffected 'Christian' style was in reality a simplicity achieved at the other side of vast sophistication. Eloquence had to be taught, self-consciously, if it was not to share in the slow erosion of Latin civilization in Africa and the West generally. But Augustine had made his career in the 370s and 380s in the great Roman towns: in his attitude to Roman culture, as in his attitude to the Roman Empire, he approached the problem with forty years of comparative security behind him; he never realized the speed with which the Western Empire collapsed in his old age. The next generations would show plainly the price Augustine had to pay for taking the survival of education for granted: the style of Possidius was simple only by being flat; and with other African clergymen, we have, not innocence of rhetoric, but the bombast of the half-educated.[2]

The old pagan world could not be ignored so easily. Educated pagans continued to see Augustine exclusively in terms of his past career.[3] As he wrote his commentary on *Genesis*, he was made constantly aware of the vast body of pagan knowledge to which the Biblical account of the creation was nonsense: subtle arguments of physics 'elaborated by men of leisure'[4] had already been mobilized by Porphyry against the Christians;[5] a whole battery of such awkward problems, *quaestiones*, formed part of the intellectual atmosphere of the late fourth century.[6]

Even the habits of thought which Augustine had hoped to use in the study of the Bible, had run too long in pagan channels. The symbolism of numbers, for instance, was irresistible to 'the mind of any gentleman'.[7] Therefore, the number 10, the number of the Ten Command-

---

[1] *de doct. christ.* IV, i, 2.

[2] v. some awful examples cited by Marrou, *Saint Augustin et la fin de la culture antique*, p. 528; J. Leclercq, 'Prédication et rhétorique au temps de S. Augustin', *Rev. bénédictine*, 57, 1947, pp. 117–131, esp. pp. 121–125.

[3] e.g. *Epp.* 90 and 117.   *de Gen. ad litt.* III, iii, 4.

[5] J. Pépin, *Théologie cosmique et théologie chrétienne*, 1964, esp. pp. 418–461.

[6] v. esp. P. Courcelle, 'Propos antichrétiens rapportés par S. Augustin', *Rech. augustin.* i, 1958, pp. 149–189, esp. pp. 185–186.

[7] *de doct. christ.* II, xvi, 25.

ments, must be particularly edifying. Unfortunately, for the educated man, the number 10 was a mere upstart; it was of no interest whatsoever compared with the number 9: for the number 9 had been fixed in their minds since childhood as the number of the Muses.[1] Augustine would have to reverse such habits. He could never obliterate them. Only a thin brick wall, for instance, separated his baptistery from a luxurious house, some hundred years old. On its mosaic pavement, the owner had placed, as was proper for an educated man, the symbols of the old culture, medallions of the Nine Muses:[2] so close did the pagan world press in around the 'basilica of the Christians at Hippo'.[3] It could not be ignored: paganism must be openly refuted; Augustine's middle age will end with his committing himself to this task with the vast labour of his *City of God*.

[1] *de doct. christ.* II, xvii, 27.　　　[2] v. sup. p. 190.　　　[3] *Ep.* 118, ii, 9.

24

'SEEK HIS FACE EVERMORE

The most important feature of Augustine's intellectual activity in his middle-age, as he himself saw it, was that it took place in a community, the Catholic Church. Such a community, in his opinion, provided a field for vigorous intellectual activity. It was, potentially, an international body: the Latin ecclesiastical literature in his library might be joined, in translation at least, by works of Greek, even of Syriac, authors.[1] It contained a body of knowledge which was destined to expand. Rites such as baptism, mysteries such as the Trinity, contained hidden depths, which could only be explored gradually by a succession of thinkers.[2] Even the ambiguities of the Bible were placed there, so Augustine believed, to provide future generations with ever new facets of the truth to be discovered:[3] for, because of the 'fertility of human reason', truth also would 'grow and multiply'.[4] In such a situation, complete uniformity of opinion was a privilege only of angels.[5] When we read Augustine's insistence, in his works against the Donatists on the authority of the Catholic Church, on the objective quality of its sacramental powers, on the divine guarantees of its cohesion, we should remember that Augustine needed to emphasize these qualities, partly so that he could believe, that his church provided an environment whose superhuman resilience was capable of surviving the tensions engendered by very human activity: diversity of opinion, protracted argument, discovery. Like every other community, the Catholic church needed a culture. Augustine was annoyed by those who claimed by seeking direct inspiration in expounding the Scriptures to dispense with the normal means of human intellectual life, the writing and the reviewing of books. 'Everything could well have been done by an angel, but the standing

---

[1] v. de Bapt. III, iv, 6.   [2] de Bapt. I, xviii, 28.   [3] Enarr. in Ps. 146, 15.
[4] Conf. XIII, xxiv, 36–37.   [5] de Bapt. II, iv, 5.

of the human race would have been devalued if God had seemed unwilling to let men act as the agents of His Word to men . . . on top of that, charity itself which binds men together in the tight knot of unity, would have no means of expressing itself, by pouring out, and as it were mixing together the souls of men, if human beings could learn nothing from their fellows.'[1]

It is not surprising that Augustine took such a robust view of his intellectual activity in the Catholic church. His middle age as a Catholic priest and bishop, was the most creative period of his life: it saw the crystallization of his ideas on grace, the writing of the *Confessions*, the slow piling-up of two masterpieces — his vast commentary on Genesis, the *De Genesi ad Litteram*, and his *De Trinitate*. Augustine's mind was set by such achievements. But they took place in a 'splendid isolation', that would have momentous consequences for the culture of the Latin church.

For Augustine remained a cosmopolitan *manqué*. His relations with an international Christian culture, especially with the Greeks, were somewhat platonic. He depended on translations: and the supply of such translations was erratic. He would never draw on Greek Christian authors in the same way as he drew constantly, deeply, and so almost imperceptibly, on his translations of Greek pagan philosophers. This is the great lacuna of Augustine's middle age. Only after 420, when confronted with a Pelagian, Julian of Eclanum, who claimed to know the traditions of Greek theology far better than he did, would he try to refute his critic by a shrewd if essentially superficial comparison of a few texts in the original Greek with their translation.[2]

Augustine was aware of this gap. He had, after all, begun his life at Hippo as the priest of a Greek bishop. So in 392, he will write to Jerome, asking for translations of Greek commentators on the Bible, above all of Origen.[3] He wished to create in Hippo and among his friends in the African church an atmosphere similar to that of Milan: the 'learned fellowship of the African churches' would, as a matter of course, draw on the Greek East, the traditional source of a high Christian culture. The plan miscarried. The commentaries did not arrive: for Origen fell out of favour, and Jerome was ruffled.[4] The 'learned fellowship' fell back on its own resources: the systematic

---

[1] *de doct. christ.* Prooem. 6.

[2] v. notably, Marrou, *S. Augustin et la fin de la culture antique*, pp. 27–46; Courcelle, *Les lettres grecques en Occident*, esp. pp. 183–194; and B. Altaner, 'Augustinus und die griechische Patristik', *Revue bénédictine*, 62, 1952, pp. 201–215, esp. pp. 211–212.

[3] *Ep.* 28, ii, 2.　　　　　　　[4] v. inf. pp. 274–275.

treatise on exegesis, which Augustine will now recommend, and from which he will derive many details and some basic ideas, was the work of an African who was even a Donatist: the '*Rules*' of Tyconius. The intervention of Tyconius at this moment was decisive. For this writer, more than any other whose influence we can discern, deflected Augustine's thought into some of its most distinctive channels: for Tyconius also was a drastic interpreter of S. Paul, a man whose thought was dominated by the idea of the Church, who already saw history in terms of the destinies of the 'City of God'.[1]

The opportunity for a leisured absorption of Christian literature from all over the Mediterranean ended only too soon for Augustine. For the Donatist controversy caught him unprepared. At Thagaste, he had debated with the Manichees as a Neo-Platonic philosopher. In such debates, the issue of authority was not raised, for Augustine would meet his opponents half-way by appealing to reason;[2] and so the traditional literature of the Catholic church was not considered relevant. From 393 onwards however, Augustine had to meet the Donatists by sinking himself into the claustrophobic world of African writings on the nature of the Church. Even Ambrose may have been forgotten until as late as 418.[3] The sudden absorption of a highly individual body of local authors, will isolate Augustine yet further from his contemporaries: *optimi Punici Christiani*, 'the African Christians are best.'[4] It is against this firm, narrow tradition that Pelagius and his truly cosmopolitan supporters would stumble.

Gradually the 'learned fellowship' would cease to feel the need for Greek books. For they had Augustine. No matter how much he might protest that he preferred to read rather than to write,[5] to listen rather than to speak,[6] Augustine found himself constantly giving. The stenographers would always be at hand, taking down some treatise from dictation.[7] His friends would always gather round him, asking questions, needing help, demanding yet more and more books. They

---

[1] v. esp. *Ep.* 41, 2, the judgements in *de doct. christ.* III, xxx, 42–xxxvii, 56, and *Ep.* 249. A. Pincherle, *La formazione teologica di S. Agostino*, pp. 185–188 and 202–205, is the best discussion of the influence of Tyconius. The difference between the two is most clearly stated by J. Ratzinger, 'Beobachtungen z. Kirchenbegriff d. Tyconius', *Rev. études augustin.*, ii, 1958, pp. 173–185. v. most recently, F. Lo Bue, *The Turin Fragments of Tyconius' Commentary on Revelation*, (Texts and Studies, n.s., vii), 1963, esp. pp. 35–38.

[2] *de mor. eccl. cath.* (I), i, 3.

[3] There are, certainly, no direct citations before that time; v. A. Paredi, 'Paulinus of Milan', *Sacris Erudiri*, xiv, 1963, esp. p. 212, who makes plain how the appeal to Ambrose was necessary to combat the Pelagians.

[4] *de pecc. mer.* I, xxiv, 34.

[5] *de Trin. III*, Prooem., '*credant qui volunt*'.

[6] *Retract.*, Prolog. 2.

[7] e.g. *Ep.* 139, 3.

would snatch his great works from him in their first draft: many such manuscripts circulated for decades in an incomplete form.[1] By 416, the bishop's library at Uzalis was filled with Augustine's works;[2] cultured Christians would come to visit it,[3] and Evodius would pester his friend for yet more treatises.[4] Augustine would always give way to such pressure. Despite his yearnings for contemplation, he had the busy man's fatal genius for generating more and more work. Greek culture did not just drain away of its own accord from Augustine's Africa. The one man who might have brought it alive there, replaced it by constantly giving and creating:

'From the few excerpts that have been translated', Augustine remarked on Greek writers on the Trinity, 'I have no doubt that they contain everything worth trying to discover. But I am, nevertheless, unable to resist my brethren when they require me, according to the law of charity by which I have become their servant, to do work for them. . . . Also, I must confess that, personally, I have learned many things I never knew before . . . just by writing.'[5]

If Augustine was isolated in Africa, at least he lived a very sheltered life there. He was the undisputed teacher of a devoted circle. The international storm of the Origenist controversy, in which the Christian aristocrats of Rome were divided for and against Jerome, passed him by: Jerome's notorious breach with Rufinus puzzled and shocked him, 'for who, then, will not fear a future enemy in every friend if things can happen, as we see them happening, with such pained surprise, between Rufinus and Jerome.'[6]

Above all, he was one of the leaders of a church united against external enemies. He had plenty of comrades-in-arms, and no enemy of the same calibre as himself. This situation was demoralizing. Fighting the Donatists, Augustine became quite punch-drunk with cheap journalism: *'Fill their countenances with shame'* had been his motto;[7] and he had applied it ruthlessly.[8] This might encourage him to be equally rude when dealing with more serious opponents. A heresy on the nature of the Vision of God, current among cultivated men in Rome and Africa, will be dismissed as 'undisciplined chatter':[9] it is not surprising that a fellow Catholic bishop was deeply offended by the manner in which Augustine had handled his opinions;[10] and that he took Augustine's protestations of wishing to learn from anyone as no more than another

---

[1] e.g. *de Trinitate*, (v. *Ep.* 174) and *de doct. christ.* (v. sup. p. 264, n. 2). [2] *Ep.* 161.
[3] v. inf. p. 399 on Florus, a monk of Hadrumetum. [4] e.g. *Ep.* 162.
[5] *de Trin. III*, Prooem. [6] *Ep.* 73, iii, 6. [7] *Ps.* 83, 16 in *C. litt. Petil.* I, xxix, 31.
[8] e.g. *Retract.* II, 51. [9] *Ep.* 92, 4. [10] *Ep.* 148, 4.

sarcastic cut.[1] It is a tribute to Pelagius that, when the time came, Augustine would treat him with greater care.

Augustine is at his most charming only at close quarters, among his friends. He could write exquisite letters. 'Eustasius has gone before us to that rest: no waves beat on it, as on your island home; nor does he pine for Caprara, your Island of Goats, for he no longer seeks to wear the goats'-hair tunic of the monk.'[2]

He knew that, as a bishop, he had been forced by pressure of work to give quick answers to big questions.[3] Yet his sensitivity never deserts him: 'We are human beings and live among men: I must confess that I am not yet among those who are no longer troubled by the problem of doing a lesser evil to avoid a worse; often in such human problems my human feelings overcome me.'[4] Men with little problems, will be reminded of first principles. Noblemen worried by the successful oracles of demons, will be expected to take the plunge at the deep end, by being asked immediately why God permits evil in the universe.[5] A fussy senator who approached Augustine for a final ruling, like any judge, will be told that 'as soon as I learnt of its nature in your letter, the "dilemma" you refer to became my own. Not that all the problems you raise there move me as you say they move you. But I must confess that to find a way of ever removing your dilemma now leaves me in a dilemma.'[6]

It is only at a distance that we can see the sharper quality of Augustine's mind. His long drawn out correspondence with Jerome, for instance, is a unique document in the Early Church. For it shows two highly-civilized men conducting with studied courtesy, a singularly rancorous correspondence. They approach each other with elaborate gestures of Christian humility.[7] They show their claws, for an instant, in classical allusions, in quotations from the poets which the recipient would complete for himself.[8] Neither will give an inch. There is no doubt that Augustine provoked Jerome; and Jerome, though treating Augustine with more respect than others who had crossed him, would not resist playing cat and mouse with the younger man. Augustine's reaction is most revealing. Jerome's handling wounded him: 'how can we engage in such discussion without bitterness of feeling, if you have made up your mind to offend me.'[9] Like many people anxious to be innocent of his own aggressive behaviour, Augustine declared himself always ready to accept criticism: 'Here I am, and in whatever I have

[1] *Ep.* 148, 4. [2] *Ep.* 48, 4. [3] *Ep.* 98, 8; cf. *Ep.* 194, x, 46. v. inf .p. 385, n. 4.
[4] *c. mend.* xviii, 36. [5] *de div. daem.* i, 2. [6] *Ep.* 47 ,1.
[7] e.g. *Ep.* 28, iv, 6. [8] *Ep.* 40, iv, 7. [9] *Ep.* 73, i,1.

spoken amiss, tread firmly on me.'[1] In fact, Augustine was unimpressed by the superior learning of Jerome when it crossed his own opinions. He would dismiss the imposing list of Greek authors with which Jerome supported his views: 'Far be it from me to feel hurt if you can prove your point with a conclusive argument.'[2] *Certa ratione*: this, typically, is what Augustine wanted; and there is little to suggest that he seriously thought that Jerome would provide it, 'for it might just possibly be the case that what you think is not the same as what the truth is.'[3] And when at last Jerome offered to bury the hatchet, and proposed (with considerable restraint, given his taste for invective), that they should 'play together harmlessly in the fields of the Scriptures', Augustine was not amused: 'As for me, I prefer to do things in earnest, not to "play". If you chose the word to imply that what we do is easy exercise, then let me tell you, frankly, that I expected more of you. . . . It is your business to help those engaged in great and exacting investigations — as if studying the Scriptures were a matter of romping around on level ground, not puffing and panting up a steep mountain-face.'[4]

Indeed, Augustine took his ideas very seriously. For him, a good book was a series of 'knots of problems'.[5] His Late Roman readers appreciated this 'knotty' quality of his own books more than we do. Rhetoric had always been connected with a legal training. The form of presentation a reader valued most was closest to that of a modern barrister. The author had to show himself capable both of commanding 'a rich flow of words' and of being 'exceptionally subtle' on small points.[6] Like the Judge in A. P. Herbert's '*Misleading Cases*', the Late Roman reader anticipated some 'jolly litigation'.[7] Little wonder, then, that most of Augustine's books read like an obstacle race. Above all, problems seemed to interest him far more than the people who propounded them. He will betray his acquaintance with important authors with studied impersonality: 'a problem arises' . . . 'some men ask . . .' 'a learned man has said. . . .'[8] One may suspect one reason for this vagueness. Augustine was no respecter of persons among his con-

---

[1] *Ep.* 73, i, 1.   [2] *Ep.* 73, i, 1.   [3] *Ep.* 73, ii, 3.
[4] *Ep.* 82, i, 2.

Both men, in fact, later drew on each other's ideas, v. most recently, Y.-M. Duval, 'Saint Augustin et le *Commentaire sur Jonas* de saint Jérôme', *Rev. études augustin.*, xii, 1966, pp. 9–40.

[5] e.g. *de Bapt.* II, i, 1.   [6] *Ep.* 138, i, 1, anticipating the writing of the *City of God*.
[7] e.g. *de doct. christ.* IV, xx, 39.

[8] v. esp. B. Altaner, 'Augustins Methode der Quellenbenutzung. Sein Studium der Väterliteratur', *Sacris Erudiri*, 4, 1952, pp. 5–17, esp. p. 7. This is notably different from the 'literary' method of Jerome, which entailed a display of 'authorities': *Ep.* 75, iii, 5–6.

temporaries; but he was intensely aware of seeming to criticize colleagues for personal reasons.[1] Very often, an opaque formula would
muffle Augustine's disagreement; and would enable this supremely
individual thinker to pass on, leaving in his wake yet another discarded
opinion of a fellow-Catholic.[2]

For in his approach to problems, Augustine stands out among his
contemporaries by reason of his philosophical training. The only lesson
that he drew from, the immediate history of his times, was that an
historical alliance existed between the Platonists and the Catholic
Church. This alliance ensured that the 'highest peak of human reason'
had found a recognized place within the 'citadel of authority'.[3]
Augustine needed to assert this view. Few of his Latin contemporaries
shared it. The rise of Christianity among men who had never had much
interest in Greek philosophy, threatened to do away with the rational
world-view of the ancients. Surprisingly sophisticated men colluded
in this betrayal of reason. Augustine did not. When he approached the
book of Genesis, for instance, Augustine had to take a firm stand
against a rising tide of fundamentalism.[4] 'It is difficult to do justice to
the discomfort and sadness which such rash claims to knowledge cause
the learned brethren.'[5]

In fact, the ancient view of the world received from Augustine a
tolerance based on lack of interest. He accepted ancient opinions
without thinking; and went on to find in Genesis his own recurrent
preoccupation with strictly philosophical problems,[6] such as simul-
taneous creation, and the relation of time and eternity. Thus, Augustine
would merely put the Greek view of the physical universe in cold
storage; but at least his sensitive horror of committing himself to
irrelevant conjectures about mere physical phenomena,[7] would provide
Galileo with a battery of extremely pertinent citations.[8]

Moreover, the average Latin clergyman had a Roman respect for
authority. As Christians, they could base this attitude on a cult of
human infirmity, and on an appeal to the lasting traditions of inverted
snobbery in the Early Church. The mysteries, they said, must be 'an
impenetrable cloud' to fallen men; and, in any case, to admit the claims
of reason would be to admit the 'expert', and so to open the leadership

---

[1] *Ep.* 95, 4.   [2] e.g. inf. p. 296 on Orosius.   [3] *Ep.* 118, v, 32–33.
[4] e.g. *Conf.* XI, xii, 14. v. esp. Pépin, ' "Caelum Caeli" ', *Bulletin du Cange*, 23, 1953,
pp. 185–274, esp. p. 234.
[5] *de Gen. ad litt.* I, xix, 39.   [6] v. esp. *de Gen. ad litt.* V, xvi, 34 — a forceful statement.
[7] A frequent theme, v. esp. *de Gen. ad litt.* I, xxi, 41; II, v, 9; ix, 20 and xvii, 38.
[8] Who cites *de Gen. ad litt.* I, x, 18, 19 and 21, and II, v, 9 and 10, in the *Lettera a
madama Cristina di Lorena* (1615).

of the church to suspect 'intellectuals', to 'orators and philosophers'.[1] Augustine would answer such a man firmly: 'Far be it from us to think that God would hate in us that which distinguishes us from the beasts.·. . .[2] Love understanding wholeheartedly.'[3]

The two great works of Augustine's middle age, the *De Genesi ad litteram* and the *De Trinitate*, are remarkable evidence of Augustine's capacity for speculation. Even slight acquaintance with these two works is sufficient to dispel the facile impression that Augustine developed his ideas only as a controversialist.[4] For in the *De Genesi* we see the first, relaxed elaboration of themes that will appear, compressed and monumental, in the *City of God*.[5] In the *De Trinitate* we have a book more radically metaphysical than that of any Greek author: throughout it we can see the tension involved in embracing, in one perspective, both the God of Abraham and Isaac and the God of the Philosophers.[6]

The needs of the Donatist controversy came as an unwelcome impingement on the elaboration of these two great works. The pressure of work made Augustine even more insistent on his priorities.[7] He would, for instance, no longer write 'play-things':[8] he would no longer think of building a Christian philosophy out of a text-book of poetry, as he had once done with his *De Musica* in Milan. For he knew that he would only have time to grapple with the basic problems of Christianity, with the Creation, and with the doctrine of the Trinity. In these books, he will show himself quite ruthless in excluding any problem he did not feel qualified to answer by his highly specialized training as a philosopher and an exegete. But within the field of philosophical enquiry, both books communicate all the excitement of sharing in a search in which no problem is avoided, no tension shelved, and in which a speculative masterpiece unfolds quite unselfconsciously before us:

'Therefore, let everyone who reads these pages proceed further with me, when he is equally certain as I am; let him make enquiries with me when he is as hesitant as I; . . . Thus let us enter together, in the path of charity, in search of Him of Whom it is said: *Seek His face evermore.*'[9]

No one has analysed the quality of Augustine's intellectual life as

---

[1] *Ep.* 119, 1.   [2] *Ep.* 120, 3.   [3] *Ep.* 120, 13.

[4] v. his own judgement on the *de Genesi ad litteram* in *Retract.* II, 50.

[5] This has been made clear in the excellent study of R. A. Markus; 'Two Conceptions of Political Authority: Augustine's *De Civ. Dei*, XIX, 14–15, and some Thirteenth-Century Interpretations', *Journ. Theol. Studies*, n.s., xvi, 1965, pp. 68–100, esp. pp. 75–76.

[6] v. esp. M. Schmaus, 'Die Denkform Augustins in seinem Werk *de Trinitate*', *Sitzungsberichte der bayer. Akad. d. Wiss.*, Philos.-hist. Klasse, 1962, no. 6.

[7] e.g. *Ep.* 261, 1; cf. *de lib. arb.* III, xxi, 60.   [8] *Ep.* 101, 4.   [9] *de Trin.* I, iii, 5.

well as Augustine himself. '*To him who has, it shall be given.* God will give more to those who use (for others) that which they have received: He will fill up and pile to the brim what He first gave. . . . Our reflections will be multiplied at His prompting, so that, in our service of Him, we will suffer no shortage, but, rather, will rejoice in a miraculous abundance of ideas.'[1]

In his middle age, Augustine spent his life giving: between 395 and 410 he wrote some 33 books and long letters. This shift to giving is highly significant. At Cassiciacum and Thagaste he had been more isolated, prepared to scale alone if needs be, the highest peaks of Wisdom. As a bishop of Hippo, depressed by human weakness, he will turn his creativity into a form of giving food: he will always present it as 'feeding' men as much in need of nourishment as he now felt himself to be.[2]

Such constant outpouring was like a vast river. It is easy to observe the speed with which it slips by, to be impressed by the endless variations of its eddies; to think of it, therefore, as something infinitely flexible, as capable of unlimited change. Yet, in Augustine's thought, his own sense of unremitting labour, his acute sensitivity to the limitations of the human mind when faced by certain problems, his constant protestations of his willingness to learn from others, are intimately related to a growing sense of certainty about essential issues: the very speed and volume of the water of this river, had carved deep, immovable channels along its bed.

For, in Augustine's middle age, his intellectual progress had come to involve the commitment of the whole personality to the Catholic church. The ideal remained the same: the 'purification' of the mind, where shadows gave way to reality. '*In the morning I shall stand before Thee and contemplate.*'[3] But the process of 'purification' itself, had become infinitely more complex. In Augustine's early works the soul needed only to be 'groomed' by obvious and essentially external methods, by a good education, by following rational demonstrations, by authority conceived of primarily as an aid to learning.[4] In his middle age, this 'purification' is treated as more difficult, for the soul itself, he thought, was more deeply 'wounded'; and, above all, the healing of the soul has come to involve more parts of the personality.[5] The problem is no longer one of 'training' a man for a task he will later accomplish: it

---

[1] *de doct. christ.* I, i, 1.   [2] *de doct. christ.* II, vii, 11.
[3] *de Trin.* IV, xviii, 24; cf. *Ep.* 242, 4.   [4] v. esp. Burnaby, *Amor Dei*, pp. 73–79.
[5] The most sound statements of this attitude are by F. Cayré, *Initiation à la Philosophie de S. Augustin*, 1947, pp. 249–250, and Holte, *Béatitude et Sagesse*, pp. 361–386.

is one of making him 'wider', of increasing his capacity, at least to take in something of what he will never hope to grasp completely in this life.[1] No one can truly understand a book, Proust has said, unless he has already been able to 'allow the equivalents to ripen slowly in his own heart'. This profoundly human truth is what Augustine will always tell his readers: they must 'look into the Scriptures, the eyes of their heart on its heart'.[2] Such a 'widening'[3] can only happen by loving what is only partially known: 'It is impossible to love what is entirely unknown, but when what is known, if even so little, is loved, this very capacity for love makes it better and more fully known.'[4]

Very briefly then, no one will love what he has no prospect of making his own by understanding: faith without the hope of understanding would be no more than compliance to authority. Yet he will not understand what he is not prepared to love. To separate 'faith' and 'reason', therefore, goes against the grain of Augustine's thought. For what concerned him was to set a process in motion: it was to 'purify', to 'heal' a damaged mind. He never doubted for a moment, that this process happened through the constant interplay of the two elements: of faith 'that works by love',[5] of understanding, 'that He may be known more clearly and so loved more fervently.'[6]

This is very much the view of a 'committed' man. Augustine was acutely aware that he took up his attitude in order to avoid alternatives, and that it had been possible for great minds to waste their lives through taking a superficial view of human nature.[7] He had been a Manichee; he had come so close to an 'autonomous' Platonism that the experience lived on powerfully in him. He had not written his *Confessions* for nothing. A middle-aged man's sense of having once wandered, of regret at having found truth so late, will harden Augustine's attitude.[8]

Augustine had come to regard his intellectual activity as dependent, also, on currents beyond his own control. For with the growth of his distinctive ideas on grace, the capacity to love, on which understanding depends, was itself a gift of God, outside a man's powers of self-determination: no 'training' could create it. Augustine felt acutely the need for some guiding principle, beyond his own mind, to direct the turbulent onrush of his thoughts. The idea that God 'inspired', 'prompted', even 'revealed' ideas to a thinker, is common in Late

---

[1] e.g. *Frang.* 2, 6, (*Misc. Agostin.*, i, pp. 196–197).   [2] *de doct. christ.* IV, v, 8.
[3] *Enarr. in Ps.* 146, 12.   [4] *Tract. in Joh.* 96, 4; cf. esp. *Enarr. xviii in Ps.* 118, 3.
[5] *Ep.* 120, 8.   [6] *de Trin.* VIII, ix, 13.   [7] e.g. *de Trin.* XV, xxiv, 44.
[8] Well put by Marrou, *St. Augustine* (Men of Wisdom), 1957, pp. 71–72.

Antiquity:[1] but with Augustine, these ideas, which were often expressed very crudely by contemporaries, are rooted in a profound sense of the momentum of psychological forces beyond his control;[2] 'I hope that God, in His mercy, will make me remain steadfast on all the truths which I regard as certain. . . .'[3] Augustine, the son of the visionary Monica, had inherited some of the unnerving certainty of his mother.

Augustine's certainties could reach down to deep, even primitive, roots. The 'custom of the Church', for instance, when allied to reason, could be used to sweep away any number of purely rational objections.[4] Augustine, for instance, regarded the sacrament of baptism as being charged with instinctive feelings of awe, feelings strong enough, in themselves to deter men from the practice of rebaptism.[5] The Pelagians will be brought up sharply against this aspect of Augustine's thought. Augustine had once hoped to understand the rite of infant baptism: 'Reason will find that out.'[6] Now he will appeal, not to reason, but to the rooted feelings of the Catholic masses.[7]

Above all, Augustine's very certainty grew out of his deep awareness of how very little a man could ever know. One can trace the development of Augustine's mind by following the strands of feeling that he picks out in the book of Wisdom. Once it was Wisdom meeting men 'cheerfully';[8] this strand will now be overshadowed, for the rest of Augustine's life by the sophisticated melancholy of a Jew of Hellenistic times: *'For the thoughts of mortal men are fearful and our counsels uncertain. For the corruptible body is a load upon the soul, and the earthly habitation presseth down the mind that museth on many things. . . .'*[9]

---

[1] It was a usual theme in etiquette to treat one's correspondent as 'inspired': e.g. *Epp.* 24, 2 (Paulinus on Augustine), and 82, 2 (Augustine on Jerome). Medieval illuminations will show Augustine being inspired by an angel, or by an angel and the Holy Ghost: e.g. Jeanne and Pierre Courcelle, 'Scènes anciennes de l'iconographie augustinienne', *Rev. études augustin.*, x, 1964, pl. XVII–XIX, and pp. 63–65.

[2] Augustine's view of the nature of the inspiration of the writers of the Bible is equally differentiated and humane: v. esp. H. Sasse, '*Sacra Scriptura*: Bemerkungen zur Inspirationslehre Augustins', *Festschr. Franz Dornseiff*, 1953, pp. 262–273. Thus, when Augustine speaks of an idea having been 'revealed' to him, he means only that he has reached the inevitable conclusion of a series of certainties (e.g. *de grat. et lib. arb.* i, 1 and *de praed. sanct.* i, 2 quoting *Phil.* 3, 15–16 — v. inf. p. 403) — an experience not unknown to speculative thinkers today: v. M. L. Cartwright, *The Mathematical Mind*, 1955. v. esp. A. C. de Veer, ' "Revelare", "Revelatio". Éléments d'une étude sur l'emploi du mot et sur sa signification chez s. Augustin', *Rech. augustin.*, ii, 1962, pp. 331–357, esp. pp. 352–354.

[3] *de Trin.* I, iii, 5.
[4] *de Bapt.* III, ii, 3: 'the safest of all reasons'.
[5] e.g. *de Bapt.* V, vi, 7.
[6] *de quant. anim.* xxxvi, 80.
[7] v. inf. p. 385.
[8] e.g. *de lib. arb.* II, xvi, 41.
[9] *de Trin.* III, x, 21.

PART IV
410-420

410 18.viii. Alaric enters Rome. Roman refugees to Africa. Pelagius passes through Hippo. 25.viii. Withdrawal of toleration for Donatists. 14.x. Edict summoning a *Collatio* at Carthage. Arrival of Marcellinus.	14.vi. XV Council of Carthage. In Carthage at intervals from 19.v, until he goes to Utica, 11.ix, an to Hippo Diarrhytus, 22.ix. Retires to a villa outside Hippo for the winter because of his health *Epistola CXVIII ad Dioscurum.* *De unico baptismo contra Petilianum* (= *Ep.* 120).
411 18.v. Donatists come to Carthage for *Collatio*. 1.vi. Opening session of the *Collatio*. 9.vi. Judgement given against Donatists by Marcellinus.	Preaching regularly at Carthage from Jan. to March, and at Cirta well as at Carthage, from April to June, against the Donatists. 1,3,8.vi. *Collatio* at Carthage with Donatists. Affair of Pinianus at Hippo. Letter from Marcellinus late in year to say that Pelagian views we spreading in Carthage, and to tell him of the condemnation Caelestius. /12 *Breviculus collationis contra Donatistas.* /12 *De peccatorum meritis et remissione.*
412 30.i. Edict against the Donatists.	14.vi. Synod at Cirta. Regularly preaching in Carthage, Sept.–Dec. *Post collationem contra Donatistas.* *De spiritu et littera.* *De gratia novi testamenti* (= ep. 140).
413 Revolt of Heraclian. Demetrias receives the veil from Aurelius. Pelagius, *Letter to Demetrias*. Defeat of Heraclian. 13.ix. Execution of Marcellinus.	In Carthage (mid-January). *De videndo Deo ad Paulinam* (= ep. 147). *De fide et operibus.* Carthage at end of June and again in August and Septemb attempting to save Marcellinus. *De civitate Dei, I–III* (written before death of Marcellinus). /15 *De civitate Dei, IV–V.* /15 *De natura et gratia.*
414 Orosius goes to Jerusalem, to remain there two years.	*De bono viduitatis ad Julianam.* *De Trinitate* appears. /16–17 *Tractatus in Joannis evangelium* (begun, perhaps, 407–408)
415 20.xii. Synod at Diospolis (Lydda) examines Pelagius.	*Ad Orosium contra Priscillianistas et Origenistas.* *De origine animae et de sententia Jacobi ad Hieronymu* (= *Epp.* 166–7). /16 *Tractatus in epistolam Joannis ad Parthos* (begun, perhap 407–408). /16 *De perfectione justitiae hominis.* /17 *De civitate Dei VI–X.*
416 Orosius comes to council in Carthage on Pelagius (September). He brings relics of S. Stephen. Settlement of Visigoths in Spain.	Attends council at Milevis (Sept.–Oct.) which condemns Pelagiu and Caelestius. *Ep.* 177 to Pope Innocent.

P.L. VOL. COL.	TRANSLATIONS
33 · 431	
43 · 595	
43 · 613	
44 · 109	(in) *The anti-Pelagian writings of St Augustine*, I, Edinburgh, 1872.
43 · 651	
44 · 201	(in) *The anti-Pelagian writings*, I, Edinburgh, 1872; *Three anti-Pelagian treatises of St Augustine*, Ld., 1887; *Basic Writings*, I, NY., 1948; *Augustine, the later works*, Ld., 1954; *On the spirit and the letter*, Ld., 1925.
43 · 538	
3 · 596	
0 · 197	(in) *Seventeen short treatises*, Oxford, 1847; *Faith and works*, NY., 1955.
1 · 13	*The city of God*, (2 vols.), Edinburgh, 1871; (in) *Basic Writings*, II (selections only), NY., 1948; *City of God*, (7 vols.), Ld., 1952–; *City of God*, NY., 1962–; *City of God*, (abridged), Ld., 1963.
4 · 247	(in) *The anti-Pelagian writings*, I, Edinburgh, 1872; *Three anti-Pelagian treatises*, Ld., 1887; *Basic Writings*, I, NY., 1948.
0 · 429	(in) *Seventeen short treatises*, Oxford, 1847; *The excellence of widowhood*, NY., 1952.
5 · 1379	*Homilies on the Gospel according to St John*, (2 vols.), Oxford, 1848/9; *On John*, (2 vols.), Edinburgh, 1873/4.
2 · 669	
3 · 720	
5 · 1977	(in) *Homilies on St John II*, Oxford, 1848; *Augustine: later works*, Ld., 1954.
4 · 291	*The anti-Pelagian writings*, I, Edinburgh, 1872.
· 764	

417 12.iii. Innocent condemns Pelagius and Caelestius.
 18.iii. Election of Zosimus.
 Before Sept. Zosimus writes to African bishops: '*Magnum pondus . . .*'
 Mid-Sept. Zosimus examines Pelagius. Writes to African bishops: '*Postquam . . .*'
	Receives Orosius's *History*.
	    De gestis Pelagii.
	 Preaching in Carthage in mid-September.
	    De correctione Donatistarum (= *Ep.* 185).
	    De praesentia Dei ad Dardanum (= *Ep.* 187).
	    De patientia
	 /18 *De civitate Dei, XI–XIII.*

418 23.iii. Third letter of Zosimus: Caelestius and Pelagius still excommunicated.
 30.iv. Expulsion of Pelagius and Caelestius from Rome.
 Death of Zosimus (Dec.)
 29.xii. Election of Boniface.
	1.v. XVI Council of Carthage. He remains in Carthage at least until middle of month.
	 Receives letter from Pinianus in Jerusalem, who has just met Pelagius.
	 Sends him *De gratia Christi et de peccato originali.*
	
	 20.ix. At Caesarea in Mauretania:
	    Gesta cum Emerito Donatistarum episcopo.
	 /19 *Contra sermonem Arianorum.*
	 /20 *De civitate Dei, XIV–XVI.*
	    Ep. 194 to Sixtus.

419 First work of Julian of Eclanum appears.	25.v. XVII Council of Carthage.
	    Locutiones in Heptateuchum.
	    Quaestiones in Heptateuchum.
	 /21 *De nuptiis et concupiscentia.*
	 /21 *De anima et ejus origine.*
	 /21 *De conjugiis adulterinis.*

420 Gaudentius of Timgad threatens to burn himself, his congregation and his basilica, on the arrival of the imperial agent Dulcitius.	*Contra mendacium.* /21 *Contra adversarium legis et prophetarum.* /21 *Contra duas epistolas Pelagianorum.* /25 *De civitate Dei, XVII.* ? Interview with tribune Boniface at Tubunae (Tobna).

P.L. VOL. · COL.	TRANSLATIONS
4 · 319	(in) *The anti-Pelagian writings, I*, Edinburgh, 1872; *Three anti-Pelagian treatises*, Ld., 1877.
3 · 792	(in) *On the Donatist controversy*, Edinburgh, 1872.
3 · 832	
0 · 611	(in) *Seventeen short treatises*, Oxford, 1847; *Patience*, NY., 1952.
4 · 359	(in) *The anti-Pelagian writings, II*, Edinburgh, 1874; *Basic Writings, I*, NY., 1948.
3 · 697	
2 · 683	
3 · 874	
4 · 485	
4 · 547	
4 · 413	(in) *The anti-Pelagian writings, II*, Edinburgh, 1874.
4 · 475	(in) *The anti-Pelagian writings, II*, Edinburgh, 1874.
0 · 451	*Adulterous marriage*, NY., 1955.
0 · 517	(in) *Seventeen short treatises*, Oxford, 1847; *Against Lying*, NY., 1952.
2 · 603	
4 · 549	(in) *The anti-Pelagian writings, III*, Edinburgh, 1876.

25

SENECTUS MUNDI

THE SACK OF ROME[1]

Towards the end of 408, Augustine wrote a long letter to Paulinus of Nola.[2] Paulinus was a lucky man: he could still afford to be otherworldly: he was a recluse, living an 'Evangelic death' to the business of the world.[3] For Augustine, the bishop, this old tradition of withdrawal was no longer enough: he had to 'live *among* men, for their benefit';[4] and, 'it seems to me that the uncertainty and difficulty that we encounter (in this), springs from the one fact that in the midst of the great variety of men's habits and opinions . . . we are having to conduct the affairs of a whole people — not of the Roman people on earth, but of the citizens of the Heavenly Jerusalem.'[5]

Here Augustine touches on a tender spot for the bishops of his age. It was a truism that the Christians belonged to a Heavenly Jerusalem: in that city only would they be 'not passers by, not resident aliens, but full citizens'.[6] In expressing this overriding loyalty to another world in terms of 'full citizenship', they had chosen the most vivid and meaningful expression that ancient men could use.[7] And yet, during the episcopate of Augustine, this group of otherworldly men had made a dramatic and violent impact on this world. For over a decade, the bishops in Africa had provoked the destruction of the old ways. Public paganism had been suppressed: the great temples were closed; the statues broken up, often by Christian mobs;[8] the proud inscriptions that had proclaimed the unshakeable alliance of the ancient cities and their protecting gods, had been used to pave the public highways.[9]

Sometimes the irritation had proved too great. In Calama, in 408,

---

[1] The most reliable studies are F. G. Maier, *Augustin und das antike Rom*, 1955, and P. Courcelle, *Histoire littéraire des grandes invasions germaniques*, 3rd ed., 1965.
[2] *Ep.* 95. [3] *Ep.* 94, 4. [4] *Ep.* 95, 2. [5] *Ep.* 95, 5.
[6] *Ephes.* 2, 19. [7] e.g. *Enarr. in Ps.* 61, 6. [8] v. sup. p. 231.
[9] Van der Meer, *Augustine*, pp. 37–43.

Possidius had tried to use his new powers under an Imperial law, to break up a traditional procession: he had almost been killed in the riots that followed[1] (Augustine had this incident in mind as he wrote to Paulinus). Augustine himself had then been approached by Nectarius, a leading townsman of Calama, who pleaded with him to intervene to modify the savage punishments that might be inflicted after such rioting.[2] The bishop of Hippo was after all a highly-educated man, and like Nectarius, he had become a local figure: could he be so insensible to love of one's home-town, 'the only love which rightly excells love of one's parents'?[3] Augustine answered flatly in Nectarius' own terms: he had found a better country to love, 'Please pardon us', he wrote, 'if *our* country, up above, has to cause trouble to your own.'[4]

It only required a public calamity to bring such a tension to a head. Calamities were not lacking. It was the time of the 'Barbarian Invasions'. On August 24th 410, the inconceivable happened: a Gothic army, led by Alaric, entered Rome.[5] On two occasions in the past two years, the Goths had besieged the sacred city, and starved the inhabitants into cannibalism. Rome was sacked for three days; and parts of it were, inevitably, burnt.

In the next few years, there would, of course, be many people anxious to minimize the disaster. It could have been worse. Alaric had lived most of his life within the frontiers of the Roman Empire. Compared with other barbarians, he was almost an Elder Statesman. He had used the destructiveness of his tribe to bargain for pensions, and for a post in the High Command of the Roman state; he and his successors depended for their position on their remaining open to negotiation with the Roman government.[6] In the next few years, politicians would realize with relief, that the potential conquerors of Europe were in reality no more than ambitious blackmailers.[7] But all this was in the future. The refugees who made their appearance in Africa in that winter could not afford the complacency of the politicians and of later historians, who would minimize the importance of the sack of their city. Pelagius, a monk from Britain, had been present: he wrote to a Roman lady when the event was still fresh in both their minds:

---

[1] *Ep.* 91, 8–10.
[2] *Ep.* 90. He may have approached Augustine successfully on another occasion: *Ep.* 38, 3.
[3] *Ep.* 90.   [4] *Ep.* 91, 2.   [5] v. esp. Courcelle, *Hist. littér.*, pp. 31–77.
[6] E. A. Thompson, 'The Visigoths from Fritigern to Euric', *Historia*, xii, 1963, pp. 105–126.
[7] Orosius, *Hist.* I, 16.

'It happened only recently, and you heard it yourself. Rome, the mistress of the world, shivered, crushed with fear, at the sound of the blaring trumpets and the howling of the Goths. Where, then, was the nobility? Where were the certain and distinct ranks of dignity? Everyone was mingled together and shaken with fear; every household had its grief and an all-pervading terror gripped us. Slave and noble were one. The same spectre of death stalked before us all.'[1]

Rome, of course, had long ceased to be the political capital of the Empire. As the residence of many important senators, however, it had remained the centre of Western society; and its refugees were particularly vocal and influential.[2] Above all, Rome was the symbol of a whole civilization: it was as if an army had been allowed to sack Westminster Abbey or the Louvre. In Rome, the protection of the gods for the Empire had been made explicit. For the conservatives of the previous century, Rome had been a sort of 'pagan Vatican': a punctiliously protected city of great temples where the religion that had guaranteed the greatness of the Empire could survive and be seen to survive.[3] The Christians had even colluded with this myth: just as Rome had assembled the gods of all nations to act as talismans, so Roman Christians had come to believe that Peter and Paul had travelled from the East to lay their holy bodies in the city.[4] The one talisman had merely replaced the other; and, after 410, Augustine had to deal with disillusioned Christians quite as much as with angry pagans.[5]

On a deeper level, Rome symbolized the security of a whole civilized way of life. To an educated man, the history of the known world culminated quite naturally in the Roman Empire, just as, to a nineteenth century man, the history of civilization culminated in the supremacy of Europe.[6] The sack of Rome by the Goths, then, was an ominous reminder of the fact that even the most valuable societies might die. 'If Rome can perish' wrote Jerome, 'what can be safe?'[7]

---

[1] Pelagius, *Ep. ad Demetriadem*, 30, (P.L. xxx, 45D).

[2] v. esp. A. Chastagnol, *La Préfecture urbaine à Rome sous le Bas-Empire*, 1960, esp. pp. 450–462.

[3] v. esp. N. H. Baynes, 'Symmachus', *Byzantine Studies*, pp. 361–365, esp. pp. 364–365.

[4] e.g. H. Chadwick, 'Pope Damasus and the Peculiar Claim of Rome to St. Peter and St. Paul', *Freundesgabe O. Cullmann*, (*Novum Testamentum*, Suppl. 6), 1962, pp. 313–318, and M. Ch. Pietri, '*Concordia apostolorum* et *renovatio urbis*. (Culte des martyrs et propagande papale)', *Mél. d'archéol. et d'hist.*, 73, 1961, pp. 275–322. Paulinus would always visit the *limina Apostolorum* every Easter season: *Ep.* 94, 1.

[5] e.g. *Serm.* 81, 8.

[6] v. esp. the admirable survey of F. Vittinghoff, 'Zum geschichtlichen Selbstverständnis der Spätantike', *Hist. Zeitschr.*, 198, 1964, pp. 529–574; esp. pp. 543 and 572.

[7] Jerome, *Ep.* 123, 16.

Augustine is the only contemporary whom we can see reacting immediately to this disaster: long sermons, closely dated, and a series of letters to leading refugees allow us to sense the complexity of his attitude.[1] In these we can see how an event whose outline and significance tends to be taken for granted by historians, can be refracted in one participant, into a surprisingly rich spectrum. We would impoverish Augustine's reaction to the sack of Rome if we were only interested in one aspect of it, in the reaction of a Christian to the general fate of the Roman Empire. This issue rarely comes to the surface: instead, there is room in Augustine's mind for all the confused emotions of any contemporary, who feels obscurely that the world he lives in can no longer be taken for granted. We will find, in Augustine's writings of this time, perspicacious comment rubbing shoulders with the expression of political vested interest; the calculated pursuit of his own authority in an atmosphere of crisis, mingling with a mounting preoccupation with elemental themes, with guilt and suffering, old age and death.

Augustine was a bishop. His contact with the outside world was through pious Christians.[2] He wished to 'weep with those who weep'; and he was genuinely annoyed that the Italian bishops had not troubled to inform him of the extent of the disaster.[3] As an African bishop, however, he was himself fully preoccupied by events nearer home. The authorities in Carthage panicked at this time: to allay discontent they issued a hasty edict of toleration for the Donatists.[4] This action dominated Augustine's life at the time of the sack of Rome. He was faced with a crisis of authority in his own town. Donatist violence had been renewed, and with it, a revival of religious 'segregation' among the Catholics: his congregation had begun to ostracize Donatist converts.[5] Augustine was partly responsible for this bad atmosphere. He had been constantly absent: he was still in Carthage on September 8th, 410, receiving urgent letters to return to Hippo.[6] On his return, he was faced with far more pressing problems than the news of the distant sack of Rome: a converted Donatist had lapsed through being cold-shouldered by the Catholics. This is what really moved him: 'At that news, I tell you, brethren, my heart was broken: yes, my heart was broken.'[7]

---

[1] v. esp. Maier, *Augustin u. Rom*, pp. 48–75, and Courcelle, *Hist. littér.*, pp. 65–77.

[2] *Serm.* 105, 12, referring to his friends in Rome.   [3] *Ep.* 99, 1.   [4] v. inf. p. 330.

[5] v. *Serm.* 296, 12, and a veiled reference to discontent among his congregation in *Ep.* 124, 2.

[6] *Frang.* 5, 6 (*Misc. Agostin.*, i, p. 218).   [7] *Serm.* 296, 12.

As a bishop, he had looked to Ravenna, where the Catholic Emperors issued the laws that protected his church, not to Rome. Thus, while Britain became independent, and Gaul fell to usurpers, Augustine and his colleagues remained loyal to the existing Emperor — Honorius. The father of this 'pale flower of the women's quarters', Theodosius the Great, will be presented as a model Christian prince in the *City of God*.[1] There were good reasons for such a superficial panegyric: a law reaffirming all previous legislation suppressing non-Catholics had emerged from the chancery at Ravenna at almost exactly the same time as the Goths entered Rome.[2]

By contrast, Rome could be represented as the black sheep of a family of loyal Christianized cities: Carthage, Alexandria and Constantinople. The siege had provoked an ostentatious pagan reaction in the city; and so, for a Catholic bishop, the Romans, who pinned their faith on false gods, had merely got what they deserved.[3] Carthage, decently purged of its great temples by Imperial commissioners,[4] was still standing, *in nomine Christi*, 'in the Name of Christ.'[5] This smug remark betrays Augustine as very much an average provincial of the Later Empire: his patriotism meant loyalty to an absolute, idealized monarch; untouched by aristocratic nostalgia for Old Rome, he would pin his faith on distant autocrats, who at least shared the same Christian prejudices as his own congregation.[6]

In an atmosphere of public disaster, men want to know what to do. At least Augustine could tell them. The traditional pagans had accused the Christians of withdrawing from public affairs and of being potential pacifists. Augustine's life as a bishop had been a continual refutation of this charge. He knew what it was to wield power with the support of the Imperial administration. Far from abandoning civil society, he had maintained what he believed to be its true basis, the Catholic religion; and in his dealings with heresy, lawlessness and immorality, he had shown not a trace of pacifism.

When he wrote to pagan and Christian members of the governing class at this time, he could approach them as a man who had gained his experience of their problems in a hard school. As a bishop he could claim to have done what no pagan god had done: he had undertaken the moral guidance of a whole community.[7] No pagan temple had ever

---

[1] *de civ. Dei*, V, 26.

[2] *Cod. Theod.* XVI, 5, 51 (25th Aug. 410), and XVI, 11, 3 (14th Oct. 410).

[3] *Serm.* 105, 12–13.   [4] *de civ. Dei*, XVIII, 54.   [5] *Serm.* 105, 12.

[6] v. esp. Augustine's references to pious visits of the Emperors to the tomb of S. Peter at Rome: *Ep.* 232, 3; *Enarr. in Ps.* 65, 4 (415) and 86, 8.

[7] *de civ. Dei*, II, 19, 12 and II, 28.

resounded to such oratory as Augustine now used, to establish his threatened authority over the Catholic 'sheep' at Hippo.[1]

There was no room for vagueness in Augustine's programme. The conservative pagans had talked nostalgically, in general terms, of imponderable past values, such as the 'old *morale*':[2] Augustine wrote unambiguously about the precise public enforcement of morality.[3] They had hankered after the military glory of their ancestors: Augustine merely turned this belligerence inwards; vice and heresy were 'inner enemies', requiring an austere 'Home Front'.[4] His ideal assumed an active powerful state: he had no use for 'empty praise of the *mos maiorum*, the ancestral way of life'; laws, revealed to men by divine authority and actively enforced, were to be the basis of his Christian empire.[5]

There were many men who would listen to such advice. Flavius Marcellinus, an Imperial commissioner who arrived in Carthage at the end of the year, was typical of a new generation of Catholic politicians: baptized, an amateur theologian, austere, completely chaste.[6] Like Augustine, such a man felt 'press-ganged' into public service: like Augustine, he could be expected to react to his position by being doubly conscientious; as in the Gospel, he must now 'walk two miles with those who had pressed him to walk one'.[7] There is a grim truth in Augustine's use of this command. In 410 and afterwards, a new type of Imperial servant walked a good two miles in the interests of the Catholic church. The final suppression of Donatism in the province by such men owed much to the mood of panic and to the need for strong action, that had accompanied the fall of Rome.[8]

But the deeper anxieties could not be avoided by calls to action: Augustine had also to make sense of suffering and political collapse on a scale that had taken his congregation by surprise.

Africa was a land of olive-trees. All through the summer, the olives hung on branches that waved freely in the breeze: at the end of the year, they would be beaten down and crushed in the olive-presses.[9] The familiar image of the olive-press, the *torcular*, will now recur in Augustine's sermons:[10] 'Now is the end of the year.... Now is the time to be pressed.'[11] This image sums up Augustine's distinctive assessment

---

[1] *de civ. Dei*, II, 4, 13. Compare the great *Sermons* 46 and 47 on Ezechiel. Augustine suggested that the Roman clergy had been punished for not sufficiently rebuking their community: *de civ. Dei*, I, 9, 37 (citing Ezech. 33, 6).

[2] *Ep.* 136, 2. [3] *Ep.* 137, v, 20. [4] *Ep.* 138, iii, 14.
[5] Implied by *de civ. Dei*, II, 7, 23. [6] v. esp. *Ep.* 151, 8–9, and inf. p. 337.
[7] *Enarr. in Ps.* 61, 8. [8] v. inf. p. 336. [9] *Enarr. in Ps.* 136, 9.
[10] e.g. *Denis* 24, 11, (*Misc. Agostin.*, i, p. 151). [11] *Enarr. in Ps.* 136, 9.

of the meaning of the sack of Rome. The disasters of the time were the *pressurae mundi*, the pressing of the whole human community.[1] No one could be exempt from such pressing. It is typical of Augustine that he should link guilt and suffering so intimately, and that he should see them as so pervasive. His reaction to the catastrophes of 410 reveals the elemental bedrock of the ideas that he had crystallized in justifying the 'controlled catastrophe' of the coercion of the Donatists: the human race as a whole needed discipline,[2] by frequent, unwelcome impingements; and so his God is a stern father, who will *'scourge the son he receives'*: 'And you, you spoilt son of the Lord: you want to be received, but not beaten.'[3]

This deeply-ingrained attitude meant, also, that Augustine refused to stand outside the disaster, as many Christians did. The Romans, for instance, were not punished for any distinctive, particular sins: unlike later Christian moralists, Augustine does not castigate in detail the vices of Roman society.[4] For him, the deep guilt of the human race as a whole was a quite sufficient reason for any of its particular tribulations. Still less did he gloat over the sack of Rome as over the collapse of an alien and hostile civilization, as may well have happened among a fringe of Christians.[5] Above all, he refused to be passive. He would not see only destruction. 'Pressing' was an active process, aimed at positive results; through it, good oil was set free to run into the vats: 'The world reels under crushing blows, the old man is shaken out; the flesh is pressed, the spirit turns to clear flowing oil.'[6] Augustine's reaction to the atmosphere of public emergency had stimulated action; his view of the corrective nature of catastrophes admitted a genuine respect for heroism.

But a man, of course, chooses his heroes from the company he keeps. Augustine looked to a narrow élite — to the 'servants of God', who,

---

[1] *Ep.* 111, 2 and *Serm.* 81, 7.

[2] *de civ. Dei*, I, 10, 32: *'experimentorum disciplina'*.

[3] *Serm.* 296, 10; cf. *Ep.* 99, 3, in which Augustine expresses hopes for the 'correction' of a family of young children at this time. v. sup. p. 237.

[4] v. esp. Salvian, *De gubernatione Dei*, (P.L. liii, 25–158), who, despite the evident dislike of many modern historians (e.g. Courcelle, *Hist. littér.*, pp. 146–154), remains their most circumstantial source for the abuses of fifth century Gaul: v. Jones, *The Later Roman Empire*, i, p. 173.

[5] v. esp. Commodian, *Carmen de duobus populis*, ed. J. Martin, *Corpus Christianorum*, ser. lat. cxxviii, 1960, e.g. ll. 921 ff., (p. 107): 'She indeed used to rejoice, but the whole earth was groaning. . . . She who bragged that she was Eternal now weeps to eternity'. The most likely hypothesis on the date and milieu of Commodian is Courcelle, 'Commodien et les invasions du ve siècle', *Rev. études latines*, xxiv, 1946, pp. 227–246, and *Hist. littér.*, pp. 319–337.

[6] *Serm.* 296, 6; cf. *Ep.* 111, 2.

like the just men of Israel, praised God and prayed, in the midst of their torments, 'for their sins and the sins of their people.'[1] His heroes were the ascetic members of the Roman aristocracy, whom he had come to know of through *Paulinus noster*, Paulinus of Nola.[2] Augustine had no illusions about the average man: 'The congregation of Hippo', he wrote, 'whom the Lord has ordained me to serve, is in great mass, and almost wholly of a constitution so weak, that the pressure of even a comparatively light affliction might seriously endanger their well-being; at the present, however, it is smitten with tribulation so overwhelming, that even if it were strong, it could hardly survive the imposition of this burden.'[3]

These *déraciné* Christian noblemen created a great stir when they arrived in Africa; but they were of little practical help. A great opportunity was missed. The Christian members of a noble family, renowned for their austerities, Melania, her husband Pinianus, and their mother Albina, had retired to their estates at Thagaste.[4] Augustine plainly hoped that a visit from such heroes of piety would restore the morale of his flock;[5] but the citizens of Hippo were more impressed by the lavish grants that the Church of Thagaste had enjoyed from their pious visitors.[6] They set upon Pinianus in church, with 'a continuous, terrifying shouting',[7] in order to force him to remain with them as a priest. The distinguished visitors left Hippo, shocked to find such turbulence among Augustine's 'sheep'.[8] The people of Hippo had intended to choose Pinianus as a wealthy patron against times of emergency.[9] Augustine did not share their views: he was prepared to allow Pinianus to leave the town, if Hippo were ever attacked by the Goths.[10] Neither Pinianus nor Augustine envisaged an alliance of great landowner and bishop against the barbarians, that would come to be so important in other provinces. For Augustine, the 'pressing of the oil' remained a secret process, and heroism, the heroism of a sufferer loyal to his distant heavenly city, not of a defender of any earthly town.[11]

Indeed, Augustine took the survival of the Roman Empire for granted. For him it was 'the world', the *mundus*, in which he had

---

[1] *Ep.* 111, 4, citing *Dan.* IX, 3–20.   [2] *de civ. Dei*, I, 10, 57–63; e.g. *Ep.* 94, 3–4.

[3] *Ep.* 124, 2.

[4] *Vie de sainte Mélanie*, ed. and tr. D. Gorce, (Sources chrétiennes, 90), 1962, c. 21, pp. 170–172.

[5] *Ep.* 124, 2.   [6] *Ep.* 126, 7.   [7] *Ep.* 125, 3 and 126, 1.

[8] *Ep.* 126, 1–2.   [9] *Ep.* 125, 4.   [10] *Ep.* 126, 4.

[11] Hence the importance, in the '*City of God*', of Regulus, who was prepared to die in a foreign country, far from home and alone, out of loyalty to his oath: *de civ. Dei*, I, 24, 14–40.

grown up for sixty years. He was quite prepared to regard the sack of Rome as an unprecedented disaster;[1] he made no attempt whatsoever to palliate the horrifying news, 'massacres, fires, looting, men murdered and tortured.'[2] He had a civilized man's distaste for the Goths: captivity among them was 'at least among human beings *even if*(!) among barbarians'.[3] He could accept the mortality of all human institutions.[4] But his whole perspective implied a belief in the resilience of the Empire as a whole. Corrective treatment fails in its purpose, if it exterminates its subject:[5] Rome, in his mature view, had been 'punished, but not replaced'.[6] Talk of the inevitability of death can so often be used deliberately to ignore a precise, unpleasant question: whether this inevitable death is now taking place. Augustine is candid with his audience: 'Do not lose heart, brethren, there will be an end to every earthly kingdom. If this is now the end, God sees. Perhaps it has not yet come to that: for some reason — call it weakness, or mercy, or mere wretchedness — we are all hoping that it has not yet come.'[7]

Men are not, however, purely passive in what they choose to take for granted: they very often insist on treating topics as 'quite natural' in order to avoid being embarrassed by them. Augustine's remarks about the Roman Empire, in his sermons and in his *City of God*, have this quality about them. As a Christian thinker, he had taken many things about the pagan past for granted in this deliberate, distinctive way.[8] He had dismissed the tremendous self-consciousness surrounding the Latin language, that had been instilled by the rhetorical schools, by claiming that good Latin could be 'picked up' in the most natural way.[9] In the same manner, and for the same reasons, he took the survival of the Roman Empire for granted, lest, in their anxiety, his congregation should again become hypnotized by the myth of Rome. So potent a symbol of purely earthly endeavour had to be neutralized, if he was to interest men in another topic, that had become all-important to him: '*Dominus aedificans Jerusalem*', 'The Lord building Jerusalem.'[10]

By 417, he would have before him a book that showed, in a Christian guise, the immense potency of the myth of Rome. This was the *History against the Pagans* by the Spanish priest, Orosius. The book

---

[1] *Serm.* 296, 9: 'pending further investigation'. [2] *de urbis excidio*, 3.
[3] *de civ. Dei*, I, 14, 7. cf. *de civ. Dei* I, 7, 13: God's Providence is shown by the very fact that such 'exceptionally bloodthirsty and brutal minds' showed respect for Christianity.
[4] *Serm.* 105, 9–10.   [5] *Serm.* 81, 9.   [6] *de civ. Dei*, IV, 7, 40.
[7] *Serm.* 105, 11.   [8] v. sup. pp. 267–268.   [9] *de doct. christ.* IV, iii, 5.
[10] *Ps.* 146, 2, in *Serm.* 105, 9.

was dedicated, humbly, to himself.[1] Yet Orosius, despite his courtesy to Augustine, had reached his own conclusions, that were very different from Augustine's.[2] Augustine shared neither Orosius' interest in palliating the barbarian invasions, nor his basic assumptions about the providential role of the Roman Empire. The *History* that had been dedicated to him, joined the many books of his contemporaries that Augustine pointedly ignored.[3] For his thought had come to rest on the future: '*Let me know mine end.*'[4]

Augustine thought of himself as living in the Sixth, the last, the old Age of the World.[5] He thought of this, not as a man living under the shadow of an imminent event; but rather, with the sadness of one for whom nothing new could happen. All that needed to be said had been said: a man is old at sixty, Augustine thought; even if he drags on, as some had done, to one hundred and twenty.[6] It was futile to calculate the end of the world: for even the shortest spell of time would seem too long for those who yearned for it.[7]

In times of disaster, men can live more avidly upon the future than on the past and the present; and it is on the future that Augustine will insist throughout his sermons in these years. He would give the Catholic official a 'mirage' of a Heavenly City, for which he could work in this life;[8] to the disillusioned, the sense that present events had been foretold a long time ago;[9] to the Christian communities, the indispensable feeling that they were still a small group, privileged to participate in a foreordained experiment in suffering.[10]

When we compare such sermons with the opinions of a pagan, such as Nectarius of Calama, we can seize the force of this preoccupation

---

[1] Orosius, *Historiarum adversus paganos libri vii*, (P.L. xxxi, 663–1174). Transl. I. W. Raymond, *Seven Books of History against the Pagans*, (Columbia University Records of Civilization, xxii), 1936.

[2] v. esp. the excellent study of E. Th. Mommsen, 'Orosius and Augustine', *Medieval and Renaissance Studies*, ed. Rice, 1959, pp. 325–348. See also K. A. Schöndorf, *Die Geschichtstheologie des Orosius*, (Diss. Munich), 1952, G. Fink-Errera, 'San Agustin y Orosio', *Ciudad de Dios*, 167, 1954, pp. 455–549, and B. Lachoix, *Orose et ses Idées*, (Université de Montreal. Publications de l'Institut d'Études médiévales, xviii), 1965.

[3] e.g. on the number of the persecutions: *de civ. Dei*, XVIII, 52, 1–5.

[4] *Ps.* 38, 5, quoted in *Ep.* 202A, vii, 16.

[5] v. esp. A. Wachtel, *Beiträge z. Geschichtstheologie*, pp. 60–63; Vittinghoff, 'Z. geschichtl. Selbstverständnis', *Hist. Zeitschr.*, 198, 1964, pp. 557–564 and A. Luneau, *L'histoire du Salut chez les Pères de l'Église: la doctrine des âges du monde*, 1964, esp. pp. 314–321. v. most recently, K. H. Schwarte, *Die Vorgeschichte der augustinischen Weltalterlehre*, 1966.

[6] *de div. qu.* LXXXIII, 58, 2. It is an attitude that greatly enhanced the importance of the Catholic Church; it was, already, the Kingdom of God, the Millenium: A. Wachtel, *Beiträge z. Geschichtstheologie*, esp. p. 127, and Luneau, *L'histoire du Salut*, p. 320.

[7] *Ep.* 199, i, 1. [8] *Enarr. in Ps.* 136, 2. [9] *Epp.* 122, 2 and 137, iv, 16. [10] *Serm.* 81, 7.

with the future, that lay in store for a world in its old age. Augustine was not just 'otherworldly': Nectarius, also, had room for another world, even for a 'heavenly city'.[1] But the heavenly city of Nectarius existed somehow over and above the static, tranquil present of a conservative. Citizens who had lived in the traditional way, performing traditional duties in the ancient towns in which they had been born and educated, would gain 'promotion' to this other city.[2] The two worlds seem distinct, self-sufficient, and untroubled; and the 'promotion' linking them, an orderly affair. Old age and death are not orderly; they link the present with the future by long, destructive processes. Such processes linked the old 'world' of Augustine to his heavenly 'city': and life itself was presented as a gradual and painful adjustment to a miraculous new growth that could happen in the midst of the horror of old age.

Destruction was only too obvious in the world after 410. On his way from Carthage that autumn, Augustine had ridden past amphitheatres whose megalomaniac style still amazes us. Nectarius, and indeed many of Augustine's own audience, would have thought that these astonishing monuments had been built by 'piety':[3] by the *pietas* that summed up the preternatural tenacity, by which the Romans of Africa and elsewhere, had sought to pass on from father to son the pattern of a way of life firmly rooted in this world. But the recent crises of the Roman state had made themselves felt in Africa. Money had become short; such public building had come to a halt; the mighty amphitheatres had already begun to crumble.[4] Augustine is not surprised to find these ruins. This past could die.

Augustine had become an old man. His health was failing.[5] His sermons on the future of a Heavenly City have the tone of a man who had been brought into contact with elemental hopes and fears:

'You are surprised that the world is losing its grip? that the world is grown old? Think of a man: he is born, he grows up, he becomes old. Old age has its many complaints: coughing, shaking, failing eyesight, anxious, terribly tired. A man grows old; he is full of complaints. The

[1] *Ep.* 103, 2. [2] *Ep.* 103, 2. [3] *Denis* 24, 13 (*Misc. Agostin.*, i, p. 153).
[4] For the effect of the financial crisis of the Later Empire on traditional standards of public entertainment: G. Ville, 'Les jeux de gladiateurs dans l'Empire chrétien', *Mél. d'archéolog. et d'hist.*, 72, 1960, pp. 273–335.
    R. P. Duncan-Jones, 'Wealth and Munificence in Roman Africa', *Papers of the British School at Rome*, xxxi, 1963, pp. 159–177, is an impressive survey of the standards of munificence current up to 244 A.D.
[5] *Ep.* 109, 3; *Ep.* 118, v, 34; 119, 1; 122, 1; 124, 2. A. M. La Bonnardière, *Rech. de chronologie augustin.* p. 62, notes a halt in Augustine's preaching on S. John around this time: 'Saint Augustin va vivre quelques années lourdes'.

world is old; it is full of pressing tribulations. . . . Do not hold on to the old man, the world; do not refuse to regain your youth in Christ, who says to you: "The world is passing away, the world is losing its grip, the world is short of breath. Do not fear, *Thy youth shall be renewed as an eagle.*" [1]

[1] *Serm.* 81, 8.

26

MAGNUM OPUS ET ARDUUM

WRITING THE 'CITY OF GOD'

By the autumn of 410, Augustine's health finally failed him. Convalescing on a friend's estate in the countryside, he could recapture, for a moment, the *otium*, the cultivated leisure, that he had once enjoyed in Cassiciacum and Thagaste.[1] He now had poignant memories of those days: 'Reading through your letters, as far as my time permits me', he had written to a young colleague, 'I am reminded of my friend Nebridius. . . . But you are a bishop, burdened with the same cares as myself. . . . While he was a man in his youth . . . able to discuss problems with me, as one man of leisure to another.'[2]

Yet Augustine could not escape his former reputation as a literary man. Alypius had even boasted of his friend's prowess as an expert on Cicero to university circles in Carthage;[3] and so Augustine was presented, on the eve of his convalescence, with a whole sheaf of literary and philosophical problems, taken from the *Dialogues* of Cicero, by Dioscurus, a Greek student about to leave the university of Carthage.[4] Here was another young man, his head crammed with bits and pieces of Cicero,[5] in a hurry to sail from Carthage to a wider world:[6] it could have been the young Augustine! The tired old bishop was annoyed: 'I wish I could snatch you away from your titillating disquisitions and ram you into the sort of cares I have to cope with.'[7] Above all, if Dioscurus had anything worth saying, surely he could say it without so much literary snobbery: 'There is no need to gain readers by flaunting a knowledge of the *Dialogues* of Cicero.'[8] Had young

---

[1] *Ep.* 109, 3. But he could not escape writing yet another pamphlet against the Donatists: v. A. C. de Veer, 'La date du *de unico baptismo*', *Rev. études augustin.*, x, 1964, pp. 35–38.

[2] *Ep.* 98, 8.

[3] *Ep.* 117. In Italy he was known for his *de Musica* (v. sup. p. 126): *Ep.* 101 and inf. p. 381.

[4] *Ep.* 118.   [5] *Ep.* 118, ii, 10.   [6] *Ep.* 117.   [7] *Ep.* 118, i, 1.   [8] *Ep.* 118, ii, 11.

Dioscurus read the great work that would begin to appear three years later — Augustine's *De Civitate Dei*, '*The City of God*', he might well have been surprised and impressed: for in it, the old bishop would flaunt, by innumerable direct citations, his own mastery of all the writings of Cicero.[1] A new audience had come to demand a new approach: for the cultured pagan noblemen of Rome had begun to make their presence felt, as refugees, in the *salons* of Carthage.

The most important member of this group was an able young man of about 30, Volusianus.[2] He belonged to an old Roman family; and had dutifully followed the religion of his pagan fathers. Yet he was in an awkward position. He already lived in a 'post-pagan' world. Augustine knew the women of the family as devout Christians: his mother was Albina, and his niece, Melania, the wife of the Pinianus, whose arrival in Hippo would cause such a stir.[3] He was the servant of Christian Emperors, and so not free to voice his opinion;[4] and, as the son of a pious mother, he was constantly approached by bishops such as Augustine, and by enthusiastic laymen, such as Flavius Marcellinus.[5]

His paganism even lacked concrete roots. He grew up when the round of pagan ceremonies performed so lovingly by his father and his father's friends, had already ebbed away from the streets and temples of Rome. Volusianus could only find the dear old religion in his books; and so he appears to Augustine as the centre of a literary circle, known for his 'cultivated, polished style, made outstanding by the charm of true Roman eloquence'.[6]

There was one book which reveals very clearly the tastes of Volusianus and his friends, the *Saturnalia* of Macrobius.[7] This was a

[1] v. esp. Testard, *S. Augustin et Cicéron*, i, esp. p. 195, and ii, pp. 36–71 and 122–124 (129 citations).

[2] v. esp. A. Chastagnol, 'Le sénateur Volusien et la conversion d'une famille de l'aristocratie romaine au Bas-Empire', *Rev. études anc.* 58, 1956, 240–253. His family owned property at Tubursicubure, not far from Hippo: *Corpus Inscript. Lat.*, VIII, 25990.

[3] v. sup. p. 294. [4] *Ep.* 136, 2.

[5] v. esp. Brown, 'Aspects of the Christianisation of the Roman Aristocracy', *Journ. Rom. Studies*, li, 1961, pp. 1–11, esp. pp. 7–8. So polite was the interchange of letters between Augustine and Volusianus, 'whom I mention with esteem and affection' (*Enchiridion*, xxxiv), that the 12th-century illuminator of Letter 132 can be excused for showing this last pagan with a monk's tonsure and a halo: Jeanne et Pierre Courcelle, 'Scènes anciennes de l'iconographie augustinienne', *Rev. études augustin.*, x, 1964, pp. 51–96; pl. II.

[6] *Ep.* 136, 1.

[7] v. esp. H. Bloch, 'The Pagan Revival in the West at the End of the Fourth Century', *The Conflict between Paganism and Christianity in the Fourth Century*, ed. Momigliano, 1963, pp. 193–218, esp. pp. 207–210 (a condensation of his fundamental treatment in *Harvard Theol. Rev.* xxxviii, 1945, 199–244).

Sir Samuel Dill, *Roman Society in the Last Century of the Western Empire*, 1898, book of 'Imaginary conversations': it portrayed the great Roman conservatives in their hey-day, around 380 — Volusianus' father, Albinus, was there: so was the orator Symmachus, his intimate friend, and the great religious expert, Praetextatus. They are shown enjoying erudite discussions during the holiday of the Saturnalia. In these conversations, however, we can sense something more than the genteel enjoyment of a great past: it is a whole culture running hard to stand still. 'The Old Tradition,' *Vetustas*, is now to be 'always adored'.[1] Like men who put their money in a safe foreign bank, these last pagans were anxious to invest their beliefs in a distant, golden past, untroubled by the rise of Christianity. The Christian Emperors had abandoned the title of *Pontifex Maximus*; but Vergil might replace them in performing this office for religious readers.[2] From being a school text-book, Vergil could become, like the Bible, an inexhaustible source of precise religious information.[3] Even the artists who were commissioned by such men would lovingly portray the smallest details of the sacrifices of Aeneas, a generation after just these sacrifices had been officially abolished.[4] We have here a strange phenomenon: the preservation of a whole way of life in the present, by transfusing it with the inviolable safety of an adored past.

This was not all. These men were deeply religious. They could compete with the Christians in their firm belief in rewards and punishments after death. Macrobius also wrote a commentary on the *Dream of Scipio*: it showed that 'the souls of those who have merited well of the commonwealth return from the body to Heaven, and there enjoy blessedness forever.'[5] For such men, Christianity appeared, as it appears to many to-day, as a religion out of joint with the natural assumptions of a whole culture. The great Platonists of their age, Plotinus and Porphyry, could provide them with a profoundly religious view of the world, that grew naturally out of an immemorial tradition. The claims of the Christian, by contrast, lacked intellectual foundation.

Book i, (Meridian Paperbacks, 1958, pp. 3–112), remains valuable. v. now the most important treatment of A. Cameron, 'The Date and Identity of Macrobius', *Journ. Rom. Studies*, lvi, 1966, pp. 25–38, which, in ascribing a late date to the *Saturnalia* — of around 430 — would seek to minimize its pagan content. I would conclude only that the text threw more light on the paganism of a Volusianus, than of a Symmachus.
[1] *Saturnalia*, III, xiv, 2. [2] *Saturnalia*, I, xxiv, 16.
[3] Bloch, 'The Pagan Revival', *The Conflict between Paganism and Christianity*, p. 210.
[4] e.g. J. de Wit, *Die Miniaturen des Vergilius Vaticanus*, 1959, pll. 32, 34 and 37, 1.
[5] Transl. W. H. Stahl, *Macrobius, Commentary on the Dream of Scipio*, (Records of Civilization, Sources and Studies, 48), 1952. v. Dill, *Roman Society*, pp. 106–111. Even the scathing Jerome is impressed by the faith of a pagan widow: *Ep.* 39, 3; v. P. Courcelle, *Les lettres grecques*, pp. 35–36.

For a man such as Volusianus to accept the Incarnation would have been like a modern European denying the evolution of the species: he would have had to abandon not only the most advanced, rationally based knowledge available to him, but, by implication, the whole culture permeated by such achievements. Quite bluntly, the pagans were the 'wise' men, the 'experts', *prudentes*; and the Christians were 'stupid'.[1]

Augustine was well-qualified to appreciate the nature of the threat presented by this literary and philosophical neo-paganism. For a time, he had seemed about to be coopted into the pagan circle: he had been patronized by Symmachus; and in Milan, he had taught the sons of Symmachus' friends, who were the exact contemporaries of Volusianus. These men were not isolated die-hards: they were the centre of a wide intelligentsia, spreading through all the provinces of the West.[2] To a man in Augustine's position, with Augustine's first-hand experience of the intellectual world of his day, the real danger, in the year after 410, came less from popular dismay at the sack of Rome,[3] as from the power of these men, who could harden a prestigious tradition against the spread of Christianity.[4] Seen in this light, the *City of God* is the last round in a long drama: written by a former protégé of Symmachus, it was to be a definitive rejection of the paganism of an aristocracy that had claimed to dominate the intellectual life of their age.

The arrival of Roman aristocrats in Africa made the issue very clear. Augustine would certainly have known the effect that their leadership might have throughout the province. The university life of Africa was still vigorous and largely pagan:[5] Augustine's own pupil, Eulogius Favonius, also wrote a commentary on the *Dream of Scipio*.[6] A man like Nectarius of Calama treasured this text: it offered an immortality in the Milky Way, to men who, like himself, did the right thing in the traditional way.[7] Behind these conservatives stood the philosophers Augustine knew so well — the *Platonici*; like himself, they were

[1] Ps. Augustini, *Quaestiones Veteris et Novi Testamenti*, cxiv, 8 (C.S.E.L. l, p. 306), v. A. Cameron, 'Palladas and Christian Polemic', *Journ. Rom. Studies*, lv, 1965, p. 25.

[2] v. sup. p. 65; v. *de civ. Dei*, I, 3, 4–6, on the public endowment of chairs of pagan literature.

[3] *Ep.* 138, ii, 9; cf. *de civ. Dei*, II, 3, 4–11.

[4] v. esp. the perceptive conclusion of A. Momigliano, 'Pagan and Christian Historiography in the Fourth Century', *The Conflict between Paganism and Christianity*, pp. 98–99.

[5] v. P. Monceaux, *Les Africains: Les païens*, 1894 and the richly-documented survey in P. Courcelle, *Les lettres grecques*, pp. 195–205.

[6] *Disputatio de Somnio Scipionis*, ed. and transl. R. E. Weddingen (Collection Latomus XXVII), 1957.

[7] v. sup. p. 297.

ascetic, otherworldly men, concerned, like himself, with the salvation of men's souls, yet standing aloof from the congregations of the Catholic church, dressed in the traditional, sober robes of their austere calling.[1]

Such men provided the opponents for the *City of God*. They had even set out to provoke Augustine in a manner worthy of Macrobius' heroes. Macrobius introduces a discussion of Vergil, his religious classic, by making an unwelcome stranger raise objections before a shocked company.[2] Volusianus, also, introduced criticisms of Christianity in exactly the same way, in a literary banquet that he describes in detail to Augustine.[3] In the *Saturnalia*, it was, of course, Symmachus, who rose first to defend the revered poet. Now it was to Augustine, the *doyen* of a new Christian literature,[4] that this fastidious audience had turned, somewhat ironically,[5] for satisfaction.

Augustine hesitated for a time, before committing himself to writing a book.[6] He had hoped that Marcellinus might circulate his open letters in the salons:[7] but Marcellinus demanded something more, a 'splendid solution'.[8] Thus, when the first three books of the *City of God* appeared, in 413, Augustine gave every promise of a monumental work: 'a great and arduous work, *magnum opus et arduum*, my dearest Marcellinus.'[9] Thirteen years later, Augustine will end this work of twenty-two books with a compact sentence that sums up the tone of massive deliberation in which he had chosen to write: 'With the help of the Lord, I seem to have paid off my debt, in this, a giant of a book.'[10]

Augustine had lived twenty years as a provincial bishop in Hippo. Now his reputation was at stake before a very different and exacting audience.[11] As a result, the *City of God* is the most self-conscious book that he ever wrote. It was planned ahead on a massive scale: five books dealt with those who worshipped the gods for felicity on earth; five,

[1] v. esp. *Ep.* 138, 19: iv, Augustine deals especially with Apuleius, 'who, as an African, is better known to us Africans'. In *de civ. Dei*, X, 29, 23, the moving address to Porphyry is designed to touch his living admirers.

[2] *Saturnalia*, I, xxiv, 6–8.

[3] *Ep.* 135, 2.   [4] *Ep.* 135, 2.   [5] *Ep.* 136, 2.   [6] *Ep.* 132.

[7] *Ep.* 138, i, 1. P. Courcelle suggests, very tentatively, that Evodius of Uzalis may have made up for his friend's hesitation by writing a literary dialogue between a pagan and a Christian, based on Augustine's *Ep.* 137: 'Date, source et génèse des "*Consultationes Zacchaei et Apollonii*"' (now in *Hist. littér.*, pp. 261–275, esp. pp. 271–275).

[8] *Ep.* 136, 2.   [9] *de civ. Dei*, I, Praef., 8.   [10] *de civ. Dei*, XXII, 30, 149.

[11] Rutilius Namatianus, a Gallic pagan senator and an admirer of Volusianus, may even have glanced through the first books of the *City of God*; but it is unlikely that he wrote his poem, *de reditu suo*, to answer its unflattering commentary on Roman history: v. Courcelle, *Hist. littér.*, pp. 104–107. Writing among men who had recently been forced to suppress a peasants' revolt, he had his own, more pressing, reasons for upholding the traditional image of Eternal Rome.

with those who worshipped them for eternal felicity; the remaining
twelve would elaborate Augustine's great theme: four would deal with
the origin of 'Two cities, one of God, the other of the world'; four
with their 'unfolding course' in the past; four with their ultimate
destinies. We even possess the letter which Augustine wrote to his
literary agent, the priest Firmus: in it, Augustine gives directions as to
how to bind up the unwieldy manuscript in accordance with its basic
plan;[1] and the free flow of the books is sign-posted by a list of chapter
headings.[2] This was no transitory pamphlet for a simple audience: it
was a book which men of leisure,[3] learned men, must be prepared to
read again and again to appreciate.[4]

The *City of God* is a monument to the literary culture of the Later
Empire, quite as distinctive in its own way as the *Saturnalia* of
Macrobius. This is evident even in its smallest details. The literary man
was supposed to be a learned man. As in the Renaissance, his arguments
had to be developed in relation to a whole range of literary authorities.
In the *City of God*, Augustine deliberately builds up his arguments, not
in the dialectical method of later schoolmen, but in such a way as to
show that he, also, could move among cumulus clouds of erudition.[5]
This approach is markedly different from that of his other writings.
His arguments against fatalism, for instance, follow the same course as
in his other works;[6] but, in the *City of God*, they are set in a framework
of great names provided by Cicero: 'Cicero says of Hippocrates, the

---

[1] Letter to Firmus, in *Corpus Christianorum, ser. lat.*, xlvii, 1955, pp. III–IV, esp. p. III,
11–22; cf. *Retract*. II, 69.

v. H. I Marrou, 'La technique de l'édition à l'époque patristique', *Vigiliae Christianae*,
3, 1949, esp. pp. 217–220. The original divisions have survived in the manuscript tradition
of the *City of God*: v. B. V. E. Jones, in *Journ. Theol. Studies*, n.s., xvi, 1965, pp. 142–145.

[2] *Breviculus, Corpus Christianorum, ser. lat.* xlvii, pp. V–XLV. This edition, with its
separate index of contents, reproduces more faithfully the original format of the work.
The insertion of 'Chapter-headings' into the free flow of each book was a disastrous
innovation of the 15th and 16th centuries, too frequently followed by modern editors:
v. esp. H. I. Marrou, 'La division en chapitres des livres de la "Cité de Dieu" ', *Mélanges
J. de Ghellinck*, i, 1951, pp. 235–249.

[3] *Ep.* 184A, i, 1.

[4] Letter to Firmus, *Corpus Christianorum*, p. III, 35.

[5] Hence the comment of Gibbon: 'His learning is too often borrowed and his arguments
are too often his own', *Decline and Fall*, chp. xxviii, note 79. For Augustine's qualities as
a writer and the literary tastes of his audience, v. esp. H. I. Marrou, *S. Augustin et la fin
de la culture antique*, esp. pp. 37–76 (with handsome afterthoughts in his *Retractatio*,
pp. 665–672). J. C. Guy, *Unité et structure logique de la 'Cité de Dieu'*, 1961, provides a
clear survey of the basic structure of the *City of God*. For a stimulating treatment of the
relation between an author's thought and his modes of exposition (a subject too often
overlooked in dealing with the *City of God*), v. H. A. Wolfson, *The Philosophy of Spinoza*,
Preface and chapters I and II (Meridian 1958, pp. vi–viii and pp. 3–60).

[6] e.g. *Conf.* VII, vi, 8 and *de doct. christ.* II, xxii, 32–33.

most notable doctor ... Posidonius the Stoic ... the notable argument of the potter's wheel ... from which Nigidius was called "Potters Wheel" Nigidius. ..."[1] The final touch of classical fastidiousness comes when Augustine mentions the Biblical twins, Esau and Jacob. They are not referred to by name: instead, they are introduced in a ponderous circumlocution such as would have delighted the literary snobbery of Augustine's audience, 'There once were born twin-boys, in the ancient memory of our fathers (I talk here of famous men). ...'[2]

Augustine's extreme sensitivity to the tastes of a specific audience also determined the strategy of his attack on the pagan cults. The *City of God* contains hardly any reference to those contemporary forms of pagan worship and feeling that interest modern scholars of late paganism — the mystery-cults, the Oriental religions, Mithraism. It seems as if Augustine were demolishing a paganism that existed only in libraries.[3] In fact Augustine believed quite rightly, that he could best reach the last pagans through their libraries. In this, the *City of God* reflects faithfully the most significant trend in the paganism of the early fifth century. The partially disinherited generation of a Volusianus had sought to invest its religion in the distant past. They were fanatical antiquarians. They preferred every form of religion and philosophy that could boast a *litterata vetustas* — an immemorial origin preserved for them in literary classics.[4] It is just this *vetustas* which Augustine dissects. He intercepts the pagans in their last retreat to the past: he will expose the tainted origins of the cults that were most ancient, and that figured most in the classics; he will play upon the inconsistencies, and hint at the secret incredulity of the writers who preserved this past, their poet, Vergil, their antiquarian, Varro.[5] His discussion of Roman history, also, gravitates around the origins of Rome. These early days had particularly interested the learned pagans of the previous century;[6] and Augustine followed their taste closely. For this remote past could be idealized in safety; and so it is only against the epic war of Rome on Alba (of the 7th century B.C.) that Augustine feels challenged to employ to the full the approach of a true radical faced with the myths of conservatism — he will indulge in the great pleasure of calling a spade a spade: 'Away with the vain screens of common opinion',[7] and 'Away with the whitewash! ...'[8]

---

[1] *de civ. Dei*, V, 2–3.   [2] *de civ. Dei*, V, 4, 1–2.

[3] But see the important remarks of N. H. Baynes, 'Lactantius', *Byzantine Studies*, p. 348.

[4] *Ep.* 118, iv, 26.   [5] e.g. *de civ. Dei*, III, 4, 1–3 on Varro.

[6] v. esp. A. Momigliano, 'Some Observations on the "Origo Gentis Romanae" ', *Secondo contributo alla storia degli studi classici*, 1960, pp. 145–178, esp. pp. 157–158.

[7] *de civ. Dei*, III, 14, 40.   [8] *de civ. Dei*, III, 14, 60.

The *City of God*, therefore, would have impressed its first readers in a very different manner from the *Confessions*. They were presented here with no startling literary novelty. Instead, they could enjoy what Macrobius had enjoyed in the conversations of the great pagans, especially in those of Praetextatus: the spectacle of an earnest man with a whole conventional culture at his finger-tips — religious lore, philosophy, history.[1] Thus, when the retiring Vicar, the Deputy for the Prefects in Africa, Macedonius, received his copies of the first three books of the *City of God*, he praised in it aspects which the modern historian often overlooks. A loyal official, he refuses to see in it a book about the sack of Rome; this 'public calamity' was treated in it no more than was strictly decent.[2] Instead, he could settle back to enjoy an intellectual feast: 'I am in a quandary as to which to admire the most: the complete religious knowledge of a priest; the range of philosophical opinions; the fullness of its historical information; the charm of a grand style.'[3]

Yet, just these qualities enabled the *City of God* to rank in Roman literature as a work of 'Christian nationalism'. Like most nationalisms, the form in which it is expressed is borrowed from its rulers; but this form is borrowed only to assert an independent alternative to the literary culture that had dominated men's minds. After twenty years of studying the Bible, Augustine was convinced that the Christians also had a literature of inexhaustible richness. '*Your*' Vergil is now deliberately juxtaposed, at every turn, with '*Our*' Scriptures.[4]

Juxtaposition, indeed, is the basic literary device that determines the structure of every book of the *City of God*. Augustine deliberately uses it to contrive a 'stereoscopic' effect. The solutions of the new Christian literature must 'stand out the more clearly'[5] by always being imposed upon an elaborately constructed background of pagan answers to the same question. It is a method calculated to give a sense of richness and dramatic tension. This accounts for the vast appeal of the *City of God* to learned men in future ages. For, in it, Augustine moves with massive and ostentatious deliberation, from the classical into the Christian world. We follow a conventional argument on the role of the emotions in a wise man, moving slowly from an anecdote about 'A Stoic in a Shipwreck' in the *Attic Nights* of Aulus Gellius, through Cicero's description of the virtues of Julius Caesar, until, at the end of this well-trodden path, we suddenly meet something new: the monumental formulation of 'what the Divine Scripture teaches,

---

[1] *Saturnalia* I, xxiv, 1; cf. I, iv, 1, on Albinus: '*quasi vetustatis promptuarium*'.
[2] *Ep.* 154, 2.   [3] *Ep.* 154, 2.   [4] v. sup. p. 263.   [5] e.g. *de civ. Dei*, XV, 8, 17 and XIX, 1, 9.

that contains the sum of Christian learning'.[1] 'In our way of thinking, *in disciplina nostra*, then, we do not ask merely whether a pious soul is angry, but why; not whether he is sad, but for what reason; not whether he feels afraid, but what it is he fears.'[2]

Writing the *City of God* forced Augustine to make up his mind about his own past as an educated man. We can see clearly, the shape which this past had taken on for him. The past of the literary man, which Augustine and his readers took for granted from their schooldays, no longer belongs to him: it is '*your*' literature, the literature of the Roman pagans. This is not so with the Platonists. He regarded them as far more formidable opponents than the conservative men of letters.[3] He re-read the treatises of Porphyry and Plotinus.[4] He evoked the dilemma of these men in so masterly a fashion, that modern interpretations of the enigmatic Porphyry still gravitate around the tenth book of the *City of God*.[5] Porphyry was the bug-bear of the average Christian: Jerome had called him 'a scoundrel, an impudent fellow, a vilifier, a sycophant, a lunatic and a mad dog'.[6] In the hands of Augustine, he achieves heroic stature: Augustine's final formulations are made to grow, majestically, from a detailed critique of Porphyry's abortive quest for a 'universal way to set free the soul';[7] and so the demolition of paganism, in the first ten books of the *City of God*, can close with the generous evocation of a magnificent failure.

It is a revealing feature: Augustine's disputes with fellow-Christians rarely rose above the level of the pamphlet-warfare so common in the Early Church; Christian heretics remained external enemies to be demolished. By contrast, Augustine's treatment of the Platonists throughout the *City of God*, shows the extent to which a part of the pagan past was still alive in Augustine, stimulating his finest thought, and challenging him to a continuous inner dialogue that would last up to his death.

An interest in the classical past could raise disquieting problems for Christians. At just this time, Augustine wrote to Evodius. Whom had Christ delivered from punishment when He had descended into Hell?[8]

---

[1] *de civ. Dei*, IX, 4.
[2] *de civ. Dei*, IX, 5, 5.
[3] *de civ. Dei*, I, 36, 17–22.
[4] Courcelle, *Les lettres grecques*, p. 168.
[5] e.g. J. O'Meara, *Porphyry's Philosophy from Oracles in Augustine*, 1959, and the important critique by P. Hadot, 'Citations de Porphyre chez Augustin', *Rev. études augustin*, vi, 1960, pp. 205–244.
[6] Epithets collected by J. Bidez, *Cambridge Ancient History*, XII, 1939, p. 634.
[7] *de civ. Dei*, X, 32.
[8] He was influenced, at the time, by an apocryphal *Apocalypse of Paul*, brought from Spain by Orosius: v. S. Merkle, 'Augustin über eine Unterbrechung d. Höllenstrafen', *Aurelius Augustinus*, 1930, pp. 197–202.

'It would be rash to lay down who they were. If we were to say that everyone in Hell had been delivered, then who would not be pleased if we could prove it? They would be particularly glad because of those men who are intimately known to us by their works, whose style and qualities of mind we have admired: not only the poets and orators, who, in many passages of their works, held up the false gods of the nations to ridicule, and sometimes even confessed the one true God (though usually following the crowd in its superstitious rites); but also those who have upheld the same opinions, not in poetry and rhetoric, but as philosophers. Then, there are those who have left no literary remains; but we have learnt from the classics, that they had lived praiseworthy lives, by their own lights. Except for the fact that they did not serve God, but erred in worshipping the vanities that were the established religion of their time . . . they can be justly held up as models of all the other virtues — of frugality, self-denial, chastity, sobriety, courageous in the face of death for their country's sake, keeping their sworn word to their fellow-citizens and even to their enemies. All these things are . . . in a sense, worthless and unprofitable; but as signs of a certain character, they please us so much that we would want those in whom they exist to be freed from the pains of Hell: but of course, it may well be that the verdict of human feeling is one thing, and the justice of the Creator, quite another.'[1]

Augustine regarded the Ancient Romans with the same intense ambivalence as we regard our Eminent Victorians. History-books had presented them to men of letters as a row of idealized 'models' of behaviour, as *exempla*.[2] In Rome, senatorial families sought out an *exemplum*, an exemplary ancestor in the distant past, from whom to claim descent.[3] Christians in Rome had also taken these *exempla* at their face value: Paulinus, visited by a Christianized clan, would spin out an elaborate comparison between these modern saints and their great ancestors; and in so doing, he would take a favourable view of the problem of pagan virtues.[4]

Augustine was less inclined to be impressed. His view of the Roman attitude to their past formed part of his more basic attitude to what he

---

[1] *Ep.* 164, ii, 4.

[2] The most sound treatment is by Maier, *Augustin u. Rom*, 1955, pp. 84–93. Apart from the intrusion of demons, Augustine's judgements on the good and bad figures in Roman history do not differ from those of any of his contemporaries with claims to classical education, e.g. Aurelius Victor, *Epitome*, XLVIII, 11–12, on the historical knowledge of Theodosius I.

[3] v. Brown, 'Aspects of Christianisation', *Journ. Rom. Studies*, li, 1961, p. 6, n. 41.

[4] Paulinus, *Carmen* XXI, 230–238.

calls the *civitas terrena*, that is, to any group of people tainted by the Fall, and so, 'of the earth, earthly.' Such a group refused to regard the 'earthly' values they had created as transient and relative. Committed to the fragile world they had created, they were forced to idealize it; they had to deny any evil in its past, and the certainty of death in its future. Even the most honest of their historians, Sallust, had lied in praising the ancient days of Rome. This was inevitable, 'for', as Augustine said, poignantly, 'he had no other city to praise.'[1]

It would be easy merely to explode the Roman conservatives' view of the past as a 'myth'. Orosius had done so. Augustine always tended to do so. He takes a grim pleasure, rather like a nineteenth-century free-thinker demolishing a religious belief, in deflating the most prestigious idea by reducing it to its bare essentials: 'Away with all this arrogant bluffing: what, after all, are men but men!'[2] In this way he refuses to regard Roman history as in any way privileged. He can reduce the rise of Rome to a simple common denominator, shared by all states: the 'lust for domination', which Sallust had mentioned 'in passing'[3] as an un-Roman vice, is fastened upon by Augustine, and generalized, with characteristic thoroughness, as a law governing the rise of every state. A successful brigandage, then, can become the basic model of any empire;[4] and Augustine can ask his readers to see their own idealized past as in a distant mirror, in the history of an entirely non-classical state, the aggressive Empire of the Assyrians.[5] Africans, indeed, were notorious debunkers.[6] Sarcasm had always been Augustine's most formidable weapon;[7] and in turning it upon the Roman past, Augustine showed a complete lack of Roman 'gravity': the flamboyant 'set piece', the *controversia*, in which he piles on innuendoes against the chastity of Lucretia, would have appeared in singularly bad taste. (Paulinus of Nola, after all, a good Roman Christian, had been proud to call his wife 'my Lucretia'!).[8]

But Augustine did not merely debunk. He agreed with his contemporaries on two important points: the moral history of the Roman people was more important than the naked 'facts of life' of the Roman conquests; and the moral qualities of the Romans had made their Empire, if not uniquely privileged and deserving to last forever (as was

[1] *de civ. Dei*, III, 17, 34–37.   [2] *de civ. Dei*, V, 17, 28.
[3] *de civ. Dei*, III, 14, 47.
[4] *de civ. Dei*, IV, 4 and 5. *Latrocinium*, 'Brigandage', was used to describe any usurpation in the Later Empire: v. R. MacMullen, 'The Roman Concept of Robber-Pretender', *Rev. intern. des Droits de l'Antiquité*, 3ᵉ sér., x, 1963, pp. 221–236.
[5] *de civ. Dei*, IV, 7, 38.   [6] v. sup. p. 32.   [7] e.g. *de civ. Dei*, III, 12.
[8] *de civ. Dei*, I, 19, 15; cf. Paulinus, *Carmen*, X, 192.

the case for pagans), at least better than any of its predecessors.[1] Much as we still think of the successes of the Victorian Age in terms of individual Eminent Victorians, so the moral qualities of the ancient Romans seemed to provide the key to the former greatness of Rome.[2] Augustine accepts this attitude: and he uses it to frame his own, highly personal and tentative[3] opinion as to why God should have permitted the Romans to create so great an Empire.[4]

By allowing himself to be challenged by these *exempla*, Augustine transforms the Roman view of their own past. He goes behind the appearance of the conduct of these noble ancestors, to find out why they actually behaved as they did. Again fastening on a fleeting hint in a classical author,[5] he emerges with a single, all-embracing explanation: the Romans had been moved to an outstanding show of virtue by one force alone, by an overweening love of praise: 'They were, therefore, *"grasping for praise, open-handed with their money; honest in the pursuit of wealth, they wanted to hoard glory."* This is what they loved so wholeheartedly; for this they lived, for this they did not hesitate to die: all other lusts, they battened down with this overwhelming desire.'[6]

This is Augustine's alternative to the flat, idealized family-portraits, that had dominated the Romans of his age. But, as Augustine realized, their's were the virtues of a narrow élite.[7] Augustine's average man was a very frail creature indeed. He was a slave to social custom.[8] Even the greatest thinkers of the pagan past, it seemed to him, had capitulated to this force: they had hidden their true views,[9] or had been driven to compromise with the beliefs of the herd.[10] The irrational is also very close: the devotion of the crowds can make idols seem to move;[11] a mysterious 'lower realm of feelings' can make a man put his own sense of being alive into a dead copy of the human form.[12] Men need 'auth-

---

[1] Vittinghoff, 'Z. geschichtl. Selbstverständnis', *Hist. Zeitschr.*, 198, 1964, pp. 545–546.

[2] e.g. *de civ. Dei*, V, 12, 1–3. This attitude to the past is typical of an age where history was no more than an aid to rhetoric, used 'to point a moral and adorn a tale': v. Marrou, *S. Augustin et la fin de la culture antique*, pp. 131–135, and esp. I. Calabi, 'Le fonti della storia romana nel "de civitate Dei" di Sant'Agostino', *Parola del Passato*, 43, 1955, pp. 274–294. Even a historian of contemporary events would appeal constantly to ancient examples: e.g. J. Vogt, 'Ammianus Marcellinus als erzählender Geschichtsschreiber d. Spätzeit', *Mainz. Akad. d. Wiss. u.d. Lit., Abh. d. geistes-u. sozialwiss. Kl.*, 1963, no. 8, pp. 820–822.

[3] *de civ. Dei*, V, 9, 52–54.   [4] v. esp. *de civ. Dei*, V, 12 and 19, 48–60.

[5] *de civ. Dei*, V, 12, 16, from Sallust, *Cat.* 7, 6.   [6] *de civ. Dei*, V, 12, 15–19.

[7] *de civ. Dei*, V, 12, 153.   [8] e.g. *Enarr. in Ps.* 64, 6; 136, 21; 138, 18.

[9] *de civ. Dei*, IV, 29, 45 and VI, 6, on Varro.   [10] *de civ. Dei*, X, 3, 3–5: the Platonists.

[11] *Ep.* 102, iii, 18; cf. *Enarr. ii in Ps.* 113, 3.

[12] *Enarr. ii in Ps.* 113, 1. v. esp. the thoughtful study of A. Mandouze, 'S. Augustin et la religion romaine', *Rech. augustin.*, i, 1958, pp. 187–223; v. also A. M. La Bonnardière, *Rech. de chronologie augustin.*, pp. 158–164.

ority': they need to be shaken from their habits and irrational tendencies, by a firm, persuasive challenge from above.[1] If this guidance does not come from God, it will come from another source.

For Augustine believed in demons: a species of beings, superior to men, living forever, their bodies as active and as subtle as the air, endowed with supernatural powers of perception; and, as fallen angels, the sworn enemies of the true happiness of the human race.[2] Their powers of influence were enormous: they could so interfere with the physical basis of the mind as to produce illusions.[3] Thrust into the turbulence of the lower air, below the moon, these condemned prisoners, awaiting sentence in the Last Judgement,[4] were always ready to swoop, like birds, upon the broken fragments of a frail and dissident humanity.[5]

In Late Roman popular belief, the methods of demons were extremely crude: they would simply take on human shape to start a plague or a riot.[6] With Augustine, by contrast, the nexus between men and demons was purely psychological. Like was drawn to like. Men got the demons they deserved; the demons, for their part, perpetuated this likeness by suggesting to the masses immoral and anarchic gods as symbols of divine power.[7]

Sallust had written the moral history of the decline of the Roman Republic: for Augustine's audience, this moral history was *the* authoritative history of the period.[8] Augustine will turn it into a religious history by introducing two alien ideas — that of authority,[9] and of demons: and so the history of Rome becomes the story of a community, deprived of the authority of Christ, and left to drift at the mercy of forces beyond the control of a fragile crust of human virtue.[10]

Augustine's final exorcism of the pagan past, however, did not stop at revealing its demonic undertow. He did something far more subtle and irreversible. The *City of God* is a book about 'glory'. In it, Augustine drains the glory from the Roman past in order to project it far beyond the reach of men, into the 'Most glorious City of God'. The virtues the Romans had ascribed to their heroes, would be realized only in the citizens of this other city; and it is only within the walls of the

---

[1] *Epp.* 137, iii,-12 and 138, iii, 17. [2] Defined, from Apuleius, in *de civ. Dei* IX, 8, 1–4.
[3] e.g. *Ep.* 9, 3, and the stories in *de civ. Dei*, XVIII, 18, 12–22.
[4] *Ep.* 102, iii, 20; *de civ. Dei*, XI, 33, 1–2. [5] *de civ. Dei*, XVI, 24, 60.
[6] e.g. Libanius, *Oratio*, xix, on the great riot at Antioch in 387. v. N. H. Baynes, 'The Hellenistic Civilisation and East Rome', *Byzantine Studies*, pp. 6–7. 'A part of man's daily, hourly fear is the demon world which besets him on every side'.
[7] e.g. *de civ. Dei*, II, 25, 5.
[8] *de civ. Dei*, I, 5, 32; v. esp. Maier, *Augustin u. Rom*, pp. 80–81.
[9] e.g. *de civ. Dei*, I, 31, 28. [10] *de civ. Dei*, II, 8, 58–73.

Heavenly Jerusalem, that Cicero's noble definition of the essence of the Roman Republic could be achieved.[1]

For we should not forget, that together with the *Confessions*, the *City of God* is one of the few books of Augustine's whose very title is significant, *de civitate Dei*. As with the *Confessions*, the theme of the title suddenly crystallized in Augustine's mind; and, once formed, it is written into every line of the book.

The *City of God* cannot be explained in terms of its immediate origins. It is particularly superficial to regard it as a book about the sack of Rome. Augustine may well have written *a* book 'On the City of God' without such an event. What this sack effected, was to provide Augustine with a specific, challenging audience at Carthage; and in this way the sack of Rome ensured that a book which might have been a work of pure exegesis for fellow Christian scholars (somewhat like the great commentary on *Genesis*, in which the idea of a book on the 'Two Cities' is raised),[2] became a deliberate confrontation with paganism. The *City of God*, itself, is not a 'tract for the times'; it is the careful and premeditated working out, by an old man, of a mounting obsession.

In a sermon which Augustine preached at Carthage in the same year that he sat down to write the *City of God*, we can sense, better than anywhere else, the force and the true direction of the momentum that would lead him to pile up this 'great and arduous work' for future generations to puzzle over. 'When, therefore, death shall be swallowed up in victory, these things will not be there; and there shall be peace — peace full and eternal. We shall be in a kind of city. Brethren, when I speak of that City, and especially when scandals grow great here, I just cannot bring myself to stop. . . .'[3]

---

[1] e.g. *de civ. Dei*, II, 21, 116–123.   [2] *de Gen. ad litt.* XI, xv, 20.
[3] *Enarr. in Ps.* 84, 10.

27

CIVITAS PEREGRINA[1]

In the years after 410, the Christians who flocked into the great basilicas of Carthage were uncertain of themselves. They had boasted of the 'Christian Era',[2] and now it had coincided with unparalleled disasters. After a generation of success, they found themselves unpopular.[3] They hankered after the old ways, especially after the pagan circus-shows, which alone in that time of crisis had seemed to maintain public confidence in the security and opulence of the old world.[4]

Augustine told them just what a demoralized group needs to hear. He gave them a sense of identity; he told them where they belonged, to what they must be loyal. In a series of great sermons,[5] he spoke to confused men, lingering in a hundred ways on the fringe of paganism, with pagan relatives, pagan neighbours, loyalties to their city that could only be expressed by pagan ceremonies.[6] He told them that they were a distinct people: 'citizens of Jerusalem.' 'O God's own people,

[1] Out of the enormous bibliography on the *City of God* (for which v. C. Andresen, *Bibliographia Augustiniana*, 1962, pp. 34-37), I have particularly appreciated the thoughtful translations of select passages with commentary in R. H. Barrow, *Introduction to St Augustine, 'The City of God'*, 1950. The bilingual edition with notes in the *Bibliothèque augustinienne*, sér. v, 33-37, 1959-1960, is also valuable.

[2] *Serm.* 81, 7 and 105, 8.

[3] *Serm.* 105, 12. Augustine is plainly anxious not to be accused on gloating over the disaster: *Enarr. in Ps.* 136, 17.

[4] v. e.g. Rutilius Namatianus, *de reditu suo*, I, 201-204. *Cod. Theod.* XV, 7, 13, of Feb. 413, mentions a '*tribunus voluptatum*' at Carthage. A fragment of an ivory tablet shows a senatorial family presiding at such games: C. Mohrmann and F. Van der Meer, *Atlas of the Early Christian World*, 1958, ill. 201, p. 81. Support for such games was closely associated with conservative paganism, as is shown by the mosaics of a rich villa at Carthage: G. Picard, 'Un palais du ive siècle à Carthage', *Comptes-Rendus de l'Acad. Inscript. et Belles Lettres*, 1964, pp. 101-118.

[5] v. esp. A. Lauras-H. Rondet, 'Le thème des deux cités dans l'œuvre de S. Augustin', Rondet and others, *Études augustiniennes*, 1953, pp. 99-162.

[6] *Enarr. in Ps.* 39, 6.

O Body of Christ, O high-born race of foreigners on earth . . . you do not belong here, you belong somewhere else.'[1]

Augustine used a theme that had already become a commonplace among African Christians:[2] he had met it first, perhaps, in the work of a Donatist, Tyconius.[3] Since the Fall of Adam, the human race had always been divided into two great 'cities', *civitates*; that is, into two great pyramids of loyalty. The one 'city' served God along with His loyal angels; the other served the rebel angels, the Devil and his demons.[4] Although the two 'cities' seemed inextricably mixed, within the church as in the world, they would be separated at the Last Judgement.[5] Christ would speak the words of judgement; the two cities — Babylon and Jerusalem — would then appear plainly, the one on the left, the other on the right.[6]

In the years after 410, Augustine took this theme; and, with deliberate showmanship, he 'spreads it out' for his audience.[7]

The Jews had once entered into captivity in Babylon. There they longed to return to Jerusalem. Their prophets had announced their return, and their Psalms had sung of the longing of a whole people for a distant homeland, and for the ruined Temple that they must repair. As Augustine presents it, it is a vision of captivity and liberation, of loss and reparation,[8] shared, in general terms by most of the great religious thinkers of Late Antiquity, by Platonists,[9] Manichees[10] and Christians alike. But in his hands, at this time, it is explored in all its nuances and ramifications, it is worked out in all its details with a great artist's passion, and, at the same time, it is fully incarnated in a particular incident in the distant history of the Jews: 'We also must know first our captivity, then our liberation: we must know Babylon and Jerusalem. . . . These two cities, as a matter of historical fact, were two cities recorded in the Bible. . . . They were founded, at precise moments, to crystallize in symbolic form, the reality of these two 'cities' that had begun in the remote past, and that will continue to the end of the world.'[11]

---

[1] *Enarr. in Ps.* 136, 13.

[2] *Enarr. in Ps.* 136, 1: 'which everyone brought up in the traditions of the holy church should know'.

[3] v. esp. T. Hahn, *Tyconius-Studien*, 1900, p. 29.

[4] *de cat. rud.* xix, 31; *Enarr. in Ps.* 61, 5–6.   [5] *de cath. rud.* xix, 31.

[6] *Enarr. in Ps.* 64, 2.   [7] *Enarr. in Ps.* 147, 2.   [8] *Enarr. in Ps.* 147, 5.

[9] e.g. H. Leisegang, 'Der Ursprung d. Lehre Augustins von d. "Civitas Dei" ', *Archiv für Kulturgesch.*, 16, 1925, 127–155.

[10] A. Adam, 'Der manichäische Ursprung d. Lehre von d. zwei Reichen bei Augustin', *Theol. Literaturzeitung*, 77, 1952, pp. 385–390.

[11] *Enarr. in Ps.* 64, 1 and 2.

The Jews had done many things in Babylon; and Augustine himself had changed his mind as to what to emphasize. They had gone obediently; they had proved peaceful subjects and loyal public servants; the prayers of their martyrs had been answered in the conversion of the King — Nebuchadnezzar.[1] In the honeymoon period of the alliance of Church and State in Africa, Augustine had emphasized these facts against pagans and Donatists.[2] Now, it is the poignant longing of the Psalms that he fastens on. Babylon had meant 'confusion' — a merging of the identity in the things of the world.[3] The citizens of Jerusalem also depended on this world, but they became distinct from Babylon by their capacity to yearn for something else: 'Now let us hear, brothers, let us hear and sing; let us pine for the City where we are citizens. . . . By pining, we are already there; we have already cast our hope, like an anchor, on that coast. I sing of somewhere else, not of here: for I sing with my heart, not my flesh. The citizens of Babylon hear the sound of the flesh, the Founder of Jerusalem hears the tune of our heart.'[4]

While other Christian moralists of this age of crisis, Pelagius most notably, were to couch their message exclusively in terms of the ineluctable approach of the Day of Judgement,[5] Augustine chose a different perspective. He deliberately turned away from the threats of the Gospels, to find in the Psalms a capacity to love the future:[6] the exhortations that Augustine chooses to notice at this time, are exhortations to sing 'serenades', *ad amatoria quaedam cantica*;[7] the emotions he plays on, are not fear, but love for a distant and immemorial country: 'the ancient City of God.' 'The origin of this city goes back to Abel, as that of the evil one to Cain. It is, therefore, an ancient city, this City of God: always enduring its existence on earth, always sighing for heaven — whose name is also Jerusalem and Sion.'[8]

This tender oratory would have left an educated pagan unmoved.[9] When seen against the background of the history he knew, the 'Christian religion' was a very parochial affair. The worship of the gods stretched back, through Rome, to the very beginnings of the human race: centuries had elapsed before Christ appeared. Nor was it possible for Christianity to extend its antiquity by claiming that God

[1] *Serm.* 51, ix, 14.   [2] *de cat. rud.* xxi, 37; *C. Faustum* XII, 36.
[3] *Enarr. in Ps.* 64, 2.   [4] *Enarr. in Ps.* 64, 3.
[5] The alternative title to Salvian's, *de gubernatione Dei* was *de praesenti iudicio*: Gennadius, *de vir. ill.* 67, (P.L. lviii, 1099).
[6] *Enarr. in Ps.* 147, 4; v. sup. p. 251.   [7] *Enarr. in Ps.* 64, 3.   [8] *Enarr. in Ps.* 142, 2.
[9] *Enarr. in Ps.* 136, 17: 'What is that "City"?'

had made provision for the human race in the Jewish law: this law had always been confined to a small tract of country in Syria.[1] A Roman conservative found Christianity particularly hard to understand: for, having received a perfectly valid religious tradition from their ancestors the Jews, the Christians had replaced this by new rites.[2] These were forceful criticisms, elaborated only a century before, with astonishing learning, by none other than Porphyry, the great Platonist: a 'universal way of salvation' such as had been claimed by the Christians, was as yet, he said, 'unknown to historical knowledge'.[3]

Augustine was forced to take up this challenge. Up to this time, his ideas on the two Cities had developed largely in relation to the human composition of the church;[4] and his justification of the relevance of the Old Testament against the Manichees had been confined to a narrow track of Jewish history. Now, these themes had to be set against a different background: Augustine was brought up against 'the whole wide sweep of the centuries'.[5]

As a historian, Augustine was quite outclassed by Porphyry.[6] But he met Porphyry's criticism on different grounds. For instance, he immediately picked on the conservative assumption, that change was always more shocking than permanence: that the religious history of the human race should have consisted in the preservation of immemorial traditions;[7] and so, that a change of rites could only be a change for the worse. Any shrewd man could see that this was untrue in the things around him.[8] Indeed, Augustine had always tried, as a philosopher, to reconcile change and permanence in the world of nature. His great commentary on *Genesis* adapts a traditional solution of this problem: God had implanted in each organism a constant, organizing principle, a *ratio seminalis*, that would ensure that change happened, not arbitrarily, but in accordance with a latent pattern laid down, once and for all, at the Creation.[9] In the same way, changes in religious institutions, such as had occurred throughout the history of Israel, need not be regarded as unnecessary and shocking reversals of ancestral custom; they could be presented as significant landmarks that

---

[1] *Ep.* 108, ii, 8.   [2] *Ep.* 136, 2.   [3] *de civ. Dei,* X, 32, 5–11.
[4] e.g. *de cat. rud.* xix, 31.   [5] *Ep.* 102, iii, 21.
[6] 'The best scholar of his time . . .', Dodds, *Pagan and Christian,* p. 126. v. esp. W. den Boer, 'Porphyrius als historicus in zijn strijd tegen het Christendom', *Varia Historica aangeboden an Professor Doctor A. W. Bijvanck,* 1954, pp. 83–96.
[7] *Ep.* 136, 2.   [8] *Ep.* 138, i, 2–3.
[9] The idea has led to a somewhat fruitless debate on whether Augustine had anticipated the idea of Evolution: e.g. H. Woods, *Augustine and Evolution,* 1924 and A. Mitterer, *Die Entwicklungslehre Augustins,* 1956.

hint at a process of growth.[1] In this process, the human race could be conceived of as a vast organism, like a single man,[2] that changed according to a pattern of growth that was inaccessible to the human mind, yet clear to God.

In his attitude to history, Augustine claimed to have gone further than the pagan Platonists. They could only grasp the immutable: content to contemplate a timeless Deity, they could answer none of the questions posed, by 'the closewoven sequence of the centuries. . . . They could not trace the long space of the ages, place landmarks on that unfolding process by which the human race flows onward like a vast river, nor seize the final culmination of its appointed ends.'[3] According to Augustine, the rare privilege of linking the 'revolution of the ages' to the immutable Wisdom of God had been reserved to the Hebrew prophets.

The whole course of human history, therefore, could be thought of as laden with meanings which might be seized, partially by the believer, in full by the seer.[4] Areas of the past that lay far beyond the range of the classical historian, could be the scene of events of prophetic significance, and so be scrutinized and defended as valuable historical territory. (Augustine would even turn archaeologist to do so: he had seen at Utica a molar tooth so big as to prove that there had been giants on the earth in the age of Cain.)[5] In his *City of God*, Augustine was one of the first to sense and give monumental expression to a new form of intellectual excitement. Plotinus, when he wrote on 'Providence', had already presented the natural world as a harmony of minutely-articulate parts. The same sense of wonder, which is so marked a feature of the way in which Plotinus speaks of the Universe — the Cosmos[6] — will flood into the language of Augustine as he speaks of the marvellous and perfectly ordered distribution of the ages.[7] 'God is the unchanging conductor as well as the unchanged Creator of all things that change. When He adds, abolishes, curtails, increases

---

[1] *Ep.* 138, i, 7–8. Augustine also uses medical imagery, citing his former acquaintance, Vindicianus (*Ep.* 138, i, 3). The image fits well with what little we know of the characteristic doctrine of Vindicianus, v. sup. p. 67.

[2] v. esp. *de civ. Dei*, X, 14, 1–5.   [3] *De Trin.* IV, xvi, 21.

[4] Vittinghoff, 'Z. geschichtl. Selbstverständnis', *Hist. Zeitschr.*, 198, 1964, p. 541, singles out this belief as the distinctive feature of the Christian writers of the age.

[5] *de civ. Dei*, XV, 9, 20.   [6] *Ennead* 3, 2, 13 cited in *de civ. Dei*, X, 14, 12.

[7] *de civ. Dei*, X, 15, 1 sq., arguing directly from Plotinus' idea of providence in the universe to his own idea of providence in history. Compare the passage in J. Burckhardt, *Weltgeschichtliche Betrachtungen*, (Bern 1941), p. 393, most appositely cited by R. Walzer as evidence of the abiding force of Platonic ideas, in 'Platonism in Islamic Philosophy', *Greek into Arabic*, 1962, p. 251.

or diminishes the rites of any age, He is ordering all events according to His providence, until the beauty of the completed course of time, whose parts are the dispensations suitable to each different period, shall have played itself out, like the great melody of some ineffable composer. . . .'[1]

Men choose words to communicate; God had chosen both words and events.[2] To Augustine, God had expressed Himself in the past like a consummate stylist in the Late Roman manner. He delighted to talk allusively, in elaborate circumlocutions. The subject hinted at with mounting degrees of explicitness, is always the same: Christ and His Church.[3] Words, however, pass away, leaving only the meaning they signify. The great 'words' of God's language, whole nations and famous cities had all been swallowed up in the bankruptcy of temporal achievements: 'Look now at the city (Jerusalem) of which these most glorious things were spoken. On earth it is destroyed: it has fallen to the ground before its enemies; now it is not what it once was. It has delineated an image: this shadow has passed its meaning on to somewhere else.'[4]

Such remarks are typical of Augustine. He had little or no sense, as he surveyed the vast tract of history, that he might have inherited something directly from the purely human achievements of the civilizations of the Near East. Seen as a whole, human history was but 'that stretch of time in which the new born oust the dying',[5] a great river, slipping towards death. What had fascinated him, however, was the language of God, distant and opaque as a liturgy. It is the significance of this language, suddenly uncovered in the appearance of Christ among men, that poured meaning into a small part at least of this disquieting inanity: 'The centuries of past history would have rolled by like empty jars, if Christ had not been foretold by means of them.'[6]

Augustine had always believed, with all the Christians of the Early Church, that what was most significant in history was that narrow thread of prophetic sayings and happenings that culminated in the coming of Christ and the present situation of the Church. As in a kaleidoscope, patterns charged with prophetic significance would suddenly crystallize, only to dissolve and be replaced by a more vivid

---

[1] *Ep.* 138, i, 5.   [2] *Ep.* 102, vi, 33.   [3] *de civ. Dei*, X, 20, 7–13.
[4] *Enarr. in Ps.* 86, 6; cf. *de civ. Dei*, XVII, 13 and XVIII, 45.
[5] *de civ. Dei*, XVI, 1, 25; v. esp. H. I. Marrou, *L'Ambivalence du Temps de l'Histoire chez S. Augustin*, 1950.
[6] *Tract. in Joh.* 9, 6.

grouping: the Ark of Noah, the Promises to Abraham, the Exodus, the Captivity of Babylon. The vast intervals of time that had elapsed between such groupings — a millennium, for instance, separates Noah from Abraham — only served to heighten, by contrast to the drab succession of events recorded by 'historical diligence', the other-worldly significance of the few moments of 'prophetic truth'.[1] As a bishop, Augustine had been absorbed in following this narrow track, along which the history of the Old Testament had pointed to the new dispensation. The longest book in any of his works[2] was written on this theme, against Faustus the Manichee.

Porphyry was a critic of a different stature from Faustus: his objections had forced Augustine, in the *City of God*, to defend Christianity as the natural, true religion of the whole human race, as the 'universal way' whose existence had been denied by Porphyry, and not a parochial aberration. The essence of Christianity had to be seized and presented in general terms in the *City of God*: this lay in re-establishing the correct relationship between all created beings and their Creator, and, consequently, between one another. Such a formulation assumed an alternative. The nature of the deranged relationship between creature and Creator had to be analysed; its origin had to be laid bare in the fall of the angels; its juxtaposition seized in terms of two 'cities', and the human race would be presented in the *City of God* as divided between two fields of force.[3]

It was Augustine's intention, in the *City of God*, to prove to his readers that hints of a division between an 'earthly' and a 'heavenly' city could be seen throughout the history of the human race.

'Prophetic' history, as Augustine had known it, could skip the centuries, by concentrating on the few oases of significance; the 'unfolding course' of the two cities, by contrast, ran through every age. Augustine would try gallantly to reconstruct 'traces' of both 'cities', century by century, in the confused narratives of early Biblical history.[4] 'Prophetic' history was exclusively religious history. Its turning points were the great sacrifices, the sacrifices of Abel, of Abraham, of Melchisedech. In these, the celebrant would appear (as he appears, for instance, in the Early Christian mosaics above the altar of S. Vitale in Ravenna) standing alone with his God. By contrast, relations between men and men played an essential part in the idea of the two cities: in its classic incidents, it is always the relationship between two men, or two groups of men, that is vividly portrayed; for instance, that

[1] *de civ. Dei*, XVI, 2, 82–85.
[2] *C. Faust.* XXII; v. *Retract.* II, 33.
[3] *de Gen. ad litt.* XI, xv, 20; *de civ. Dei*, XIV, 28.
[4] e.g. *de civ. Dei*, XVI, 3.

of a whole nation in an alien land, as with the Jews in Babylon. And men are interested in more things than sacrifices: they seek all the 'goods' of this earth.[1] Augustine regards the social good of peace in an organized community as the most representative of such goods.[2] Thus the narrow tract of religious history must be widened: there is room, in Augustine's view of the past, for the consideration of whole societies, not only for a stately procession of just men; the *civitas terrena*, the 'city' of men pursuing earthly things, had to be seen to draw its strength from a history that stretched far beyond the Bible.[3] A view of history that had been content to follow a string of events to their culmination, is now immeasurably enriched by the need to trace, in every age, the way in which men's lives had crystallized around two basic alternatives.

This tension was 'published'[4] at the very onset of the human race, by being concentrated in one of the most elemental of human relationships, the relationship of a younger to an elder brother.[5] Augustine (himself the younger brother of Navigius) brings out to the full the charged and paradoxical quality of the whole of human history in terms of the single incident of Cain and Abel.[6] Cain, the elder brother, is the true son of his father, Adam. He is the 'natural' man after the Fall. He is a 'citizen of this world', because he is fully rooted and at home in it: even his name means 'full ownership'. He hoped for no more than he could see;[7] so, he founded the first city.[8] (The modern historian of civilization, indeed, would find Cain and his family, among them the first blacksmith and the first musician,[9] of absorbing interest.) Abel, by contrast, built no city; his son, Enoch, stands out in marked contrast to the rooted life of his cousins, men 'not out of place in this world, content with the peace and felicity of passing time',[10] by hoping for something else: *speravit invocare nomen Domini*, 'he *waited upon the name of the Lord.*'[11]

Augustine treats the tension between Cain and Abel as universal, because he can explain it in terms applicable to all men. All human society, he says, is based on a desire to share some good.[12] Of such goods, the most deeply felt by human beings is the need for 'peace': that is, for a resolution of tensions, for an ordered control of unbalanced appetites in themselves, and of discordant wills in society.[13] No man can

---

[1] *de civ. Dei*, XVIII, 2.
[2] e.g. *de civ. Dei*, XV, 4.
[3] in *de civ. Dei*, Book XVIII.
[4] *de civ. Dei*, XV, 21, 5.
[5] *de civ. Dei*, XV, 1, 29–41; cf. *Enarr. in Ps.* 61, 7: 'magnum mysterium'.
[6] *de civ. Dei*, XV, 17–18.
[7] *de civ. Dei*, XV, 17, 47; cf. *Enarr. in Ps.* 136, 2.
[8] *de civ. Dei*, XV, 17, 8.
[9] *Gen.* 4, 18 sq., in *de civ. Dei*, XV, 17, 32–38.
[10] *de civ. Dei*, XV, 17, 8–10.
[11] *Gen.* 4, 26: *de civ. Dei*, XV, 18, 2.
[12] e.g. *de civ. Dei*, XV, 4, 3.
[13] e.g. *de civ. Dei*, XIV, 1, 18.

exempt himself from such needs; but the members of the *civitas terrena*, that is, fallen men, tend to regard their achievement of such peace in society as sufficient in itself.[1] They make it a closed system, that admits no higher aims; and they view with envy those who possess an alternative to their own ideal of happiness.[2]

It was envy, therefore, that had made Cain slay Abel. Augustine did not find this surprising. He passed on immediately to the founding of Rome: here also, Romulus had slain his brother Remus, though this time out of rivalry.[3] The foundation of the state best known to Augustine's readers, therefore, 'measured up exactly to the first example: this was what is called in Greek an "Archetype", a unique pattern of behaviour'.[4]

Previously, in his *Contra Faustum*, Augustine had been content to see the incident of Cain and Abel as an allegory of Christ slain by the Jews.[5] It was the symbolic outline of the event that had then pre-occupied him. Now, Augustine will draw from it a pattern of the archetypal motives that sway real men, in all ages and in all countries: it is like coming from the unearthly, symbolic figures of Type and Antetype that face each other in the stained-glass windows along the walls of a Gothic cathedral, to the charged humanity of a religious painting by Rembrandt: 'in a wide world inhabited by so many different peoples, with divergent religions and manners, infinitely divided in their language, armaments and clothing, there have, never-theless, arisen no more than two kinds of groups of human beings, which we can call two "*cities*", according to the special usage of our Scriptures.'[6]

This, then, is Augustine's contribution to a new view of the past. A universal sweep, a universal explanation of men's basic motives, a certainty of the existence, in every age, of a single, fundamental tension. A more superficial man would have immediately turned such intuitions into a neatly-patterned Christian 'Universal History'.[7]

---

[1] *de civ. Dei*, XV, 4, 27; cf. *Enarr. in Ps.* 136, 2.   [2] *de civ. Dei*, XV, 4, 18 and 5, 24.
[3] *de civ. Dei*, XV, 5, 26–35.
[4] *de civ. Dei*, XV, 5, 6–7. In so doing, Augustine has dismissed the tradition by which Romulus was only indirectly responsible for the death of Remus (v. *de civ. Dei*, III 6, 6–9). Medieval illuminators show the slaying of Remus as an exact echo of the slaying of Abel, until Petrarch re-established the tradition that was more favourable to Romulus and, hence, to Rome: v. esp. E. Th. Mommsen, 'Petrarch and the Decoration of the "Sala Virorum Illustrium" ', *Medieval and Renaissance Studies*, ed. Rice, 1959, pp. 130–174, esp. pp. 158–159, and Ill. 12 and 33.
[5] *C. Faust.* XII, 9; *de civ. Dei*, XV, 7, 118.   [6] *de civ. Dei*, XIV, 1, 12–18.
[7] As did Orosius, v. sup. p. 296, so earning the comment of J. B. Bury: 'Perhaps it deserves more than any book to be described as the first attempt at a universal history, and it was probably the worst', *History of the Later Roman Empire*, i, 1923, (Dover Edition, p. 306).

Augustine did not. When he treated the 'courses' of the two 'cities' in one entire book, he was content merely to point to some unflattering comparisons between the principles reflected in the history of pagan states known to his learned readers, and the 'consecrated common-wealth' of Israel;[1] and, in suggesting a few points in which their destinies were related, he did no more than follow a picture of the past, that most educated Christians of his age had already come to take for granted.[2]

We should not expect such a 'Universal History' from Augustine. We do so, in part, because we expect him to have time to interest himself in other cities than his 'City of God'.[3] Augustine knew very well that he could not afford to do so. To his pagan readers, the only real history was the account of the glorious achievements of their own civilizations. Augustine had to show that there was an alternative to the busy, rooted life of the states known to ancient men.[4] Within the obvious 'city' of fallen men, with its obvious necessities and achieve-ments and its well-recorded history, there had always been room for another group, for men, like Abel, who could long for something else, who could be aware of the transience of the conventional life of their fellows. It is a message that crystallized deeply-rooted ideas. What wa. at stake, in the *City of God* and in Augustine's sermons, was the capacity of men to 'long' for something different, to examine the nature of their relationship with their immediate environment; above all, to establish their identity by refusing to be engulfed in the un-thinking habits of their fellows. With such a message, the parts of the *City of God* that deal with the past could never be a mere sketch of 'Universal History'. They are a brisk journey through the past, in which Augustine points out the precise and vivid 'traces', *vestigia*,[5] of an alternative to the normal, all-embracing aims of fallen men.

This history must, of course, concentrate on the symbols around which a sense of a separate identity had formed: the compact par-

---

[1] *de civ. Dei*, X, 32, 92 and XV, 8, 17.

[2] e.g. *de civ. Dei*, XVIII, 27, 23 on Rome and Babylon.

[3] He regarded the Holy Spirit as sharing his preferences in recording the narratives of the Old Testament, e.g. *de civ. Dei*, XV, 15, 36. For Augustine, the Bible was the only truly reliable history-book, because not written by men alone (*Ep.* 101, 2) and because the choice of what is significant had been correctly made. Contrast J. B. Bury, *History of the Later Roman Empire*, i, 1923, (Dover) p. 305: 'To a modern, and possibly also to an ancient enquirer, Augustine's work would have been more interesting if he had seriously addressed himself to an historical study of the Babylonian and Roman Empires'. But this was an age in which the educated man's grasp even of the Roman past had become extremely feeble: v. A. Momigliano, 'Pagan and Christian Historiography', *The Conflict between Paganism and Christianity*, pp. 85–86.

[4] esp. *de civ. Dei*, XV, 8, 7–20.

[5] *de civ. Dei*, XVI, 1, 1.

ticularism of Israel[1] and the world-wide unity of the Catholic Church are shadows of the Heavenly City. But membership of them cannot in itself make men perfect: the dividing-line between the two 'cities' is invisible, because it involves each man's capacity to love what he loves.[2]

For Augustine, both past and present remain largely opaque; but he could, throughout, see the outlines of a choice. Men are inextricably 'merged' by the needs of their common, mortal life.[3] But ultimately, the only thing that matters, is to transcend this insidious symbiosis: men must be prepared to be 'distinct'.[4]

Augustine was only a learned bishop. A man inspired by God would see, behind the confused events on which Augustine's tenacious mind had fastened, the terrible simplicity of the alternatives between which men had gravitated throughout their history. Such a man was the Evangelist, John:

'In the spirit, he could realize this division: as a human being, he could see only an inseparable mixture. What could not yet be seen as separate in space, he separated out with his mind, with the glance of his heart: he saw just two peoples, the faithful, the faithless. . . .'[5]

The need to save one's identity as a citizen of Heaven, is therefore the centre of gravity of Augustine's idea of the relationship of the two 'cities' in this world. The normal human society has to make room for a group of men who must remain aware of being different, for a *civitas . . . peregrina*;[6] for resident strangers.

Peregrinatio is the word which Augustine uses to sum up the situation. The category of *peregrini*, of 'resident aliens', was well-known to ancient men. Augustine himself had experienced such a situation in Milan: his stormy residence in a great capital had been a *peregrinatio*,[7] (and how narrowly the young African had escaped absorption at that time!).

---

[1] *Ep.* 102, iii, 15; *de civ. Dei*, XV, 8, 10, and XVI, 3, 70.

[2] v. esp. *Enarr. in Ps.* 64, 2; v. Y. M. J. Congar, ' "Civitas Dei" et "Ecclesia" chez S. Augustin', *Rev. études augustin.*, iii, 1957, 1–14.

[3] v. esp. H.-I. Marrou, 'Civitas Dei, Civitas terrena: num tertium quid?' (Studia Patristica, ii) *Texte und Untersuchungen*, 64, 1957, pp. 342–350.

[4] *Enarr. in Ps.* 64, 2: 'They are set apart by a holy yearning'.

[5] *Tract. in Joh.* 14, 8.   [6] *de civ. Dei*, XVIII, 1, 3: *etiam ista peregrina*.

[7] *Conf.* V, xiii, 23. v. the prudent discussion of Guy, *Unité et structure logique*, pp. 113–114. But with the spread of Roman citizenship, the term had lost its precise legal meaning, and now meant simply 'foreigner', 'outsider', 'stranger': v. e.g. *Conf.* I, xiv, 23, Greek is a *lingua peregrina*; *Tract. in Joh.* 40, 7, *peregrini*, 'strangers', bring Arian beliefs into Hippo, the *civitas*; cf. *Coll. Carthag.* iii, 99 (P.L. xi, 1381 A), where *peregrini* means 'non-Africans'. v. esp. J. Gaudemet, 'L'étranger au Bas-Empire', *Recueils Soc. Jean Bodin*, ix, 1958, pp. 207–235.

If we can seize the nuances of this term as used by Augustine, we can gain an impression of an essential theme in his religion as an old man. A sensitive *peregrinus* would, of course, feel homesick, almost a 'captive' sighing for release, like the Jews in Babylon.[1] He would feel uprooted, a passing stranger in the comfortable, settled life around him. We can translate *peregrinus* by 'pilgrim': but only if we realize that Augustine detested travelling,[2] and that his 'pilgrim' is far closer, in his romantic discontent and yearning, to *Der Wanderer* of Schubert's song than to the jovial globe-trotters of the *Canterbury Tales*. The image, therefore, could provide a radically otherworldly man with a language of incomparable richness and tenderness: the 'authentic philosopher' of Plotinus, endowed with 'the soul of a lover', also sighing for a distant country,[3] is the first-cousin of the *peregrinus* of Augustine.

Yet Augustine went beyond Plotinus. He grappled with a problem which Plotinus had not felt challenged to face. For the *peregrinus* is also a temporary resident. He must accept an intimate dependence on the life around him: he must realize that it was created by men like himself, to achieve some 'good' that he is glad to share with them, to improve some situation, to avoid some greater evil;[4] he must be genuinely grateful for the favourable conditions that it provides.[5] In fact, Augustine had come to expect the Christian to be aware of the tenacity of the links that would always bind him to this world. The thought of his middle-age is marked by a growing appreciation of the value of such links.[6] So the *City of God*, far from being a book about flight from the world, is a book whose recurrent theme is 'our business within this common mortal life';[7] it is a book about being other-worldly in the world.

Augustine the young convert could not have written such a book. Indeed, in the letters and sermons of Augustine's middle age, we can see how much the harshness of the young man had mellowed. He has become far more open to the reality of the bonds that unite men to the world around them. He had, for instance, once told Nebridius that the wise man could 'live alone with his mind';[8] now he will pray to have friends:[9] 'For when we are harassed by poverty, saddened by bereavement, ill and in pain . . . let good men visit us — men who can not only rejoice with those that rejoice, but weep with those that weep, and who know how to give useful advice and how to win us to express

---

[1] *Enarr. in Ps.* 61, 6; 85, 11; 148, 4. [2] v. sup. p. 210.
[3] e.g. *Ennead* V, 9, 1–2, (transl. MacKenna 2 p. 434–5). [4] v. esp. *de civ. Dei*, XV, 4, 16.
[5] v. esp. *de civ. Dei*, XIX, 17, 11–25 and XIX, 26, 4–10. [6] e.g. *de doct. christ.* I, xxxv, 39.
[7] *de civ. Dei*, XV, 21, 15. [8] *Ep.* 10, 1. [9] Denis, 16, 1, (*Misc. Agostin.*, i, p. 75)

our own feelings in conversation. . . .'[1] He had come to know what it was to exercise authority in an organized community. The measured paternalism that he suggests as an ideal quality of government in the *City of God*, reflects his own practice as a bishop.[2] His bitter campaigns had taught him how much he needed an external peace: the man who had once come to Hippo to persuade an Imperial agent to become a monk,[3] will now travel into the depths of Numidia, to persuade a general not to do so.[4]

The men of Augustine's sermons are not mere 'dust and ashes'. They are sturdy sinners, who enjoy what they do. The sheer tenacity of their feelings astonishes him: think of highwaymen, who stick out against all tortures rather than reveal the names of their accomplices; 'They could not have done this without a great capacity for love.'[5] 'The world is a smiling place.'[6] Little wonder that it is enjoyed immoderately. 'I do not blame you; I do not criticize you, even if this life is what you love. . . . You can love this life all you want, as long as you know what to choose. Let us therefore be able to choose our life, if we are capable of loving it.'[7] The deadly perfectionism of the Pelagians was distasteful to him: he also was trying to be perfect; but 'in their exhortations, let them urge the higher virtues; but without denigrating the second-best'.[8]

The members of the *civitas peregrina*, therefore, maintain their identity not by withdrawal, but by something far more difficult: by maintaining a firm and balanced perspective on the whole range of loves of which men are capable in their present state: 'It is because of this, that the Bride of Christ, the City of God, sings in the *Song of Songs: "ordinate in me caritatem"*, "Order in me my love".'[9]

Augustine had come to a firmly-rooted idea of the essential goodness of created things, and so of human achievements. These good things were 'gifts': *bona . . . dona* is a key-phrase throughout the *City of God*; and God is thought of mainly as Creator and, even more, as a *largitor*, as a lavisher of gifts.[10]

The only piece of genuine poetry that we possess of Augustine's is concerned with just this theme. It is a poem in praise of the Easter Candle (and we know how much Augustine loved light of all kinds).[11] He will quote it in the *City of God*, when dealing, of all subjects, with the exceptional beauty of the first women of the earthly city:

[1] *Ep.* 130, ii, 4.　　[2] e.g. *de civ. Dei*, XIX, 14, 35–51.　　[3] v. sup. p. 136.
[4] v. inf. p. 422.　　[5] *Serm.* 169, 14.　　[6] *Serm.* 158, 7.
[7] *Serm.* 297, 4 and 8.　　[8] *Ep.* 157, iv, 37.
[9] *Cant.* 2, 4, in *de civ. Dei*, XV, 22, 29; cf. *de doct. christ.* I, xxvii, 28. v. esp. Burnaby, *Amor Dei*, pp. 104–109.
[10] esp. *de civ. Dei*, XIX, 13, 57–75.　　[11] e.g. *Serm.* 88, 15.

*Those things are Yours, O God. They are good, because You created
them.
None of our evil is in them. The evil is ours if we love them
At the expense of Yourself — these things that reflect Your design.*[1]

'Suppose brethren, a man should make a ring for his betrothed, and
she should love the ring more wholeheartedly than the betrothed who
made it for her. . . . Certainly, let her love his gift: but, if she should
say, "The ring is enough. I do not want to see his face again" what
would we say of her. . . . The pledge is given her by the betrothed just
that, in his pledge, he himself may be loved. God, then, has given you
all these things. Love Him who made them.'[2]

The relation between God and the goods enjoyed by created beings
is conceived of as a relation between an utterly gratuitous giver and a
recipient. Augustine could not have seized upon a more difficult and
ambivalent relationship. The acknowledgment of dependence, and
with it, the capacity to be grateful, does not come easily, in Augustine's
opinion; and he will unravel the origin and relationship of the two
'cities' precisely in terms of this basic relationship of giver and recipient.

The Devil had wished to enjoy what he had been given, as if it were
his own: he had wished no other source of goodness than himself.[3]
Such usurped omnipotence could only diminish him. It altered his
relations with his fellows: it caused him to assert this omnipotence by
dominating his equals;[4] it made him view with envy those who
possessed a source of goodness, a felicity outside his own.[5]

Augustine, who had watched so closely even the jealousy of one
baby for another, was not likely to underrate the power of envy, in
determining the relations of the 'city' of the fallen with the 'City' of
God: envy of the human race, for instance, determines the impingement of the demons on mankind, and, so, the course of the religious
history of paganism, that plays such a large part in the *City of God.*
The 'lust to dominate' is an equally potent force among the fallen
beings: Augustine will see it everywhere in a history that had, significantly, become for him a history only of the great Empires of the
ancient world.[6] But above all, there is pride: an omnipotent denial of
dependence characterizes the attitude of the 'earthly city' to the quite

---

[1] *de civ. Dei,* XVII, 15.   [2] *Tract. in Ep. Joh.* 2, 11.   [3] *de civ. Dei,* XII, 6, 1–14.
[4] *de civ. Dei,* XIV, 28, 3–10 and XIX, 12, 87–89.   [5] *de civ. Dei,* XV, 5, 19–32.
[6] e.g. *de civ. Dei,* XIV, 28, 7–10. Cf. *de civ. Dei,* XVIII, 2, 16–25: the 2 great Empires are
Rome and Assyria. v. R. Drews, 'Assyria in Classical Universal Histories', *Historia,* xiv,
1965, pp. 129–142, esp. pp. 137–138.

genuine values its members had created: its heroisms, its culture, its periods of peace. Throughout the *City of God*, it is to this basic denial of dependence, and so of gratitude, that Augustine will point, in politics,[1] in thought, in religion.[2]

Augustine, therefore, will demolish with quite exceptional intellectual savagery, the whole of the ancient ethical tradition: 'those theories of mortal men, in which they have striven to make for themselves, by themselves, some complete happiness within the misery of this life.'[3] He thought of such theories as leading to a closed circle, calculated to deny a relationship of giving and receiving. To this tradition he will oppose an idea that involves just such a relationship: faith, and above all, 'hope'.[4] He will search hard among the genuine good things which men enjoy, for some hint of what happiness men may yet '*hope*' for at the hands of a lavish Creator.[5]

Augustine's thought was always in a state of tension. In the *City of God*, we can most clearly see why it was sharpened to such an intense pitch in the other writings of his old age. For, if the material world, and with it, the human body had been a perfect gift of God, it could never be treated as a second-best. It had not just 'run out' ineluctably from some higher perfection, as Plotinus had thought. Augustine, therefore, had to face with new eyes the problem of evil in the world. For he had once thought, somewhat like Plotinus, that Adam and Eve had 'fallen' into a physical state:[6] that the prolific virtues they would have engendered in a purely 'spiritual' existence had declined, with the Fall, into the mere literal flesh and blood of human families.[7] He now no longer thought like this. Augustine will look back at Adam with particular poignancy: Adam, also, had been a man of flesh and blood like himself; he had eaten, he had enjoyed the sights of the world, he would have raised a family by intercourse with his wife;[8] why was it that the 'natural' enjoyments of Adam in his Paradise were accompanied in Augustine by emotional overtones that were a source of such unbearable tension: 'what is it that has sown this war in me?'[9]

Against Julian of Eclanum, an optimist, Augustine would justify the

---

[1] e.g. *de civ. Dei*, XV, 7, 36–49.

[2] v. esp. G. Madec, 'Connaissance de Dieu et action de grâces', *Rech. augustin.*, ii, 1962, pp. 273–309.

[3] *de civ. Dei*, XIX, 1, 4–5.   [4] *de civ. Dei*, XIX, 1, 6.

[5] *de civ. Dei*, XIX, 11, 26–33 and 20, 11.

[6] v. *Enarr. in Ps.* 9, 14. v. R. J. O'Connell, 'The Plotinian Fall of the Soul in St. Augustine', *Traditio*, 19, 1963, pp. 1–35.

[7] *de Gen. c. Man.* II, xix, 29; v. *Retract.* II, 9, 3.   [8] *de civ. Dei*, XIV, 26, 16–22.

[9] *C. Jul.* V, vii, 26.

collective punishment by which God had pursued the single sin of Adam in the bodies of all his descendants. These terrible pages reflect Augustine's dilemma.[1] He was a man who could no longer take physical evil for granted. For, if the life of the senses cannot be assumed to be an inevitable 'second best', below an existence of 'pure spirit', then the difficulties of the body — its horrible diseases and the unpleasant emotional concomitants of its most normal physical acts — could no longer be taken for granted either. Such difficulties could only be thought of as the result of the derangement of an order in which material and spiritual could have been harmoniously joined.[2] Such a derangement, again, could only be thought of as the result of a precise, unilateral action on the part of the recipient of God's gifts; and the untold misery of the human race had to be ascribed to a calculated and awesome act of justice on the part of God, the giver, whatever the cost to human feelings. For only some 'unspeakable sin' could have caused so omnipotent and generous a Creator to mingle such great pain with the flow of good things.

As Augustine wrote the last book of the *City of God*, when he was seventy-two years old, he included a passage that is the final elaboration of an argument that had recurred frequently towards the end of the work. It is an argument for hope.

'"*Lord, I have loved the beauty of Thy house.*" ... From His gifts, which are scattered to good and bad alike in this, our most grim life, let us, with His help, try to express sufficiently what we have yet to experience.[3]

'In its collective origin, from the evidence of this life itself, a life so full of so many and such various evils that it can hardly be called living, we must conclude that the whole human race is being punished. . . .'[4] There are the horrors of the education of small children;[5] the gratuitous accidents of daily life;[6] the merciless elements: 'I know of peasants whose excellent harvest has been swept away, from out of their barns, by a sudden water-race;'[7] the bizarre and humiliating effects of rare diseases;[8] the sudden terrors of dreams.[9]

---

[1] v. inf. pp. 394–397.

[2] v. *Retract.* I, 10, 2, on *de Musica*, VI, iv, 7.

v. most recently, H. I. Marrou, *The Resurrection and St. Augustine's Theology of Human Values*, 1966 (= 'Le dogme de la résurrection', *Rev. études augustin.*, xii, 1966, pp. 111–136, esp. pp. 126–129.

[3] *de civ. Dei*, XXII, 21, 26.   [4] *de civ. Dei*, XXII, 22, 1.

[5] *de civ. Dei*, XXII, 22, 34.   [6] *de civ. Dei*, XXII, 22, 74.

[7] *de civ. Dei*, XXII, 22, 82.   [8] *de civ. Dei*, XXII, 22, 94.

[9] *de civ. Dei*, XXII, 22, 100.

Yet so much good still flows beside the evil 'as in a vast, racing river'.[1] Think of the intimate wonders of the human body, even, the quite gratuitous ornament of a male beard![2] The force of reason shown in the sheer proliferation of invention; 'And, last of all' (and this from Augustine, the Catholic bishop), 'who can possibly do full justice to the intellectual brilliance displayed by philosophers and heretics in defending their errors and incorrect opinions.'[3]

And there is the world around him, as always, a play of light and colour: 'the extraordinary brilliance and surface effects of the light itself, in sun and moon and stars, in the dark shades of a glade, in the colours and scents of flowers, in the sheer diversity and abundance of chirruping, painted birds. . . . And' (perhaps, at this point, the old bishop turned to look out over the wide bay of Hippo) 'there is the grandeur of the spectacle of the sea itself, as it slips on and off its many colours like robes, and now is all shades of green, now purple, now sky-blue. . . . And all these are mere consolations for us, for us unhappy, punished men: they are not the rewards of the blessed. What can these be like, then, if such things here are so many, so great, and of such quality. . . .'[4]

[1] de civ. Dei, XXII, 24, 11. [2] de civ. Dei, XXII, 24, 160.
[3] de civ. Dei, XXII, 24, 109. [4] de civ. Dei, XXII, 24, 175 sq.

28

UNITY ACHIEVED[1]

In the disastrous years of 409 and 410, Alaric had marched back-
wards and forwards over Italy. The Roman government lost
interest in Africa; its support was withdrawn from the Catholic
church; the campaign to repress Donatism foundered. The
Donatist bishop returned in triumph to Hippo. Augustine became a
marked man, 'a wolf, to be slain.'[2] He found himself at this time faced
with the prospect of ending his life as a martyr.[3] Only the mistake of a
guide in choosing the wrong road saved him from an ambush laid by
the Circumcellions.[4] His flock was demoralized. He would need all his
determination: 'I have no fear of you. You cannot overturn the
Judgement Seat of Christ and set up that of Donatus. I shall continue
to call back the wandering; I shall seek out the lost. Even if the
branches of the wood tear me in my search, I shall still force my way
through every narrow path. In as much as the Lord, Who drives me to
this task by His terror, gives me strength, I shall go through everything.'[5]

For a dramatic period, from late 409 to August 410, the Imperial
laws against heresy were suspended.[6] They could not be reimposed
now, without some public gesture. For the Catholic Emperor,
Honorius, it was a matter of *reculer pour mieux sauter*: only a full
official enquiry into the origin of the Donatist schism would eclipse the
vacillations of Imperial policy in the previous years. On August 25th,

---

[1] The best treatments are Frend, *Donatist Church*, pp. 275–299, and Crespin, *Ministère
et Sainteté*, pp. 77–103. (E. L. Grasmück, *Coercitio: Staat und Kirche im Donatistenstreit*,
1964, adds little).

[2] *Vita*, IX, 4.

[3] *Guelf* 28, 7–8: preached possibly at Utica on 14th Sept. 410, (*Misc. Agostin.*, i, p. 542).

[4] *Vita*, XII, 2.   [5] *Serm.* 46, 14.

[6] v. esp. Frend, *Donatist Church*, pp. 269–274, on the fluctuations of policy from 408 to
411.

410, therefore, he summoned the bishops of both churches to a conference. It would be called a *Collatio*, a 'comparison', of the legal claims of both parties, to be the true Catholic church. The *Collatio* was to be finished in four months. It would be conducted by Flavius Marcellinus, a man who, as we have seen, was a devout Catholic.[1]

The Emperor had ordered what Augustine and his colleagues had always wanted: a public confrontation with the Donatist leaders. Such a confrontation was particularly welcome at the time. For the Catholic Church had come to contain too many half-convinced converts from Donatism. Only a fully-publicized, definitive examination of the issues would persuade such men that the cause of Donatism was irretrievably lost.[2] In the *Collatio* of 411, therefore, the bishops of both sides would argue passionately, less to convince each other than to impress this influential body of waverers.[3]

Augustine hardly expected the conference to be an occasion for eirenic negotiation. It was an official inquiry, in which the justice that had already been done a century before in favour of the Catholics, would be seen to be done. For, as he never tired of telling his rivals, it was the Donatists who had first appealed to Constantine to arbitrate between themselves and Caecilian.[4] Constantine had declared that the party of Caecilian was the Catholic church; and all later Imperial laws against Donatism merely stemmed directly from this fateful decision.[5] The matter was as simple as that.[6]

The Donatists, of course, did not come for a clear-cut legal decision. They thought of themselves as the authentic Christian church in Africa: public opinion, traditional views of the church, not legal documents, were the mainstay of their case. They would play to the gallery. On May 18th, 411, they even entered Carthage in a solemn procession, some 284 bishops from all over Africa.[7]

The compact mass of the Donatist bishops dominated the first

---

[1] *Gesta Collationis Carthaginensis*, i, 4 (P.L. xi, 1260–1261). The more tactful *Edictum* of Marcellinus is the better source for the protocol envisaged: *Coll. Carth.* i, 5–10, (P.L. xi, 1261–1266). v. esp. Crespin, *Ministère et Sainteté*, pp. 81–82.

[2] *Ep.* 185, vii, 30; cf. *Ep.* 97, 4.

[3] As would happen later in Caesarea, when Augustine held a debate with the former Donatist bishop in order to convince waverers: *Gesta cum Emerito*, 2. One must add that Augustine may have been genuinely disillusioned by the meagre results of mere suppression in the period 405–408: v. Crespin, *Ministère et Sainteté*, pp. 75–76.

[4] *Ep.* 89, 2.   [5] *Ep.* 88, 5.

[6] *Ep.* 88, 10: 'We do not want to have a second final decision, but to have it made known as already settled to those who meanwhile are not aware that it is so'.

[7] *ad Don. post. Coll.* XXV, 45. v. Frend, *Donatist Church*, pp. 280–281, on the type of conference envisaged by the Donatists.

sessions of the Conference. Their leader, Petilian of Constantine, won all the opening moves. He forced the burden of proof back on the Catholics: for if the conference was a proper trial, a *cognitio*, he argued, the Catholics had to establish their identity as the accusers;[1] they had to prove that they, and not the Donatists, were the true Catholic Church. At a stroke, the conference became a general debate on the nature of the true church: and for this debate the Donatists had prepared an impressive manifesto.[2] For two-and-a-half sessions, Petilian managed to steer the proceedings away from the awkward 'case of Caecilian'.[3] Once the narrow issue of Constantine's decision in favour of Caecilian was raised, his case would be shipwrecked. For he had taken the measure of Marcellinus. Marcellinus was a scrupulously conscientious man, willing to put up with any amount of chicanery and insult,[4] prepared to make substantial concessions on his own initiative,[5] in order to obtain a fair decision: but, at bottom, he was a good, Roman bureaucrat. The 'case of the church' was general and confusing. By contrast, the case of Caecilian had been summed up for him by the Catholics, in a dossier of impressive official documents.[6] Little wonder that, with such a man presiding, the Donatists shied away from the appearance of this dossier 'as demons recoil in horror at the approach of an exorcist'.[7]

The Conference lasted for 3 sessions, on the 1st, 3rd and 8th of June, 411. It was recorded verbatim by stenographers. In the large part that has survived, we can follow word for word the spoken Latin of the fifth century A.D.; we can hear stubborn, clever men, versed in rhetoric and legal argument, manoeuvring for position over an issue on which their careers would depend.[8]

Marcellinus had arranged that only two delegations of 7 bishops from each side should appear before him in the great hall of a public

---

[1] The legal acumen of Petilian has been made plain by the study of A. Steinwenter, 'Eine kirchliche Quelle d. nachklassischen Zivilprozesses', *Acta congressus iuridici internationalis*, 2, 1935, pp. 123–144.

[2] *Coll. Carthag.* iii, 258, (P.L. xi, 1408–1414).

[3] Frend, *Donatist Church*, pp. 285–286.

[4] e.g. *Coll. Carthag.* i, 7, (P.L. xi, 1265), where he offers to stand down if not acceptable to either party.

[5] e.g. *Coll. Carthag.* i, 5, (P.L. xi, 1262): he had returned confiscated Donatist basilicas pending a decision.

[6] *Coll. Carthag.* iii, 144 and 176, (P.L. xi, 1389 and 1394). Such documents were treated with great reverence in Late Roman and Byzantine times: v. F. Dölger, 'Die Kaiserurkunde der Byzantiner', *Hist. Zeitschrift.*, 159, 1938/9, pp. 229–250.

[7] *Ad Don. post. Coll.* xxv, 44.

[8] v. esp. E. Tengström, *Die Protokollierung d. Collatio Carthaginensis*, (Studia Graeca et Latina Gothoburgensia, xiv), 1962.

bath, the *Thermae Gargilianae*.[1] But when the session opened, the whole Donatist episcopate trooped into the hall, and stood, immovable, behind their champions.[2] Marcellinus rose to greet the bishops with frigid politeness: he said he wished that an inquiry had not been necessary.[3] The Donatist bishops would not take a seat: they would stand, 'like Christ before Pilate'. As a layman, Marcellinus would not resume his seat in the presence of standing bishops: and so the business began, with the president standing rigid, in an attitude of defiant humility.[4]

Next, Petilian would only accept the procedure laid down by Marcellinus, if the Catholics could prove that they were a sufficiently large body to be represented by a delegation. He accused them of bluffing, by creating 'shadow' bishoprics in the time of persecution.[5] So the Catholic bishops were assembled from all over Carthage, to undergo an identity parade. Both sides stood around on a hot summer's afternoon, as each Donatist bishop recognized his Catholic rival. Tempers soon became frayed. Memories of violence broke into the monotony of the roll-call. 'Here I am. Put it down. Does Florentius recognize me? He should: he put me in prison for four years, and would have had me executed. . . .'[6] 'I recognize my persecutor. . . .'[7] 'I have no rival, for there is the body of Lord Marculus, for whose blood the Lord will exact retribution on the last day.'[8] By now the lights are lit. A single incident threatens to steer the whole proceedings into a *cul de sac*: had the Donatists signed on behalf of a dead bishop? 'It is only human to die,' Petilian had said. 'It may be human for a man to die,' Alypius snapped back: 'but it is unworthy of a man to lie.'[9]

Two days later, the Donatists gained another point. They obtained a postponement of five days to check the shorthand record of the first session: they gained time to prepare their brief. Augustine had taken no part in these manoeuvres. He now urged Marcellinus to grant this request. *Humanum est*: 'It is only fair,' that they should be given time to make up their minds.[10] He had once treated a Manichaean missionary in the same way.[11] Confident of winning his case, he saw no reason why

---

[1] v. esp. Frend, *Donatist Church*, p. 277 n. 7, who emphasizes, with his characteristic shrewdness, the poor ventilation of such a bath.

[2] *Coll. Carthag.* i, 2 and 14, (P.L. xi, 1259 and 1266).

[3] *Coll. Carthag.* i, 3, (P.L. xi, 1259).

[4] *Coll. Carthag.* i, 144–145, (P.L. xi, 1319). The incident was repeated at the next session: ii, 3–7 (P.L. xi, 1354).

[5] *Coll. Carthag.* i, 61 and 65, (P.L. xi, 1274).   [6] *Coll. Carthag.* i, 142, (P.L. xi, 1318A).

[7] *Coll. Carthag.* i, 143, (P.L. xi, 1318A).   [8] *Coll. Carthag.* i, 187, (P.L. xi, 1329A).

[9] *Coll. Carthag.* i, 208, (P.L. xi, 1345B).   [10] *Coll. Carthag.* ii, 56, (P.L. xi, 1361A).

[11] *Gesta cum Felice* I, 20.

the Donatists should not be given enough rope to hang themselves with.

His colleagues had been less remote. Possidius was excited and deliberately rude.[1] Alypius, though more dignified, had entered with gusto into the trial of strength of the previous day. He had always judged the policy of repression by its results. He was a proud and successful man: 'Would that other towns could rejoice in the ancient, established unity of Thagaste.'[2]

It was only in the last session, on June 8th, that Augustine came into his own. He was determined, now, to force a decision on the main business: 'How much longer is the populace going to wait? Their soul is at stake: yet we use delaying-tactics, so that the end, the discovery of the truth, may never come.'[3] At last the Catholics manoeuvred persistently towards the heart of the matter. With the whole Catholic case at his finger-tips, Augustine answered, impromptu, the carefully-prepared manifesto of the Donatists.[4] It must have been an astonishing and heartening performance. Marcellinus, who until then had stood aloof, now took the bit between his teeth. He brushed aside demands for a separate judgement on the 'case of the Church'.[5] He insisted on finding the 'cause of dissension':[6] that is, he steered for a safe port among the official documents of the 'case of Caecilian'. The Catholics were left to reconstruct from the documents the exact history of the schism in its first year.[7] This was all that Marcellinus had required in order to reach a final decision. The delegations were recalled, and by torchlight, in the early morning of June 9th, Marcellinus delivered judgement: the Donatists had no case; 'Let falsehood, once detected, bow its neck to truth made manifest.'[8]

In the next years, Donatism would be repressed with exceptional thoroughness. The laws against Donatists became coercive in the true sense of the word: they punished laymen for *not* becoming Catholics. In 405, the Donatist church had merely been 'disbanded': it had been deprived of its bishops, of its churches, and of its funds; its members lost certain civic rights. From 412, by contrast, a tariff of exceptionally heavy fines was applied to laymen of all classes who failed to join the Catholic church.[9]

[1] *Coll. Carthag.* ii, 29, (P.L. xi, 1336). [2] *Coll. Carthag.* i, 136, (P.L. xi, 1316A).
[3] *Coll. Carthag.* iii, 20, (P.L. xi, 1366).
[4] *Coll. Carthag.* iii, 267, (P.L. xi, 1415C); v. iii, 261–281, (P.L. xi, 1414–1418).
[5] *Brev. Collat.* III, xi, 23. [6] *Brev. Collat.* III, xi, 21.
[7] *Brev. Collat.* III, xii, 24–xxiv, 42.
[8] *Coll. Carthag.* Sententia cognitoris, (P.L. xi, 1418–1420, 1419A).
[9] *Cod. Theod.* XVI, 5, 52 (412) and 54 (414), (in P.L. xi, 1420–1428): v. Brown, 'Religious Coercion', *History*, xlviii, 1963, p. 290.

In Augustine's writings and sermons, from 405 to 409, and after 411,[1] we can catch glimpses of a great church driven underground: Donatists had to resort to ingenious legal devices to save the validity of their wills;[2] men were afraid to offer hospitality to their former bishops.[3] Like any desperate group, the Donatists had fallen back on wild hopes and legends. They would console themselves that Simon of Cyrene, who had been forced by the Romans to carry the Cross of Christ, had been an African: it is a touching image.[4] They would remember, how in the days of glory, their great bishops had heard voices from Heaven, had performed miracles.[5] The Circumcellion movement might have formed the backbone of the Donatist resistance.[6] But their bands were now deprived of leadership from the bishops of the towns, perhaps, also, of material support:[7] the fanatical aggression that had once been turned outwards, against the 'unclean' Catholics, was now turned inwards in these despairing men, in a horrible epidemic of suicides.[8]

Augustine will only mention these events in passing. He had become involved in the Pelagian controversy, and was increasingly impatient of resistance in Africa. Long experience of violence had hardened him. A stranger might be shocked by the suicides of the Circumcellions: for Augustine, they were 'part of their accustomed behaviour'.[9] A passionate and sensitive campaigner, Augustine will show himself a hard victor.

In 420, Gaudentius, the successor of the great Optatus as Donatist bishop of Timgad, had retired to his magnificent basilica on the approach of the Imperial officials, and had threatened to burn himself with his congregation.[10] The Imperial agent, Dulcitius, was a pious man, his brother was a priest in Rome.[11] He was, not unnaturally, taken aback by the ferocity of the ecclesiastical politics of Africa. Here, after all, was a Christian congregation, sharing the same form of worship as himself, barricaded against him in a splendid sacred building. Augustine will now find it only too easy to answer this worried man; the fearful doctrine of predestination had armed him against feeling: 'Seeing that God, by a hidden, though just, disposition, has predestined some to

---

[1] v. esp. A. M. La Bonnardière, *Rech. de chronologie augustin.*, pp. 19–62.

[2] *Serm.* 47, 13.   [3] *C. Gaud.* I, xviii, 19.   [4] *Serm.* 46, 41.   [5] *Tract. in Joh.* 13, 17.

[6] For a most stimulating treatment of this phase of the suppression of Donatism, v. E. Tengström, *Donatisten u. Katholiken*, pp. 165–184. (But v. my reserves on Dr. Tengström's tempting hypothesis in *Journ. Rom. Studies*, lv, 1965, p. 282.)

[7] *Ep.* 185, ix, 36.   [8] *Ep.* 185, iii, 12.   [9] *Ep.* 185, iii, 12.

[10] v. Frend, *Donatist Church*, p. 296. The *Contra Gaudentium* is noticeably the most heartless of Augustine's writings in defence of the suppression of the Donatists.

[11] Laurentius, the recipient of the *Enchiridion: de VIII Dulcitii quaestionibus*, 10.

the ultimate penalty (of Hellfire), it is doubtless better that an over-whelming majority of the Donatists should have been collected and reabsorbed ... while a few perish in their own flames: better, indeed, than that all Donatists should burn in the flames of Hell for their sacrilegious dissension.'[1]

After the sack of Rome, Africa had become the sheet anchor of the fortunes of the Emperor Honorius. Loyalty had its price. The African landowners immediately extorted tax-concessions.[2] The bishops also had got what they wanted: the resolute imposition of a Catholic 'unity' throughout the provinces.

What the administrators gained from this policy of repression, was imponderable but very welcome. In a time of unparalleled confusion throughout the Western Empire, they came to a province, where a highly articulate body of men thought they were doing exactly the right thing to save the State. They would return to Italy with presen-tation-copies of the *City of God*.[3] Augustine had told them, that the disasters of the Roman Empire had come not from neglect of the old rites, but from tolerating paganism, heresy and immorality in the new Christian Empire.[4] Such men would believe him. They were no longer pagans, no longer neutral arbitrators in religious affairs. This new generation of politicians were good 'sons of the Church', who could be expected to share the same feelings as their bishops.[5] He will even urge one such man to be baptized. The times had changed. In the strange crisis of otherworldliness that had robbed the Roman administration of so much talent in the 380's, Augustine and his friends had plainly tended to identify baptism with retirement from public life. Now baptism would merely appear to him as a guarantee that a Roman governor would set about his duties in enforcing Catholicism with greater vigour.[6]

Yet this Christian Roman Empire had come to be ruled by a small group of men, violent, petty and corrupt. Even upright Christians led a double life. Dardanus, a retired Prefect of Gaul, had christened the village he owned in the Alpes Maritimes, Theopolis, 'City of God.'[7] In his philosophical leisure, he will receive compliments from Jerome, and will be enlightened by Augustine on the nature of the presence of God.[8] Yet, a few years previously, he had waylaid and 'disposed of' with his

---

[1] *Ep.* 204, 2.   [2] e.g. *Cod. Theod.* XI, xxviii, 5.

[3] e.g. The *Vicarius* Macedonius: *Epp.* 152, 3 and 154, 1.

[4] *Ep.* 137, v, 20; and implied in *de civ. Dei*, XVIII, 41.

[5] v. esp. *Ep.* 96, 1: Augustine speaks to the leading politician of the Western Empire, Olympius, as a 'fellow servant', praising his 'religious obedience'.

[6] *Ep.* 151, 14.   [7] v. sup. p. 116.   [8] v. inf. p. 360.

own hands a political prisoner on his way, under escort, to Ravenna.[1]

The pious Marcellinus, of all people, fell victim to the violence of the politicians. A revolt led by Heraclian, the Count (the military commander-in-chief) of Africa, was suppressed, and in the 'purge' that followed, Marcellinus was arrested and eventually executed, on September 13th, 413.[2] This was a cruel blow to Augustine, both personally and because it showed how little the established Catholic church in Africa was able to cope with the society in which it lived. All the machinery of the church as the protector of prisoners was set in motion only to be cynically flouted: a bishop had been sent to Ravenna to appeal for mercy; officials had sworn solemn oaths before the altar; the news that Marcellinus had been judged in a summary trial was greeted with satisfaction, for the next day was the Feast of S. Cyprian, a suitable occasion for an amnesty.[3] Augustine had been with Marcellinus in the previous days. Marcellinus had been able to assure him, on oath, that he had never once been unchaste.[4] At dawn, on the day of the Feast, Marcellinus was led out, taken to a corner of the public park, and beheaded. The church had failed to protect its most devoted son.

At this crucial moment, Augustine showed that he was no Ambrose: he lacked the streak of obstinacy and confidence that he could control events, that is so marked in the great ecclesiastical politicians of his age. He left Carthage in a hurry, lest he be forced to join his colleagues in pleading for the release of other political suspects, who had fled to sanctuary in the churches of the city. He would not demean himself before the man who had committed the judicial murder of his friend.[5]

Thus, only three years after his triumph at the Conference, Augustine left Carthage determined not to return for a long time.[6] The incident, also, marks, on a deeper level, the end of a period of Augustine's life. For, paradoxically, he had lost his enthusiasm for the alliance between the Roman Empire and the Catholic Church, at just the time when it had become effectively cemented. The alliance remained as a practical necessity, a *sine qua non* of the organized life of his church; it would be invoked against other heretics, the Pelagians;[7] but there is little trace, now, of the heady confidence of the 400's. For now that he no longer needed to convince others, Augustine seems to have lost conviction himself: he fell back on more sombre views. Bishops in other provinces might still be unduly impressed by the sudden conversion of the Emperors:[8] Augustine would tell one of them, that this did not in any

[1] Olympiodorus, fgt. 19, ed. Müller, *Fragm. Hist. Graec.*, iv, p. 61.
[2] v. esp. Frend, *Donatist Church*, pp. 292–293. [3] *Ep.* 151, 5–6. [4] *Ep.* 151, 9.
[5] *Ep.* 151, 3. [6] *Ep.* 151, 13. [7] v. inf. pp. 361–363. [8] *Ep.* 198, 6.

way mean that the Gospel had been preached 'to the uttermost ends of the earth'.[1] The public Christianization of the Roman Empire, indeed, did nothing to relieve Augustine's reserves about the chances of salvation of the majority of the human race:[2] this salvation had come to rest on a narrow core of the 'elect'. Nor had the Christian congregations benefited notably from their alliance with the state: far from being a source of improvement, this alliance was a source of 'greater danger and temptation'.[3]

Augustine had become more cautious. In his letters around 410, the need to reassure Roman officials such as Marcellinus had led him to make the facile claim that the existing Christian Empire was the best possible state: for the Christian churches in the Empire were acting as a school of citizenship, as 'holy lecture-halls';[4] their teachings of honesty and brotherly love could turn out men as austere and as public-spirited as the ancient Romans, with the benefit of eternal life thrown in.[5] Even when he wrote the first books of the *City of God*, Augustine had come to qualify these singularly rash claims: given the state of the world, the good Christian citizen and governor would have to 'stick out' his present existence, without much hope of bringing about a fully Christian society.[6] The examples of the ancient Romans could never be 'brought up to date' through Christian teaching: they had been used by God only to encourage the members of a 'City of God' established in another world, not to bring about some magical moral renewal of the present Roman Empire.[7]

Augustine, indeed, now felt old and ineffective. He travelled back to Hippo, to a safe backwater among his books.[8] 'I have resolved', he wrote, 'to devote my time entirely, if the Lord will, to the labour of studies pertaining to ecclesiastical learning: in doing which I think that I may, if it please the mercy of God, be of some service even to future generations.'[9]

Augustine had begun a new phase of his career. He already knew that he would not be allowed to finish his life as a secluded provincial bishop. He had seized on a new opportunity for active controversy.

---

[1] *Ep.* 199, xii, 46–47. [2] e.g. *Enarr. in Ps.* 61, 10.
[3] *de perf. just.* xviii, 35. [4] *Epp.* 91, 2 and 138, ii, 9.
[5] *Ep.* 138, ii, 9 and iii, 17. For the importance of hopes of reform by a return to the 'ancient virtues', v. Vittinghoff, 'Z. geschichtl. Selbstverständnis', *Hist. Zeitschr.*, 198, 1964, p. 566.
[6] *de civ. Dei* II, 19. [7] *de civ. Dei* V, 18; v. sup. pp. 311–312.
[8] Later, he could only begin to write a book when safely away from Carthage: *de VIII Dulcitii quaestionibus*, Praef.; cf. *de gratia Christi*, i, 1.
[9] *Ep.* 151, 13.

Even at the time of the Conference, he had already caught a few glimpses of the face of a man[1] roughly the same age as himself, like himself a 'servant of God', held in high esteem by the Roman aristocrats who had fled to Carthage after the Gothic sack; a man who was said to be the inspirer of the radical views that already troubled the friends of Marcellinus — the British monk, Pelagius.

[1] *de gest. Pel.* xxii, 46.

29

PELAGIUS AND PELAGIANISM[1]

(I)

After 410, the Roman Empire had become full of refugees. The noble families of Rome had found themselves driven for a moment to Augustine's doorstep. They would be forced to spend some years in this safe, provincial backwater: to the biographer of one such family, Thagaste appeared as 'small and very poor'.[2]

The provincials were duly impressed by such a remarkable group of men and women. Augustine met, for the first time, elderly Christian noblewomen, such as Proba, the widow of the richest man in the Empire, the mother and aunt of consuls. The younger generation was no less remarkable. At the age of fourteen, the grand-niece of Proba, Demetrias, would throw over the prospect of a politic marriage in order to become a nun, and so outdo the men of her family in the eyes of delighted bishops.[3] A few years previously, a young couple from another family, Melania and Pinianus, had set the Roman Senate by the

---

[1] The foundations of modern scholarship on Pelagius have been laid by G. de Plinval, *Pélage: ses écrits, sa vie et sa réforme*, 1943. Despite de Plinval's attempt at a characterization, Pelagius himself remains elusive: de Plinval, *Pélage*, esp. pp. 17–46, ascribes most 'Pelagian' writings to Pelagius himself; contrast the more cautious list of S. Prete, *Pelagio e il Pelagianesimo*, 1961, pp. 191–193, and the valuable critical studies of R. F. Evans, 'Pelagius, Fastidius and the pseudo-Augustinian ,'de Vita Christiana"', *Journ. Theol. Studies*, n.s., xiii, 1962, pp. 72–98 and, particularly, of J. Morris, 'Pelagian Literature', *Journ. Theol. Studies*, n.s., xvi, 1965, pp. 26–60, esp. pp. 26–40. The critical notes of Caspari, *Briefe, Abhandlungen u. Predigten*, 1894, pp. 223–389, remain of great value, as do the 7 *Dissertationes* of Jean Garnier (1673), printed as the Second Appendix to Marius Mercator: P.L. xlviii, 255–698. A. Hamman, P.L. *Supplementum*, 1958, 1101 sq., provides a complete edition of the surviving works ascribed to Pelagius and his followers; and R. S. T. Haslehurst, *The Works of Fastidius*, 1927, has edited and translated the vivid Pelagian texts discovered by Caspari.

[2] *Vie de Sainte Mélanie*, ed. transl. Gorce, (Sources chrétiennes, 90), c. 21, p. 170.

[3] On this important family, v. esp. de Plinval, *Pélage*, pp. 214–216; Brown, 'Aspects of Christianisation', *Journ. Rom. Studies*, li, 1961, p. 9, and Chastagnol, *Les Fastes de la Préfecture urbaine*, 1962, p. 291, (a family-tree).

ears by liquidating their vast estates to give to the poor.[1] And, as we have seen, the arrival of these eccentric millionaires caused great excitement at Hippo.

The arrival of magnificent strangers stirred up a society that had turned in upon itself. In 410–411, Augustine was fully preoccupied with the Donatist schism, a purely local issue. Within the next few years, the pagan members of the Roman aristocracy would provoke the *City of God*;[2] and Pelagius, a man who had moved among their Christian neighbours and relatives, would lead Augustine into the controversy that was to secure for him a truly international reputation.

We know very little about Pelagius.[3] Like Augustine, he was a provincial: he had come from Britain to Rome at much the same time as Augustine had first arrived in Italy to seek his fortune. But while Augustine had returned to his native land after only four years, Pelagius had remained in Rome. Augustine had lived the life of a serious baptized layman for some four years, Pelagius, for over thirty. Augustine had settled into a life dedicated to local, pastoral problems, and in his intellectual activities he had been content with a splendid isolation. Pelagius, by contrast, had continued to live in a town frequently visited by monks from the eastern Mediterranean, and troubled by theological issues from all over the world.[4] Above all, this layman and his supporters, could have heard priests keeping an open mind on issues which an African bishop had long come to treat as closed.[5] Thus, at exactly the same time as Augustine was to throw himself into a narrow ecclesiastical controversy, as a bishop with other bishops, Pelagius reached his peak, in Rome, in a world where cultivated Christian laymen exercised more influence than at any time previously.[6] Laymen and women had become prominent as apostles of the new ascetic movement: they were the illustrious recipients of letters from Paulinus of Nola, Augustine and Jerome; their theological views were respected; their patronage sought; their mansions put at the disposal of holy men and pilgrims from all over the world. Pelagius had joined such men in discussions on S. Paul. These discussions had formed the basis of his *Expositions of the Letters of St. Paul*, the most

---

[1] *Vie de Sainte Mélanie*, c. 19, p. 166.   [2] v. sup. pp. 300–303.

[3] v. esp. de Plinval, *Pélage*, pp. 47–71.

[4] For Rufinus, a Syrian, v. F. Refoulé, 'La datation du premier concile de Carthage contre les Pélagiens et du *Libellus fidei* de Rufin', *Rev. études augustin.*, xi, 1963, pp. 41–49, esp. p. 49. For Pelagius' reading, v. esp. de Plinval, *Pélage*, pp. 72–97; and for the importance of the revival of Origenism in Rome, v. esp. T. Bohlin, *Die Theologie d. Pelagius u. ihre Genesis*, (Uppsala Universitets Årsskrift, 9), 1957, pp. 77–103.

[5] *de pecc. orig.* iii, 3.   [6] v. esp. de Plinval, *Pélage*, pp. 210–216.

PELAGIUS AND PELAGIANISM

sure source of his theological views;[1] and, in addressing such men, he had perfected an art ideally suited to communicating his ideas, the difficult art of writing formal letters of exhortation.[2] These letters were admired in exactly the same circles as would have read Augustine and Jerome. Augustine always paid handsome tributes to Pelagius' exhortations: they were noted for being 'well written and straight to the point', for their '*facundia*' and their '*acrimonia*'.[3] *Le style, c'est l'homme.* Indeed, we have come to know Pelagius far better through the literary quality of his letters, above all for the *acrimonia* that sets the tone of the whole Pelagian movement, than we once did through the theological propositions for which he was to earn his reputation as a heretic.[4]

The long letter which Pelagius wrote to Demetrias, in 413, on the occasion of her decision to become a nun, was a calculated and widely-publicized declaration of his message.[5] This message was simple and terrifying: 'since perfection is possible for man, it is obligatory.'[6] Pelagius never doubted for a moment that perfection was obligatory; his God was, above all, a God who commanded unquestioning obedience. He had made men to execute his commands; and He would condemn to hell-fire anyone who failed to perform a single one of them.[7] But what Pelagius was concerned to uphold with especial fervour, was that man's nature had been created for such perfection to be achieved: 'Whenever I have to speak of laying down rules for behaviour and the conduct of a holy life, I always point out, first of all, the power and functioning of human nature, and show what it is capable of doing ... lest I should seem to be wasting my time, by calling on people to embark on a course which they consider impossible to achieve.'[8]

Pelagius was prepared to fight for his ideal, and in the gregarious world of the Later Empire, he was never alone. He attracted patrons; Paulinus of Nola was among them.[9] He fired disciples, especially young men of good family who had come to Rome like himself, to make their

[1] Ed. A. Souter, *Pelagius' Expositions of 13 Epistles of St. Paul*, (Texts and Studies, 9, 2), 1923: Hamman, *P.L. Supplem.* 1110–1374. v. esp. de Plinval, *Pélage*, pp. 121–166.

[2] v. de Plinval, *Essai sur le style et la langue de Pélage*, 1947.　　[3] *Ep.* 188, iii, 13.

[4] *de gest. Pel.* xxv, 50: 'vehement and, in their way, burning exhortations to a good life'.

[5] in P.L. xxx, 15–45.

[6] E. Portalié, *A Guide to the Thought of St. Augustine*, (transl. Bastian), 1960, p. 188.

[7] *de gest. Pel.* iii, 9 and 11.　　[8] Pelagius, *ad Demetriadem*, 2, (P.L. xxx, 17B).

[9] v. inf. p. 384 and Courcelle, *Les Confessions*, pp. 590–595. The Christian aristocracy of Rome had already been bitterly divided between Jerome and Rufinus on the Origenist controversy. Paulinus, loyal to Rufinus and his lay patrons, had broken with Jerome, (v. Courcelle, 'Paulin de Nole et Saint Jérôme', *Rev. études lat.*, xxv, 1947, pp. 274–279). The followers of Pelagius, a man violently attacked by Jerome, could well expect support from Paulinus.

careers as lawyers in the Imperial bureaucracy. This distinctive world, half university half civil service, was far more familiar to Alypius, who had lived in it, than to Augustine. A legal training produced skilled debaters, excellent tacticians; it caused serious young men to be genuinely preoccupied with problems of responsibility and freedom and, not surprisingly, to be puzzled by the God of the Old Testament, Whose equity, in His collective punishments and His deliberate 'hardening' of the hearts of individuals, was far from obvious.[1] Caelestius, destined to be the *enfant terrible* of the movement, was just such a young man: a boy from a noble family, he was early impressed by Pelagius; he had abandoned the world and had written urgent letters, *On the Monastery*, to his parents.[2]

Pelagius had no patience with the confusion that seemed to reign on the powers of human nature. He and his supporters wrote for men 'who want to make a change for the better'.[3] He refused to regard this power of self-improvement as having been irreversibly prejudiced; the idea of an 'original sin', that could make men incapable of not sinning even more, struck him as quite absurd.[4] He was annoyed by the way in which Augustine's masterpiece, the *Confessions*, seemed merely to popularize the tendency towards a languid piety. He had almost fallen foul of a bishop — was it Paulinus? — in a discussion that had followed a reading of the tender passages in Book Ten, 'Command what You will: give what You command.'[5] Such a phrase seemed to blur, by personal acts of favouritism, the incorruptible majesty of God the Lawgiver. A feeling that the tide of opinion was fast turning against him towards a tolerance of sin as 'only too human', drew from him an angry and outspoken pamphlet, *On Nature*.[6] Later, Augustine would treat this book as a prize-exhibit in his case against Pelagius.

But, for Augustine, these debates were very distant in 410. He had, indeed, had surprisingly little contact with the intellectual life of the Roman families before the Gothic sack;[7] and, when the scandal

---

[1] de Plinval, *Pélage*, p. 212. Their best-informed Roman opponent, Marius Mercator, came from a similar background.

[2] Morris, 'Pelagian Literature', *Journ. Theol. Studies*, n.s., xvi, 1965, pp. 41–43, reviews the evidence, concluding in favour of a British origin; de Plinval, *Pélage*, p. 212 and esp. n. 1 — Campania or Africa. Both views are conjectures.

[3] *de induratione cordis Pharaonis*, in de Plinval, *Essai*, p. 139, (Hamman, *P.L. Supplem.* 1507).

[4] in *de nat. et gratia*, xx, 23.

[5] *de dono persev.* xx, 53; v. Courcelle, *Les Confessions*, p. 580.

[6] Reconstructed in P.L. xlviii, 599–606.

[7] e.g. *Ep.* 92, 6, where he canvasses his views to Italica with great caution, even diffidence.

caused by these ideas broke out in Carthage in late 411, he was busy in Hippo. He was dependent for his information on letters from Count Marcellinus, his usual source at this time for the grievances and perplexities of the Roman refugees.[1]

Pelagius had even berthed at Hippo on his arrival in Africa; but Augustine was absent at the time.[2] Augustine answered the letter that announced his safe arrival politely, but cautiously.[3] Later he was to say that this short reply had implied a warning to Pelagius, and an invitation to come and visit him for a discussion.[4] One wonders what would have happened if Pelagius had been exposed to the charm of the old bishop. In a year, Pelagius was gone again, to the Holy Land: he would only be known by his books, to Augustine, above all, by the *On Nature*, and to the family and acquaintances of Demetrias, by his *Letter*, which evidently impressed them. It is a baffling double-image: to Augustine he was the optimistic theologian of the *On Nature*; to the family of Demetrias, an ardent ascetic who had written an urgent admonition for their daughter.

It was Caelestius who provoked the crisis in Africa, not Pelagius. As soon as he arrived in Carthage, he had intervened confidently in contemporary debates, that seem to have touched on the perennial mystery of the origin of the soul, and moved to the kindred problems of the solidarity of the human race in the sin of Adam: for how, for instance, could the 'brand new' soul of an individual be held to be guilty of the distant act of a different person?[5] These discussions had touched on the necessity of infant baptism. It was here that the Pelagian arguments met their first serious check. Bishops who had spent years upholding the absolute necessity and uniqueness of the baptism conferred by themselves in the Catholic church, and who could consult, in the library of the Bishops of Carthage, a letter of S. Cyprian insisting upon the baptism of newborn babies,[6] were in no mood to tolerate such speculations. Caelestius was denounced when he applied to become a priest.[7] The six condemned propositions which he refused to withdraw[8] were to form, with Pelagius' *On Nature*, the basis of Augustine's

---

[1] *de gest. Pel.* xi, 23 and v. sup. p. 303.

[2] v. esp. J. H. Koopmans, 'Augustine's first contact with Pelagius and the Dating of the Condemnation of Caelestius at Carthage', *Vigiliae Christianae*, 8, 1954, pp. 149–153, rectified by F. Refoulé, 'Datation', *Rev. études augustin.*, ix, 1963, esp. pp. 41–44.

[3] *Ep.* 146. [4] *de gest. Pel.* xxv, 51. [5] e.g. *Ep.* 166, iv, 10.

[6] *de pecc. mer.* III, 10: Letter 64 of Cyprian to Fidus.

[7] Not by an African, however, but by Paulinus, a deacon of Milan: on whom, v. inf. p. 409, n. 2.

[8] *de pecc. orig.* iii–iv, 3: Bonner, *St. Augustine*, pp. 321–322, translates this vivid interview.

case against Pelagius. To Augustine they were the *capitula capitalia*:[1] for these propositions would be enough to 'hang' Pelagius if ever it could be accepted that the radicalism of Caelestius, the disciple, was only the logical extension of the secret opinions of his master.[2]

Augustine was in Hippo at that time, and knew little of the local meeting that had condemned Caelestius. When Marcellinus wrote to him, in the winter of 411, these ideas were just 'in the air' at Carthage, with all the uncertainty and irritation that occurs when two fashions of thought are obscurely felt to conflict. It is extremely difficult to identify the opinions and pamphlets that provided Augustine with the material for his first coherent picture of the ideas he would later ascribe directly to Pelagius.[3]

The letter of Marcellinus reached Hippo when Augustine was snowed under with the work that had followed the suppression of Donatism: his notaries were unable to cope with his demands; he was having to summarize for his flock the enormous verbatim record of the Conference; he was 'press-ganged' by the requests of local men for favours and arbitration.[4] Yet Augustine wrote back immediately. As usual, he jumped to conclusions before he had even read everything that he had been sent.[5] The answer shows a quite astonishing grasp of the new problem. What had appeared in Carthage as disquieting and disparate straws in the wind, came together for the first time in this work of Augustine's to form a coherent system: 'See where it leads to . . .' is a constant refrain.[6] It is a refrain that will be repeated throughout Augustine's writings of the next years. Indeed, Pelagian*ism* as we know it, that consistent body of ideas of momentous consequences, had come into existence; but in the mind of Augustine, not of Pelagius.

(II)

For Augustine, Pelagianism was always a body of ideas, of *disputationes*, 'arguments'. He was in no doubt as to the intellectual quality of these arguments. For the first time in his career as a bishop, he was confronted by opponents of the same calibre as himself, before an audience capable of judging a case on its purely intellectual merits: 'These points are raised by great and shrewd minds: it would be a confession of failure, on my part, to avoid them by not mentioning them, and a sign of intellectual conceit, to pass them over as not worth

[1] *de gest. Pel.* xiii, 30.   [2] *de gest. Pel.* xxiv, 65; *de gratia Christi*, xxxiii, 36.
[3] v. esp. Refoulé, 'Datation', *Rev. études augustin.*, ix, 1963, pp. 47–48.   [4] *Ep.* 139, 3.
[5] *de pecc. mer.* III, i, 1.   [6] v. esp. de Plinval, *Pélage*, pp. 261–263.

mentioning.'[1] But in Rome, such ideas had set off a 'movement'.[2] Pelagius had a tenacious and well-placed body of supporters. They ensured that his letters would circulate with surprising rapidity;[3] that he should be determined to seek a place for his ideas within the Catholic church.[4] They would provide enthusiasts who formed Pelagian 'cells' as far apart as Sicily, Britain and Rhodes.[5] We can now appreciate the motives of such men; and so we can assess the role which Pelagianism played in one of the most dramatic crises in the Christian church in the West.

Pelagianism had appealed to a universal theme: the need of the individual to define himself, and to feel free to create his own values in the midst of the conventional, second-rate life of society. In Rome, the weight of convention was particularly oppressive. The families, whose members Pelagius addressed, had lapsed gradually into Christianity by mixed-marriages and politic conformity.[6] This meant that the conventional 'good man' of pagan Rome had quite unthinkingly become the conventional 'good Christian' of the fifth century. The flamboyant courtesies of Late Roman etiquette could pass as 'Christian humility';[7] the generosity traditionally expected of an aristocrat, as 'Christian almsgiving'. '*It is better to give than to receive*' was a popular tag; but, like all Biblical citations used to ease the conscience, no one could quite remember where it came from![8] Yet these 'good Christians', 'true believers,' were still members of a ruling class committed to maintaining the Imperial laws by administering brutal punishments.[9] They were

---

[1] *Ep.* 186, v, 13.

[2] One is particularly indebted to the fascinating studies of J. N. L. Myres, 'Pelagius and the End of Roman Rule in Britain', *Journ. Roman Studies*, l, 1960, pp. 21–36, and of J. Morris, 'Pelagian Literature', *Journ. Theol. Studies*, n.s., xvi, 1965, esp. at pp. 43–60, for having drawn attention to the possible social repercussions of certain aspects of Pelagianism. I cannot, however, follow them in their main hypothesis, that the Pelagian teachings can be related to a precise social movement; nor am I convinced that Britain was the 'storm-centre' of such a movement. For a shrewd criticism of the thesis of Myres, v. W. Liebeschütz, 'Did the Pelagian Movement have Social Aims?' *Historia*, xii, 1963, pp. 227–241.

[3] *de gest. Pel.* xx, 45 and xxx, 55; and *Ep.* 183, 3. [4] *de gest. Pel.* xxx, 54 and *Ep.* 172, 1.

[5] On Pelagianism in Britain, v. esp. J. N. L. Myres, 'Pelagius', *Journ. Rom. Studies*, l, 1960, pp. 34–36, and Morris, 'Pelagian Literature', *Journ. Theol. Studies*, n.s., xvi, 1965, pp. 56–59. In Rhodes: Jerome, *Comm. in Hierem.* Praef. 4; in Sicily, v. esp. *Ep.* '*Honorificentiae tuae*', 5, (Caspari, p. 12), and *Ep.* 156, at Syracuse. Sicily, a land of great estates and splendid villas, had a long tradition, in the Later Empire, of learned *otium* such as might shelter such groups: v. sup. 115.

[6] v. Brown, 'Aspects of Christianisation', *Journ. Rom. Studies*, li, 1961, pp. 9–11.

[7] Pelagius, *ad Dem.* 20 and 21, (P.L. xxx, 36A and D).

[8] *Ep.* '*Honorificentiae tuae*', 4, (Caspari, p. 10). The citation figures on an inscription at Nola: Diehl, *Inscript. Lat. Christ*, i no. 2474.

[9] *de divitiis*, vi, 1, (Caspari, p. 31): transl. Haselhurst, pp. 30–107.

prepared to fight tooth and nail to protect their vast properties,[1] and were capable of discussing at the dinner-table both the latest theological opinion, on which they prided themselves as experts,[2] and the kind of judicial torture they had just inflicted on some poor wretch.[3]

In this confusion, the harsh, firm message of Pelagius came as a deliverance. He would offer the individual absolute certainty through absolute obedience. We can see this in the letter of a man who had suddenly fallen under the influence of a noble lady, the dominating figure of a group of Pelagian enthusiasts in Sicily. 'When I lived at home, I thought that I was being a worshipper of God. . . . Now for the first time, I have begun to know how I can be a true Christian. . . . It is easy to say: I know God, I believe in God, I fear God, I serve God. But you do not know God, if you do not believe in Him; and you do not believe in Him, unless you love Him; and you cannot say you love Him, unless you fear Him; you cannot say you fear Him, unless you serve Him; and you cannot be said to serve Him if you disobey Him in any single point. . . . *Who believes in God, attends to His commandments. This is love of God; that we do what He commands.'*[4]

It was a serious age. The Emperors use the same desperate language when insisting that their laws must be observed, that Pelagius will use when speaking of the laws of his God.[5] The men who read the Pelagian writings had just witnessed a series of events that had shattered the confidence of a whole class: brutal purges, the ruin of whole families, spectacular political assassinations,[6] and later the terrors of barbarian invasion.[7] But while some might be driven into retirement by such catastrophes, the Pelagians seemed determined to turn outwards, to reform the whole Christian church. This is the most remarkable feature in their movement: the narrow stream of perfectionism that had driven the noble followers of Jerome to Bethlehem, had led Paulinus to Nola and Augustine from Milan to a life of poverty in Africa, is suddenly turned outwards in the Pelagian writings, to embrace the whole Christian church: 'Surely it is not true that the Law of Christian behaviour has not been given to everyone who is called a Christian? . . . Do you think that the fires of Hell will burn any less hotly for men licensed (as governors) to give vent to their sadism, and will be made hotter only for those whose professional duty it is to be pious. . . .

[1] *de divitiis*, iv, 1, (Caspari, p. 27). [2] *de divitiis*, vi, 2, (Caspari, p. 32).
[3] *de divitiis*, vi, 2, (Caspari, p. 32).
[4] *Ep. 'Honorificentiae tuae'*, 1, (Caspari, p. 4): transl. Haslehurst, pp. 2–17.
[5] Pelagius, *ad Dem.* 16, (P.L. xxx, 31D–32). [6] *de vita Christiana*, 3, (P.L. xl, 1035).
[7] Pelagius, *ad Dem.* 30, (P.L. xxx, 45).

There can be no double-standard in one and the same people.'[1] This is the most pungent protest in all Late Roman literature, against the subtle pressure, which Augustine had experienced in Hippo, to leave the Christian life to recognized saints and to continue to live as ordinary men, like pagans.[2] Pelagius wanted every Christian to be a monk.[3]

For the Pelagians still thought of the Christian church as if it were a small group in a pagan world. They were concerned to give a good example: the 'sacrifice of praise', that is such an intimate matter for Augustine, means for the Pelagian the praise of pagan public opinion that would be gained by the Christian church as an institution made up of perfect men.[4]

It is here, of course, that the Pelagian movement intimately affected Augustine. To him it seemed that the new claims made by the Pelagians, that they could achieve a church 'without spot or blemish', merely continued the assertion of the Donatists, that only they belonged to just such a church.[5] He was in no mood to tolerate the *coteries* of 'perfect' Christians, that had sprung up in Sicily and elsewhere under Pelagian influence.[6] For this reason, the victory of Augustine over Pelagius was also a victory for the average good Catholic layman of the Later Empire, over an austere, reforming ideal. Augustine describes just the sort of man that he had found a place for in the Catholic church: a man with a few good works to his name, who slept with his wife, *faute de mieux*, and often just for the pleasure of it; touchy on points of honour, given to vendettas; not a landgrabber, but capable of fighting to keep hold of his own property, though only in the bishop's court; and, for all that, a good Christian in Augustine's sense, 'looking on himself as a disgrace, and giving the glory to God.'[7]

But the victory of Augustine over the Pelagians was fought out in very different circumstances from the Donatist schism. He was now involved in one of those mysterious and dramatic 'crises of piety', which sometimes affect the members of a governing class.[8] Among the Roman refugees in Africa the two rival views were juxtaposed:

[1] *de divitiis*, vi, 3, (Caspari, pp. 32–33).   [2] v. sup. pp. 248–249.

[3] Pelagius, *ad Dem.* 10, (P.L. xxx, 26B).   [4] *de vita christiana*, 9, (P.L. xl, 1038).

[5] v. esp. *de gest. Pel.* xii, 27–28; cf. *Ep.* 185, ix, 38, for a natural importation, into an anti-Donatist letter, of anti-Pelagian arguments.

[6] Hilarius had approached Augustine for his opinion on the nature of the church 'in this world': *Ep.* 157, iv, 40.

[7] *c. Epp. Pel.* III, v, 14.

[8] One might instance Jansenism, which also proved attractive to a class threatened, like the Later Roman aristocracy, with political impotence: v. the fascinating and differentiated treatment of L. Goldmann, *The Hidden God*, (trans. Thody), 1964, pp. 89–141.

Timasius, for instance, a young man who had abandoned the world under the influence of Pelagius, was a friend of Pinianus, the young nobleman who had almost become a priest of Augustine at Hippo.[1]

Pelagius had chosen his recipients well. Demetrias, Melania and Pinianus, had all of them shown the remarkable strength of their wills by making a complete break with 'the world', in the face of the oppressive family-feeling of Late Roman aristocratic society.[2] The extraordinary pig-headedness of these young nobles seemed a sure omen for future progress in perfection.[3] Having used their will-power to such powerful effect, they might easily have become zealous followers of Pelagius. They would have given the blessing of the most influential class of Christian laymen in the Roman world to his reforming movement. For Pelagianism could appear as a movement with a definite programme of action. Augustine, for whom communication was always an inscrutable mystery, and the inner life of prayer and self-examination the centre of Christian devotion, was faced by people, who believed that they could by urgent exhortations, exercise an immediate influence on the behaviour of society.[4]

For the Pelagians, man had no excuse for his own sins, nor for the evils around him. If human nature was essentially free and well-created, and not dogged by some mysterious inner weakness, the reason for the general misery of men must be somehow external to their true selves; it must lie, in part, in the constricting force of the social habits of a pagan past. Such habits could be reformed. Thus few writers in the Later Empire are so outspoken in their criticisms of Roman society. The most tender passages in the cold exhortations of the Pelagians are those which describe the horror of public executions,[5] and urge the Christian to 'feel the pain of others as if it were his own, and to be moved to tears by the grief of other men'.[6] This emotive quality is very different from the philosophical detachment with which Augustine can view the infliction of physical pain.[7] Job was the hero of the Pelagians: here was a man suddenly stripped of the heavy artifice of society, and capable of showing to the world the raw bones of a heroic individuality.[8]

It is no coincidence that such ideas should have circulated among men who had wanted to strip themselves of their vast wealth. The past decades had been full of such spectacular renunciations. This radicalism, however, was checked and canalized as soon as the young aristocrats

[1] *Ep.* 126, 6. [2] Pelagius, *ad Dem.* I, (P.L. xxx, 16B): 'the sword of the will'.
[3] Pelagius, *ad Dem.* 10, (P.L. xxx, 27C). [4] *de bono vid.* xviii, 22.
[5] *de divitiis*, vi, 2, (Caspari, p. 31). [6] *de vita christiana*, 14, (P.L. xl, 1045).
[7] v. sup. p. 232. [8] Pelagius, *ad Dem.* 6, (P.L. xxx, 22C).

came into contact with the established church in Africa: Aurelius, Augustine and Alypius succeeded in persuading Melania and Pinianus to endow the Catholic monasteries with permanent lands, rather than cut the Gordian knot of their guilty fortune by scattering it among the poor.[1] In giving such advice, Augustine only practised what he was preaching against the Pelagians.[2] To a Sicilian bishop, worried by Pelagian assertions that a rich man was surely damned, he replied that, like the massive hierarchy of the Empire, the church, also, must find room both for its 'higher civil servants' and its 'tax-payers' — in this case, for the rich landowners on whose endowments and influence the monks and clergy had come to depend.[3]

Like many reformers, the Pelagians placed the terrifying weight of complete freedom on the individual: he was responsible for his every action; every sin, therefore, could only be a deliberate act of contempt for God.[4] Augustine was less sure that a fallen human nature could bear so great a weight: 'Many sins are committed through pride, but not all happen proudly . . . they happen so often by ignorance, by human weakness; many are committed by men weeping and groaning in their distress. . . .'[5] The Catholic church existed to redeem a helpless humanity; and once the essential grace was given, he could accept with ease in his congregation the slow and erratic processes of healing.[6] The Pelagians, with their optimistic views on human nature, seemed to Augustine to blur the distinction between the Catholic church and the good pagans;[7] but they did so only in order to establish an icy puritanism as the sole law of the Christian community.[8] Paradoxically, therefore, it is Augustine, with his harsh emphasis on baptism as the only way to salvation, who appears as the advocate of moral tolerance: for within the exclusive fold of the Catholic church he could find room for a whole spectrum of human failings.[9] Augustine's writings against the Pelagians follow closely on his campaign against the Donatists. Between them, they are a significant landmark in that process by which the Catholic church had come to embrace, and so to tolerate, the whole lay society of the Roman world, with its glaring inequalities of wealth and the depressing resilience of its pagan habits.

---

[1] *Vie de St. Mélanie*, ed. Gorce, (Sources chrétiennes, 90), c. 20, p. 170; cf. *Ep.* 157, iv, 38.

[2] e.g. *Enarr. in Ps.* 71, 3.   [3] *Ep.* 157, iv, 37.

[4] Pelagius, *ad Dem.* 9, (P.L. xxx, 25B), and in *de nat. et gratia* xxix, 33.

[5] *de nat. et gratia*, xxix, 33.   [6] *de nat. et gratia*, lxviii, 82.

[7] e.g. in *de nat. et gratia*, i, 2.

[8] Clearly seen by E. Portalié, *A Guide to the Thought of S. Augustine*, pp. 188–189.

[9] e.g. *de spiritu et littera*, xxviii, 48.

In these years Augustine will write to two noble ladies, affected by Pelagian ideas: Proba and Juliana.[1] They are the most mature and sympathetic statements of his ideal of the Christian life. For it is the inner tensions of the individual that concern him: in advocating continence to a rich widow, he can add, 'I have, however, often observed this fact of human behaviour that, with certain people, when sexuality is repressed avarice seems to grow in its place. . . .'[2] In all their shrill denunciations of the 'way of the world',[3] the Pelagian writings can offer nothing so shrewd.

But this concern with the inner life could seem to accept too readily the existing state of Roman society as the unalterable backdrop to a life of intimate aristocratic piety. Augustine's letters to Proba would seem to encourage this attitude: the heiress of a vast agricultural empire, acquired by rapine[4] and maintained with a selfishness that had aggravated the miseries and resentments of the Gothic disaster,[5] was allowed to remain unchanged in the midst of such wealth. It was enough that she should be oppressed by thoughts on the corruptibility of human things,[6] and detached from the accumulated magnificence that surrounded her by an orientation of the inner self so deep and so mysterious, that no man might judge it.[7] But after 410, Africa was one of the only provinces where the social *status quo* could be taken for granted. It may be more than a coincidence that the Pelagian ideas seem to have had the greatest resonance in just those provinces where the old ways of life had been dislocated by the barbarian invasions: in Britain;[8] in Southern Italy, where Julian of Eclanum, Augustine's brilliant adversary, had gained a reputation for the measures he had taken, to combat the famine that had followed in the wake of the Gothic army;[9] and in Gaul, where, after 'a decade of slaughter', a Pelagian poet could look out upon a ruined land and still know that the citadel of his free soul had remained unshaken.[10]

As we have seen, the difference between Augustine and Pelagius was capable of ramifying from the most abstract issues of freedom and responsibility, to the actual role of the individual in the society of the Later Empire. The basic difference between the two men, however, is

---

[1] *Ep.* 130 (412), to Proba, and the *de bono viduitatis* (414), to Juliana.
[2] *de bono vid.* xx, 26.
[3] e.g. *de castitate*, (Caspari, pp. 122–167): transl. Haslehurst, pp. 200–285.
[4] Ammianus Marcellinus, *Res gestae*, xxx, 5, 4–10.   [5] Zosimus, *Historia Nova*, VI, 7.
[6] *Ep.* 131.   [7] *Ep.* 130, iii, 8.
[8] As suggested by Myres, 'Pelagius', *Journ. Rom. Studies*, l, 1960, p. 36.
[9] v. inf. p. 381.
[10] Orientius, *Carmen de Providentia*, (P.L. li, 616–638); v. de Plinval, *Pélage*, p. 404.

to be found in two radically different views on the relation between man and God. It is summed up succinctly in their choice of language. Augustine had long been fascinated by babies: the extent of their helplessness had grown upon him even since he wrote the *Confessions*;[1] and in the *Confessions*, he had had no hesitation in likening his relation to God to that of a baby to its mother's breast, utterly dependent, intimately involved in all the good and evil that might come from this, the only source of life.[2]

The Pelagian, by contrast, was contemptuous of babies.[3] 'There is no more pressing admonition than this, that we should be called *sons* of God.'[4] To be a 'son' was to become an entirely separate person, no longer dependent on one's father, but capable of following out by one's own power, the good deeds that he had commanded. The Pelagian was *emancipatus a deo*;[5] it is a brilliant image taken from the language of Roman family law: freed from the all-embracing and claustrophobic rights of the father of a great family over his children, these sons had 'come of age'. They had been 'released', as in Roman Law, from dependence on the *pater familias* and could at last go out into the world as mature, free individuals, able to uphold in heroic deeds the good name of their illustrious ancestry: '*Be ye perfect, even as Your Father in Heaven is perfect.*'[6]

[1] e.g. *de pecc. mer.* I, 65–68, and *de nat. et gratia*, xxi, 23. [2] e.g. *Conf.* IV, i, 1.
[3] Ps. Jerome, *Ep.* 32, 3, (P.L. xxx, 247D). [4] Pelagius, *ad Dem.* 17, (P.L. xxx, 32C).
[5] *Op. Imp.* I, 78.
[6] *Matth.* 5, 48: *Ep. de possibilitate non peccandi*, iv, 2, (Caspari, p. 119).

30

CAUSA GRATIAE[1]

Not every man lives to see the fundamentals of his life's work challenged in his old age. Yet this is what happened to Augustine during the Pelagian controversy. At the time that the controversy opened, he had reached a plateau. He was already enmeshed in a reputation that he attempted to disown with characteristic charm: 'Cicero, the prince of Roman orators', he wrote to Marcellinus, in 412, 'says of someone that "He never uttered a word which he would wish to recall". High praise indeed! — but more applicable to a complete ass than to a genuinely wise man. . . . If God permit me, I shall gather together and point out, in a work specially devoted to this purpose, all the things which justly displease me in my books: then men will see that I am far from being a biased judge in my own case. . . . For I am the sort of man who writes because he has made progress, and who makes progress — by writing.'[2]

Behind this candour, there lies a formidable sense of achievement. Augustine often uses the word 'progress' during his old age. But we have seen, that for him it did not mean the prospect of unrestricted change and adaptation: rather, it implies a consciousness of having left behind the superfluous, and of having become increasingly certain of the essential.[3] He felt that he was on a steady course, carried by the momentum of 20 years of unremitting intellectual labour as a Catholic bishop.

The emergence of Pelagianism as a threat to his ideas, marks the end of a period of Augustine's intellectual life. Around 414, he had become aware of the extent to which he had once given rein to his love of speculation: there had been a time when he had 'discussed off the beaten track',[4] four possible views of the origin of the soul; he had just

---

[1] v. esp. de Plinval, *Pélage*, pp. 252–355, and Bonner, *St. Augustine*, pp. 320–346, who provides a sound account.
    [2] *Ep.* 143, 2 and 3.   [3] v. sup. pp. 279–280.   [4] *Ep.* 143, 5.

attempted to seize the essence of the Trinity; he was known to educated Christians for his definite opinions on the nature of the vision of God,[1] and for his academic disagreements with another scholar, with Jerome.[2] Yet this speculation had placed a strain on him. With characteristic intellectual sensitivity, he had hesitated for years before finally making up his mind to publish the great works of his middle age, the *Commentary on Genesis* and the book *On the Trinity*: such books, he thought, contained too many 'extremely perilous problems'.[3] Now, with the challenge of Pelagianism, this speculation suddenly comes to a halt. Evodius, always avid for erudite and esoteric subjects, will be treated abruptly, 'You are asking many things of a very busy man;'[4] and would be told that the profound speculations included in the *De Trinitate* had suddenly become irrelevant, 'If Christ had died only for those who could with certainty apprehend these matters, we are virtually wasting our time in the Church.'[5] Jerome would receive similar treatment. He had speculated about the origin of the soul, positing that it was newly-created in each individual. Augustine's suspicions were immediately aroused: might this not seem to deny the solidarity of all human souls in the sin of Adam?[6] With great courtesy, he will firmly warn the old man off the subject: 'this opinion of yours, if it is not opposed to the most firmly established faith, it can be mine also; if it is opposed, then let it not be yours.'[7] *Fundatissima fides* 'the most firmly established faith', is what Augustine thought he was defending against the Pelagians. The matter was unambiguous. *Fundata ista res est*:[8] he had a cast-iron case. Thus, after a decade of profound, inconclusive and highly personal speculations, Augustine will suddenly pour his ideas into a solid mould. He will identify them entirely with the unquestioned faith of the Catholic church, and will set about conducting what he called the *causa gratiae*, the 'case for grace'. It is one of the mysterious inner changes, that are so characteristic of the man: perhaps the inner tension that made Augustine need to act as the champion of the obvious after years of probing the unknown, is part of the secret of his genius as a polemist.

This *causa gratiae* will be the high-water mark of Augustine's literary career. As early as 411, he had constructed a coherent picture of Pelagianism, that would link Pelagius and Caelestius, two widely different persons in the eyes of the world, within the same body of ideas; and he would consistently treat these ideas as a totality that cut

[1] e.g. *Epp*. 92, 147 and 148.   [2] *Epp*. 143, 5 and 180, 5.   [3] *Ep*. 143, 4.   [4] *Ep*. 162, 1.
[5] *Ep*. 169, i, 4.   [6] *Ep*. 166, iv, 10.   [7] *Ep*. 166, viii, 25.
[8] *Serm*. 294, 20.

at the foundations of the Catholic faith. He knew Pelagius only as an author,[1] and he combated him by books: the hostile review, the marked copy and the drawing up of doctrinal 'tests' — these, the sure signs of a heresy-hunt in the world of ideas, are the landmarks of the Pelagian controversy as viewed from Carthage and Hippo. *Scripta manent*: by the time that the *causa gratiae* had been won, the Roman world was littered with works of Augustine; pamphlets, formal declarations of faith, letters that summed up the 'Augustinian system' in its most extreme form, had come to recipients as far apart and as various, as a retired governor in Provence,[2] a priest and a lawyer in Rome,[3] Paulinus in Nola,[4] a bishop in Syracuse,[5] and the Latin *émigrés* in Jerusalem.[6] Seeing that at this time he thought that the only people who could read all his books, were monks who enjoyed complete leisure,[7] it is amazing that Augustine could write as much as he did. Why should he detain his readers on such an issue? 'First and foremost', he told Paulinus, 'because no subject gives me greater pleasure. For what ought to be more attractive to us sick men, than grace, grace by which we are healed; for us lazy men, than grace, grace by which we are stirred up; for us men longing to act, than grace, by which we are helped?'[8]

Augustine saw the problem of Pelagianism differently from many of his contemporaries. Many bishops, as events would show, wanted to treat Pelagius on his merits. Here was a sincere Christian, anxious to remain in the Catholic church: they needed only to be reassured that the opinions which Pelagius now held were consistent with traditional orthodoxy. Pelagius, for his part, was anxious to reassure such men. As the head of a reforming movement within the Catholic church, he was particularly anxious that his austere message should not be outlawed by being declared heretical. Like many groups in such a situation, the Pelagians felt that the church needed their services: it was rather for them to tolerate the moral laxity of the Catholic church, whose rank and file would always label any disagreeable opinion as a 'heresy'.[9]

It was difficult for the average man to decide whether the language used by Pelagius was 'heretical'. 'Heresy' meant errors on the nature of the Trinity, such as had provoked the Arian controversy; and on this issue, the Pelagians were blameless. The noble Roman Christians who

---

[1] *de gest. Pel.* xxi, 46. [2] *Ep.* 187. [3] *Epp.* 194 and 193. [4] *Ep.* 186.
[5] *Ep.* 157. For all these, v. the meticulous study of H. Ulbrich, 'Augustins Briefe z. entscheidender Phase d. pelagianischen Streites', *Rev. études augustin.*, ix, 1963, pp. 51–75, and 235–258.
[6] *de gratia Christi* and *de pecc. orig.*: to Pinianus and Melania, v. sup. p. 294.
[7] *Ep.* 184A, i, 1. [8] *Ep.* 186, xii, 39. [9] *de malis doctoribus*, xvii, 2, (Caspari, p. 101).

had read the '*Letter to Demetrias*' with pleasure, were frankly unimpressed by the dire warnings of Augustine and Alypius. Demetrias' mother, Juliana, will put these fussy, provincial bishops firmly in their place: her family had never been touched by any heresy — 'not even by the most trivial'(!)[1] A good Christian of the Later Empire, 'heresy' to her had meant Greek errors on the Godhead, not African scruples on grace and freewill.[2]

Even more was at stake in this controversy than two different approaches to the nature of religious error. In Africa, Augustine felt absolutely certain of his case: nobody in Carthage could doubt for a moment that views that could claim S. Cyprian as their patron, could possibly be wrong. But this very certainty was a source of weakness. The Pelagians always threatened to appeal to the Eastern churches, with their very different, more liberal traditions.[3] Seen from outside, the *fundatissima fides* of Augustine, might seem to express merely the narrow rigour of an isolated church. Would this impressive ecclesiastical culture be left in splendid isolation? Or would the ideas formed in its distinctive climate come to dominate the Latin West?[4]

At first it seemed as if Africa could be safely ignored. Pelagius had arrived in the Holy Land as a man with a past; but only an 'expert' as skilled as Augustine could have persuaded the local bishops of this fact. Augustine's allies on the spot were plainly unable to do so. The new controversy descended on the amazing group of Latin *émigrés* settled in Jerusalem: this was a community with a liveliness and a capacity for resentment similar to that of the White Russians in Paris in the 1920's.[5] It threatened to turn the Holy Places into a theological bear-garden. Jerome was settled in the Mount of Olives, in an attitude of contemptuous hostility to the bishop, John of Jerusalem. Orosius, who had been sent by Augustine to join Jerome, knew no Greek; and, like many men incapable of getting on with foreigners, he may have blamed the results of his own tactlessness on the difficulties of the language. He was joined, in hunting Pelagius, by two Gallic bishops, Heros and Lazarus, who had 'left their country for their country's good', having been deposed from their sees for collaboration with a

---

[1] *Ep.* 188, i, 3.

[2] Pelagius told a similar couple that his error was 'civil' not 'criminal': *de pecc. orig.* xxiii, 26.

[3] *de gest. Pelag.* xi, 25. Seen clearly by Bonner, *St. Augustine*, pp. 323–324.

[4] Augustine expected all Catholics to agree with him against Pelagius: *de gest. Pel.* xxxv, 66.

[5] v. esp. de Plinval, *Pélage*, pp. 271–292 and pp. 306–307, and G. D. Gordini, 'Il monachesimo romano a Palestina nel iv sec.', *Studia Anselmiana*, 46, 1961, pp. 85–107.

usurping Emperor. By the time a synod of 14 bishops met in Diospolis (Lydda) on December 20th 415, it was plain that they had not come to 'try' Pelagius, as Orosius had hoped; they merely wanted to be reassured about him. Pelagius reassured them. With a lack of scruple, common in men of high principles, he condemned his own disciple, Caelestius, and explained away the passages in his own works which had made him seem an *enfant terrible* in the West. He had a serious mission to fulfil, and so shook off his accusers with contempt: the distant Augustine; Jerome, whose personal grudges were notorious; Orosius, 'a young man set upon me by my enemies;' and the two ambiguous bishops.[1] It was a crushing defeat for the 'experts': 'There are', Augustine wrote, 'very few men versed in the Law of the Lord.'[2]

If the acceptance of Pelagius seemed quite regular in the East, it did cause a great stir in the West. The mysterious network of supporters of Pelagius now ensured that his account of the synod of Diospolis should travel with amazing speed to the Latin world. The conspiracy to do him wrong had been turned to confusion; he had been given a 'clean slate';[3] his opinion, that men could be without sin, had been approved by bishops in the Holy Places.[4] Augustine had to suffer the humiliation of receiving a copy of this tendentious pamphlet unaccompanied by any personal letter of salutation from its author.[5]

It was now the turn of the isolated church of Africa to stage a counter-demonstration. This was impressive. Orosius arrived in Carthage in September 416, to find a council waiting in the city; another, dominated by Augustine and Alypius, came together rapidly in Milevis. The discipline learnt during the campaign against the Donatists had borne fruit: only in Africa could three hundred Catholic bishops come together, and agree unanimously to decrees drafted by unquestioned experts.[6]

The African bishops were afraid that Pelagius would try to canvass the support of Innocent, the bishop of Rome. He was known to have well-placed supporters, even among the proud clerical oligarchy of the city: Sixtus, a future pope, was said to be his protector.[7] For the Africans, only the prestige of Rome could eclipse the judgement of an Eastern synod. Thus, at the end of 416, Innocent received a quite unaccustomed sheaf of documents from Africa: two closely reasoned

---

[1] Pelagius, *Ep. ad Innocentium papam*, (P.L. xlviii, 610B).   [2] *de gest. Pel.* i, 3.
[3] *de gest. Pel.* xix, 45.   [4] *de gest. Pel.* xxx, 54.   [5] *de gest. Pel.* i, 1.
[6] v. Prosper of Aquitaine, *Carmen de ingratis*, i, 72–92, (P.L. li, 100–102).
[7] *Ep.* 191, 1.

condemnations of Pelagian ideas, from the two Catholic synods of Milevis and Carthage; and a long personal letter from Aurelius, Augustine and Alypius.[1] This letter enclosed a marked copy of the notorious *On Nature*,[2] and a letter to Pelagius, the implication being that the proud layman would not deign to open correspondence addressed to him by Augustine.[3]

The decisions of the two synods were framed with studious courtesy. They claimed to be merely *relationes*, that is 'reports' by local officials, that required the sanction of a higher authority.[4] In fact, they were framed in order to alarm Innocent. For the first time, Pelagius and Caelestius were condemned together, and the ultimate consequences of their ideas shown to cut at the roots of episcopal authority. For if human nature was so perfect that it did not need to pray for help, what would happen to the benediction of the bishop? What, above all, to the special prayer of Christ for Peter 'that your faith shall not fail'?[5] The documents claimed that by appeasing the Pelagians the Catholic church would lose the vast authority it had begun to wield as the only force that could 'liberate' men from themselves.[6]

These documents had all the marks of a 'witch-hunt'. The Africans had attempted to impose a rigid 'test' of orthodoxy: and they had even hinted that more people were involved than 'just the one Pelagius' — indeed, that the most respectable see in Christendom was being undermined by a secret movement.[7]

Augustine was prepared to abandon one of the rules of Late Roman courtesy in order to make his point — that one correspondent should not intrude upon another without the preliminary occasion of a formal letter of greeting. The letters to Innocent, could at least be disguised as official minutes; but the letter by which he now approached John of Jerusalem directly, to demand a copy of the proceedings at Diospolis and to warn him to love Pelagius with due caution, bordered on insolence: 'I would not dare to take it amiss that I have received no letter from your holiness: I would rather believe that you had no bearer to carry it, than that I should dream of thinking that your reverence had deliberately ignored me.'[8]

Innocent was an old man, confident of his authority. He could afford to be generous to the Africans without committing himself too specifically. In a studiously vague bombast, copied from the Imperial chancery, he made their grievances his own:[9] if such ideas existed, they must, of course, be condemned. But he would rather believe that they

---

[1] *Ep.* 177. [2] *Ep.* 177, 6. [3] *Ep.* 177, 15. [4] *Ep.* 186, i, 2. [5] *Ep.* 175, 5.
[6] *Ep.* 175, 2. [7] *Ep.* 177, 2 and 3. [8] *Ep.* 179, 1. [9] e.g. *Ep.* 181, 4–5.

were not held by anyone at all! By summoning Pelagius and Caelestius, he perhaps expected to be reassured yet again.[1]

Now it was the turn of the Africans to pin all their hopes on this one, ambiguous judgement. Innocent died on March 12th, 417. His successor Zosimus was a man who hated muddles. Unlike Innocent, he was a weak man who was determined to get his way, even by gross favouritism and rudeness.[2] He may also have been a Greek, and so might have been impressed by the support that Pelagius had gained in the Holy Land.[3] The formidable Caelestius appeared in the city. Pelagius hastened to obey the summons of the Roman bishop; he had been preceded by a glowing testimonial from the bishop of Jerusalem. His accusers, the bishops Heros and Lazarus, were personal enemies of Zosimus;[4] and the two young men, Timasius and Jacobus, who had once betrayed Pelagius' *On Nature* to Augustine, were nowhere to be found.[5] All the Africans could do was to ignore this ominous change. Augustine preached in Carthage on September 23rd; '*Causa finita est*', 'the matter is closed'.[6] He, at least, was certain of himself. In his book *On the Proceedings concerning Pelagius*, he had already strengthened the authority of Aurelius with 'the pen of my industrious insignificance'.[7] Paul had spoken; Augustine had understood. That should be enough: 'For this reason, O blessed Paul, great preacher of grace, I can speak out straight. I shall have no qualms. For who shall object least to my saying such things than you, Paul, who said that they should be said, and taught that they should be taught.'[8]

Meanwhile, Zosimus had been preparing his solution to this untidy business. Caelestius was first examined in the new basilica of S. Clement, chosen in order to remind those present of the disciple of S. Peter who had 'cleared up' so many errors, as Zosimus intended to do. In a formal session, Zosimus refused to press Caelestius too far, and so could declare himself satisfied. Pelagius received an even warmer welcome in mid-September. Peace had returned to the City and the world. 'If only you had been present, my beloved brethren', Zosimus told the Africans, '... How deeply each one of us was moved! Hardly anyone present could refrain from tears at the thought

---

[1] v. esp. E. Caspar, *Geschichte d. Papsttums*, i, 1930, pp. 331–337.

[2] v. esp. E. Caspar, *Geschichte d. Papsttums*, i, pp. 344–356. G. Langgärtner, *Die Gallien-politik d. Päpste in den v u. vi. Jhten.*, (Theophaneia, 16), 1964, esp. pp. 24–52, reviews more favourably a particularly questionable episode in the policy of Zosimus.

[3] v. Bonner, *St. Augustine*, p. 341.

[4] Zosimus, *Ep.* '*Postquam*', 2, (P.L. xlv, 1721.) v. inf. p. 360, n. 8.

[5] Zosimus, *Ep.* '*Postquam*', 3, (P.L. xlv, 1722.)   [6] *Serm.* 131, X, 10.

[7] *de gest. Pel.* xxxiv, 59.   [8] *de gest. Pel.* xiii, 34.

that persons of such genuine faith could have been slandered.'[1]

In Roman Law, a false accusation was supposed to recoil on the head of the accuser. This was a fact which Augustine had stressed with considerable relish in his writings against the Donatists. It was now his turn to be lectured: 'It is the symptom of a decent mind to believe evil with difficulty.'[2] As for what Augustine considered to be the *fundatissima fides*, Zosimus will turn on both sides of the controversy all the ingrained dislike of a conservative politician for the fanaticism of clever men: 'this hairsplitting and these pointless debates . . . all pour out of an infectious curiosity, when each and all abuse their intellectual powers and give vent to their uncontrolled eloquence at the expense of the Scriptures. Not even the greatest minds', he went on to say, 'are immune from this. Their writings, in the course of time, are afflicted with the same dangerous lack of judgement. So God has prophesied: "*From many words thou shalt not escape sin,*" and holy David asked for "*a gate of prudence before his lips*".'[3]

The Africans could only wait. Augustine had to write even more. Paulinus of Nola was approached with a passionate and quite unsolicited theological treatise;[4] and Dardanus, a retired Prefect of Gaul, also received an oblique attack on Pelagian ideas.[5] Dardanus was a devout Christian, a man of vast prestige[6] and of odious reputation among the local population.[7] As the chief agent of the political purges that had recently taken place in Gaul after the suppression of the usurper, Constantine III, he may well have shared the dislike of Zosimus for the unfortunate bishops Heros and Lazarus, who had accused Pelagius; for they also had been involved with Constantine.[8] But the most significant letter of this time, seemed to have nothing to do with the Pelagian controversy: it was the pamphlet, *On correcting the Donatists*,[9] in which Augustine had persuaded waverers in the provincial government of Africa, to apply the full rigour of the laws against Donatist heretics.[10] It is a symbolic coincidence: for the Imperial

---

[1] Zosimus, *Ep.* '*Postquam*', 1, (P.L. xlv, 1721).

[2] Zosimus, *Ep.* '*Magnum pondus*', 4, (P.L. xlv, 1720).

[3] Zosimus, *Ep.* '*Magnum pondus*', 5, (P.L. xlv, 1720). For a sympathetic treatment of the position of Zosimus, v. esp. T. G. Jalland, *The Church and the Papacy*, 1944, pp. 286–288, and F. Floeri, 'Le pape Zosime et la doctrine augustinienne du péché originel', *Aug. Mag.*, ii, 1954, pp. 755–761.

[4] *Ep.* 186. v. Courcelle, *Les Confessions*, pp. 590–595.   [5] e.g. *Ep.* 187, xiii, 40.

[6] *Ep.* 187, i, 1.

[7] v. esp. J. Sundwall, *Weströmische Studien*, 1915, pp. 9–11 and 67–68.

[8] They had been involved in the usurpation of Constantine III: Zosimus, *Ep.* '*Postquam*', 2, (P.L. xlv, 1721); v. Langgärtner, *Die Gallienpolitik d. Päpste*, pp. 24 and 34.

[9] *Ep.* 185.   [10] *Retract.* II, 74.

Court at Ravenna, which administered these laws, will be the source of the next move out of the impasse caused by Pope Zosimus.

One cannot know exactly why the Imperial Court intervened at this precise moment. It would be misleading to be too precise. The Pelagians had made as many enemies in Italy as they had gained supporters.[1] News had come of the bloody rioting in which they seemed to have been involved among the Latin community of Jerusalem.[2] An intimate agent of Augustine's, Firmus, was at that time acting as factotum for one of the senatorial ladies in the group around Jerome.[3] He had visited Ravenna on business, and may have set about making contacts. Another mysterious figure had converged on the court, the Praetorian Prefect Palladius. Was he the same man as the 'honourable son', whom Augustine had recommended to a Sicilian bishop: an eminent politician, sailing from Hippo to take up high office in Italy, and well briefed by Augustine on 'the new heresy, hostile to the grace of Christ, that is trying to rise up against the church of Christ, and is not yet plainly cut off from this church'?[4]

Then, riots suddenly broke out in Rome. Pelagian supporters set upon a retired official.[5] This was too much. At the time of the Gothic sack, the Emperor Honorius had been living safely behind the marshes of Ravenna: he had been believed to be capable of mistaking 'Rome' for a pet cock of the same name.[6] After the disaster, he felt under a particular obligation to care for his 'Most Sacred City': at least he could protect it from rioting and heresy.[7] On April 30th 418, Palladius received a 'law to outdo the laws of every age'. It is the most depressing edict in the Later Roman Empire: Pelagius and Caelestius, the new disturbers of the Catholic faith, it said, 'think that it is a mark of lower class pettiness to agree with everybody else, and think that they are exceptionally knowledgeable, because they destroy what is agreed upon by the whole community'.[8] Pelagius and Caelestius were to be expelled from Rome; anyone who spoke in their favour was to be brought before the authorities.[9] Zosimus, already caught in this swing

[1] Bonner, *St. Augustine*, pp. 344–345.   [2] Bonner, *St. Augustine*, p. 344

[3] *Ep.* 172, 2. Marrou, 'La technique de l'édition', *Vigiliae Christianae*, 3, 1949, p. 218, n. 36.

[4] *Ep.* 178, 1. On this important person: v. L. Cantarelli, 'L'iscrizione onoraria di Giunio Quinto Palladio', *Bulletino Comunale di Roma*, liv, 1926, pp. 35–41.

[5] Prosper, *Chron.*, ad ann. 418, (P.L. li, 592A).   [6] Procopius, *de bellis*, III, ii, 25–26.

[7] This may be part of a general concern to reestablish the prestige of Rome after the Gothic Sack of 410. The official triumph of Honorius on suppressing a usurper had taken place in Rome in the previous year: Prosper, *Chron.*, ad ann. 417, (P.L. li, 592A).

[8] in P.L. xlviii, 379–386, with commentary, 386–392.

[9] in P.L. xlviii, 392–394. The exceptional severity of these laws is stressed by Morris, 'Pelagian Literature', *Journ. Theol. Studies*, n.s., xvi, 1965, pp. 52–53.

of feeling against the Pelagians, condemned the heresy: his famous condemnation, the *Epistula tractatoria*, now strengthened by the Imperial attitude, was to be signed by the Italian bishops, and technically promulgated, like the Imperial law, throughout the Roman world.[1]

Even this was not sufficient. The death of Zosimus, in December 418, paralysed the Church of Rome, and so gave the supporters of Pelagius the chance to reopen their case. This small group was now brilliantly led by a young man, Julian, bishop of Eclanum. They were respectable bishops of Italian towns. They rallied to uphold the Catholic faith — that is, the essential goodness of God's creation, the value of human endeavour; and they rejected as absurd determinism in any form. They would sum up their message as 'The Five Praises': praise of creation, of marriage, of God's law, of free will, and of the hardwon merits of the holy men of old.[2]

Without a qualm, Augustine, Alypius, and their agents, turned the laymen at the court against the Italian bishops. Count Valerius, a court general, blocked the Pelagians' appeal to have their case heard in Ravenna,[3] and helped to obtain a law to coerce any bishop suspected of Pelagian leanings.[4] This man, *plus catholique que le pape*, a reader of the works of Augustine, proud to have bishops among his clients,[5] his whole house a deadly enemy of heretics,[6] was related to a great landowner in Hippo.[7] Was he also an African? and if so, had Augustine and his friends put pressure on their fellow-countrymen at the court? In any case, such diplomacy was known to be costly. On one mission, Alypius had carried with him the promise of eighty Numidian stallions, fattened on the estates of the church, as *douceurs* for the cavalry-officers, whose views on grace had proved decisive.[8] Once again, the African bishops had the pleasure of knowing that '*The heart of the King is in the hand of God*'.[9]

The Italians might well be shocked: the Roman clergy felt bullied; the cultured bishops were convinced that such a resort to force was a confession of intellectual impotence.[10] Augustine, with fifteen years of repression behind him in Africa, was quite unmoved by the denial of freedom of discussion: 'Far be it from the Christian rulers of the earthly commonwealth that they should harbour any doubts on the

---

[1] v. Bonner, *St. Augustine*, p. 345.
[2] v. their appeal in P.L. xlviii, 509–526; de Plinval, *Pélage*, pp. 336–341.
[3] *Op. Imp.* I, 10.   [4] Edict in *Ep.* 201.   [5] *Ep.* 206.   [6] *Ep.* 200, 2.
[7] The Romulus of *Ep.* 247: v. Chastagnol, *Les Fastes de la Préfecture urbaine*, p. 290.
[8] *Op. Imp.* I, 42.   [9] Letter of Aurelius: P.L. xlviii, 401A.   [10] *C. Jul.* III, 5.

ancient Catholic faith ... certain and firmly-grounded on this faith, they should, rather, impose on such men as you are, fitting discipline and punishment.'[1] Sixtus, the Roman priest who had abandoned the lost cause of Pelagíus, would learn from Augustine what victory could mean: 'Those whose wounds are hidden are not for that reason to be passed over in the doctor's treatment. . . . They are to be taught; and, in my opinion, this can be done with greater ease, when the teaching of truth is aided by the fear of severity.'[2]

As in his dealings with the Donatists, Augustine showed himself a stern victor. In a sermon that he preached to a simple audience, he dismissed the Pelagians and Caelestians: these 'wind bags', puffed up with pride, had dared, in the face of the thunderous words of the Apostle, to deny that 'nobody in this flesh, nobody in this corruptible body, nobody on the face of this earth, in this malevolent existence, in this life full of temptation — nobody can live without sin'.[3] 'Let them and their cleanliness be outside.'[4]

Now was the time for Augustine to reap the harvest of congratulation. Jerome was delighted. Throughout the *causa gratiae*, Augustine had showed qualities that Jerome had always greatly relished in himself. He had maintained an obstinate isolation, 'you preferred, as far as you could, to free yourself alone from Sodom rather than tarry with those who perished.' He was a well-hated man, 'a sign of greater glory, all heretics detest you.' For the first time in his life Augustine was acclaimed as a truly international figure by another: *conditorem antiquae rursus fidei*. He had 'set up anew the ancient faith'.[5]

A small incident shows the state of Augustine's mind at that time. On a visit to Mauretania, he had heard of a young man, a small-town intellectual called Vincentius Victor, who held definite views on the origin of the soul. Augustine, he said, had sat on the fence on this issue. This is true: Augustine had gained his certainty in facing the Pelagians by shelving this highly speculative issue. His silence had worried many well-educated men who had been accustomed, in Later Antiquity, to deal with the problem of human destiny and the origin of evil, precisely in terms of the origin of the soul and of its relation to the world of material things.[6] But, as Victor hinted, a bishop, 'a man set in honour,' was not supposed to be clever.[7]

Augustine's immediate reaction is rather touching: if only the young

---

[1] *Op. Imp.* I, 9.   [2] *Ep.* 191, 2.   [3] *Serm.* 181, 1.   [4] *Serm.* 181, 3.   [5] *Ep.* 195.
[6] e.g. *Ep.* 167, i, 2. Augustine, also, had been affected by such speculations: R. J. O'Connell, 'The Plotinian Fall of the Soul in St. Augustine', *Traditio*, 19, 1963, pp. 1–35.
[7] *de anim. et eius orig.* IV, ii, 2.

man would come and talk with him, there was so much that he could tell him about his thoughts on this mystery, far, far more than he could possibly put on paper.[1] But it is also the reaction of an elderly bishop, whose sense of authority was learnt in a hard school. Victor was a newly-converted Donatist; he had even adopted his first name, Vincentius, in honour of the Donatist bishop of Cartennae, to whom Augustine had first justified his attitude to religious coercion, in 408.[2] Augustine could not overlook this fact. To him, a bishop's duties were not only 'pastoral'; they had also become 'medicinal'.[3] Laymen who pontificated to the clergy would be well to remember this 'tonic' of authority. Augustine intended to 'correct' Victor, not to follow him.[4]

This attitude gives poignancy to the situation that will develop in Augustine's last years. Young Victor had rushed in when 'my old man's fears, my son' had held Augustine back.[5] Now another young man, able, obstinate and unscrupulous, would badger him on the issues on which he felt most certain until his death, Julian, bishop of Eclanum.

---

[1] *de anim. et eius orig.* III, xiv, 20.
[2] *de anim. et eius orig.* III, i, 2.
[3] *de anim. et eius orig.* III, i, 2.
[4] *de anim. et eius orig.* III, i, 1.
[5] *de anim. et eius orig.* IV, ix, 16.

31

FUNDATISSIMA FIDES

Throughout the course of the Pelagian controversy, Augustine was able to expound in packed churches his alternative to the ideal of the Christian life that Pelagius had advocated in letters to select individuals. The basic conviction of Pelagius and his followers, was that man's nature was certain and fundamentally unchanging. Originally created good by God, the powers of human nature had, admittedly, been constricted by the weight of past habits and by the corruption of society. But such constriction was purely superficial. The 'remission of sins' in baptism, could mean for the Christian, the immediate recovery of a full freedom of action, that had merely been kept in abeyance by ignorance and convention.[1]

Augustine's audience, by contrast, would be told repeatedly that even the baptized Christian must remain an invalid: like the wounded man, found near death by the wayside in the Parable of the Good Samaritan, his life had been saved by the rite of baptism; but he must be content to endure, for the rest of his life, a prolonged and precarious convalescence in the 'Inn' of the Church.[2] For, to Augustine, man's nature was at a nadir of uncertainty: it had been dramatically impaired by an event in the distant past; and it would be cured, in an equally distant future, only by a transformation so total and so glorious, that, in its light, the least symptom of man's present collapse, must always be regarded as a cause of profound sadness.[3]

For Augustine, the individual was involved in this collapse and in this recovery on a level that went far beyond his conscious choice. The Pelagian man was essentially a separate individual: the man of Augustine is always about to be engulfed in vast, mysterious solidarities. For Pelagius, men had simply decided to imitate Adam, the first sinner: for

---

[1] v. esp. Bohlin, *Die Theologie d. Pelagius*, pp. 29–39, esp. pp. 35–37.
[2] *Serm.* 131, 6; cf. *Serm.* 151, 4–5.   [3] *Serm.* 155, 14.

Augustine, they received their basic weakness in the most intimate and irreversible manner possible; they were born into it by the mere fact of physical descent from this, the common father of the human race.[1] (The idea of an hereditary obligation seemed quite natural to the supporters of Augustine, who lived in an age which had come to regard the ineluctable inheritance of social duties, especially of the more unpleasant, as the basis of an organized community.)[2]

Behind this ominous sinking of the individual, however, there lies a deep sense of the nature of human evil. For Pelagius, human sin was essentially superficial: it was a matter of choice. Wrong choices might add some 'rust' to the pure metal of human nature;[3] but a choice, by definition, could be reversed.[4] For Augustine, the nature of the imperfection of man was sensed as a profound and permanent dislocation: as a *discordia*, a 'tension', that strove, however perversely, to seek resolution in some balanced whole, in some *concordia*.[5] Because of this view, the cure for sin had to be far more radical than that proposed by Pelagius. For Pelagius, self-control was sufficient: it was sufficient to guard the citadel of free decision[6] by choosing good and rejecting evil. Augustine was less sure. Self-control was essential and laudable;[7] but could it ever be enough? For even the frontiers of such self-control were dangerously ill-defined.[8] Not all consent to evil promptings need be fully-conscious: indeed, Augustine can envisage unconscious consent to the 'desires of sin' as betraying itself in a slip of the tongue;[9] and, in so doing, he anticipates Freud in seeing in this seemingly harmless phenomenon, the constant activity of unconscious desires. 'Even if I do not consent to it, there is still in me both something dead and something alive. Surely you cannot deny that this dead part of you belongs to you?'[10] Only the transformation of this deadness could heal men of the deep cause of their sins.[11] Thus the Resurrection is one of the central preoccupations of Augustine at this time. The old man, unrivalled in his sense of the frailty of human flesh, will never cease to feel poignantly attached to that rebel province, his own body: 'I want to be healed completely, for I am a complete whole.'[12] 'Take away death, the last enemy, and my own flesh shall be my dear friend throughout eternity.'[13]

---

[1] e.g. *de pecc. mer.* III, viii, 15; *Serm.* 294, 15.
[2] e.g. Marius Mercator, *Liber subnotationum*, ii, 2, (P.L. xlviii, 124–125).
[3] Pelagius, *ad Dem.* 8, (P.L. xxx, 24).
[4] Pelagius, *ad Dem.* 3, (P.L. xxx, 18c); summed up in *Ep.* 186, x, 34.   [5] *Serm.* 151, 4.
[6] Pelagius, *ad Dem.* 4, (P.L. xxx, 20B).   [7] *Serm.* 155, 2.
[8] e.g. *de pecc. mer.* II, viii, 10.   [9] *de perf. just.* xxi, 44.   [10] *Serm.* 154, 14.
[11] *Serm.* 45, 10.   [12] *Serm.* 30, 4; cf. 30, 6.   [13] *Serm.* 155, 15.

Thus, the Christian life, as seen by Augustine, could only be a long process of healing. To convey some impression of this gradual and precarious transformation, Augustine even uses the verb 'to run' in an unusual, technical sense found in Roman medical jargon — to describe the way in which new, healthy tissue 'runs' over the scar.[1] To him, the controversial statements of the Pelagians can be dismissed as an unseemly brawl in a sanatorium: 'O what a ridiculous illness! The Doctor is calling out for men to come to Him, and the sick man is wrapped up in his arguments.'[2]

Augustine could hold his audience spellbound on such themes. They were so identified with his feelings, that they would even burst into sudden shouts of terror at an abrupt mention of the wrath of God.[3] In his letters, also, he felt sure of public opinion: the Pelagians had been 'smashed to pieces by the absolutely unanimous agreement of all Christian peoples on the faith'.[4] 'Let us hold on to what we have all just sung', he would say, ' "*Have mercy on me, O Lord, have mercy on me*".'[5]

Augustine was right in feeling that public opinion was on his side. A mentality of dependence; an emphasis on the absolute necessity of humility, on the idea of a 'general collapse' of the human race above which no man might dare to claim to raise himself by his own merits; these are the ideas that will dominate the early Middle Ages.[6] For, no matter how self-consciously Christian the Pelagian movement had been, it rested firmly on a bed rock of the old ethical ideals of paganism, especially on Stoicism.[7] Its moral exhortations had appealed to a classical sense of the resources and autonomy of the human mind. For this reason, the victory of Augustine's ideas over those of Pelagius are one of the most important symptoms of that profound change that we call 'The End of the Ancient World and the Beginning of the Middle Ages'. Yet, while Augustine's ideas would be dominant, Pelagianism would remain endemic. At the very end of the fifth century, an elderly bishop in Picenum, called appropriately enough Seneca, a man 'not untouched by classical learning', would reach his own conclusions without any

---

[1] *de perf. just.* xx, 43.   [2] *Serm.* 30, 8.   [3] e.g. *Serm.* 131, 5; v. sup. p. 252.
[4] *Ep.* 194, vii, 31.   [5] *Serm.* 165, 9.
[6] The letter to Demetrias ascribed to Pope Leo, will be entitled 'On Humility': P.L. lv, 161–180.
[7] But v. the pertinent remarks of Prete, *Pelagio*, pp. 49–53, and Refoulé, 'Julien d'Éclane', *Rech. sc. relig.*, 52, 1964, pp. 233–241. For the ease with which a collection of pagan sayings achieved immense popularity in a Christianized edition, v. the excellent study of H. Chadwick, *The Sentences of Sixtus: A Contribution to the History of Early Christian Ethics*, (Texts and Studies, n.s., v), 1959, esp. pp. 118–122 — on their use by Pelagius — and p. 138.

knowledge of the great Pelagian authors.[1] He, also, thought that babies were made by God, and so were good; that they could not be damned for not being baptized; 'that man can achieve happiness by his free choice, supported by the goodness of human nature;' and he had even put his faith in human nature to the test by refusing to segregate the monks and virgins of his diocese. 'While,' wrote the pope indignantly, 'the minds of spiritual men, even when mixed company is avoided, are plagued with . . . beguiling imaginations.'[2]

Pelagius and Augustine were both religious geniuses. Both made unambiguous sense of a conglomerate of ideas and attitudes which men of a previous age had been content to leave undefined. Both men were revolutionaries, and the controversy which followed their disagreement, far from being a purely academic wrangle, was a crisis in which the spiritual landscape of Western Christendom can be clearly seen for the first time.[3]

The nature of baptism provided the great watershed separating the two men.[4] Here Pelagius felt he could speak for the conventional, adult Christian convert. For such a man, baptism was a dramatic 'fresh start', the beginning of a heroic life of action. The biographer of S. Cyprian had quite unconsciously begun the 'true' life of his hero with his baptism.[5] It is Augustine, whose clinical examination of past and present failings in the *Confessions* seems almost to take the rite of baptism for granted, who marks a new departure.[6] Yet if we turn to the works of Augustine's first years as a Catholic, we can still see a frame of mind not very different from that which Pelagius expected his readers to have: 'conversion' and baptism had meant a sudden relief of tension, and a happy, unclouded sense of serious purpose. The Pelagian communities in Sicily and elsewhere, would not have been very different from the little groups that had formed round Augustine in Cassiciacum, Ostia and Thagaste. His occasional sharp remark against

[1] Pope Gelasius to the bishops of Picenum: c.2, (P.L. xlv, 1766–1767).
[2] ibid. c.8, (P.L. xlv, 1770–1771).
[3] 'We can observe here, if anywhere, the "logic" of history. There has never, perhaps, been another crisis of equal importance in Church history in which the opponents have expressed the principles at issue so clearly and abstractly': A. Harnack, *History of Dogma*, v, (Dover), p. 169.
[4] The dialogue in *Serm.* 131, 6 is of great importance.
[5] v. sup. p. 177: e.g. *Ep.* 1, 3–4, (P.L. iv, 201–205). Pelagius owed much to Cyprian: v. de Plinval, *Pélage*, pp. 75–78. v. *de gest. Pel.* vi, 16: Christian perfection would not, of course, be reached by a child, but was, Pelagius insisted, possible for an adult 'converted from his past sins'; cf. *de nat. et gratia*, lii, 60–liv, 64. For a marked streak of perfectionism, associated with the 'Mystery' of Baptism, in the Early Church v. sup. p. 177 and, especially, the excellent remarks of K. E. Kirk, *The Vision of God*, 1931, pp. 229–234.
[6] v. sup. p. 177.

those who would persuade men, as the pagan philosophers had done, that they could achieve a 'complete life', a *beata vita*, in this world,[1] shows how Augustine, himself the author of an exhortation *On the Complete Life* derived from a pagan Platonist, understood, from his own experience as a young convert, the latent perfectionism of the Pelagian movement. In this we can see a parting of the ways. It is Augustine who had come to abandon the old hopes of the Christian convert; and the certainty with which he picked out the weaknesses of the idealistic message of Pelagius, is perhaps a symptom of the silent ferocity with which Augustine had continued to criticize his own past.

Seen from the outside, however, the alternative offered by Augustine, the heroic endurance of unresolved tensions, might seem to mock all Christian hopes for a new life. Augustine might be able to afford such an attitude in Africa. There, Christianity was well-established. But Pelagius and his supporters came from provinces where the Christian church still lived as a 'missionary' group. Conscientious bishops in the predominantly pagan provinces of Italy and Gaul, spent much of their energies pleading with their congregations to enter into the great 'mystery' of baptism. They could hardly support views that might seem to encourage pagan converts, who had at last taken the momentous step of becoming full Christians, to settle back into the moral torpor of a confirmed invalid.[2]

Augustine, indeed, had seemed to take the extent of evil almost for granted. This was a dangerous attitude among men who had hardly liberated themselves from the utter passivity engendered by astrological beliefs. The desperate prayer of Augustine's Christian, '*lest iniquity perchance have the domination over me*,' seemed to admit, once again, a tyranny as flat and ineluctable as that still exercised, in the mind of ancient men, by the stars.[3]

Above all, how could the permanent tension, the *discordia*, of 'flesh' and 'spirit', stressed by Augustine, fail to resemble the permanent dichotomy of evil flesh and good mind, posited by the Manichees? Augustine's sermons against the Pelagians are, significantly, often openly directed against the Manichees. In Africa and elsewhere, the tide had turned away from Manichaeism among educated men, largely through the intervention of Augustine: there was a real danger that this tide should turn again towards Manichaeism, as a result of the

[1] *Ep.* 186, x 1,37.   [2] e.g. *Op. Imp.* II, 8 and IV, 114 and 119.

[3] *Ps.* 118, 133: *de pecc. mer.* II, vi, 7; cf. *Epp.* 157, ii, 8 and 194, ii, 5: the inscrutable 'Wisdom' of God, essential to Augustine's ideas on predestination, is always presented as the antithesis of 'Fate'.

dangerous armaments assembled by Augustine against his new opponents.[1] Many of Augustine's former friends had remained Manichees. One of them, Honoratus, had held discussions with Julian of Eclanum around 410.[2] Such personal knowledge of the 'Manichaean Problem' may well have strengthened the resolution of young Julian not to surrender the cause of Pelagius to the Africans. It certainly provided him with scope for his journalistic talents. Julian would play brilliantly on the fears of his Italian readers, who had far less direct acquaintance with Manichaeism as it really was, than an African bishop would have had.[3] In the most notable 'scoop' of his whole controversy with Augustine, he even had better luck than he realized. He had found what purported to be a letter of Mani to a Persian princess, Menoch.[4] In actual fact, it was something far more damaging, because far closer to the world of Augustine: it was a fragment of a commentary on Paul by a Latin Manichee, designed to prove from Paul, as unambiguously as Augustine had proved it, that concupiscence existed as a permanent evil force.[5] In 405, Secundinus the Manichee had claimed, that had Augustine remained a Manichee, he would have become 'the Paul of our times'.[6] Julian and his readers, contemplating the vast edifice raised by Augustine on his interpretation of the Apostle, might well have felt that the hopes of Secundinus had come only too true. For a sensitive man of the fifth century, Manichaeism, Pelagianism, and the views of Augustine were not as widely separated as we would now see them: they would have appeared to him as points along the same great circle of problems raised by the Christian religion. Thus, this so-called 'Letter to Menoch', written by a Latin as certain as Augustine that he had understood the message of S. Paul, was a

[1] v. esp. *Serm.* 153, 2, where the Manichee is presented as 'encouraged' by what Augustine has just said.

[2] *Op. Imp.* V, 26. Honoratus was either the recipient of *Ep.* 140, in which anti-Pelagian views are canvassed, or of *de utilitate credendi* of 392, (and so must have remained unimpressed by his friend's anti-Manichaean arguments). Furthermore, Firmus, Augustine's 'literary agent' in Italy at that time, and an intimate friend of Count Valerius, Augustine's patron at the Court, (v. sup. p. 304 n. 1) may well be the same person as the Manichaean merchant converted by Augustine: *Vita*, XV, 5.

[3] v. inf. p. 393.

[4] Cited in *Op. Imp.* III, 136–137. The arguments do, indeed, bear a remarkable resemblance to those used by Augustine, as they draw on identical arguments, notably on the 'facts' of shame and loss of control in intercourse and on the 'fact' of infant baptism. The highly pejorative antithesis of 'spiritual' generation by baptism and 'physical' procreation is used both by Faustus the Manichee, (*C. Faust.* XXIV, 1), and, repeatedly, by Augustine: e.g. *Serm.* 294, 16.

[5] v. G. J. D. Aalders, 'L'Épître à Menoch attribuée à Mani', *Vigiliae Christianae*, 14, 1960, pp. 245–249.

[6] *Ep. Secundini ad Aug.*

warning to contemporaries that they lived on a round world; and that, behind the *fundatissima fides* of Augustine there stood, always ready to rise again above the horizon, the Paul of the Manichees.

Others were less alarmist. One, Anianus of Celeda, shows the state of mind of a cultured Pelagian cleric. Depressed and shocked by the modern mystique of human incapacity, he had set himself to translate into Latin the homilies of S. John Chrysostom. Here were very different sermons from those of Augustine: they spoke of the moral achievements of S. Paul; they castigated all thoughts of a fatality of evil, and had upheld, in this darkening world, the nobility of man, and the capacity of his nature to fulfil the perfect message of the Gospels.[1]

Augustine, however, saw the basic difference between himself and Pelagius in a different light. What he criticized immediately in Pelagianism, was far less its optimism about human nature, as the fact that such optimism seemed to be based upon a transparently inadequate view of the complexity of human motivation. The two men disagreed radically on an issue that is still relevant, and where the basic lines of division have remained the same: on the nature and sources of a fully good, creative action. How could this rare thing happen? For one person, a good action could mean one that fulfilled successfully certain conditions of behaviour, for another, one that marked the culmination of an inner evolution. The first view, was roughly that of Pelagius; the second, that of Augustine.

The good Pelagian was a 'good citizen'. He was treated as a responsible person, capable of carrying out a just code of laws. In Paradise, Adam and Eve had shown towards God a *devotio*, a conscientious loyalty, such as was expected by a Late Roman Emperor of his tax payers.[2] Pelagius' treatises read at times like works of rational political theory. His God is an Enlightened Despot; and the Christians are well provided for by His copious legislation.[3] Pelagius was indignant that men should continue to fail to fulfil the commands of so reasonable and well-intentioned a sovereign: 'After so many notices drawing your attention to virtue; after the giving of the Law, after the Prophets, after the Gospels, after the Apostles, I just do not know how God can show indulgence to you, if you wish to commit a crime.'[4] Pelagius constantly assumes that the provision of a good environment can directly influence men for the better. According to him, men's wills could be 'stunned'

[1] v. esp. in P.L. xlviii, 626–630.
[2] It is a virtue required in 39 edicts of the Theodosian Code.
[3] v. esp. Pelagius, *ad Dem.* 16, (P.L. xxx, 31D–32).
[4] Ps. Jerome, *Ep.* 13, 6, (P.L. xxx, 172D).

into action by the good example of Christ, and by the terrible sanction of Hell-fire.[1] Such a view inevitably placed a great emphasis on the fear of punishment. There is a cold streak in the mentality of the whole Pelagian movement. Adam had suffered the death-penalty for breaking one single prohibition; and even he was less to blame than ourselves, for he had not had the great benefit of the previous execution of a human being to deter him.[2] It is Pelagius, not Augustine, who harps on the terrors of the Last Judgement: to which Augustine simply remarked that 'a man who is afraid of sinning because of Hell-fire, is afraid, not of sinning, but of burning'.[3]

Thus the book which Augustine himself regarded as his most fundamental demolition of Pelagianism, is entitled *On the Spirit and the Letter*.[4] The clear code of laws enforced by sanctions, that had been welcomed by the Pelagians as a sufficient stimulus to good action, is dismissed by Augustine as the '*Letter that killeth*', as the Old Law. Only God could give the '*Spirit that makes alive*': the capacity to love goodness for itself that will ensure that a man will grow rather than wither in the harsh environment of God's commands.[5] 'You enumerate', he says later, 'many ways in which God helps us — the commands of the Scriptures, blessings, healings, chastenings, excitations and inspirations; but that He gives us *love* and helps us in this way, this you do not say.'[6]

Thus, we come to two different views of the way in which men are able to act, and so to two different views of freedom. For Pelagius, freedom could be taken for granted: it was simply part of a common-sense description of a human being. He was assumed to be responsible (or how could his sins be called sinful?); he was conscious of exercising choice; therefore, Pelagius insisted, he was free to determine his actions. '*In the beginning, God set man and left him in his own counsel. . . . He placed before you water and fire, to what you wish, stretch out your hand.*'[7]

For Augustine, this description might suit an ideal human being. What concerned him was not 'planning human nature, but how to heal it'.[8] Therefore, freedom for Augustine was something that had to be

---

[1] in *de grat. Christi*, x, 11.　　[2] *Ep.* 'Honorificentiae tuae', 1, (Caspari p. 7).

[3] *Ep.* 145, 4.

[4] *Retract.* II, 63. This work is translated with an excellent introduction, by J. Burnaby, *Augustine: Later Works*, (Library of Christian Classics, viii), 1955, pp. 182-250.

[5] In the imagery of *Serm.* 155, 6, as the people stand far away from Sinai, so the Law is external to them.

[6] *Op. Imp.* III, 106.　　[7] *Eccles.* 15, 14 sq., cited by Caelestius: *de perf. just.* xix, 40.

[8] *de nat. et gratia*, x, 12.

achieved. He will always speak of freedom in comparatives, of 'greater freedom', 'fuller freedom', 'perfect freedom'.[1] Pelagius and Caelestius by contrast, thought that they could argue directly from the agreed facts of choice and responsibility, to complete human self-determination:[2] 'It is the easiest thing in the world', wrote Caelestius, 'to change our will by an act of will.'[3] For them, the difference between good and bad men was quite simple: some chose the good, some the bad.[4] To which Augustine replied: 'I could say with absolute truth and conviction (that men were not sinless) because they did not want to be sinless. But if you were to ask me *why* they did not want to be so, then we are getting out of our depth — *imus in longum*.'[5]

Men choose in a way more complex than that suggested by the hallowed stereotypes of common-sense. For an act of choice is not just a matter of knowing what to choose: it is a matter in which loving and feeling are involved. And in men, this capacity to know and to feel in a single, involved whole, has been intimately dislocated: 'The understanding flies on ahead, and there follows, oh, so slowly, and sometimes not at all, our weakened human capacity for feeling.'[6] Men choose because they love; but Augustine had been certain for some twenty years, that they could not, of themselves, choose to love.[7] The vital capacity to unite feeling and knowledge comes from an area outside man's powers of self-determination. 'From a depth that we do not see, comes everything that you can see.'[8] '*I know, O Lord, that the way of a man is not in his power; nor is it for him to walk and direct his own steps.*'[9]

Thus, for Augustine freedom can only be the culmination of a process of healing.[10] Augustine will turn the whole of Psalm 118, ostensibly a thoroughly 'Pelagian' Psalm, containing as it does a static code of precepts for the life of the good man, into a treatise on the dynamic transformation of the will.[11] The most fitting image of the 'freed' will, will be one full of motion, the baffling resilience and activity

[1] e.g. *Ep.* 157, ii, 8.   [2] e.g. in *de nat. et gratia*, xxx, 34.
[3] in *de perf. just.* vi, 12.   [4] e.g. Pelagius, *ad Dem.* 8, (P.L. xxx, 24A).
[5] *de pecc. mer.* II, xvii, 26; cf. *de perf. just.* xix, 41.   [6] *Enarr. viii in Ps.* 118, 4.
[7] v. sup. p. 154; cf. *de spir. et litt.* xxxiv, 60.   [8] *Serm.* 165, 3.
[9] *Jerem.* 10, 23, in *de pecc. mer.* II, xvii, 26.
[10] v. esp. the lucid summary in the form of Scriptural citations, in which each step follows the other 'like links in a chain': *de spir. et litt.* xxx, 52.
[11] e.g. *Enarr. x in Ps.* 118, 1 and 6: 'the prayer of a man developing'. v. esp. C. Kannengiesser, 'Enarratio in Psalmum CXVIII: Science de la révélation et progrès spirituel', *Rech. augustin.*, ii, 1962, pp. 359–381 and A. M. La Bonnardière, *Rech. de chronologie augustin.*, pp. 119–141.

of a great fire, that can roar up again when beaten by the winds of adversity.[1]

The healing process by which love and knowledge are reintegrated, is made possible by an inseparable connection between growing self-determination and dependence on a source of life that always escapes self-determination.[2] The healed man enjoys a more acute sense of responsibility, clearer knowledge, a greater ease of choice.[3] He has had to achieve all that Pelagius had thought he possessed from the start.[4] The idea that we depend for our ability to determine ourselves, on areas that we cannot ourselves determine, is central to Augustine's 'therapeutic' attitude to the relation between 'grace' and 'free will'. It is the connection of the two, in a single healing process, that occupied all Augustine's attention:[5] any attempt to dissect such a living relationship, to see a contrast where he saw only a vital interdependence, frankly puzzled him: 'Some men try hard to discover in our will what good is particularly due to ourselves, that owes nothing to God: how they can find this out, I just do not know.'[6]

Freedom, therefore, for Augustine, cannot be reduced to a sense of choice: it is a freedom to act fully. Such freedom must involve the transcendance of a sense of choice. For a sense of choice is a symptom of the disintegration of the will: the final union of knowledge and feeling would involve a man in the object of his choice in such a way that any other alternative would be inconceivable.

Throughout his sermons against the Pelagians, Augustine repeats this as his fundamental assertion on the relation of grace and freedom: that the healthy man is one in whom knowledge and feeling have become united; and that only such a man is capable of allowing himself to be 'drawn' to act by the sheer irresistible pleasure of the object of his love. The notorious tag of Vergil, *Trahat sua quemque voluptas*, 'Let each man's pleasure draw him,' occurs, surprisingly, in a sermon by the old man on the Gospel of S. John: 'And have the senses of the body their delights, while the soul is left devoid of pleasures? If the soul does not have pleasures of its own, why is it written: "*The soul of men shall hope under the shadow of Thy wings; they shall be made drunk with the fullness of Thy house; and of the torrents of Thy pleasures Thou wilt give them to drink; for in Thee is the Fountain of Life, and in Thy*

---

[1] *Enarr. xvii in Ps.* 118, 2.
[2] *Enarr. xvii in Ps.* 118, 2: 'and these two are so linked to one another that the one cannot exist without the other'.
[3] *Enarr. xvii in Ps.* 118, 7.
[4] e.g. *de nat. et gratia*, lviii, 68.
[5] e.g. *Ep.* 186, iii, 10.
[6] *de pecc. mer.* II, xviii, 28.

Light shall we see the light"? Give me a man in love: he knows what I mean. Give me one who yearns; give me one who is hungry; give me one far away in this desert, who is thirsty and sighs for the spring of the Eternal country. Give me that sort of man: he knows what I mean. But if I speak to a cold man, he just does not know what I am talking about. . . .'[1]

[1] *Tract. in Joh.* 26, 4.

PART V
421-430

P.L. VOL. · COL.	TRANSLATIONS
43 · 707	
44 · 641	*Against Julian*, NY., 1957.
40 · 231	*The Enchiridion*, Edinburgh, 1873; *The Enchiridion to Laurentius*, Oxford, 1885; *Enchiri* of *St Augustine, addressed to Laurentius*, Ld., 1887; *Faith, Hope and Charity*, NY., 1 *Faith, Hope and Charity*, Ld., 1947; *St Augustine's Enchiridion*, Ld., 1953; *Enchiri* Ld., 1955; (in) *Seventeen short treatises*, Oxford, 1847; *Basic Writings I*, NY., 1948.
40 · 591	(in) *Seventeen short treatises*, Oxford, 1847; *How to help the dead*, Ld., 1914; *The care* taken for the dead, NY., 1955.
40 · 147	*The eight questions of Dulcitius*, NY., 1952.
39 · 1568	
44 · 881	(in) *The anti-Pelagian writings III*, Edinburgh, 1876; *Basic Writings I*, NY., 1948.
44 · 915	(in) *The anti-Pelagian writings III*, Edinburgh, 1876; *Admonition and grace*, NY., 1947.
32 · 583	
42 · 709	
42 · 743	
42 · 21	
44 · 959	*The anti-Pelagian writings III*, Edinburgh, 1876; *Basic Writings I*, NY., 1948.
45 · 993	(in) *The anti-Pelagian writings III*, Edinburgh, 1876.
42 · 51	*An answer to the Jews*, NY., 1955.
45 · 1049	

Enquiry into Manichees at Carthage, about the middle of the year.	/22 *Contra Gaudentium Donatistarum episcopum.* 13.vi. XVIII Council of Carthage. *Contra Julianum.* /23 *Enchiridion ad Laurentium.* /24 *De cura pro mortuis gerenda.*
4.ix. Death of Boniface. Election of Pope Celestine (–27.vii.432).	/25 *De VIII Dulcitii quaestionibus.*
	Affair of Antonius of Fussala.
Eraclius builds *memoria* to S. Stephen at Hippo.	
Valentinian III becomes Emperor in the West. Bishops of Gaul face enquiry to detect Pelagian sympathizers.	*De civitate Dei XVIII.* /27 *De civitate Dei XIX–XXII.* Scandal at Hippo: Sermons 355–6 (Dec.–Jan.).
	Death of Severus of Milevis. Visits Milevis to regulate succession. Nominates his successor, the priest Eraclius. /27 *De gratia et libero arbitrio.* /27 *De correptione et gratia.* /27 *Retractationes.*
Revolt of Boniface.	/28 *Collatio cum Maximino Arianorum episcopo.*
	Contra Maximinum Arianorum episcopum. *De haeresibus ad Quodvultdeum.* Receives letters from Prosper and Hilary. /29 *De praedestinatione sanctorum.* /29 *De dono perseverantiae.*
Vandals from Spain approaching along the coast of Mauretania (Summer). Darius comes to Africa to reconcile Boniface and the Empress.	/30 *Tractatus adversus Judaeos.* /30 *Contra secundam Juliani responsionem opus imperfectum.*
Ravaging of Numidia by Vandals.	28.viii. Death and burial of Augustine.

32

JULIAN OF ECLANUM[1]

(I)

In 408, Augustine was approached by bishop Memor, a member of
the circle of Paulinus of Nola.[2] Memor asked for a copy of his *De
Musica*. Augustine found that he had little time for 'such play-
things':[3] oppressed by his bitter campaign against the Donatists in
Africa, the request for such a text-book must have seemed to come to
him from an old world of cultivated, leisured Christians, with time to
pursue the 'liberal' training of a gentleman.[4] Yet this old world was
still very much alive in Southern Italy. Memor saw nothing strange in
a Christianized text-book of classical poetry. He had a brilliant son to
educate: Julian, the future bishop of Eclanum, the most devastating
critic of Augustine in his old age.[5]

Augustine and Julian were separated by a gulf far wider than the
Mediterranean. They belonged to different worlds. Julian's family
boasted noble birth. His father was a bishop: he himself married, as a
priest, the daughter of another bishop, Aemilius of Beneventum. A
generation before, Beneventum had been a pagan town, whose public-
spirited nobility had impressed Symmachus.[6] Now these virtues would
be continued in new, clerical dynasties: Julian will sell his estates to
relieve a famine.[7] Hospitality, wise words, fair judgement: these were
the virtues which such men culled from the Scriptures to place on

---

[1] F. Refoulé, 'Julien d'Éclane, théologien et philosophe', *Recherches de sciences religieuses*,
52, 1964, pp. 42–84 and 233–247, though unhistorical in approach and open to criticism
(v. F-J. Thonnard in *Rev. études augustin.*, xi, 1965, pp. 296–304), marks what one hopes
will be a fresh start towards a more perceptive treatment of Julian. v. also A. Bruckner,
Julian v. Eclanum, (Texte u. Untersuchungen, 15, 3), 1897 and the list of works attributed
to Julian in Hamman, *P.L. Supplement*, i, 1571–1572.

[2] *Ep.* 101 answers this letter. [3] *Ep.* 101, 3.
[4] *Ep.* 101, 1. [5] *Ep.* 101, 4.
[6] Symmachus, *Ep.* I, 3, (A.D. 375).
[7] Gennadius, *De viris illustribus*, 45, (P.L. lviii, 1084).

inscriptions[1] — very different inscriptions from the fighting-slogans placed in the African churches.[2]

We can even see a charming strain of 'primitivism' in Julian. His picture of the state of Adam in Paradise, the 'harmless farmer of a pleasant plot'[3] with God as a friendly landlord,[4] is one of a long series of idealized pictures of peasant life, such as had appealed to sophisticated men in the ancient world: it was particularly appropriate in a young man who had grown up near the landscape that had inspired the *Georgics* of Vergil.[5] For a Pelagian, this pastoral idyll was a serious matter. For the Pelagians believed that the happiness that had existed in the past, could, with an effort of will, be made to happen again in the present. No irreversible Fall of Man,[6] only a thin wall of corrupt manners stood between Julian and the delightful innocence of man's first state.[7] Even when Julian married, Paulinus of Nola could bless this simple, clerical occasion, untouched by the vulgarity of a fashionable wedding, as an attempt to recapture the *simplicitas*, the unaffected innocence[8] of Adam and Eve.

The ideals of Pelagius took such a young man by storm. He became the lifelong ally of Caelestius. When the condemnation of his heroes became official, in 418, it was Julian, now aged about 35 and a popular figure among the monks and noblemen of his neighbourhood, who led the resistance of a group of 18 Italian bishops.[9] Driven from Italy next year, he found himself more at home in the Greek East. For, unlike Augustine, he came from a cosmopolitan family[10] and had learnt Greek.[11] He was sympathetically received by Theodore of Mopsuestia in Cilicia;[12] and, with Caelestius, he would try his fortune at Constantinople. As late as 439, he almost succeeded in reinstating himself as a bishop in Italy. He died in Sicily, having spent almost half his life in exile, a 'marked man', the 'Cain of our times', teaching the Latin alphabet to the children of a Pelagian family. On his tomb, his friends

---

[1] Diehl, *Inscript. Lat. Christ. vet.*, i, 2474.

[2] e.g. Diehl, *Inscript. Lat. Christ. vet.*, i, 2489.   [3] *Op. Imp.* VI, 12.

[4] *Op. Imp.* VI, 20.   [5] Cited frequently: e.g. *Op. Imp.* III, 129; IV, 38; V, 11.

[6] *Op. Imp.* VI, 26.   [7] Hence the citation of Juvenal, (*Sat.* I, 5, 119), in *Op. Imp.* VI, 29.

[8] Paulinus, *Carmen*, XXV, esp. l. 102.   [9] v. sup. p. 362.

[10] If his father-in-law was Aemilius of Beneventum, who had distinguished himself on a mission to Constantinople.

[11] Gennadius, *de vir. ill.*, 45, (P.L. lviii, 1084). Bruckner, *Julian*, p. 77, finds little trace of Greek in his writings against Augustine.

[12] On the sympathy of the two men, which, however, need not amount to 'Pelagian' influence on Theodore, v. J. Gross, *Entstehungsgeschichte d. Erbsündendogmas*, i, 1960, pp. 190–204. v. *Op. Imp.* IV, 88: it is Jerome, not Augustine who is criticized by Theodore.

would place a final challenge to his victors: 'Here lies Julian, the *Catholic* bishop.'[1]

Julian was not a sympathetic person. Writing a Biblical commentary, for instance, he would go out of his way to shine at the expense of the expert, in this case Jerome, now safely dead: the old man's work, Julian said, had been so 'puerile', so unenterprising, so unoriginal, so arbitrary, that 'the reader can scarcely refrain from laughing'.[2] Julian devoted himself to ridiculing the ideas of his elders: Augustine, who treated him with a heavy-handed paternal touch, constantly urging the young man to remember his late father, an unexceptionable Catholic bishop, may well have hit on a sore spot in Julian's character.[3]

But it was not Julian's business to be pleasant. For twenty years, almost single-handed, he carried on a deadly feud against men who had foisted their own opinions on the church, who had denied him free discussion of his own views, who had exiled him from a bishopric in which he had been active and popular. *'Fill their countenance with ignominy'* had been Augustine's frank motto in conducting his own pamphlet-war against the Donatists.[4] Now this Biblical citation will be invoked against him by Julian,[5] in repeated waves of well-argued invective, that threatened to wash the ideas of Augustine out of the minds of educated Italians: *Patronus asinorum*, 'The lord of all donkeys.'[6]

For Julian, Augustine was always 'the African' — the *Poenus*. He waged his campaign against Augustine as a Punic War of the mind.[7] He saw to it, that his readers should treat his case as a defence of Italy against the *latrocinium*, the *Putsch*, by which a small party of well-organized Africans, headed by Augustine, seconded by Alypius, had imposed upon the Italian church a set of dogmas genuinely foreign to the spirit of the Christianity of their land.[8]

Julian had chosen his target carefully. Pelagianism had been condemned by the Pope and the Emperors. But it was one thing to condemn a heresy, quite another to set about suppressing it. The Africans had insisted on suppression: Alypius, in his diplomatic missions to the court of Ravenna, had imported into Italy the harsh methods that he had learnt in the campaign against the Donatists in Africa — the denial of free discussion, the exile of bishops.[9] Once organized opposition had

[1] The evidence for the last decades of the life of Julian is assembled by Vignier in P.L. xlv, 1040–1042 and accepted by Bruckner, *Julian*, esp. p. 72.

[2] v. Morin, in *Revue bénédictine*, 30, 1916, p. 4.   [3] e.g. *C. Jul.* I, iv, 11 and vii, 35.

[4] *Ps.* 82, 17. Cited in *C. litt. Petil.* I, xxix, 31.   [5] *Op. Imp.* V, 15.

[6] *Op. Imp.* IV, 46.   [7] e.g. *Op. Imp.* VI, 18.   [8] e.g. *Op. Imp.* I, 42 and 74.

[9] v. de Plinval, *Pélage*, pp. 341–347.

been crushed in this way, waverers would be 'taught' by Augustine. Sixtus, an influential Roman clergyman, had already received his treatise:[1] but Julian would see to it that there were many more, who needed urgently to be taught. Julian had active supporters in Rome;[2] Paulinus of Nola will still take Pelagian arguments seriously;[3] even non-Christians were involved: Volusianus, the sceptical pagan whose genteel incredulity had done much to provoke the *City of God*, will find himself forced, as Prefect of Rome, to carry out harsh measures against the Christian enemies of Augustine![4] Now Julian would tell such men that 'the helm of reason has been wrenched from the Church, so that opinions of the mob can sail ahead with all flags flying';[5] that the supporters of the Africans in Italy were the innocent (or the timorous) fellow-travellers of the Manichees; and that Augustine, in 'bellowing' the doctrine of original sin in all its fantastic and disgusting ramifications, was merely recalling from memory the teachings he had imbibed from Mani.[6]

Julian wrote at leisure in a foreign country. (It was a favourable environment for a polemist, as the example of Jerome had shown.)[7] He would produce, from 419 onwards, open letters, manifestoes on behalf of his colleagues, four great volumes ostentatiously demolishing one short work of Augustine's. Later, eight more volumes would have to be hastily forwarded in instalments from Rome by Alypius.

Augustine's 'teaching' of the terrorized Italians quickly degenerated into a personal duel with Julian. The duel was a dingy, rushed affair, and it lasted until Augustine's death. At Nola, Paulinus could die in peace, having allowed the Pelagians in the neighbourhood, friends and allies of his old friends, Memor and young Julian, to rejoin the Church.[8] In Hippo, Augustine will plod on, amid the destruction of his life's work in Africa, defending himself against a man young enough to be his son.

Augustine was a hardened campaigner. His works against Julian have the cold competence of an old, tired man, who knew only too well how to set about the harsh business of ecclesiastical controversy.

---

[1] *Ep.* 194 on which v. inf. p. 399.

[2] v. esp. H. v. Schubert, *Der sogenannte Praedestinatus*, (Texte u. Untersuchungen, 24, 4), 1903, esp. pp. 82–85.

[3] *de cura ger. pro mort.* 2: citing II Cor. 5, 10 in favour of individual responsibility as opposed to blind faith in the intercession of saints.

[4] in P.L. xlv, 1750–1751; v. A. Chastagnol, *La Préfecture urbaine à Rome*, pp. 170–171.

[5] *Op. Imp.* II, 1.   [6] *Op. Imp.* III, 170.

[7] Unfortunately, D. S. Wiesen, *St. Jerome as a Satirist*, 1964, is disappointing.

[8] Uranius, *de obitu sancti Paulini*, (P.L. iii, 859).

Julian had appealed to a 'high-brow' audience.[1] Augustine, shrewdly, will render him impotent by appealing to the 'middle-brows'. He assured his readers that Julian was an 'intellectual', bent on troubling the faith of simple military men, such as Count Valerius; that he was a man who thought himself above the healthy feelings of the man in the street,[2] a secular dilettante whose work could be understood only by those who had enjoyed the luxury of a university education.[3]

To move his readers in this way, Augustine will fall back on firmly entrenched positions, will appeal to dangerously primitive layers of feeling. Once again, for instance, he will find himself defending his own interpretation of the concrete rite of baptism. The bishops of Africa had long been accustomed, in their fierce controversies, to pinning precise and rigid doctrines on a rite that had pushed such deep roots in the feelings of their congregations.[4] Julian sensed rightly, that the widespread practice of infant baptism 'for the remission of sins', was Augustine's trump-card, the secret of his sinister demagogy.[5] Augustine will merely answer, that such a topic could not 'escape the notice of the people';[6] and, seeing that he had fought for all of 25 years to bring the masses of Africa over to his view of Catholic baptism, he spoke to his new Italian readers from bitter experience.

Not far from Hippo, at Uzalis, stories were already circulating which show how, working in Africa, Augustine had come to tap exceedingly primitive levels of feeling. A child had died as a mere catechumen, without baptism. In despair at his eternal damnation, his mother had taken him to the shrine of S. Stephen; he was raised from the dead merely in order to be baptized and then to die again, in the certainty of having avoided 'the second death' of Hell.[7] Even more revealing is the widespread sense of guilt and the insistence that a man could be saved only through such a visible rite of expiation. A noble lady will remain ill, until she dreams of a black dragon hovering unseen above her head. This dragon was the *reatus*, the abiding guilt of a long-forgotten sin: it is an echo in popular imagery, of that element of invisible, unconscious guilt, that plays such a part in Augustine's own doctrine of original sin.[8]

---

[1] *C. Jul.* II, x, 36 and V, i, 4; *Op. Imp.* II, 36. [2] e.g. *C. Jul.* V, i, 2.

[3] e.g. *C. Jul.* VI, xx, 64; *Op. Imp.* II, 51.

[4] e.g. *Op. Imp.* III, 199, an argument from the ceremony of exorcism as drastic as that of Optatus, *de schism. Don.*, IV, 6, (P.L. xi, 1037). Augustine admits that this is an argument which he uses for lack of time to elaborate any 'more subtle or shrewd' argument: *Ep.* 194, x, 46; cf. *Ep.* 193, ii, 4.

[5] e.g. *Op. Imp.* III, 137 and 138. [6] *C. Jul.* I, vii, 31.

[7] *de miraculis sancti Stephani*, I, xv, 1, (P.L. xli, 842). Augustine repeats this story to his own congregation: *Serm.* 323, 3 and 324.

[8] *de miraculis sancti Stephani*, II, ii, 6, (P.L. xli, 846–847).

In appealing to the average Catholic, Augustine had found Julian's weak point. Julian was clever, well-educated, he knew his Scriptures well; but he belonged to an earlier age. He had trained himself as a philosopher. Like the young Augustine, (whose philosophical works he had read), he was one of a considerable number of men of largely secular philosophical culture, who had found a niche for themselves in the Catholic hierarchy as hammers of the Manichees. Indeed, he depended for his success on making Augustine appear a Manichee, in order to demolish him with the weapons he could best command, with logic and a philosopher's concept of freedom.[1] He may have persuaded some modern scholars of the truth of his charges; but the average Italian clergyman was unimpressed.

For the times had changed. Augustine had not written his *de Doctrina Christiana* for nothing. A bishop of the fifth century would be moved by the authority of a great name such as Ambrose (whom Augustine will quote frequently). He felt that he belonged to a professional caste, possessing truths that had been passed on and elaborated through a chain of great 'experts', from Cyprian, through Hilary of Poitiers, to Ambrose.[2] As for the laymen of the court and aristocracy, bishops were increasingly important for them: they played a vital role in their intrigues, in the crisis-ridden society of Gaul and Italy; a man such as Valerius was proud, perhaps anxious, to have such influential local figures among his clients.[3] He would believe implicitly what the experts told him. He, and the bishops he patronized, would be duly shocked to hear that Julian, in discussing music, had mentioned Pythagoras and not David:[4] though it was Augustine, the author of the *de Musica*, a patently Pythagorean exercise in Christian guise,[5] from which the name David is notably absent, who pointed this out! Julian died teaching the classics to small children. To his smug adversaries, the punishment suited the crime: 'mundane' wisdom seemed out of place in a bishop.[6] In fact, Augustine had beaten Julian by two generations to the 'gold of the Egyptians', to the riches of pagan philosophy; and, in the receding culture of the Latin West, what little was left was now grudged to the greatest writer in the Pelagian cause.

---

[1] v. esp. Refoulé, 'Julien d'Éclane', *Rech. sc. relig.*, 52, 1964, esp. p. 241 f.: he was, of course, well-equipped by Augustine's own anti-Manichaean tract, *de ii animabus*, 14–15.

[2] Julian, significantly, skirts round Augustine's citations from Ambrose: *Op. Imp.* IV, 110–113.

[3] *Ep.* 206.   [4] *C. Jul.* V, v, 23.

[5] v. sup. p. 126. Memor was aware of the omission when he had asked about the metre used by David.

[6] Fulgentius in P.L. xlv, 1041–1042.

Julian had been a singularly challenging opponent. We have only begun to appreciate the extent of his learning and originality. Though he wrote as a Latin for Latins, the 'learned reader' of his heart's desire existed not in Rome but in Antioch and Cilicia. In his use of Aristotle, he anticipates a Christian humanism such as would only be realized 700 years later. The 'Council of the Aristotelians', which Augustine jeeringly dismissed as the last court of appeal of the Pelagians,[1] would meet — in the university of Paris, in the thirteenth century: and it would include S. Thomas Aquinas, whose humane synthesis Julian had anticipated on many points.[2]

Yet only a modern scholar is sufficiently distant from the controversy, to handle the highly-provocative statements of Julian without feeling the blisters he originally intended to inflict. Augustine, thrown on to the defensive by so vehement an attack, could only save himself by refusing to recognize the value of Julian's ideas. A great opportunity was missed. Compared with the sensitive dialogue which Augustine was quite prepared to enter into with pagan Platonists in the *City of God*, before much the same cultivated audience as Julian now addressed, his treatment of the challenge of Julian, a fellow-Christian bishop, was an unintelligent slogging-match. There is an element of tragedy in this encounter. Seldom in the history of ideas has a man as great as Augustine or as very human, ended his life so much at the mercy of his own blind-spots.

(II)[3]

'You ask me why I would not consent to the idea that there is a sin that is part of human nature?', Julian wrote of Augustine's doctrine of original sin, 'I answer: it is improbable, it is untrue; it is unjust and impious; it makes it seem as if the Devil were the maker of men. It violates and destroys the freedom of the will ... by saying that men are so incapable of virtue, that in the very wombs of their mothers they are filled with bygone sins. You imagine so great a power in such a sin, that not only can it blot out the new-born innocence of nature, but, forever afterwards, will force a man throughout his life into every form of viciousness.... (And) what is as disgusting as it is blasphemous,

[1] *C. Jul.* II, x, 37.

[2] Refoulé, 'Julien d'Éclane', *Rech. sc. relig.*, 52, 1964, esp. p. 72 on 'concupiscence' in Julian and S. Thomas; but with reservations (e.g. p. 62). v. the remarks of Thonnard, *Rev. études augustin.*, xi, 1965, pp. 298–304.

[3] On the position of Augustine, I am particularly indebted to the brilliant exposition of Burnaby, *Amor Dei*, esp. pp. 184–214.

this view of yours fastens, as its most conclusive proof, on the common decency by which we cover our genitals.'[1]

The idea that some great sin lay behind the misery of the human condition was shared by pagans[2] and Christians[3] in Late Antiquity. Augustine had met it early in his life as a Catholic: 'The Ancient Sin: nothing is more obviously part of our preaching of Christianity; yet nothing is more impenetrable to the understanding.'[4] Now that the Pelagians had hedged this mystery with hostile questions, Augustine would give them drastic answers. Thus, while many Catholics in Africa and in Italy[5] already believed that the 'first sin' of Adam had somehow been inherited by his descendants, Augustine will tell them precisely where they should look in themselves for abiding traces of this first sin. With the fatal ease of a man who believes that he can explain a complex phenomenon, simply by reducing it to its historical origins, Augustine will remind his congregation of the exact circumstances of the Fall of Adam and Eve. When they had disobeyed God by eating the forbidden fruit, they had been 'ashamed': they had covered their genitals with fig-leaves.[6] That was enough for Augustine: '*Ecce unde*. That's the place! That's the place from which the first sin is passed on.'[7] This shame at the uncontrollable stirring of the genitals was the fitting punishment of the crime of disobedience.[8] Nothing if not circumstantial, Augustine will drive his point home by suddenly appealing to his congregation's sense of shame at night-emissions.[9]

Augustine lived in an ascetic age, where the sensitive man already felt humiliated by his body[10] and where his clerical readers would have been increasingly celibate.[11] But compared with the hot shame of a man such as Ambrose,[12] Augustine will develop his views with a cold, clinical precision. Sexual feeling as men now experience it, was a penalty. Because it was a penalty for disobedience, it was itself disobedient, 'a torture to the will:'[13] thus it is the element of loss of control in the sexual act, that is isolated. Because it was a permanent

[1] *Op. Imp.* III, 67 sq.

[2] e.g. Cicero cited in *C. Jul.* IV, xiii, 78; v. esp. Dodds, *Pagan and Christian*, pp. 23–24.

[3] v. esp. the surveys of N. P. Williams, *The Idea of the Fall and of Original Sin*, 1927 and J. Gross, *Entstehungsgeschichte d. Erbsündendogmas*, i, 1960.

[4] *de mor. eccl. cath.* (I), xxii, 40.

[5] v. esp. Williams, *The Idea of the Fall*, pp. 294–310. In a late third-century Gallic sarcophagus, the rite of baptism is shown in close relation to a picture of the Fall of Adam; v. F. Van der Meer, 'À propos du sarcophage du Mas d'Aire', *Mélanges Christine Mohrmann*, 1963, pp. 169–176.

[6] *Serm.* 151, 5.   [7] *Serm.* 151, 5.   [8] *Serm.* 151, 5.   [9] *Serm.* 151, 8.
[10] v. Dodds, *Pagan and Christian*, pp. 29–30.   [11] e.g. *de grat. et lib. arb.* iv, 7.
[12] Cited in *C. Jul.* II, vi, 15.   [13] *de nupt. et concup.* I, xxiv, 27.

punishment, it was presented as a permanent tendency, as an instinctual tension that could be resisted, but which, even when repressed, would remain active,[1] imprisoning a man in the sexual element of his imagination: it manifested itself in dreams;[2] it held a man away from the contemplation of God by the sheer quality of his thoughts, by 'a pressing throng of desires'.[3]

This is a strictly psychological view. It emphasized subjective elements — tensions caused by shame, by loss of control, by the imagination.[4] In this, Augustine meticulously avoided appearing as a Manichee or an extreme Platonist: the life of the senses, he insisted, was not in itself evil, only the tension that arose when the will, directed by reason, clashed with the appetites. But of all the appetites, the only one that seemed to Augustine to clash inevitably and permanently with reason, was sexual desire. Augustine knew himself to be potentially a very greedy man:[5] but greed could be controlled; in the High Table atmosphere of Augustine's monastery, it had been possible to 'entertain and discuss serious matters' at dinner,[6] but not, Augustine thought, in bed — 'for in that business, what man is able to entertain any thought at all, let alone of Wisdom. . . .'[7] Thus at one stroke, Augustine will draw the boundary between the positive and the negative elements in human nature along a line dividing the conscious, rational mind from the one 'great force', that escaped its control.[8]

Augustine was a polemist determined to convince the average man. Such a polemist is inevitably a sorcerer's apprentice: for he can canonize, on paper, the fears and prejudices that the average man accepts unconsciously. Thus, writing to a common married man like Count Valerius, he will claim that this invidious isolation of sexuality was not only demonstrated 'by subtle reasoning': it was confirmed by the 'facts', by 'universally-accepted opinion'.[9] Such 'facts' included the shame surrounding intercourse,[10] the frequent condemnation of passion in ancient authors,[11] even the manner in which men cover their genitals when alone.[12]

Like so many men who claim in public controversy to be speaking as 'realists', Augustine had come to rest his case on the hoary stereotypes of popular opinion. He was accustomed to such tricks. Writing

[1] e.g. C. Jul. IV, ii, 10.   [2] C. Jul. IV, ii, 10.   [3] C. Jul. VI, xviii, 56 cf:
[4] Augustine is sometimes consistent enough to treat impotence as being as significant as passion: e.g. de pecc. mer. I, xxix, 57.
[5] v. sup. p. 179.   [6] C. Jul. IV, xiii, 71.   [7] C. Jul. IV, xiii, 71.
[8] C. Jul. IV, xiii, 71.   [9] de nupt. et concup. I, vii, 8.
[10] de nupt. et concup. I, xxi, 24.   [11] e.g. C. Jul. IV, xii, 59.
[12] de civ. Dei, XIV, 17.

to justify religious coercion to men not very different from Valerius, he will argue in favour of suppressing heresy from the dangerous analogy of social restraint on all levels.[1] Now Augustine will come to erect a highly-sophisticated view of the psychological tension between reason and instinct in sexuality, upon the murky foundations of traditional Roman attitudes to intercourse in marriage. Views on such a subject have usually been among the least-dusted corners of common moral attitudes: and nowhere more than in the appalling insensitivity of some ancient Romans, who treated sexual passion in a wife with contempt.[2]

Yet, given the harsh moral climate of the age, (in which, for instance, the princess Galla Placidia, a dominant figure at the court of Ravenna, held strong views on clerical celibacy — [3] a fact which Valerius could hardly afford to ignore), Augustine was a moderate man. He expected that, ideally, intercourse should take place only to conceive children; but this was no more than austere pagans had demanded. He considered that the extreme views of some Christians, that marriage should be a competition in continence, was not applicable to the average man;[4] and he knew very well that it was positively harmful if used by one partner against the other.[5] Yet, twenty years previously, in the mellow mood that had coincided with the writing of the *Confessions*, Augustine had even gone so far as to suggest, with great sensitivity, that the quality of sexual intercourse itself might be modified and transformed by the permanent friendship of two people in marriage.[6] Now, however, he will isolate sexual intercourse as an element of evil encapsulated in every marriage, an element whose significance is grotesquely magnified by being so carefully fenced in by a heavy frame of the virtues and joys of respectable Catholic wedlock: Valerius might have fidelity, friendship, children, 'but when it comes to the act itself. . . .'[7] Augustine, after all, had always isolated this element in himself. When he had contemplated marriage, he had seen himself 'not as an admirer of the idea of marriage, but a slave of lust': he plainly regarded with horror the prospect of being accompanied into 'a wife's kingdom' — the *regnum uxorium* — by what, for him, were compulsive sexual habits.[8]

Julian spoke boldly of the sexual instinct as a sixth sense of the body, as a neutral energy that might be used well, of man as a microcosm,

---

[1] v. sup. pp. 239–240.   [2] The attitude of Cato, cited in *de nupt. et concup.* I, xv, 17.
[3] e.g. *Cod. Theod.* XVI, 2, 44 of 420.
[4] v. Dodds, *Pagan and Christian*, p. 32. He had few illusions as to the difficulties which married couples experienced in adhering to this rule: *de bono coniug.* xiii, 15.
[5] *de bono coniug.* vii, 6 and *Ep.* 262.   [6] *de bono coniug.* iii, 3.
[7] *de nupt. et concup.* I, xxiii, 27.   [8] *Conf.* VI, xvi, 25.

delicately poised between reason and animal feeling.[1] Augustine would not listen. He refused to believe that the young man could stop at anything: it is the tragic and highly unpleasant manner of a man whose convictions were based upon a savage denial of all his opponent had seemed to propose: 'Really, really: is that your experience? So you would not have married couples restrain that evil — I refer, of course, to your favourite good? So you would have them jump into bed whenever they like, whenever they feel tickled by desire. Far be it from them to postpone this itch till bedtime: let's have your "*legitimate union of bodies*" whenever your "*natural good*" is excited. If this is the sort of married life you led, don't drag up your experience in debate. . . .'[2]

It is easy for the modern man to feel involved in this aspect of the clash between Augustine and Julian. Julian has often been dismissed as a great 'might have been', as a man whose optimistic view of human nature fitted him for any century but his own.[3] In a sense, this is a back-handed compliment to Julian: it tends to minimize the challenge he presented. For he spoke very well the language of his own age, and of the Early Latin Church on one essential point: he upheld with passion the equity of God. Both protagonists were entirely religious men. They both treated their views on sexuality as secondary:[4] it was not the nature of man alone that interested them, it was the nature of God. *Deus Christianorum*,[5] 'The God of the Christians', had only recently been established in the imagination of ancient men: Latin Christians stood at a cross-roads, between Julian and Augustine, deciding in which way to view their God.

The God of Augustine was a God Who had imposed a collective punishment for the sin of one man. ' "*Tiny babies*", you say, "*are not weighed down by their own sin, but they are being burdened with the sin of another.*" Tell me then', Julian will ask Augustine, 'tell me: who is this person who inflicts punishment on innocent creatures. . . . You answer: God. God, you say! God! He Who *commended His love to us*, Who *has loved us*, Who *has not spared His own Son for us*. . . . He it is, you say, Who judges in this way; He is the persecutor of new-born children; He it is who sends tiny babies to eternal flames. . . . It would be right and proper to treat you as beneath argument: you have come so far from religious feeling, from civilized thinking, so far, indeed, from mere common sense, in that you think that your Lord God is

---

[1] Notably in *Op. Imp.* IV, 39–41.   [2] *C. Jul.* III, xiv, 28.
[3] e.g. Harnack, *History of Dogma*, v, (Dover), p. 170.   [4] e.g. Julian in *Op. Imp.* VI, 1.
[5] *Op. Imp.* V, 64. Significantly, this forms the title of an excellent study of Tertullian, by R. Braun, '*Deus Christianorum*'. *Recherches sur le vocabulaire doctrinal de Tertullien*, 1962.

capable of committing a crime against justice such as is hardly conceivable even among the barbarians.'[1]

The Lord is just, He has loved justice, His countenance has looked favourably upon equity.[2] This sums up the religion of Julian. It was God's justice that made him 'the holiest of beings':[3] a justice that weighed the deeds of each separate individual separately, 'without fraud or favour.' Justice was the 'crowning virtue'. It was the image of God in man.[4] A God that was not just, therefore, was so far beyond natural reason that He could not exist:[5] 'It would be better by far to take our necks away from beneath the yoke of religious belief, than to wander abandoned by all sense of justice, through such disastrous, such odious opinions.'[6] The punishment of others for the sin of their father, the condemnation of helpless babies, the passing of sentence on men who had been unable to act otherwise; the whole Christian revelation was a measured and authoritative declaration against such *iniquitas*, such corrupt dealing.[7]

Julian represents one peak of Roman civilization. What he defended in God was the rationality and universal force of law.[8] He saw in the God of Augustine not what a modern man might tend to see — the creator of a Hell filled with small children:[9] what he attacked was the tyrannical governor of a long Roman tradition, a divine Verres, standing trial again for the massive proscription of the innocent.[10]

This was a cause that Julian's readers could understand. He could look back to the very beginnings of Latin Christianity to find a kindred spirit in the great Tertullian, 'one of the formative minds of European civilization,'[11] and, like Julian, a passionate advocate of the legal nature of the bonds between God and man.[12] What Julian said was intelligible and relevant to his contemporaries: for the cultivated Italian bishop found himself confronted, not by an enlightened pagan humanism, but by dark ideas that robbed men of their freedom and their separate identity — by astrology, by magic, by the Manichees.[13] Julian's 'thunderbolt' could blast the whole system of Augustine:[14] for only a burning sense of the traditional norms of justice could treat each

---

[1] *Op. Imp.* I, 48 sq.   [2] *Ps.* 10, 8.   [3] *Op. Imp.* I, 49.   [4] *Op. Imp.* I, 37.
[5] *Op. Imp.* I, 28.   [6] *Op. Imp.* III, 27.   [7] *Op. Imp.* I, 14.
[8] v. esp. the technical language of Roman legislation constantly applied to the Bible: *Op. Imp.* II, 136; III, 34 and 43.
[9] Not without some regret: e.g. *Ep.* 166, vi, 16; and insisting on the 'lightest of all penalties': *C. Jul.* V, xi, 44.
[10] *Op. Imp.* I, 48.   [11] W. H. C. Frend, *Martyrdom and Persecution*, p. 366.
[12] v. the most instructive study of J. H. Baxter, 'Notes on the Latin of Julian of Eclanum', *Bulletin du Cange*, 21, 1949, pp. 5–54, esp. p. 12.
[13] *Op. Imp.* I, 82.   [14] *Op. Imp.* III, 20.

man as free, as responsible for his actions, as a person separate from the sinister mass into which the God of Augustine had fused the human race: *'The righteousness of the righteous shall be upon his own head, and the wickedness of the wicked man shall be upon himself alone.'*[1]

'I am amazed', Julian would write, 'that anyone should entertain the slightest doubt as to the equity of God.'[2] 'You must distinguish', Augustine would reply, 'you must distinguish the justice of God from human ideas of justice.'[3] For Julian, the Bible contained a single, utterly consistent message: like a noble family, no part of it was 'bastard or low-born';[4] there were no pockets of primitive vengeance, no supports for theories of blood guilt. Augustine was not so sure. Far above the sunlit surface of Julian's Bible, the God of Augustine had remained the ineffable God of the Neo-Platonic mystic. The justice of God was as inscrutable as any other aspect of His nature,[5] and human ideas of equity as frail as 'dew in the desert'.[6] Far below human ideas of innocence, the guilt of Adam had been incurred by an 'unspeakable' sin, a sin that 'far surpassed the experience of men today': a sin beyond reason, inherited in a way that was 'frankly speaking, marvellous'.[7] Julian might use his reason to define a newborn baby as innocent. The eyes of God, in the Scriptures, saw deeper. The thin crust of human equity trembled at such statements as *'I shall visit the sins of the father on the children'*:[8] all Augustine could know, was that God's omniscience would not err, as mere human vengeance might err, as He pursued His awesome blood-feud against the family of Adam.[9]

Julian accused Augustine of being a Manichee. As we have seen, this was partly good tactics on his part.[10] Julian, indeed, did not have the same mastery of Manichaean doctrine as Augustine. Mani's great *Letter of the Foundation* lay to hand on the bookshelves of Hippo, its margins filled with critical notes:[11] thus equipped, it was as easy for Augustine as it is for a modern scholar of Manichaean literature to see the difference between his own system and that of Mani, and to shrug off Julian's accusations as a caricature of both.[12]

Yet the quality of a religious system depends perhaps less on its specific doctrine, than on the choice of problems that it regards as important, the areas of human experience to which it directs attention.

---

[1] *Ezech.* 18, 20, cited in *Op. Imp.* III, 49. [2] *Op. Imp.* III, 7. [3] *Op. Imp.* III, 27.
[4] *Op. Imp.* I, 4. [5] *Serm.* 341, 9. [6] *Ad Simplicianum de div. quaest.* qu. ii, 16.
[7] *de nupt. et concup.* I, xix, 21; cf. *C. Jul.* III, xix, 37.
[8] e.g. *Exod.* 34, 7 and the other Old Testament citations in *Op. Imp.* I, 50 and III, 12–15.
[9] e.g. *C. Jul.* VI, xxv, 82.   [10] v. sup. p. 386.   [11] *Retract.* II, 28.
[12] e.g. *Op. Imp.* I, 97 corrects Julian on the implications of Manichaean dualism.

Writing against Julian, Augustine found himself agreeing whole-heartedly with Mani. Christianity was a religion of salvation: whether for the soul alone, or for soul and body, Christ had come as a saviour.[1] Man's present life was an insubstantial shadow, a nadir of existence, intelligible only in terms of a great Myth of Fall and Restoration. Mesopotamia, that land fertile in myths contrasting the first state of man with his present misery, had provided both Augustine with the opening chapters of the book of *Genesis*, and Mani with his vision of the present human race as a horrible outcome of the War of the Two Kingdoms. To justify this view of religion, both men will insist that the desperate problem of suffering was the first issue that a religious thinker had to face.[2] 'The most blatant misery of the human race' forces itself to the foreground in Augustine's later works against Julian. When he rounds on Julian for blandly defining away the extent of human unhappiness, we can at last sense an upsurge of genuine feeling, of moral outrage, a refusal to abandon hopes for something better, to deny unpleasant facts for the sake of intellectual comfort that has flowed towards pessimism in many sensitive thinkers.[3] If Paul had been forced to prove his assertions on original sin, Augustine believed he would have turned his readers' attention, as Augustine did, to the extent of suffering in this world.[4]

The Manichaean missionaries had certainly done this in order to publicize their myth.[5] It is perhaps significant, that Augustine should have turned to the *Hortensius* of Cicero to make his case against Julian. He recognized in this book, the quintessence of pagan wisdom on the wretchedness of the human condition.[6] Had Augustine wandered back in his memory to the months, when as a young student in Carthage, he had stepped from reading these grim citations in the *Hortensius* of Cicero into the conventicles of the Manichaeans? He was still asking: *Unde hoc malum?* 'Whence comes all this evil?'[7]

A religion that places the problem of suffering in the centre of its message to the world, has to face in a particularly acute form, the problem of the relation between God and evil. Mani had cut off God from the horror of human existence. Julian remarked that at least such a God was 'utterly divorced from all cruelty'. Augustine would reply immediately, that in preserving the innocence of God, Mani had made Him 'cruelly weak'.[8] Augustine would never dare to commit himself again to the feelings of helpless violation by alien forces, of desolation

[1] *de nupt. et concup.* II, iii, 9.
[2] *de nupt. et concup.* II, xxix, 50.
[3] e.g. *C. Jul.* IV, xiii, 83.
[4] *Op. Imp.* I, 25.
[5] e.g. *de mor. Man.* (II), ix, 14.
[6] e.g. *C. Jul.* IV, xiii, 72.
[7] *Op. Imp.* V, 16.
[8] *Op. Imp.* I, 120

and profound loneliness, which play so large a part in the religious feelings of the Manichees.[1] God to him was now omnipotent: this, he reminds Julian, was 'the opening-declaration of our faith'.[2] But if God is absolutely omnipotent, nothing happens unless he causes it to happen or permits it to happen: and as He is absolutely just, the appalling sufferings of the human race could only be permitted, because He was angry.[3] For why else could the omnipotent possibly permit the evils that Augustine saw around him?[4] '*He has sent upon them the anger of his indignation, indignation and rage and tribulation, and possession by evil spirits.*'[5]

God had plainly allowed the human race to be swept by His wrath: and this human race, as Augustine presents it in his works against Julian, is very like the invaded universe of Mani. Augustine had always believed in the vast power of the Devil: God had shown His omnipotence most clearly in restraining this superhuman creature,[6] whose aggressive force was so great that he would obliterate the whole Christian church if released.[7] Now this Devil will cast his shadow over mankind: the human race is 'the Devil's fruit-tree, his own property, from which he may pick his fruit',[8] it is a 'plaything of demons'.[9] This is evil, thought of much as the Manichees had done, as a persecutory force. The demons may now have been enrolled as the unwitting agents of a superior justice: but it is they who are seen as active, and man as merely passive. Small babies are exposed to 'invasion' by them in the form of fits, and men in general, to every imaginable temptation, disease and natural catastrophe.[10] Disease, and those disasters before which men were helpless, had always been used by the Manichees as evidence, *par excellence*, of an active and overwhelming force of evil.[11] So when Augustine returns to this theme of suffering as a passive state in the 'small-scale Hell' of the world,[12] we can catch an echo, if not of the great myths of Mani himself, at least of the sombre homilies of the Manichaean Elect.

The world, in the Later Empire as now, is only too easily filled with invisible persecutors. Envious powers hover around the newborn child

---

[1] v. sup. pp. 51–53.   [2] *Op. Imp.* I, 49.

[3] e.g. *de civ. Dei*, XXI, 24, 78: 'for this life, for mortals, is "*The Wrath of God*".'

[4] v. the very revealing comment that if men were in a position to stop the evils around them and did not do so, they would be held guilty of them: *C. Jul.* V, iii, 14.

[5] *Ps.* 77, 49, cited in *C. Jul.* V, iii, 8; cf. *C. Jul.* VI, viii, 31.

[6] e.g. *de civ. Dei*, XX, 8, 41.

[7] *Enarr. in Ps.* 61, 20 and *Denis* 21, 6, (*Misc. Agostin.*, i, p. 130).

[8] *de nupt. et concup.* I, xxiii, 26.   [9] *C. Jul.* VI, xxi, 67.   [10] v. *de civ. Dei*, XXII, 22.

[11] v. Chavannes-Pelliot, *Journal asiatique*, sér. X, xviii, 1911, p. 517, note 2.

[12] *Op. Imp.* VI, 30.

in many societies. Augustine's contemporary, John Chrysostom was
no optimist, yet he had to insist that small babies were innocent: for his
congregation believed that newborn babies could be killed by sorcery,
and their souls possessed by demons.[1] His protest at least preserved a
tiny oasis of personal responsibility. But Augustine will flood the
world with uncontrollable powers, under the shadow of the justice of
his God.

For, if suffering is seen only as the just reward of guilt, it is drained
of its value. Twenty years previously, Augustine had rallied whole
congregations, shaken by the sack of Rome, in brave sermons on the
necessity, the purpose, the opportunity for new growth presented by
suffering.[2] Now such suffering has become flat and sinister: for those
who are not the elect, (and this would include babies who had died
without baptism), suffering was merely 'torture inflicted as a punishment',[3] a visible reminder of the future penalties of Hell,[4] a horrible
overture to the terror of the Last Judgement.

For in the last resort, there was much that Augustine had refused to
accept in the life around him: areas of experience had become unbearable to him, because they had been too long denied. He will react with
horror to the suggestion of Julian, that life in Paradise would have been
much like life as it was now lived. If this was so, Augustine repeatedly
insisted, terrible things would have to be admitted into that encapsuled,
unviolated area of past innocence. It would include the inexplicable
sufferings of small children, the horrors of the deformed and the
mentally defective: but far worse, a whole world of rejected and
devalued experience would sidle in around Augustine, as he imagined
this 'Paradise of the Pelagians': the invisible stirrings of lust, the
degradations of pregnant women,[5] intercourse untrammelled and —
why not? — in every imaginable manner.[6] Last of all, Julian would
'fill this sheltered garden of perfect, measured and complete delight
with ill-omened and repulsive sights: with the funerals of dead
men....'[7]

Augustine wrote this last sentence in the days before a fever caught
him. The last work against Julian remained unfinished. Its last pages

---

[1] John Chrysostom, *Hom. 28 in Matthaeum*, (*Patrologia Graeca*, lvii, 353).

[2] e.g. *Enarr. in Ps.* 136, 9: 'a therapy, not a punishment'; v. esp. *de Gen. ad litt.* XI,
xxxv, 48 where 'the whole grinding-down of this existence', the shameful quality of
sexuality after the Fall included, is treated as a discipline leading to self-knowledge and
humility.

[3] *de corrept. et gratia*, xiv, 43. [4] *C. Jul.* III, vi, 12.

[5] e.g. *Op. Imp.* III, 154. [6] *de nupt. et concup.* II, xxxv, 59.

[7] *Op. Imp.* VI, 41.

are a tragic revelation of one facet of the old man, of the fearsome intensity with which he had driven the problem of evil into the heart of Christianity: 'This is the Catholic view: a view that can show a just God in so many pains and in such agonies of tiny babies.'[1]

[1] *Op. Imp.* I, 22.

33

PREDESTINATION[1]

Julian knew only too well that he was a voice crying in a deafened world.[2] His Latin colleagues had been silenced. An elderly friend of Paulinus of Nola had 'sinned by speaking' in favour of the Pelagians:[3] it was a 'sin' which men now thought more prudent to avoid. For Augustine had on his bookshelf a personal copy of an Imperial law threatening deposition and exile to any bishop convicted of Pelagian views;[4] and in 425, the bishops of S. Gaul had been summoned at the behest of the Italian authorities, to face an enquiry designed to detect Pelagian sympathizers.[5] It is not surprising that, in such an atmosphere, the supporters of Julian in Rome had to content themselves with the all-too-easy task of turning the works that Augustine had poured in upon them, into a caricature.[6]

The Pelagian controversy, however, had been decided exclusively among the bishops of the Latin church. One vital area had not been touched: the monasteries. The Mediterranean had come to be ringed with dynamic little communities: in Africa, at Hadrumetum, along the southern coast of Gaul, at Marseilles and Lérins. Such monasteries were often led by men of totally different background from Augustine. John Cassian, for instance, at Lérins, had come from the Balkans, had been a monk in Egypt, had become a disciple of John Chrysostom at Constantinople. He was a living representative, in the midst of the Latin world, of views that Augustine had never absorbed, of the opti-

---

[1] I am particularly indebted to the most stimulating discussions of Augustine's position in Burnaby, *Amor Dei*, pp. 226–241, and R. Lorenz, 'Der Augustinismus Prospers v. Aquitanien', *Zeitschrift für Kirchengeschichte*, 73, 1962, pp. 217–252, esp. pp. 238–250.

[2] *Op. Imp.* II, 102. [3] Gennadius, *de vir. ill.*, 19, (P.L. lviii, 1073).

[4] in *Ep.* 201. [5] in P.L. xlv, 1751.

[6] v. Schubert, *Der sogennante Praedestinatus*, esp. p. 21. Book III of the *Praedestinatus* is a brilliant caricature, (P.L. liii, 627–672).

mistic traditions of Origen.[1] Even the libraries of such monasteries had remained splendidly innocent of the controversies of their bishops: the great diplomatic documents — the doctrinal decisions of the African councils, the answers of the Popes, the closely-reasoned manifestoes of Augustine — were not to be found on the shelves of the abbot of Hadrumetum.[2] The monks had enjoyed the freedom, the lack of interest in past issues, even the irresponsibility, of a generation that had grown up after a Great War. They would tend to judge the works of Augustine strictly on their own merits, in terms of their implications for men pursuing the perfect life. They would not be impressed when Augustine spoke to them as a veteran of the Great War:[3] when he justified himself by carrying its spirit into peacetime, by writing in terms of the causes and strategies of a past struggle and by insisting that the traditional enemy of the Catholic faith was still the Pelagianism that had been defeated ten years previously.

Nine years after the official decision against Pelagius, that is in 427, a monk of Hadrumetum, Florus, visited the library of Evodius at Uzalis. He returned to his community with a copy of Augustine's long letter to the priest Sixtus, (Letter 194), which had closed the Pelagian controversy in the Roman church. Far from making Florus popular, this document caused an uproar of protest.[4] It is the beginning of a 'revolt of the monasteries', which will occupy Augustine for the rest of his life.[5]

The Letter 194 to Sixtus had been a manifesto of unconditional surrender written in the heat of controversy. Sixtus should remain in no doubt as to the implications of the defeat of Pelagius. It was God alone who determined the destinies of men, and these destinies could only be seen as an expression of His Wisdom.[6] The Wisdom of God, for the old Augustine, bruised human reason.[7] The first stirring of men's own wills was 'prepared' by God, and God, in His timeless Wisdom, had decided to 'prepare' only the wills of a few.[8]

---

[1] O. Chadwick, *John Cassian*, 1950, and esp. P. Munz, 'John Cassian', *Journ. Eccles. Hist.*, xi, 1960, pp. 1–22.

[2] *Ep.* 215, 2.   [3] e.g. *de dono persev.* xxi, 55.   [4] *Ep.* 216, 3.

[5] v. esp. J. Chéné, 'Les origines de la controverse semi-pélagienne', *Année théol. augustin.*, 13, 1953, pp. 56–109.

[6] 'Wisdom', the antithesis of 'Fate' or 'Fortune', is central to the Augustinian idea of predestination: e.g. *Ep.* 194, ii, 5. For the very different reaction of Augustine from that of Origen, even of S. Paul, to the idea of the 'depth' of the Wisdom of God, v. esp. M. Pontet, *L'Exégèse de S. Augustin*, p. 499, and esp. p. 513: '"O altitudo" reste chez lui un cri de terreur plus que d'amour débordant et stupéfait'.

[7] As in *Ep.* 190, iii, 12.

[8] *Ep.* 194, ii, 3–4. v. A. Sage, '"Praeparatur voluntas a Deo"', *Rev. études augustin.*, x, 1964, pp. 1–20. The classic statement of Augustine's position is O. Rottmanner, *Der Augustinismus*, 1892, (French transl. in *Mélanges de science religieuse*, vi, 1949, pp. 31–48).

This was a dangerous document to bring to monks. Such men always lived on the borderline of eccentricity: for, in the Early Church as in Byzantium and Russia, a monk's life could easily be treated as a training for complete passivity to the supernatural.[1] A strong tradition of prayer, 'in the spirit', for instance, had already encouraged some African monks to devalue other, more pedestrian and commonsense activities: in 400, they would not work;[2] in 427, they would not be rebuked by their abbot — for the opponents of Florus at Hadrumetum would argue that, if their wills depended upon God, the abbot should refrain from rebuking them, and should content himself with praying to God for their amendment. Passivity to the supernatural had usually been preceded by human effort: but in Augustine's doctrine, this passivity seemed to be robbed of any human context. If God had decided beforehand to deal only with a 'fixed quota' of men, His activity would seem utterly divorced from a monk's hopes and strivings.[3] 'A man is living badly', Augustine had said, 'and perhaps in the predestination of God he is light: another lives well, and perhaps he is as black as night.'[4]

In a monastic community, each monk was concerned with reaching a high goal, to establish his identity as an 'imitator of Christ'. Augustine placed this future identity far above human knowledge: and in a community that was particularly sensitive to just this issue, he seemed to condemn men to uncertainty, to despair, to an anxious paralysis of effort: 'There was once a man in my monastery', Augustine admitted, 'who, when rebuked by the brethren for doing things he should not have done and for not doing what he should do, replied: "Whatever I may be now, I shall be what God knows I will be".'[5]

In 428, Augustine received letters from two worried admirers in Southern Gaul, from Prosper and Hilary.[6] In their letters, we can see

---

This has been challenged in favour of a more optimistic interpretation, by F-J. Thonnard, in *Rev. études augustin.*, ix, 1963, pp. 259–287 and x, 1964, pp. 97–123. G. Nygren, *Das Prädestinationsproblem i.d. Theologie Augustins*, (Studia Theologica Lundensia, 12), 1956, is a very interesting evaluation. Pontet, *L'Exégèse de S. Augustin*, pp. 480–501, provides a brilliant characterization of the idea in Augustine's sermons.

[1] 'The mind is taken captive by Another's strength'; Meyendorff and Baynes, 'The Byzantine Inheritance in Russia', *Byzantium*, ed. Baynes and Moss, 1948, p. 380, (on the thought of Nil Sorski).

[2] v. G. Folliet, 'Les moines euchites à Carthage en 400–401', (Studia Patristica, ii), *Texte u. Untersuchungen*, 64, 1957, pp. 386–399.

[3] *Ep.* 225, 3 and *de praed. sanct.* x, 21.   [4] *Guelf.* 18, 1, (*Misc. Agostin.*, i, p. 499).

[5] *de don. persev.* xv, 38.

[6] *Epp.* 225 and 226. The letter of Prosper and his other writings are translated and commented by P. De Letter, *St. Prosper of Aquitaine, Defense of St. Augustine*, (Ancient Christian Writers, xxxii), 1963.

how the natural scruples of the monks widened in scope by crossing the Mediterranean. For monks from the communities of Lérins and Marseilles were already becoming bishops. Consequently, the quality of Christianity in Gaul was at stake. This was a Christianity confident both that the world needed it, and that the world felt this need.[1] Like Christ, it confronted men, saying: *'Believe and ye shall be made whole.'*[2] These men, so the Gallic monks and bishops thought, were free to respond to this challenge of their own free will: not, of course, like the strapping volunteers of the army of Pelagius, but at least in the manner of the sick men who had pressed in around Christ 'in terror, with a beseeching will'.[3] To say, as Augustine said, that men felt their need for salvation only when stirred to do so by God, and that He had decided to stir only a few, appeared to counsel the blackest pessimism: it drew a line across the human race as immovable as the division of Good and Evil Natures proposed by Mani.[4]

In Southern Gaul, the monasteries of the Côte d'Azur were being filled with new converts. These converts had every intention of becoming complete 'slaves' of God: but total obedience lost its obvious traditional meaning, if such men had not once been free to abandon their freedom.[5] Their experience of conversion may not have been like that of Augustine. They may have experienced no mysterious resolution of deep inner conflicts. Many of them were noblemen, shaken by the disasters that had overtaken their country, ruined by barbarian war-bands: they had come to the monasteries as 'suppliant sinners', but they plainly came of their own free will.[6]

Even the frontier of the Roman world had fallen open to such men. Christianity had come to the tribes that had entered the Roman Empire from the North;[7] in this generation, it would spill over into Scotland and Ireland. The response of utterly foreign peoples to the message of Christianity reassured men, that God *'wishes all men to be saved'*.[8] Augustine was concerned to explain away this passage,[9] Prosper to treat it as a 'trite objection',[10] but a simple faith in its truth will lead S. Patrick out of Roman Britain to the terrible Irish.[11]

---

[1] v. esp. the concise and suggestive remarks of J. M. Wallace-Hadrill, 'Gothia and Romania', *The Long-Haired Kings*, 1962, pp. 35–36.

[2] *Ep.* 226, 2. One should remember how frequently scenes showing Christ's miracles of healing appear on Early Christian sarcophagi as symbols of spiritual healing.

[3] *Ep.* 226, 2.   [4] *Ep.* 225, 3.   [5] e.g. *Ep.* 225, 6.

[6] e.g. the *Epigramma Paulini*, esp. l.1, (*Corpus Scriptorum Ecclesiae Latinorum*, xvi, pp. 503–506).

[7] *de vocatione omnium gentium*, ii, 16, (P.L. li, 704A).   [8] e.g. *Ep.* 225, 5.

[9] e.g. *de corrept. et gratia*, xiv, 44.   [10] Prosper, *Ep. ad Rufinum*, xiii, 14, (P.L. li, 85A).

[11] Patrick, *Confessio*, 16, (P.L. liii, 809–810).

In Africa, Augustine's faith was not bolstered by exciting missionary activities. His world had come to a stand-still. In the south, Christianity had never crossed the Roman frontier.[1] In the prosperous 'Christian Africa of the coastline, the great basilicas had been packed too long: 'What joy have we in such crowds? Hear me, you few. I know that many listen to me, few take any notice.'[2]

Valentinus, the abbot of Hadrumetum, wrote to his neighbours for their advice when first challenged by the issues raised among his monks by the views of Augustine. The answers of Evodius of Uzalis and of a priest, Januarianus, survive.[3] They are depressing documents. It was a monk's business, Evodius wrote, to weep for his imperfections, not to ask questions.[4] It was 'abominable', 'a devilish prompting' to question what had been laid down by a full council of the African Church.[5] '*A servant of God should not argue*',[6] Januarianus had added, with the shrewd advice that Valentinus should in future be more careful in deciding which books his monks should be allowed to read.[7] Both men were anxious to be 'tiny little men', 'mere babies'[8] — narrow men, that is, content to echo the view of their elders and betters. '*Ask thy father, and he shall show you, and thy elders and they shall tell you.*'[9]

Augustine, when he was approached by Valentinus, reacted very differently. He frankly admitted that he had raised 'a particularly difficult problem, which only a few can understand'.[10] Florus must come to Hippo to be helped.[11] Later Augustine wrote back to Valentinus: he had been ill when Florus arrived, and regretted not having seen as much of him as he had wished; perhaps Florus might return to continue his discussions?[12] This is the vehement opponent of Julian of Eclanum!

For Augustine felt at his ease among Catholic monks. His last works to them were the fruit of patient interviews, conducted at a time when, if not in bed, he was frequently physically too exhausted to meet visitors.[13] He would answer the community at Hadrumetum, as he will meet the questions of Prosper and Hilary, with complete confidence that they would understand him. At the time, he was summing up a life-time of theological speculation, by reviewing his own works, by writing his *Retractations*. As he saw himself in this review[14] he felt that he

---

[1] *Ep.* 199, xii, 46.   [2] *Serm.* III, 1.
[3] Ed. G. Morin in *Rev. bénédictine*, 18, 1901, pp. 241–256.
[4] *Rev. bén.*, 18, 1901, p. 255.   [5] *Rev. bén.*, 18, 1901, p. 256.
[6] *Rev. bén.*, 18, 1901, p. 247 (2 *Tim.*, 2, 24).   [7] *Rev. bén.*, 18, 1901, p. 253.
[8] *Rev. bén.*, 18, 1901, p. 249.
[9] *Rev. bén.*, 18, 1901, p. 256, citing *Deut.* 32, 7; cf. *Ep.* 46, v. sup. p. 274.
[10] *Ep.* 215, 6.   [11] *Ep.* 215, 8.   [12] *Rev. bén.*, 18, 1901, p. 243.
[13] *Ep.* 220, 2.   [14] *de dono persev.* xxi, 56; v. inf. p. 428.

had 'progressed' towards the particular truths that the monks had challenged. He felt deeply, that *'our thoughts and words'* were *'in the hand of God'*, and if a problem arose he was not the man to shirk 'approaching and solving' it.[1] All he had done, he told his readers, had been to throw up with greater urgency and precision than any of his predecessors, a fortification designed to protect the central truths of Christianity from the unprecedented onslaughts of Pelagius: even his giddy doctrine of predestination, as expounded with the sober zeal of a great military architect, was merely another 'impregnable bastion' of the Catholic faith.[2] Evodius might tell the monks that there were many questions that had to be postponed to the next life.[3] Such an answer was utterly alien to Augustine: he saw no reason whatsoever why men as well-intentioned as his correspondents, should be content to call a halt at this particular chasm; they already had so much in common; what remained would be 'revealed' to them, as it had been 'revealed' to Augustine.[4] The ideas themselves, he admitted, were exceptionally difficult and open to abuse.[5] The Apostle Peter had said as much of the ideas of S. Paul: and when 'so great an Apostle' had issued 'so terrible a warning', this warning had been against the men who had wilfully misunderstood these truths,[6] not, Augustine implied (with a hint of iron beneath the velvet glove of monastic courtesy), not against the men who had propounded them. It is the 'serene intransigence'[7] of a man who was sure of the heart of his message.

In Prosper and his friends, Augustine had won disciples who called themselves 'the fearless lovers of all-or-nothing grace'. These 'fearless lovers' agreed with their master that 'men place the initiative in their salvation on a wrong footing by placing it in themselves'.[8] They were not the last men to sacrifice the initiative of the individual in a desperate age. What they gained was a belief that the world around them was intelligible, even if on a plane that surpassed human reason and strained human feeling; and the certainty that they would remain active and creative. Even if they were merely agents, they were at least the agents of forces which guaranteed achievements greater than their own frail efforts could ever have brought about.[9]

For Augustine's doctrine of predestination, as he elaborated it, was a doctrine for fighting men. A monk might waste his leisure worrying

---

[1] *de corrept. et gratia*, x, 26.   [2] *de dono persev.* xxi, 54.   [3] *Rev. bén.*, 18, 1901, p. 254.
[4] *de grat. et lib. arb.* i, 1; *de praed. sanct.* i, 2, citing *Phil.* 3, 15–16; v. sup. p. 280, n. 2.
[5] *Ep.* 215, 2.   [6] *Ep.* 214, 6–7.
[7] Chéné, 'Les origines', *Année théol. augustin.*, 13, 1953, p. 109.
[8] *Ep.* 225, 7.   [9] *de corrept. et gratia*, ii, 4.

about his ultimate identity: to Augustine, such an anxiety was misplaced. A doctrine of predestination divorced from action, was inconceivable to him. He had never written to deny freedom, merely to make it more effective in the harsh environment of a fallen world. This world demanded, among other things, unremitting intellectual labour to gain truth, stern rebuke to move men. Augustine, as a bishop, had thrown himself into both activities. When some men claimed that they could obtain a supernatural understanding of the Scriptures without effort and without culture, Augustine ridiculed them.[1] He would now dismiss, in the same way, those who thought they could live among men without the unpleasantness of being rebuked.[2] Ever sensitive to his critics, he will now avoid the charge of passivity, by compiling a meticulous code of good and evil actions from the Scriptures: his 'Mirror' for the active Christian.[3] Thus when a man such as Prosper rallied to Augustine's views, he did so, not, as some have suggested,[4] because they made men safely passive, but because in an age that seemed to mock the practicability of any purpose, such doctrines offered the creative man the absolute certainty of belonging to a group whose purpose was effective: *'Say not in thy heart: My strength and the power of my hand has wrought this great wonder: but thou shalt remember the Lord thy God, for He it is Who gives the strength to do great deeds.'*[5]

What is more, such views made the world readily intelligible. The doctrine of predestination was developed by Augustine mainly as a doctrine, in which every event was charged with a precise meaning as a deliberate act of God, of mercy for the elect, of judgement for the damned.[6] Vague popular beliefs in the judgements of God[7] re-emerge in the work of the old Augustine, as the hard fibre from which all human history is woven.[8] Had Augustine been able to see 'in the spirit', he would have seen the troubled history of his own times just as the prophet Micheas had seen his own: *'He saw the Lord God sitting on His throne, and all the hosts of Heaven stood around Him. . . . And the Lord said: Who shall seduce Ahab King of Israel that he may go up and be slain at Ramoth Galaad.'*[9] A precise judgement of God was respon-

---

[1] *de doct. christ.*, Prooem. 5. [2] *de corrept. et gratia*, v, 7; cf. *de doct. christ.* IV, xvi, 33.
[3] *Vita*, XXVIII, 3.
[4] Morris, 'Pelagian Literature', *Journ. Theol. Studies*, n.s., xvi, 1965, pp. 59–60.
[5] *Deut.* 8, 77 in *de gratia et lib. arb.* vii, 16. [6] e.g. *de dono persev.* xii, 31.
[7] *C. Jul.* VI, xii, 38.
[8] Rightly stressed by Lorenz, 'Der Augustinismus Prospers', *Zeitschr. f. Kirchengesch.*, 73, 1962, p. 246.
[9] I. *Reg.* 22, 19, in *C. Jul.* V, iii, 13.

sible for every check in the activity of the human agents of His church: a hidden judicial decision explained away the long age of pagan incredulity;[1] as we have seen, it even hardened Augustine's heart against the pathetic resistance of a few Donatist fanatics.[2] Similarly, every tribulation of the elect was a calculated mercy. This alone was no small thing: for in the anthology of the works of Augustine, later compiled by Prosper,[3] the opening book of the *City of God*, with the record of the still-distant news of unburied corpses, of nuns raped, of the enslavement of prisoners of war, will now appear as relevant to the everyday experience of a man of the fifth century.[4]

Augustine had lived for over 40 years as a 'servant of God'. He could overlook the completed course of many men's lives. What he had seen had not reassured him: 'For no one is known to another so intimately as he is known to himself, and yet no one is so well known even to himself that he can be sure as to his conduct on the morrow.'[5] When Augustine wrote the *Confessions*, such a sense of the unknown areas in the personality had appeared to him as a guarantee of humility.[6] Now this uncertainty has hardened into an acute fear. 'Who is not aghast'[7] at the sudden crevasses that might open in the life of a dedicated man?[8] 'When I was writing this (work against Julian), we were told that a man of 84, who had lived a life of continence under religious observance with a pious wife for 25 years, has gone and bought himself a music-girl for his pleasure. . . .'[9] If the angels were left to their own free-will, even they might lapse, and the world be filled with 'new devils'.[10] What preoccupied Augustine, therefore, was no longer the mobilization of love that caused a man to act, but the mysterious resilience that would enable some men to maintain this love for the full course of their lives.[11] For many did not: 'It might appear obvious to men that all who are plainly good, faithful Christians deserve to receive the gift of persevering to the end: God, however, has judged it better that some who will not persevere should be mingled with the fixed number of the saints.'[12] Thus, for the old Augustine, the idea that a divine decree had already established 'an unshakeable number of the elect', that the sons of God were 'permanently inscribed in the archive of

---

[1] e.g. *de dono persev.* ix, 22.   [2] *Ep.* 204, 2; v. sup. pp. 335–336.

[3] In P.L. li, 427–496. v. esp. the masterly analysis and conclusions of Lorenz, 'Der Augustinismus Prospers', *Zeitschr. f. Kirchengesch.*, 73, 1962, pp. 218–232.

[4] e.g. *Sent.* 50, 51 and 53.   [5] *Ep.* 130, ii, 4.

[6] v. sup. p. 178, and *de sancta virg.*, xlii, 43.   [7] *de grat. et lib. arb.* xx, 42.

[8] *de corrept. et gratia*, viii, 18, and *de dono persev.* ix, 21.   [9] *C. Jul.* III, x, 22.

[10] *Op. Imp.* V, 57.   [11] e.g. *de corrept. et gratia*, viii, 17.

[12] *de dono persev.* viii, 19.

the Father'[1] was desperately welcome; for it provided men with what he knew they could never create for themselves: a permanent core of identity, mysteriously free from those vertiginous chasms whose presence in the soul he had always felt so acutely. It is not surprising that, at this time, Augustine should have circulated his *Confessions*,[2] that he should have appealed to them as his most popular work. For in the *Confessions*, we already see how much this very anxious man had needed to see his youth as a preordained process, dominated by the relentless Monica:[3] the harsh consequences of this attitude were but a small price to pay for the sense that, among the shapeless and volatile chaff of the human race, it had been possible for a man to be a 'tiny speck of gold' exquisitely worked upon by a master-goldsmith.[4]

Augustine claimed that this doctrine had always been proclaimed in the church. In a limited sense, he was right: for in Augustine's attitude to predestination we can feel the arctic current of specifically African views of the church. Cyprian had already presented the church as a group of 'saints', whom God alone could enable to survive the bitter hostility of the 'world'.[5] Augustine will fall back on this idea. For him, also, the most difficult task that faced a man was simply to survive. He had always insisted, against the Donatists, that the survival of the Catholic church was guaranteed: now, the iron backbone of a church whose permanence rested on the 'predestinate plan of God', is merely introjected to form the core of the identity of each member of the elect.[6]

This was a hard message for a hard age. In such works we can already feel an autumn chill, almost the presage of a great catastrophe. Augustine's last books, *On the Predestination of the Saints* and *On the Gift of Perseverance*, were sent across the Mediterranean towards the end of 429. Throughout that summer, a great army of Vandals from Spain slowly approached along the coastline of Mauretania. Next year, they would ravage Numidia.[7] When Augustine's friends met again around his table, they would meet as refugees, who had seen their life's work disappear within a few months. They no longer needed Augustine to warn them that the judgements of God were 'such as make the soul shudder'.[8]

An ancient terror had suddenly come back to these civilized bishops: fear of the wholesale lapse of the faithful under persecution, fear of massacre, of subtle propaganda, of ingenious torture. Augustine had

---

[1] *de corrept. et gratia*, ix, 20.   [2] e.g. *Ep.* 231, 6.   [3] *de dono persev.* xx, 53.
[4] *Serm.* 15, 5.   [5] e.g. *de dono persev.* iii, 4; vii, 13 and xxii, 60–62.
[6] v. sup. p. 221; v. esp. *de dono persev.* xii, 63.   [7] v. inf. pp. 424–425.
[8] *Vita*, XXVIII, 13.

ordered the bishops to stay by their flocks: as the Vandals closed in around Hippo, he would pray that he and his congregation might be able to persevere through what lay ahead.[1]

The 'gift of perseverance', he had said, was the greatest of God's gifts to the individual. For it bestowed on frail human beings the same unshakeable stability as the human nature in Christ had enjoyed: by this gift, a man was joined forever to the Divine, could be confident that the '*hand of God*' would be stretched above him to shield him, unfailingly, against the world.[2] 'Human nature could not have been raised higher.'[3]

But the elect received this gift so that they, also, could tread the hard way of Christ.[4] It was for this that they needed 'a liberty . . . protected and made firm by the gift of perseverance, that this world should be overcome, the world, that is, in all its deep loves, in all its terrors, in all its countless ways of going wrong'.[5]

Now, in the early months of 430, Augustine will appear in church to tell panic-stricken crowds what he had already written to a few monks: that they would have to 'persevere' although love of life was still strong in them. For Augustine had lost none of his capacity to feel. In these few last sermons we realize that the old man's horror at the evils of existence, so powerfully marshalled against Julian, was the obverse of his deep-rooted loves: he still knew what it was to love life whole-heartedly, and thus he could convey how much it had cost the martyrs to overcome this love.[6] Like the martyrs, Augustine's hearers, also, might have to follow in the footsteps of Christ's Passion.[7] Predestination, an abstract stumbling-block to the sheltered communities of Hadrumetum and Marseilles, as it would be to so many future Christians, had only one meaning for Augustine: it was a doctrine of survival, a fierce insistence that God alone could provide men with an irreducible inner core.

Augustine died, mercifully, from a sudden fever. He had already provided his friends with a way of understanding himself and his times. The last works had left a deep impression on Augustine's circle: Possidius, his biographer, could now only think of his dead friend as 'Bishop Augustine . . . a man predestinate . . . brought forward in our time . . . a man among those who have gained their end, who have persevered up to the day of their death.'[8]

[1] *Vita*, XXIX, 1.   [2] *de dono persev.* vii, 14.   [3] *de praed. sanct.* xiv, 31.

[4] Clearly seen by Pontet, *L'Exégèse de S. Augustin*, pp. 502–510.

[5] *de corrept. et gratia*, xii, 35.   [6] *Serm.* 344, 4, (translated inf. p. 431).

[7] *Serm.* 345, 6.   [8] *Vita*, Praef., 2.

34

OLD AGE

On September 26th, 426, Augustine had assembled his clergy and a large congregation in the *Basilica Pacis* to witness a solemn decision. He nominated his successor, the priest Eraclius; and he arranged that, in the meanwhile, Eraclius would take over the judicial business, that he had for a long time found so irksome.[1]

'In this life', he told them, 'we are all bound to die; and for everyone, his last day is always uncertain. Yet, as babies, we can look forward to being boys; and, as boys, to youth; as youths, to being grown up, and, as young men, to reaching our prime, and, in our prime, to growing old. Whether this will happen is uncertain; but there is always something to look forward to. But an old man has no further stage of life before him. Because God wished it, I came to this town in my prime: I was a young man then, now I have grown old.'[2] After the decision had been recorded, Eraclius stood forward to preach, while the old Augustine sat behind him on his raised throne: 'The cricket chirps,' Eraclius said, 'the swan is silent.'[3]

To an African clergyman such as Eraclius, Augustine was not the writer whose thought had aroused admiration and concern around the Mediterranean: he was, above all, a bishop who had practised what he preached.[4] The Christian bishop was now an important figure throughout the Roman world: visits to his residence had become a normal part of the social life of most towns.[5] Augustine sensed this change: he was particularly concerned with the 'image' that a bishop should present to the outside world. His own hero was Ambrose. At a time when he himself felt in need of reassurance after the misbehaviour of one of his protégés,[6] he urged a Milanese deacon, Paulinus, to write a life of

[1] *Ep.* 213, 5. [2] *Ep.* 213, 1. [3] Sermon of Eraclius in P.L. xxxix, 1717.
[4] P.L. xxxix, 1717–1719. [5] Guelf. 32, 4, (*Misc. Agostin.*, i, p. 566). [6] v. inf. p. 412.

Ambrose.[1] Ambrose had been dead for twenty-five years; and seen at that distance by a man such as Paulinus, he appeared very different from the Ambrose that we meet in Augustine's *Confessions*. The Ambrose of Paulinus is a man of action, who had cut a furrow through his contemporaries: no less than six people suffer crushing divine punishments for standing in his way or for criticizing him, among them quite ordinary African clergymen.[2] Paulinus plainly felt that, at the Last Judgement, men would still be divided between those who admired Ambrose, and those who heartily disliked him.[3] When Augustine's friend, Possidius, came to write his *Life of Augustine*,[4] the picture was very different. Possidius will dwell, rather, on the life that Augustine had created for himself and others in his bishop's house: on how he had written verses on the table to prohibit malicious gossip;[5] on how anyone who swore would forfeit his glass of wine;[6] on how they ate with silver spoons, but off simple crockery, 'not because they were too poor, but on purpose'.[7]

It is easy to dismiss Possidius as a simple man, who failed to seize the complexity of his hero. In reality, this biography mirrors very exactly the anxieties of Augustine and his circle in their old age.[8] For they had to maintain, in changed circumstances, among younger men, the exacting ideals according to which they had lived their daily life for almost forty years.

The focus of Augustine's ideal had been the common life of absolute poverty lived by himself and his clergy in the bishop's house. The citizens of Hippo could well be proud of this: 'Under bishop Augustine, everyone who lives with him, lives the life described in the Acts of the Apostles.'[9] Augustine had made the acceptance of this life, a condition of serving him as a member of his clergy: anyone who defaulted from this agreement would be deprived of holy orders.[10] Many of Augustine's colleagues thought that he was too strict;[11] and, characteristically,

[1] On the influence of the example of Ambrose on Augustine, v. Courcelle, *Les Confessions*, pp. 617–621, and, generally, Van der Meer, *Augustine*, pp. 570–572.

[2] v. the excellent edition, translation and introduction of M. Pellegrino, *Paolino di Milano, Vita di S. Ambrogio*, (Verba Seniorum, n.s. 1), 1961, and, most recently, A. Paredi, 'Paulinus of Milan', *Sacris Erudiri*, xiv, 1963, pp. 206–230.

[3] Paulinus, *Vita*, c.55 (ed. Pellegrino, pp. 128–129).

[4] v. esp. the two excellent editions, with translation and commentary of H. T. Weisskotten, *Sancti Augustini Vita scripta a Possidio episcopo, Edition with Revised Text, Introduction, Notes and an English Version*, 1919, and M. Pellegrino, *Possidio, Vita di Agostino*, (Verba Seniorum, 4), 1955.

[5] *Vita*, XXII, 6.   [6] *Vita*, XXV, 2.   [7] *Vita*, XXII, 5.

[8] e.g. *Vita* XXIV, 1–17, on the financial caution of Augustine.   [9] *Serm.* 356, 1.

[10] *Serm.* 355, 6.   [11] *Serm.* 355, 4 and 6.

Augustin⸱ had been content, having imposed this rule, to believe that it would not be circumvented. The scandal that came to light in 424 took him completely by surprise. One of his clergy had not given all his money to the church: he had kept some back under false pretences, and, on his death, his heirs fought for this personal property.[1]

Augustine dealt with the affair with a characteristic mixture of charm and determination. He had been too strict, he told his congregation; his clergy might be forced to stoop to such pretences out of fear of losing their holy orders: 'Look. Before the eyes of God and you all, I change my mind. Whoever wants private means, whoever is not satisfied with God and his Church, let him reside where he wants: I will not deprive him of his holy orders. I do not want any hypocrites. . . . If he is prepared to live off God through His Church, and to have nothing of his own . . . let him stay with me. Whoever does not want this, let him have his freedom: but he shall see for himself whether he can have his eternal happiness. . . .'[2]

'I have spoken a lot: please forgive me. I am a long winded old man, and ill-health has made me anxious. As you see, I have grown old with the passing years; but, for a long time now, this ill-health has made an old man of me. But, if God is pleased with what I have just said, He will give me strength: I will not desert you.'[3]

A short time later, the affair was cleared up. Augustine himself took the *codex* of the Acts of the Apostles from his reader, and read out in church the passage on which the life of his clergy had been based.[4] With the holy book on his knees, he launched into an amazingly precise account of the financial operations of each one of his clergy: it is a vivid document of the life of little men in a Late Roman town.[5] Even Augustine's attitude to his clothes emerges with engaging candour: 'Somebody comes with a present of a rich silk robe. It might suit a bishop, but not Augustine, not a poor man, born of poor parents. Men would only say that I had now come into expensive clothes, such as I could never have had in my father's house, or in my secular career. I tell you, an expensive robe would embarrass me: it would not suit my profession, nor my principles; and it would look strange on these old limbs, with my white hairs.'[6]

After this, anyone found pretending to have left all his property would be degraded on the spot: 'Let him appeal to a thousand councils against me, let him sail to court wherever he wants, let him do what he

[1] *Serm.* 355, 3.   [2] *Serm.* 355, 6.   [3] *Serm.* 355, 7.
[4] *Serm.* 356, 1.   [5] Used as such by Jones, *The Later Empire*, ii, p. 771.
[6] *Serm.* 356, 13.

can, when he can: God will help me; where I am bishop, he will not be priest.'[1]

His severity had made him unpopular in Hippo; but he had no wish to be a martyr to public opinion: 'We do not want to gain this great merit at your expense. Let me have a loss of it here, and so I can enter the Kingdom of Heaven with all of you.'[2]

This scandal was not an isolated event. Many incidents point to a vague malaise that throws as much light on Augustine and his circumstances in the African church as do the violent campaigns of his middle age. There was a personal element in this situation. Augustine and his friends were now old men. They had always formed a close, dominating group; now they were in danger of becoming isolated. Severus of Milevis, for instance, had caused great and unnecessary trouble in his town, by keeping his choice of a successor a secret between himself and his clergy; Augustine had to intervene, to pacify the conflict created by his friend's behaviour.[3] Old loyalties had been undermined: the monastery of women, that had been governed by Augustine's own sister, seems to have deteriorated once the family-link was broken.[4] It would, in any case, be difficult to find bishops who could replace this brilliant generation. Eraclius, for instance, was a very different sort of man from Augustine: popular, efficient, passing for rich, he had a taste for building, which Augustine had never shared.[5]

Augustine's brilliance had even tended to smother local talent. Absorbed in the international controversy on Pelagianism, he had tended, in his old age, to dismiss the intellectual life nearer home. A bishop, for instance, who complained that his opinions on the origin of the soul were not appreciated by the 'herd of country-bumpkins of clergymen' among whom he was forced to live, was handled sarcastically.[6]

Yet, Augustine's great work on the elaboration of Christian scholarship, the *de Doctrina Christiana*, would soon be completed. In a sense, it was already out of date. For it had deliberately taken for granted things which, after the barbarian invasions, could no longer be taken for granted. It had assumed that men could still receive a sufficiently sound primary education in the Roman schools to be able to speak good Latin unselfconsciously without the affected polish of the rhetoricians. It had looked forward to continued intellectual

---

[1] *Serm.* 356, 14. [2] *Serm.* 356, 15. [3] *Ep.* 213, 1. [4] *Ep.* 211, 4.
[5] *Serm.* 356, 4. v. P. Verbraken, 'Les deux sermons du prêtre Éraclius d'Hippone', *Rev. bénédictine*, 71, 1961, pp. 3–21.
[6] e.g. *Ep.* 202A, iii, 7.

interchange between scholars in the different parts of the Christian world.[1] In fact, it would have been impossible for a provincial, in 420, to make the same career as Augustine had made in the 370's. There were no classical bookshops in Hippo;[2] and Augustine was evidently glad of any contribution to the costs of his own library.[3] Even in Carthage, it was impossible to find a translator for a simple Greek text.[4] Worst of all, the new generation of African clergy were content merely to turn to Augustine. In 428, Quodvultdeus, a deacon (and, later, a bishop) of Carthage,[5] could turn to Augustine to extract from him a mere pot-boiler, a brief handbook of heresies.[6] Only Augustine, it seemed, knew of previous compilations of heresies, in Latin and Greek.[7] While Augustine had gallantly attempted to achieve a cosmopolitan culture by learning some Greek, and would go to the trouble to translate a short Greek text for this book,[8] Quodvultdeus seems to represent the dangers of a stagnant and self-satisfied provincial culture, hiding under a great name: good 'African bread' was all he needed.[9]

Moreover, in many areas, the Catholic Church had not recovered from the violence of the suppression of Donatism. Many bishops found themselves placed, by the Imperial laws, at the head of reluctant, passive communities.[10] Augustine preached one of his most urgent sermons on the duties of a bishop at one such place, Fussala, which until recently, had been a violent Donatist stronghold.[11] And it was just at Fussala that another terrible scandal took place.[12] The village was in Augustine's diocese. Augustine had gained an unchallenged right to choose bishops for such a place from his own community. When his first choice refused, he presented the villagers with another, disastrous, candidate, Antoninus. Young Antoninus behaved like a petty tyrant, and when condemned, he refused to relinquish his see.[13] He went to fight his case in Rome. Even the African bishops were divided;[14] and Augustine, who felt himself to blame, had to write a passionate, and, at the same time, highly diplomatic letter to the new bishop of Rome, Celestine, in order to quash Antoninus' machinations,[15] which had plainly been quite successful. Had the young man succeeded, a situation would have been created similar to that of only a decade before: 'For threats are being made to the people . . . of legal processes and

---

[1] v. sup. p. 270. [2] *Ep.* 118, ii, 9. [3] *Ep.* 231, 7. [4] *Epp.* 222, 1 and 223, 4.
[5] On whom v. esp. the excellent introduction of R. Braun, to *Quodvultdeus, Livre des Promesses et des Prédictions de Dieu*, (Sources chrétiennes, 101), 1964, i, pp. 88–112.
[6] *Ep.* 221, 3. [7] *Ep.* 222, 1. [8] v. esp. Courcelle, *Les lettres grecques*, pp. 192–194.
[9] *Ep.* 223, 3. [10] v. Brown, 'Religious Coercion', *History*, xlviii, 1963, pp. 292–293.
[11] *Guelf*, 32, (*Misc. Agostin.*, i, pp. 563–575). [12] *Ep.* 209.
[13] *Ep.* 209, 4. [14] *Ep.* 209, 6. [15] *Ep.* 209, 5.

public officials and pressure from the military. . . . In consequence, these unfortunate people, though Catholic Christians, are in dread of heavier punishment from a Catholic bishop than they feared from the laws of Catholic emperors when they were heretics.'[1] It is an ugly reminder of the price of unity.

But Fussala, a remote, Punic-speaking village, was perhaps rather an exception: in Hippo, the strong Catholic minority would have changed gradually into a majority. Such a process of absorption might well have affected the quality of the religious life with which Augustine came into contact. There is evidence that the tenacious popular feeling that had once crystallized around the Donatist leaders, had come to bear on Augustine. Dreams commanding baptism, for instance, were a common feature of popular Christianity in the ancient world, as indeed in many missionary areas today. Augustine had once mocked Donatist claims based on such revelations.[2] Now, he was the object of just such excitements: a poor man from an outlying village had come into Hippo to be baptized by Augustine as the result of just such a dream.[3] Augustine knew that he had played a role in the dreams of many people.[4] In his reaction to this, he shows himself very much the son of his mother Monica.[5] On his death-bed, a sick man was brought to him to be healed. His first reaction was to joke: 'If I had the gift you say I have, I would be the first to try it on myself'; but, as soon as he heard that the man had been told to come to him by a dream, he laid his hands on him.[6]

In his last year, indeed, Augustine had to deal with miracles on his doorstep. When Orosius returned to Africa, in 416, he brought with him from Jerusalem, relics of the newly-discovered body of S. Stephen. In the next years, *memoriae* — little chapels containing caskets of the holy dust — sprang up in many towns and country-estates round Hippo: Possidius had one at Calama, and Evodius at Uzalis. Other *memoriae*, especially those of the Milanese martyrs discovered by S. Ambrose, Gervasius and Protasius, were already in existence.[7]

These *memoriae* crystallized feelings that had been strong in Catholic and Donatist alike. In the Late Roman towns, men had come to need and to expect the protection of powerful men: S. Stephen settled in Uzalis as the spiritual equivalent of such earthly patrons; he appeared to a farmer, dressed as a resident senator.[8] Above all, there was the sense

[1] *Ep.* 209, 9. [2] *Ep. ad cath.* xix, 49–50. [3] *de cura ger. pro mort.* xii, 15.
[4] *Serm.* 322 and 323, 2. [5] v. sup. pp. 29 and 33. [6] *Vita*, XXIX, 5.
[7] v. esp. *de civ. Dei*, XXII, 8. [8] *de miraculis S. Stephani*, I, 14, (P.L. xli, 841).

of the charged physical presence of a holy body:[1] out of twelve cures effected at *memoriae*, nine happened through direct contact with the shrine, or with objects that had touched it.[2]

Augustine had spoken scathingly of such popular beliefs whenever they appeared to him as bulwarks of the Donatist church. 'They worship every bit of dust from the Holy Land',[3] he had said. Now, he found himself preaching to huge crowds drawn by just such a 'little bit of dust'.[4] Evodius had even made use of these new relics to strengthen his own position. He placed them in the confiscated Donatist basilica, the 'Regained' Basilica, in order to cement the loyalty of its former congregation.[5] Around Hippo, also, the new *memoriae* had sprung up around country-churches, which, a decade previously, had been harried by the Circumcellions.[6] All this is hardly surprising. Africa had always been full of such holy bodies.[7] What was new, however, was the sudden wave of miraculous cures associated with them: seventy would take place in Hippo within the space of two years.[8]

The historian will probably never penetrate to the roots of such a sudden crisis of feeling. What we can trace, however, is the way in which Augustine reacted to these miraculous events.[9] Up to 424, there had been no *memoria* of S. Stephen in Hippo. It was built by Eraclius[10] at his own expense, and decorated with mosaics showing the death of Stephen, and with verses written by Augustine.[11] Once involved in this movement, Augustine's contribution was characteristically thorough. Miracles had remained a matter of vague popular feeling: those who had experienced them, treated them as intimate, personal revelations;[12] those who heard them, quickly forgot or garbled their accounts.[13] Augustine decided both to examine and record each instance, and to give verified cures a maximum of publicity. In Hippo, he insisted on receiving a written report from the healed person, a *libellus*; and this document would then be read out in church, in the presence of the

---

[1] *Ep.* 78, 3.   [2] in *de civ. Dei*, XXII, 8.   [3] *Ep.* 52, 2.   [4] *Serm.* 317, 1.

[5] *de miraculis S. Stephani*, I, 7, (P.L. xli, 839).

[6] v. the convenient table of H. J. Diesner, 'Die Circumcellionen v. Hippo Regius', *Kirche und Staat im spätrömischen Reich*, 1963, p. 79.

[7] *Ep.* 78, 3.

[8] v. Quodvultdeus, *Livre des promesses*, VI, vi, 11, ed. Braun, ii, p. 609, a Catholic description of the miracles of a rival healer: 'tricks based on pure imagination', by which 'the crowds thought they had regained their sight and ability to walk'.

[9] v. the excellent study of J. de Vooght, 'Les miracles dans la vie de S. Augustin', *Recherches de Théologie ancienne et médiévale*, xi, 1939, pp. 5–16.

[10] *Serm.* 356, 4.   [11] *Serm.* 316, 5.

[12] e.g. *de civ. Dei*, XXII, 8, 164–168.   [13] *de civ. Dei*, XXII, 8, 400.

writer, and later would be stored in the bishop's library.[1] He tried, not very effectively, to recommend this system to his colleague Evodius, whose own collection of miracles is a vivid record of the trivialities of life in Uzalis, but hardly a very impressive argument for the supernatural.[2] There was a sense of urgency in this move of Augustine's: he was 'genuinely annoyed' that a noble Carthaginian lady had failed to use her rank and influence to publicize a cure effected on her.[3] His aim was to draw together these scattered incidents, until they formed a single corpus, as compact and compelling as the miracles that had assisted the growth of the Early Church.[4] It is not the first time that Augustine had appealed to the 'facts' of popular belief. He had rallied equally tenacious feelings surrounding infant baptism in Africa, in order to 'smash' the Pelagians.[5] The aim of this new campaign, as it is applied in the last book of the *City of God*, is also to 'bend' the 'shocking hardness'[6] of the reasonable pagans, many of whom were eminent doctors,[7] by a direct appeal to the astonishing things happening in the Christian communities all around them.

Yet, when Augustine wrote *On the True Religion* in 390, he had stated, explicitly, that miracles such as had happened in the times of the Apostles were no longer allowed to take place;[8] and he had repeated this view, by implication, in many other books and sermons.[9] At the same time, however, he had actually witnessed, and accepted, the cures associated with the spectacular discovery of the bodies of Gervasius and Protasius in Milan. Thus, Augustine's sudden decision to give a maximum of publicity to miraculous cures in Africa, should not be regarded as a sudden and unprepared surrender to popular credulity.[10] It is, rather, that, within the immensely complex structure of Augustine's thought, the centre of gravity had shifted; modern miracles, which had once been peripheral, now become urgently important as supports to faith.

In this evolution, indeed, we have a microcosm of the deep change that separates the religion of the young Augustine from that of the

---

[1] v. the masterly studies of H. Delehaye, 'Les premiers "libelli miraculorum"', *Analecta Bollandiana*, 29, 1910, pp. 427–434, and 'Les recueils antiques des miracles des saints', *Analecta Bollandiana*, 43, 1925, pp. 74–85.

[2] Jones, *The Later Empire*, ii, p. 963: 'such silly stories . . .'.

[3] *de civ. Dei*, XXII, 8, 160. [4] *de civ. Dei*, XXII, 8, 350–353. [5] v. sup. p. 385.

[6] *de civ. Dei*, XXII, 8, 568. Their attitude was justified by the whole intellectual climate of Later Antiquity: v. esp. H. I. Marrou, (en collaboration avec A. M. La Bonnardière), 'Le dogme de la résurrection des corps et la théologie des valeurs humains selon l'enseignement de saint Augustin', *Rev. études augustin.*, xii, 1966, pp. 111–136, esp. pp. 115–119.

[7] *Ep.* 227. [8] *de vera relig.* xxv, 47. [9] *Retract.* I, 13, 7.

[10] Implied by Jones, *The Later Roman Empire*, ii, pp. 963–964.

old man. Like most Late Antique men, Augustine was credulous without necessarily being superstitious. When remarkable events happened at holy places, he was thoroughly well-armed, as a philosopher, against crude interpretations of the event, but not against the event itself.[1] He was not prepared to deny what reliable men told him; but he would tenaciously criticize any explanation of such events, or any religious practice, that seemed unworthy of a correct view of God and the soul.[2]

Even the natural world was full of unique and surprising happenings. As a full-grown man, he was 'greatly startled' by first seeing a magnet.[3] The wise men of the ancient world had failed to map out the whole world of nature. Augustine, in his old age, was acutely aware of their failures. He was confronted by two men confident of the rational categories available to classical men: the learned Porphyry had dismissed the Resurrection and Ascension of Christ as incompatible with ancient physics;[4] Julian of Eclanum had held that the idea of an inherited original sin was contradicted by logic.[5] Against both, Augustine will array a catalogue of inexplicable amazing facts: among them, the inheritance of acquired characteristics[6] and the behaviour of grafted olives.[7] It is the silent rebellion of the 'pockets of resistance' left uncovered by natural science:[8]

> *There are more things in heaven and earth, Horatio,*
> *Than are dreamt of in your philosophy.*[9]

A 'miracle' for Augustine was just such a reminder of the bounds imposed on the mind by habit. In a universe in which all processes happen by the will of God, there need be nothing less remarkable in the slow, habitual processes of nature. We take for granted the slow miracle by which water in the irrigation of a vineyard becomes wine: it is only when Christ turns water into wine, 'in quick motion' as it were, that we are amazed.[10]

Sudden amazements did not play a great role in the religious ideas of Augustine the young Platonist. Then he had regarded the essence of religion as a striving to rise away from habitual ways of thinking, that were tainted by our commerce with the sensible world. Constant miracles, he thought, would only have dulled the awareness of the

---

[1] Rightly emphasized by Van der Meer, *Augustine*, pp. 527–557.

[2] e.g. *de cura pro mort. ger.* xvi, 19. [3] *de civ. Dei*, XXI, 4, 81.

[4] *de civ. Dei*, XXII, 11. [5] *C. Jul.* V, xiv, 51. [6] e.g. *C. Jul.* VI, vi, 15.

[7] *de nupt. et concup.* I, xix, 21. [8] v. esp. *C. Jul.* VI, vi, 17–18.

[9] Cited by Marrou, *S. Augustin et la fin de la culture antique*, pp. 151–157, in a brilliant characterization of this attitude.

[10] e.g. *Ep.* 137, iii, 10.

human race: because a miracle would cease to be marvellous as soon as it became habitual.[1] For the contemplative, the marvellous, the bizarre, the unexpected, tended to fade into the background of a harmonious, rational universe, like dim lights against the sun. The rational mind could rise gradually and in an uninterrupted ascent, from 'laws' of 'nature' that were merely the subjective registration of accustomed happenings, to the true law, a law more plainly harmonious, regular and reasonable.[2] With the old Augustine, this attitude had become a little less firmly rooted. He had defended with passion and conviction doctrines that ran contrary to all habitual processes of reasoning. Human ideas of equity, for instance, found themselves in unresolved conflict with the fact of the collective punishment of the human race for one man's sin.[3] Augustine had tacitly withdrawn the frontiers of the human mind before such problems: the contemplative's universe is now surrounded by a fringe of incomprehensible happenings.

These local miracles, moreover, were purely physical cures. As an old man, Augustine had also abandoned much of the Platonist's one-sided preoccupation with the mind. To 'heal the eyes of the heart', remained the essence of religion;[4] but Augustine had now made room, also, for the fate of the body: he would pray for good health;[5] and expected that men would always be afraid of death.[6] A God Whose generosity had scattered so much purely physical beauty on the earth, could not neglect physical illness.[7] Augustine, indeed, had been led into an acute awareness of the extent of the purely physical suffering of the human race. These miracles had sprouted from the desperation of men afflicted 'by more diseases than any book of medicine could hold'.[8] The evident horrors of human existence, its *miseria*, assumed an urgent need for some relief, for some few *solacia*.[9] These reliefs were some slight hint, like thin rays of sunshine entering a darkened room, of the final transformation, the glorious resurrection, of the bodies of the elect.[10]

For it is this urgent need for faith in an unbelievable, distant transformation, that determines Augustine's final attitude to the miracles around him. As a younger bishop, he had considered that men no longer needed such spectacular proofs for their faith. His thought at this time moved around the unity of faith that 'glowed' so marvellously in the universal Catholic Church.[11] The miracles of the Early Church

[1] *de util. cred.* xvi, 34.   [2] *C. Faust.* XXVI, 3.   [3] v. sup. p. 393.   [4] *Serm.* 88, 5.
[5] v. esp. Burnaby, *Amor Dei*, pp. 113–114.   [6] *Serm.* 299, 8 and 355, 4.
[7] *Serm.* 317, 3.   [8] *de civ. Dei*, XXII, 22, 90.
[9] *de cura ger. pro mort.* xvi, 20.   [10] *Serm.* 317, 1.   [11] *Serm.* 88, 2.

had started, even 'boosted', this marvellous diffusion, which had been largely realized in his own time. Against the solid, undemonstrative unity of the Catholic Church, the miracles of Donatist popular belief could be dismissed as histrionic tricks.[1] Behind this attitude there had lurked the assumption, that with the rapid Christianization of the Roman world, men in general had in some way advanced beyond the incredulity of pagan times, and so did not have to be moved by the force of miracle.

Now, Augustine is less sure: the human race had remained much the same, always frail, always in need of compelling authority. The 'God of our fathers is our God also':[2] His mysterious omnipotence linked the wonders of the Old Testament with the modern world, just as, in Augustine's attitude to coercion, it had linked the harsh sanctions of the Old Israel to the enforced unity established in the African church. God could fully determine, for Himself, without the advice of a Platonist, how often miracles should or should not occur.[3] All the hopes of the people of God were now pinned on the future — on the resurrection of the body. The martyrs had died for this impossible belief; their dead bodies, also, could be allowed to witness to it.[4] This is the attitude which Augustine had reached when, in the twenty-second book of the *City of God*, he attempted, by an unwieldy and picturesque catalogue of strange occurrences in Hippo, Carthage, Calama, Uzalis, Fussala and little churches in the countryside, to persuade men reared on ancient physics, that the pure, uncontaminated Empyrean of their imagination might yet find room for the substance of their human flesh: '*God knows the cogitations of the wise, that they are vain.*'[5]

[1] *Tract. in Joh.* 13, 17.   [2] *de VIII Dulcitii quaest.* vii, 3.   [3] *Serm.* 286, 5.
[4] *de civ. Dei*, XXII, 9.   [5] *Ps.* 93, 11, in *de civ. Dei*, XXII, 4.

35

THE END OF ROMAN AFRICA[1]

'Not only along the frontiers,' Augustine had once written to a Roman senator, 'but throughout all the provinces (of Africa), we owe our peace to the sworn oaths of the barbarians.'[2] Augustine seldom mentions this world of the 'African barbarians'.[3] To the south and west of Hippo the great mountain ranges — the Kabylie, the Hodna, the Aures — were inhabited by semi-nomadic tribes. Living near starvation-level, they constantly pressed downwards into the civilized plains. The cavalry of their raiding-parties ranged widely: a niece of Severus of Milevis was kidnapped near Sitifis (Sétif) in one such raid.[4] Farther to the south and east, the true nomads had made themselves felt wherever the Roman frontier touched on the desert. It was a world of scattered forts, of semi-independent chieftains, of fortified farmsteads, built up in storeys; unlike the peaceable, sprawling villas of the coast, they stood guard, like medieval castles, over estates of olive-trees, held precariously against the ways of the desert.[5] This vast hinterland had little to do with the Roman Africa known to Augustine: only slaves on the estates around Hippo would remind him of a world hardly controlled by Roman arms, and impervious to the spread of Christianity.[6]

As a bishop, Augustine had not greatly changed his habits since his student days. Carthage remained the centre of his world: he had travelled there thirty-three times in thirty years,[7] and only once into the wilder province of Mauretania.[8] He would spend whole months in

[1] Outstandingly the best study is by Chr. Courtois, Les Vandales et l'Afrique, 1955.
[2] Ep. 47, 2.   [3] Ep. 220, 7.   [4] Ep. 111, 7
[5] B. H. Warmington, The North African Provinces, pp. 20–26.
[6] Ep. 199, xii, 46.   [7] v. sup.p. 193.
[8] v. sup. p. 363; v. G. Bonner, 'Augustine's Visit to Caesarea in 418', Studies in Church History, i, ed. Dugmore and Duggan, 1964, pp. 104–113.

the city, engaged in hectic business with his colleagues,[1] visiting important people, apparently dining well (on roast peacock, a change from his vegetarian diet in the monastery of Hippo).[2] In Carthage, the old life had persisted. Proconsular Africa had remained an oasis of almost unbelievable prosperity at a time when the rest of the Western Empire had been ravaged by barbarians. It was the 'sheet anchor' of the fortunes of the Western Emperors; its great landowners had been wooed by frequent concessions, ranging from favourable tax-adjustments to the right to hunt lions;[3] inscriptions continued to praise the generosity and integrity of the aristocratic Proconsuls, who came to a Carthage that was still 'Rome in Africa'.[4]

Yet, Africa had merely enjoyed a sheltered existence for the past thirty years. It was a strangely divided and inert society. The great local landowners seldom entered the service of the Emperors.[5] They exercised their power outside the normal machinery of government. Their main concern was their estates, the yield of their crops,[6] the quality of their wine,[7] the pleasures of the hunt.[8] They were isolated and envied: '*Isti soli vivunt.*' 'They are the only ones who live at all.'[9]

The bishops, also, stood apart. They had become the courtiers *par excellence.* Their business took them frequently to Ravenna. Alypius negotiated in Rome right up to the end of Augustine's life: he had learnt to remain sensitive to Italian opinion, and knew how to pay his way among the courtiers.[10] The Catholic bishops now had the advantage, in the eyes of visiting officials, of being some of the oldest and most respected members of provincial society. It is not at all surprising that the last letters we have of Augustine's, were polished, diplomatic notes.[11] Yet the bishops had been active only for themselves and their protégés.[12] They had left the laymen to fend for themselves. For these laymen, continued prosperity meant also the continuance of the façade of pagan life: they would join pagan literary circles, would patronize great circus shows; they would even claim tax-exemption from the Catholic Emperors, as priests of the pagan Imperial cult.[13] Compared

---

[1] v. sup. p. 230 and p. 338.   [2] *de civ. Dei,* XXI, 4, 15.   [3] e.g. *Cod. Theod.* XV, 11, 1.

[4] Salvian, *de gubernatione Dei,* VII, 16, (P.L. liii, 143).   [5] v. sup. p. 25.

[6] *Enarr. in Ps.* 136, 3.

[7] *Enarr. in Ps.* 136, 5; cf. *de miraculis S. Stephani,* II, iii, 9, (P.L. xli, 849).

[8] *Mai* 126, 12, (*Misc. Agostin.* i, p. 366).   [9] *Serm.* 345, 1.

[10] v. sup. p. 362 and p. 383.   [11] *Epp.* 229-231.

[12] Rightly emphasized by Frend, *Donatist Church,* p. 329.

[13] e.g. *Cod. Theod.* VII, xiii, 22 (428), addressed, significantly, to the pagan Volusianus (v. sup. p. 300) v. the interesting study of T. Kotula, *Zgromadzenia prowincjonalne w rzymskiej Afryce w epoce późnego Cesarstwa,* 1965, esp. pp. 161–166, (French resumé: *Les Assemblées provinciales dans l'Afrique romaine sous le Bas-Empire,* pp. 171–179), which,

with such men, the bishops were still small fry: in Rome, it was quite possible for people to believe that Augustine had acted as the tool of a great landowner, anxious to rid his estate of a troublesome bishop.[1] The nexus of bishop and great landowner, which was to be so important for the morale of the Roman populations of Gaul, Spain and N. Italy, had plainly not happened in Africa. Imperceptibly then, the control of the African provinces slipped from its civilian inhabitants into the hands of sinister outsiders — to the succession of military commanders, who, as Counts of Africa, protected the civilized coastline from its vast hinterland. The military establishment of Africa was dangerously small, scattered, and universally unpopular. Augustine had no illusions about them: the prime joy of a soldier's life consisted in bullying the local farmers.[2] His congregation plainly agreed; for they once lynched the commander of their garrison.[3] The officers, who now appeared in Africa, were a reminder of the troubled world North of the Mediterranean. One such man was buried in Cartennae (Ténès), far to the west of Hippo. He had become rich: his uniform-cloak was pinned with magnificent golden brooches; but these brooches had been made, perhaps by Germanic craftsmen certainly from Germanic models, in the distant Rhineland.[4]

Augustine could not avoid contact with these men. The army was the only effective police-force; it was indispensable to him in applying the policy of suppression against the Donatists.[5] It was just this concern for the application of the laws against heretics, and for the security of the Catholic church in Mauretania and Southern Numidia, that brought Augustine into contact with one of the most colourful, and certainly the most fateful, of the new generation of professional soldiers, with Boniface.[6]

When we first meet Boniface, in 418, his career had already taken him from the Danube to Marseilles. He had lived among barbarians all his life. Now he was stationed, at the head of a band of Gothic mercenaries, on the southern frontier of Africa, perhaps near Vescera (Biskra). The suppression of the Donatists may well have been a duty

perhaps, exaggerates the decline of such institutions in the last decades of Roman Africa. It is now possible to see Macrobius, the author of the *Saturnalia*, as a product of this African environment: v. sup. p. 300, n. 7.

[1] *Ep.* 209, 5.

[2] *Enarr. in Ps.* 136, 3; cf. *de div. quaest.* LXXXIII, 79, 4, on the requisitioning of horses.
[3] *Serm.* 302, 16.   [4] J. Heurgon, *Le trésor de Ténès*, 1958.

[5] e.g. *Cod. Theod.* XVI, 2, 31; v. Brown, 'Religious Coercion', *History*, xlviii, 1963, p. 288.

[6] v. esp. H. J. Diesner, 'Die Laufbahn des *Comes Africae* Bonifatius und seine Beziehungen zu Augustin', *Kirche und Staat im spätrömischen Reich*, 1963, pp. 100–126.

that puzzled him: his own troops, as Goths, were Arian Christians; and so, technically, also 'heretics'.[1] But, with a pious Catholic wife, he was a man whom Augustine could approach with a long open letter justifying such suppressions.[2] Influential local commanders were sorely needed as allies by the bishops. Boniface seemed to be just such a man. When his wife died at some time around 420, Boniface even thought of entering a monastery.[3] Yet of all people it was Augustine and Alypius who dissuaded him from doing so. Thirty years before, Augustine had travelled from Thagaste to Hippo in order to persuade a member of the Imperial secret service to become a monk;[4] now, he undertook a quite unprecedentedly long journey to Tubunae (Tobna) in the depths of Numidia, in order to keep a general at his post.[5] He had come to realize the urgent need for security. In the *City of God* he had explored and justified the value of purely 'earthly' peace;[6] in Southern Numidia, he may well have appreciated for the first time, how much 'earthly peace', which he could take for granted at home, meant in this wild land. The Catholic communities needed a strong man to act as their protector against the lightning raids of the nomads.[7]

Augustine and Alypius, therefore, had appealed for protection direct to a general on the frontier, as they had so often appealed to the Emperors in Ravenna. But they were out of date in their estimate of a man like Boniface. The great Moorish general of their younger days, Gildo, may well have been unpopular, but at least he was a local man, with great estates in the provinces he defended.[8] Boniface, by contrast, was a career-general. His fortune depended on participating in events as far apart as the Danube and Southern Spain. He belonged to a class of men who were becoming the king-makers of the inglorious Emperors of the West. To remain at his post in an out-of-the-way frontier of Africa, would have meant renouncing the world quite as surely as if he had become a monk. Augustine expected him to make this sacrifice: it was simply his duty as a devout Christian of ascetic leanings, to obey a bishop's counsel to be poor, just and celibate.[9] This pastoral advice meant, in fact, that Boniface should abandon all hope of advancement.

The influence of Boniface's dead wife soon waned. By 423, he had made himself *de facto* Count of Africa; by 426, he had made his position certain by a visit to the court. This visit marked the end of Augustine's

[1] *Ep.* 185, i, 1. For the sudden spread of Arianism in Africa among such soldiers and their bishops, v. esp. La Bonnardière, *Rech. de chronologie augustin.*, pp. 94–97.

[2] *Retract.* II, 73. [3] *Ep.* 220, 2 and 12. [4] v. sup. p. 136.

[5] *Ep.* 220, 3. [6] v. sup. p. 325. [7] *Ep.* 220, 3.

[8] Warmington, *The North African Provinces*, pp. 10–12. [9] *Ep.* 220, 3 and 5.

illusions. Boniface returned with a rich heiress, and with concubines to console him for this politic match.[1] He had even compromised with the religion of so many of the barbarian chieftains turned Roman generals; his wife was an Arian, and he allowed his daughter to be baptized by the heretics.[2] Worst of all for the province, he was a Count of Africa who had to use his army to protect his position against attack from Italy. Carthage, of all places, was fortified[3] against attack from Rome, while in the hinterland, the 'African barbarians' were restless.[4]

Augustine was dismayed by this. So many provinces had paid for their sins by the scourge of a barbarian invasion: in Africa, it now appeared to him, there were enough sins — and certainly enough barbarians — to make a disaster inevitable.[5]

Yet Boniface expected the bishops to support him. He claimed that his cause was just;[6] he had attended church when Augustine preached;[7] he had even gone out of his way to pay a respectful visit to the old man, only to find him too tired to communicate.[8] In the winter of 427/8, however, he received a letter from Augustine, sent by a highly confidential messenger.[9] This studiously unpolitical letter was both a pastoral reminder of his abandoned ideals, and a tacit withdrawal of support. Augustine, to the last, was a civilian. He was horrified by news of a rebellion of the tribes:[10] he castigates the *atrocitas* — the outrageous behaviour — of the armed retainers of the Count;[11] instinctively loyal to the court, he refuses to judge the issue that divided Boniface from Ravenna.[12] An old man, he was in no position now to offer any political advice.[13] He had just re-read the history of the Kings of Israel in the Old Testament: what had impressed him most in this history, was the manner in which the hidden ways of God had caused the most reasonable policies to miscarry.[14] Had not his own relations with Boniface been marked by the same fatality? All he would advise, was to love peace: it was a policy he would praise also in the Imperial commissioner, Darius, who would come, in the next year, to negotiate an agreement with the Count.[15]

This mixture of military blackmail and diplomacy still belongs to the old, sheltered world of African politics. But not for long. While the general, the bishops and the courtiers exchanged carefully-weighed

---

[1] *Ep.* 220, 4. [2] *Ep.* 220, 4. [3] Diesner, 'Bonifatius', *Kirche und Staat*, p. 111.
[4] *Ep.* 220, 7. [5] *Ep.* 220, 8. [6] *Ep.* 220, 5. [7] *Serm.* 114.
[8] *Ep.* 220, 2. [9] *Ep.* 220, 1–2. [10] *Ep.* 220, 7. [11] *Ep.* 220, 6.
[12] *Ep.* 220, 5. [13] *Ep.* 220, 1 and 9.
[14] v. esp. A. M. La Bonnardière, 'Quelques remarques sur les citations scripturaires du *de gratia et libero arbitrio*', *Rev. études augustin.*, ix, 1963, pp. 77–83.
[15] *Ep.* 220, 12; cf. *Ep.* 229, 2.

letters, their divisions were being watched from the far end of the Mediterranean. Only the Straits of Gibraltar and the long, empty coastline of Mauretania lay between this, the richest province of the West, and a new man, recently established as head of a tribe that had always remained outside the network of Roman diplomacy. He was a cripple, 'deep in his designs, speaking little, contemptuous of luxury, given to mad fits of rage, greedy for wealth, a master of the art of intrigue among the tribes, always ready to sow the seeds of division, to conjure up new hatreds'[1] — Genseric, the king of the Vandals.

The whole tribe, as they crossed the Straits of Gibraltar, numbered eighty thousand. The warriors formed 'an enormous band'.[2] They had been joined by adventurers from other tribes, by Alans and Goths: for this was the conquest of which all barbarians had dreamed and had never succeeded in achieving. The Vandals were also Arian Christians, who believed that the God of Battles was on their side. They had fought the Romans with the Gothic Bible of Ulfilas at their head.[3]

Roman rule in Africa simply collapsed.[4] In the summer of 429 and the spring of 430, the Vandals suddenly and swiftly overran Mauretania and Numidia. There is no record of resistance by the population: no Catholic communities rallied behind their bishops, as had been the case in Spain, to resist and harry the barbarians. The Catholic bishops were divided and demoralized, their flock passive. Faced with 'overthrowers of the Roman world',[5] they lost their taste for martyrdom. Augustine had once taunted the Donatists: when persecuted, they should take the advice of the Gospel and 'flee to another city'.[6] The tasteless jibe now recoiled: his colleagues would use this text to justify an infectious panic.[7] 'If we stay by our churches', one wrote, 'I just cannot see how we can be of any use, to ourselves or our people: we would only stay to witness, before our very eyes, men struck down, women raped, churches going up in flame; and we would be tortured to death for wealth we do not possess.'[8]

Augustine answered these arguments in a typically conscientious and differentiated letter.[9] His decision was plain: his ideal was at stake; the bonds that bound a bishop to his flock must hold. 'Let no one dream

[1] Jordanes, *Getica*, 33.   [2] *Vita*, XXVIII, 4.

[3] Salvian, *de gubernatione Dei*, VII, 11, (P.L. liii, 138).

[4] v. esp. H. J. Diesner, 'Die Lage der nordafrikan. Bevölkerung im Zeitpunkt der Vandaleninvasion', *Historia*, xi, 1962, pp. 97–111, (*Kirche und Staat*, pp. 127–139), and P. Courcelle, *Histoire littéraire des grandes invasions*, pp. 115–139.

[5] *Vita*, XXX, 1.   [6] e.g. *C. litt. Petil.* II, xix, 42–43.   [7] *Ep.* 228, 2 and 4.

[8] *Ep.* 228, 4.   [9] *Ep.* 228 is included by Possidius in the *Vita*, (XXX, 3–51).

of holding our ship so cheaply, that the sailors, let alone the captain, should desert her in time of peril. . . .'[1]

Hippo was a fortified town. By a paradoxical turn of fortune, Boniface commanded the defence: the great Count of Africa was again a mere commander of Gothic mercenaries.[2] Bishops who had fled, or had lost their flocks, trooped into the town for safety. Among them was poor Possidius: 'So we were all thrown together, with the terrifying judgements of God before our very eyes: we could only think of them and say: "*Thou art just, O God, and Thy judgement is righteous.*"'[3]

That winter, the Vandals surrounded the town: their fleet held the sea. Sixteen years previously, Augustine had described from the pages of Livy, the horrors of the siege of Saguntum: how would 'a Christian people' have behaved, he had asked?[4] The Vandals had already tortured two Catholic bishops to death outside their captured towns.[5] 'One day when we were with him at table and were talking, he said to us: "You should know that I have prayed to God either that He should deliver this city, beleaguered by the enemy, or, if He thought otherwise, that He should make His servants strong enough to endure His will, or, even, that He should receive me out of this existence." '[6]

Augustine lived to see violence destroy his life's work in Africa. '*He who puts on wisdom, puts on grief; and a heart that understands cuts like rust in the bones.*' 'The man of God saw whole cities sacked, country villas razed, their owners killed or scattered as refugees, the churches deprived of their bishops and clergy, and the holy virgins and ascetics dispersed; some tortured to death, some killed outright, others, as prisoners, reduced to losing their integrity, in soul and body, to serve an evil and brutal enemy. The hymns of God and praises in the churches had come to a stop; in many places, the church-buildings were burnt to the ground; the sacrifices of God could no longer be celebrated in their proper place, and the divine sacraments were either not sought, or, when sought, no one could be found to give them. . . .'[7]

'In the midst of these evils, he was comforted by the saying of a certain wise man: "He is no great man who thinks it a great thing that sticks and stones should fall, and that men, who must die, should die." '[8]

[1] *Ep.* 228, 11. [2] *Vita*, XXVIII, 12. [3] *Vita*, XXVIII, 13.
[4] *de civ. Dei*, III, 20, 39.
[5] Victor Vitensis, *Historia persecutionis Vandalicae*, I, iii, 10, (P.L. lviii, 185); v. Courtois, *Les Vandales*, p. 163.
[6] *Vita*, XXIX, 1. [7] *Vita*, XXVIII, 6-8. [8] *Vita*, XXVIII, 11.

The 'certain wise man', of course, is none other than Plotinus.[1] Augustine, the Catholic bishop, will retire to his deathbed with these words of a proud pagan sage.

[1] Plotinus, *Ennead* I, iv, 7, (MacKenna 2, pp. 46–47); v. Pellegrino, *Possidio*, p. 226, n. 14, and Courcelle, *Hist. littéraire*, pp. 277–282.

36

DEATH

In the winter before the disaster — in 428–429 — Augustine had received a highly complimentary note from Count Darius, the Imperial agent sent to negotiate with Boniface.[1] In his reaction to the bejewelled eulogies contained in this letter, we can catch an indirect glimpse of Augustine for the last time — polished, exceedingly literate, charmingly preoccupied with the temptations of his own reputation.[2] Darius was plainly well-educated, and had sung Augustine's praises: 'Someone, then, might say, "Do not these things delight you?" Yes, indeed they do: "For my heart", as the poet says, "is not made of horn" that I should either not observe these things, or observe them without delight.'[3]

The *Confessions*, of course, are Augustine's answer to such reflections. He sends Darius a copy: 'In these behold me, that you may not praise me beyond what I am; in these believe what is said of me, not by others, but by myself; in these contemplate me, and see what I have been, in myself by myself. . . . For *"He hath made us and not we ourselves"*, indeed, we had destroyed ourselves, but He who made us has made us anew. . . .'[4]

He reminded Darius that Themistocles, also, had loved to hear his own praises.[5] Why? Here was a man whose art had been 'to make a small city great'.[6] At first sight, a reference to the remarkable Athenian seems out of place in the last days of Roman rule in Africa. But Augustine had created his own empire of the mind; and Darius had recognized it: he had sent money for 'my library, that I may have the means to edit new books and repair the old'.[7]

Augustine had been able to live for the past three years in his library. As always, Augustine intended to spend his leisure, 'exercising

[1] *Ep.* 230.   [2] *Ep.* 231.   [3] *Ep.* 231, 2.   [4] *Ep.* 231, 6.   [5] *Ep.* 231, 3.
[6] *Ep.* 231, 3; cf. *Ep.* 118, iii, 13.   [7] *Ep.* 231, 7.

myself in the Holy Scriptures.'[1] He seems to have concentrated, in his reading, on the historical books of the Old Testament. Previously, his views on grace and free-will had been developed in terms of the thought of Paul — of the personal moral struggle, of the renewing power of Christ. Now, Augustine will show that, at the age of seventy-two, he was still capable of pouring his ideas into yet another and stranger mould. What for the Pelagians had been a straightforward collection of examples of good and evil actions becomes, with Augustine, a history tinged with mystery. Self-conscious human intention carries so far and no farther, in public as well as in private action. In the history of Israel, he will see the mass-panics that suddenly fall on victorious armies, the unpredictable outcome of sound policies, the sudden changes in the hearts of kings.[2]

This scheme was silted over by the steady flood of books, which Augustine still had to write in answer to immediate questions and attacks: the silent rebellion of the monasteries;[3] the venom of Julian;[4] the standing challenge of the Jewish communities;[5] and the sudden, ominous appearance in the wake of the armies, of confident Arian bishops, the trusted representatives of Germanic generals, who now knew that their hour had come.[6]

But above all, it was the library itself that claimed his attention. On the shelves, in the little cupboards that were the book-cases of Late Roman men,[7] there lay ninety-three of his own works, made up of two hundred and thirty-two little books, sheafs of his letters, and, perhaps, covers crammed with anthologies of his sermons, taken down by the stenographers of his admirers.[8]

Some of these manuscripts were in need of editing;[9] some were incomplete drafts;[10] many reminded him of work of which he had allowed copies out of his hands before they reached their final form.[11] He would not live much longer. Just as he had taken the care to nominate a successor, so he must now put his vast literary inheritance in order.

Augustine worked hard at this task right up to his death. Through-

---

[1] *Ep.* 213, 1. [2] v. esp. La Bonnardière, in *Rev. études augustin.*, ix, 1963, pp. 77–83.
[3] v. sup. pp. 398 sq. [4] v. sup. p. 384.
[5] Hence the *Tractatus adversus Judaeos*. [6] *Collatio cum Maximino*, esp. I, 1.
[7] v. B. Altaner, 'Die Bibliothek des heiligen Augustinus', *Theologische Revue*, 1948, pp. 73–78. We know far more about other Later Roman libraries, e.g. H. I. Marrou, 'Autour de la bibliothèque du pape Agapet', *Mél. d'archéol. et d'hist.*, 48, 1931, pp. 124–169.
[8] e.g. *Retract.* II, 39. [9] e.g. *Retract.* II, 30, on the *de doctrina christiana*.
[10] e.g. *Retract.* I, 17. [11] *Retract.*, Prolog. 3.

out all the disasters, he would read his old works at night; and in the daytime, he would still be in the library, dictating answers to the importunate Julian.[1] We have only the results of his reading of his main works — his *Retractationes*.[2] This is a catalogue of titles, arranged in chronological order. Augustine usually gives the occasion, and a brief note of the content of the work, along with his comments. These invaluable remarks of the old man are partly in self-criticism, but more often they are attempts to explain himself.[3] The work against Julian kept Augustine from dictating what would have interested us even more: his commentary on his letters, and, above all, some comment on the hundreds of sermons, whose chronology still baffles us, and whose very spontaneity seemed to have caused the old bishop some concern; for in church, he admits, he had seldom been able to be '*quick to listen and slow to speak*'.[4]

In his preface to the *Retractationes*, Augustine was well aware that he was writing a new kind of book.[5] His reasons, though not explicit, are clear enough. Here was a huge library, full of books whose impact among Catholics he had been able recently to appreciate.[6] 'What is written, "*From much words thou shalt not escape sin*" frightens me considerably. It is not that I have written so much. . . . Heaven forbid that things that have had to be said should be called "*much words*", no matter how long and exhausting; but I am afraid of this judgement of the Scriptures, because I have no doubt that, from my works, which are so many, it would be possible to collect much, which, if not false, would seem to be, or be revealed to be, unnecessary.'[7]

Augustine wanted to see his works as a whole, that might be read, in future, by men who had reached the same certainty as himself, by mature Catholic Christians. Such men must appreciate the long journey which Augustine had taken to reach his present views. This is why, instead of being arranged by subjects, the books are deliberately criticized in chronological order.[8] These criticisms, however, are not profound autobiographical comments. There is the occasional flash of an active mind, which shows that, as a philosopher at least, Augustine

---

[1] *Ep.* 224, 3.

[2] v. esp. A. Harnack, 'Die Retractationen Augustins', *Sitzungsber. preuss. Akad. der Wiss.*, 1905, 2, pp. 1096–1131.

[3] v. esp. J. Burnaby, 'The "Retractations" of St. Augustine: Self-criticism or Apologia?', *Aug. Mag.*, i, 1954, pp. 85–92.

[4] *Retract.*, Prolog. 3.   [5] *Retract.*, Prolog. 1.

[6] v. sup. Prosper of Aquitaine, for instance, had already appealed to the 'Complete Works' of Augustine against the mere 'lectures' of the Semi-Pelagians: *ad Rufinum*, iv, 5, (P.L. li, 80).

[7] *Retract.*, Prolog. 2.   [8] *Retract.*, Prolog. 3.

was aware that his life had taken him into new horizons.[1] But Augustine's main intention was, rather, to help the reader to read even the least satisfactory of his works 'profitably', that is, through Augustine's present eyes.[2] For the same reason, many books that Augustine had been inclined to suppress as too involved or incomplete, are spared; for they might contain some argument or other, that was 'necessary', and not to be found elsewhere.[3]

Augustine, therefore, was not a man living in his past. His eyes were on the present. His contemporaries, for instance, seemed to have lost touch with the problems that had faced him in his defence of the freedom of the will against the Manichees.[4] That extraordinary generation of Manichaean 'fellow travellers' among the intellectuals of Africa had passed away; it was Pelagius, not Mani, who would interest a man of the 430's.

Augustine's colleagues plainly shared this sense of urgency; for they had urged him to write down as soon as possible, that part of the *Retractationes* that we now possess — the catalogue of his formal works. By that time, the future was too uncertain to hesitate further. No province of the Western Empire could consider itself safe. Augustine provided the Catholic church with what, in future centuries, it would need so much: an oasis of absolute certainty in a troubled world: here was the library of a man, whose life could be regarded as a steady progression towards 'the ecclesiastical norm'[5] of Catholic orthodoxy.

On the whole, the writing of the *Retractationes* was a dry business. It shows the extraordinary, myopic tenacity expected in the work of Late Roman learned men: commenting on 'flying creatures' in *Genesis*, he had forgotten to mention grasshoppers;[6] writing against Julian of Eclanum, he had given a name to a king of Cyprus, where Soranus, the standard text-book of medicine, had given none.[7] There is only one oasis of feeling:

'Thirteen books of my *Confessions*, which praise the just and good God in all my evil and good ways, and stir up towards Him the mind and feelings of men: as far as I am concerned, they had this effect on me when I wrote them, and they still do this, when now I read them. What others think is their own business: I know at least, that many of the brethren have enjoyed them, and still do.'[8]

---

[1] e.g. *Retract.* I, 10, 2, on *de Musica*, and II, 41, 2, on the *de Trinitate*: v. the most interesting study of R. A. Markus ' "Imago" and "Similitudo" in Augustine', *Rev. études augustin.*, xi, 1964, pp. 125–143.

[2] e.g. *Retract.*, Prolog. 3, on his works at Cassiciacum.

[3] e.g. *Retract.* I, 26.   [4] e.g. *Retract.* I, 8.   [5] *Vita*, XXVIII, 1.

[6] *Retract.* II, 41, 3.   [7] *Retract.* II, 88, 2.   [8] *Retract.* II, 32.

The spirit of the *Confessions* is not so very far from the surface of this meticulous work: 'Therefore, what remains for me to do, is to judge myself under my single Master, whose Judgement I desire to escape, for all my offences.'[1]

In his last months, Augustine would appear, still active in mind and body,[2] in a church packed with the demoralized remnants of a once-splendid Roman society. Rich men, who had lived in unapproachable affluence, now mingled with the beggars who had envied them. The Vandals had extorted, by torture and ransom, all the wealth that Christ and His poor had never received.[3] It was a theme for a popular moralist; yet it is not the only theme that Augustine finds important. The two remarkable sermons from this time are very different from his reaction to the distant catastrophes that had once afflicted Rome. In 410, he had spoken, repeatedly and coherently, of the indiscriminate scourging of God, of the value of suffering, of the inevitable decay of all material things, of the grim approach of the old age of the world.[4] Now, in the very midst of disasters, he will talk quite differently. The sudden descent of war-bands on a fertile province had made people realize, not that the world was ugly and unsure, but had caused them to experience the sheer, desperate tenacity of their love of life: they had learnt this vividly in themselves, as they had looked anxiously in their safe cupboard for money, as they had offered their whole patrimony to men who tortured them, as they reached the safe walls of Hippo, penniless, naked, yet alive.[5] It is the gnarled force of this love of the world of the living, that the disaster had taught the refugees; and Augustine is fully in touch with the feelings of the men he spoke to now:

'*When you are old, another will bind you, and take you, and will carry you to where you will not want to go.*' (*John* 21, 18)

The heroism of the martyrs had consisted of just this: 'They really loved this life; yet they weighed it up. They thought of how much they should love the things eternal; if they were capable of so much love for things that pass away. . . .

'I know you want to keep on living. You do not want to die. And you want to pass from this life to another in such a way that you will not rise again, as a dead man, but fully alive and transformed. This is what you desire. This is the deepest human feeling: mysteriously, the soul itself wishes and instinctively desires it. . . .'[6]

In August 430, Augustine fell ill with a fever. He knew he would die.

[1] *Retract.*, Prolog. 2.   [2] *Vita*, XXXI, 4.   [3] *Serm.* 345, 2.
[4] v. sup. pp. 292–293 and 297–298.   [5] *Serm.* 345, 2.   [6] *Serm.* 344, 4.

Far away, in Italy, Paulinus was also dying; but in the profound peace of a provincial town, receiving the courteous visits of his friends.[1] Augustine wanted to die alone.

'Whoever does not want to fear, let him probe his inmost self. Do not just touch the surface; go down into yourself; reach into the farthest corner of your heart. Examine it then with care: see there, whether a poisoned vein of the wasting love of the world still does not pulse, whether you are not moved by some physical desires, and are not caught in some law of the senses; whether you are never elated with empty boasting, never depressed by some vain anxiety: then only can you dare to announce that you are pure and crystal clear, when you have sifted everything in the deepest recesses of your inner being'[2]

'Indeed, this holy man ... was always in the habit of telling us, when we talked as intimates, that even praiseworthy Christians and bishops, though baptized, should still not leave this life without having performed due and exacting penance. This is what he did in his own last illness: for he had ordered the four psalms of David that deal with penance to be copied out. From his sick-bed he could see these sheets of paper every day, hanging on his walls, and would read them, crying constantly and deeply. And, lest his attention be distracted from this in any way, almost ten days before his death, he asked us that none should come in to see him, except at those hours when the doctors would come to examine him or his meals were brought. This was duly observed: and so he had all that stretch of time to pray. ...'[3]

Augustine died, and was buried, on August 28th, 430.

A year later, Hippo was evacuated and partly burnt. Yet it seems that the library had marvellously escaped the destruction.[4] Possidius had taken with him Augustine's last letter to the bishops, in which he urged them to stay at their post. He would include it in his *Life of Augustine*: it was, he said, 'extremely useful and relevant.'[5] Possidius lived a few years among the ruins. Then the new Arian Christian rulers of Carthage drove him from Calama, as Possidius had once driven out his fellow-Christian, the Donatist bishop.[6]

---

[1] Uranius, *de obitu sancti Paulini*, 3, (P.L. liii, 861).   [2] *Serm.* 348, 2.

[3] *Vita*, XXXI, 1–3.

[4] v. H. V. M. Dennis, 'Another note on the Vandal occupation of Hippo', *Journ. Rom. Studies*, xv, 1925, pp. 263–268. Within a generation, the Suebian wife of a Vandal will be buried in the main basilica of Augustine: Marec, *Les Monuments*, pp. 62–63. Frend, *Donatist Church*, pp. 229–230, may be unduly pessimistic about the survival of Augustine's memory in Hippo: v. H. I. Marrou, 'Épitaphe chrétienne d'Hippone à réminiscences virgiliennes', *Libyca*, i, 1953, pp. 215–230.

[5] *Vita*, XXX, 1.   [6] Prosper, *Chron.*, ad ann. 438, (P.L. li, 547).

There was nothing left of Augustine now but his library. Possidius compiled a full list of his works;[1] he thought that no man could ever read them all.[2] All future biographers of Augustine have come to feel something of what Possidius felt in that empty room:

'Yet I think that those who gained most from him were those who had been able actually to see and hear him as he spoke in Church, and, most of all, those who had some contact with the quality of his life among men.'[3]

[1] Ed. A. Wilmart, *Misc. Agostin.*, ii, pp. 149–233.
[2] *Vita*, XVIII, 9.   [3] *Vita*, XXXI, 9.

BIBLIOGRAPHY

G. J. D. AALDERS, 'L'Épître à Menoch attribuée à Mani,' *Vigiliae Christianae*, 14, 1960, pp. 245–249.

A. ADAM, 'Der manichäische Ursprung von den zwei Reichen bei Augustin,' *Theologische Literaturzeitung*, 77, 1952, pp. 385–390.

A. ADAM, *Texte zum Manichäismus*, (Kleine Texte für Vorlesungen und Übungen, 175), 1954.

A. ADAM, 'Das Fortwirken des Manichäismus bei Augustinus,' *Zeitschrift für Kirchengeschichte*, 69, 1958, pp. 1–25.

A. ADAM, 'Manichäismus,' *Handbuch der Orientalistik*, (1. Abteilung: Der Nahe und der Mittlere Osten; viii Bd. 2), 1961, pp. 102–119.

P. ALFARIC, *L'Évolution intellectuelle de S. Augustin*, 1918.

A. ALFÖLDI, *A Conflict of Ideas in the Later Roman Empire*, 1952.

C. R. C. ALLBERRY, *A Manichaean Psalmbook*, (Part II), (Manichaean Manuscripts in the Chester Beatty Collection, vol. ii), 1938.

B. ALTANER, 'Die Bibliothek des heiligen Augustinus,' *Theologische Revue*, 1948, pp. 73–78.

B. ALTANER, 'Augustinus und die griechische Patristik,' *Revue bénédictine*, 62, 1952, pp. 201–215.

B. ALTANER, 'Augustins Methode der Quellenbenützung. Sein Studium der Väterliteratur,' *Sacris Erudiri*, 4, 1952, pp. 5–17.

C. ANDRESEN, *Bibliographia Augustiniana*, 1962.

P. ANTIN, 'Autour du songe de S. Jérôme,' *Revue des études latines*, 41, 1963, pp. 350–377.

A. H. ARMSTRONG, 'Salvation, Plotinian and Christian,' *The Downside Review*, 75, 1957, pp. 126–139.

J. P. ASMUSSEN, $X^u\bar{A}STV\bar{A}N\bar{I}FT$. Studies in Manichaeism, (Acta Theologica Danica, vii), 1965.

P. AUBIN, *Le problème de la 'conversion'*, 1963.

A. AUDOLLENT, *Carthage romaine*, 1901.

E. AUERBACH, 'Sermo humilis', *Literary Language and its Public in Late Latin Antiquity and in the Middle Ages*, (transl. Manheim), 1965, pp. 27–66.

BIBLIOGRAPHY

R. H. BARROW, *Introduction to St. Augustine, 'The City of God'*, 1950.

Chr. BAUR, *Das manichäische Religionssystem*, 1831.

J. H. BAXTER, 'Notes on the Latin of Julian of Eclanum,' *Bulletin du Cange*, 21, 1949, pp. 5–54.

N. H. BAYNES, *Byzantine Studies and Other Essays*, 1955.

M.-F. BERROUARD, 'S. Augustin et le ministère de la prédication,' *Recherches augustiniennes*, ii, 1962, pp. 447–501.

H. BLOCH, 'The Pagan Revival in the West at the End of the Fourth Century,' *The Conflict between Paganism and Christianity in the Fourth Century*, ed. Momigliano, 1963, pp. 193–218.

A. BÖHLIG, 'Christliche Wurzeln im Manichäismus,' *Bulletin de la société d'archéologie copte*, xv, 1960, pp. 41–61.

W. den BOER, 'Porphyrius als historicus in zijn strijd tegen het Christendom,' *Varia Historica aangeboden an Professor Doctor A. W. Bijvanck*, 1954, pp. 83–96.

T. BOHLIN, *Die Theologie des Pelagius und ihre Genesis*, (Uppsala Universitets Årsskrift, 9), 1957.

G. BONNER, *St. Augustine of Hippo: Life and Controversies*, 1963.

G. BONNER, 'Augustine's Visit to Caesarea in 418,' *Studies in Church History*, i, ed. Dugmore and Duggan, 1964, pp. 104–113.

Mary BOYCE, *The Manichaean Hymn Cycle in Parthian*, 1954.

R. BRAUN, *'Deus Christianorum'. Recherches sur le vocabulaire doctrinal de Tertullien*, 1962.

R. BRAUN, Introduction: *Quodvultdeus, Livre des Promesses et des Prédictions*, (Sources chrétiennes, 101), 1964.

E. BRÉHIER, *La Philosophie de Plotin*, revised ed. 1961.

J.-P. BRISSON, *Autonomisme et christianisme dans l'Afrique romaine*, 1958.

P. R. L. BROWN, 'Religious Dissent in the Later Roman Empire: the case of North Africa,' *History*, xlvi, 1961, pp. 83–101.

P. R. L. BROWN, 'Aspects of the Christianisation of the Roman Aristocracy,' *Journal of Roman Studies*, li, 1961, pp. 1–11.

P. R. L. BROWN, 'Religious Coercion in the Later Roman Empire: the case of North Africa,' *History*, xlviii, 1963, pp. 283–305.

P. R. L. BROWN, 'St. Augustine's Attitude to Religious Coercion,' *Journal of Roman Studies*, liv, 1964, pp. 107–116.

A. BRUCKNER, *Julian von Eclanum*, (Texte und Untersuchungen, 15, 3), 1897.

J. BURNABY, *Amor Dei: A Study of the Religion of St. Augustine*, 1938.

J. BURNABY, 'The "Retractations" of St. Augustine: Self-criticism or Apologia?', *Augustinus Magister*, i, 1954, pp. 85–92.

BIBLIOGRAPHY

J. Burnaby, *Augustine: Later Works*, (Library of Christian Classics, viii), 1955.

J. B. Bury, *History of the Later Roman Empire*, i, 1923.

I. Calabi, 'Le fonti della storia romana nel "de civitate Dei" di Sant' Agostino,' *Parola del Passato*, 43, 1955, pp. 274–294.

A. Cameron, 'The Roman Friends of Ammianus,' *Journal of Roman Studies*, liv, 1964, pp. 15–28.

A. Cameron, 'Palladas and Christian Polemic,' *Journal of Roman Studies*, lv, 1965, pp. 17–30.

A. Cameron, 'Wandering Poets: a literary movement in Byzantine Egypt,' *Historia*, xiv, 1965, pp. 470–509.

A. Cameron, 'The Date and Identity of Macrobius,' *Journal of Roman Studies*, lvi, 1966, pp. 25–38.

H. von Campenhausen, *The Fathers of the Latin Church*, transl. 1964.

L. Cantarelli, 'L'iscrizione onoraria di Giunio Quarto Palladio,' *Bulletino Comunale di Roma*, liv, 1926, pp..35–41.

P. G. Caron, 'Les *Seniores Laici* de l'Église africaine,' *Revue internationale des Droits de l'Antiquité*, vi, 1951, pp. 7–22.

C. P. Caspari, *Briefe, Abhandlungen und Predigten*, 1894.

E. Caspar, *Geschichte des Papsttums*, i, 1930.

F. Cayré, *Initiation à la Philosophie de s. Augustin*, 1947.

A. K. Clarke, 'Licentius, *Carmen ad Augustinum*, ll. 45 seqq., and the Easter Vigil,' (Studia Patristica, viii), *Texte und Untersuchungen*, 93.

H. Chadwick, *The Sentences of Sixtus. A Contribution to the History of Early Christian Ethics*, (Texts and Studies, n.s., v), 1959.

H. Chadwick, 'Pope Damasus and the Peculiar Claim of Rome to St. Peter and St. Paul,' *Freundesgabe O. Cullmann*, (*Novum Testamentum*, Suppl. 6), 1962, pp. 313–318.

O. Chadwick, *John Cassian*, 1950.

A. Chastagnol, 'Le sénateur Volusien et la conversion d'une famille de l'aristocratie romaine au Bas-Empire,' *Revue des études anciennes*, 58, 1956, pp. 240–253.

A. Chastagnol, *La Préfecture urbaine à Rome sous le Bas-Empire*, 1960.

A. Chastagnol, *Les Fastes de la Préfecture urbaine*, 1962.

A. Chavannes–P. Pelliot, 'Un traité manichéen retrouvé en Chine,' *Journal asiatique*, sér. X, xviii, 1911, pp. 99–199, and sér. XI, i, 1913, pp. 177–196.

BIBLIOGRAPHY

J. Chéné, Les origines de la controverse semi-pélagienne,' *Année théologique augustinienne*, 13, 1953, pp. 56–109.

Y. M. J. Congar, ' "Civitas Dei" et "Ecclesia" chez S. Augustin,' *Revue des études augustiniennes*, iii, 1957, pp. 1–14.

P. Courcelle, 'Quelques symboles funéraires du néoplatonisme latin,' *Revue des études anciennes*, 46, 1944, pp. 65–93.

P. Courcelle, 'Commodien et les invasions du Vᵉ siècle,' *Revue des études latines*, 24, 1946, pp. 227–246.

P. Courcelle, 'Paulin de Nole et saint Jérôme,' *Revue des études latines*, 25, 1947, pp. 274–279.

P. Courcelle, *Les lettres grecques en Occident de Macrobe à Cassiodore*, 1948.

P. Courcelle, *Recherches sur les 'Confessions' de S. Augustin*, 1950.

P. Courcelle, 'Les lacunes dans la correspondance entre s. Augustin et Paulin de Nole,' *Revue des études anciennes*, 53, 1951, pp. 253–300.

P. Courcelle, 'Les sages de Porphyre et les "viri novi" d'Arnobe,' *Revue des études latines*, 31, 1953, pp. 257–271.

P. Courcelle, 'S. Augustin "photinien" à Milan: *Conf.* VII, 19, 25,' *Ricerche di storia religiosa*, i, 1954, pp. 225–239.

P. Courcelle, 'Nouveaux aspects du platonisme chez saint Ambroise,' *Revue des études latines*, 34, 1956, pp. 220–239.

P. Courcelle, 'Propos antichrétiens rapportés par S. Augustin,' *Recherches augustiniennes*, i, 1958, pp. 149–189.

P. Courcelle, 'De Platon à saint Ambroise par Apulée,' *Revue de Philologie*, n.s., xxxv, 1961, pp. 15–28.

P. Courcelle, 'Anti-Christian arguments and Christian Platonism,' *The Conflict between Paganism and Christianity in the Fourth Century*, ed. Momigliano, 1963.

P. Courcelle, *Les Confessions de S. Augustin dans la tradition littéraire: Antécédents et Postérité*, 1963.

Jeanne et Pierre Courcelle, 'Scènes anciennes de l'iconographie augustinienne,' *Revue des études augustiniennes*, x, 1964, pp. 51–96.

P. Courcelle, *Histoire littéraire des grandes invasions germaniques*, 3rd ed. 1965.

Chr. Courtois, 'S. Augustin et la survivance de la Punique,' *Revue africaine*, 94, 1950, pp. 239–282.

Chr. Courtois, *Les Vandales et l'Afrique*, 1955.

E. Cranz, 'The Development of Augustine's ideas on Society before the Donatist Controversy,' *Harvard Theological Review*, 47, 1954, pp. 255–316.

BIBLIOGRAPHY

R. Crespin, *Ministère et Sainteté: Pastorale du clergé et solution de la crise donatiste dans la vie et la doctrine de S. Augustin*, 1965.

F. L. Cross, 'History and Fiction in the African Canons,' *Journal of Theological Studies*, n.s., xii, 1961, pp. 227–247.

K. Deichgräber, 'Vindicianus,' *Pauly-Wissowa Reallexikon*, IX, A.1, (ii, xvi), 1961, coll. 29–36.

H. Delehaye, 'Les premiers "libelli miraculorum",' *Analecta Bollandiana*, 29, 1910, pp. 427–434.

H. Delehaye, 'Les recueils antiques des miracles des saints,' *Analecta Bollandiana*, 43, 1925, pp. 74–85.

H. V. M. Dennis, 'Another note on the Vandal occupation of Hippo,' *Journal of Roman Studies*, xv, 1925, pp. 263–268.

H. J. Diesner, 'Die Lage der nordafrikanischen Bevölkerung im Zeitpunkt der Vandaleninvasion,' *Historia*, xi, 1962, pp. 97–111 (= *Kirche und Staat im spätrömischen Reich*, 1963, pp. 127–139).

H. J. Diesner, 'Die Laufbahn des *Comes Africae* Bonifatius und seine Beziehungen zu Augustin,' *Kirche und Staat im spätrömischen Reich*, 1963, pp. 100–126.

H. J. Diesner, 'Die Circumcellionen von Hippo Regius,' *Kirche und Staat im spätrömischen Reich*, 1963, pp. 78–90.

Sir Samuel Dill, *Roman Society in the Last Century of the Western Empire*, 1898, (Meridian 1958).

E. R. Dodds, 'Augustine's Confessions: a study of spiritual maladjustment,' *Hibbert Journal*, 26, 1927–1928, pp. 459–473.

E. R. Dodds, 'Tradition and Personal Achievement in the Philosophy of Plotinus,' *Journal of Roman Studies*, l, 1960, pp. 1–7.

E. R. Dodds, *Pagan and Christian in an Age of Anxiety*, 1965.

F. Dölger, 'Die Kaiserurkunde der Byzantiner,' *Historische Zeitschrift*, 159, 1938/9, pp. 229–250.

H. Dörrie, 'Porphyrius als Mittler zwischen Plotin und Augustin,' *Miscellanea Medievalia I: Antike und Orient im Mittelalter*, 1962, pp. 26–47.

R. Drews, 'Assyria in Classical Universal Histories,' *Historia*, xiv, 1965, pp. 129–142.

U. Duchrow, ' "SIGNUM" und "SUPERBIA" beim jungen Augustin,' *Revue des études augustiniennes*, vii, 1961, pp. 369–372.

U. Duchrow, 'Zum Prolog v. Augustins "De Doctrina Christiana",' *Vigiliae Christianae*, 17, 1963, pp. 165–172.

R. P. Duncan-Jones, 'Wealth and Munificence in Roman Africa,' *Papers of the British School at Rome*, xxxi, 1963, pp. 159–177.

BIBLIOGRAPHY

Y.-M. Duval, 'Saint Augustin et le *Commentaire sur Jonas* de saint Jérôme,' *Revue des études augustiniennes*, xii, 1966, pp. 9–40.

R. F. Evans, 'Pelagius, Fastidius and the pseudo-Augustinian "de Vita Christiana",' *Journal of Theological Studies*, n.s., xiii, 1962, pp. 72–98.

P. Fabre, *S. Paulin de Nole et l'amitié chrétienne*, 1949.

Favonius Eulogius: *Disputatio de Somnio Scipionis*, ed. and transl. R. E. van Weddingen, (Collection Latomus, xxvii), 1957.

G. Fink-Errera, 'San Agustin y Orosio,' *Ciudad de Dios*, 167, 1954, pp. 455–549.

F. Floeri, 'Le pape Zosime et la doctrine augustinienne du péché originel,' *Augustinus Magister*, ii, 1954, pp. 755–761.

G. Folliet, 'La typologie du sabbat chez s. Augustin,' *Revue des études augustiniennes*, ii, 1956, pp. 371–390.

G. Folliet, 'Les moines euchites à Carthage en 400–401,' (Studia Patristica, ii), *Texte und Untersuchungen*, 64, 1957, pp. 386–399.

G. Folliet, 'Aux origines de l'ascétisme et du cénobitisme africain,' *Studia Anselmiana*, 46, 1961, pp. 25–44.

G. Folliet, ' "Deificari in otio", Augustin, *Epistula*, X, 2,' *Recherches augustiniennes*, ii, 1962, pp. 225–236.

W. H. C. Frend, 'The Revival of Berber Art,' *Antiquity*, 1942, pp. 342–352.

W. H. C. Frend, 'A note on the Berber background in the life of Augustine,' *Journal of Theological Studies*, xliii, 1942, pp. 188–191.

W. H. C. Frend, *The Donatist Church: a movement of protest in Roman North Africa*, 1952.

W. H. C. Frend, 'The *cellae* of the African Circumcellions,' *Journal of Theological Studies*, n.s., iii, 1952, pp. 87–89.

W. H. C. Frend, 'The Gnostic-Manichaean Tradition in Roman North Africa,' *Journal of Ecclesiastical History*, iv, 1953, pp. 13–26.

W. H. C. Frend, 'Manichaeism in the Struggle between St. Augustine and Petilian of Constantine,' *Augustinus Magister*, ii, 1954, pp. 859–866.

W. H. C Frend, 'The *Seniores Laici* and the origins of the Church in N. Africa,' *Journal of Theological Studies*, n.s., xii, 1961, pp. 280–284.

W. H. C. Frend, 'The Roman Empire in the eyes of Western Schismatics during the 4th century,' *Miscellanea Historiae Ecclesiasticae*, 1961, pp. 9–22.

W. H. C. Frend, *Martyrdom and Persecution in the Early Church*, 1964.

J. GALLAY, ' "Dilige et quod vis fac",' *Recherches de sciences religieuses*, xliii, 1955, pp. 545–555.

J. GAUDEMET, *L'Église dans l'Empire romain*, (*IV–Vᵉ s.*), (Histoire du droit et des institutions de l'Église en Occident, III), 1958.

J. GAUDEMET, 'L'étranger au Bas-Empire,' *Recueils de la Société Jean Bodin*, ix, 1958, pp. 207–235.

J. GIBB and W. MONTGOMERY, *The Confessions of St. Augustine*, (Cambridge Patristic Texts), 1908.

S. GIET, 'Basile, était-il sénateur?' *Revue d'Histoire ecclésiastique*, 60, 1965, pp. 429–443.

G. D. GORDINI, 'Il monachesimo romano in Palestina nel IV secolo,' *Studia Anselmiana*, 46, 1961, pp. 85–107.

M. GRABMANN, 'Der Einfluss des heiligen Augustinus auf die Verwertung und Bewertung der Antike im Mittelalter,' *Mittelalterliches Geistesleben*, ii, 1936, pp. 1–24.

E. L. GRASMÜCK, *Coercitio: Staat und Kirche im Donatistenstreit*, 1964.

W. M. GREEN, 'A Fourth Century Manuscript of Saint Augustine?' *Revue bénédictine*, 69, 1959, pp. 191–197.

J. GROSS, *Entstehungsgeschichte des Erbsündendogmas*, i, 1960.

J. C. GUY, *Unité et structure logique de la Cité de Dieu*, 1961.

P. HADOT, 'Citations de Porphyre chez Augustin (à propos d'un livre récent),' *Revue des études augustiniennes*, vi, 1960, pp. 205–244.

P. HADOT, Introduction: *Marius Victorinus, Traités théologiques sur la Trinité*, (Sources chrétiennes, 68), 1960.

P. HADOT, *Plotin ou la simplicité du regard*, 1963.

T. HAHN, *Tyconius-Studien*, 1900.

R. HARDER, *Kleine Schriften*, 1960.

L. HARMAND, *Le Patronat sur les collectivités publiques des origines au Bas-Empire*, 1957.

A. HARNACK, 'Die Retractationen Augustins,' *Sitzungsberichte der preussischen Akademie der Wissenschaften*, 1905, 2, pp. 1096–1131.

A. HARNACK, *History of Dogma*, v, (Dover Books, 1961).

R. S. T. HASLEHURST, *The Works of Fastidius*, 1927.

P. HENRY, *Plotin et l'Occident*, (Spicilegium Sacrum Lovaniense, 15), 1934.

P. HENRY, *La Vision d'Ostie. Sa place dans la vie et l'œuvre de S. Augustin*, 1938.

L. HERRMANN, 'Hierius et Domitius,' *Latomus*, xiii, 1954, pp. 37–39.

J. HEURGON, *Le trésor de Ténès*, 1958.

BIBLIOGRAPHY

O. HILTBRUNNER, 'Die Schrift "de officiis ministrorum" des hl. Ambrosius und ihr ciceronisches Vorbild,' *Gymnasium*, 71, 1964, pp. 174–189.

K. HOLL, 'Augustins innere Entwicklung,' *Abhandlungen der preussischen Akademie der Wissenschaften. Philosophische-historische Klasse*, 1923, pp. 1–51. (= *Gesammelte Aufsätze zur Kirchengeschichte*, iii, 1928, pp. 54–116).

R. HOLTE, *Béatitude et Sagesse: S. Augustin et le problème de la fin de l'homme dans la philosophie ancienne*, 1962.

F. HOMES-DUDDEN, *The Life and Times of St. Ambrose*, 2 vols, 1935.

H. JAEGER, 'L'examen de conscience dans les religions non-chrétiennes et avant le Christianisme,' *Numen*, vi, 1959, pp. 176–233.

H. JAEGER, 'Justinien et l'episcopalis audientia,' *Revue Historique de Droit français et étranger*, 4ᵉ sér., xxxviii, 1960, pp. 214–262.

H. JAEGER, 'La preuve judiciaire d'après la tradition rabbinique et patristique,' *Recueils de la Société Jean Bodin*, xvi, 1964, pp. 415–594.

T. G. JALLAND, *The Church and the Papacy*, 1944.

A. H. M. JONES, *The Later Roman Empire*, 3 vols, 1964.

B. V. E. JONES, 'The Manuscript Tradition of Augustine's *De Civitate Dei*,' *Journal of Theological Studies*, n.s., xvi, 1965, pp. 142–145.

I. KAJANTO, *Onomastic Studies in the Early Christian Inscriptions of Rome and Carthage*, (Acta Instituti Romani Finlandiae, ii, 1), 1963.

C. KANNENGIESSER, 'Enarratio in Psalmum CXVIII: Science de la révélation et progrès spirituel,' *Recherches augustiniennes*, ii, 1962, pp. 359–381.

T. KATÔ, 'Melodia interior. Sur le traité *De pulchro et apto*,' *Revue des études augustiniennes*, xii, 1966, pp. 229–240.

K. E. KIRK, *The Vision of God*, 1931.

C. KLEGEMAN, 'A psychoanalytic study of the Confessions of St. Augustine,' *Journal of the American Psychoanalytic Association*, v, 1957, pp. 469–484.

G. N. KNAUER, *Die Psalmenzitate in Augustins Konfessionen*, 1955.

G. N. KNAUER, 'Peregrinatio Animae. (Zur Frage der Einheit der augustinischen Konfessionen),' *Hermes*, 85, 1957, pp. 216–248.

J. H. KOOPMANS, 'Augustine's first contact with Pelagius and the Dating of the Condemnation of Caelestius at Carthage,' *Vigiliae Christianae*, 8, 1954, pp. 149–153).

T. KOTULA, *Zgromadzenia prowincjonalne w rzymskiej Afryce w epoce późnego Cesarstwa*, (French resumé: *Les Assemblées provinciales dans l'Afrique romaine sous le Bas-Empire*), 1965.

A. M. La BONNARDIÈRE, 'Quelques remarques sur les citations scripturaires du *de gratia et libero arbitrio*,' *Revue des études augustiniennes*, ix, 1963, pp. 77–83.

A. M. La BONNARDIÈRE, *Recherches de chronologie augustinienne*, 1965.

A. M. La BONNARDIÈRE, 'Le combat chrétien. Exégèse augustinienne d'*Éphés*. 6, 12,' *Revue des études augustiniennes*, xi, 1965, pp. 235–238.

B. LACHOIX, *Orose et ses Idées*, (Université de Montréal. Publications de l'Institut d'Études Mediévales, xviii), 1965.

É. LAMIRANDE, 'Un siècle et demi d'études sur l'ecclésiologie de S. Augustin,' *Revue des études augustiniennes*, viii, 1962, pp. 1–124.

É. LAMIRANDE, *L'Église céleste selon S. Augustin*, 1963.

G. LANGGÄRTNER, *Die Gallienpolitik der Päpste in den V^{ten} und VI^{ten} Jahrhunderten. Eine Studie über dem apostolischen Vikariat von Arles*, (Theophaneia, 16), 1964.

A. LAURAS–H. RONDET, 'Le thème des deux cités dans l'œuvre de S. Augustin,' *Études augustiniennes*, (Rondet and others), 1953, pp. 99–162.

G. LAZZATI, *Il valore letterario dell'esegesi ambrosiana*, (Archivio ambrosiano, xi), 1960.

J. LECLERCQ, 'Prédication et rhétorique au temps de S. Augustin,' *Revue bénédictine*, 67, 1947, pp. 117–131.

B. LEGEWIE, *Augustinus: Eine Psychographie*, 1925.

B. LEGEWIE, 'Die körperliche Konstitution und Krankheiten Augustins,' *Miscellanea Agostiniana*, ii, 1930, pp. 5–21.

H. LEISEGANG, 'Der Ursprung der Lehre Augustins von der "Civitas Dei",' *Archiv für Kulturgeschichte*, 16, 1925, pp. 127–155.

H. LEWY, *Chaldaean Oracles and Theurgy. Mysticism, Magic and Platonism in the Later Roman Empire*, 1956.

LIBANIUS: *Autobiography: (Oration I)*, ed. and transl. A. F. NORMAN, 1965.

W. LIEBESCHÜTZ, 'Did the Pelagian Movement have social aims?', *Historia*, xii, 1963, pp. 227–241.

F. LO BUE, *The Turin Fragments of Tyconius' Commentary on Revelation*, (Texts and Studies, n.s., vii), 1963.

M. LÖHRER, *Der Glaubensbegriff des heiligen Augustins in seinen ersten Schriften bis zu den 'Confessiones'*, 1955.

H. P. L'ORANGE, 'The Portrait of Plotinus,' *Cahiers archéologiques. Fin de l'Antiquité et Moyen-Âge*, v, 1951, pp. 15–30.

BIBLIOGRAPHY

H. P. L'Orange, 'Plotinus–Paul,' *Byzantion*, 25–27, 1955–1957, pp. 473–483.

R. Lorenz, 'Die Wissenschaftslehre Augustins,' *Zeitschrift für Kirchengeschichte*, 67, 1956, pp. 29–60.

R. Lorenz, 'Der Augustinismus Prospers von Aquitanien,' *Zeitschrift für Kirchengeschichte*, 73, 1962, pp. 217–252.

R. Lorenz, 'Gnade und Erkenntnis bei Augustinus,' *Zeitschrift für Kirchengeschichte*, 75, 1964, pp. 21–78.

R. Lorenz, 'Die Anfänge des abendländischen Mönchtums im 4. Jahrhundert,' *Zeitschrift für Kirchengeschichte*, 77, 1966, pp. 1–61.

A. Luneau, *Histoire du Salut chez les Pères de l'Église: La doctrine des âges du monde*, (Théologie Historique, 2), 1964.

R. MacMullen, 'The Roman Concept of Robber-Pretender,' *Revue internationale des Droits de l'Antiquité*, 3ᵉ sér., x, 1963, pp. 221–226.

M. A. MacNamara, *Friendship in St. Augustine*, (Studia Friburgensia), 1958.

Macrobius: W. H. Stahl, *Macrobius' Commentary on the Dream of Scipio*, (Records of Civilisation; sources and studies, 48), 1952.

G. Madec, 'Connaissance de Dieu et action de grâces,' *Recherches augustiniennes*, ii, 1962, pp. 273–309.

F. G. Maier, *Augustin und das antike Rom*, 1955.

H. Maisonneuve, 'Croyance religieuse et contrainte: la doctrine de S. Augustin,' *Mélanges de science religieuse*, xix, 1962, pp. 49–68.

A. Mandouze, 'L'extase d'Ostie: possibilités et limites de la méthode de parallèles textuels,' *Augustinus Magister*, i, 1954, pp. 67–84.

A. Mandouze, 'S. Augustin et la religion romaine,' *Recherches augustiniennes*, i, 1958, pp. 187–223.

R. A. Markus, ' "Imago" and "Similitudo" in Augustine,' *Revue des études augustiniennes*, xi, 1964, pp. 125–143.

R. A. Markus, 'Two Conceptions of Political Authority: Augustine's *De Civ. Dei*, XIX, 14–15 and some Thirteenth-Century Interpretations,' *Journal of Theological Studies*, n.s., xvi, 1965, pp. 68–100.

E. Marec, 'Deux mosaïques d'Hippone,' *Libyca*, i, 1953, pp. 95–108.

E. Marec, *Hippone-la-royale: antique Hippo Regius*, 1954.

E. Marec, *Monuments chrétiens d'Hippone*, 1958.

H. I. Marrou, 'Autour de la bibliothèque du pape Agapet,' *Mélanges d'archéologie et d'histoire*, 48, 1931, pp. 124–169.

H. I. Marrou, *MOYCIKOC ANHP. Études sur les scènes de la vie intellectuelle figurants sur les monuments funéraires romains*, 1938.

BIBLIOGRAPHY

H. I. Marrou, *S. Augustin et la fin de la culture antique*, 1st ed. 1938, and '*Retractatio*', 1949.

H. I. Marrou, 'Survivances païennes dans les rites funéraires des donatistes,' *Extrait de la Collection Latomus*, ii, 1949, pp. 193–203.

H. I. Marrou, 'La technique de l'édition a l'époque patristique,' *Vigiliae Christianae*, 3, 1949, pp. 217–224.

H. I. Marrou, *L'Ambivalence du Temps de l'Histoire chez S. Augustin*, 1950.

H. I. Marrou, 'La division en chapitres des livres de la "Cité de Dieu",' *Mélanges J. de Ghellinck*, i, 1951, pp. 235–249.

H. I. Marrou, 'Épitaphe chrétienne d'Hippone à réminiscences virgiliennes,' *Libyca*, i, 1953, pp. 215–230.

H. I. Marrou, 'Un lieu dit "Cité de Dieu",' *Augustinus Magister*, i, 1954, pp. 101–110.

H. I. Marrou, *History of Education in the Ancient World*, (transl. 1956).

H. I. Marrou, *St. Augustine*, (Men of Wisdom), (transl. 1957).

H. I. Marrou, 'Civitas Dei, civitas terrena: num tertium quid?', (Studia Patristica, ii), *Texte und Untersuchungen*, 64, 1957, pp. 342–350.

H. I. Marrou, 'La Basilique chrétienne d'Hippone d'après le résultat des dernières fouilles,' *Revue des études augustiniennes*, vi, 1960, pp. 109–154.

H. I. Marrou, 'Synesius of Cyrene and Alexandrian Neo-Platonism,' *The Conflict between Paganism and Christianity in the Fourth Century*, ed. Momigliano, 1963, pp. 126–150.

H. I. Marrou (and A. M. La Bonnardière), 'Le dogme de la résurrection et la théologie des valeurs humains selon l'enseignement de saint Augustin,' *Revue des études augustiniennes*, xii, 1966, pp. 111–136 (= *The Resurrection and St. Augustine's Theology of Human Values*, Villanova University Press, 1966).

F. Martroye, 'S. Augustin et la compétence de la juridiction ecclésiastique au Vᵉ siècle,' *Mémoires de la société nationale des antiquaires de France*, 7ᵉ sér., x, 1911, pp. 1–78.

G. Mathew, *Byzantine Aesthetics*, 1963.

F. Masai, 'Les conversions de S. Augustin et les débuts du spiritualisme de l'Occident,' *Le Moyen Âge*, 67, 1961, pp. 1–40.

S. Mazzarino, 'Sull' *otium* di Massiminiano Erculio,' *Rendiconti dell'Accademia dei Lincei*, ser. 8, viii, 1954, pp. 417–421.

R. Meiggs, *Roman Ostia*, 1960.

BIBLIOGRAPHY

MELANIA: *Vie de sainte Mélanie*, ed. tr. D. GORCE, (Sources chrétiennes, 90), 1962.

P. J. MENASCE, 'Augustin manichéen,' *Freundesgabe für Ernst Robert Curtius*, 1956, pp. 79–93.

S. MERKLE, 'Augustin über eine Unterbrechung der Höllenstrafen,' *Aurelius Augustinus*, 1930, pp. 197–202.

E. MERSCH, *Le corps mystique du Christ*, ii, 3rd ed. 1951.

L. MINIO-PALUELLO, 'The Text of the *Categoriae*: the Latin Tradition,' *Classical Quarterly*, 39, 1945, pp. 63–74.

A. MITTERER, *Die Entwicklungslehre Augustins*, 1956.

Christine MOHRMANN, 'Le latin commun et le latin des Chrétiens,' *Vigiliae Christianae*, 1, 1947, pp. 1–12.

Chr. MOHRMANN, 'Comment s. Augustin s'est familiarisé avec le latin des Chrétiens,' *Augustinus Magister*, i, 1954, pp. 111–116.

Chr. MOHRMANN and F. VAN DER MEER, *Atlas of the Early Christian World*, 1958.

Chr. MOHRMANN, 'Augustine and the Eloquentia,' *Études sur le latin des Chrétiens*, i, 1958, pp. 351–370.

Chr. MOHRMANN, 'S. Augustin écrivain,' *Recherches augustiniennes*, i, 1958, pp. 43–66.

A. MOMIGLIANO, 'Some Observations on the "Origo Gentis Romanae",' *Secondo contributo alla storia degli studi classici*, 1960, pp. 145–178.

A. MOMIGLIANO, 'Pagan and Christian Historiography in the Fourth Century,' *The Conflict between Christianity and Paganism in the Fourth Century*, ed. Momigliano, 1963, pp. 79–99.

E. Th. MOMMSEN, 'Petrarch and the Decoration of the "Sala Virorum Illustrium" in Padua,' *Medieval and Renaissance Studies*, ed. Rice, 1959, pp. 130–174.

E. Th. MOMMSEN, 'Orosius and Augustine,' *Medieval and Renaissance Studies*, ed. Rice, 1959, pp. 325–348.

P. MONCEAUX, *Les Africains: Les Païens*, 1894.

P. MONCEAUX, *Histoire littéraire de l'Afrique chrétienne*, v-vii, 1920–1923.

P. MONCEAUX, 'Le manichéen Fauste de Milev: Restitution de ses "capitula",' *Mémoires de l'Académie des Inscriptions et Belles Lettres*, 1924.

P. MONCEAUX, 'S. Augustin et S. Antoine,' *Miscellanea Agostiniana*, ii, 1931, pp. 61–89.

J. MORRIS, 'Pelagian Literature,' *Journal of Theological Studies*, n.s., xvi, 1965, pp. 26–60.

P. Munz, 'John Cassian,' *Journal of Ecclesiastical History*, xi, 1960, pp. 1–22.

J. N. L. Myres, 'Pelagius and the End of Roman Rule in Britain,' *Journal of Roman Studies*, l, 1960, pp. 21–36.

A. D. Nock, *Conversion: the old and the new in religion from Alexander the Great to Augustine of Hippo*, 1933.

J. Nørregaard, *Augustins Bekehrung*, 1923.

G. Nygren, *Das Prädestinationsproblem in der Theologie Augustins*, (Studia Theologica Lundensia, 12), 1956.

R. J. O'Connell, 'Ennead VI, 4 and 5 in the Works of St. Augustine,' *Revue des études augustiniennes*, ix, 1963, pp. 1–39.

R. J. O'Connell, 'The Plotinian Fall of the Soul in St. Augustine,' *Traditio*, 19, 1963, pp. 1–35.

R. J. O'Connell, 'The Riddle of Augustine's "Confessions": A Plotinian Key,' *International Philosophical Quarterly*, iv, 1964, pp. 327–372.

J. O'Meara, *St. Augustine: Against the Academics*, (Ancient Christian Writers, 12), 1950.

J. O'Meara, *The Young Augustine*, 1954.

J. O'Meara, 'Augustine and Neo-Platonism,' *Recherches augustiniennes*, i, 1958, pp. 91–111.

J. O'Meara, *Porphyry's Philosophy from Oracles in Augustine*, 1959.

Orosius: transl. I. W. Raymond, *Seven Books of History against the Pagans*, (Columbia University Records of Civilization, xxii), 1936.

B. Parodi, *La catachesi di S. Ambrogio*, 1957.

A. Paredi, 'Paulinus of Milan,' *Sacris Erudiri*, 14, 1963, pp. 206–230.

M. Pellegrino, *Possidio, Vita di Agostino*, (*Verba Seniorum*, 4), 1955.

M. Pellegrino, *Les Confessions de S. Augustin*, 1960.

M. Pellegrino, *Paolino di Milano, Vita di S. Ambrogio*, (*Verba Seniorum*, n.s., 1), 1961.

J. Pépin, 'Recherches sur le sens et les origines de l'expression "caelum caeli" dans le livre XII des Confessions de saint Augustin,' *Bulletin du Cange*, 23, 1953, pp. 185–274.

J. Pépin, 'À propos de l'histoire de l'exégèse allégorique: l'absurdité, signe de l'allégorie,' (Studia Patristica, i), *Texte und Untersuchungen*, 63, 1957, pp. 395–413.

J. Pépin, *Mythe et Allégorie*, 1958.

BIBLIOGRAPHY

J. PÉPIN, 'S. Augustin et la fonction protréptique de l'allégorie,' *Recherches augustiniennes*, i, 1958, pp. 243–286.

J. PÉPIN, *Théologie cosmique et théologie chrétienne*, (*Ambroise, Éxaém.* I, 1, 1–4), 1964.

O. PERLER, 'Les voyages de S. Augustin,' *Recherches augustiniennes*, i, 1958, pp. 5–42.

O. PERLER, 'Das Datum der Bischofsweihe des heiligen Augustinus,' *Revue des études augustiniennes*, xi, 1965, pp. 25–37.

E. de la PEZA, 'El significado de "cor" en San Augustin,' *Revue des études augustiniennes*, vii, 1961, pp. 339–368.

E. de la PEZA, *El significado de 'cor' en San Augustin*, 1962.

G. Ch. PICARD, *La civilisation de l'Afrique romaine*, 1959.

G. Ch. PICARD, 'Un palais du IVe s. à Carthage,' *Comptes-Rendus de l'Académie des Inscriptions et Belles Lettres*, 1964, pp. 101–118.

G. CH. PICARD, *La Carthage de saint Augustin*, 1965.

M. Ch. PIETRI, '*Concordia apostolorum* et *renovatio urbis*. (Culte des martyres et propagande papale),' *Mélanges d'archéologie et d'histoire*, 73, 1961, 275–322.

M. Ch. PIETRI, 'Le Serment du Soldat chrétien,' *Mélanges d'archéologie et d'histoire*, 74, 1962, pp. 649–664.

A. PIGANIOL, *L'Empire chrétien*, (Histoire romaine, IV, 2), 1947.

A. PINCHERLE, *La formazione teologica di S. Agostino*, 1947.

L. F. PIZZOLATO, *La 'Explanatio Psalmorum XII'. Studio letterario sulla esegesi di Sant'Ambrogio*, (Archivio Ambrosiano, xvii), 1965.

G. de PLINVAL, *Pélage: ses écrits, sa vie et sa réforme*, 1943.

G. de PLINVAL, *Essai sur le style et la langue de Pélage*, 1947.

PLOTINUS, *Enneads*: transl. S. MacKENNA, *Plotinus, The Enneads*, 2nd edition, 1956.

H. J. POLOTSKY, *Manichäische Homilien*, 1934.

M. PONDET, *L'Exégèse de S. Augustin prédicateur*, 1945.

E. PORTALIÉ, *A Guide to the Thought of St. Augustine*, (transl. BASTIAN), 1960.

S. PRETE, *Pelagio e il Pelagianesimo*, 1961.

PROSPER: P. de LETTER, *St. Prosper of Aquitaine: Defense of St. Augustine*, (Ancient Christian Writers, xxxii), 1963.

H. C. PUECH, 'Der Begriff der Erlösung im Manichäismus,' *Eranos Jahrbuch*, 1936, pp. 183–286.

H. C. PUECH, *Le Manichéisme: son fondateur, sa doctrine*, (Musée Guimet. Bibliothèque de diffusion, lvi), 1949.

H. C. PUECH, 'Plotin et les gnostiques,' *Les Sources de Plotin*, (Entretiens: Fondation Hardt, v), 1960, pp. 161–174.

BIBLIOGRAPHY

J. QUASTEN, ' "Vetus superstitio et nova religio" ', *Harvard Theological Review*, xxxiii, 1940, pp. 253–266.

A. RAGONA, *Il proprietario della villa romana di Piazza Armerina*, 1962.

A. RATTI, 'Il più antico ritratto di S. Ambrogio,' *Ambrosiana*, ch. xiv, 1897.

J. RATZINGER, *Volk und Haus Gottes*, 1954.

J. RATZINGER, 'Originalität und Überlieferung in Augustins Begriff der "Confessio",' *Revue des études augustiniennes*, iii, 1957, pp. 375–392.

J. RATZINGER, 'Beobachtungen zum Kirchenbegriff des Tyconius,' *Revue des études augustiniennes*, ii, 1958, pp. 173–185.

F. REFOULÉ, 'La datation du premier concile de Carthage contre les Pélagiens et du *Libellus fidei* de Rufin,' *Revue des études augustiniennes*, xi, 1963, pp. 41–49.

F. REFOULÉ, 'Julien d'Éclane, théologien et philosophe,' *Recherches de sciences religieuses*, 52, 1964, pp. 42–84 and 233–247.

J. RIES, 'Introduction aux études manichéennes,' *Ephemerides Theologicae Lovanienses*, 33, 1957, pp. 453–482, and 35, 1959, pp. 362–409.

J. RIES, 'La Bible chez S. Augustin et chez les manichéens,' *Revue des études augustiniennes*, ix, 1963, pp. 201–215.

J. RIES, 'Jésus-Christ dans la religion de Mani. Quelques éléments d'une confrontation de saint Augustin avec un hymnaire christologique manichéen copte,' *Augustiniana*, 14, 1964, pp. 437–454.

H. RONDET, 'Richesse et pauvreté dans la prédication de S. Augustin,' *Revue d'ascétisme et mystique*, xxx, 1954, pp. 193–231.

O. ROTTMANNER, *Der Augustinismus*, 1892 (trans. LIEBAERT, 'L'Augustinisme,' *Mélanges de science religieuse*, vi, 1949, pp. 31–48).

J. ROUGÉ, 'Une émeute à Rome au IVᵉ s.,' *Revue des études anciennes*, 63, 1963, pp. 59–77.

L. RUGGINI, 'Ebrei e orientali nell' Italia settentrionale (iv–vi s.),' *Studia et Documenta Historiae et Juris*, xxv, 1959, pp. 186–308.

L. RUGGINI, *Economia e società nell' Italia annonaria*, 1962.

A. SAGE, ' "Praeparatur voluntas a Deo" ', *Revue des études augustiniennes*, x, 1964, pp. 1–20.

G. SANDERS, *Licht en Duisternis in de christelijke Grafschriften*, 2 vols. (Verhandelingen van de koninklijke Vlaamse Academie voor Wetenschappen, Letteren en schone Kunsten van België. Klasse der Letteren, Jaargang xxvii, nr. 56), 1965.

BIBLIOGRAPHY

H. Sasse, '*Sacra Scriptura*: Bemerkungen zur Inspirationslehre Augustins,' *Festschrift Franz Dornseiff*, 1953, pp. 262–273.

Ch. Saumagne, 'Ouvriers agricoles ou rôdeurs de celliers? Les circoncellions d'Afrique,' *Annales d'Histoire écon. et sociale*, 6, 1934, pp. 351–364.

M. Schmaus, 'Die Denkform Augustins in seinem Werk *de Trinitate*,' *Sitzungsberichte der bayerischen Akademie der Wissenschaften, Philosophische-historische Klasse*, 1962, no. 6.

K. A. Schöndorf, *Die Geschichtstheologie des Orosius*, (Diss. Munich), 1952.

H. v. Schubert, *Der sogenannte Praedestinatus*, (Texte und Untersuchungen, 24, 4), 1903.

K. H. Schwarte, *Die Vorgeschichte der augustinischen Weltaltulehre*, 1966.

M. Simon, 'Le judaïsme berbère dans l'Afrique ancienne,' *Revue d'histoire et de philosophie religieuses*, xxvi, 1946, pp. 1–31 and 105–145 (= *Recherches d'Histoire Judéo-Chrétienne*, 1962, pp. 30–87).

M. Simon, 'Punique ou berbère?' *Annuaire de l'Institut de Philologie et d'Histoire Orientales et Slaves*, xiii, 1955, pp. 613–629 (= *Recherches d'Histoire Judéo-Chrétienne*, 1962, pp. 88–100).

A. Solignac, 'Doxographies et manuels dans la formation philosophique de S. Augustin,' *Recherches augustiniennes*, i, 1958, pp. 113–148.

A. Solignac, Introduction and notes to *Les Confessions*, transl. Tréhorel-Bouissou, (Bibliothèque augustinienne, sér. ii, 13–14), 1962.

A. Steinwenter, 'Eine kirchliche Quelle des nachklassischen Zivilprozesses,' *Acta congressus iuridici internationalis*, 2, 1935, pp. 123–144.

G. Strauss, *Schriftgebrauch, Schriftauslegung und Schriftbeweis bei Augustin*, (Beiträge zur Geschichte der biblischen Hermeneutik, 1), 1959.

J. Sundwall, *Weströmische Studien*, 1915.

M. Tajo, 'Un confronto tra s. Ambrogio e s. Agostino a proposito dell' esegesi del Cantico dei Cantici,' *Revue des études augustiniennes*, vii, 1961, pp. 127–151.

E. Tengström, *Die Protokollierung der Collatio Carthaginensis*, (Studia Graeca et Latina Gothoburgensia, xiv), 1962.

E. Tengström, *Donatisten und Katholiken: soziale, wirtschaftliche und politische Aspekte einer nordafrikanischen Kirchenspaltung*, (Studia Graeca et Latina Gothoburgensia, xviii), 1964.

M. TESTARD, *S. Augustin et Cicéron*, 2 vols, 1958.

W. THEILER, rev. COURCELLE, *Recherches sur les 'Confessions'*, *Gnomon*, 75, 1953, pp. 113–122.

E. A. THOMPSON, 'The Settlement of the Barbarians in Southern Gaul,' *Journal of Roman Studies*, xlvi, 1956, pp. 65–75.

E. A. THOMPSON, 'The Visigoths from Fritigern to Euric,' *Historia*, xii, 1963, pp. 105–126.

F.-J. THONNARD, 'La prédestination augustinienne et l'interprétation de O. Rottmanner,' *Revue des études augustiniennes*, ix, 1963, pp. 259–287.

F.-J. THONNARD, 'La prédestination augustinienne. Sa place en philosophie augustinienne,' *Revue des études augustiniennes*, x, 1964, pp. 97–123.

F.-J. THONNARD, 'L'aristotélisme de Julien d'Éclane et saint Augustin,' *Revue des études augustiniennes*, xi, 1965, pp. 296–304.

J. TOUTAIN, *Les cultes païens dans l'Empire romain*, iii, 1920.

H. ULBRICH, 'Augustins Briefe zur entscheidender Phase des pelagian-ischen Streites,' *Revue des études augustiniennes*, ix, 1963, pp. 51–75 and 235–258.

T. VAN BAVEL, *Répertoire bibliographique de S. Augustin, 1950–1960*, (Instrumenta Patristica, III), 1963.

F. VAN der MEER, *Augustine the Bishop*, (transl. BATTERSHAW and LAMB), 1961.

F. VAN der MEER, 'À propos du sarcophage du Mas d'Aire,' *Mélanges Christine Mohrmann*, 1963, pp. 169–176.

A. C. de VEER, ' "Revelare", "Revelatio". Éléments d'une étude sur l'emploi du mot et sur sa signification chez s. Augustin,' *Recherches augustiniennes*, ii, 1962, pp. 331–357.

A. C. de VEER, 'La date du *de unico baptismo*,' *Revue des études augustiniennes*, x, 1964, pp. 35–38.

A. C. de VEER, 'L'exploitation du schisme maximianiste par S. Augustin dans sa lutte contre le Donatisme,' *Recherches augus-tiniennes*, iii, 1965, pp. 219–237.

P. VERBRAKEN, 'Les deux sermons du prêtre Éraclius d'Hippone,' *Revue bénédictine*, 71, 1961, pp. 3–21.

G. VILLE, 'Les jeux de gladiateurs dans l'Empire chrétien,' *Mélanges d'archéologie et d'histoire*, 72, 1960, pp. 273–335.

BIBLIOGRAPHY

F. VITTINGHOFF, 'Zum geschichtlichen Selbstverständnis der Spätantike,' *Historische Zeitschrift*, 198, 1964, pp. 529–574.

J. VOGT, 'Ammianus Marcellinus als erzählender Geschichtsschreiber der Spätzeit,' *Mainzer Akademie der Wissenschaften und der Literatur. Abhandlungen der geistes- und sozial-wissenshaftlichen Klasse*, 1963, no. 8.

J. de VOOGHT, 'Les miracles dans la vie de S. Augustin,' *Recherches de Théologie ancienne et médiévale*, xi, 1939, pp. 5–16.

A. WACHTEL, *Beiträge zur Geschichtstheologie des Aurelius Augustinus*, 1960.

P. G. WALSH, 'Massinissa,' *Journal of Roman Studies*, lv, 1965, pp. 149–160.

R. WALZER, 'Platonism in Islamic Philosophy,' *Greek into Arabic*, 1962.

R. WALZER, 'Porphyry and the Arabic Tradition,' *Porphyre*, (Entretiens: Fondation Hardt, xii), 1965, pp. 275–299.

B. H. WARMINGTON, *The North African Provinces from Diocletian to the Vandal Conquest*, 1954.

H. T. WEISSKOTTEN, *Sancti Augustini Vita scripta a Possidio episcopo*, (Edition with Revised Text, Introduction, Notes and an English Version), 1919.

Rebecca WEST, *St. Augustine*, 1933.

G. WIDENGREN, *Mani and Manichaeism*, (transl. KESSLER), 1965.

N. P. WILLIAMS, *The Idea of the Fall and of Original Sin*, 1927.

J. de WIT, *Die Miniaturen des Vergilius Vaticanus*, 1959.

H. WOODS, *Augustine and Evolution*, 1924.

A. WUCHERER-HULDENFELD, 'Mönchtum und kirchlicher Dienst bei Augustinus nach dem Bilde des Neubekehrtens und des Bischofs,' *Zeitschrift für Katholische Theologie*, 82, 1962, pp. 182–211.

INDEX

Abel, peccadilloes of, 199–200

Adam and Eve:
  Capital punishment of Adam, 372
  Common kinship in Adam, 224
  Eve not given to Adam for company, 62
  Eve the 'active', Adam the 'contemplative' parts of the soul, 205
  Eve, the temptress, in all women, 63
  Fall of, in third-century sarcophagus, 388 n. 5
  fortunate to work in a garden, 143
  Guilt of, 'unspeakable', 393
  Idyllic description of, by Julian of Eclanum, 382
  Indirect knowledge after the Fall, 261
  Pelagius and Augustine on the sin of Adam, 365–366
  Shame of, after the Fall, 388
  Simple marriage of, praised by Paulinus of Nola, 382
  State before the Fall, 327

Adeodatus, son of Augustine, 39, 62, 118, 130, 135

Africa:
  and Italy, 24–25, 145, 383–384, 420
  army in, 192, 421–422
  ecclesiastical culture of, 23, 161–162, 271–273, 356, 383
  extension of Christianity in, 402, 419
  landowners, 20, 191–193, 241, 336, 362, 420
  loyalty of, after 410, 291, 336
  olives, 20, 191, 292, 419
  pagan classical culture in, 23, 24 n. 5, 302, 420 n. 13
  prosperity of, 19, 420

Africans:
  African accent of Augustine, 88
  at court, 24–25, 362, 420
  Christian popular beliefs, 33, 196, 413–414
  evil eye, 32
  irony, 32, 309
  lawyers, 23
  love of puns and acrostics, 22, 254
  pagan religious beliefs, 32–33
  personal relationships, 31
  position of mothers, 247–248
  sense of honour, 31, 203

Alaric, king of the Goths, 288, 330

Allegory, 154, 252–255, 259–263

Alypius, friend of Augustine, later bishop of Thagaste, 54, 67–68, 90, 107–109, 124, 133, 140 n. 6, 144, 162, 174, 201, 233, 299, 334, 362, 384, 420, 422

Ambrose, bishop of Milan, 27, 70–72, 79–87, 88, 89, 103, 111, 112, 124, 125–126, 153, 261, 272 n. 5, 408

Ammianus Marcellinus, last historian of Rome, 69 n. 4, 310 n. 2, 351 n. 4

Astrology, 57–58, 67, 369, 392

Augustine:
  and music, songs and poetry, 35, 36, 61, 67, 117, 119, 126, 141, 179, 258, 325–326
  and natural beauty, 35, 117–118, 259, 329
  and the theatre, 39, 171

INDEX

Augustine *continued*:

and travelling, 152, 191, 202, 234

and winter, 193, 210

and yearning, 156–157, 161, 210–211

as a polemist, 134, 141, 228–229, 273, 305, 354, 384–385, 389–390

as a preacher, 139, 142, 231, 233, 251–252, 253–255, 256, 291–292, 313–315, 359, 367, 431

attitude to his intellectual progress, 59, 112, 277–278, 279–280, 353, 403, 429–430

close relations with relatives, 32, 199, 227, 411

cousins uneducated, 21, 119, 267

education, 36–37

friends, 61, 63, 180, 200–202, 411

health, 109–110, 117, 297, 299, 402, 410, 417, 423, 431

ideal of episcopal authority, 206

knowledge of Greek, 38, 271, 412,

knowledge of philosophy, 57 n. 3, 94–95, 276, 307

love of light, 35, 180, 325

memory in Hippo, 432 n. 4

of poor family, 21, 410

on anger, 53, 205, 206, 209

on babies, 28–29, 171, 326, 352

on communication, 161, 256

on dreams, 413

on dress, 21, 193, 410

on envy, 32, 326

on gardening, 21, 143

on greed, 179, 389

on his schooldays, 35, 38, 171, 238, 328

on love of praise, 32, 206, 427

on mourning, 171–172

opinions of enemies and critics, 23, 195, 203–204, 233, 242–243, 330, 383

psychological interpretations of, 31 n. 4

sarcasm, 29, 118–119, 208, 273–274, 309

Thought:

authority, 42, 49, 54, 80, 216, 238, 239 n. 7, 272, 276, 278, 310–311, 418

'City of God' (and related themes), 161, 251, 287–288, 296–297, 313–315, 319, 320, 321, 322–323, 338

disciplina, 236–237, 293

faith and reason, 111–113, 276–277, 278–279

free will, 148

grace and free-will, 154–155, 234–235, 275, 373–374, 405

habit, 149, 173–174, 207, 250, 310, 416

Hell (and Hellfire), 247, 307–308, 336, 372, 392 n. 9, 395, 396

History: Roman history, 308–311

general, 316–323

Last Judgement, 198–199, 249–250, 251, 314–315, 372, 396

marriage, 38, 142, 248, 390

predestination, 175, 221, 234–235, 335, 338, 399, 403–407

unity of the human race, 224–225

Changes in Augustine's thought:

Church and State, 231–232, 315, 337–338

coercion, 230, 235–238

contemplative and active life, 204–205, 325

death, fear of, 133, 417, 431

education, 264, 269

friendship, 155–156, 161, 209–211, 324–325

ideals (A.D. 386–396), 146–147

intellectual programme: at Thagaste, 134–135

in middle age, 278–280

miracles, 415–418

rôle of feeling, 154–155, 257–258

spiritual progress of the human race, 237–238, 418

suffering, 292–293, 327

the Fall, 327

INDEX

Aurelius, bishop of Carthage, 143–147, 163, 164, 206–207, 227
Ausonius, 27, 66

Baptism:
  Ambrose on, 107
  and conversion, 177
  and the Fall, 388 n. 5
  and the Remission of sins, 365
  Associations of, in Milan, 106
  Augustine: image of convalescence, 365
  Effect on a friend, 63–64
  in Africa, 212
  in Italy and Gaul, 369
  in the 'Confessions', 222
  in the congregation at Hippo, 246
  Miracles surrounding, at Uzalis, 385
  of Augustine, 124
  of infants, 280, 344, 385
  Pelagius and Augustine on, 368 n. 5
  previously associated with retirement, 336
  Progress in understanding of, 270
  repetition of, 280
  urged on a governor, 336
Bethlehem, 202, 347
Bishop:
  and the Scriptures, 42–43, 112, 139–140, 162
  position in African society, 133, 194–198, 242, 408, 420–421
  position in the African Church, 33, 140, 143–144, 203, 210, 220, 408, 412, 424
Boniface, Count of Africa, 422–423, 425
Britain, 291, 341, 346 n. 2, 351

Caecilian, bishop of Carthage, 215, 331, 332, 334
Caelestius, disciple of Pelagius, 344–345, 359
Cain and Abel, 315, 320, 321, 322
Carthage:
  a 'cauldron', 38, 64, 72
  arrival of Caelestius in, 344
  Arrives at, in 403, 233
  attends Catholic church at, 41
  Augustine leaves, in 413, 337–338
  Augustine's first arrival at, 38
  Augustine's return from Italy, 131
  Bookstalls, 65
  Collatio with Donatists, in 411, 331–334
  Council at, in 416, 357
  Delays in, in 410, 290
  Dines on roast peacock at, 420
  fortified, 423
  in the fourth century, 65
  Journeys from Hippo, 193, 419–420
  Known as a student at, 242
  Manichees in, 43, 44, 54, 134
  Paganism and circus-shows at, 313 n. 4
  Pagan salons at, after 410, 300
  Pelagian ideas at, 344–345
  Preaches at, in 399, 230–231
  Proconsuls, 65–66, 420
  Second arrival at, 64
  sees Pelagius at, 339
  too busy to write at, 338 n. 8
Cassiciacum: Cassiago(?), near Lake Como:
  as an image of Paradise, 164
  as described by Licentius, 116, 163
  as remembered, in 410, 299
  Augustine retires to, in autumn 386, 111
  compared with Augustine's life at Thagaste (A.D. 388–391), 132
  cultured retirement at, 115–117
  similarity of Pelagian groups, 368
  text-books at, 113
Celer, Donatist landowner, 241
Christ:
  and predestination, 407
  as the 'Wisdom of God', 41–42
  Crucifixion in the sermons of Augustine, 246, 257
  in Manichaeism, 43–44, 52
  'sleeps' in the soul, 245
Cicero:
  and Jerome, 265
  and the established religion, 80

INDEX

Cicero *continued*:
  and the Fall of the Soul, 388 n. 2
  and the 'New Academy', 79–80
  Augustine's knowledge of, 36, 57, 299–300
  Hortensius, 40, 107, 394
  not sold in Hippo, 189
  on fathers and sons, 135
  on the pleasures of the body, 50
  on the wretchedness of man, 394
Circumcellions, 229, 330, 335, 414
Claudian, poet, 71 n. 7, 198 n. 9, 230 n. 7
Concubinage, 62, 248
Concubine, of Augustine, 30, 39, 61–63, 88–90
Confessions:
  Ambrose, as seen in, 162
  and Apuleius, 23
  and the *Ad Simplicianum de diversis quaestionibus*, 155
  and the traditional idea of conversion, 177–178
  and traditional biography, 173
  as the history of Augustine's feelings, 169–172
  audience, 159–160
  Augustine's self-portrait in, 179–180
  challenging perspective of, 28
  conscientia in, 210
  conversion to Manichees, as seen in, 162
  description of Augustine's conversion in, compared with his early works, 114
  emergence of the main themes of, 148
  evolution of Augustine's ideas on spiritual substance, as described in, 86, 167
  force of habit in, 173–174
  historical value of, 158 n. 1
  ideal of monastic bishop in, 162
  influence of Plotinus in, 168–169, 178
  judgement on, in the *Retractions*, 430
  meaning of *confessio*, 175
  motives for writing, 163–165, 202
  perspective of, after baptism in Milan, 126
  philosopher's prayer in, 165–166
  predestination in, 175, 406
  problem of evil in, compared with the *de Ordine*, 175–176
  psychological studies of, 31 n. 4
  reading of Neo-Platonic books, as described in, 94
  reveal Augustine's intellectual activity as a bishop, 162, 180–181, 262
  sent to Count Darius, 427
  significance of use of the Psalms in, 174–175
  style of, influenced by Augustine's preaching, 256
  treatment of adolescence in, 172
  wandering of the soul in, 168–169
Consentius, Spanish priest, 240
Constantine, Emperor, 106, 331
Cyprian, S., 153, 159, 177 n. 2, 212 n. 4, 213, 214, 216, 219, 225, 251, 337, 344 n. 6, 368, 406

Dardanus, Prefect of Gaul, 116, 336–337, 360
Darius, Count, Imperial ambassador, 423, 427
Demetrias, grand-niece of Proba, recipient of letter of Pelagius, 340, 342, 344, 356, 367 n. 6
Demons:
  and paganism, 311
  commence with, 265–266
  John Chrysostom on, 396
  World shared by man with, 41, 244–245
Devil:
  as the 'Lord of this World', 244
  Fall of, 326
  man 'his own devil', 245
  vast power of, 395
Dioscurus, Greek student at Carthage, 65 n. 7, 299–300
Diospolis (Lydda), synod, 357

Donatism, Donatists:

attitudes revealed in the 'Acts' of their martyrs, 217–218

Augustine's attitude to, 207, 216–217, 226

bishops, 144

Christianity as a 'Law' in, 218, 239

criticize Augustine, 235–236

effects of suppression, 412

idea of ritual purity in, 218–219

idea of the Church, compared with that of Augustine, 214, 221–225, 239

image of the Ark of Noah in, 221, 224

methods of suppression extended to the Pelagians, 383–384

modern explanations of, 217 n. 4

predominant in and around Hippo, 139, 226–227

refuse to coexist with 'impure' colleagues, 209, 222–223

sinlessness of the Church, 213–214

suppression of, 234, 240–242, 334–336, 360, 421

use of popular songs, 141

Dreams, 29, 33, 53, 91, 109, 119, 131, 175, 244, 385, 413

Dulcitius, Imperial agent, 335, 338 n. 8

Education:

and paganism, 302, 307

and social advancement, 21

Augustine's views on, 264–268

in Augustine's monastery in Hippo, 198, 267

in Augustine's programme in Milan, 113, 120, 122

in Carthage, 65

in Rome, 68

of Augustine, 29, 36–37

survival of, taken for granted by Augustine, 267–268, 411

Emperor, 25, 54, 69, 71, 81, 224, 225, 241, 300, 330, 336, 360–361, 420

and the establishment and expansion of Christianity, 231–232, 234, 291, 337–338

Donatist attitude to, 239

Eraclius, priest and successor of Augustine at Hippo, 408, 411, 414

Eulogius Favonius, pupil of Augustine, 131, 302

Evodius, bishop of Uzalis, 126, 130, 136, 152, 153 n. 1, 201, 273, 303 n. 7, 307, 402

Faustus of Milevis, Manichaean leader, 58, 86, 264, 319, 370 n. 4

Felix, Manichaean missionary, 242, 333

Filastrius, bishop of Brescia, 125

Firmus, priest, literary agent of Augustine, 304, 361

possibly a convert from Manichaeism, 370 n. 2

Florus, monk of Hadrumetum, 273 n. 3, 399, 402

Fonteius, pagan Platonist of Carthage, 133

Fortunatus, Manichaean friend of Augustine, 140 n. 6, 141, 148, 149, 150, 242

Freud:

and Augustine, on a 'fall' of consciousness, 261

on slips of the tongue, 366

Fu-Kien, Manichaeism in, 44, 54

Fussala, village in Augustine's diocese, 412

Galileo, cites Augustine, 276

Gaudentius, Donatist bishop of Timgad, 335

Genseric, King of the Vandals, 424–425

Gildo, Moorish Count of Africa, 230, 422

Heraclian, Count of Africa, 337

Hermogenianus, 90, 128 n. 6

Heros, Gallic bishop, 356–357, 359, 360

Hippo Diarrhytos, 240

Hippo Regius:
  after the death of Augustine, 432 n. 4
  Augustine's congregation at:
    attitudes to wealth and poverty of, 198–199, 250–251
    Augustine as arbitrator among, 195–197, 226, 408
    lynch the commander of the garrison, 192, 421
    moral attitudes of, 247–250
    popular religious customs of, 207, 234
    reaction to the sack of Rome, 290, 294
    'senior' laymen of, 197
  Augustine's monastery at, 136, 140, 142–144, 198–200, 224–225, 267, 409–410
  Augustine travels to, 136
  besieged by the Vandals, 425
  Christian basilica of, 190
  economy of, 191–192
  relations with the countryside, 191, 193, 241, 413
  relations with the sea, 191
  Roman buildings of, 189–190
  state of the Catholic community in, 139–140, 190, 194, 226–227, 234, 241–242, 413
  visitors to Augustine at, 158, 200
Honorius, Emperor, 230, 330, 361 n. 7

Innocent, pope, 200 n. 8, 357, 358, 359

Jacobus, former disciple of Pelagius, 359
Jansenism, 348 n. 8
Januarius, a priest, 402 n. 3
Jerome, 27 n. 3, 162, 202, 208, 265, 271, 273, 342, 356
  acrimonious correspondence with Augustine, 274–275
Jerusalem, Latin émigrés at, 356 n. 5, 361
John, bishop of Jerusalem, 356

Julian, Pelagian bishop of Eclanum:
  accuses Augustine of Manichaeism, 370, 386, 393
  and Augustine, on the collective punishment of the human race, 327
  and Roman Law, 392
  and Tertullian, 392
  anticipates S. Thomas Aquinas, 387 n. 2
  appeals to 'high-brow' audience, Augustine to 'middle-brow', 385
  Culture of, 387
  family and background of, 381–382
  marriage of, celebrated by Paulinus of Nola, 382
  on Adam and Eve, 382
  on Augustine's view of God, 391–392
  on Augustine's views on original sin, 387–388, 416
  on sexual instinct, 390–391
  on the equity of God, 392–393, 417
  pamphlet warfare with Augustine, 383–384
  preoccupies Augustine's last years, 428, 429
  rallies Pelagian bishops, 362, 382
  sells his property to relieve a famine, 351, 381
Juliana, mother of Demetrias, patron of Pelagius, 351 n. 1, 356
Justin, Christian convert of the second century; attracted to Platonism, 103
Justina, mother of Valentinian II, 81

Lazarus, Gallic bishop, 356–357, 359, 360
Lazarus, image of man under the 'mass of habit', 149, 177
Leo, pope, on concubinage, 88–89
Leontius, saint, first martyr-bishop of Hippo, 207
Libanius:
  on demons, 311 n. 6
  on his concubine, 62 n. 5

INDEX

Licentius, pupil of Augustine, son of Romanianus, 90, 118–119, 145, 163

Macarius, Count, suppresses Donatism around 347, 215–216, 230, 233

Macrobius, author of the 'Saturnalia', 300, 301, 303, 420 n. 13

Madaura (or Madauros), university town, 38, 135

Manichaeism:
  and astrology, 57 n. 1, 58
  and the problem of suffering, 394–395
  answer to the problem of evil, 46–48, 148–150
  as a gnosis, 59, 79–80, 111–112
  as a reaction to the African Church, 42–43
  as radical Christians, 43–44, 55, 58
  Augustine accused of, 203–204, 370, 386, 393
  discovery of Manichaean liturgies, 46 n. 5
  dualism in, 47–48, 369, 393 n. 12
  expansion of, 44–45
  passivity of the good in, 52–53, 98–99, 394–395
  propaganda in Carthage, 43, 54
  rationalism of, 48–49
  rejection of Jehovah, and of the paternal severity in God in, 50, 53, 394
  scriptures of, 53–54
  social composition of, 54–55
  use of religious debates, 43, 48, 141 n. 5
  views on the physical universe, 56–58

Manlius Theodorus, Milanese Platonist, 71 n. 8, 90, 92, 116, 117, 125

Marcellinus, Flavius, Imperial Commissioner, 292, 300, 303, 331, 332, 333, 334, 337, 344, 345

Marius Victorinus, professor at Rome, translator of the Neo-Platonic books, 70, 92, 103, 151

Mauretania, 363, 406, 419, 424

Maximus, usurper, 128

Maximus, pagan professor at Madaura, 135

Megalius, bishop of Calama, 203–204

Melania, Roman noblewoman, 294, 300, 340 n. 2, 340 n. 1, 350 n. 1

Milan, 70, 71–72, 81, 86, 87, 88, 90, 92, 93, 101, 102, 103, 113, 116, 117, 121, 124–126, 128, 132, 153, 162, 163, 173, 180, 196, 205, 209, 216, 225, 271, 344 n. 7, 415

Milton, and the tradition of the philosopher's prayer, 166

Miracles:
  Augustine acquainted with, in Milan, 125, 415
  Augustine credulous, not superstitious, 416
  Augustine on the function of, 416–417
  Augustine publicises cures, 414–415
  continued need for, 418
  healing, 414 n. 8
  healing and the Resurrection, 417
  worked by physical contact with relics, 413

Monica, mother of Augustine, 29–31, 38, 39, 53, 68, 81, 87, 109, 111, 118, 121, 127, 129, 164, 174, 175, 200 n. 10, 220, 226, 239, 264, 280, 406, 413

Mosaics:
  aesthetics of, 117, 175
  in Africa, 23, 24 n. 5
  in Hippo, 190, 197, 259
  not noticed by Augustine, 269

Navigius, brother of Augustine, 118, 129, 320

Nebridius, friend of Augustine, 67–68, 90, 96, 133, 134, 135, 136, 299, 324

Nectarius, leading citizen of Calama, 296–297, 302

Newman, J. H.:
  Manichaean remarks of, 50 n. 2
  image of the 'harbour' in conversion, 177

Optatus, bishop of Milevis, 26 n. 3, 212 n. 7, 215 n. 5, 216, 219 n. 6, 266 n. 6
Optatus, Donatist bishop of Timgad, 230, 335
Orientius, Gallic poet, 351 n. 10
Origen, of Alexandria, 129, 154, 169 n. 1, 271, 273
Origenism, and Pelagius, 341 n. 4
  Origenist controversy, 273, 342 n. 9
Original Sin (and the Fall):
  and Augustine's views on society, 238
  appeal to popular attitudes in isolation of sexuality in, by Augustine, 389–390
  associated with baptism on a third-century sarcophagus, 388 n. 5
  isolation of sexuality in, by Augustine, 388–389
  Mesopotamian myth of the Fall, in Manichaeism and *Genesis*, 394
  widespread idea of, in Late Antiquity, 388
Orosius, Spanish priest, 230 n. 8, 288 n. 7, 295–296, 307 n. 8, 309, 321 n. 7, 356, 413

Paganism:
  Ambrose uses pagan authors, 112
  and the circle of Symmachus, 67
  and the circus-shows, 199, 313 n. 4
  and the Manichees, 46, 54, 70
  and the young Augustine, 41
  conflict of pagan and Christian Neo-Platonism, 102
  in the '*City of God*', 300–312
  pagan criticisms of Christianity, 268–269, 314–315
  pagan 'fundamentalism' and the classics, 265

pagan philosophers and Christian saints, 146
pagan religious sentiment, 133
pagan riot at Calama in 408, 242, 287–288
politic conversions of pagans, 231, 234
privileges of pagan priests, 420 n. 13
shrines closed in 399, 231
survival of pagan gods, 247
Palladius, Praetonian Prefect, 361
Patricius, father of Augustine, 21, 30, 31, 161, 208
Patricius, nephew of Augustine, 201
Paul, S.:
  and Ambrose, 153–154
  and Augustine's ideal of authority, 206
  and Pelagius, 151, 341–342
  and the Manichees, 55, 105, 151, 370–371
  and the proof of original sin, 394
  Augustine and African exegetes of, 153, 272
  Augustine lectures on, in 394, 151–152
  Augustine's first impression of, 105
  exegesis of, in the fourth-century, 151
  in the *Soliloquia*, 123
Paulinus, deacon of Milan, 85 n. 5, 272 n. 3, 344 n. 7, 408–409
Paulinus, bishop of Nola:
  and human frailty, 152–153
  approached by Augustine and Alypius, 144
  as patron of Pelagius, 342 n. 9
  attitude of Augustine to his conversion, 163
  attitude to friendship, compared with Augustine, 160–161
  attitude to monastic bishops, 162
  Augustine wishes to talk with, 164
  Augustine 'yearns' to see him, 210
  breaks off relations with Augustine, 204
  calls his wife 'my Lucretia', 309

INDEX

correspondence of Augustine with, on Pelagianism, 355, 360

death of, 432

favourable views on pagan virtue, 308

leaves Aquitaine to become a monk, 27

letter of Augustine to, in 409, 213

life of a recluse, envied by Augustine, 287

relations with Julian of Eclanum, 381, 382, 384

two friends of, visit Hippo, 158

Peasantry:

and the suppression of Donatism, 241

in Augustine's diocese, 192–193

revolt of, 21

Pelagianism:

and the Latin translation of John Chrysostom, 371

as finally dismissed by Augustine, 363

as first presented by Augustine, 345

as presented to pope Innocent, 358

attitude of Augustine to, 354–355

attitude of other bishops to, 355–356

Augustine's attitude to, not shared by monks, 399

in the late fifth-century, 367–368

Pelagius:

and Augustine, on Psalm 118, 373 n. 11

and the African ecclesiastical tradition, 272, 356

and the Day of Judgement, 315

and the Fall of Rome, 288–289

annoyed by the *Confessions*, 177, 343

appeal of his ideas, 346–351

as a *servus Dei*, 132

attitude to 'heresy', 355–356

attitude to his critics at the Synod of Diospolis, 357

career in Rome, 341–343

cites Augustine *'On Free Will'*, 148

criticism of, by Augustine, 369

difference with Augustine on motivation, 371

expelled from Rome, in 418, 361

hears the *'Confessions'* of Augustine, 160

lectures on S. Paul in Rome, 151, 341–342

on baptism, 368

on erie, 366

on Hell-fire, 372

on man's nature, 365

perfectionism of, 325

protectors in Rome, 357

returns to Rome, in 417, 358

Petilian, Donatist bishop of Cirta, 231, 235 n. 2, 332, 333

Pinianus, Roman nobleman, 294, 300, 340, 349, 355 n. 6

Plotinus, Greek philosopher:

a 'convert' from Gnosticism, 99 n. 5

and Augustine's idea of history, 317 n. 7

and Augustine's idea of the Church, 222

and Augustine's reading at Cassiciacum, 122 and n. 9

and spiritual autonomy, 102, 104

and the *'Confessions'*, 168

and the inner world, 178–179

and the *peregrinus* of Augustine, 324

and the preparation of the *'City of God'*, 307

and the problem of evil, 327

and the spiritual ideas of Augustine, 245–246

in the last remarks of Augustine, 426 n. 1

life and character, 26–27, 91

'On Beauty', 95–98

on the Good as active, 99

on the Intellect as a mediating principle, 98

portrait of, at Ostia, 129

Ponticianus, Imperial agent, 71, 107, 159

Pontius, biographer of S. Cyprian, 159

INDEX

Porphyry, Greek philosopher:
  and the 'Universal Way', 92 n. 3,
    106, 316
  criticism of *Genesis*, 268
  historical criticism of Christianity,
    316, 319
  inspires pagan resistance to Chris-
    tianity, 301, 303 n. 1
  life and character, 91
  retirement in Sicily, 115
  treatment of, by Augustine com-
    pared with Jerome, 307
Possidius, bishop of Calama, bio-
    grapher of Augustine, 143, 201,
    242, 266, 268, 288, 334, 407,
    425, 432, 433
Praetextatus, pagan senator, 27, 301,
    306
Proba, great-aunt of Demetrias, 340,
    351
Profuturus, friend of Augustine, 144,
    201
Punic, 22 n. 2, 139, 192, 241, 257,
    272, 383, 413

Quintilian, 254 n. 8, 259 n. 6

Ravenna, 291, 361
Rhodes, 346
Romanianus, patron of Augustine,
    21, 54, 90, 101, 116, 117, 134,
    142, 144, 241 n. 2
Rome:
  Augustine in, 58, 68–69, 131,
    132
  Augustine's attitude to the Sack
    of, 291, 295
  Augustine's relations with the
    Christian aristocracy of, 128,
    190, 191, 273, 290, 294,
    343
  protected by SS. Peter and Paul,
    289
  refugees from, in Africa, 294, 300,
    340–341
  repercussions of the Sack, 289
  Romanianus and Licentius return
    to, 145
  Sack of Rome, 288

senators as patrons of talent, 66,
    302
the Sack of, and the suppression
    of Donatism, 292

Sacraments, as military 'tattoos',
    224 n. 2
Sallust, 36, 309, 311
Sarcophagi, Christian iconography
    of, 42, 72, 146, 224 n. 2, 388 n. 5,
    401 n. 2
Scriptures:
  and Augustine's '*Mirror*' of Chris-
    tian behaviour, 404
  and classical Latin, 42
  and preaching, 252
  and the authority of the African
    bishops, 42, 140
  as the basis of a culture, 263, 267–
    268
  as the only reliable history-book,
    322 n. 3
  as the 'Word of God', 252
  Augustine's study of, in his last
    years, 423, 428
  in the African Church, 42
  juxtaposed with pagan literature,
    306
  understanding of, as an intellectual
    activity, 162, 180, 263–264
  veiled by God, 261
Secundinus, Roman Manichee, 70,
    160, 370
Seneca, Pelagian bishop in Picenum,
    367–368
Severus, bishop of Milevis, 144, 201,
    230, 411, 419
Sicily, 115, 346, 347, 368, 382
Simplicianus, priest, later bishop of
    Milan, 93, 103, 106, 153
Symmachus, pagan senator, 66–71,
    195, 301, 302

Thagaste, 19, 31, 32, 38, 132, 133,
    134, 135, 136, 140, 193, 216,
    233 n. 4, 294, 334, 368
Theodosius, Emperor, 128, 291,
    308 n. 2
Thubursicum Bure, 230, 300 n. 2

INDEX

Thysdrus, 19

Timasius, disciple of Pelagius, 249, 359

Timgad, 19, 220, 230, 335

Turfan, 44

Tyconius, Donatist layman and exegete, 140, 151, 153, 226 n. 6, 272, 314

Valerius, bishop of Hippo, 138–140, 206

Valerius, Count, 362, 385, 389, 390

Verecundus, Milanese professor, 90, 106, 116

Vergil, 36, 266, 303, 305, 374

Vincentius, Donatist bishop of Cartennae, 242, 364

Vindicianus, 67, 317 n. 1

Volusianus, Roman pagan senator, 300, 301, 303, 384, 420 n. 13

Zenobius, Milanese friend of Augustine, 90, 117

Zosimus, pope, 359 n. 2, 360